CAPITAL MARKETS

INSTITUTIONS AND INSTRUMENTS

CAPITAL MARKETS

INSTITUTIONS AND INSTRUMENTS

Frank J. Fabozzi
Sloan School of Management
Massachusetts Institute of Technology

Franco Modigliani
Sloan School of Management
Massachusetts Institute of Technology

Prentice Hall, Englewood Cliffs, New Jersey   07632

To our wives, Dessa Fabozzi and Serena Modigliani

Library of Congress Cataloging-in-Publication Data

Fabozzi, Frank J.
   Capital markets: institutions and instruments / Frank J. Fabozzi,
Franco Modigliani.
      p.   cm.
   Includes bibliographical references and index.
   ISBN 0-13-601436-4
   1. Capital market.   I. Modigliani, Franco.   II. Title.
HG4523.F33   1991
332'.0414—dc20

91-18056
CIP

Acquisition Editor: Leah Jewell
Editorial / Production Supervision: The Total Book
Copy Editor: Patricia B. Peat
Designer: Brand X Studios / Robin Hessel Hoffmann
Cover Photo: Larry Keenan / The Image Bank
Cover Designer: Donna Wickes
Prepress Buyer: Trudy Pisciotti
Manufacturing Buyer: Robert Anderson
Supplements Editor: David Scholder
Editorial Assistant: Diane DeCastro

© 1992 by Prentice-Hall, Inc.
A Simon & Schuster Company
Englewood Cliffs, New Jersey 07632

Printed in the United States of America
10 9 8 7 6 5 4 3 2 1

ISBN 0-13-601436-4

Prentice-Hall International (UK) Limited, *London*
Prentice-Hall of Australia Pty, Limited, *Sydney*
Prentice-Hall Canada Inc., *Toronto*
Prentice-Hall Hispanoamericana, S. A., *Mexico City*
Prentice-Hall of India Private Limited, *New Delhi*
Prentice-Hall of Japan, Inc., *Tokyo*
Simon & Schuster of Southeast Asia Pte. Ltd., *Singapore*
Editora Prentice-Hall do Brasil, Ltda., *Rio de Janeiro*

CONTENTS
IN BRIEF

Frank J. Fabozzi is Visiting Professor of Finance at the Sloan School of Management at MIT where he has been a full-time faculty member since 1986. He is the editor of *The Journal of Portfolio Management* and *Advances in Futures and Options Research*. Professor Fabozzi has authored and edited several widely acclaimed books in finance. He is on the board of directors of six closed-end investment companies listed on the New York Stock Exchange and on the board of supervisory directors of three offshore funds, all specializing in mortgage-backed securities products. He holds a doctorate in economics in 1972 from The Graduate Center of the City University of New York and is a Chartered Financial Analyst.

Franco Modigliani is Institute Professor and Professor of Finance and Economics at MIT. He is an Honorary President of the International Economic Association, a former President of the American Economic Association, the American Finance Association, and the Econometric Society. Professor Modigliani has authored numerous books and articles in economics. In October 1985 he was awarded the Alfred Nobel Memorial Prize in Economic Sciences. He has served as a consultant to the Federal Reserve System, the U.S. Treasury Department, and a number of European Banks. Professor Modigliani received a Doctor of Jurisprudence in 1939 from the University of Rome and a Doctor of Social Science in 1944 from the New School for Social Research, as well as several honorary doctorates.

CONTENTS

SECTION III
THE EQUITY MARKET

SECTION IV
INTEREST RATE DETERMINATION

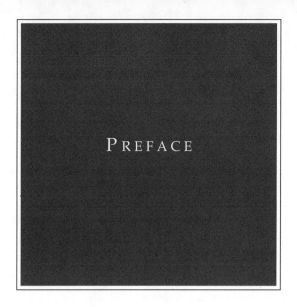

PREFACE

The revolution that has taken place in the world financial markets was aptly described by a noted economist, Henry Kaufman, in the 1985 Annual Report of Phibro-Salomon:

> If a modern-day Rip Van Winkle had fallen asleep twenty years ago, or for that matter even ten years back, on awakening today, he would be astonished as to what has happened in the financial markets. Instead of a world of isolated national capital markets and a preponderance of fixed-rate financing, he would discover a world of highly integrated capital markets, an extensive array of financing instruments, and new methods of addressing market risk.

The purpose of this book is to describe the wide range of instruments for financing, investing, and controlling risk that are available in today's financial markets. New financial instruments are not created simply because someone on Wall Street believes that it would be "fun" to introduce an instrument with more "bells and whistles" than existing instruments. The demand for new instruments is driven by the needs of borrowers and investors based on their asset/liability management situation, regulatory constraints (if any), financial accounting considerations, and tax considerations. For these reasons, to comprehend the financial innovations that have occurred and are expected to occur in the future, a general understanding of the asset/liability management problem of major institutional investors is required. Therefore, in addition to coverage of the markets for all financial instruments, we provide an overview of the asset/liability management problem faced by major institutional investors and the strategies they employ.

We believe that the coverage provided in this book on the institutional investors and financial instruments is as up-to-date as possible in a market facing rapid changes in the characteristics of the players and those making the rules as to how the game can be played. New financial instruments are introduced on a regular basis; however, armed with an understanding of the needs of institutional investors and the attributes of existing financial instruments, the reader will be able to recognize the contribution made by a new financial instrument.

This book deviates in several ways from the traditional capital markets textbook. One important way is in our coverage of derivative markets (futures, options, swaps, etc.). These markets are an integral part of the global capital market. They are not—as often categorized by the popular press and some of our less informed congressional representatives and regulators—''exotic'' markets. These instruments permit a mechanism by which market participants can control risk—borrowers can control borrowing costs and investors can control the market risk of their portfolio. It is safe to say that without the derivative markets, there would not be an efficient global capital market.

In addition, it is important to appreciate the basic principles of option theory not only as a stand-alone instrument, but because many financial instruments have embedded options. Also, the liabilities of many financial institutions have embedded options. Thus, it is difficult to appreciate the complex nature of assets and liabilities without understanding the fundamentals of option theory.

While we recognize that many colleges offer a specialized course in derivative markets, our purpose here is not to delve deeply into the various trading strategies and the nuances of pricing models that characterize such a course. Instead, we provide the fundamentals of the role of these instruments in financial markets, the principles of pricing them, and a general description of how they are used by market participants to control risk. We describe many interest rate control instruments that are customized for clients by commercial banks and investment banking firms that are often not covered in a derivative markets course.

A special feature of this book is the extensive coverage of the mortgage market and the securitization of assets. Asset securitization refers to the creation of securities whose collateral is the cash flow from the underlying pool of assets. The process of asset securitization is radically different from the traditional system for financing the acquisition of assets. By far the largest part of the securitized asset market is the mortgage-backed securities market, where the assets collateralizing the securities are mortgage loans. Securitized assets backed by non-real estate mortgage loans are a small but growing part of the market.

Another key feature of this book is emphasis on the role played by foreign investors in the U.S. market. Although the bulk of this book covers the U.S. financial markets, we discuss other major financial markets in the last chapter, particularly the Japanese market.

One of the difficulties we had in deciding the topics to cover is discriminating between what belongs in a course on capital markets and what is the province of investment management. Oftentimes, because the needs of institutional investors dictate the need for financial instruments with certain investment characteristics or for a particular strategy employing a capital market instrument, we had to cross the line.

The topics included in this book are those we cover in the course we have taught at MIT: Modigliani's Capital Markets and Institutions course and Fabozzi's Investment Banking and Markets course. We doubt if an instructor will have the luxury of covering all of the chapters in this book in a one semester course. The table on page xxiv gives our suggested chapter coverage if the focus of a one semester course is a description of the institutions and instruments. The approach taken in this book makes it adaptable for a course in investment banking.

This book can be used as a supplementary book for a derivative markets (options and futures) course and an investment (portfolio) management course. The suggested chapter coverage for each course is given in the table.

For readers who adopt the book, we would be interested in seeing your course outline.

Acknowledgements

We are indebted to many individuals for providing us with various forms of assistance in this project. Our teaching assistants, Steve Boxer and Arun Muralidhar, provided us with helpful comments on most of the chapters in the book. Laurence Siegel (R. G. Ibbotson Associates) reviewed many of the chapters and provided insightful comments, as well as encouragement. Others who have read portions of the manuscript and provided feedback include: Joseph Bencivenga (Salomon Brothers), Anand Bhattacharya (Prudential-Bache Capital Funding), Mark Castelino (Rutgers University), Daniel T. Coggin (Virginia Retirement System), Bruce Collins (Western Connecticut State University), Dessa Fabozzi (Merrill Lynch Capital Markets), Michael Ferri (George Mason University), Jack Clark Francis (Baruch College, CUNY), Gary L. Gastineau (Salomon Brothers), Robert L. Gilligan II (Brokers &

POTENTIAL USES AND CHAPTER COVERAGE FOR FABOZZI AND MODIGLIANI, *CAPITAL MARKETS: INSTITUTIONS AND INSTRUMENTS*

Chapter	One Semester Course Focusing on Institutions and Instruments	Supplementary Book for Course on:	
		Derivative Markets (Options and Futures)	Investment (Portfolio) Management
1 Introduction	X		
2 Depository Institutions	X		
3 Investment Banking	X		
4 Insurance Companies, Pension Funds, and Investment Companies	X		X
5 Risk/Return and Asset Pricing Models	(a)	(a)	X
6 Introduction to Financial Futures Markets	X	X	X
7 Introduction to Option Markets	X	X	X
8 Common Stock Market	X		X
9 Stock Options Market	X(b)	X	X
10 Stock Index Options and Futures Markets	X	X	X
11 Theory of Interest Rate Determination and Bond Valuation: I		X(e)	X(e)
12 Theory of Interest Rate Determination and Bond Valuation: II		X	X
13 Money Market Instruments	X		
14 Treasury and Agency Securities Markets	X		X
15 Corporate Senior Securities Market	X		X
16 Municipal Securities Market	X		X
17 The Mortgage Market	X(c)		
18 The Market for Mortgage Pools and Other Securitized Assets	X		X
19 Interest Rate Futures and Options	X(d)	X	X
20 Customized Interest Rate Control Contracts		X	X
21 Foreign Exchange Markets		X	
22 Global Financial Markets	X	X(f)	X

Notes: (a) Coverage of this chapter depends on whether students have covered this topic in another course. (b) Only the first section on features of exchange-traded options. (c) Omit the discussion of PLAMs and dual-rate mortgages. (d) Omit the discussion of option pricing models. (e) Omit the first section of this chapter. (f) The sections in this chapter on derivative contracts.

Reinsurance Markets Association), K.C. Ma (Texas Tech), Antonio Mello (MIT), Scott Richard (Goldman Sachs), and Uzi Yaari (Rutgers University).

We used the manuscript in our courses at MIT and received helpful comments from many of our students. In particular, we wish to thank Barbara Addo, Alan Gerstein, and Stefano Roscini.

We also benefitted from discussions with the following individuals on various topics: Robert Arnott (First Quadrant), Paul Asquith (MIT), Peter L. Bernstein (Peter L. Bernstein Inc.), David Canuel (Aetna Life and Casualty), Michael Coppola (Merrill Lynch Money Markets), John H. Carlson (Daiwa Securities America), Peter Carrill (Daiwa Securities America), Andrew S. Carron (First Boston), Glen Carter (U.S. Central Credit Union), Peter E. Christensen (PaineWebber), Ravi Dattatreya (Sumitomo Bank Capital Markets), William Dunn (Bear Stearns), Sylvan Feldstein (Merrill Lynch Capital Markets), Henry Gabbay (Blackstone Financial Management), Sean Gallop (J.P. Morgan Securities), Kevin E. Grant (Aetna Life and Casualty), Hal Hinkle (Goldman Sachs), Jane Howe (Pacific Investment Management Company), David P. Jacob (J.P. Morgan Securities), Frank J. Jones (Guardian Life Insurance Company), Andrew Kalotay (Fordham University), Robert Kulason (Salomon Brothers), Barbara Laico (Merrill Lynch Money Markets), Martin Leibowitz (Salomon Brothers), Matt Mancuso (Bear Stearns), Nick Mencher (BARRA), Ed Murphy (Merchants Mutual Insurance Company), Scott Pinkus (Goldman Sachs), Mark Pitts (Lehman Brothers), Chuck Ramsey (MMAR Group), Sharmin Mossavar-Rahmani (Fidelity Management Trust Company), Frank Ramirez (MMAR Group), Blaine Roberts (Bear Stearns), Michael Rosenberg (Merrill Lynch Capital Markets), Dexter Senft (EJV Partners), and Richard Wilson (Fitch Investors Service).

In our end-of-chapter questions, we used excerpts from *Institutional Investor* and several weekly publications of Institutional Investor Inc., *Wall Street Letter*, *Bank Letter*, *BondWeek*, *Corporate Financing Week*, *Money Management Letter*, and *Portfolio Letter*. We are grateful to Lauren Winer of *Institutional Investor* and Tom Lamont, editor of the weekly publications, for permission to use the material. Simon G. Davidson of Ferguson & Co. (Washington, D.C.) provided data on the largest U.S. bank holding companies reported in Chapter 2. The data source for the largest world banks reported in the same chapter is EURASTAR, a division of Sleigh Corporation (Franklin Lakes, N.J.). Jan D. Slee and Elaine H. Robbins furnished the information. Patricia Sce and Judith Otterman of Salomon Brothers provided the data for the size of the U.S. bond market in Chapter 14. Dana Schmidt of Morgan Stanley supplied us with the latest information from various publications of *Morgan Stanley Capital Perspective* that we used in Chapter 22. Beth Preiss of Federal Home Loan Mortgage Corporation furnished us with the latest information from *Database* published in *Secondary Mortgage Market* that we used in Chapters 17 and 18. Gary Gastineau of Salomon Brothers provided information about the various non-U.S. stock index derivative contracts reported in Chapter 22.

In addition, the authors would like to thank the following reviewers: John S. Strong (College of William and Mary), Michael G. Ferri (George Mason University), Jim Kolari (Texas A & M University), William A. Kracaw (Purdue University), Peter Williamson (Dartmouth College), Don M. Chance (Virginia Polytechnic Institute & State University), Peggy Fletcher (Northeastern University), Robert E. Lamy (Wake Forest University), Colleen Pantalone (Northeastern University), Mark Castelino (Rutgers University), and Andrea Heuson (University of Miami).

Administrative assistance was provided by Jeanne-Marie DeJordy, Ed Garlicki, Mae Nigohosian, Marie Southwick, and Nate Weiss. Pat Peat provided editorial assistance.

Last, but certainly not least, we wish to thank our families for their patience in allowing us to allocate our limited time to completion of this project.

Frank J. Fabozzi
Franco Modigliani

LEARNING OBJECTIVES

After reading this chapter you will understand:

- what a financial asset is and the principal economic functions of financial assets.

- the seven properties of financial assets: moneyness, divisibility and denomination, reversibility, yield and return, term to maturity, liquidity, and predictability or risk.

- the general principles for determining the price of a financial asset.

- the distinction between financial (or intangible) assets and tangible assets.

- what a derivative instrument is and the role of derivative instruments.

- what a financial market is and the principal economic functions it performs.

- the differences between the primary and secondary markets.

  - the differences between auction, over-the-counter, and intermediated markets.

- the difference between a broker, market maker, dealer, and financial intermediary.

  - the role of financial intermediaries.

- the different ways that governments regulate markets.

  - the primary reasons for financial innovation.

I n a market economy, the allocation of economic resources is driven by the outcome of many private decisions. Prices are the signals that direct economic resources to their best use. The types of markets in an economy can be divided into (1) the market for products (manufactured goods and services), or the product market, and (2) the market for the factors of production (labor and capital), or the factor market.

Our purpose in this book is to focus on one part of the factor market, the market for financial assets, or, more simply, the financial market. It is in this market that the cost of capital is determined. In this chapter we will look at the basic characteristics of the financial market: the "things" that are traded (that is, bought and sold), and the participants who trade them or who facilitate their trade.

FINANCIAL ASSETS

We begin with a few basic definitions. An asset is, broadly speaking, any possession that has value in an exchange. Assets can be classified as tangible or intangible. A tangible asset is one whose value depends on particular physical properties—examples are buildings, land, or machinery. Tangible assets may be classified further into reproducible assets such as machinery, or non-reproducible assets such as land, a mine, or a work of art.

Intangible assets, by contrast, represent legal claims to some future benefit. Their value bears no relation to the form, physical or otherwise, in which the claims are recorded. Financial assets, financial instruments, or securities are intangible assets. For these instruments, the typical future benefit is a claim to future cash. This book deals with the markets for and valuation of financial assets.

The entity that has agreed to make future cash payments is called the *issuer* of the financial asset; the owner of the financial asset is referred to as the *investor*. Here are just three examples of financial assets:

- a loan by a commercial bank (investor) to an individual (issuer/borrower) to purchase a car
- a U.S. Treasury bond
- the common stock of General Motors

In the case of the car loan, the terms of the loan establish that the borrower must make specified payments to the commercial bank over time. The payments include repayment of the amount borrowed plus interest. The cash flow for this asset is made up of the specified payments that the borrower must make.

In the case of a U.S. Treasury bond, the U.S. government (the issuer) agrees to pay the holder or the investor the bond interest payments every six months until the bond matures, then at the maturity date repay the amount borrowed. The common stock of General Motors entitles the investor to receive dividends distributed by the company. The investor in this case also has a claim to a pro rata share of the net asset value of the company in case of liquidation of the company.

Debt versus Equity Claims

The claim that the holder of a financial asset has may be either a fixed dollar amount or a varying, or residual, amount. In the former case, the financial asset is referred to as a *debt instrument*. The car loan and the U.S. Treasury bond cited above are examples of debt instruments requiring fixed dollar payments.

A residual or equity claim obligates the issuer of the financial asset to pay the holder an amount based on earnings, if any, after holders of debt instruments have been paid. Common stock is an example of an equity claim. A partnership share in a business is another example.

Some securities fall into both categories. Preferred stock, for example, is an equity claim that entitles the investor to receive a fixed dollar amount. This payment is contingent, however, due only after payments to debt instrument holders are made. Another "combination" instrument is convertible bonds, which allow the investor to convert debt into equity under certain circumstances. Both debt and preferred stock that pays a fixed dollar amount are called *fixed-income instruments* or *money-fixed instruments*.

The Price of a Financial Asset and Risk

A basic economic principle is that the price of any financial asset is equal to the present value of its expected cash flow, even if the cash flow is not known with certainty.[1] We elaborate on this principle throughout this book as we discuss several theories for the pricing of financial assets. Directly related to the notion of price is the expected return on a financial asset. Given the expected cash flow of a financial asset and its price, we can determine its expected rate of return.

The type of financial asset, whether debt instrument or equity instrument, and the characteristics of the issuer determine the degree of certainty of the expected cash flow. For example, assuming that the U.S. government never defaults on the debt instruments it issues, the cash flow of U.S. Treasury securities is known with certainty. What is uncertain, however, is the purchasing power of the cash flow received.

In the case of the automobile loan, the ability of the borrower to repay presents some uncertainty about the cash flow. But, if the borrower does not default on the loan obligation, the holder (the bank) knows what the cash flow will be.

The holder of General Motors common stock is uncertain as to the amount and the timing of dividend payments. Dividend payments will be related to company profits, though, and because those profits are possibly tied to the rate of inflation, it may be argued that while the amount and timing are uncertain, the cash flow and the value of the principal may to some extent be protected from inflation.

While there are various types of risks that we will discuss in this chapter and those to follow, we can see two of them in these three examples. The first is the risk attached to potential purchasing power of the expected cash flow.

---

[1] By cash flow we mean the stream of cash payments over time.

This is called *purchasing power risk,* or *inflation risk.* The second is the risk that the issuer or borrower will default on the obligation. This is called *credit risk,* or *default risk.*

Financial (Intangible) Assets versus Tangible Assets

A tangible asset such as plant or equipment purchased by a business entity shares at least one characteristic with an intangible financial asset: both are expected to generate future cash flow for their owner.

Financial assets and tangible assets are linked. Ownership of tangible assets is financed by the issuance of some type of financial asset—either debt instruments or equity instruments. Ultimately, therefore, the cash flow for an intangible financial asset is generated by some tangible asset.

Derivative Instruments

Some contracts give the contract holder either the obligation or the choice to buy or sell a financial asset. The price of any such contract derives its value from the price of the underlying financial asset. Consequently, these contracts are called *derivative instruments.*

The two basic types of derivative instruments are options contracts and futures/forward contracts. An options contract gives the owner of the contract the right, but not the obligation, to buy (or sell) a financial asset at a specified price from (or to) another party. The buyer of the contract must pay the seller a fee, which is called the option price.

A futures or forward contract is an agreement whereby two parties agree to transact with respect to some financial asset at a predetermined price at a specified future date. One party agrees to buy the financial asset, the other agrees to sell the financial asset. Both parties are obligated to perform, and neither party charges a fee. The distinction between a futures and forward contract is explained in Chapter 6.

Transactions using derivative instruments are not limited to financial assets. There are derivative instruments involving commodities and precious metals. Our focus in this book, however, is on derivative instruments where the underlying asset is a financial asset or some financial benchmark such as a stock index or an interest rate, or foreign exchange.

The Role of Financial Assets

So what is the economic function of financial assets? They have two principal economic functions. The first is to transfer funds from those who have surplus funds to invest to those who need funds to invest in tangible assets. The second economic function is transferring funds in such a way as to redistribute the unavoidable risk associated with the cash flow generated by tangible assets among those seeking and those providing the funds. However, the claims held by the final wealth holders are generally different from the liabilities issued by the final demanders of funds because of the activity of financial intermediaries who seek to transform the final liabilities into different financial assets which the public prefers (see below).

To illustrate these two economic functions, consider three situations.

1. Joe Grasso has obtained a license to manufacture Teenage Mutant Ninja Turtles wristwatches. Joe estimates that he will need $1 million to purchase plant and equipment to manufacture the watches. Unfortunately, he has only $200,000 to invest, and that is his life savings, which he does not want to invest, even though he has confidence that there will be a receptive market for the watches.

2. Susan Carlson has recently inherited $730,000. She plans to spend $30,000 on some jewelry, furniture, and a few cruises, and to invest the balance, $700,000.

3. Larry Stein, an up-and-coming attorney with a major New York law firm, has received a bonus check that after taxes has netted him $250,000. He plans to spend $50,000 on a BMW and invest the balance, $200,000.

Suppose that, quite by accident, Joe, Susan, and Larry meet in New York City. Sometime during their conversation, they discuss their financial plans. By the end of the evening, they agree to a deal. Joe agrees to invest $100,000 of his savings in the business and sell a 50% interest to Susan for $700,000. Larry agrees to lend Joe $200,000 for four years at an interest rate of 18% per year. Joe will be responsible for operating the business without the assistance of Susan or Larry. Joe now has his $1 million to manufacture the watches.

Two financial claims came out of this meeting. The first is an equity instrument issued by Joe and purchased by Susan for $700,000. The other is a debt instrument issued by Joe and purchased by Larry for $200,000. Thus, the two financial assets allowed funds to be transferred from Susan and Larry, who had surplus funds to invest, to Joe, who needed funds to invest in tangible assets in order to manufacture the watches. This transfer of funds is the first economic function of financial assets.

The fact that Joe is not willing to invest his life savings of $200,000 means that he wanted to transfer part of that risk. He does so by selling Susan a financial asset that gives her a financial claim equal to one-half the cash flow from the business. He further secures an additional amount of capital from Larry, who is not willing to share in the risk of the business (except for bankruptcy risk), in the form of an obligation requiring payment of a fixed cash flow, regardless of the outcome of the venture. This shifting of risk is the second function of financial assets.

The Role of Derivative Instruments

So far it should not be difficult to understand the economic functions of financial assets. But why do derivative instruments exist? What we shall see in later chapters, as we describe the details of these contracts, is that they allow market participants to control the risk associated with a portfolio of financial assets or the risk associated with the issuance of financial assets.

Properties of Financial Assets[2]

Financial assets have certain properties that add to or detract from their attractiveness to different classes of investors and issuers. An examination of these properties is very useful in understanding the structure of asset values as well as the role of intermediation—the activity of transforming financial assets with certain properties into financial assets with different properties.

Moneyness.   Some financial assets are used as a *medium of exchange* or in settlement of transactions. These assets are called *money*. In the United States they consist of currency and all forms of deposits that permit check writing. Other assets, although not money, are very close to money in that they can be transformed into money at little cost, delay, or risk. They are referred to as *near money*. In the case of the U.S., these include time and savings deposits and U.S. Treasury bills. Moneyness is clearly a desirable property for investors.

Divisibility and Denomination.   Divisibility relates to the minimum size in which a financial asset can be liquidated and exchanged for money. The smaller the size, the more the financial asset is divisible. A financial asset such as a deposit is typically infinitely divisible (down to the penny), but other financial assets have varying degrees of divisibility depending on their denomination, which is the dollar value of the amount that each unit of the asset will pay at maturity. Thus many bonds come in $1,000 denominations, commercial paper in $25,000 units, and certain types of certificates of deposit in $100,000 and more. In general, divisibility is desirable for investors but not for borrowers.

Reversibility.   Reversibility (round-trip cost) refers to the cost of investing in a financial asset and then getting out of it and back into cash again. A financial asset such as a deposit is obviously highly reversible because usually there is no charge for adding to or withdrawing from it. Other transaction costs may

---

[2] This section draws from James Tobin, "Properties of Assets," undated manuscript, New Haven, Yale.

be unavoidable, but these are small. For financial assets traded in organized markets or with "market makers" (discussed later), the most relevant component of round-trip cost is the so-called bid-ask spread, to which might be added commissions and the time and cost, if any, of delivering the asset. The spread charged by a market maker varies sharply from one financial asset to another, reflecting primarily the amount of risk the market maker is assuming by "making" a market.

This risk can be related to two main forces. One is the variability of the price as measured, say, by some measure of dispersion of the relative price over time, such as the standard deviation of relative price changes. Clearly, the greater the variability, the greater the probability of incurring a loss in excess of a stated bound between the time of buying and reselling the financial asset. The variability of prices differs widely across financial assets. Treasury bills, for example, have a very stable price, for reasons examined in Chapter 12, while a speculative stock will exhibit much larger short-run variations.

Another determining factor is what is commonly referred to as the *thickness* of the market; by this is meant essentially the prevailing rate at which buying and selling orders reach the market maker (i.e., the frequency of transactions). Clearly, the greater the frequency of order flows, the shorter the time that the security will have to be held in the market maker's inventory, and hence the smaller the probability of an unfavorable price movement while held.

Thickness too varies from market to market. The three-month U.S. Treasury bill is easily the thickest market in the world. In contrast, trading in stock of small companies is not thick, but rather is said to be thin. Because Treasury bills dominate other instruments both in price stability and thickness, the bid-ask spread tends to be the smallest in the market. A low turnaround cost is clearly a desirable property of a financial asset, and as a result thickness itself is a valuable property. This explains the potential advantage of large over smaller markets (economies of scale), and a market's endeavor to standardize the instruments offered to the public.

Yield and Return.   The cash yield of a financial asset per unit of time consists of all the cash distributions that the financial asset will pay its owners; this includes dividends on shares and coupon payment on bonds and other fixed-income instruments. The total yield includes also non-cash payments, such as stock dividends and options to purchase additional stock, or the distribution of other securities. The yield can be computed gross or net of taxes; in the latter case, the same instrument may have different yields for different investors.

The return is the sum of the yield and any capital gains or losses that may have been incurred during the period. Generally the (net of tax) return is the more useful measure because it tells us how much the holding of that financial asset contributed to changing our net worth.

In a world of non-negligible inflation, it is further important to distinguish between *nominal* and *real* return. The net real return is the (nominal) return as defined above, but after adjustment for the loss of purchasing power of the financial asset as a result of inflation, as explained in Chapter 11.

Term to Maturity.   This is the length of the interval until the date at which the instrument is scheduled to make its final payment, or the owner is entitled to demand liquidation. Instruments for which the creditor can ask for repayment at any time, such as checking accounts and many savings accounts, are called *demand instruments.* Maturity is an important characteristic of nominal or fixed assets such as bonds or standard mortgages, and can range from one day to a few decades. In the United Kingdom, there is one well-known type of bond that promises to pay a fixed amount per year indefinitely and not to repay the principal at any time; such an instrument is called a *perpetuity,* or a *consol.* Many other instruments, including equities, have no maturity and are thus of the nature of a perpetuity.

It should be understood that even a security with stated maturity may terminate before its stated maturity. This may occur for several reasons, including bankruptcy or reorganization, or because of "call" provisions entitling the debtor to repay in advance, usually at some penalty and only after a number of years from issue. Sometimes the lender may have the privilege of asking for early repayment, called a put option. All these circumstances are discussed in the chapters following.

Liquidity.   This is an important and widely used notion, although there is at present no uniformly accepted definition of liquidity. A useful way to think of liquidity and illiquidity, proposed by Professor James Tobin, is in terms of how much sellers stand to lose if they wish to sell immediately as against engaging in a costly and time-consuming search.[3]

The best example of a quite illiquid asset is a large and unusual house, or a work of art of a lesser artist, for which the market is extremely thin, and one must search for one of a very few suitable buyers. Less suitable buyers, including speculators and market makers, may be located more promptly, but will have to be enticed to invest in the illiquid financial asset by an appropriate discount.

For many other financial assets, liquidity is determined by contractual arrangements. Ordinary deposits, for example, are perfectly liquid because the bank has a contractual obligation to convert them at par on demand.

---

[3] Tobin, "Properties of Assets," pp. 2–10.

Securities of private pension funds may be regarded on the other hand as totally illiquid, because these can be cashed only at retirement. In the case of financial assets that are traded in the market, in particular where there are market makers, the cost that must be incurred to dispose of an asset is basically the bid-ask spread plus commissions, and neither of these is affected by the time allowed or other preparations undertaken for a sale. Hence the financial asset can be regarded as fully liquid.

Liquidity may depend not only on the financial asset but also on the quantity one wishes to sell (or buy). While a small quantity may be quite liquid, a large lot may run into illiquidity problems. Note that liquidity is again closely related to whether a market is thick or thin. Thinness always has the effect of increasing the turnaround cost, even of a liquid financial asset. But beyond some point it becomes an obstacle to the formation of a market, and has a direct effect on the illiquidity of the financial asset.

Predictability or Risk.   This is a basic property of financial assets, in that it is a major determinant of their value. Assuming investors are risk averse, the riskiness of an asset can be equated with the uncertainty or unpredictability of its return. We will see in Chapter 5 how the unpredictability of future returns can be measured and how it is related to the variability of past returns. But whatever measure of volatility we use, be it the standard deviation of expected returns or the range within which the outcome can be expected to fall with some stated probability, it is obvious that volatility varies greatly across financial assets. There are several reasons for this.

First recall that the value of a financial asset depends on the cash flow expected and on the interest rate used to discount this cash flow. Hence volatility will be a consequence of the uncertainty about future interest rates and future cash flow. Now the future cash flow may be contractual, in which case the sole source of its uncertainty is the reliability of the debtor with regard to fulfilling the obligation; or it may be in the nature of a residual equity claim, as is the case for the cash flow generated by the equity of a corporation.

The cash flow from U.S. government securities are the only cash flows generally regarded as altogether riskless. Corporate debt and corporate stock cash flows are generally riskier than cash flows of U.S. government securities. Corporate equities represent a wide range of risk, from public utilities to highly speculative issues.

As for a change in interest rates, it will in principle affect all prices in the opposite direction, but the effect is much larger in the case of the price of a financial asset with a long maturity than one with a short remaining life (see Chapter 12). Thus, on this account also, short-term U.S. government securities such as Treasury bills tend to be the safest asset, except for cash (if properly insured). For individual stocks the interest effect is generally swamped by cash flow uncertainty, although movements in interest rates have the characteristic of affecting all stocks in the same direction, while change in expected cash flow is largely idiosyncratic. In general, uncertainty about returns and future prices can be expected to increase as investment horizon lengthens.

What has been said so far relates to the predictability of *nominal returns*. Usually what is relevant, however, is *real returns*, i.e., returns corrected for gains or losses of purchasing power attributable to inflation. Of course, if inflation is absent or small, as was the case in the U.S. from the late forties to the mid-sixties, the determinants of real and nominal uncertainty and risk coincide. But in the presence of highly unpredictable inflation (which usually goes together with high inflation), the relative predictability of real and nominal returns (or real and nominal risk) may change quite drastically, in particular as between nominal and real assets. Indeed, as inflation becomes increasingly unpredictable, the returns from nominal assets may become more uncertain than those from some real assets.

FINANCIAL MARKETS

A financial market is a market where financial assets are exchanged (i.e., traded). Although the existence of a financial market is not a necessary condition for the creation and exchange of a financial asset, in most economies financial assets are created and subsequently traded on some type of organized financial market.

The market in which a financial asset trades for immediate delivery is called the *spot* or *cash market*. Derivative instruments also trade in established markets.

Role of Financial Markets

We explained above the two primary economic functions of financial assets. Financial markets provide three additional economic functions.

First, the interactions of buyers and sellers in a financial market determine the price of the traded asset. Or, equivalently, the required return on a financial asset is determined. As the inducement for firms to acquire funds depends on the required return that investors demand, it is this feature of financial markets that signals how the funds in the economy should be allocated among financial assets. This is called the *price discovery process*. Whether these signals are correct or not is an issue that we discuss in Chapter 8 when we examine the efficiency of financial markets.

Second, financial markets provide a mechanism for an investor to sell a financial asset. Because of this feature, it is said that a financial market offers liquidity, an attractive feature when circumstances either force or motivate an investor to sell. In the absence of liquidity, the owner will be forced to hold a debt instrument until it matures and an equity instrument until the company is either voluntarily or involuntarily liquidated. While all financial markets provide some form of liquidity, the degree of liquidity is one of the factors that characterize different markets.

The third economic function of a financial market is that it reduces the cost of transacting. There are two costs associated with transacting: search costs and information costs.

Search costs represent explicit costs, such as the money spent to advertise the desire to sell or purchase a financial asset, and implicit costs, such as the value of time spent in locating a counterparty. The presence of some form of organized financial market reduces search costs. Information costs are those entailed with assessing the investment merits of a financial asset, that is, the amount and the likelihood of the cash flow expected to be generated. In an efficient market, prices reflect the aggregate information collected by all market participants.

Role of Futures Markets

Derivative instruments such as futures contracts can be used to control risk. Market participants who wish to alter the risk exposure of their portfolio of financial assets can use the market for these contracts. As we will see in later chapters, the market for many futures contracts has at least three advantages over the corresponding cash (spot) market for the financial asset.

First, the cost of executing a transaction in order to adjust the risk exposure of a portfolio to new economic information is, usually, less in the futures market than it would be to make that adjustment in the cash market. Second, the speed at which a transaction can be accomplished is typically faster in the futures market. Third, the futures market typically can absorb a greater dollar transaction without an adverse effect on the price of the futures contract; that is, the futures market is more liquid than the cash market.

For these reasons, market participants often choose to use the futures market. As a result, new economic information is embodied in the futures market before it is reflected in the cash market. Hence, whenever a futures market exists for a financial asset, the futures market is generally the price discovery market. How are the prices in the futures market ultimately reflected in the cash market? As we explain in Chapter 7, this occurs through a process called arbitrage.

Types of Financial Markets

There are many ways to classify financial markets. One way is by the type of financial claim, such as debt markets and equity markets. Another is by the maturity of the claims. For example, there is a financial market for short-term debt instruments, called the *money market*, and one for longer maturity financial assets, called the *capital market*. Financial markets can be categorized as those dealing with financial claims that are newly issued, called the *primary market*, and those for exchanging financial claims previously issued, called the *secondary market*, or the market for seasoned instruments. There is also the cash market and the derivative instrument market.

Finally, a market can be classified by its organizational structure. These organizational structures can be classified as auction markets, over-the-counter markets, and intermediated markets. In an auction market there is some form of centralized trading facility where there is open competitive bidding for financial assets. All trades of that financial asset take place in the centralized trading facility.

At one time, this centralized trading facility had to be a place where buyers and sellers, or their agents, called *brokers*, would gather to exchange financial claims for their customers. Brokers do not buy or sell for their own account, but in return for their services as agents, they receive compensation called *commissions*. The auctioneer in an auction market is called the *market maker*. Market makers may or may not take a position in the financial asset being traded, i.e., buy for or sell from their own accounts (inventory). When they do, the market maker is referred to as a *dealer*.

With the advances in computer technology, a physical facility that houses the centralized trading activities is unnecessary. The key is that all orders are executed in the centralized trading facility. In an over-the-counter market, there is no centralized trading facility. The market consists of dealers who are willing to buy or sell the financial asset from or to any counterparty.

In contrast to auction markets and over-the-counter markets is an intermediated market. In this market, an entity called a *financial intermediary* issues financial claims against itself. With the funds it receives, it purchases financial assets. We discuss financial intermediaries later in this chapter.

There are basic differences between a dealer and a financial intermediary. Unlike a dealer, a financial intermediary creates a claim against itself. A dealer simply buys and sells financial assets, smoothing out short-term price fluctuations. By contrast, typically a financial intermediary plans to hold the financial asset in order to achieve a desired long-term asset/liability objective.

MARKET PARTICIPANTS

The participants in U.S. financial markets that issue and purchase financial claims include households, business entities (corporations and partnerships), the U.S. government and its agencies, state and local governments, and foreign entities. The last category includes foreign governments (called *sovereigns*), supranational agencies (such as the World Bank and the Asian Development Bank), foreign corporations, and individuals.

Finally, while we have focused on market participants who create and/or exchange financial assets, a broader definition of market participants would include regulators of financial markets. We discuss regulation later in this chapter.

Financial Institutions

Business entities include non-financial and financial enterprises. Non-financial enterprises manufacture products (e.g., cars, steel, computers) and/or provide non-financial services (e.g., transportation, utilities, computer programming). Financial enterprises, more popularly referred to as *financial institutions*, provide services related to one or more of the following:

1. transforming financial assets acquired through the market and constituting them into a different, and more widely preferable, type of asset— which becomes their liability. This is the function performed by *financial intermediaries*, the most important type of financial institution (and also the oldest, except for pawn shops).
2. exchanging of financial assets on behalf of customers
3. exchanging of financial assets for their own account
4. assisting in the creation of financial assets for their customers and then selling those financial assets to other market participants
5. providing investment advice to other market participants
6. managing the portfolios of other market participants

Financial intermediaries include depository institutions (commercial banks, savings and loan associations, savings banks, and credit unions), who acquire the bulk of their funds by offering their liabilities to the public mostly in the form of deposits; insurance companies (life and property and casualty companies); pension funds; and finance companies. Deposit-accepting, or depository institutions, are discussed in the next chapter. The other financial intermediaries are covered in Chapters 3 and 4.

The second and third services in the list above are the broker and dealer functions discussed earlier. The fourth service is referred to as underwriting. As will be explained in Chapter 3, typically a financial institution that provides an underwriting service also provides a brokerage and/or dealer service.

Some non-financial enterprises have subsidiaries that provide financial services. For example, many large manufacturing firms have subsidiaries that provide financing for the parent company's customer. These financial institutions are called *captive finance companies*. Examples include General Motors Acceptance Corporation (a subsidiary of General Motors) and General Electric Credit Corporation (a subsidiary of General Electric).

Role of Financial Intermediaries

As we have seen, financial intermediaries obtain funds by issuing financial claims against themselves to market participants, then investing those funds. The investments made by financial intermediaries—their assets—can be in loans and/or securities. These investments are referred to as *direct investments.* Market participants who hold the financial claims issued by financial intermediaries are said to have made *indirect investments.*

Two examples will illustrate this. Most readers of this book are familiar with what a commercial bank does. Commercial banks accept deposits and may use the proceeds to lend funds to consumers and businesses. The deposits represent the IOU of the commercial bank and a financial asset owned by the depositor. The loan represents an IOU of the borrowing entity and a financial asset of the commercial bank. The commercial bank has made a direct investment in the borrowing entity; the depositor effectively has made an indirect investment in that borrowing entity.

As a second example, consider an investment company, a financial intermediary such as we focus on in Chapter 4, which pools the funds of market participants and uses those funds to buy a portfolio of securities such as stocks and bonds. Investors providing funds to the investment company receive an equity claim that entitles the investor to a pro rata share of the outcome of the portfolio. The equity claim is issued by the investment company. The portfolio of financial assets acquired by the investment company represents a direct investment that it has made. By owning an equity claim against the investment company, those who invest in the investment company have made an indirect investment.

We have stressed that financial intermediaries play the basic role of transforming financial assets that are less desirable for a large part of the public into other financial assets—their own liabilities—which are more widely preferred by the public. This transformation involves at least one of four economic functions:

Providing Maturity Intermediation. In our example of the commercial bank, two things should be noted. First, the maturity of at least a portion of the deposits accepted is typically short term. For example, certain types of deposit are payable upon demand. Others have a specific maturity date, but most are less than two years. Second, the maturity of the loans made by a commercial bank may be considerably longer than two years. In the absence of a commercial bank, the borrower would have to borrow for a shorter term or find an entity that is willing to invest for the length of the loan sought, and/or investors who make deposits in the bank would have to commit funds for a longer length of time than they want. The commercial bank by issuing its own financial claims in essence transforms a longer-term asset into a shorter-term one by giving the borrower a loan for the length of time sought and the investor/depositor a financial asset for the desired investment horizon. This function of a financial intermediary is called *maturity intermediation*.

Maturity intermediation has two implications for financial markets. First, investors have more choices concerning maturity for their investments; borrowers have more choices for the length of their debt obligations. Second, because investors are reluctant to commit funds for a long period of time, they will require that long-term borrowers pay a higher interest rate than on short-term borrowing. In contrast, a financial intermediary will be willing to make longer-term loans, and at a lower cost to the borrower than an individual investor would, by counting on successive deposits providing the funds until maturity (although at some risk—see below). Thus, the second implication is that the cost of longer-term borrowing is likely to be reduced.

Providing Risk Reduction via Diversification.   Consider the example of the investor who places funds in an investment company. Suppose that the investment company invests the funds received in the stock of a large number of companies. By doing so, the investment company has diversified and reduced its risk.[4] Investors who have a small sum to invest would find it difficult to achieve the same degree of diversification because they would not have sufficient funds to buy shares of a large number of companies. Yet by investing in the investment company for the same sum of money investors can accomplish this diversification, thereby reducing risk.

This economic function of financial intermediaries—transforming more risky assets into less risky ones—is called *diversification*. While individual investors can do it on their own, they may not be able to do it as cost-effectively as a financial intermediary, depending on the amount of funds they have to invest. Attaining cost-effective diversification in order to reduce risk by purchasing the financial assets of a financial intermediary is an important economic benefit for financial markets.

Reducing the Costs of Contracting and Information Processing.   Investors purchasing financial assets should take the time to develop skills necessary to understand how to evaluate an investment. Once those skills are developed, investors should apply them to the analysis of specific financial assets that are candidates for purchase (or subsequent sale). Investors who want to make a loan to a consumer or business will need to write the loan contract (or hire an attorney to do so).

While there are some people who enjoy devoting leisure time to this task, most prefer to use that time for what it is intended—leisure. Most of us find

---

[4] An explanation of how a certain type of risk can be reduced by diversification is presented in Chapter 5.

that leisure time is in short supply, so to sacrifice it, we have to be compensated. The form of compensation could be a higher return that we obtain from an investment.

In addition to the opportunity cost of the time to process the information about the financial asset and its issuer, there is the cost of acquiring that information. All these costs are called *information processing costs.* The costs of writing loan contracts are referred to as *contracting costs.* And there is another dimension to contracting costs, the cost of enforcing the terms of the loan agreement.

With this in mind, consider our two examples of financial intermediaries—the commercial bank and the investment company. Their staffs include investment professionals who are trained to analyze financial assets and manage them. In the case of loan agreements, either standardized contracts can be prepared, or legal counsel can be part of the professional staff to write contracts involving more complex transactions. The investment professionals can monitor compliance with the terms of the loan agreement and take any necessary action to protect the interests of the financial intermediary. The employment of such professionals is cost-effective for financial intermediaries because investing funds is their normal business.

In other words, there are economies of scale in contracting and processing information about financial assets, because of the amount of funds managed by financial intermediaries. The lower costs accrue to the benefit of the investor who purchases a financial claim of the financial intermediary and to the issuers of financial assets, who benefit from a lower borrowing cost.

Providing a Payments Mechanism. While the previous three economic functions may not have been immediately obvious, this last function should be. Most transactions made today are not done with cash. Instead, payments are made using checks, credit cards, debit cards, and electronic transfers of funds. These methods for making payments are provided by certain financial intermediaries.

At one time, non-cash payments were restricted to checks written against non-interest-bearing accounts at commercial banks. Similar check writing privileges were provided later by savings and loan associations and savings banks, and by certain types of investment companies. Payment by credit card was also at one time the exclusive domain of commercial banks, but now other depository institutions offer this service. Debit cards are offered by various financial intermediaries. A debit card differs from a credit card in that, in the latter case, a bill is sent to the credit cardholder periodically (usually once a month) requesting payment for transactions that have been made in the past. With a debit card, funds are immediately withdrawn (i.e., debited) from the purchaser's account at the time the transaction takes place.

The ability to make payments without the use of cash is critical for the functioning of a financial market. In short, depository institutions transform assets that cannot be used to make payments into other assets that offer that property.

REGULATION OF FINANCIAL MARKETS

Because financial markets play a prominent role in any economy, governments have deemed it necessary to regulate certain aspects of these markets. In the U.S., regulation occurs at the federal or state level, and in some cases both. Regulation has taken three forms: (1) regulating the disclosure of information that issuers must supply potential investors, (2) regulating the trading activities in some financial markets, and (3) regulating various aspects of financial institutions.

The regulatory structure in the United States is largely the result of financial crises that have occurred at various times. Most regulatory mechanisms are the product of the stock market crash of 1929 and the Great Depression in the 1930s. Some of the regulations that exist today may make little economic sense in today's financial market, but they can be traced back to some abuse that legislators encountered, or thought they encountered, at one time.

It is the regulatory system that has separated the activities performed by different financial institutions. Today, however, it is very difficult to pigeonhole a company in the financial services business as a particular type of financial institution. Regulatory reform gradually has permitted financial institutions to offer a wider range of financial services, so that today there exist "financial supermarkets." One of the major focuses of current and prospective regulatory reform is the distinction between commercial banking and investment banking, a separation that was made in the 1930s. We'll discuss this in the next chapter.

Regulatory Reform

Regulatory reform is driven by several factors. First, as we note above, a financial crisis brings about regulatory reform. Here are three examples since the 1930s. At one time, the maximum interest rate that depository institutions were permitted to pay on certain deposit accounts was set by government regulation. When interest rates rose above the ceiling, deposits inevitably were withdrawn from deposit institutions and used to purchase securities, that is, to make direct investments. (This process is referred to as *disintermediation*.) When this threatened the economic well-being of depository institutions, these interest rate ceilings were phased out.[5]

---

[5] This change hurt depository institutions at the same time by raising the cost of their funds.

The savings and loan crisis is a second example. Because of the widespread financial difficulties encountered by these financial intermediaries, federal legislation was passed in 1989 that changed the regulatory structure of deposit-accepting institutions. Finally, the stock market crash of October 1987 produced some regulatory reform with respect to trading in the stock market and the market for derivative stock market instruments (stock index futures and stock index options).

A second motivation for regulatory reform is the development of new financial products (financial assets and derivative instruments), which has forced the introduction of new regulations with respect to the trading of these products and their use by regulated financial institutions. An example of the former is introduction in the early 1980s of derivative instruments based on a stock index. Permission to invest in low investment-grade (or junk) bonds by savings and loan associations and the subsequent withdrawal of this permission in 1989 is an example of the latter.

Globalization of the world financial markets is the third reason. Regulations established in the U.S. are enforceable only in the U.S. If certain regulations have little economic merit and simply impede an otherwise worthwhile financial transaction, market participants can sidestep those regulations by transacting outside the U.S. As financial activities move outside the U.S., a reexamination of the questionable regulations forces reform.

Another impact of globalization is that it prevents financial institutions in countries that have such regulations from competing effectively for business. Here a good example is regulation of the Japanese financial market. While at one time Japanese banks had sufficient funds to provide funding for non-Japanese domiciled multinational companies, regulations prevented them from capitalizing on these financial opportunities. Lifting of these regulations permitted them to compete effectively with major non-Japanese banks.

FINANCIAL INNOVATION

Since the 1960s, there has been a surge in significant financial innovations. Observers of financial markets have categorized these innovations in different ways. Here are just three ways suggested to classify these innovations.

The Economic Council of Canada classifies financial innovations into the following three broad categories:[6]

---

[6] *Globalization and Canada's Financial Markets* (Ottawa, Canada: Supply and Services Canada, 1989), p. 32.

- *market-broadening instruments*, which increase the liquidity of markets and the availability of funds by attracting new investors and offering new opportunities for borrowers;

- *risk-management instruments*, which reallocate financial risks to those who are less averse to them or who have offsetting exposure, and who are presumably better able to shoulder them; and

- *arbitraging instruments and processes*, which enable investors and borrowers to take advantage of differences (or "spreads") in costs and returns between markets, and which reflect differences in the perception of risks, as well as in information, taxation, and regulations.[7]

Another classification system of financial innovations based on more specific functions has been suggested by the Bank for International Settlements: *price-risk-transferring innovations, credit-risk-transferring instruments, liquidity-generating innovations, credit-generating instruments,* and *equity-generating instruments*.[8] Price-risk-transferring innovations are those that provide market participants with more efficient means for dealing with price or exchange rate risk. Reallocating the risk of default is the function of credit-risk-transferring instruments. Liquidity-generating innovations do three things: (1) they increase the liquidity of the market, (2) they allow borrowers to draw upon new sources of funds, and (3) they allow market participants to circumvent capital constraints imposed by regulations. Instruments to increase the amount of debt funds available to borrowers and to increase the capital base of financial and non-financial institutions are the functions of credit-generating and equity-generating innovations, respectively.

Finally, Professor Stephen Ross suggests two classes of financial innovation: (1) new financial products (financial assets and derivative instruments) better suited to the circumstances of the time (e.g., to inflation) and to the markets in which they trade, and (2) dynamic trading strategies that primarily use these financial products.[9]

---

[7] The Council also notes that: "Most instruments will contribute simultaneously to the broadening of markets, the management of risks, and arbitraging between markets. The classification above is based on the major role played by an instrument. For example, while an instrument may increase the liquidity of markets and assist in the management of risk, if it is mainly used to arbitrage between two markets, it will fall in the third category."

[8] Bank for International Settlements, *Recent Innovations in International Banking* (Basle: BIS, April 1986).

[9] Stephen A. Ross, "Institutional Markets, Financial Marketing, and Financial Innovation," *Journal of Finance* (July 1989), p. 541.

One of the purposes of this book is to explain these financial innovations. For now, let's look at why financial innovation takes place.

There are two extreme views of financial innovation.[10] There are some who believe that the major impetus for innovation has been the endeavor to circumvent (or "arbitrage") regulations and find loopholes in tax rules.[11] At the other extreme, some hold that the essence of innovation is the introduction of financial instruments that are more efficient for redistributing risks among market participants.

It would appear that many of the innovations that have passed the test of time and have not disappeared have been innovations that provided more efficient mechanisms for redistributing risk. Other innovations may just represent a more efficient way of doing things. Indeed, if we consider the ultimate causes of financial innovation,[12] the following emerge as the most important:

1. increased volatility of interest rates, inflation, equity prices, and exchange rates

2. advances in computer and telecommunication technologies

3. greater sophistication and educational training among professional market participants

4. financial intermediary competition

5. incentives to get around existing regulation and tax laws

6. changing global patterns of financial wealth

With increased volatility comes the need for certain market participants to protect themselves against unfavorable consequences. This means new or more efficient ways of risk-sharing in the financial market are needed. Many of the financial products require the use of computers to create and continually monitor them. To implement trading strategies using these financial products also requires computers, as well as telecommunication networks. Without advances in computer and telecommunication technologies, some innovations would not have been possible. Although financial products and trading strategies created by some market participants may be too complex for other market participants to use, the level of market sophistication, particu-

---

[10] Ian Cooper, "Financial Innovations: New Market Instruments," *Oxford Review of Economic Policy* (November 1986).

[11] Merton H. Miller, "Financial Innovation: The Last Twenty Years and the Next," *Journal of Financial and Quantitative Analysis* (December 1986), pp. 459–471.

[12] Cooper, "Financial Innovations," Table 9. We add inflation to the first category described.

larly in terms of mathematical understanding, has risen, permitting the acceptance of some complex products and trading strategies.[13]

As we discuss in the next two chapters, competition among financial institutions has brought forth and fostered the development of new products and markets. Regulations that impede the free flow of capital and competition among financial institutions (particularly interest rate ceilings) have fostered the development of financial products and trading strategies to get around these restrictions. Finally, the global pattern of financial wealth has transformed financial markets from local markets into global ones—that is, internationalized financial markets. Through technological advances and the reduction in trade and capital barriers, surplus funds in one country can be shifted more easily to those who need funds in another country. As a result, there has arisen a need for financial products and trading strategies to protect more efficiently against the adverse movements of foreign currencies.

As you read the chapters on the various sectors of the financial markets that we review in this book, be sure you understand the factors behind any innovations in that market.

SUMMARY

In this chapter we have explained the characteristics of financial assets and the markets where they are traded, and provided an overview of market participants. A financial (or intangible asset, or financial instrument or security) entitles the owner to future cash flows to be paid by the issuer as well as to the liquidation value of the asset. The claim can be either an equity or debt claim. The price of any financial asset is equal to the present value of the cash flow expected. Because of uncertainty about the cash flow, in nominal and inflation-adjusted dollars, there is risk in investing in financial assets. A derivative instrument is a contract whose value depends on the value of the underlying financial asset.

The two principal economic functions of a financial asset are (1) transferring funds from those who have surplus funds to invest to those who need funds to invest in tangible assets, and (2) transferring funds in such a way that redistributes the unavoidable risk associated with the cash flow generated by tangible assets among those seeking and those providing the funds. The chief economic function of a derivative instrument is to provide ways to control risk.

---

[13] Large compensation packages offered in some sectors of the financial market have attracted "rocket scientists" from the manufacturing and service industries to the financial services industry.

Financial markets provide the following three additional functions beyond that of financial assets themselves: (1) they provide a mechanism for determining the price (or, equivalently, the required return) of financial assets, (2) they make assets more liquid, and (3) they reduce the costs of exchanging assets. The costs associated with transacting are search costs and information costs.

Typically, futures markets offer three advantages over spot (cash) markets: (1) lower transactions costs, (2) faster speed at which transactions can be completed, and (3) greater liquidity. For these reasons, transactions typically take place first in the futures markets; hence, the futures market is often the price discovery market.

Financial assets possess varying degrees of properties that either add to or detract from their attractiveness to different classes of investors and issuers. These properties are classified as moneyness, divisibility and denomination, reversibility, yield and return, term to maturity, liquidity, and predictability or risk.

There are various ways to classify financial markets: money (or short-term) versus capital markets, debt versus equity markets, primary versus secondary markets, and cash versus derivative markets. Another classification is based on the type of organizational structure: auction versus over-the-counter versus intermediated markets.

Participants in financial markets include households, business entities, the U.S. and state and local governments, and foreign entities, as well as regulators. Financial institutions provide various types of financial services: broker and dealer functions and underwriting functions.

A special group of financial institutions are called financial intermediaries. These entities obtain funds by issuing claims to market participants and use these funds to purchase financial assets. Intermediaries transform assets they acquire into assets—their liabilities—that are more attractive to the public in four ways: (1) providing maturity intermediation, (2) providing risk reduction via diversification at lower cost, (3) reducing the cost of contracting and information processing, and (4) providing a payments mechanism.

Many of the regulations in the U.S. financial market have their origins in the economic and financial crises of the 1930s. Regulation has taken three forms: (1) regulating the disclosure of information that must be reported, (2) regulating trading activities in financial markets, and (3) regulating the permissible activities of financial institutions. There has been significant regulatory reform in the 1980s.

Financial innovation has increased dramatically since the 1960s, particularly in the late 1970s. While financial innovation can be the result of arbitrary regulations and tax rules, innovations that persist after regulations or tax rules have been changed to prevent exploitation are frequently those that have provided a more efficient means for redistributing risk.

QUESTIONS

1. In September 1990 a study by the U.S. Congress, Office of Technology Assessment, entitled "Electronic Bulls & Bears: U.S. Securities Markets and Information Technology," included this statement:

   Securities markets have five basic functions in a capitalistic economy:

   1. they make it possible for corporations and governmental units to raise capital;
   2. they help to allocate capital toward productive uses;
   3. they provide an opportunity for people to increase their savings by investing in them;
   4. they reveal investors' judgments about the potential earning capacity of corporations, thus giving guidance to corporate managers; and
   5. they generate employment and income.

   For each of the functions cited above, explain how financial markets (or securities markets, in the parlance of this Congressional study) perform each function.

2. Your broker is recommending you purchase U.S. government bonds. Here is the pitch:

   Listen, in these times of uncertainty, with many companies going bankrupt, it makes sense to play it safe and purchase long-term government bonds. They're issued by the U.S. government, so they are risk-free.

   How would you respond to the broker?

3. You just inherited 30,000 shares of a company you have never heard of, ABC Corporation. You call your broker to find out if you have finally struck it rich. After several minutes she comes back on the telephone and says: "I don't have a clue about these shares. It's too bad they are not traded in a financial market. That would make life a lot easier for you." What does she mean by this?

4. You are at a dinner party with a friend from business school. After graduation, you have both decided to accept positions at a commercial bank. At the party, someone says to you both: "What worthless jobs. Those institutions add nothing of value to society." Walking away, you whisper to your friend: "This guy obviously doesn't appreciate the role of financial intermediaries." Explain what you mean.

5. In a 1989 study entitled "Globalization and Canada's Financial Markets," a research report prepared for the Economic Council of Canada, the following was reported:

    An important feature of the increasing significance of some aspects of financial activity is the greater use of financial markets and instruments that intermediate funds directly—a process called "market intermediation," which involves the issuance of, and trading in, securities such as bonds or stocks—as opposed to "financial intermediation," in which the financial institution raises funds by issuing a claim on itself and provides funds in the form of loans.

    a. What are the implications of the shift from financial intermediation to market intermediation for commercial banks?

    b. What do you think some of the obstacles are in market intermediation?

6. An article in the January 1989 issue of *Institutional Investor* stated that:

    In a business where First Boston introduces a new product on Monday and Salomon wants to be trading it by Wednesday and Goldman will issue its own version by Friday, the ability to develop systems to support such products is of great bottom line significance.

    As this quotation suggests, advances in computer technology and systems have been important causes of financial innovation. Discuss other causes of financial innovation.

2

DEPOSITORY INSTITUTIONS

LEARNING OBJECTIVES

After reading this chapter you will understand:

- the role of depository institutions.

- how a depository institution generates income.

- differences between commercial banks, savings and loan associations, savings banks, and credit unions.

- the asset/liability problem all depository institutions face.

- how several financial innovations have helped the asset/liability management problem of depository institutions.

- who regulates commercial banks and thrifts and the types of regulations imposed.

- the funding sources available to commercial banks and thrifts.

- the capital requirements imposed on commercial banks and savings and loan associations.

Depository institutions include commercial banks (or simply banks), savings and loan associations (S&Ls), savings banks, and credit unions. All are financial intermediaries that accept deposits. These deposits represent the liabilities (debt) of the deposit-accepting institution. With the funds raised through deposits and other funding sources, depository institutions both make direct loans to various entities and invest in securities. Their income is derived from two sources: the income generated from the loans they make and the securities they purchase, and fee income.

It is common to refer to S&Ls, savings banks, and credit unions as "thrifts," which are specialized types of depository institutions. Traditionally, thrifts have not been permitted to accept deposits transferable by check (negotiable), or, as they are more popularly known, checking accounts. Instead, they have obtained funds primarily by tapping the savings of households. Since the early 1980s, however, thrifts have been allowed to offer negotiable deposits entirely equivalent to checking accounts, although they bear a different name (NOW accounts, share drafts). By law, the investments that thrifts are permitted to make have been much more limited than those permitted to banks. Recent legislation, however, has expanded the range of investments allowed by thrifts so that they can compete more effectively with banks.

Depository institutions are highly regulated because of the important role that they play in the country's financial system. Demand deposit accounts are the principal means that individuals and business entities use for making payments, and government monetary policy is implemented through the banking system. Because of their important role, depository institutions are afforded special privileges such as access to federal deposit insurance and access to a government entity that provides funds for liquidity or emergency needs. For example, the deposits of most depository institutions are currently insured up to $100,000 per account. We'll give examples of how depository institutions have access to emergency funds later in this chapter.

In this chapter we will look at depository institutions—the nature of their liabilities, where they invest their funds, and how they are regulated. Before we examine the specific institutions, we begin with an overview of the asset/liability problem that a depository institution must manage.

ASSET/LIABILITY PROBLEM OF DEPOSITORY INSTITUTIONS

The asset/liability problem that depository institutions face is quite simple to explain—although not necessarily easy to solve. A depository institution seeks to earn a positive spread between the assets it invests in (loans and securities) and the cost of its funds (deposits and other sources). The spread is referred to as *spread income* or *margin.* The spread income should allow the institution to meet operating expenses and earn a fair profit on its capital.

In generating spread income a depository institution faces several risks. These include *credit risk, regulatory risk,* and *funding* (or *interest rate) risk.* Credit risk, also called *default risk,* refers to the risk that a borrower will default on a loan obligation to the depository institution or that the issuer of a security that the depository institution holds will default on its obligation. Regulatory risk is the risk that regulators will change the rules so as to impact the earnings of the institution unfavorably.

Funding Risk

Funding risk can be explained best by an illustration. Suppose that a depository institution raises $100 million by issuing a deposit account that has a maturity of one year and by agreeing to pay an interest rate of 7%. Ignoring for the time being the fact that the depository institution cannot invest the entire $100 million because of reserve requirements, which we discuss later in this chapter, suppose that $100 million is invested in a U.S. government security that matures in 15 years paying an interest rate of 9%. Because the funds are invested in a U.S. government security, there is no credit risk in this case.

It seems at first that the depository institution has locked in a spread of 2% (9% minus 7%). This spread can be counted on only for the first year, though, because the spread in future years will depend on the interest rate this depository institution will have to pay depositors in order to raise $100 million after the one-year time deposit matures. If interest rates decline, the spread will increase because the depository institution has locked in the 9% rate. If interest rates rise, however, the spread income will decline. In fact, if this depository institution must pay more than 9% to depositors for the next 14 years, the spread will be negative. That is, it will cost the depository institution more to finance the government securities than it will earn on the funds invested in those securities.

In our example, the depository institution has borrowed short (borrowed for one year) and lent long (invested for 15 years). This policy will benefit from a decline in interest rates but be disadvantaged if interest rates rise. Suppose the institution could have borrowed funds for 15 years at 7% and invested in a U.S. government security maturing in one year earning 9%—borrowed long (15 years) and lent short (one year). A rise in interest rates will benefit the depository institution because it can then reinvest the proceeds from the maturing one-year government security in a new one-year government security offering a higher interest rate. In this case a decline in interest rates will reduce the spread. If interest rates fall below 7%, there will be a negative spread.

All depository institutions face this funding problem. Managers of a depository institution who have particular expectations about the future direction of interest rates will seek to benefit from these expectations. Those who expect interest rates to rise may pursue a policy to borrow funds for a long time horizon (i.e., borrow long) and lend funds for a short time horizon (i.e., lend short).[1] If interest rates are expected to drop, managers may elect to borrow short and lend long.

The problem of pursuing a strategy of positioning a depository institution based on expectations is that considerable adverse financial consequences will result if those expectations are not realized. The evidence on interest rate forecasting suggests that it is a risky business. We doubt if there are managers of depository institutions who have the ability to forecast interest rate moves so consistently that the institution can benefit should the forecast be realized. The goal of management is to lock in a spread as best as possible, not to wager on interest rate movements.

Inherent in any balance sheet of a depository institution is funding risk exposure. Managers must be willing to accept some exposure, but they can take various measures to address the interest rate sensitivity of the institution's liabilities and its assets. A depository institution will have an asset/liability committee that is responsible for monitoring the interest rate risk exposure. There are several asset/liability strategies for controlling interest rate risk. While a discussion of these strategies is beyond the scope of this chapter, we can point out here that development of particular financial instruments reflects the asset/liability problem that depository institutions seek to solve. Three examples are floating-rate notes, adjustable-rate mortgages, and interest rate swaps.

Financial Innovations and Asset/Liability Management

Floating-Rate Notes.   Depository institutions, primarily banks, have been the major issuers of floating-rate notes. As we will explain in Chapter 15, a floating-rate note is a debt instrument whose interest rate changes periodically according to some interest rate benchmark. A common benchmark is the London Interbank Offered Rate (LIBOR), which is an interest rate that reflects the marginal, overnight, or short-term wholesale cost of funds for the global banking system. Suppose that a bank borrows $50 million by issuing five-year

---

[1] A financial innovation that we describe later in this chapter, interest rate swaps, lets a depository institution accomplish this.

floating-rate notes. The interest rate on these notes resets every six months on the basis of LIBOR at the time plus a risk premium. Ignoring reserve requirements, suppose also that the bank makes a loan to a corporation where the interest rate on the loan resets at LIBOR plus 2% every six months. Holding aside credit risk, the bank has locked in a spread of 2%.

Adjustable-Rate Mortgages. Another type of instrument developed by depository institutions to address funding risk is the adjustable-rate mortgage. A mortgage is a pledge of real estate to secure the payment of a loan. Prior to the 1980s, the interest rate on mortgage loans was fixed throughout the life of the loan, typically for between 15 and 30 years. Because the funds obtained to make mortgage loans are typically short-term, the interest rate risk exposure that the depository institution faces is substantial. In the 1980s, adjustable-rate mortgages became popular. With this type of mortgage the interest rate on the loan adjusts periodically—every month, six months, year, two years, or three years—according to a spread on some benchmark interest rate.

Suppose that the funds raised by a depository institution to invest in mortgages are from deposits that have a maturity of roughly one year and for which the interest rate paid depositors is usually around 0.5% above the interest rate on a U.S. government security with a maturity of one year. The institution then might reset the adjustable-rate mortgage interest rate every year at a level 1.5% above the interest rate on a one-year U.S. government security. Then, once again holding aside credit risk, the depository institution has locked in a spread. In this example it is 1%. We provide more information on adjustable-rate mortgages in Chapter 17.

Interest Rate Swaps. As a final example of a financial innovation to improve asset/liability management, consider a depository institution that raises $100 million for 10 years at a fixed interest rate of 8% and then lends that money to a corporation for 10 years. The loan calls for an interest rate that changes every year. The interest rate that the corporation agrees to pay is LIBOR plus 2.5%. Suppose LIBOR is 7.5% when the loan is initiated. This means that in the first year the corporation will pay 10% (LIBOR of 7.5% plus 2.5%). The depository institution locks in a spread of 2% for the first year.

The interest rate risk exposure for this depository institution is that interest rates, and therefore LIBOR, will decline. Should LIBOR fall below 5.5%, the interest rate for the loan for that one-year period would be less than the depository institution must pay on the money it borrowed at 8%. Thus, the depository institution would realize a negative spread for that period.

Suppose that the depository institution could find another party that would be willing to enter into a transaction so that: (1) every year it will pay the depository institution 7.5% of $100 million, and (2) at the same time the depository institution will pay the other party LIBOR plus 1% of $100 million. Each year the outcome of this transaction, coupled with the fixed interest rate that the depository institution must pay on the money it borrowed and the interest income it receives on the loan it made to the corporation, is as follows:

1. depository institution pays 7.5% of $100 million
2. depository institution receives from other party 8% of $100 million
3. depository institution receives LIBOR plus 2.5% of $100 million from loan to corporation
4. depository institution pays LIBOR plus 1% of $100 million to other party

The net result is that, regardless of what happens to LIBOR, the depository institution has locked in a spread of 1% on the $100 million.

The arrangement that we have described between the depository institution and the other party is called an *interest rate swap*. This simple illustration demonstrates how it can be employed for asset/liability management. Probably you have questions such as: Who would be willing to take the other side of this transaction? How does one find this other party? How are the terms of the transaction determined? Why couldn't this depository institution just issue a floating-rate note rather than issue a fixed-rate note? We'll answer these questions in Chapter 20 when we discuss interest rate swaps more fully.

Liquidity Concerns

Besides facing credit risk and interest rate risk, a depository institution must be prepared to satisfy withdrawals of funds by depositors and to provide loans to customers. There are several ways that a depository institution can accommodate withdrawal and loan demand: (1) attract additional deposits, (2) use existing securities as collateral for borrowing from a federal agency or other financial institution such as an investment bank, (3) sell securities that it owns, or (4) raise short-term funds in the money market.

The first alternative is self-explanatory. The second has to do with the privilege we mentioned earlier. Banks are allowed to borrow at the discount window of the Federal Reserve Banks. The fourth alternative primarily includes using marketable securities owned as collateral for raising funds in the repurchase agreement market. This will be clear when we discuss the money market in Chapter 13.

The third alternative, selling securities that it owns, requires that the depository institution invest a portion of its funds in securities that are both liquid and have little price risk. By price risk we refer to the prospect that the selling price of the security will be less than its purchase price, resulting in a loss. For example, as we explain in Chapters 12 and 14, while a 30-year U.S. government security is a highly liquid security, its price would change dramatically as interest rates rise. A price decline of, say, 25% would not be uncommon in a volatile interest rate environment. A 30-year government bond is therefore highly liquid, but exposes the depository institution to substantial price risk.

In general, as we explain in Chapter 12, short-term securities entail little price risk. It is therefore short-term, or money market, debt obligations that a depository institution will hold as an investment to satisfy withdrawals and customer loan demand. It does this chiefly by lending federal funds, an investment vehicle that we will discuss later in this chapter. The term to maturity of the securities it holds affect the amount that depository institutions can borrow from some federal agency because only short-term securities are acceptable collateral.

Securities held for the purpose of satisfying net withdrawals and customer loan demands are sometimes referred to as "secondary reserves."[2] A disadvantage of holding secondary reserves is that securities with short maturities offer a lower yield than securities with a longer maturity in most interest rate environments. The percentage of a depository institution's assets held as secondary reserves will depend both on the institution's ability to raise funds from the other sources and on its management's risk preference for liquidity (safety) versus yield.

Depository institutions hold liquid assets not only for operational purposes, but also because of the regulatory requirements that we discuss below.

COMMERCIAL BANKS

In 1988, there were about 13,500 commercial banks in the U.S. A commercial bank can be chartered either by the state (state-chartered banks) or by the federal government (national banks). Of the 13,500 banks, about 60% were state-chartered. All national banks must be members of the Federal Reserve System and must be insured by the Bank Insurance Fund (BIF), which is administered by the Federal Deposit Insurance Corporation (FDIC). While federal depository insurance has existed since the 1930s, and the insurance

---

[2] Roland I. Robinson, *The Management of Bank Funds* (New York: McGraw-Hill, 1962), p. 15. The term secondary reserves is used because primary reserves are the reserves required by the Federal Reserve Board that we will discuss later. If you looked at the balance sheet of a depository institution, you will not see the term "secondary reserves" on it. A depository institution invests in short-term or money market instruments for reasons other than liquidity and does not report the purpose for which it acquires securities.

program is administered by the FDIC, BIF was created early in 1989 by the Financial Institutions Reform, Recovery, and Enforcement Act of 1989 (FIRREA). Coverage is currently $100,000 per account. However, there have been several proposals to restructure deposit insurance coverage, which we will discuss later.

State-chartered banks may elect to join the Federal Reserve System. Their deposits may be insured by BIF or by some other non-federal insurance program. While most banks elect to have their deposits insured by the BIF, a minority elect to be members of the Federal Reserve System. In 1988, of the approximately 9,000 state-chartered banks, only about 1,000 are Federal Reserve member banks. In spite of the large number of banks that elect not to be members of the Federal Reserve System, banks that are members hold more than 70% of all deposits in the U.S. Moreover, with the passage of the Depository Institutions Deregulation and Monetary Control Act of 1980 (DIDMCA), the reserve requirements that we shall discuss below for banks that are members of the Federal Reserve System apply also to state-chartered banks.

The size of banks in the U.S. varies greatly as can be seen from Table 2-1,

TABLE 2-1	DISTRIBUTION OF FDIC COMMERCIAL BANKS BY SIZE AS OF DECEMBER 1988			
ASSET SIZE (IN MILLIONS)	NUMBER OF BANKS	% OF BANKS	ASSETS (IN BILLIONS)	% OF ASSETS
Less than $5.0	185	1.4	$ 0.6	<0.05
$ 5.0–$ 9.9	731	5.6	5.7	0.2
$ 10.0–$ 24.9	3,225	24.5	56.2	1.8
$ 25.0–$ 49.9	3,383	25.7	122.1	3.9
$ 50.0–$ 99.9	2,784	21.2	194.1	6.2
$100.0–$499.9	2,249	17.1	440.2	14.1
$500 or more	582	4.4	2,311.8	73.8
Total	13,139	100.0	$3,130.7	100.0

Source: The data for this table come from Table No. 799, Selected Financial Institutions—Number and Assets, by Asset Size: 1988, *Statistical Abstract of the United States: 1990* (Department of Commerce, Bureau of the Census).

TABLE 2-2	TEN LARGEST U.S. BANK HOLDING COMPANIES AS OF AUGUST 1991 RANKED BY TOTAL ASSETS AS OF MARCH 1991*

| | | IN MILLIONS | |
RANKING	BANK	TOTAL ASSETS	EQUITY CAPITAL
1	Citicorp	$216,914	$10,416
2	BankAmerica Corp.[1]	195,030	11,069
3	Chemical Banking Corp.[2]	137,259	7,433
4	Nations Bank[3]	116,280	6,259
5	Chase Manhattan Corp.	98,089	4,811
6	J. P. Morgan & Co., Inc.	93,835	5,401
7	Wells Fargo & Co.	55,691	3,282
8	First Interstate Bancorp	50,402	2,874
9	First Chicago Corp.	49,677	2,842
10	PNC Financial Corp.	44,546	2,654

*The rankings reflect three mergers in 1991 indicated below.

[1]After the merger of BankAmerica and Security Pacific.

[2]After the merger of Chemical Banking Corporation and Manufacturers Hanover.

[3]Entity resulting from the merger of NCNB Corporation and C&S/Sovran Corporation.

Source: Data provided by Simon G. Davidson of Ferguson & Co. (Washington, D.C.).

which shows the distribution for FDIC banks as of December 1988. Also shown in the same table are total assets for each asset size. As can be seen, while less than 5% of the banks have total assets in excess of $500 million, these banks hold almost three-quarters of the total assets. The ten largest U.S. bank holding companies as of August 1991, in terms of total assets, are listed in Table 2-2. (A bank holding company is a corporation that owns stock in one or more banks.) The rankings reflect three major bank mergers in 1991.

Table 2-3 shows as of September 1991 the ten largest banks in the world measured in U.S. dollars and ranked in terms of total assets. Seven of the ten largest banks in the world are Japanese, two are French, and one is German. The listing in Table 2-3, however, is misleading because regulations differ across countries. Specifically, U.S. regulations prevent greater degrees of leverage for large banks; Japanese regulation does not apply this brake.

TABLE 2-3   TEN LARGEST BANKS IN THE WORLD AS OF SEPTEMBER 1991 RANKED BY TOTAL ASSETS

		IN MILLIONS OF U.S. DOLLARS	
RANK	BANK NAME (COUNTRY)	TOTAL ASSETS	TOTAL EQUITY
1	Dai-Ichi Kangyo Bank (Japan)	$406,404	$11,874
2	Mitsui Taiyo Kobe Bank (Japan)*	405,581	11,653
3	Mitsubishi Bank Ltd (Japan)*	379,209	12,096
4	Sumitomo Bank Ltd (Japan)	370,438	12,981
5	Fuji Bank (Japan)	365,064	11,454
6	Sanwa Bank (Japan)	356,453	11,130
7	Credit Agricole (France)	302,984	13,258
8	Industrial Bank of Japan (Japan)*	287,847	9,508
9	Credit Lyonnais (France)	285,238	13,843
10	Deutsche Bank AG (Germany)	265,049	10,040

*Fiscal year end March 31, 1991. All others are fiscal year end 1990.

Source: The data was provided by Jan D. Slee and Elaine Robbins of the EURASTAR Division of Sleigh Corporation, Franklin Lakes, New Jersey.

Bank Services

Commercial banks provide numerous services in our financial system. The services can be broadly classified as follows: (1) individual banking, (2) institutional banking, and (3) global banking.[3] Of course, different banks are more active in certain of these activities than others. For example, money center banks (defined later) are more active in global banking.

Individual banking encompasses consumer lending, residential mortgage lending, consumer installment loans, credit card financing, automobile and boat financing, brokerage services, student loans, and individual-oriented financial investment services such as personal trust and investment services. Interest and fee income are generated from mortgage lending and credit card financing. Mortgage lending is more popularly referred to as mortgage banking. We'll discuss this activity and how fee income is generated in

---

[3] This classification of activities and their components is adapted from the 1988 Annual Report Part Two of The Chase Manhattan Corporation, p. 92.

Chapter 17. Fee income is generated from brokerage services and financial investment services.

Loans to non-financial corporations, financial corporations (such as life insurance companies), and government entities (state and local governments in the U.S. and foreign governments) fall into the category of institutional banking. Also included in this category are commercial real estate financing, leasing activities[4] and factoring.[5] In the case of leasing, a bank may be involved in leasing equipment either as lessors,[6] as lenders to lessors, or as purchasers of leases. Loans and leasing generate interest income, and other services that banks offer institutional customers generate fee income. These services include management of the assets of private and public pension funds, fiduciary and custodial services, and cash management services such as account maintenance, check clearing, and electronic transfers.

It is in the area of global banking that banks have begun to compete head-to-head with another financial institution discussed in the next chapter, investment banking firms. Global banking covers a broad range of activities involving corporate financing and capital market and foreign exchange products and services. Most global banking activities generate fee income rather than interest income.

Corporate financing involves two components. First is the procuring of funds for a bank's customers. This can go beyond traditional bank loans to involve the underwriting of securities. As we shall explain later, legislation in the form of the Glass–Steagall Act limits bank activities in this area. In assisting its customers in obtaining funds, banks also provide bankers acceptances, letters of credit, and other types of guarantees for their customers. That is, if a customer has borrowed funds backed by a letter of credit or other guarantee, its lenders can look to the customer's bank to fulfill the obligation. The second area of corporate financing involves advice on such matters as strategies for obtaining funds, corporate restructuring, divestitures, and acquisitions.

Capital market and foreign exchange products and services involve transactions where the bank may act as a dealer or broker in a service. Some banks, for example, are dealers in U.S. government or other securities. Customers who wish to transact in these securities can do so through the

---

[4] Leasing programs offered by some banks include vendor leasing, direct leasing, and leveraged leasing. For a discussion of these programs and the restrictions imposed on banks with respect to leasing activities, see Peter K. Nevitt, Frank J. Fabozzi, and Edmond J. Seifried, *Equipment Leasing for Commercial Bankers* (Philadelphia, PA: Robert Morris Associates, 1987).

[5] The factoring business involves a bank's purchase of accounts receivable.

[6] This means that the bank buys the equipment and leases it to another party. The bank is the lessor and the party that uses the leased equipment is the lessee.

government desk of the bank. Similarly, some banks maintain a foreign exchange operation, where foreign currency is bought and sold. Bank customers in need of foreign exchange can use the services of the bank.

In their role as dealers, banks can generate income in three ways: (1) the bid-ask spread, (2) capital gains on the securities or foreign currency they have transacted in, and (3) in the case of securities, the spread between interest income by holding the security and the cost of funding the purchase of that security.

The financial products that banks have developed to manage risk also yield income. These products include interest rate swaps, interest rate agreements, currency swaps, forward contracts, and interest rate options. We will discuss interest rate swaps and interest rate agreements in Chapter 20, currency swaps in Chapter 21, forward contracts in Chapter 6, and interest rate options in Chapter 19. Banks can generate either commission income (that is, brokerage fees) or spread income from selling such products.

Bank Funding

In describing the nature of the banking business, we have focused so far on how banks generate income. Now let's take a look at how a bank raises funds. There are three sources of funds for banks: (1) deposits, (2) non-deposit borrowing, and (3) common stock and retained earnings. Banks are highly leveraged financial institutions, which means that most of their funds come from borrowing—the first two sources we refer to. Included in non-deposit borrowing are borrowing from the Federal Reserve through the discount window facility, borrowing reserves in the federal funds market, and borrowing by the issuance of instruments in the money and bond markets.

Deposits.   There are several types of deposit accounts. Demand deposits (checking accounts) pay no interest and can be withdrawn upon demand. Deposit accounts that look very similar to demand deposits and that do pay interest include the so-called negotiable order of withdrawal (NOW) accounts and share drafts offered by credit unions (discussed below). Savings deposits pay interest, typically below market interest rates, do not have a specific maturity, and usually can be withdrawn upon demand.

Time deposits, also called *certificates of deposit*, have a fixed maturity date and pay either a fixed or floating interest rate. Some certificates of deposit that we shall describe in Chapter 13 can be sold in the open market prior to their maturity if the depositor needs funds. Other certificates of deposits cannot be sold. If a depositor elects to withdraw the funds from the bank prior to the maturity date, a withdrawal penalty is imposed. A *money market demand account* is one that pays interest based on short-term interest rates. The market for short-term debt obligations is called the money market, which is how these deposits get their name. They are designed to compete with money market mutual funds, which we will describe in Chapter 4.

Reserve Requirements and Borrowing in the Federal Funds Market. A bank cannot invest $1 for every $1 it obtains in deposit. All banks must maintain a specified percentage of their deposits in a non-interest bearing account at one of the 12 Federal Reserve Banks. These specified percentages are called *reserve ratios,* and the dollar amounts based on them that are required to be kept on deposit at a Federal Reserve Bank are called *required reserves.* The reserve ratios are established by the Federal Reserve Board (the "Fed"). The reserve ratio differs by type of deposit. The Fed defines two types of deposits: transactions and non-transactions deposits. Demand deposits and what the Fed calls "other checkable deposits" (primarily NOW accounts) are classified as transactions deposits. Savings and time deposits are non-transactions deposits. Reserve ratios are higher for transactions deposits relative to non-transactions deposits.

To arrive at its required reserves, a bank does not simply determine its transactions and non-transactions deposits at the close of each business day and then multiply each by the applicable reserve ratio. The determination of a bank's required reserves is more complex. Here we'll give a rough idea of how it is done. First, to compute required reserves, the Federal Reserve has established a two-week period called the *deposit computation period.* Required reserves are the average amount of each type of deposits held at the close of each business day in the computation period, multiplied by the reserve requirement for each type.

Reserve requirements in each period are to be satisfied by *actual* reserves, which are defined as the average amount of reserves held at the close of business at the Federal Reserve Bank during each day of a two-week *reserve maintenance period,* beginning on Thursday and ending on Wednesday two weeks later. For transactions deposits, the deposit computation period leads the reserve period by two days. For non-transactions deposits, the deposit computation period is the two-week period four weeks prior to the reserve maintenance period.

If actual reserves exceed required reserves, the difference is referred to as *excess reserves.* Because reserves are placed in non-interest bearing accounts, there is an opportunity cost associated with excess reserves. At the same time, there are penalties imposed on banks that do not satisfy the reserve requirements. Thus, banks have an incentive to manage their reserves so as to satisfy reserve requirements as precisely as possible.

Banks temporarily short of their required reserves can borrow reserves from banks that have excess reserves. The market where banks can borrow or lend reserves is called the *federal funds market.* The interest rate charged to borrow funds in this market is called the *federal funds rate.*

Borrowing at the Fed Discount Window.   The Federal Reserve Bank is the banker's bank—or, to put it another way, the bank of last resort. Banks temporarily short of funds can borrow from the Fed at its discount window. Collateral is necessary to borrow, but not just any collateral will do. The Fed establishes (and periodically changes) the type of collateral that is eligible. Currently it includes (1) Treasury securities, federal agency securities, and municipal securities, all with a maturity of less than six months, and (2) commercial and industrial loans with 90 days or less to maturity.

The interest rate that the Fed charges to borrow funds at the discount window is called the *discount rate*. The Fed changes this rate periodically in order to implement monetary policy.[7] Bank borrowing at the Fed to meet required reserves is quite limited in amount, despite the fact that the discount rate generally is set below the cost of other sources of short-term funding available to a bank. This is because the Fed views borrowing at the discount window as a privilege to be used to meet short-term liquidity needs, and not a device to increase earnings.

Continual borrowing for long periods and in large amounts is thereby viewed as a sign of a bank's financial weakness or as exploitation of the interest differential for profit. If a bank appears to be going to the Fed frequently to borrow, relative to its previous borrowing pattern, the Fed will make an *informational call* to ask for an explanation for the borrowing. If there is no subsequent improvement in the bank's borrowing pattern, the Fed then makes an *administrative counseling call* in which it tells the bank that it must stop its borrowing practice.

Other Non-Deposit Borrowing.   Most deposits have short maturities. Bank borrowing in the federal funds market and at the discount window of the Fed is short-term. Other non-deposit borrowing can be short-term in the form of issuing obligations in the money market, or intermediate- to long-term in the form of issuing securities in the bond market. An example of the former is the repurchase agreement (or "repo") market, which we discuss in Chapter 13. An example of intermediate- or long-term borrowing is floating-rate notes and bonds, the subject of Chapter 15.

Banks that raise most of their funds from the domestic and international money markets, relying less on depositors for funds, are called *money center banks*. Eight of the ten banks listed in Table 2-2 are money center banks. A *regional bank* by contrast is one that relies primarily on deposits for funding and makes less use of the money markets to obtain funds. The largest regional bank is Nations Bank. In recent years, larger regional banks have been

---

[7] While altering the discount rate is a tool to implement monetary policy, along with open market operations and the changing of reserve ratios, today it is not viewed as a primary tool.

merging with other regional banks to form so-called "superregional banks." Nations Bank is the result of a merger between NCNB of Charlotte, North Carolina and C&S/Sovran of Norfolk, Virginia. With their greater size, these superregional banks can compete in certain domestic and international financial activities that were once the domain of money center banks.

Regulation

Because of the special role that commercial banks play in the financial system, banks are regulated and supervised by several federal and state government entities. At the federal level, supervision is undertaken by the Federal Reserve Board, the Office of the Comptroller of the Currency, and the Federal Deposit Insurance Corporation. While much of the legislation defining these activities dates back to the late 1930s, the nature of financial markets and commercial banking has changed in the past 20 years. Consequently, rethinking of regulation is taking place as this chapter is written. Moreover, bank regulation is becoming international in nature.

Here we will review some of the major regulations concerning the activities of commercial banks. The regulations historically cover four areas:

1. ceilings imposed on the interest rate that can be paid on deposit accounts
2. geographical restrictions on branch banking
3. permissible activities for commercial banks
4. capital requirements for commercial banks

Regulation of Interest Rates. While regulation of the interest rates that banks can pay has been all but eliminated for accounts other than demand deposits, we discuss it because of its historical relevance. Federal regulations prohibit the payment of interest on demand (checking) accounts. Regulation Q at one time imposed a ceiling on the maximum interest rate that could be paid by banks on deposits other than demand accounts.

Until the 1960s, market interest rates stayed below the ceiling (except those on checking deposits), so Regulation Q had virtually no impact on the ability of banks to compete with other financial institutions to obtain funds. As market interest rates rose above the ceiling and ceilings were extended to all depository institutions after 1966, these institutions found it difficult to compete with other financial institutions—such as the money market funds that we will discuss in Chapter 4—to attract funds. As a result, there was "disintermediation"—funds flowed out of commercial banks and thrift institutions and into the other financial institutions.

To circumvent the ceilings on time deposits and recapture the lost funds, banks developed the negotiable certificate of deposit, which in effect had a higher ceiling, and eventually no ceiling at all, as we shall discuss in Chapter

13. They also opened branches outside the U.S., where no ceilings were imposed on the interest rate they could offer. As all depository institutions found it difficult to compete in the 1970s, federal legislation in the form of the Depository Institutions Deregulation and Monetary Control Act of 1980 gave banks relief. With a few exceptions, the 1980 act phased out the ceilings on interest rates on time deposits and certificates of deposit. The Garn–St. Germain Act of 1982 permitted banks to offer money market accounts, accounts that were similar to those offered by money market funds.

Geographical Restrictions.   Each state has the right to set its own rules on intrastate branch banking, which was established by the McFadden Act, passed by Congress in 1926. This rather outdated legislation was intended to prevent large banks from expanding geographically and thereby forcing out or taking over smaller banking entities, possibly threatening competition. There are some states where banks cannot establish branches statewide—so-called *unit-banking states*. There are also *limit branch banking states*, which permit some statewide branches, and other states that have virtually no restrictions on statewide branching. Recently, some states are permitting out-of-state banks to establish branches within their state, usually under regional compacts based on reciprocity. Federal legislation is under consideration to permit interstate banking.

Permissible Activities for Commercial Banks.   The activities of banks and bank holding companies are regulated by the Federal Reserve Board. The Fed was charged with the responsibility of regulating the activities of bank holding companies by the Bank Holding Company Act of 1956, subsequently amended in 1966 and 1970. The act states that the permissible activities of bank holding companies are limited to those that are viewed by the Fed as "closely related to banking."

Early legislation governing bank activities developed against the following background:

1. Certain commercial bank lending was believed to have reinforced the stock market crash of 1929.
2. The stock market crash itself led to the breakdown of the banking system.
3. Transactions between commercial banks and their securities affiliates led to abuses. For example, it was discovered that banks were underwriting securities and then selling those securities to customers whose investment accounts they managed or advised.[8]

---

[8] We'll discuss the underwriting of securities in the next chapter.

Against this background, Congress passed the Banking Act of 1933, which, among other provisions, created the Federal Deposit Insurance Corporation. Four sections of the 1933 act foreclosed commercial bankers from certain investment banking activities—Sections 16, 20, 21, and 32. These four sections are popularly referred to as the *Glass–Steagall Act.*

For banks that are members of the Federal Reserve System, Section 16 provides that:

> business of dealing in securities and stock by a national bank shall be limited to purchasing and selling such securities and stock without recourse, solely upon the order, and for the account of customers, and in no case for its own account, and the (national bank) shall not underwrite any issue of securities or stock.

Banks can neither (1) underwrite securities and stock, nor (2) act as dealers in the secondary market for securities and stock, although Section 16 does provide two exceptions. Banks were permitted to underwrite and deal in U.S. government obligations and "general obligations of any state or any political subdivisions thereof." (The latter securities are municipal bonds, which we shall discuss in Chapter 16. The exemption applies to one type of municipal security, general obligation bonds, not another type, revenue bonds.) Section 16 also restricts the activities of banks in connection with corporate securities such as corporate bonds and commercial paper, and securities such as mortgage-backed and asset-backed securities (which we discuss in Chapter 18).

These restrictions were imposed on activities of commercial banks in the U.S., not overseas. Commercial banks are not barred from underwriting or dealing in corporate bonds outside the U.S., nor are they restricted from aiding in the private placement of corporate securities. More recently developed instruments are not specifically forbidden to commercial banks. A good example is swaps—currency and interest rate swaps, which we discuss in Chapters 19 and 21.

Commercial banks that are members of the Federal Reserve System are prohibited from maintaining a securities firm by Section 20, which states that no member bank shall be affiliated:

> with any organization, association, business trust, or other similar organization engaged principally in the issue, flotation, underwriting, public sale, or distribution at wholesale or retail or through syndicate participation of stocks, bonds, debentures, notes or other securities.

Section 21 prohibits any "person, firm, corporation, association, business trust, or other similar organization" that receives deposits—that is, depository institutions—from engaging in the securities business as defined in Section 16. Section 32 further prevents banks from circumventing the restrictions on securities activities. It does so by prohibiting banks from placing bank employees or board members in positions with securities firms so that they can obtain indirect but effective control.

Subsequent legislation, court rulings, and regulatory decisions have whittled away at the barriers against commercial banks' engagement in investment banking activities. Here is a brief rundown of the significant events. In June 1987, the Fed granted approval to three bank holding companies—Citicorp, Bankers Trust, and J.P. Morgan Guaranty—to underwrite securities that were prohibited by the 1933 act: commercial paper, certain municipal revenue bonds, mortgage-backed securities, and asset-backed securities. To do so, the bank holding company must set up a separately capitalized subsidiary to underwrite these securities and must comply with rules established by the Fed regarding limits on market share, income, and revenue. The Comptroller of the Currency ruled subsequently that the 1933 act does permit national banks to underwrite mortgage-backed securities.

Court rulings in the 1980s granted commercial banks opportunities to act as investment advisors and furnish brokerage services. The Supreme Court ruled in 1981 that bank holding companies are allowed to serve as advisors to investment companies. Three years later, the Court ruled that, as long as a bank does not offer investment advice, it could provide discount brokerage services. A Federal Court of Appeals, however, has ruled since that a bank subsidiary could operate a brokerage firm even though it offered investment advice.

The legal distinction between commercial banks and investment banks seems to have been weakened further by a ruling by the Fed in November 1986 that permitted a Japanese bank, Sumitomo Bank Ltd., to invest $500 million in an investment banking firm, Goldman Sachs. While the Fed did impose restrictions to assure that Sumitomo could not exert control over the management of Goldman Sachs' operations, the action set a precedent nonetheless. In the next chapter, we will return to the issues surrounding the Glass–Steagall Act and the deregulation of commercial banking.

Beyond legislation, regulators have placed restrictions of their own on the types of securities that a bank can take a position in for its own investment portfolio. For example, while we pointed out earlier in this chapter that adjustable-rate mortgages are attractive investments, given the asset/liability problem of depository institutions, permission to invest in such mortgages had to be granted. The most recent example is the Comptroller of the

Currency's restrictions on investing in certain mortgage-backed securities that we will discuss in Chapter 18.

Capital Requirements for Commercial Banks. The capital structure of banks, like that of all corporations, consists of equity and debt (i.e., borrowed funds). Commercial banks, just like the other depository institutions that we discuss in this chapter, and investment banks, which we discuss in the next chapter, are highly leveraged institutions. That is, the ratio of equity capital to total assets is low, typically less than 8% in the case of banks. This gives rise to regulatory concern about potential insolvency resulting from the low level of capital provided by the owners. An additional concern is that the amount of equity capital is even less adequate because of potential liabilities that do not appear on the bank's balance sheet. These so-called off-balance sheet obligations include commitments such as letters of credit and obligations on customized interest rate agreements (such as swaps, caps, and floors).

Currently there are dual capital adequacy standards. The first set of standards consists of two tests. The first test involves the ratio of "primary capital" to total assets, with primary capital defined as common stock, retained earnings, and undivided profit and reserves established for loan losses. For national banks, this ratio must be at least 5.5%. The second test is based on the ratio of "total capital" to total assets, where total capital is defined as the sum of primary capital and subordinated debt. The minimum ratio is now 6%.

In 1986, the Federal Reserve Board, the Office of the Comptroller of the Currency, and the Federal Deposit Insurance Corporation began to review risk-based capital requirements. In January 1989, the Federal Reserve issued final guidelines to implement risk-based capital requirements, the second set of capital adequacy standards that we referred to above. They are to be phased in between now and the end of 1992. The guidelines are based on a framework adopted in July 1988 by the Basle Committee on Banking Regulations and Supervisory Practices, which consists of the central banks and supervisory authorities of the G-10 countries.[9]

The principal objectives of the guidelines are as follows. First, regulators in the U.S. and abroad have sought greater consistency in the evaluation of the capital adequacy of major banks throughout the world. Second, regulators have tried to establish capital adequacy standards that take into consideration the risk profile of the bank. Consider, for example, two banks, A and B, with $1 billion in assets. Suppose that both invest $400 million in

---

[9] The G-10 countries include Belgium, Canada, France, Germany, Italy, Japan, Netherlands, Sweden, Switzerland, United Kingdom, and United States.

identical assets, but the remaining $600 million in different assets. Bank A invests $500 million in U.S. government bonds and $100 million in business loans. Bank B invests $100 million in U.S. government bonds and $500 million in business loans. Obviously, the exposure to default losses is greater for Bank B. While the capital adequacy standards take this greater credit risk into account, they do not recognize liquidity factors or the market price sensitivity to which a bank may be exposed. Capital adequacy standards do give explicit recognition to off-balance sheet items.

The risk-based capital guidelines attempt to recognize credit risk by segmenting and weighting requirements. First, capital is defined as consisting of Tier 1 and Tier 2 capital. Minimum requirements are established for each tier. Tier 1 capital is considered *core capital*; it consists basically of common stockholders' equity, certain types of preferred stock, and minority interest in consolidated subsidiaries. Tier 2 capital is called *supplementary capital*; it includes loan-loss reserves, certain types of preferred stock, perpetual debt (debt with no maturity date), hybrid capital instruments and equity contract notes, and subordinated debt.

Second, the guidelines establish a credit risk weight for all assets. The weight depends on the credit risk associated with each asset. There are four credit risk classifications for banks in the U.S.: 0%, 20%, 50%, and 100%, arrived at on no particular scientific basis. Listed below are a few examples of assets that fall into each credit risk classification.

RISK WEIGHT	EXAMPLE OF ASSETS INCLUDED
0%	U.S. Treasury securities Mortgage-backed securities issued by the Government National Mortgage Association
20	Municipal general obligation bonds Mortgage-backed securities issued by the Federal Home Loan Mortgage Corporation or the Federal National Mortgage Association
50	Municipal revenue bonds Residential mortgages
100	Commercial loans and commercial mortgages LDC loans Corporate bonds Municipal IDA bonds

The way the credit risk weights work is as follows. The book value of the asset is multiplied by the credit risk weight to determine the amount of core and supplementary capital that the bank will need to support that asset. For example, suppose that the book values of the assets of a bank are as follows:

ASSET	BOOK VALUE (IN MILLIONS)
U.S. Treasury securities	$400
Municipal general obligation bonds	100
Residential mortgages	200
Commercial loans	300

The risk-weighted assets are calculated as follows:

ASSET	BOOK VALUE (IN MILLIONS)	RISK WEIGHT	PRODUCT (IN MILLIONS)
U.S. Treasury securities	$400	0%	$ 0
Municipal general obligation bonds	100	20	20
Residential mortgages	200	50	100
Commercial loans	300	100	300
Risk-weighted assets			$420

The risk-weighted assets for this bank would be $420 million.

Before explaining how this procedure is used to determine the amount of capital required by the bank, we should mention how off-balance sheet items are handled. A bank may have acquired a position in interest-sensitive contracts and/or foreign exchange-related products that is not reported on the balance sheet (that is, the investments are off-balance sheet items). Under the guidelines, these are considered in determining the risk-weighted assets. As we do not discuss such instruments until later in this book, here we just cite the basic treatment, which involves two steps. The guidelines establish a *credit equivalent amount* that converts the off-balance sheet items into an amount that should be used in the calculation of the risk-weighted assets. Then the credit equivalent amount is multiplied by the credit risk weight.

The capital requirement guidelines are to be phased in between 1990 and 1992. There are different requirements between 1990 and 1992 (the transitional period). From year-end 1992 and thereafter, the minimum core (Tier 1) capital is 4% of the risk-weighted assets; the minimum total capital (core plus supplementary) capital is 8% of the risk-weighted assets. To see how this works, consider the hypothetical bank we used earlier to illustrate the calculation of risk-weighted assets. For that bank the weighted risk assets are $420 million. The minimum core capital is $16.8 million (0.04 times $420 million); the minimum total capital is $33.6 million (0.08 times $420 million).[10]

One implication of the new capital guidelines is that it will encourage banks to sell off their loans in the open market. By doing so, the bank need not maintain capital for the loans (assets) sold off. While the secondary market for individual bank loans has been growing, it has not reached the stage where a bank can efficiently sell large amounts of loans. An alternative is for a bank to pool loans and issue securities that are collateralized by the pool of loans. This process is referred to as "asset securitization." We'll have more to say about this process in the next chapter and Chapter 18.[11]

Federal Deposit Insurance

Because of the important economic role played by banks, the U.S. government sought a way to protect them against depositors who because of what they thought were either real or perceived problems with a bank would withdraw funds in a disruptive manner. Bank panics occurred frequently in the early 1930s, resulting in the failure of banks that might have survived economic difficulties had it not been for massive withdrawals. The mechanism the U.S. government devised in 1933 to prevent a "run on a bank" was to create federal deposit insurance. The insurance was provided through a new agency, the Federal Deposit Insurance Corporation. A year later, federal deposit insurance was extended to savings and loan associations with the creation of the Federal Savings and Loan Insurance Corporation.

In 1933, federal deposit insurance covered accounts up to $2,500. This amount has been subsequently raised to its current level of $100,000. Prior to FIRREA, the premium banks paid for this insurance was 0.083% of deposits. Currently it is 0.15% of deposits.

While federal deposit insurance did achieve its objective of preventing a run on banks, it unfortunately created incentives that encourage managers of depository institutions to take on excessive risks. If highly risky investments work out, the benefits accrue to the stockholders and management; however, if they do not, it is the depositors who are supposed to absorb the losses. Yet, depositors will have little concern about the risks that a depository institution is taking on because their funds are insured by the federal government. From

---

[10] Other minimum standards imposed by the guidelines cover limitations on supplementary capital elements.

[11] For a discussion of the development of the market for senior bank loans, see Frank J. Fabozzi and John Carlson (eds.), *The Trading and Securitization of Senior Bank Loans* (Chicago: Probus Publishing, 1992).

a depositor's perspective, so long as the amount deposited does not exceed the insurance coverage, one depository institution is as good as another.

There have been several proposals to revise federal deposit insurance to overcome the incentive for excessive risk taking while preserving substantial deposit protection.[12] One proposal is to charge an insurance premium based on the riskiness of the bank's assets. The problem with this approach is quantifying the riskiness of assets. A system similar to the risk-based capital guidelines has been suggested. Another proposal is to make depositors discipline the management of depository institutions by either lowering the amount covered by insurance, or limiting the amount that any individual can be insured for, not in one account at one depository institution but in all depository institutions. Whether depositors have the ability to assess the risks associated with depository institutions and thereby discipline management is questionable.

SAVINGS AND LOAN ASSOCIATIONS

S&Ls represent a fairly old institution. The basic motivation behind creation of S&Ls was provision of funds for financing the purchase of a home. The collateral for the loans would be the home being financed.

S&Ls are either mutually owned or have corporate stock ownership. "Mutually owned" means there is no stock outstanding, so technically the depositors are the owners. To increase the ability of S&Ls to expand the sources of funding available to bolster their capital, legislation facilitated the conversion of mutually-owned companies into a corporate stock ownership structure.

Like banks, S&Ls may be chartered under either state or federal statutes. At the federal level, the primary regulator of S&Ls is, at present, the Director of the Office of Thrift Supervision (DOTS), created in 1989 by FIRREA. Prior to the creation of DOTS, the primary regulator was the Federal Home Loan Bank Board (FHLBB). While the FHLBB still exists, its responsibilities have been limited to the credit-facilitating function, that is, making loans (advances) to S&Ls.

Like banks, S&Ls are now subject to reserve requirements on deposits established by the Fed. Prior to the passage of FIRREA, federal deposit insurance for S&Ls was provided by the Federal Savings and Loan Insurance Corporation (FSLIC). The Savings Association Insurance Fund (SAIF) has replaced FSLIC. SAIF is administered by the FDIC.

---

[12] For a summary of the various proposals to restructure federal deposit insurance, see Loretta J. Mester, "Curing Our Ailing Deposit-Insurance System," *Business Review*, Federal Reserve Bank of Philadelphia (September–October 1990), pp. 13–24.

Assets

Traditionally, the only assets in which S&Ls were allowed to invest have been mortgages, mortgage-backed securities (which we will discuss in Chapter 18), and government securities. Mortgage loans include fixed-rate mortgages, adjustable-rate mortgages, and other types of mortgages such as graduated-payment mortgages. While most mortgage loans are for the purchase of homes, S&Ls do make construction loans. Historically, S&Ls have received favorable tax benefits from such investments, in order to encourage investment in mortgages and mortgage-related securities. As of December 31, 1988, of the $1,350 billion of assets held by S&Ls, $727 billion were invested in mortgages and $214 billion in mortgage-related securities.[13]

As the structures of S&L balance sheets and the consequent maturity mismatch led to widespread disaster and insolvency, the Garn–St. Germain Act of 1982 expanded the types of assets in which S&Ls could invest. The acceptable list of investments now includes consumer loans (loans for home improvement, automobiles, education, mobile homes, and credit cards), non-consumer loans (commercial, corporate, business, or agricultural loans), and municipal securities.

While S&Ls had a comparative advantage in originating mortgage loans, they lacked the expertise to make commercial and corporate loans. Rather than make an investment in acquiring those skills, S&Ls took an alternative approach and invested in corporate bonds because these bonds were classified as corporate loans. More specifically, S&Ls became one of the major buyers of non-investment-grade corporate bonds, more popularly referred to as "junk" bonds or "high-yield" bonds. Under FIRREA, S&Ls will no longer be permitted to invest new money in junk bonds and must divest themselves of their current holdings by August 1994.

S&Ls invest in short-term assets for operational (liquidity) and regulatory purposes. All S&Ls with federal deposit insurance must satisfy minimum liquidity requirements. These requirements are specified by the FHLBB. Acceptable assets include cash, short-term government agency and corporate securities, certificates of deposit of commercial banks,[14] other money market assets described in Chapter 13, and federal funds. In the case of federal funds, the S&L is lending excess reserves to another depository institution that is short of funds.

---

[13] U.S. Office of Thrift Supervision, *Savings and Home Financing Source Book,* annual.

[14] The S&L is an investor when it holds the CD of a bank, but the CD represents the liability of the issuing bank.

Funding

Prior to 1981, the bulk of the liabilities of S&Ls consisted of passbook savings accounts and time deposits. The interest rate that could be offered on these deposits was regulated. S&Ls were given favored treatment over banks with respect to the maximum interest rate they could pay depositors. They were permitted to pay an interest rate 0.5% higher, later reduced to 0.25%. With the deregulation of interest rates discussed earlier in this chapter, banks and S&Ls now compete head-to-head for deposits. Deregulation also expanded the types of accounts that may be offered by S&Ls—NOW accounts and money market deposit accounts (MMDA).

In the 1980s, S&Ls have been more active in raising funds in the money market. For example, they have been able to use the repurchase agreement market to raise funds. Some larger S&Ls have issued commercial paper as well as medium-term notes.[15] They can borrow in the federal funds market and they have access to the Fed's discount window. S&Ls can also borrow from the Federal Home Loan Banks. These borrowings, called *advances*, can be short-term or long-term in maturity, and the interest rate can be fixed or floating.

Regulation

Federal S&Ls are chartered under the provisions of the Home Owners Loan Act of 1933. Federally chartered S&Ls are now supervised by the Office of Thrift Supervisor. State-chartered banks are supervised by the respective state. A further act in 1933 established the Federal Savings and Loan Insurance Corporation, which at that time insured the deposits of federally chartered S&Ls up to $5,000 and allowed state-chartered S&Ls that could qualify to obtain the same insurance coverage. We discuss some of the important legislation and the players below. There is further discussion in Chapter 14 where we cover federal agency securities and in Chapter 17 where we discuss the development of the mortgage market.

As in bank regulation, S&Ls historically have been regulated with respect to the maximum interest rates on deposit accounts, geographical operations, permissible activities (types of accounts and types of investments), and capital adequacy requirements. In addition, there have been restrictions on the sources of non-deposit funds and liquidity requirements. We mentioned liquidity requirements earlier.[16]

---

[15] The medium-term note market is discussed in Chapter 14.

[16] Liquidity requirements are not imposed on banks because the majority of their assets are of less than five years maturity.

The maximum interest rate that is permitted on deposit accounts has been phased out by the Depository Institutions Deregulation and Monetary Control Act of 1980 (DIDMCA). While this allowed S&Ls to compete with other financial institutions to raise funds, it also raised their funding costs. For reasons to be described later, while banks also faced higher funding costs, their balance sheets were better constituted than those of S&Ls to cope with the higher costs resulting from interest rate deregulation.

Besides phasing in the deregulation of interest rates on deposit accounts, DIDMCA was significant in several other ways. First, it expanded the Fed's control over the money supply by imposing reserve deposit requirements on S&Ls. In return, S&Ls were permitted to offer negotiable order of withdrawal (NOW) accounts.

Subsequent legislation, the Garn–St. Germain Act, not only granted thrifts the right to offer money market demand accounts so that S&Ls could compete with money market funds, but also broadened the types of assets in which S&Ls could invest. While S&Ls were first given permission by the FHLBB in 1979 to originate and invest in adjustable-rate mortgage loans, restrictions on the interest rate and other terms stymied their use. Two years later, the FHLBB removed some major impediments.

Permission to raise funds in the money market and the bond market was granted by the Federal Home Loan Bank Board in 1975 (when it allowed the issuance of mortgage pass-through securities by S&Ls) and in 1979 (when it allowed the issuance of commercial paper and Eurodollar issues). FHLBB permission to form finance subsidiaries was granted in 1984. Through these subsidiaries, S&Ls were able to broaden their funding sources by the issuance of mortgage-related securities known as *collateralized mortgage obligations.*

There are two sets of capital adequacy standards for S&Ls as for banks. For S&Ls there are also two ratio tests based on "core" capital and "tangible" capital. The risk-based capital guidelines are similar to those for banks. Instead of two tiers of capital, however, there are three: Tier 1—tangible capital, Tier 2—core capital, and Tier 3—supplementary capital.

Geographical operations of S&Ls were restricted until 1981, when the FHLBB permitted thrifts to acquire thrifts in other states.

The S&L Crisis

The story of the growth of the S&L industry since the late 1960s and the ensuing S&L crisis can't be described in one short chapter, but a basic understanding of the downfall of this industry is possible.

Until the early 1980s, S&Ls and all other lenders financed housing through traditional mortgages at interest rates fixed for the duration of the loan. The period of the loan was typically long, frequently up to 30 years.

Funding for these loans, by regulation, came from deposits having a maturity considerably shorter than the loans. As we explained earlier in this chapter, this is the funding problem of lending long and borrowing short. It is extremely risky—although regulators took a long time to understand it. There's no problem, of course, if interest rates are stable or declining, but if interest rates rise above the interest rate on the mortgage loan, a negative spread will result, which must result eventually in insolvency. Regulators at first endeavored to shield the S&L industry from the need to pay high interest rates without losing deposits by imposing a ceiling on the interest rate that would be paid by S&Ls and by their immediate competitors, the other depository institutions. But the approach did not and could not work.

With the high volatility of interest rates in the 1970s, followed by the historically high level of interest rates in the early 1980s, all depository institutions began to lose funds to competitors exempt from ceilings, such as the newly-formed money market funds; this development forced some increase in ceilings. The ceilings in place since the middle of the 60s did not protect the S&Ls; they began to suffer from diminished profits and increasingly from operating losses. A large fraction of S&Ls became technically insolvent as rising interest rates eroded asset market values to the point where they fell short of the liabilities.

But regulators, anxious to cover up the debacle of their empire, let them continue to operate, worsening the problem by allowing them to value their mortgage assets at book value. Profitability worsened with deregulation of the maximum interest rate that S&Ls could pay on deposits. While deregulation allowed S&Ls to compete with other financial institutions for funds, it also raised funding costs. Banks were better equipped to cope with rising funding costs because bank portfolios were not dominated by old, fixed-rate mortgages as S&Ls were. A larger portion of bank portfolios consisted of shorter-term assets and other assets whose interest rate reset to market interest rates after short time periods.

The difficulty of borrowing short and lending long was only part of the problem faced by the industry. As the crisis progressed, and the situation of many S&Ls became hopeless, fraudulent management activities were revealed. Many S&Ls facing financial difficulties also pursued strategies that exposed the institution to greater risk, in the hope of recovering if these strategies worked out. What encouraged managers to pursue such high risk strategies was that depositors were not concerned with the risks associated with the institution where they deposited funds because the U.S. government, through federal deposit insurance, guaranteed the deposits up to a predetermined amount. Troubled S&Ls could pay existing depositors through attracting new depositors by offering higher interest rates on deposits than financially stronger S&Ls. In turn, to earn a spread on the higher cost of funds, they had to pursue riskier investment policies.

SAVINGS BANKS

Savings banks are institutions similar to, although much older than, S&Ls. They can be either mutually owned (in which case they are called *mutual savings banks*) or stockholder owned. While conversion of mutual to corporate structure was made easier by the Garn–St. Germain Act, most savings banks are of the mutual form. Only 16 states in the eastern portion of the U.S. charter savings banks. In 1978, Congress permitted the chartering of federal savings banks.

While the total deposits at savings banks are less than those of S&Ls, savings banks are typically larger institutions. Asset structures of savings banks and S&Ls are similar. The principal assets of savings banks are residential mortgages. Because states have permitted more portfolio diversi-fication than was permitted by federal regulators of S&Ls, savings bank portfolios weathered funding risk far better than S&Ls. Included in savings bank portfolios are corporate bonds, Treasury and government agency securities, municipal securities, common stock, and consumer loans.

The principal source of funds for savings banks is deposits. Typically, the ratio of deposits to total assets is greater for savings banks than for S&Ls. Savings banks offer the same types of deposit accounts as S&Ls. Deposits can be insured by either the BIF or SAIF.

CREDIT UNIONS

Credit unions are the smallest and the newest of the depository institutions. Credit unions can obtain either a state or federal charter. Their unique aspect is the "common bond" requirement for credit union membership. According to the statutes that regulate federal credit unions, membership in a federal credit union "shall be limited to groups having a common bond of occupation or association, or to groups within a well-defined neighborhood, community, or rural district." They are either cooperatives or mutually owned. There is no corporate stock ownership. The dual purpose of credit unions is therefore to serve their members' saving and borrowing needs.

Technically, because credit unions are owned by their members, member deposits are called *shares*. The distribution paid to members is therefore in the form of dividends, not interest. Since 1970, the shares of all federally-chartered credit unions have been insured by the National Credit Union Share Insurance Fund (NCUSIF) for up to $100,000, the same as other depository institutions. State-chartered credit unions may elect to have NCUSIF coverage; for those that do not, insurance coverage is provided by a state agency.

Federal regulations apply to federally-chartered credit unions and state-chartered credit unions that have elected to become members of NCUSIF. Most states, however, specify that state-chartered institutions must be subject to the same requirements as federally-chartered ones. Effectively, therefore, most credit unions are regulated at the federal level. The principal federal regulatory agency is the National Credit Union Administration (NCUA).

Credit unions obtain their funds primarily from deposits of their members. With deregulation, they can offer a variety of accounts, including share drafts, which are similar to checking accounts but that pay interest. Playing a role similar to the Fed, as the lender of last resort, is the Central Liquidity Facility (CLF) which is administered by NCUA. CLF provides short-term loans to member credit unions with liquidity needs.

Credit union assets consist primarily of small consumer loans to their members. They also provide credit card loans.

SUMMARY

Depository institutions (commercial banks, savings and loan associations, savings banks, and credit unions) accept various types of deposits. With the funds raised through deposits and other funding sources, they make loans to various entities and invest in securities. The deposits usually are insured by a federal agency. Income is derived from investments (loans and securities) and fee income. Thrifts (savings and loan associations, savings banks, and credit unions) are specialized types of depository institutions. Historically, they have not been authorized to accept demand accounts, but more recently thrifts have been offering some types of deposits equivalent to checking accounts.

A depository institution seeks to earn a positive spread between the assets it invests in and the cost of its funds. In generating spread income, a depository institution faces credit risk and funding or interest rate risk. Financial instruments such as floating-rate notes, adjustable-rate mortgages, and interest rate swaps have been used to control funding or interest rate risk.

A depository institution must be prepared to satisfy net withdrawals of funds by depositors and provide loans to customers. A depository institution can accommodate withdrawals or loan demand by attracting additional deposits, using existing securities as collateral for borrowing from a federal agency, selling securities that it owns, or raising short-term funds in the money market.

All national banks must be members of the Federal Reserve System.

State-chartered banks may elect to join the Federal Reserve System. The services provided by commercial banks can be broadly classified as individual banking, institutional banking, and global banking.

There are three sources of funds for banks: (1) deposits, (2) non-deposit borrowing, and (3) retained earnings and sale of equity. Banks are highly leveraged financial institutions, meaning that most of their funds are obtained from deposits and non-deposit borrowing, which includes borrowing from the Fed through the discount window facility, borrowing reserves in the federal funds market, and borrowing by the issuance of instruments in the money and bond markets.

Banks must maintain reserves at one of the 12 Federal Reserve Banks, according to reserve requirements established by the Fed. Banks temporarily short of their required reserves can borrow reserves in the federal funds market or borrow temporarily from the Fed at its discount window.

There is both federal and state regulation of banks. At the federal level, supervision of banks is the responsibility of the Federal Reserve Board, the Office of the Comptroller of the Currency, and the Federal Deposit Insurance Corporation. Recent legislation has altered the regulatory structure. The major regulations involve geographical restrictions on branch banking, which are administered by the state and therefore vary widely, activities that are permissible for commercial banks, and capital requirements.

Like banks, S&Ls may be chartered under either state or federal statutes. At the federal level, the primary regulator of S&Ls is the Director of the Office of Thrift Supervision. S&Ls are subject to reserve requirements on deposits established by the Fed. Federal deposit insurance for S&Ls is provided by the Savings Association Insurance Fund.

Much as in the case of bank regulation, S&Ls are regulated with respect to geographical operations, permissible activities, and capital adequacy requirements. S&Ls invest principally in mortgages and mortgage-related securities. Recent deregulation has expanded the types of investments that S&Ls are permitted to make, as well as expanding the types of deposit accounts that may be offered and the available funding sources.

The asset structures of savings banks and S&Ls are similar. As some states have permitted greater portfolio diversification than is permitted by federal regulators of S&Ls, this is reflected in savings bank portfolios. The principal source of funds for savings banks is deposits. Deposits can be federally insured by either the BIF or SAIF.

Credit unions are depository institutions that have a "common bond" requirement for membership. They are owned by their members. Although they can be state- or federally-chartered, most credit unions effectively are regulated at the federal level by the National Credit Union Administration. The assets of credit unions consist primarily of small consumer loans to their members and credit card loans.

QUESTIONS

1. You and a friend are discussing the savings and loan crisis. She states that "the whole mess started in the early '80s. When short-term rates skyrocketed, S&Ls got killed—their spread income went from positive to negative. They were borrowing short and lending long."

    a. What does she mean by "borrowing short and lending long"?

    b. Are higher or lower interest rates beneficial to an institution that borrows short and lends long?

    c. How could adjustable-rate mortgages alleviate this situation for an S&L?

2. An article on bank funding in the October 15, 1990, issue of *Bank Letter* states:

    > The steep rise in deposit insurance next year may trigger a growing preference for note issuance over wholesale deposits by top-tier banks, according to treasurers and a recent report by Keefe, Bruyette & Woods. . . . Investor skittishness over credit quality has kept most banks out of the wholesale funding [note issuance] market, but when investor sentiment improves, higher quality issuers will make increased use of uninsured vehicles such as note issuance. . . .

    Discuss this quotation. In your answer be sure to mention the three sources of bank funding.

3. Discuss this quotation from the October 29, 1990, issue of *Corporate Financing Week:*

    > Chase Manhattan Bank is preparing its first asset-backed debt issue, becoming the last major consumer bank to plan to access the growing market, Street asset-backed officials said. . . . Asset-backed offerings enable banks to remove credit card or other loan receivables from their balance sheets, which helps them comply with capital requirements.

4. The Chairman of the Federal Reserve Board told the U.S. Senate on July 12, 1990:

    > As you know, the Board has long supported repeal of the provisions of the Glass–Steagall Act that separated commercial and investment banking. We still strongly advocate such repeal because we believe that technology and globalization have continued to blur the distinctions among credit markets, and have eroded the franchise value of the classic bank intermediation process. Outdated constraints will

only endanger the profitability of banking organizations and their contribution to the American economy.

a. What does Mr. Greenspan mean when he says that the value of the bank intermediation process has been eroded by technology and globalization?

b. What are some of the major benefits and risks of repealing key provisions of the Glass-Steagall Act?

5. Consider this headline from *The New York Times* of March 26, 1933:

Bankers will fight Deposit Guarantees. . . . Bad Banking would be encouraged

a. What do you think this headline was getting at?

b. Discuss the pros and cons of whether deposits should be insured by the U.S. government.

6. Comment on this statement:

The risk-based guidelines for commercial banks attempt to gauge the interest-rate risk associated with a bank's balance sheet.

LEARNING OBJECTIVES

After reading this chapter you will understand:

- the nature of the investment banking business.

- the revenue-generating activities of investment banks.

- the activities of investment banking firms that require them to commit their own capital.

- the role investment bankers play in the underwriting of securities.

- the different types of underwriting arrangements.

- SEC Rule 415 ("shelf registration").

- the distinction between riskless arbitrage and risk arbitrage.

- the advantages and disadvantages from an issuer's perspective of a private placement.

- Rule 144A and its potential impact on the private placement market.

- what is meant by the securitization of assets.

- the various roles investment bankers play in mergers and acquisitions.

- what is meant by merchant banking.

- why investment banking firms create and trade risk control instruments.

- how investment banking firms are classified.

- the measures commonly used to rank investment banking firms and the pitfalls of these measures.

- the competition and challenges facing investment banking firms in the 1990s.

Defining what constitutes investment banking is no longer a simple matter. Basically, investment bankers perform two general functions. For corporations, U.S. government agencies, state and local governments, and foreign entities (sovereigns and corporations) that need funds, investment bankers assist in obtaining those funds. For investors who wish to *invest* funds, investment banking firms act as brokers or dealers in the buying and selling of securities.

Robert Kuhn suggests four definitions of investment banking, ranging from broadly inclusive of wide-ranging financial services to a narrow traditionalist definition (some of the terms used below will be clarified later):

1. The broadest definition includes virtually all activities of major Wall Street firms, from international corporate underwriting to retail branch marketing to a host of other financial services (e.g., real estate and insurance).

2. The next broadest definition envisions investment banking as covering all capital market activities, from underwriting and corporate finance, to mergers and acquisitions (M&A) and fairness opinions, to fund management and venture capital. Excluded, for example, are the selling of securities to retail customers, consumer real estate brokerage, mortgage banking, insurance products, and the like. Included is merchant banking, when investment bankers work and invest for their own account. Also included is the nonretail trading of blocks of securities for financial institutions.

3. Here investment banking is defined to include only *some* capital market activities, stressing underwriting and mergers and acquisitions. Excluded, for example, are fund management, venture capital, commodities, aspects of risk management, and the like. Depending on firm orientation, research may also be excluded if it is used primarily to support retail sales. (Note that the changing profile of investment banking would now include merchant banking in this definition.)

4. The narrowest definition takes investment banking back to its historical foundations, limiting the field strictly to underwriting and raising of capital in the primary markets, and the trading of securities (broker/dealer) in the secondary market. (It is hard to conceive of a contemporary definition of investment banking that would exclude M&A, so this one is for historians and purists.)[1]

The definition with which we basically agree is the second definition. That is, investment banking involves all capital market activities except those involving retail-oriented sales. There are firms in the financial services business that buy or sell securities only for customers (retail or institutional) but are not involved in the fund-raising function. These firms are called securities or brokerage firms.

According to this definition of investment banking, it would seem that many investment banking activities are similar to those performed by the larger commercial banks. This is true. As we stressed in the previous chapter,

---

[1] Robert Lawrence Kuhn, *Investment Banking: The Art and Science of High-Stakes Dealmaking* (New York: Harper & Row, 1990), pp. 5–6.

the wall between commercial banking and investment banking is being chipped away by financial deregulation.

NATURE OF THE BUSINESS

Investment banking firms are highly leveraged firms. Table 3-1 lists the total consolidated capital, equity capital, and long-term debt of the larger investment banking firms in the U.S. as of the end of 1989. The degree of leverage is even greater than that shown in the table because firms rely on considerable short-term borrowing as well. As we explain the activities that these firms are engaged in, you will see why investment banking firms have had an appetite for capital. The increasing need for capital has resulted in consolidation of firms in the industry and a change in many firms from the partnership structure to the corporate structure, the latter giving firms easier access to public funds.

In addition to needing long-term sources of capital, investment banking firms borrow on a short-term basis to finance their inventory of securities. The primary means for borrowing on a short-term basis is the repurchase agreement. We'll discuss this in Chapter 13.

Investment banking firms generate revenue from commissions, fee income, spread income, and principal activities. After we describe the various activities of investment banking, we'll show the revenue breakdown of two well-known U.S. investment banking firms.

TABLE 3-1 CAPITAL STRUCTURE OF SEVERAL INVESTMENT BANKING FIRMS (IN MILLIONS, AS OF END OF 1990)			
FIRM	TOTAL CONSOLIDATED CAPITAL	EQUITY CAPITAL	LONG-TERM DEBT
Merrill Lynch & Co.	$9,567.0	$3,225.4	$6,341.6
Shearson Lehman Brothers	7,499.0	2,027.0	5,472.0
Salomon Brothers Holding Co.	7,162.0	4,442.0	2,720.0
Goldman, Sachs & Co.	4,700.0	2,477.0	2,223.0
Morgan Stanley Group	3,380.4	2,171.5	1,208.9
CS First Boston	1,612.0	707.0	905.0
PaineWebber Group	1,552.9	895.9	657.0
Dean Witter Reynolds	1,405.0	908.0	497.0
Bear, Stearns & Co.	1,387.7	1,004.3	383.4
Smith Barney, Harris Upham & Co.	1,012.0	773.0	239.0
Donaldson, Lufkin & Jenrette	919.0	294.0	625.0

Source: Adapted from "Ranking America's Biggest Brokers," Institutional Investor (April 1991), p. 139.

According to our working definition of investment banking, the activities of firms in this business can be divided into specific revenue-generating activities:

- Public offering (underwriting) of securities
- Trading of securities
- Private placement of securities
- Securitization of assets
- Mergers and acquisitions
- Merchant banking
- Trading and creation of risk control instruments
- Money management

Not all investment banking firms are involved in each of these activities. In the 1980s, the philosophy in the industry was to throw people, money, and other resources at developing a market share in each of these activities—that is, to provide a full line of services. This will not be the philosophy of investment banking firms in the 1990s, as firms have reevaluated the economics of being in certain lines of businesses.[2]

Public Offering (Underwriting) of Securities

The traditional role associated with investment banking is the underwriting of securities. Entities that issue securities include agencies of the U.S. government, state and local governments, corporations, supranational entities such as the World Bank and the Asian Development Bank, foreign governments, and foreign corporations.

The typical underwriting process involves three functions: (1) advising the issuer on the terms and the timing of the offering, (2) buying the securities from the issuer, and (3) distributing the issue to the public. The advisor role may require investment bankers to design a security structure that is more palatable to investors than a particular traditional instrument. For example, the high interest rates in the U.S. in the late 70s and early 80s increased the cost of borrowing for issuers of even the highest quality rating. To reduce the cost of borrowing for their clients, investment bankers designed securities with characteristics that were more attractive to investors but not onerous to

---

[2] For an excellent discussion of the evolution of investment banking from its beginnings to today's global financial markets, see Samuel L. Hayes III and Philip M. Hubbard, *Investment Banking: A Tale of Three Cities* (Boston: Harvard Business School Press, 1990).

issuers. They also designed security structures for low-quality bond issues, so-called high-yield or junk bond structures. We'll give several examples of these financial innovations in Chapters 15 and 16.

The underwriting process need not involve the second function—buying the securities from the issuer. When the investment banking firm agrees to buy the securities from the issuer at a set price, the underwriting arrangement is referred to as a *firm commitment*. The risk that the investment banking firm accepts in a firm commitment underwriting arrangement is that the price it pays to purchase the securities from the issuer will be less than the price it receives when it reoffers the securities to the public. In contrast, in a *best efforts* underwriting arrangement, the investment banking firm agrees only to use its expertise to sell the securities—it does not buy the entire issue from the issuer.

The fee earned from underwriting a security is the difference between the price paid to the issuer and the price at which the investment bank reoffers the security to the public. This difference is called the *gross spread*, or the *underwriter discount*. There are numerous factors that affect the size of the gross spread.[3] Typical gross spreads for common stock offerings, initial public offerings (IPOs), and fixed-income offerings are shown in Table 3-2. IPOs are typically common stock offerings issued by companies that had not previously issued common stock to the public. Because of the risk associated with pricing and then placing IPOs, the gross spread is higher.

The typical underwritten transaction involves so much risk of capital loss that for a single investment banking firm to undertake it alone would expose it to the danger of losing a significant portion of its capital. To share this risk, an investment banking firm forms a syndicate of firms to underwrite the issue. The gross spread is then divided among the lead underwriter(s) and the other firms in the underwriting syndicate. The lead underwriter manages the deal (runs the books for the deal). In many cases there may be more than one lead underwriter, in which case the lead underwriters are said to colead or comanage the deal. In a bond transaction, the lead underwriters customarily receive 20% of the gross spread as compensation for managing the deal.[4]

To realize the gross spread, the entire securities issue must be sold to the public at the planned reoffering price. This usually requires a great deal of marketing muscle. Investment banking firms have an investor client base (retail and institutional) to which they attempt to sell the securities. To increase the potential investor base, the lead underwriter will put together a selling group. This group includes the underwriting syndicate plus other

---

[3] For a discussion of these factors, see G. Clyde Buck, "Spreads and Fees in Investment Banking," Chapter 5 in Robert Lawrence Kuhn (ed.), *The Library of Investment Banking*, Volume II (Homewood, IL: Dow Jones-Irwin, 1990), pp. 146–147.

[4] Ernest Block, *Inside Investment Banking* (Homewood, IL: Dow Jones-Irwin, 1989), p. 323.

firms that are not in the syndicate. Members of the selling group can buy the security at a concession price (i.e., a price less than the reoffering price). The gross spread is thereby divided among the lead underwriter, members of the underwriting syndicate, and members of the selling group.

Underwriting activities are regulated by the Securities and Exchange Commission (SEC). Regulation covers not only information that must be disclosed to the public about the issue and the issuing entity, but also the subsequent market making activities.

Variations in the Underwriting Process.   Not all deals are underwritten using the traditional syndicate process we have described. Variations include the "bought deal" for the underwriting of bonds, the auction process, and the standby arrangement for underwriting common stock.

The bought deal was introduced in the Eurobond market in 1981 when Credit Suisse First Boston purchased from General Motors Acceptance Corporation a $100 million issue without lining up an underwriting syndicate prior to the purchase. Thus, Credit Suisse First Boston did not use the traditional syndication process to diversify the capital risk exposure associated with an underwriting that we described earlier.

The mechanics of a bought deal are as follows. The lead manager or a group of managers offers a potential issuer of debt securities a firm bid to purchase a specified amount of the securities with a certain interest (coupon) rate and maturity. The issuer is given a day or so (it might even be a few hours) to accept or reject the bid. If the bid is accepted, the investment banking firm has bought the deal. It can, in turn, sell the securities to other investment banking firms for distribution to their clients and/or distribute the securities to its clients. Typically, the investment banking firm that buys the deal will have presold most of the issue to its institutional clients.

The bought deal appears to have found its way into the U.S. in mid-1985 when Merrill Lynch did a bond deal in which it was the only underwriter. The gross spread on the bond, a $50 million issue of Norwest Financial, was 0.268%. This is far less than the 0.7% gross spread indicated in Table 3-2. Merrill Lynch offered a portion of the securities to investors and the balance to other investment banking firms. For the portion of the issue it sold to other investment banking firms, it kept about 25% of the gross spread.

There are several reasons why some investment banking firms have found the bought deal attractive. First, in 1982 the SEC approved Rule 415, popularly referred to as the *shelf registration rule*, which permits *certain* issuers to issue securities on very short notice. Prior to establishment of Rule 415, there was a lengthy period required before a security could be sold to the public. While Rule 415 gave certain issuers timing flexibility to take advantage of "windows" of opportunities in the global marketplace, it required that investment banking firms be prepared to respond on short notice to commit funds to a deal. This meant the investment banking firm had very little time

TABLE 3-2	TYPICAL GROSS SPREADS BY OFFERING SIZE

COMMON STOCK OFFERING*		INITIAL PUBLIC OFFERING	
SIZE (IN MILLIONS)	GROSS SPREAD	SIZE (IN MILLIONS)	GROSS SPREAD
$ 10	6.0–8.0%	$ 5	8.0–10.0%
15	5.0–7.5	10	7.5– 9.0
20	5.0–7.0	15	7.0– 8.0
30	3.5–5.0	20	6.5– 7.0
50	2.0–5.0	30	5.5– 7.0
100	2.0–4.5	50	5.0– 7.0
150	2.0–4.0		
200	2.0–4.0		

FIXED INCOME OFFERING[†]

SIZE (IN MILLIONS)	GROSS SPREAD
$ 20	1.3%
25	1.2
30	1.0
50	0.7
100	0.7
150	0.7
200	0.7

* For industrial companies not utilities.

† Typical offering of A-rated corporate debt with 10 years to maturity.

Source: Adapted from Figures 1, 2, and 3 of G. Clyde Buck, "Spreads and Fees in Investment Banking," Chapter 5 in Robert Lawrence Kuhn (ed.), *The Library of Investment Banking*, Volume II (Homewood, IL: Dow Jones-Irwin, 1990).

to line up a syndicate, favoring the bought deal. However, a consequence of this is that investment banking firms needed to expand their capital so that they could commit greater amounts of funds to such deals.

The risk of capital loss in a bought deal may not be as great as it may first appear. There are some deals that are so straightforward that a large investment banking firm may have enough institutional investor interest that the risks of distributing the issue at the reoffering price are small. Moreover, in the case of bonds, there are hedging strategies using the interest rate risk control tools that we will discuss in Chapters 19 and 20 that reduce the risk of realizing a loss of selling the bonds at a price below the reoffering price.

Another variation for underwriting securities is the auction process. In this method, the issuer announces the terms of the issue, and interested parties submit bids for the entire issue. The auction form is mandated for certain securities of regulated public utilities and many municipal debt obligations. It is more commonly referred to as a *competitive bidding* underwriting. In a variant of the process the bidders indicate the price they are willing to pay and the amount they are willing to buy. As we explain in Chapter 14, this process is used exclusively in the issuance of U.S. Treasury securities.

A corporation can issue new common stock directly to existing shareholders via a *preemptive rights offering*.[5] A preemptive right grants existing shareholders the right to buy some proportion of the new shares issued at a price below market value. This insures that they may maintain their proportionate equity interest in the corporation. For the shares sold via a preemptive rights offering, the underwriting services of an investment banker are not needed. However, the issuing corporation will use the services of an investment banker for the distribution of common stock that is not subscribed to. A *standby* underwriting arrangement will be used in such instances. This arrangement calls for the underwriter to buy the unsubscribed shares. The issuing corporation pays a standby fee to the investment banking firm. In the U.S., the practice of issuing common stock via a preemptive rights offering is uncommon. In other countries it is much more common; in some countries, it is the only means by which a new offering of common stock may be sold.

Global Offerings.   The underwriting of securities is not limited to offerings in the U.S. An issuer can select among many foreign securities markets to identify the one in which to offer securities so as to reduce its cost of funds. Indeed, some securities have been offered simultaneously in several markets throughout the world. This will be discussed further in Chapter 22.

Privatization.   Investment bankers have assisted in offering the securities of government-owned companies to private investors. This process is referred to as *privatization*. An example in the U.S. is the initial public offering of the U.S. government-owned railroad company Conrail in March of 1987. More than 58 million shares were sold, raising a total of $1.65 billion. This is the largest IPO in the history of the U.S.[6] Non-U.S. examples include the U.K.'s

---

[5] For a description of the mechanics of this underwriting arrangement, see Richard A. Brealey and Stewart C. Myers, *Principles of Corporate Finance* (New York: McGraw-Hill, 1991), Chapter 15.

[6] Prior to the Conrail IPO, AT&T had raised $1.5 billion in 1983.

British Telecom, Chile's Pacifica, and France's Paribas. In the case of British Telecom (the government-owned telephone company of the United Kingdom), the amount raised was $4.7 billion. This offering was a global offering; that is, it was offered simultaneously in several countries.

In the 1990s, the role of investment bankers in placing the securities of government-owned companies into the hands of private investors will increase. Eastern Europe, for example, is following a major program of privatization. It has been estimated that the combined capitalization of now government-owned firms there will be around $200 billion.[7] Revenue for investment bankers will be generated from several sources, including underwriting fees, fees from finding joint venture partners, and advisory fees.

Trading of Securities

We have noted that a successful underwriting of a security requires a strong institutional sales force. The sales force provides feedback on advance interest in the deal, and the traders (or market makers) provide input in pricing the deal as well.

It would be a mistake to think that once the securities are all sold the investment banking firm's ties with the deal are ended. In the case of bonds, those who bought the securities will look to the investment banking firm to make a market in the issue. This means that the investment banking firm must be willing to take a principal position in secondary market transactions. Revenue from this activity is generated through (1) the bid–ask spread, and (2) appreciation of the price of the securities held in inventory. Obviously, if the securities depreciate in price, there will be a reduction in revenue. To protect against a loss, investment banks engage in hedging strategies.

There are various strategies that are employed by traders to generate revenue from positions in one or more securities: riskless arbitrage, risk arbitrage, and speculation.

Riskless Arbitrage. Of the two types of arbitrage transactions (riskless arbitrage and risk arbitrage), *riskless arbitrage* calls for a trader to find a security trading at different prices in two different markets. For example, as we explain in Chapter 8, there are common stocks of companies that trade in more than one location within the U.S. Also, as we explain in Chapter 22, common stock of some multinational companies trades in both the U.S. and on an exchange in one or more foreign countries. If there are price discrepancies in the various markets, it may be possible to lock in a profit after

---

[7] David Fairlamb, "The Privatizing of Eastern Europe," *Institutional Investor* (April 1990), p. 172.

transactions costs by selling the security in the market where it is priced higher and buying it in the market where it is priced lower. In the case of a security priced in a foreign currency, the price must be converted based on the exchange rate.

Traders don't hold their breath waiting for such situations to occur, because they are rare. While they do exist periodically in financial markets, riskless arbitrage opportunities are short-lived. There are, however, situations where packages of securities and derivative contracts, combined with borrowing, can produce a payoff identical to another security, yet the two are priced differently. The key point is that a riskless arbitrage transaction does not expose the investor to any adverse movement in the market price of the securities in the transaction.

We'll give examples of this in future chapters because the concept of riskless arbitrage provides the underlying process by which assets are priced. For now, a simple example should suffice.

Consider three securities A, B, and C that can be purchased today, and for which one year from now there are only two possible outcomes (State #1 and State #2):

Security	Price	Payoff in State #1	Payoff in State #2
A	$70	$50	$100
B	60	30	120
C	80	38	112

Let W_A and W_B be the quantity of security A and B, respectively, in the portfolio. Then the payoff (i.e., the terminal value of the portfolio) under the two states can be expressed mathematically as follows:

if State #1 occurs: $\$\ 50\ W_A + \$\ 30\ W_B$

if State #2 occurs: $\$100\ W_A + \$120\ W_B$

Can we create a portfolio consisting of A and B that will reproduce the payoff of C regardless of the state that occurs one year from now? That is, we want to select W_A and W_B such that:

if State #1 occurs: $\$\ 50\ W_A + \$\ 30\ W_B = \$\ 38$

if State #2 occurs: $\$100\ W_A + \$120\ W_B = \$112$

The dollar payoff on the right-hand side of the two equations is the payoff of C in each state.

We can solve these two equations algebraically, obtaining a value of 0.4 for W_A and 0.6 for W_B. Thus, a portfolio consisting of 0.4 of security A and 0.6 of security B will have the same payoff as security C. How much will it cost us to construct this portfolio? As the prices of A and B are $70 and $60, respectively, the cost is:

$$0.40\ (\$70) + 0.60\ (\$60) = \$64$$

Note that the price of C is $80. Thus, for only $64 an investor can obtain the same payoff as C. This is a riskless arbitrage opportunity that can be exploited by buying A and B in the proportions given above and shorting (selling) C. This lets the investor lock in a profit of $16 today regardless of what happens one year from now. By selling C, the investor must pay $38 if State #1 occurs and $112 if State #2 occurs. The investor will obtain the dollars necessary to make either payment from the payoff of A and B.

Risk Arbitrage.   Another type of arbitrage is called *risk arbitrage*. There are two types of risk arbitrage. The first arises in the case of exchange offers for securities of corporations coming out of a bankruptcy proceeding. For example, suppose that company A is being reorganized, and one of its bonds is now selling in the market for $200. If the trader believes that the outcome of the bankruptcy proceedings will be the exchange of three securities with an estimated value of $280 for the existing bond worth $200, then the trader will buy the existing bond. The trader will realize a profit of $80 if in fact the final exchange offer is as anticipated, and the value of the package is worth $280.

The spread between the $280 potential package and the $200 price for the bond reflects two risks: the risk that the exchange will not take place on the terms that the trader believes, and the risk that the value of the package of three securities that will be received will be less than $200. The "risk" in this risk arbitrage transaction reflects these two risks.

The other type of risk arbitrage occurs when a merger or acquisition is announced. The merger or acquisition can involve only a cash exchange, an exchange of securities, or a combination of both. First let's consider a cash exchange. Suppose that company X announces that it plans to make an offer to buy company Y's common stock for $100 per share at a time when company Y's common stock is selling for $70. One would expect that the market price of company Y's common stock would rise to around $100. There is, however, a chance that company X will, for whatever reason, withdraw its planned purchase of the stock. The price of company Y's common stock consequently may rise to, say, $90 rather than $100. The $10 difference is the market's assessment of the likelihood of the planned purchase not being completed. An investor who buys the common stock of Y can lock in a profit of $10 if the purchase occurs at $100. The risk is that it will not occur and that the price will decline below $90.

The various takeover attempts of UAL Corp. (the parent company of United Airlines) give a classic example of the risk associated with this type of risk arbitrage. In September 1989 there was a $300 per share bid for UAL's stock made by a group consisting of pilots and management. While the board of UAL Corp. approved the offer, the bidders could not obtain the necessary financing to complete the transaction. During this time, the stock had reached a peak of $296 per share. In mid-October, when it was determined that the transaction would not take place, the stock fell in a matter of a few days by almost 50%. In January 1990, there was once again a bid for UAL Corp. for $201 per share, the bidder this time being the union. Once again, the financing for the takeover could not be obtained, resulting in a plunge in the market price. It has been estimated that these failed takeover attempts resulted in losses to risk arbitrageurs of over $1 billion.

When the transaction involves the exchange of securities rather than cash, the announced terms of the exchange will not be reflected immediately in the price of the securities involved. For example, suppose that company B announces that it plans to acquire company T. Company B is called the *b*idding or acquiring firm and company T the *t*arget firm. Company B announces that it intends to offer one share of its stock in exchange for one share of company T stock. At the time of the announcement, suppose that the prices of the stock of B and T are $50 and $42, respectively. If the acquisition does take place as announced, a trader who acquires one share of company T for $42 can exchange it for stock worth $50, a spread of $8. This spread reflects three risks: (1) the acquisition may not be consummated for one reason or another and then T's stock may have to be sold, possibly at a loss, (2) there is a time delay, which means that there will be a cost to financing the position in T's stock, and (3) the price of B's stock can decline in value so that when T's stock is exchanged for B's, less of a spread is realized.

The way to protect against this last risk is for the trader to buy shares of T and sell short an equal number of shares of B (recall the transaction is a one-for-one share exchange), in order to lock in a spread of $8 if the transaction is consummated. Let's look at what happens now if the price of B's stock changes at the time the transaction is consummated. At that time, the price of the stock of both B and T will be the same. Suppose the price of B's stock falls from $50 to $45. Then, when the trader exchanges one share of stock T for stock B, there will be a profit of $3 at the purchase price of $42 for stock T. The short sale of one share of stock B for $50 can now be covered by buying it back for $45, realizing a profit of $5. The trader's overall profit will be $8, the spread that the trader wanted to lock in.

Suppose instead that at the time the exchange is consummated one share of stock B is worth $60 per share. By exchanging stock T, which was purchased at $42, for one share of stock B, which is now worth $60, a profit of $18 is realized on this leg of the transaction. However, because stock B was sold short for $50 and must now be purchased for $60 to cover the short position, a loss of $10 is realized on the second leg of the transaction. Overall, a profit of $8 still is realized.

Thus, risk arbitrage to lock in a spread, *if the exchange is consummated on the announced terms*, involves buying the shares of the target company and shorting the shares of the acquiring or bidding company. The number of shares depends on the exchange terms. Our example assumes a one-for-one exchange, so one share of B was shorted for every share of T purchased. Had the exchange been one share of B for every two shares of T, then one share of B would be shorted for every two shares of T purchased.

There remains the first risk: the risk that the deal will not be consummated. To reduce this risk, the trader or research department must carefully examine the likelihood of a successful takeover or merger.[8]

Speculation.   Speculative trading is one in which the trader positions the capital of the investment banking firm to take advantage of a specific anticipated movement of prices or a spread between two prices. The benefits of being right, particularly with a highly leveraged position, are rewarding. We read in the popular press that some investment banking firms have reaped millions of dollars from a certain speculative position; remember, however, that just as often we read about large trading losses from speculative strategies.

Execution of Trades for Clients.   Commissions are generated by executing trades for investors, both retail and institutional investors. Two common institutional trades that investment bankers are called upon to execute are *block trades* and *program* (or *basket*) *trades*. These trades are discussed in Chapter 8.

Prior to May 1975, commissions charged by brokers for executing stock trades were fixed by the exchange on which the stock was traded. Now that they are negotiable, competition has reduced the commissions that brokers charge.

Research and Trading.   To encourage clients to use a firm to execute transactions so that commissions or the bid–ask spread income can be generated, investment banks provide research for clients. Typically, the research is provided free for clients that generate a certain amount of trades. For those that do not, the research is sold.

---

[8] Of course, there is always the Dennis Levine/Ivan Boesky risk reduction approach to risk arbitrage: through illegal means acquire material non-public information (called "inside information") about merger and acquisition transactions. This is, of course, not an approach we recommend.

There is some research that a firm will restrict to its own traders. The purpose is to provide strategies or information that the firm's trader may be able to use to improve performance.

Private Placement of Securities

In addition to underwriting securities for distribution to the public, investment banking firms place securities with a limited number of institutional investors such as insurance companies, investment companies, and pension funds. Private placement is distinguished from the "public" offering of securities that we have described so far. The size of the private placement market is estimated to be $200 billion.[9]

Public and private offerings of securities differ in terms of the regulatory requirements that must be satisfied by the issuer. The Securities Act of 1933 and the Securities Exchange Act of 1934 require that all securities offered to the general public must be registered with the SEC, unless there is a specific exemption.

The Securities Acts allow three exemptions from federal registration. First, intrastate offerings—that is, securities sold only within a state—are exempt. Second, there is a small-offering exemption (Regulation A). Specifically, if the offering is for $1 million or less, the securities need not be registered. Finally, Section 4(2) of the 1933 Act exempts from registration "transactions by an issuer not involving any public offering." At the same time, the 1933 Act does not provide specific guidelines to identify what is a private offering or placement.

In 1982, almost a half century after the passage of the 1933 Act, the SEC adopted Regulation D, which sets forth the specific guidelines that must be satisfied to qualify for exemption from registration under Section 4(2). The guidelines require that, in general, the securities cannot be offered through any form of general advertising or general solicitation that would prevail for public offerings. Most importantly, the guidelines restrict the sale of securities to "sophisticated" investors. Such "accredited" investors are defined as those who (1) have the capability to evaluate (or who can afford to employ an advisor to evaluate) the risk and return characteristics of the securities, and (2) have the resources to bear the economic risks.[10]

---

[9] John W. Milligan, "Two Cheers for 144A," *Institutional Investor* (July 1990), p. 117.

[10] Under the current law, an accredited investor is one who satisfies either a net worth test (at least $1 million excluding automobiles, home, and home furnishings) or an annual income test (at least $200,000 for a single individual, $300,000 for a couple for the last two years, with expectations of such income to continue for the current year).

The exemption of an offering does not mean that the issuer need not disclose information to potential investors. The issuer must still furnish the same information deemed material by the SEC. This is provided in a private placement memorandum, as opposed to a prospectus for a public offering. The distinction between the private placement memorandum and the prospectus is that the former does not include information deemed by the SEC as "non-material" whereas such information is required in a prospectus. Moreover, unlike a prospectus, the private placement memorandum is not subject to SEC review.

Investment banking firms assist in the private placement of securities in several ways. They work with the issuer and potential investors on the design and pricing of the security. Often it has been in the private placement market that investment bankers first design new security structures. Field testing of many of the innovative securities that we describe in this book occurred in the private placement market.[11]

The investment bankers may be involved with lining up the investors as well as designing the issue. Or, if the issuer has already identified the investors, the investment banker may serve only in an advisory capacity. Work as an advisor generates fee income, as does arranging the placement with investors. An investment banker can also participate in the transaction on a best efforts underwriting arrangement.

It is in the private placement market that securities for risky emerging companies are placed. Investment banking firms work with these clients in developing a business plan and advise them how to raise funds. They also negotiate on behalf of their clients with venture capital firms—that is, firms that specialize in acquiring equity interest in risky emerging companies.

The fees for arranging a private placement vary depending on the issuance amount and the complexity of the transaction. Fees for the placement of an issue of senior debt might be as follows:[12]

SIZE OF PLACEMENT (IN MILLIONS)	FEE
$ 5–10	1.5–4.0%
10–25	1.0–3.0
25–50	0.7–2.0
>50	0.5–1.5

---

[11] For example, zero-coupon corporate bonds were first publicly issued by corporations in April 1981. (The first issue was by J.C. Penney.) Prior to that there was a private offering by PepsiCo.

[12] Buck, "Spreads and Fees in Investment Banking," p. 149.

For risky subordinated debt, the fee would be higher.

In the case of fund raising for risky emerging companies, the average fee might be 5% to 6%, higher for small transactions.[13] Moreover, in raising venture capital for clients, investment bankers are frequently offered the opportunity to share in the prosperity of the company. This opportunity typically comes in the form of an option to buy a specified number of shares at a price that is set at a time the funds are raised. An arrangement that allows the investment banking firm to benefit from the company's success is referred to as an "equity kicker."

Rule 144A.   One restriction imposed on buyers of privately placed securities is that they may not be resold for two years after acquisition. Thus, there is no liquidity in the market for that time period. Buyers of privately placed securities must be compensated for the lack of liquidity.

In April 1990, however, SEC Rule 144A became effective. This rule eliminates the two-year holding period by permitting large institutions to trade securities acquired in a private placement among themselves without having to register these securities with the SEC. Under Rule 144A, a large institution is defined as one holding at least $100 million of the security.

It is too early to assess the impact of this new rule on the growth of the private placement market.[14] Some believe that it will encourage non-U.S. corporations to issue securities in the U.S. private placement market for two reasons. First, it will attract new large institutional investors into the market who were unwilling previously to buy private placements because of the requirement to hold the securities for two years. Such an increase in the number of institutional investors may encourage non-U.S. entities to issue securities. Second, foreign entities have been unwilling to raise funds in the U.S. prior to establishment of Rule 144A because they had to register their securities and furnish the necessary disclosure set forth by U.S. securities laws. Private placement requires less disclosure. Rule 144A also improves liquidity, reducing the cost of raising funds.

---

[13] Buck, "Spreads and Fees in Investment Banking," p. 150.

[14] The difference of opinion as to the likely outcome of Rule 144A can be illustrated in comments by two investment bankers, both of the First Boston Corporation. Curtis Welling, head of capital markets, believes that the rule is nothing short of revolutionary. In his words: "I think it will be viewed in 10 years as equal to or greater than the creation of the Eurobond market or Rule 415." His colleague, Thomas Keaveney, managing director for private finance, says: "It's awfully hard to get excited about something like that." (Milligan, "Two Cheers for 144A," p. 117.)

Securitization of Assets

Securitization of assets refers to the issuance of securities that have a pool of assets as collateral. The securitization of home mortgage loans to create mortgage pass-through securities (which we discuss in Chapter 18) is the first example of this process. The bulk of these securities are backed by the U.S. government or an agency of the U.S. government. More recently, investment banking firms and commercial banks have created mortgage pass-through securities that are not guaranteed by the U.S. government or a government agency. These securities are called *private label* pass-through securities.

Since 1985, non-mortgage assets have been securitized as well. The securities thus created are called *asset-backed securities.* The two most common type of asset-backed securities are those collateralized by automobile loans and credit card receivables, although there are securities backed by boat loans, recreational vehicle loans, computer leases, and accounts receivable. Mortgage pass-through securities and asset-backed securities, as well as the implications of asset securitization for financial markets, are discussed fully in Chapter 18.

Asset securitization generates revenue in one of two ways. First, when an investment banking firm securitizes assets on behalf of a client, and then underwrites the issue, it receives the gross spread, just as in any other underwriting. Second, if the investment banking firm buys the underlying assets, creates the securities, and then sells the securities, it realizes a profit on the difference between what it sells the entire issue for and the price it paid for the assets.

Mergers and Acquisitions

Investment banking firms are active in mergers and acquisitions (M&A). Under M&A activity are also included leveraged buyouts (LBOs), restructuring and recapitalization of companies, and reorganization of bankrupt and troubled companies. There has been significant activity in the M&A business in the U.S. in the 1980s, and it is expected that merger, LBO, and restructuring activities will be substantial in Europe in the 1990s.

Investment bankers may participate in M&A activity in one of several ways: (1) finding M&A candidates, (2) advising acquiring companies or target companies with respect to price and non-price terms of an exchange, or helping target companies fend off an unfriendly takeover attempt, and (3) assisting acquiring companies in obtaining the necessary funds to finance a purchase.

Fees charged by investment bankers in M&A work depend on the extent of their participation and the complexity of the activities they are asked to perform. An investment banker may simply receive an advisory fee or retainer. More likely, an investment banker will receive a fee based on a percentage of the selling price. The fee structure in this case can be of one of three types: (1) the percentage can decline, the higher the selling price, (2) the percentage can be the same regardless of the selling price, or (3) the percentage can be fixed with addition of an incentive fee if the price is better than a specified amount. An example of the first fee structure is what is called the 5-4-3-2-1 "Lehman formula." In this fee structure that some firms have adopted, the fee would be 5% of the first $1 million, 4% of the second $1 million, 3% of the third $1 million, 2% of the fourth $1 million, and 1% for any excess amount. A typical flat percentage is 2% to 3% of the selling price.

Participating in an LBO can generate several fees. LBOs call for a firm to be acquired using mostly debt funds and taken private. The debt raised is from one of two sources: senior bank debt and unsecured junior debt (called subordinated debt, or mezzanine financing). An investment banking firm can earn fees from (1) proposing the acquisition, (2) arranging the financing, (3) arranging *bridge financing* (that is, temporary funds loaned until permanent debt financing is completed), and (4) other advisory fees.

Under "other advisory fees" we would find fees charged by investment banking firms for providing a valuation of a firm that is the subject of a takeover or a merger, and for rendering a *fairness opinion*. The question of fairness arises in such a transaction because there is an issue as to whether the purchasers of the company may have access to information that allows them to acquire the firm at a price less than its true market value. This situation is of increasing concern in LBOs, particularly management-led LBOs—that is, where the current management of the firm makes an offer to purchase the company. An investment banking firm is typically engaged by the board of directors of the company that is the subject of the takeover to render an independent and expert opinion as to the fairness of the price being offered for the shares. Fees for a fairness opinion range from $50,000 for a transaction involving a few million dollars to $1 million or more for large transactions.[15]

An investment banking firm may provide its own capital for bridge financing. This is one type of merchant banking, the activity that we turn to next.

Merchant Banking

When an investment banking firm commits its own funds by either taking an equity interest or creditor position in companies, this activity is referred to as merchant banking. If an equity interest is taken, there is usually substantial

---

[15] Buck, "Spreads and Fees in Investment Banking," p. 153.

upside potential. The interest rate charged on debt funding provided to a client, particularly for bridge financing, is high, reflecting the high risk associated with such lending activities.

First Boston Corporation's bridge loan of $450 million to Ohio Mattress Co. to finance an LBO illustrates the risk of bridge financing for an investment banking firm. After the LBO was completed and Ohio Mattress sought to acquire permanent debt financing to refinance the bridge loan, First Boston could not sell the securities. As a result, First Boston was stuck with the loan.[16]

Bridge financing is seen as important not only for its potential source of interest income, but also as a financing vehicle that can be used to attract clients who are considering an LBO.

Trading and Creation of Risk Control Instruments

Futures, options, interest rate swaps, and customized interest rate agreements are examples of instruments that can be used to control the risk of an investor's portfolio, or, in the case of an issuer, the risk associated with the issuance of a security. Risk control instruments allow an investment banking firm to realize revenue in several ways. Customers generate commissions from the exchange-traded instruments they buy and sell. This is no different from the commissions generated by the brokerage service performed for customers when stocks are bought and sold.

Second, there are certain risk control instruments that an investment banking firm *creates* for its clients where it acts as a counterparty to the agreement. These are called over-the-counter or dealer-created instruments. An example is an interest rate swap, which we discussed briefly in the previous chapter. (Others will be described in Chapter 20.) There is the risk of loss of capital whenever an investment banking firm is a counterparty, because the investment banker becomes a principal to the transaction. To protect against capital loss, an investment banking firm will seek another party to take the other side of the transaction. When this occurs, spread income is generated.

Risk control instruments are also used to protect an investment bank's own position in transactions. Here are just two examples. Suppose an investment banking firm underwrites a bond issue. The risk that the firm is exposed to is a decline in the price of the bonds purchased from the issuer,

---

[16] Eventually the parent company of First Boston, Credit Suisse First Boston, provided assistance by buying the bridge loan from First Boston.

which are to be reoffered to the public. (As we explain in Chapter 11, this tends to occur if interest rates rise.) Using either interest rate futures or options, the subject of Chapter 19, the investment banking firm can protect itself. As a second example, an investment banking firm has many trading desks with either long or short positions in a security. Risk control instruments can be used by the trading desks to protect the firm against an adverse price movement.

Money Management

- Investment banking firms have created subsidiaries that manage funds for either individual investors or institutional investors such as pension funds. Examples include First Boston Asset Management, a subsidiary of the investment banking firm of First Boston Corporation; Blackstone Financial Management, a subsidiary of the Blackstone Group, an investment banking firm; and Nomura Investment Management Company, a subsidiary of Nomura Securities, a Japanese investment banking firm. Money management activities generate fee income based on a percentage of the assets under management.

Fees

Now that we have reviewed the activities of investment banking firms, let's look at the fees generated by two investment banking firms. In Tables 3-3 and 3-4 we present the revenue in 1989 of two firms, Merrill Lynch and Bear Stearns, both of which are involved in all the activities we discussed above. (The entry "Investment Banking" in the tables means underwriting.)

TABLE 3-3 1989 REVENUE OF MERRILL LYNCH (IN MILLIONS)	
Commissions	$ 1,798,783
Interest and Dividends	5,489,283
Principal Transactions	1,225,015
Investment Banking	1,108,462
Insurance	553,521
Asset Management and Custodial Fees	598,250
Other	561,892
Total Revenues	$11,325,206

Source: 1989 Annual Report.

TABLE 3-4	1989 REVENUE OF BEAR STEARNS (IN MILLIONS)
Commissions	$ 346,515
Principal Transactions	518,159
Investment Banking	235,795
Interest and Dividends	1,253,919
Other Income	10,349
Total Revenues	$2,364,737

Source: 1989 Annual Report.

CURRENT INDUSTRY STRUCTURE

As we noted earlier, not all investment banking firms are involved in every activity described above. One way to classify firms in the investment banking business is by the types of activities that they are involved in, or, more appropriately, the types of activities that they emphasize.

Within an activity area, firms that specialize in the area can be ranked by some measure of market share. Depending on the activity area, there are several potential measures. As an example, consider underwriting activity. Market share can be measured by one of the following: the number of deals done in a year, or the total dollar volume of all deals done in a year. Even this isn't simple. Recall that in an underwriting an investment banking firm may be the lead manager, comanager, or just a member of the underwriting syndicate. Consequently, ranking by number of deals or total dollar volume of deals can be made by giving full credit only to the lead manager or some proportional credit to each manager.

Moreover, adding to the complication, even within an activity area, such as underwriting, a firm may not be active within all segments of a given market. For example, a firm may have a major presence in the underwriting of high-quality corporate bonds, but it may not be involved in the underwriting of commercial paper, high-yield (junk) bonds, or municipal bonds.

Some industry observers believe that measures such as the number of deals and the total dollar volume of deals are not completely adequate. One reason is that it is necessary to know how a transaction translates into profits. To draw an analogy to manufacturing, having the largest market share for a product doesn't necessarily mean the largest profit, particularly if the product is underpriced and/or the cost structure reflects operating inefficiencies. Returning to investment banking firms, the assembly of high-priced human capital coupled with a desire to buy market share by accepting lower gross spreads in the underwriting of some types of securities may have caused some firms to be ranked number one in that area using the measures we have described. This income may not necessarily flow through to the bottom line, however. As an example, Salomon Brothers Inc was frequently ranked at the top in the underwriting of municipal securities. Yet, it dropped out of this business.

Investment bankers point to "reputation" as a non-quantifiable measure of the relative importance of an investment banking firm within a business activity. While ranking by the measures we have discussed may be a proxy for reputation, there are some observers who feel that in some activities there is not necessarily a high correlation.

A popular classification of U.S. firms is as follows: bulge-bracket firms, major bracket firms, submajor bracket firms, regional firms, specialized firms, research firms, and merchant banks.[17]

Bulge-bracket firms are those that are viewed as the premier investment banking firms because of their size, reputation, presence in key markets, and customer base. Included in this exclusive group are First Boston Corporation; Goldman Sachs & Co.; Merrill Lynch; Morgan Stanley, Salomon Brothers Inc; and Lehman Brothers (formerly Shearson Lehman Hutton). Large investment banking firms that do not have the same status as the bulge-bracket firms but nevertheless provide full-line services are called major bracket firms. Included in this group are Bear Stearns & Co.; Smith Barney, Harris Upham; Kidder Peabody; PaineWebber; Donaldson, Lukfin & Jenrette; Dean Witter; and Prudential-Bache Capital Funding.

Submajor bracket firms are frequently New York-based firms that cater to special investor groups and smaller issuing companies. Firms located outside New York and that serve regional issuers (corporate and local governments) are classified as regional firms.

There are also firms that specialize in one major activity. These firms are referred to as "boutiques." Research firms, as the name suggests, specialize in various research products used by investors or issuers of securities. A firm that is classified as a "specialized" firm is one that concentrates on the issuance of securities in certain industries, high technology, say.

Merchant banks are investment banking firms that focus on M&A and fund-raising activities. Examples include the Blackstone Group and Wasserstein, Perella & Co. Japanese investment banking firms have entered into joint ventures with the better-known merchant banking firms. There is a joint venture, for example, between the Blackstone Group and Nikko Securities and between Wasserstein, Perella & Co. and Nomura Securities.

---

[17] Kuhn, p. 20.

COMPETITION AND CHALLENGES FOR INVESTMENT BANKING FIRMS

Investment banking firms face competition from several directions, and will have to rethink the types of activities they wish to dedicate resources to in the future.

Competition

In the previous chapter, we reviewed the Glass–Steagall Act and the separation between commercial banking and investment banking. As we emphasized, the barriers between the two are being eroded. U.S. investment banking firms face not only actual and potential competition from commercial banks (both domestic and foreign), but also competition from foreign investment banking firms. This competition will put pressure on fees and spreads from all activities.

Competition is coming in other forms. Trading technology that may allow institutional investors to trade among themselves without the use of brokers or a need for dealers threatens the sales and trading revenue of investment banking firms. Examples of automated transaction systems are Instinet, the Cross Network, and POSIT. Trading technologies will be discussed in Chapter 8.

Underwriting revenues could be diminished if corporate issuers can succeed in placing newly issued debt obligations directly with institutional investors. One step in this direction is the services provided by CapitaLink Securities. This firm is linking issuers directly to institutional investors using computerized auctions. In 1989, CapitaLink was successful in offering a new corporate bond issue directly to institutional investors via a computerized auction.[18] At the end of 1990, there were 125 major institutions and 16 prospective issuers that had joined the service.[19] In February 1988, Great Northern Nekoosa was able to place $75 million in publicly registered bonds directly with Metropolitan Life Insurance Company.[20] This was not a private placement; the bonds were registered.

In June 1989, Metropolitan Life actually attempted to go head-to-head with investment banking firms to bid on a $100 million bond offering of Carolina Power & Light Co. Although Metropolitan Life did not actually get to bid on the issue because it insisted on a provision that would protect it

---

[18] Beth Selby, "End-Running the Underwriters," *Institutional Investor* (June 1989), p. 27.

[19] Chris Welles and Monica Roman, "The Future of Wall Street," *Business Week* (November 5, 1990), p. 122.

[20] Beth Selby, "End-Running the Street," *Institutional Investor* (September 1989), p. 181.

against certain risks, the event was a clear indication that the Great Northern Nekoosa transaction was not a one-time transaction but part of a longer-term plan by Metropolitan Life to deal directly with issuers for publicly registered debt securities, thereby bypassing investment banking firms. It has been estimated that in 1989 Metropolitan Life bought directly several dozen publicly registered debt obligations with an estimated par value of $1 billion.[21]

Investment bankers' response to the practice of direct purchase of publicly registered securities is that as intermediaries they add value by searching their institutional client base, which increases the likelihood that the issuer will incur the lowest cost, after adjusting for the underwriting fees. By dealing with just a few institutional investors, investment bankers argue, issuers cannot be assured of obtaining funds at the lowest cost. In addition, investment bankers often provide another important role: they make a secondary market in the securities they issue. This improves the perceived liquidity of the issue and, as a result, reduces the cost to issuers.

The question of whether investment bankers can obtain lower cost funding (after accounting for underwriting fees) to issuers compared to a direct offering is an interesting empirical question. In July 1989, Corning Corporation asked its investment bankers (Goldman Sachs & Co. and Lazard Frères & Co.) to bid on a traditional public offering of $100 million in bonds, and invited Metropolitan Life and another institutional investor to bid on a private placement of $100 million in bonds.[22] Although the traditional public offering was selected, this does not indicate that Corning chose the cheapest offering mechanism, because one was a public offering and the other a proposed private placement. As we explained earlier, investors typically want a higher yield in a private placement because of the lack of liquidity.

This example may suggest the future road that some corporate issuers will take in soliciting bids for an offering. Moreover, Rule 144A will provide liquidity in the private placement market, driving down the yields demanded by institutional investors. In fact, insurance companies such as Prudential-Bache and Cigna have established units that will bid on private placements and distribute the obligations to other institutional investors.

Investment bankers also face competition from the more sophisticated corporations that are establishing in-house groups to perform some of the activities traditionally done by investment banking firms. Here are just two examples.[23] British Petroleum established an in-house investment bank, BP

---

[21] Selby, "End-Running the Street," p. 181.

[22] Selby, "End-Running the Street," p. 182.

[23] David Zigas, Gary Weiss, Ted Holden and Richard A. Melcher, "Corporate America's End Run," *Business Week* (November 5, 1990), pp. 124–130.

Finance. The activities this group has performed for its parent company are: (1) advising on multibillion dollar divestiture transactions, (2) directly issuing British Petroleum commercial paper, and (3) handling all foreign exchange trading. DuPont has set up an M&A unit that does an average of 20 deals a year, ranging from $5 million to $500 million.

Reassessing the Business

The biggest problem the managers of investment banks face, however, is determining which lines of business are the most beneficial to pursue. While investment bankers receive high marks in the creation of new financial products and strategies, many would receive failing marks in managerial economics/managerial accounting. We refer to topics such as product pricing and cost allocation, subjects that investment bankers apparently felt they did not need in the glory days of the 1980s.

Investment banks typically have done little study to determine how costs could be controlled. Fixed overhead costs were often incurred with no concern for long-run implications for profits. In turn, overhead costs typically were arbitrarily allocated among activities, thereby masking the true costs of creating products or providing services. This caused misallocation of resources to products or services that were either unprofitable or did not generate an adequate return relative to the resources committed.

Subsidizing unprofitable or less profitable activities with profits from other activities has caused dissension among investment bankers. In fact, several of the boutique firms were started when key investment bankers at a firm became disenchanted with the distribution of profits to the various business units. The merchant banking boutique, Wasserstein, Perella & Co., for one, was created by two former M&A investment bankers at First Boston who were dissatisfied when the large M&A fees generated were used to subsidize other firm activities, particularly unprofitable trading activities. The goal of a "financial supermarket" may be one that investment bankers will find it uneconomic to pursue.

Investment banking firms must take several steps to remain profitable. Costs have to reflect the true cost of delivering products or services, which requires examining existing products and services to determine what costs are and how they can be reduced. Investment banking firms are taking that step.

SUMMARY

Investment bankers provide two general functions: raising funds for clients and assisting clients in the sale or purchase of securities. In this chapter we have explained the various activities of investment banking and how these activities generate revenue. The activities include public offering of securities, public trading of securities, private placement of securities, securitization of assets, mergers and acquisitions, merchant banking, trading and creation of risk control instruments, and money management.

Not all firms are active participants in each activity. The premier firms, because of their size, reputation, presence in key markets, and customer base are called bulge-bracket firms. Major bracket firms do not have the same high status as the bulge-bracket firms but nevertheless provide full-line services. Submajor bracket firms, typically located in New York, focus on special investor groups and smaller issuing companies. Regional firms are located outside New York and serve regional issuers. Research firms, specialized firms, and merchant banks specialize in one activity and are referred to as boutiques.

Investment banking firms are facing increased competition that has forced them to reconsider their long-term business strategies. Competition comes not only from commercial banks, but also from new trading technologies, which are allowing institutional investors to execute trades without using investment banking firms as intermediaries, and the direct purchase by institutional investors of publicly registered securities from issuers.

QUESTIONS

1. Explain at least three circumstances when investment banking firms must commit their own capital.

2. **a.** What is meant by a bought deal?

   b. Why do bought deals expose investment banking firms to greater capital risk than traditional underwriting?

3. The following quotation appeared in the December 10, 1990, issue of *Portfolio Letter:*

   Arb desks across the Street were biting off big chunks of NCR last week as AT&T unveiled an all cash $90 a share hostile tender offer for the computer company. While unanimous in their view that NCR will be acquired by AT&T, the arbs were divided on the duration of the struggle and the price NCR will eventually fetch.

   What type of investment banking activity is being discussed here, and what are the opportunities and risks inherent in such activities?

4. *The Economist* of September 22, 1990, provided this description of recent activities of investment bankers:

> Ever since the Berlin Wall came down, the airlines, hotels and taxi ranks of Eastern Europe have been filled with business-suited Westerners hoping to make money in the wake of its collapse. In the first few months, many came, saw and left shaking their heads in disbelief at the mess. But fast on their heels came the professional advisers—accountants, management consultants, investment bankers—for whom the mess itself is money. Or may one day be.

   a. What types of functions can investment banks provide in restructuring the economies of Eastern Europe?

   b. What kinds of investment banking skills will be required?

   c. Can you think of potential problems that investment banks will face?

5. The following statements come from the December 24, 1990, issue of *Corporate Financing Week:*

> As in the public market, growth in the private placement market was slowed this year by a rise in interest rates that pushed many issuers to the sidelines, by the Mideast crisis and by a flight to quality by investors. . . . Foreign private placements saw a marked increase due to Rule 144A.

   a. What are the key distinctions between a private placement and a public offering?

   b. Why would Rule 144A have increased foreign private placements?

6. The quotation following is taken from the February 11, 1991, issue of *Bondweek:*

> Dai Ichi Kangyo Bank, the world's largest bank, and other Japanese banks are eyeing securitization of their U.S. corporate loan portfolios, among other strategies, to help stay within international capital guidelines. . . .

   a. What "international capital guidelines" does this sentence refer to?

   b. What do you think this article means by "securitization of their U.S. corporate loan portfolios," and why would this help in meeting the international capital guidelines?

7. The quotations below come from an *Institutional Investor* article entitled "The Reeducation of Wall Street" in the January 1990 issue. Following each one there is a question to answer.

a. In finance, size has no advantage. The most important thing is what you do *not* do. (Michel David-Weill, senior managing partner at the investment banking firm of Lazard Frères & Co.)

Discuss this assertion and indicate whether you agree or disagree.

b. Market share is a proxy for how active we are in the market, and unless we're in the top group in our principal business we won't be credible enough with our customers. (Stephen Friedman, vice chairman and chief executive officer of Goldman Sachs & Co.)

How is market share measured, and do you agree with the statement?

c. For all their protestations that they are getting costs under control, so far most Wall Street executives are still ignoring basic above-the-line questions. As a body, the industry has attacked expenses and overcapacity only through layoffs. What it needs to do is analyze the real costs of a transaction or deal—or even a business line—by parsing it and coming up with a price for each of the component parts that go into servicing a client, from clearing to research to overhead to management.

Why is it necessary for investment banks to go through this process?

8. How do you think the trends enumerated below will impact the investment banking industry? As a senior manager at a bulge-bracket investment bank, how would you respond to these trends?

a. Major multinational corporations increasingly set up their own in-house investment banks. These companies have in-house expertise on all major investment banking activities.

b. Technological innovations such as CapitaLink that allow institutional investors to deal directly, in the absence of intermediaries, become increasingly common.

c. Deregulation of financial markets eliminates the distinctions imposed by the Glass–Steagall Act between investment and commercial banking activities. J.P. Morgan, Bankers Trust, and other major banks are permitted to become major underwriters of corporate debt and equities.

INSURANCE COMPANIES, PENSION FUNDS, AND INVESTMENT COMPANIES

LEARNING OBJECTIVES

After reading this chapter you will understand:

- the nature of the liabilities faced by financial institutions.

- the nature of the business of insurance companies.

- the differences between the nature of the liabilities of life insurance companies and those of property and casualty insurance companies.

- how the insurance business has changed and the factors contributing to those changes.

- the different types of life insurance policies.

- the different types of pension plans.

- the various financial services provided to pension funds.

- the principal provisions of the Employee Retirement Income Security Act of 1974.

- the different types of investment companies.

- how share prices of mutual funds and closed-end funds are determined.

- the different types of investment companies by investment objective.

I n this chapter we continue our coverage of financial institutions. The four that we discuss here are life insurance companies, property and casualty companies, pension funds, and investment companies. We begin with an overview of the asset/liability management problem for these institutions.

OVERVIEW OF ASSET/LIABILITY MANAGEMENT FOR FINANCIAL INSTITUTIONS

In Chapter 2 we emphasized that the nature of the liabilities dictates the investment strategy a financial institution will pursue. Depository institutions seek to generate income by the spread between the return that they earn on assets and the cost of their funds. That is, they are spread businesses. Two of the four financial institutions that we shall discuss in this chapter—life insurance companies and, to a certain extent, property and casualty insurance companies—are in the spread business.

Pension funds are not in the spread business in that they do not raise funds themselves in the market. They seek to cover the cost of pension obligations at a minimum cost that is borne by the sponsor of the pension plan. Investment companies face no explicit costs for the funds they acquire and must satisfy no specific liability obligations, except in the case of one type of investment company that agrees to repurchase shares at any time.

Nature of Liabilities

By the liabilities of a financial institution we mean the amount and timing of the cash outlays that must be made to satisfy the contractual terms of the obligations issued. The liabilities of any financial institution can be categorized according to four types as shown in Table 4-1. The categorization in the table assumes that the entity that must be paid the obligation will not cancel the financial institution's obligation prior to any actual or projected payout date.

The descriptions of cash outlays as either known or uncertain are undoubtedly broad. When we refer to a cash outlay as being uncertain, we do not mean that it cannot be predicted. There are some liabilities where the "law of large numbers" makes it easier to predict the timing and/or amount of cash outlays. This is the work typically done by actuaries, but even actuaries have difficulty predicting natural catastrophes such as floods and earthquakes.

As we describe the various financial institutions in this chapter, keep these risk categories in mind. For now, let's illustrate each one.

Type-I Liabilities.   Both the amount and timing of the liabilities are known with certainty. A liability where a financial institution knows that it must pay $50,000 six months from now would be an example. We've already encountered financial institutions that have Type-I liabilities. Banks and thrifts know the amount that they are committed to pay (principal plus interest) on the maturity date of a fixed-rate deposit, assuming that the depositor does not withdraw funds prior to the maturity date.

Type-I liabilities, however, are not limited to depository institutions. A major product sold by life insurance companies is a guaranteed investment contract, popularly referred to as a GIC. The obligation of the life insurance company under this contract is that, for a sum of money (called a *premium*), it will guarantee an interest rate up to some specified maturity date. For example, suppose a life insurance company for a premium of $10 million

| TABLE 4-1 | NATURE OF LIABILITIES OF FINANCIAL INSTITUTIONS | |

LIABILITY TYPE	AMOUNT OF CASH OUTLAY	TIMING OF CASH OUTLAY
Type I	known	known
Type II	known	uncertain
Type III	uncertain	known
Type IV	uncertain	uncertain

issues a five-year GIC agreeing to pay 10% compounded annually. The life insurance company knows that it must pay $16.11 million to the GIC policyholder in five years.[1]

A GIC doesn't seem to be very different from a CD, or another instrument discussed later in this book called a zero-coupon bond, and in fact it is not.[2] Nor does a GIC seem like a product that we would associate with a life insurance company, because the policyholder doesn't have to die in order for someone to be paid. Yet as we shall see later when we discuss life insurance companies, a major group of insurance company financial products are in the pension benefit area. A GIC is one such product.

Type-II Liabilities.   The amount of cash outlay is known, but the timing of the cash outlay is uncertain. The most obvious example of a Type-II liability is a life insurance policy. There are many types of life insurance policies that we shall discuss later, but the most basic type is that, for an annual premium, a life insurance company agrees to make a specified dollar payment to policy beneficiaries upon the death of the insured.

Type-III Liabilities.   With this type of liability, the timing of the cash outlay is known, but the amount is uncertain. A two-year floating-rate CD where the interest rate resets quarterly based on three-month LIBOR is an example. Not surprisingly, there are also floating-rate GICs; these also fall into the Type-III liabilities category.

Type-IV Liabilities.   There are numerous insurance products and pension obligations where there is uncertainty as to both the amount and the timing of the cash outlay. Probably the most obvious examples are automobile and home insurance policies issued by property and casualty insurance companies. When, and if, a payment will have to be made to the policyholder is uncertain. Whenever damage is done to an insured asset, the amount of the payment that must be made is uncertain.

As we will discuss later, sponsors of pension plans can agree to various types of pension obligations to the beneficiaries of the plan. There are plans

---

[1] This amount is determined as follows: $10,000,000 (1.10)^5$.

[2] In fact, banks and S&Ls have offered generic depository time deposits called *bank investment contracts* (BICs) that have the characteristics of GICs and are issued to qualified retirement plans. At the time of this writing, regulators are considering whether these contracts should qualify for deposit insurance.

For Canadian students, we should point out that Canadian banks issue obligations that they call GICs. In this case, it stands for "guaranteed interest certificate."

where retirement benefits depend on the participant's income for a specified number of years before retirement and the total number of years the participant worked. This will affect the amount of the cash outlay. The timing of the cash outlay depends on when the employee elects to retire, and whether the employee remains with the sponsoring plan until retirement. Moreover, both the amount and the timing will depend on how the employee elects to have payments made—over only the employee's life or those of the employee and spouse.

Liquidity Concerns

Because of uncertainty about the timing and/or the amount of the cash outlays, a financial institution must be prepared to have sufficient cash to satisfy its obligations. Also keep in mind that our discussion of liabilities assumes that the entity that holds the obligation against the financial institution may have the right to change the nature of the obligation, perhaps incurring some penalty. For example, in the case of a CD, the depositor may request the withdrawal of funds prior to the maturity date. Typically, the deposit-accepting institution will grant this request, but assess an early withdrawal penalty. In the case of certain types of investment companies, shareholders have the right to redeem their shares at any time.

Some life insurance products have a cash-surrender value. This means that, at specified dates, the policyholder can exchange the policy for a lump sum payment. Typically, the lump sum payment will penalize the policyholder for turning in the policy. There are some life insurance products that have a loan value, which means that the policyholder has the right to borrow against the cash value of the policy.

In addition to uncertainty about the timing and amount of the cash outlays, and the potential for the depositor or policyholder to withdraw cash early or borrow against a policy, a financial institution has to be concerned with possible reduction in cash inflows. In the case of a depository institution, this means the inability to obtain deposits. For insurance companies, it means reduced premiums because of the cancellation of policies. For certain types of investment companies, it means not being able to find new buyers for shares.

Regulations and Taxation

As we explained in Chapter 1, there are regulations and tax considerations that influence the investment policies that financial institutions pursue. In Chapter 2, we discussed those that are important to depository institutions. As we discuss the financial institutions covered in this chapter, we will highlight any key regulations and tax factors.

LIFE INSURANCE COMPANIES

Insurance companies are financial intermediaries that, for a price, will make a payment if a certain event occurs. They function as risk bearers. There are two types of insurance companies: life insurance companies and property and casualty insurance companies. The principal event that the former insure against is death. Upon the death of a policyholder, a life insurance company agrees to make either a lump sum payment or a series of payments to the beneficiary of the policy. Life insurance protection is no longer the only financial product sold by these companies; a major portion of the business of life insurance companies is now in the area of providing retirement benefits. In contrast, property and casualty insurance companies insure against a wide variety of occurrences. Two examples are automobile and home insurance, and we'll discuss others in the next section.

The key distinction between life insurance and property and casualty insurance companies lies in the difficulty of projecting whether a policyholder will be paid off and how much the payment will be. While this is no easy task for either type of insurance company, it is easier from an actuarial perspective for a life insurance company. The amount and timing of claims on property and casualty insurance companies are more difficult to predict because of the randomness of natural catastrophes and the unpredictability of court awards in liability cases. This uncertainty about the timing and amount of cash outlays to satisfy claims has an impact on the investment strategies of the funds of property and casualty insurance companies compared to life insurance companies.

While we have distinguished the two types of insurance companies here because of the nature of the events they insure against, most large insurance companies do underwrite both life insurance and property and casualty insurance policies. Usually a parent company has a life insurance company subsidiary and a property and casualty insurance company subsidiary.

Nature of the Business

In 1988, the total premium income of life insurance companies in the U.S. was $252 billion. Their "admitted assets," defined as all assets approved by state insurance departments as existing property in the ownership of the company, totaled $1.2 trillion.[3]

The contractual commitment made by a life insurance company is only as good as the issuing company's ability to make the contractual payments. There is no government entity, state or federal, that steps in should the

---

[3] *Best's Insurance Reports—Life/Health*, 1988, p. vii.

issuing company fail to satisfy its obligations. Consequently, the pricing terms that life insurance companies offer on policies are related directly to their financial ratings. Most market participants rely on the rating system of A.M. Best, which measures an insurance company's performance in terms of three critical areas: profitability, leverage, and liquidity.

The nature of the life insurance business has changed dramatically since the 1970s, as a result of high and variable inflation rates and increased domestic and global competitive pressures resulting from financial deregulation throughout the world.

Moreover, investor sophistication increased, forcing life insurance companies to offer more competitive products. For example, consider two common forms of life insurance policies: term insurance and whole life insurance. Term insurance requires payment of a premium to the insurance company periodically. Assuming that the insured does not die by the end of the policy period, the policy has no value. In contrast, whole life insurance has two features: (1) it pays off a stated amount upon the death of the insured, and (2) it accumulates a cash value that the policyholder can call on. The first feature is an insurance protection feature—the same feature that term insurance provides. The second is an investment feature because the policy accumulates value.

Life insurance companies compete with other life insurance companies in providing insurance protection. When it comes to the investment feature, however, life insurance companies compete not only with other life insurance companies but also with other financial institutions that provide investment instruments and with direct market investment in securities. The interest rate effectively paid on whole life insurance policies is typically below market interest rates. In fact, a popular saying is "buy term and invest the difference." This means that the policyholder would be better off obtaining insurance protection by purchasing term insurance and investing the cost savings that results from buying term rather than whole life insurance. The underlying principle here is that the policyholder/investor can unbundle the features offered by insurance policies.

As inflation and interest rates escalated in the 1970s, people became more aware of the dangers of nominally fixed contracts relying on nominal rates and more sensitive to the rates they were earning on the funds they invested. With persistent and volatile inflation, insurance products such as whole life lost value in real terms and generated uncertainty of the purchasing power of the terminal amount promised by the contract; it thus became less attractive, thereby reducing the number of policies written. An additional drain on the cash flow of life insurance companies was that the older whole life insurance policies in force permitted the policyholder to borrow from the insurance company against the cash value of the policy at interest rates related to those at which interest was being credited to the policy. These rates soon became considerably less than prevailing rates. Policyholders took advantage of the low borrowing costs and invested the funds borrowed in alternative market instruments.

This cash outflow from life insurance companies is referred to as disintermediation, a process we discussed in Chapter 2 when describing the net outflow of deposit funds from depository institutions. To survive, life insurance companies had to develop new, more attractive products.

Types of Policies

Policies issued by life insurance companies can be classified as one of four types: (1) pure insurance protection against risk of death, (2) a package consisting of life insurance protection and an investment vehicle, (3) insurance against the risk of life (annuities), primarily designed for pension programs, and (4) pure investment-oriented vehicles (such as GICs). We have already discussed the prevalent form of pure insurance protection, term policies, and one form of insurance/investment policy, whole life policies. Below we describe other types of insurance/investment policies, annuities, and pure investment-oriented policies.

Insurance against the Risk of Life.   Consider a person who retires with a given amount of resources to be spread evenly over her remaining life. Clearly, she faces a problem because the length of life is a random variable, largely unknown to her. A life insurance company, relying on the fact that the average length of life of a (random) group can be estimated rather accurately, can offer the person a fixed annuity as long as she lives, thus relieving her of the risk of outliving her resources. Annuities are one of the oldest types of insurance contracts. At present they are used primarily in connection with a pension fund.

In a *single-premium deferred annuity*, the sponsor of a pension plan pays a single premium to the life insurance company, which in turn agrees to make lifelong payments to the employee (the policyholder) when that employee retires. Most policies give the policyholder the right to take the benefits in a lump sum rather than a payout over time.

Insurance/Investment Policies.   Two principal policies fall into the insurance/investment category: universal life and variable life.

The universal life policy, introduced in the early 1980s, pays a dividend that is tied to market interest rates. Insofar as market rates reflect inflation,[4]

---

[4] See the discussion of Fisher's Law in Chapter 11.

this protects the insured against real losses from inflation. Because it pays a competitive interest rate, universal life has all but replaced the traditional whole life policy. Essentially, the cash value of a universal life policy builds and is used to buy term insurance. A variable life insurance contract provides a death benefit that depends on the market value of the investment at the time of the insured's death. The securities that the premiums are invested in are typically common stock, and hence such policies are referred to as equity-linked policies. While the death benefits are variable, there is a guaranteed minimum death benefit that the insurer agrees to pay regardless of the market value of the portfolio.

Pure Investment-Oriented Policies. The policy that falls into the investment-oriented category is the guaranteed investment contract (GIC). These policies typically are purchased by pension plan sponsors as an investment. In a GIC, a life insurance company agrees, for a single premium, to pay a dollar amount at the maturity of the GIC. The dollar amount will be equal to the premium paid plus accumulated interest. An interest rate guaranteed by the life insurance company is specified in the policy. For example, a $10 million five-year GIC guaranteeing an interest rate of 10% means that, at the end of five years, the life insurance company is guaranteeing a payment of $16,105,100.[5]

The maturity of a GIC can vary from 1 year to 20 years. The interest rate guaranteed depends on market conditions and the rating of the life insurance company. The interest rate will be some spread above the yield offered on U.S. Treasury securities of the same maturity. The lower the rating of the life insurance company, as classified by A.M. Best, the higher the yield it must offer to attract policyholders.

The GIC that we described above is called a *bullet contract*; it is the most common type. Of other types of GIC policies, we describe just two: the window contract and the floating-rate contract.[6] In a *window contract*, instead of accepting a lump-sum payment, the life insurance company agrees to accept deposits over some future designated time period, usually between 3 to 12 months. All deposits made are guaranteed the same interest rate.[7] This type of contract is used by a pension sponsor that will make periodic contributions on behalf of employees and wishes to lock in an interest rate. The risk that the life insurance company faces is that, if interest rates decline

---

[5] Determined as follows: $10,000,000 (1.10)^{10} = $16,105,100$.

[6] There are *"if" and "but" contracts, participating contracts, bank investment contracts,* and *pooled GIC funds.* For a detailed description of GICs, see Kenneth L. Walker, *Guaranteed Investment Contracts: Risk Analysis and Portfolio Strategies* (Homewood, IL: Dow Jones-Irwin, 1989).

[7] The amount of the deposits may or may not be fixed in advance.

below the interest rate guaranteed on the window contract, any new deposits must be invested at a lower interest rate than the life insurance company has agreed to pay. Of course, if interest rates rise above the contract rate, the life insurance company will be able to invest the new deposits at a higher rate, thereby increasing its spread income. Nevertheless, to protect against a decline in interest rates, the interest rate offered on window contracts will be below that offered on bullet contracts with the same maturity.

A *floating-rate contract* is a GIC where the guaranteed interest rate is tied to some predetermined market benchmark such as a specific-maturity Treasury yield. The interest rate will be at some spread to the index. The spread will reflect market conditions and the rating of the life insurance company—the lower the rating, the greater the spread.

Investments

Most investments made by life insurance companies are in debt obligations. The distribution of assets of U.S. life insurance companies in 1988 is summarized in Table 4-2.

In fact, life insurance companies are the largest buyers of corporate bonds. They invest not only in publicly traded bonds, but also provide direct

TABLE 4-2   DISTRIBUTION OF ASSETS OF U.S. LIFE INSURANCE COMPANIES: 1988

ASSET	AMOUNT (000,000)	PERCENT
Government securities	$ 144,035	12.3
Corporate securities		
Bonds	423,703	36.2
Common stock	44,272	3.8
Preferred stock	9,555	0.8
Total corporate securities	477,530	40.8
Mortgages	229,263	19.6
Real estate	27,318	2.3
Policy loans	54,146	4.6
Cash	4,154	0.4
Short-term investments	32,188	2.8
All others	201,459	17.2
Total admitted assets	$1,170,093	100.0

Source: A.M. Best Company, *Best's Insurance Reports—Life/Health,* 1988, p. vii.

commercial loans and invest in private placements. As we explained in the previous chapter, interest in private placements can be expected to grow in the future due to Rule 144A. Because of the tax advantages granted to life insurance companies, there is no benefit to investment in tax-advantaged securities such as tax-exempt municipal bonds.

As can be seen from Table 4-2, in 1988 bonds plus mortgages constituted some 70% of total life insurance company assets. A life insurance company's decision to allocate most of its funds to long-term debt obligations is a result of the nature of its liabilities. As most contracts written by life insurance companies are based on some contractually fixed interest rate that will be paid to a policyholder after a long stretch of years, long-term debt obligations are a natural investment vehicle for an insurance company to use to hedge its commitments (match maturities).[8] Moreover, there is an incentive to invest in bonds rather than equities because of restrictions on portfolio composition imposed by regulation, which plays an important role for life insurance companies. Regulations require a life insurance company buying equity to report any decline in the value of the equity in the periodic financial statement that must be supplied to regulators. A bond by contrast is carried at acquisition cost; if a bond's market value declines, the reduction in value is not recognized.

Regulation

Life insurance companies are regulated primarily at the state level as a result of a 1945 federal statute, the McCarran–Ferguson Act. They must also comply with regulations as set forth by the Employee Retirement Income Security Act of 1974 (ERISA) for the portion of their business that deals with pension funds. We'll have more to say about ERISA when we cover pension funds. Life insurance companies whose stock is publicly traded must comply with the federal regulations set forth by the Securities and Exchange Commission. Our focus here is on state regulation.

Each state establishes its own regulations with respect to (1) the types of securities that are eligible for investment, and (2) how the value of those securities must be shown for regulatory reporting purposes. As for eligible investments, a state will typically restrict the percentage of funds allocated to common stock investments to the lesser of 10% of assets (in some states 20%) or 100% of surplus. It will also restrict investments in bonds and preferred stock to those of a certain quality rating. A "basket provision" usually permits

---

[8] Or, more precisely, match the "duration" of their liabilities. The concept of "duration" is discussed in Chapter 12.

investments of about 5% of assets in any type of vehicle that is not explicitly prohibited by law.

To insure compliance with its regulations, life insurance companies licensed to do business in a state are required to file an annual statement and supporting documents with the state's insurance department. States also conduct periodic on-site examinations of companies.

The annual statement, referred to as the *convention statement*, shows the assets, liabilities, and surplus of the reporting company. The surplus is closely watched by regulators and A.M. Best because it determines the amount of business that an insurance company can underwrite.

The convention statement must be prepared in accordance with certain accounting principles that are the same for all states. They require that common stock and lower-quality bonds be valued at the lower of cost or market. In contrast, high-quality bonds are carried at acquisition cost. Consequently, if $10 million is invested in a U.S. Treasury security whose market value declines to $7 million because interest rates have increased, the securities continue to be reported at $10 million. This accounting requirement has two important implications. First, it encourages life insurance companies to allocate only a small portion of their funds to stock and lower quality-rated bonds because a decline in the market value of those assets below cost will reduce the life insurance company's surplus. Second, it may discourage managers of life insurance companies from trying to take advantage of perceived or real opportunities in the bond market. For example, suppose an insurance company that has invested $10 million in a U.S. Treasury security recognizes that it can improve its asset/liability position if it swaps out of these U.S. Treasury securities and into a different U.S. Treasury issue. It would be discouraged to do so if the market value of the U.S. Treasury securities it owns is less than $10 million, because once these securities are sold in order to purchase the new Treasury issue, a loss must be recognized. This would result in a reduction in the life insurance company's surplus.

For regulatory reporting purposes, all life insurance companies have general accounts, and most have one or more separate accounts. A separate account is one where the life insurance company reports for specific types of insurance contracts. The benefit of separate accounts is that they give the life insurance company greater latitude to match the assets with the specific nature of the liability created by the insurance contracts.

PROPERTY AND CASUALTY INSURANCE COMPANIES

Property and casualty (P&C) insurance companies provide a broad range of insurance protection against:

1. loss, damage, or destruction of property
2. loss or impairment of income-producing ability

3. claims for damages by third parties because of alleged negligence

4. loss resulting from injury or death due to occupational accidents

Nature of the Business

Property and casualty insurance products can be classified as either "personal lines" or "commercial lines." Personal lines include automobile insurance and homeowner insurance. Commercial lines include product liability insurance, commercial property insurance, and malpractice insurance.

The price that the insured pays for coverage is called a premium. The amount of the liability coverage is specified in the policy. The premium is invested until, and if, the insured makes a claim on the entire amount or a fraction of the amount of the policy, and that claim is validated. For some lines of business, the P&C company will know immediately that it has incurred a liability from a policy it has underwritten; when the claim will have to be paid and the amount of the claim may not be known at that time, however.

To illustrate this, suppose that in 1991 an automobile policy is written that provides $1 million liability coverage for Bob Smith. The policy covers him against claims by other parties resulting from an automobile accident. Let's suppose that in 1991, Bob Smith does in fact get into an automobile accident that results in the permanent disability of Karen Lee, the driver of the other car. The P&C company recognizes that it has a liability, but how much will it have to pay Karen Lee? It may be several years before the injured party and the company settle the matter, and a trial may be necessary to determine the monetary damages that the P&C company must pay.

There are some lines of business where a claim is not evident until several years after the policy period. For example, suppose that for the years 1987 through 1989 a P&C company wrote a product liability policy for a toy manufacturing company. It may not be until 1991 that it is discovered that one of the products manufactured by the toy company was defective, causing serious injury to children.

Thus, the costs of the policies underwritten by a P&C company consist of (1) claims for losses that have been incurred and are reported during the year, and (2) actuarially estimated claims on policies written during the year that will not be paid until later years. P&C companies must by law establish reserves to satisfy the actuarially estimated claims. Reserves are increased or decreased depending on whether actual claims are above or below those actuarially estimated.

A P&C company's revenue for a year is generated from two sources. First is the premium income for policies written during the year. Second is investment income resulting from the investment of both the reserves established to pay off future claims and the P&C's surplus (assets less liabilities).

The profit of a P&C company is calculated by subtracting from the revenue for the year (as defined in the previous paragraph) each of the following: (1) funds that must be added to reserves for new claims for policies written during the year (called *claim expenses*), (2) funds that must be added to reserves because of underestimates of actuarially projected claims from previous years (called *claim adjustment expenses*), (3) taxes, and (4) administrative and marketing expenses associated with issuing policies. If revenue for the year exceeds (1) through (4), then the surplus of the P&C company is increased; it is decreased if the reverse occurs. Surplus also changes when funds are distributed to shareholders.

As in the case of life insurance companies, surplus is important because it is the surplus that ultimately can be drawn upon to pay policyholders. The growth of the surplus of a P&C company will determine how much future business it can underwrite. The ability of a P&C company to take on risk is measured by the ratio of the annual premium to the capital plus surplus. Usually, this ratio is kept at between two-to-one and three-to-one. Consequently, $2 to $3 in annual premium can be supported for each $1 increase in surplus.

If annual premiums exceed the sum of claim expenses, claim adjustment expenses, and administrative and marketing expenses, the difference is said to be the underwriting profit; an underwriting loss results if claim expenses and claim adjustment expenses exceed annual premiums. A common measure reported by P&C companies is a *combined ratio*,[9] which is calculated by dividing the sum of claim expenses, claim adjustment expenses, and administrative and marketing expenses by annual premiums. A ratio of less than 100% means that a P&C company realized an underwriting profit; a ratio of greater than 100% means that the P&C company realized an operating loss.

Between 1950 and 1973, the overall industry combined ratio exceeded 100% only nine times.[10] Unlike the 1950–1973 period, between 1974 and 1989 the combined ratio was below 100% for only two years. The industry combined ratio reached a peak of 120% in 1984.

Pricing pressure in the business has come not only from intercompany competition but also from large non-insurance corporations that have established insurance captives in tax havens such as Bermuda or in low-tax

---

[9] It is called a combined ratio because it depends on two other ratios, an *expense ratio* and a *loss ratio*. The former is the ratio of administrative and marketing expenses to annual premiums. The latter is the ratio of the sum of claim expenses and claim adjustment expenses to annual premiums. The combined ratio is the sum of these two ratios.

[10] Frank D. Campbell, "Asset-Liability Management for Property-Casualty Insurers," Chapter 47 in Frank J. Fabozzi (ed.), *The Handbook of Fixed Income Securities* (Homewood, IL: Business One-Irwin, 1991), p. 1006.

states such as Vermont. (As of 1990, Vermont had more than 160 insurance captives.)[11] These insurance captives self-insure the corporation. To reduce their risks, they lay off some of the insurance risks to non-captive insurance companies, a process known as "reinsurance." Additional pressure was put on the P&C industry when the biggest insurance brokerage firm, Marshall & McLennan, created an alternative insurance outlet by pooling the liability risks of large corporations. It has been estimated that these alternative insurance markets have taken away $50 billion in premiums (almost 35% of the market) from traditional P&C companies.[12]

Because of competitive pressure, today there is better coordination between the insurance and investment sides of the business when pricing insurance policies. Firms do this by establishing an asset/liability committee consisting of the actuaries and investment managers.

Regulation

As with life insurance companies, P&C companies are regulated at the state level. States regulate P&C companies in several ways. First, they regulate the prices that may be charged for insurance coverage. Competitive pressures, however, have made the need for price regulation less important. In instances where states have imposed prices that insurers feel are uneconomic, companies have withdrawn from offering insurance.

Second, to reduce the likelihood of insolvency, states establish regulations governing eligible investments that P&C companies may make. While life insurance companies are constrained as to eligible assets, P&C companies have greater leeway for investing. For example, a P&C company might be required to invest a minimum in eligible bonds and mortgages. As long as this minimum is satisfied, however, a P&C company is free to allocate its investments any way it pleases among eligible assets in the other asset classes.

PENSION FUNDS

A pension plan is a fund that is established for the payment of retirement benefits. The entities that establish pension plans—called the plan sponsors—are private business entities acting for their employees; state and local entities on behalf of their employees; unions on behalf of their members; and individuals for themselves.

---

[11] Fredric Dannen, "The Incredible Shrinking Insurance Industry," *Institutional Investor* (January 1990), p. 68.

[12] Ibid., p. 68.

The total assets of U.S. pension funds have grown rapidly since World War II. They almost tripled in the 1980s. By 1989, pension fund total assets were about $2.47 trillion. The top 20 pension funds as measured by assets as of September 30, 1989, account for more than 25% of all pension assets. The assets of corporate-sponsored pension plans in 1990 were about $1.1 trillion, while those of government-sponsored pension plans totaled about $0.7 trillion.[13]

Pension funds are financed by contributions by the employer and/or the employee; in some fund plans employer contributions are matched in some measure by employees. The great success of private pension plans is somewhat surprising because the system involves investing in an asset (i.e., the pension contract) that for the most part has been and is largely illiquid. It cannot be used—not even as collateral—until retirement. The key factor explaining pension fund growth despite this serious limitation is that the employer's contributions and up to a specified amount of the employee's contributions, as well as the earnings of the fund's assets, are tax-exempt. In essence a pension is a form of employer remuneration for which the employee is not taxed until funds are withdrawn. Pension funds also have served traditionally to discourage employees from quitting, as usually the employee lost at least the accumulation resulting from the employer contribution, i.e., pension benefits have not been portable. As we will discuss later, portability of pension benefits has increased somewhat as a result of federal legislation (the Employee Retirement Income Security Act of 1970).

Types of Pension Plans

There are two types of pension plans: *defined contribution plans* and *defined benefit plans.* In a defined contribution plan, the plan sponsor is responsible only for making specified contributions into the plan on behalf of qualifying participants. The amount contributed is typically either a percentage of the employee's salary or a percentage of profits. The plan sponsor does not guarantee any certain amount at retirement. The payments that will be made to qualifying participants upon retirement will depend on the growth of the plan assets; that is, payment is determined by the investment performance of the funds. Defined pension plans come in several legal forms: money

---

[13] *1990 Money Market Directory.* According to a study on pension funds by Columbia University Law School, the three largest corporate-sponsored pension funds as of September 30, 1989, are AT&T ($42.7 billion), General Motors ($40.9 billion), and IBM ($25.8 billion). The two largest government-sponsored pension funds are California Public Employees ($54.0 billion) and New York State/Local Employees ($44.2 billion). The largest pension fund by far is TIAA/CREF, with total assets as of September 31, 1989, of $81 billion.

purchase pension plans, 401(k) plans, and employee stock ownership plans (ESOP).

In a defined benefit plan, the plan sponsor agrees to make specified dollar payments to qualifying employees at retirement (and some payments to beneficiaries in case of death before retirement). The retirement payments are determined by a formula that usually takes into account the length of service of the employee and the earnings of the employee. The pension obligations are effectively the debt obligation of the plan sponsor, who assumes the risk of having insufficient funds in the plan to satisfy the contractual payments that must be made to retired employees.

A plan sponsor establishing a defined benefit plan can use the payments made into the fund to purchase an annuity policy from a life insurance company. Defined benefit plans that are guaranteed by life insurance products are called *insured plans*;[14] those that are not are called *non-insured plans*. An insured plan is not necessarily safer than an uninsured plan, as the former depends on the ability of the life insurance company to make the contractual payments.

Whether a private pension plan is insured or non-insured, a federal agency, the Pension Benefit Guaranty Corporation (PBGC), insures the *vested* benefits of participants. Benefits become vested when an employee reaches a certain age and completes enough years of service so that he or she meets the minimum requirements for receiving benefits upon retirement. The payment of benefits is not contingent upon a participant's continuation with the employer or union.

Regulation

Because pension plans are so important for U.S. workers, Congress passed comprehensive legislation in 1974 to regulate pension plans. The legislation, the Employee Retirement Income Security Act of 1974 (ERISA), is fairly technical in its details. For our purposes, it is necessary only to understand the major provisions of ERISA.

First, ERISA establishes minimum funding standards having to do with the minimum contributions that a plan sponsor must make to the pension plan to satisfy the actuarially projected benefit payments. Prior to enactment of ERISA, many corporate plan sponsors followed a "pay-as-you-go" funding policy. That is, when an employee retired, the corporate plan sponsor took

---

[14] Life insurance companies also manage pension funds without guaranteeing a specified payout. In this case they are acting only as money manager, and the funds they manage are not insured plans.

the necessary retirement benefits out of current operations. Under ERISA, such a practice is no longer allowed.

Second, ERISA establishes fiduciary standards for pension fund trustees, managers, or advisors. Specifically, all parties responsible for the management of a pension fund are guided by the judgment of a mythical "prudent man" in seeking to determine which investments are proper.[15] Because a trustee takes care of other people's money, it is necessary to make sure that the trustee takes the role seriously. In fulfillment of responsibilities, a trustee must use the care of a reasonably prudent person to acquire and use the information that is pertinent to making an investment decision.

Third, minimum vesting standards were established by ERISA. For example, after five years of employment a plan participant is entitled to 25% of accrued pension benefits. The percentage increases to 100% after ten years.

Finally, ERISA created the PBGC to insure vested benefits. The insurance program is funded from annual premiums that must be paid by pension plans.

Responsibility for administering ERISA is delegated to the Department of Labor and the Internal Revenue Service. To ensure that a pension plan is in compliance with ERISA, periodic reporting and disclosure statements must be filed with the Department of Labor and the Internal Revenue Service.

It is important to recognize that ERISA does not require that a corporation establish a pension plan. If a corporation does establish a defined benefit plan, however, it must comply with the regulations set forth in ERISA.

Financial Reporting Requirements.   While the selection of assets to include in a pension fund is dictated by the actuarially projected pension obligations, another important consideration is the financial reporting requirements. Corporations report to shareholders on the basis of generally accepted accounting principles (GAAP). The reporting requirement for pension obligations is promulgated by Financial Accounting Standard Board (FASB) No. 87.

This controversial accounting standard basically requires that a corporation do the following for each pension plan it has established (a corporation may establish more than one pension plan for different categories of workers or employees of different subsidiaries). Each year it must determine the present value of the projected liabilities of the plan and compare this to the market value of the pension assets. If the market value of the assets exceeds the present value of the liabilities, there is a surplus; such a surplus is *not* shown on the corporation's balance sheet. On the other hand, if the present

---

[15] The prudent-man rule developed as part of trust law.

value of the liabilities exceeds the market value of the assets, there is a deficit, which must then be reported on the balance sheet as a liability. This liability must be reported even if the corporation has surpluses in all of the other plans it has established, and the surpluses exceed the deficit. That is, no offsetting is permitted.

Opponents of FASB No. 87 argue that this financial reporting requirement does not reflect the economics of the pension obligations.[16] While full consideration of the nuances of FASB No. 87 is not appropriate here, suffice it to say that it has implications for a sponsor's decision to allocate plan assets between common stock and bonds. Specifically, FASB No. 87 encourages corporate pension plan managers to hedge the risk that the surplus will be affected adversely by a change in interest rates by holding a portfolio of bonds with certain investment characteristics.[17]

Tax Considerations. Qualified pension funds are exempt from federal income taxes. Thus, fund assets can accumulate tax-free. Consequently, pension funds do not find tax-advantaged investments beneficial. While there have been recent proposals to make any profits realized from short-term trading taxable, no real action has been taken.

Investments

The aggregate asset mix of the 1,000 top defined benefit pension plans is summarized in Table 4-3. As can be seen, almost 80% is allocated between equities and fixed-income securities. Note in the allocation of assets for defined contribution plans the large proportion of assets placed in GICs.

Participants in the Non-Insured Pension Fund Business

While we refer to pension funds as financial institutions, there are many types of entities in the financial services business that are involved in the pension fund business. We have already discussed the role of life insurance companies. Below, we describe other participants in the non-insured pension fund business.

---

[16] See Keith P. Ambachtsheer, "Fixing the Accounting Standards for Pension and Health Care Benefits: Advice for FASB," Chapter 14 in Frank J. Fabozzi (ed.), *Pension Fund Investment Management* (Chicago: Probus Publishing, 1990).

[17] See Jo Ann Corkran and Michael Peskin, "Decreasing the Financial Risk of Pension Plans," Chapter 16 in Frank J. Fabozzi (ed.), *Portfolio & Investment Management* (Chicago: Probus Publishing, 1989).

TABLE 4-3	AGGREGATE ASSET MIX FOR TOP 1,000 PENSION FUNDS IN 1990

ASSET	PERCENT
DEFINED BENEFIT PLANS	
Equity	46.6
Fixed income	33.3
Cash equivalents	8.9
Real estate equity	4.1
Mortgages	1.1
GIC/BIC	3.2
Annuities	0.6
Other	2.2
DEFINED CONTRIBUTION PLANS	
Company stock	23.2
Other stock	18.7
Fixed income	11.7
Cash equivalents	7.3
GIC/BIC	35.7
Annuities	0.7
Other	2.7

Source: As reported in *Pension & Investment Age,* January 22, 1990, p. 16.

A corporate plan sponsor can do one of the following with the pension assets under its control: (1) manage all the pension assets itself (i.e., use in-house management), (2) distribute the pension assets to one or more money management firms to manage, or (3) combine alternatives (1) and (2).

Professional money management firms obtain their income from a fee charged to manage the assets. The fee can range from 0.75% of assets under management to as little as 0.01% of assets under management. The percentage charged depends on (1) the type of investment strategy pursued by the professional money management firm, and (2) the amount of the assets under management. By investment strategy, we mean whether the money management firm is following an active strategy to try to beat some benchmark or an indexing strategy where it attempts to match an index.[18]

---

[18] These strategies are discussed in Chapter 8.

Much lower percentage fees are charged in the latter case. As for the amount managed, the percentage charged declines as the amount the firm is asked to manage increases. More recently, some plan sponsors have been entering into management fee contracts based on performance rather than according to a fixed percentage of assets under management.[19]

In addition to money management firms, there are advisors to plan sponsors. Advisors help the plan sponsor in several ways:

- developing plan investment policy and asset allocation among the major asset classes
- actuarial advising (liability modeling and forecasting)
- designing of benchmarks (called "normal portfolios") that the fund's money managers will be measured against
- measuring and monitoring the performance of the fund's money managers
- measuring trading costs and analysis of those costs
- index fund construction when a pension plan elects to manage indexed funds internally
- searching for and recommending money managers to pension plans
- providing specialized research

Frank Russell Associates, SEI, BARRA, Wilshire, Callan, and Rogers, Casey are a few examples of the better-known consultants to pension funds.

INVESTMENT COMPANIES

Investment companies are financial intermediaries that sell shares to the public and invest the proceeds in a diversified portfolio of securities. Each share that they sell represents a proportionate interest in the portfolio of securities owned by the investment company. The type of securities purchased depends on the company's investment objective.

Types of Investment Companies

There are three types of investment companies: open-end funds, closed-end funds, and unit trusts.

---

[19] See Arjun Divecha and Nick Mencher, "Manager Fees from the Performance Viewpoint," Chapter 9 in Fabozzi, *Pension Fund Investment Management*, op. cit.

Open-End Funds.   These funds, more popularly referred to as *mutual funds*, continually stand ready to sell new shares to the public and to redeem their outstanding shares on demand at a price equal to an appropriate share of the value of their portfolio, which is computed daily at the close of the market.

A mutual fund's share price is based on its *net asset value per share*, which is found by subtracting from the market value of the portfolio the mutual fund's liabilities and then dividing by the number of mutual fund shares outstanding. For example, suppose that a mutual fund with 10 million shares outstanding has a portfolio with a market value of $215 million and liabilities of $15 million. In this case the net asset value per share is $20 [($215 million − $15 million) divided by 10 million].

The share price is quoted on a bid–offer basis. The offer price is the price at which the mutual fund will sell the shares. It is equal to the net asset value per share plus any sales commission that the mutual fund may charge. The sales commission is referred to as a "load." The commission or load typically ranges from 8.5% on small amounts invested down to 1% on amounts of $500,000 or over. A mutual fund that does not impose a sales commission is called a *no-load fund*. No-load mutual funds compete directly with load funds and appeal to investors who object to paying a commission (particularly because there is no empirical evidence that suggests that load funds have outperformed no-load funds after accounting for the load charge). The relative attraction of no-load funds has forced many mutual funds to convert to no-load status. For no-load funds, the offer price is the same as the net asset value per share.

Even though a fund does not charge a commission for share purchases, it may still charge investors a fee to sell (redeem) shares. Such funds, referred to as *back-end load funds*, may charge a commission of 4% to 6%. Some back-end load funds impose a full commission if the shares are redeemed within a designated time period after purchase, such as one year, reducing the commission the longer the investor holds the shares.

There are mutual funds that do not charge an upfront or a back-end commission but instead take out up to 1.25% of average daily fund assets each year to cover the costs of selling and marketing shares. SEC Rule 12b-1 allows mutual funds to use such an arrangement for covering selling and marketing costs; such funds are referred to as *12b-1 funds*.

The number of mutual funds increased fourfold in the 1980s, from 250 in 1980 to more than 1,000 in 1990. The amount controlled by funds increased from $100 billion to more than $1 trillion over the same period.

Closed-End Funds.   In contrast to mutual funds, closed-end funds sell shares like any other corporation and usually do not redeem their shares. Shares of closed-end funds sell on either an organized exchange, such as the New York Stock Exchange, or in the over-the-counter market. The price of a share is determined by supply and demand, so the price can fall below or rise above the net asset value per share. Investors who wish to purchase closed-end funds must pay a brokerage commission at the time of purchase and again at the time of sale.

Unit Trust.   A unit trust is similar to a closed-end fund in that the number of unit certificates is fixed. Unit trusts typically invest in bonds. Unit trusts differ in several ways from both mutual funds and closed-end funds that specialize in investing in bonds. First, there is no active trading of the bonds in the portfolio of the unit trust. Once the unit trust is assembled by the sponsor (usually a brokerage firm or bond underwriter) and turned over to a trustee, the trustee holds all the bonds until they are redeemed by the issuer. Usually the only time the trustee can sell an issue in the portfolio is if there is a dramatic decline in the issuer's credit quality. This means that the cost of operating the trust will be considerably less than costs incurred by either a mutual fund or a closed-end fund. Second, unit trusts have a fixed termination date, while mutual funds and closed-end funds do not.[20] Third, unlike the mutual fund and closed-end fund investor, the unit trust investor knows that the portfolio consists of a specific collection of bonds and has no concern that the trustee will alter the portfolio.

All unit trusts charge a sales commission. The initial sales charge for a unit trust is 3.5% to 5.5%. There is often a commission of 3% to sell units, but trusts sponsored by some organizations do not charge a commission when the units are sold. In addition to these costs, there is the spread that an investor indirectly pays. When the brokerage firm or bond underwriting firm assembles the unit trust, the price of each bond to the trust includes the dealer's spread.

We focus in the balance of our discussion on open-end (mutual) funds and closed-end funds. We shall refer to both as simply "funds."

Structure of a Fund

A fund is structured with a board of directors, an advisor responsible for managing the portfolio, and a distributing and selling organization. Funds enter into contracts with a financial advisor to manage the fund, typically, a company that specializes in the management of funds.

The financial advisor to the fund charges an advisory fee. This fee, which is one of the largest costs of administering a fund, is usually equal to 0.5% to

---

[20] There are exceptions. The Blackstone Target Term Trust, a closed-end fund listed on the New York Stock Exchange, terminates in the year 2000. This fund was introduced in 1988. In 1991, another closed-end fund with a termination date was issued, the Blackstone 1998 Term Trust.

1.5% of the fund's average assets, but the fee per dollar of assets managed is determined on a sliding scale that declines as the dollar amount of the fund increases. The advisory fee should reflect the difficulty of managing the particular fund.[21]

Funds incur other costs in addition to the advisory fee. We have already mentioned the costs of selling and marketing in the case of an open-end fund. Beyond these the fund is charged fees for custodial and accounting services and board of director fees. And, of course, there are transactions costs associated with the implementation of the fund's investment strategy. All cost information on managing and operating a particular fund is publicly available.

Types of Funds by Investment Objective

A wide range of funds with different investment objectives are available. The investment objective is set forth in the fund's prospectus. There are funds that invest exclusively in equities, and others in bonds. Even within an asset class, there are funds with different objectives. In the case of funds that invest exclusively in equities, for example, the investment objective of one fund may be to emphasize stable income, another capital gains, or growth, and still another a combination of income and growth. Some limit investments to specific industries so that the fund manager can presumably specialize and achieve better selection and timing. A few funds offer participation in potentially glamorous new research companies by investing in fields such as electronics, oceanography, and telecommunications. There are funds that restrict their investment to small firms and some that invest in foreign stocks. For investors who wish to achieve maximum diversification, the latest development in the mutual fund area is indexed funds that hold a portfolio mimicking the composition of a broad index such as the S&P 500.

Funds that specialize in bond investments also have a wide menu of funds. U.S. government bond funds invest only in U.S. government bonds. There are corporate bond funds, which can have very different investment objectives. Some funds invest only in high-quality corporate bonds, while others invest primarily in low-quality (junk) corporate bonds. Convertible securities funds invest in convertible bonds and convertible preferred stock. Investors interested in mortgage-backed securities can turn to a fund that specializes in those securities.

---

[21] The advisory fee must be approved by members of the board of directors who are classified as "disinterested" directors. A disinterested director is one with little or no economic interest in the advisory company.

There is a wide range of funds that invest exclusively in municipal bonds. Some funds specialize in municipal bond issuers within a given state so that investors can take advantage of the exemption of interest income from state and local taxes. Residents of New York State and California, for example, can choose from a dozen or more mutual funds that invest in bonds of issuers within their home state; interest income is then exempt from state taxes.

Money market mutual funds invest in securities with a maturity of one year or less, called money market instruments. We discussed these types of mutual funds in Chapter 2, when we mentioned investors withdrawing savings from depository institutions to invest them in these funds. There are three types of money market funds. General money market funds invest in taxable money market instruments such as Treasury bills, short-term U.S. government agency issues, commercial paper, and negotiable certificates of deposit. U.S. government short-term funds invest only in Treasury bills or U.S. government agency securities. The third type of money market mutual fund is the short-term municipal fund.

A balanced fund is one that invests in both stocks and bonds. While there are often limits as to how much a fund manager may allocate to an asset class, there is room to modify the asset mix to take advantage of what the fund manager expects will be the better-performing asset class.

Economic Motivation for Funds

Recall from Chapter 1 that financial intermediaries obtain funds by issuing financial claims against themselves and then investing those funds. An investment company is a financial intermediary because it pools the funds of market participants and uses those funds to buy a portfolio of securities. Also recall the special role in the financial markets played by financial intermediaries. They provide at least one of the following four economic functions: (1) maturity intermediation, (2) risk reduction via diversification, (3) lower costs of contracting and information processing, and (4) a payments mechanism. Let's look at which of these economic functions a fund provides.

Consider first maturity intermediation. An investor with a short-term investment horizon wishing to invest in either stocks or debt obligations with a maturity greater than the planned investment horizon faces the risk that the securities may have to be sold at a time when their market value is less than the price paid. However, this is true even if a share of a fund is purchased because the net asset value per share will fluctuate with market conditions. Consequently, maturity intermediation is not an economic function provided by a fund.

Consider next the risk reduction through diversification function. By investing in a fund, an investor can obtain broad-based ownership of a sufficient number of securities either within a sector of the financial market or across market sectors to reduce portfolio risk. (We'll be more specific about the type of risk that is reduced in Chapter 5.) While an individual investor may be able to acquire a broad-based portfolio of securities, the degree of diversification will be limited by the amount available to invest. By investing in the investment company, however, the investor can effectively achieve the benefits of diversification at lower cost even if the amount of money available to invest is not large.

Beyond risk reduction via diversification offered by funds, there are reduced costs of contracting and information processing because an investor purchases the services of a presumably skilled financial advisor at less cost than if the investor directly negotiated with an advisor. The advisory fee is lower because of the larger size of assets managed, as well as reduced costs of searching for an investment manager and obtaining information about the securities. Also, the costs of transacting in the securities are reduced because a fund has more clout in negotiating transactions costs, and custodial fees and bookkeeping costs are less for a fund than for an individual investor.

Finally, money market funds generally provide payment services by allowing investors to write checks drawn on the fund, although this facility is limited in various ways.

Regulation

All investment companies are regulated at the federal level according to the Investment Company Act of 1940 and subsequent amendments to that legislation. The securities they issue must be registered with the SEC. Moreover, investment companies must provide periodic financial reports and disclose their investment policies to investors. The act prohibits changes in the nature of an investment company's investment policies without the approval of shareholders.

Regulations are also imposed on the advertisements or claims made by mutual funds. In particular, the return performance advertised must not be misleading. Unfortunately, there have been past abuses in the case of bond funds, which have tended to report yield numbers rather than return numbers.[22] Effective May 1, 1988, the SEC set forth new rules for the yield measures that mutual funds may use in advertising in order to "prevent misleading performance claims by funds and permit investors to make more meaningful comparisons among fund performance claims in advertisements."[23]

---

[22] The distinctions between the two are explained in Chapter 11.

[23] Securities and Exchange Commission, Release Number 33-6753, February 2, 1988, p. 6.

SUMMARY

Four financial institutions are discussed in this chapter: life insurance companies, property and casualty insurance companies, pension funds, and investment companies. The nature of their liabilities, as well as regulatory and tax considerations, determines the investment strategy pursued by all financial institutions. The liabilities of all financial institutions will generally fall into one of the four types shown in Table 4-1.

Life insurance companies and property and casualty insurance companies are financial intermediaries that function as risk bearers. While the principal event that life insurance companies insure against is death, since the 1970s a major portion of their business has been in providing lifetime benefits in the form of retirement policies.

Life insurance policies can be classified as one of four types: (1) pure insurance protection against risk of death (for example, term insurance), (2) a package consisting of insurance protection and an investment vehicle (for example, whole life, universal life, and variable life), (3) insurance against the risk of life (annuities), and (4) an investment-oriented vehicle, primarily designed for pension programs (for example, guaranteed investment contracts). Life insurance companies are regulated primarily at the state level; they must also comply with ERISA requirements when they deal in the pension fund area.

Property and casualty insurance companies insure against a wide variety of occurrences. Revenue is generated from two sources: premium income for policies written during the year, and investment income resulting from the investment of both the reserves established to pay off future claims and the P&C's surplus. Today well-managed companies attempt some integration of the insurance and investment sides of the business when pricing insurance policies. P&C companies are regulated at the state level but are afforded greater latitude than life insurance companies in their investment choices.

A pension plan is a fund that is established by private employers, governments, or unions for the payment of retirement benefits. Pension plans have grown rapidly largely because of favorable tax treatment. Qualified pension funds are exempt from federal income taxes, as are employer contributions. The two types of pension funds are defined contribution plans and defined benefit plans. In the former plan the sponsor is responsible only for making specified contributions into the plan on behalf of qualifying employees but does not guarantee any specific amount at retirement. A defined benefit plan sponsor agrees to make specified payments to qualifying employees at retirement. There is federal regulation of pension funds, as embodied in the Employee Retirement Income Security Act of 1974 (ERISA).

Investment companies sell shares to the public and invest the proceeds in a diversified portfolio of securities, with each share representing a proportionate interest in the underlying portfolio of securities. There are three types of investment companies: open-end or mutual funds, closed-end funds, and unit trusts. A wide range of funds with different investment objectives are available, with investment objectives as set forth in a fund's prospectus. Mutual funds and closed-end funds provide two economic functions associated with financial intermediaries—risk reduction via diversification and lower costs of contracting and information processing. Money market funds allow shareholders to write checks against their shares, thus providing a payments mechanism, another economic function of financial intermediaries. Regulation is at the federal level, with the key legislation being the Investment Company Act of 1940.

QUESTIONS

1. The quotation following is from a recent survey in *The Economist* on the American insurance industry:

   > Life insurers, like bankers, learnt the hard way about inflation and interest rates a decade ago. Insurance was a fairly straightforward business in the old days. As late as 1979, more than 80% of new premiums were for "whole life" policies with fixed premiums, benefits and surrender values; almost all the rest was "term" insurance which pays out only on death. . . .
   >
   > That comfortable world had begun to change even before inflation went into double-digits in the late 1970s. Customers realized that the cash values piling up in their insurance companies did not compare favorably with returns on other instruments. Issuers had to offer policies like universal life and variable life and permutations of the two. These gave customers market-related returns, often above a guaranteed minimum, and more flexibility.

   a. What is meant by whole life, universal life, and variable life insurance policies?

   b. In general, what have been the consequences of life insurance companies having to offer market-related returns?

2. When medical waste washed up on the beaches of New Jersey and New York in several separate incidents in 1988, the public was disgusted and scared. Many oceanfront resort operators and workers who depend on the allure of the beach for their livelihood were nearly

ruined. But the financial losses from that lost summer of 1988 pale in comparison with the economic havoc that improperly handled medical waste can wreak on America's health care providers. . . .

To date, no medical facility has been sued for injuries or damages caused by the disposal of medical waste, but given today's consciousness of this issue and the trend in environmental legislation, such litigation is inevitable. Clearly, the eventuality represents both an emerging liability coverage issue and a thorny challenge for the commercial insurance industry.

Discuss this excerpt from *Best's Review* of June 30, 1990. Your answer should address these issues:

a.   The type of insurance company that would underwrite coverage for medical waste.

b.   Some of the problems that such companies have in estimating their liabilities to policyholders.

c.   The likelihood that insurance companies will be eager to start underwriting insurance for medical waste.

3.   Comment on this quotation from an article by Kenneth Black, Jr., in the June 30, 1990, issue of *Best's Review:*

The industry has had to develop competence in asset/liability management, having learned that the traditional long-term nature of individual life-insurance contracts could really be short-term in light of the call and put options . . . in many products. The integration of investment processes and product design and management is a most significant recent development. A company can no longer be functionally compartmentalized and survive.

a.   Give an example of the options inherent in products that Black mentions.

b.   What does he mean when he says that "a company can no longer be functionally compartmentalized and survive"?

4.   This excerpt is from the 1989 Annual Report of Merrill Lynch & Co.

In 1988, the Corporation terminated, in accordance with the applicable provisions of ERISA, its defined benefit pension plan, which covered substantially all eligible U.S. employees. Following termination, a portion of the plan assets were used to purchase a group annuity contract from Metropolitan Life Insurance Company to guarantee the payment of benefits vested under the terminated plan.

Explain ERISA, a defined-benefit plan, and an annuity contract.

5. Here is a quotation from the May 1, 1990, issue of *Forbes:*

    Which is a better buy, the $352 million American Capital Harbor Fund
    or the closed-end $77 American Capital Convertible Securities? At
    first glance, it's hard to choose. They're both balanced funds. James
    Behrman, 45, runs both. . . . Yet Behrman has done much better
    with the closed-end fund. Measured by the performance of its
    portfolio (that is on net asset value, rather than on the trading price
    of the fund's shares), American Capital Convertible has returned
    11.5% a year over the past five years. Harbor has returned only 8.7%
    a year.

    a. What are open- and closed-end funds, and what are the major
        differences between the two?

    b. What is meant by net asset value?

    c. Can you think of a reason why a closed-end fund would outperform
        an open-ended fund composed of similar securities?

6. What types of services do advisors provide to pension sponsors?

LEARNING OBJECTIVES

After reading this chapter you will understand:

- the fundamental principles of portfolio theory.

- how to calculate the historical single-period investment return for a security or portfolio of securities.

- how to calculate the expected return and variability of expected return of a portfolio.

- the components of a portfolio's total risk: systematic risk and unsystematic risk.

- what the beta of a stock measures.

- why diversification eliminates unsystematic risk.

- the capital asset pricing model, the relevant measure of risk in this model, and the limitations of the model.

- the development of the multifactor capital asset pricing model.

- the difficulty of empirically testing the capital asset pricing model.

- the fundamental principles underlying the arbitrage pricing theory model.

- the empirical difficulties in testing the arbitrage pricing theory model.

Portfolio theory deals with the selection of optimal portfolios by rational risk-averse investors: that is, by investors who attempt to maximize their expected portfolio returns consistent with individually acceptable levels of portfolio risk. Capital markets theory deals with the implications for security prices of the decisions made by these investors: that is, what relationship should exist between security returns and risk if investors behave in this optimal fashion. Together, portfolio and capital markets theories provide a framework to specify and measure investment risk, to develop relationships between expected security return and risk (and hence between risk and required return on investment), and to measure the performance of managed portfolios such as mutual funds and pension funds.

The purpose of this chapter is to introduce portfolio and capital markets theories. We begin with the basic concepts of portfolio theory and then build upon these concepts to develop the theoretical relationship between the expected return on a security and risk. Because the risk and return relationship indicates how much expected return a security should generate, given its relevant risks, it also tells us how assets should be priced. Hence the risk and return relationship is also referred to as an *asset pricing model*.

The three asset pricing models that we present in this chapter are those that dominate financial thinking today: the capital asset pricing model, the multifactor capital asset pricing model, and the arbitrage pricing theory model. Our focus is on the key elements underlying portfolio theory and asset pricing theory. We will not attempt to provide a rigorous mathematical presentation of these theories.

PORTFOLIO THEORY

In designing a portfolio, investors seek to maximize the expected return from their investment, given some level of risk they are willing to accept.[1] Portfolios that satisfy this requirement are called *efficient* (or *optimal*) portfolios. To construct an efficient portfolio, it is necessary to understand what is meant by "expected return" and "risk." The latter concept, risk, could mean any one of many types of risk. We shall be more specific about its meaning as we proceed in the development of portfolio theory. We begin our exploration of portfolio theory with the concept of investment return.

Investment Return

The return on an investor's portfolio during a given interval is equal to the change in value of the portfolio plus any distributions received from the portfolio, expressed as a fraction of the initial portfolio value. It is important that any capital or income distributions made to the investor be included, or the measure of return will be deficient. Another way to look at return is as the amount (expressed as a fraction of the initial portfolio value) that can be withdrawn at the end of the interval while maintaining the principal intact. The return on the investor's portfolio, designated R_p, is given by

$$R_p = \frac{V_1 - V_0 + D_1}{V_0} \tag{1}$$

where V_1 = the portfolio market value at the end of the interval.
V_0 = the portfolio market value at the beginning of the interval.
D_1 = the cash distributions to the investor during the interval.

The calculation assumes that any interest or dividend income received on the portfolio securities and not distributed to the investor is reinvested in the

---

[1] Alternatively stated, investors seek to minimize the risk that they are exposed to given some target expected return.

portfolio (and thus reflected in V_1). Further, the calculation assumes that any distributions occur at the end of the interval, or are held in the form of cash until the end of the interval. If the distributions were reinvested prior to the end of the interval, the calculation would have to be modified to consider the gains or losses on the amount reinvested. The formula also assumes no capital inflows during the interval. Otherwise, the calculation would have to be modified to reflect the increased investment base. Capital inflows at the end of the interval (or held in cash until the end), however, can be treated as just the reverse of distributions in the return calculation.

Thus, given the beginning and ending portfolio values, plus any contributions from or distributions to the investor (assumed to occur at the end of an interval), Equation (1) lets us compute the investor's return. For example, if the XYZ pension fund had a market value of $100,000 at the end of June, benefit payments of $5,000 made at the end of July, and an end-of-July market value of $103,000, the return for the month would be 8%.

$$R_p = \frac{103,000 - 100,000 + 5,000}{100,000} = 0.08$$

In principle, this sort of calculation of returns could be carried out for any interval of time, say, for one month or ten years. Yet there are several problems with this approach. First, it is apparent that a calculation made over a long period of time, say, more than a few months, would not be very reliable because of the underlying assumption that all cash payments and inflows are made and received at the end of the period. Clearly, if two investments have the same return as calculated from the formula above, but one investment makes cash payment early and the other late, the one with early payment will be understated. Second, we cannot rely on the formula above to compare return on a one-month investment with that on a ten-year return portfolio. For purposes of comparison the return must be expressed per unit of time—say, per year.

In practice, we handle these two problems by first computing the return over a reasonably short unit of time, perhaps a quarter of a year or less. The return over the relevant horizon, consisting of several unit periods, is computed by averaging the return over the unit intervals. There are three generally used methods of averaging: (1) the arithmetic average return, (2) the time-weighted rate of return (also referred to as the geometric rate of return), and (3) the dollar-weighted return. The averaging yields a measure of return per unit of time period. The measure can be converted to an annual or other period yield by standard procedures.

The *arithmetic average rate of return* is an unweighted average of the returns achieved during a series of such measurement intervals. The general formula is:

$$R_A = \frac{R_{P1} + R_{P2} + \ldots + R_{PN}}{N}$$

where R_A = the arithmetic average return

R_{Pk} = the portfolio return in interval k as measured by Equation (1), $k = 1, \ldots, N$

N = the number of intervals in the performance evaluation period

For example, if the portfolio returns were -10%, 20%, and 5% in July, August, and September, respectively, the arithmetic average monthly return is 5%.

The arithmetic average can be thought of as the mean value of the withdrawals (expressed as a fraction of the initial portfolio value) that can be made at the end of each interval while maintaining the principal intact. In the example above, the investor must add 10% of the principal at the end of the first interval and can withdraw 20% and 5% of the initial value per period.

The *time-weighted rate of return* measures the compounded rate of growth of the initial portfolio during the performance evaluation period, assuming that all cash distributions are reinvested in the portfolio. It is also commonly referred to as the "geometric" rate of return. It is computed by taking the geometric average of the portfolio returns computed from Equation (1). The general formula is:

$$R_T = [(1 + R_{P1})(1 + R_{P2}) \cdots (1 + R_{PN})]^{1/N} - 1$$

where R_T is the time-weighted rate of return, and R_{Pk} and N are as defined earlier.

For example, if the portfolio returns were -10%, 20%, and 5% in July, August, and September, as in the example above, then the time-weighted rate of return is:

$$R_T = [(1 + (-0.10))(1 + 0.20)(1 + 0.05)]^{1/3} - 1$$
$$= [(0.90)(1.20)(1.05)]^{1/3} - 1 = 0.043$$

As the time-weighted rate of return is 4.3% per month, one dollar invested in the portfolio at the end of June would have grown at a rate of 4.3% per month during the three-month period.

In general, the arithmetic and time-weighted average returns do not provide the same answers. This is because computation of the arithmetic average assumes the amount invested to be maintained (through additions or withdrawals) at its initial value. The time-weighted return, on the other hand, is the return on a portfolio that varies in size because of the assumption that all proceeds are reinvested. We can use an example to show how the two averages fail to coincide. Consider a portfolio with a $100 market value at the end of 1988, a $200 value at the end of 1989, and a $100 value at the end of 1990. The annual returns are 100% and -50%. The arithmetic return is 25%, while the time-weighted average return is 0%. The arithmetic average return consists of the average of the $100 withdrawn at the end of 1989 and the $50 replaced at the end of 1990. The compound rate of return is clearly zero, however, the 100% in 1989 being exactly offset by the 50% loss in 1990 on the larger investment base. In this example, the arithmetic average exceeds the time-weighted average return. This always proves to be true, except in the special situation where the returns in each interval are the same, in which case the averages are identical.

The *dollar-weighted rate of return* (also called the *internal rate of return*) is computed by finding the interest rate that will make the present value of the cash flows from all the interval periods plus the terminal market value of the portfolio equal to the initial market value of the portfolio. The internal rate of return calculation, as explained in Chapter 11, is calculated exactly the same way the yield to maturity on a bond is. The general formula for the dollar-weighted return is:

$$V_0 = \frac{C_1}{(1 + R_D)} + \frac{C_2}{(1 + R_D)^2} + \ldots + \frac{C_N + V_N}{(1 + R_D)^n}$$

where R_D = the dollar-weighted rate of return
V_0 = the initial market value of the portfolio
V_N = the terminal market value of the portfolio
C_k = the cash flow for the portfolio (cash inflows minus cash outflows) for interval k, $k = 1, \ldots, N$

For example, consider a portfolio with a market value of $100,000 at the end of 1987, capital withdrawals of $5,000 at the end of 1988, 1989, and 1990, and a market value at the end of 1990 of $110,000. Then $V_0 = \$100,000$; $N = 3$; $C_1 = C_2 = C_3 = \$5,000$; $V_3 = \$110,000$; and R_D is the interest rate that satisfies the equation:

$$\$110,000 = \frac{\$5,000}{(1 + R_D)} + \frac{\$5,000}{(1 + R_D)^2} + \frac{\$5,000 + \$110,000}{(1 + R_D)^3}$$

It can be verified that the interest rate that satisfies this expression is 8.1%. This is the dollar-weighted return.

Under special conditions, both the dollar-weighted return and the time-weighted return produce the same result. This will occur when no further additions or withdrawals occur, and all dividends are reinvested.

Throughout this chapter we generally use rate of return to refer to an appropriately standardized measure.

Portfolio Risk

The definition of investment risk leads us into less-explored territory. Not everyone agrees on how to define risk, let alone measure it. Nevertheless, there are some attributes of risk that are reasonably well accepted.

An investor holding a portfolio of Treasury securities until the maturity date faces no uncertainty about monetary outcome. The value of the portfolio at maturity of the securities will be identical with the predicted value; the investor bears no monetary risk. In the case of a portfolio composed of common stocks, however, it will be impossible to predict the value of the portfolio at any future date. The best an investor can do is to make a best-guess or most-likely estimate, qualified by statements about the range and likelihood of other values. In this case, the investor does bear risk.

One measure of risk is the extent to which future portfolio values are likely to diverge from the expected or predicted value. More specifically, risk for most investors is related to the chance that future portfolio values will be less than expected. That is, if the investor's portfolio has a current value of $100,000, and an expected value of $110,000 at the end of the next year, what matters is the probability of values less than $110,000.

Before proceeding to the quantification of risk, it is convenient to shift our attention from the terminal value of the portfolio to the portfolio rate of return, R_p, because the increase in portfolio value is related directly to R_p.[2]

Expected Portfolio Return. A particularly useful way to quantify the uncertainty about the portfolio return is to specify the probability associated with each of the possible future returns. Assume, for example, that an investor has identified five possible outcomes for the portfolio return during the next year. Associated with each return is a subjectively determined probability, or relative chance of occurrence. The five possible outcomes are:

---

[2] The transformation changes nothing of substance because

$$\tilde{M}_T = (1 + \tilde{R}_p)M_0$$
$$= M_0 + M_0\tilde{R}_p,$$

where $\tilde{M}_T$ is the terminal portfolio value and $\tilde{R}_p$ is the portfolio return. (The tilde (˜) above a variable indicates that it is a random variable.) Because $\tilde{M}_T$ is a linear function of $\tilde{R}_p$, any risk measures developed for the portfolio return apply equally to the terminal market value.

OUTCOME	POSSIBLE RETURN	SUBJECTIVE PROBABILITY
1	50%	0.1
2	30	0.2
3	10	0.4
4	−10	0.2
5	−30	0.1

Note that the probabilities sum to 1 so that the actual portfolio return is confined to assume one of the five possible values. Given this probability distribution, we can measure the expected return and risk for the portfolio.

The expected return is simply the weighted average of possible outcomes, where the weights are the relative chances of occurrence. In general, the expected return on the portfolio, denoted $E(R_p)$, is given by

$$E(R_p) = P_1R_1 + P_2R_2 + \ldots + P_nR_n$$

$$E(R_p) = \sum_{j=1}^{n} P_jR_j \tag{2}$$

where the R_j's are the possible returns, the P_j's the associated probabilities, and n the number of possible outcomes.

The expected return of the portfolio in our illustration is:

$$\begin{aligned} E(R_p) &= 0.1(50.0) + 0.2(30.0) + 0.4(10.0) \\ &\quad + 0.2(-10.0) + 0.1(-30.0) \\ &= 10\% \end{aligned}$$

Variability of Expected Return. If risk is defined as the chance of achieving returns less than expected, it would seem logical to measure risk by the dispersion of the possible returns below the expected value. Risk measures based on below-the-mean variability are difficult to work with, however, and moreover are unnecessary as long as the distribution of future return is reasonably symmetric about the expected value. Figure 5-1 shows three probability distributions: the first symmetric, the second skewed to the left, and the third skewed to the right. For a symmetrical distribution, the dispersion of returns on one side of the expected return is the same as the dispersion on the other side of the expected return.

Empirical studies of realized rates of return on diversified common stock

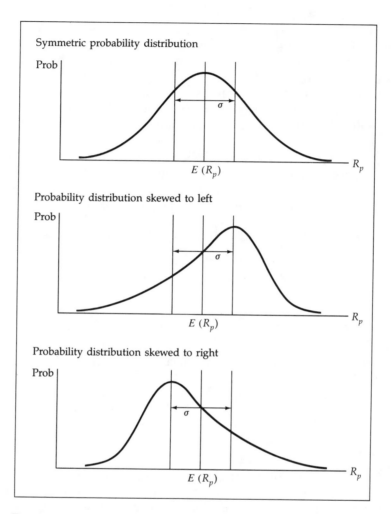

FIGURE 5-1
Possible Shapes for Probability Distributions

portfolios show that skewness is not a significant problem.[3] If future distributions are shaped like historical distributions, it makes little difference whether we measure variability of returns on one or both sides of the expected return. If the probability distribution is symmetric, measures of the

[3] For example, see Marshall E. Blume, "Portfolio Theory: A Step Toward its Practical Application," *Journal of Business* 43 (April 1970), pp. 152–173.

total variability of return will be twice as large as measures of the portfolio's variability below the expected return. Thus, if total variability is used as a risk surrogate, the risk ranking for a group of portfolios will be the same as when variability below the expected return is used. It is for this reason that total variability of returns has been used so widely as a surrogate for risk.

It now remains to choose a specific measure of total variability of returns. The most commonly used measures are the variance and standard deviation of returns.

The variance of return is a weighted sum of the squared deviations from the expected return. Squaring the deviations ensures that deviations above and below the expected value contribute equally to the measure of variability regardless of sign. The variance for the portfolio, designated σ_p^2, is given by

$$\sigma_p^2 = P_1[R_1 - E(R_p)]^2 + P_2[R_2 - E(R_p)]^2 + \ldots + P_n[R_n - E(R_p)]^2$$

or

$$\sigma_p^2 = \sum_{j=1}^{n} P_j[R_j - E(R_p)]^2 \tag{3}$$

In the previous example, the variance for the portfolio is

$$\begin{aligned} \sigma_p^2 &= 0.1(50.0 - 10.0)^2 + 0.2(30.0 - 10.0)^2 \\ &\quad + 0.4(10.0 - 10.0)^2 + 0.2(-10.0 - 10.0)^2 \\ &\quad + 0.1(-30.0 - 10.0)^2 \\ &= 480\% \text{ squared.} \end{aligned}$$

The standard deviation (σ_p) is defined as the square root of the variance. It is equal to 22% in our example. The larger the variance or standard deviation, the greater the possible dispersion of future realized values around the expected value, and the larger the investor's uncertainty. As a rule of thumb for symmetric distributions, it is often suggested that roughly two-thirds of the possible returns will lie within one standard deviation either side of the expected value, and that 95% will be within two standard deviations.

Figure 5-2 shows the historical return distributions for a diversified portfolio. The portfolio is composed of approximately 100 securities, with each security having equal weight. The month-by-month returns cover the period from January 1945 through June 1970. Note that the distribution is approximately, but not perfectly, symmetric. The arithmetic average return for the 306-month period is 0.91% per month. The standard deviation about this average is 4.46% per month.

Figure 5-3 gives the same data for a single security, National Department

FIGURE 5-2
Distribution of Monthly Returns for a Portfolio of 100 Securities (equally weighted),
January 1945–June 1970

	RANGE		FREQ.	1...5...10...15...20...25...30...35...40...45...50.
1	−13.6210	−12.2685	1	*
2	−12.2685	−10.9160	2	**
3	−10.9160	−9.5635	2	**
4	−9.5635	−8.2110	3	***
5	−8.2110	−6.8585	8	********
6	−6.8585	−5.5060	9	*********
7	−5.5060	−4.1535	17	*****************
8	−4.1535	−2.8010	18	******************
9	−2.8010	−1.4485	27	***************************
10	−1.4485	−0.0960	28	****************************
11	−0.0960	1.2565	30	******************************
12	1.2565	2.6090	50	**
13	2.6090	3.9615	35	***********************************
14	3.9615	5.3140	33	*********************************
15	5.3140	6.6665	18	******************
16	6.6665	8.0190	14	**************
17	8.0190	9.3715	4	****
18	9.3715	10.7240	2	**
19	10.7240	12.0765	2	**
20	12.0765	13.4290	3	***

Average return = 0.91% per month.
Standard deviation = 4.46% per month.
Number of observations = 306.

Stores. Note that the distribution is highly skewed. The arithmetic average return is 0.81% per month over the 306-month period. The most interesting aspect, however, is the standard deviation of month-by-month returns—9.04% per month, more than double that for the diversified portfolio. We discuss this result further below.

Thus far we have confined our discussion of portfolio risk to a single-period investment horizon such as the next year. That is, the portfolio is held unchanged and evaluated at the end of the year. An obvious question relates to the effect of holding the portfolio for several periods—say, for the next 20 years. Will the one-year risks tend to cancel out over time? Given the random walk nature of security prices,[4] the answer to this question is no. If

---

[4] By random walk, we mean that the expected value of future price changes is independent of past price changes.

the risk level (standard deviation) is maintained during each year, the portfolio risk for longer horizons will increase with the horizon length. The standard deviation of possible terminal portfolio values after N years is equal to $\sqrt{N}$ times the standard deviation after one year.[5] Thus, the investor cannot rely on the "long run" to reduce the risk of loss.

A final remark before leaving portfolio risk measures. We have assumed implicitly that investors are risk-averse; that is, they seek to minimize risk for a given level of return. This assumption appears to be valid for most investors in most situations. The entire theory of portfolio selection and capital asset pricing rests on the assumption that investors on the average are risk-averse.

Diversification

When we compare the distribution of historical returns for the 100-stock portfolio (Figure 5-2) with the distribution for National Department Stores (Figure 5-3), we discover a curious relationship. While the standard deviation of returns for the security alone is double that of the portfolio, the stock average return is less than the portfolio return. Is the market so imperfect that over a long period of time (25 years) it rewarded substantially higher risk with lower stock return?

Not so. The answer lies in the fact that not all of the security's risk is relevant. Much of the total risk (standard deviation of return) of National Department Stores was diversifiable. That is, if that investment had been combined with other securities, a portion of the variation in its returns could have been smoothed or canceled by complementary variation in the other securities. The same portfolio diversification effect accounts for the low

---

[5] This result can be illustrated as follows. The portfolio market value after N years, $\tilde{M}_N$, is equal to

$$\tilde{M}_N = M_0[(1 + \tilde{R}_{p1})(1 + \tilde{R}_{p2}) \cdots (1 + \tilde{R}_{pN})],$$

where M_0 is the initial value, and R_{pt} ($t = 1, \ldots, N$) is the return during year t (as given by Equation [1]). For reasonably small values of the annual returns, this expression can be approximated by

$$\tilde{M}_N = M_0[1 + \tilde{R}_{p1} + \tilde{R}_{p2} + \ldots + \tilde{R}_{pN}].$$

Now, if the annual returns, $\tilde{R}_{pt}$, are independently and identically distributed with variance σ^2, the variance of $\tilde{M}_N$ will equal $(M_0)^2 N\sigma^2$, or N times the variance after one year. Therefore, the standard deviation of the terminal value will equal $\sqrt{N}$ times the standard deviation after one year. The key assumption of the independence of portfolio returns over time is realistic because security returns appear to follow a random walk through time.

A similar result could be obtained without the restriction on the size of the $\tilde{R}_{pt}$ if we had dealt with continuously, as opposed to annually, compounded rates of return. This is a more complicated analysis.

FIGURE 5-3
Distribution of Monthly Returns for National Department Stores, January
1945–June 1970

	RANGE		FREQ.	1...5...10...15...20...25...30...35...40...45...50.
1	−32.3670	−29.4168	1	*
2	−29.4168	−26.4666	0	
3	−26.4666	−23.5163	0	
4	−23.5163	−20.5661	1	*
5	−20.5661	−17.6159	1	*
6	−17.6159	−14.6657	3	***
7	−14.6657	−11.7155	13	*************
8	−11.7155	−8.7653	11	***********
9	−8.7653	−5.8151	39	***************************************
10	−5.8151	−2.8649	47	***
11	−2.8649	0.0853	45	***
12	0.0853	3.0355	34	**********************************
13	3.0355	5.9857	28	****************************
14	5.9857	8.9359	25	*************************
15	8.9359	11.8861	17	*****************
16	11.8861	14.8363	17	*****************
17	14.8363	17.7865	9	*********
18	17.7865	20.7366	8	********
19	20.7366	23.6868	5	*****
20	23.6868	26.6370	2	**

Average return = 0.81% per month.
Standard deviation = 9.04% per month.
Number of observations = 306.

standard deviation of return for the 100-stock portfolio. In fact, the portfolio standard deviation was lower than that of the typical security in the portfolio. Much of the total risk of the component securities had been eliminated by diversification. As long as much of the total risk can be eliminated simply by holding a stock in a portfolio, there is no economic requirement for the return earned to be in line with the total risk. Instead, we should expect realized returns to be related to that portion of security risk that cannot be eliminated by portfolio combination—so-called systematic risk (more on risk/return relationships later in this chapter).

Diversification results from combining securities whose returns are less than perfectly correlated in order to reduce portfolio risk. As noted above, the portfolio return is simply a weighted average of the individual security returns, no matter the number of securities in the portfolio. Therefore, diversification will not systematically affect the portfolio return, but it will reduce the variability (standard deviation) of return. In general, the less the correlation among security returns, the greater the impact of diversification on reducing variability. This is true no matter how risky the securities of the portfolio are when considered in isolation.

Theoretically, if we could find sufficient securities with uncorrelated returns, we could eliminate portfolio risk completely. Unfortunately, this situation is not typical in real securities markets, where returns are positively correlated to a considerable degree because they tend to respond to the same set of influences (e.g., business cycles and interest rates). Thus, while portfolio risk can be reduced substantially by diversification, it cannot be eliminated entirely. This can be demonstrated very clearly by measuring the standard deviations of randomly selected portfolios containing various numbers of securities.

In a study of the impact of portfolio diversification on risk, Wayne Wagner and Sheila Lau divided a sample of 200 New York Stock Exchange (NYSE) stocks into six subgroups based on the Standard & Poor's stock quality ratings as of June 1960.[6] The highest-quality ratings (A+) formed the first group, the second-highest rating (A) the next group, and so on. Randomly selected portfolios containing from 1 to 20 securities were then formed from each of the subgroups. The month-by-month portfolio returns for the 10-year period through May 1970 were then computed for each portfolio (portfolio composition remaining unchanged). The exercise was repeated 10 times to reduce the dependence on single samples. The values for the 10 trials were then averaged.

Table 5-1 shows the average return and standard deviation for portfolios from the first subgroup (A+ quality stocks). The average return is unrelated to the number of issues in the portfolio. Yet the standard deviation of return declines as the number of holdings increases. On the average, approximately 40% of the single-security risk is eliminated by forming randomly selected portfolios of 20 stocks. It is also evident, however, that additional diversification yields rapidly diminishing reduction in risk. The improvement is slight when the number of securities held is increased beyond, say, 10. Figure 5-4 shows the results for all six quality groups. The figure shows the rapid decline in total portfolio risk as the portfolios are expanded from 1 to 10 securities.

Returning to Table 5-1, note from the second-to-last column in the table that the return on a diversified portfolio follows the market very closely. The degree of association is measured by the correlation coefficient (R) of each

---

[6] Wayne H. Wagner and Sheila Lau, "The Effect of Diversification on Risk," *Financial Analysts Journal* (November–December 1971), pp. 2–7.

| | | STANDARD | CORRELATION WITH MARKET | |
NUMBER OF SECURITIES IN PORTFOLIO	AVERAGE RETURN (%/MO.)	DEVIATION OF RETURN (%/MO.)	R	R^2
1	0.88	7.0	0.54	0.29
2	0.69	5.0	0.63	0.40
3	0.74	4.8	0.75	0.56
4	0.65	4.6	0.77	0.59
5	0.71	4.6	0.79	0.62
10	0.68	4.2	0.85	0.72
15	0.69	4.0	0.88	0.77
20	0.67	3.9	0.89	0.80

TABLE 5-1   RISK VERSUS DIVERSIFICATION FOR RANDOMLY SELECTED PORTFOLIOS OF A + QUALITY SECURITIES (JUNE 1960–MAY 1970)

Source: Wayne H. Wagner and Sheila Lau, "The Effect of Diversification on Risk," *Financial Analysts Journal* (November–December 1971), Table C, p. 53.

portfolio with an unweighted index of NYSE stocks (perfect positive correlation results in a correlation coefficient of 1.0).[7] The 20-security portfolio has a correlation of 0.89 with the market. The implication is that the risk remaining in the 20-stock portfolio is predominantly a reflection of uncertainty about the performance of the stock market in general. Figure 5-5 shows the results for the six quality groups.

Correlation in Figure 5-5 is represented by the correlation coefficient squared, R^2 (possible values range from 0 to 1.0). The R^2 coefficient has a useful interpretation: it measures the proportion of portfolio return variability (variance) that is attributable to variability in market returns. The remaining variability is risk that is unique to the portfolio and, as shown in Figure 5-4, that can be eliminated by proper diversification of the portfolio. Thus, R^2 measures the degree of portfolio diversification. A poorly diversified portfolio will have a lower R^2 (0.30–0.40). A well-diversified portfolio will have a much

---

[7] Two securities with perfectly correlated patterns will have a correlation coefficient of 1.0. Conversely, if the return patterns are perfectly negative correlated, the correlation coefficient will equal -1.0. Two securities with uncorrelated (i.e., statistically unrelated) returns will have a correlation coefficient of zero. The average correlation coefficient between returns for NYSE securities and the S&P 500 Stock Index during the 1945–1970 period was approximately 0.5.

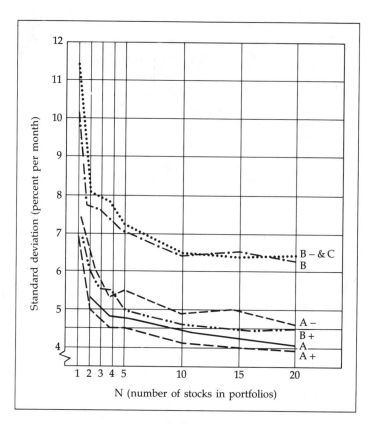

Figure 5-4
Standard Deviation versus Number of Issues in Portfolio.
Source: Wayne H. Wagner and Sheila Lau, "The Effect of Diversification on Risks,"
Financial Analysts Journal (November–December 1971), Exhibit 1, p. 50.

higher R^2 (0.85–0.95). A perfectly diversified portfolio will have an R^2 of 1.0;
that is, all the risk in such a portfolio is a reflection of market risk.

Figure 5-5 shows the rapid gain in diversification as each of the portfolios
increases in size from 1 security to 2 securities and on up to 10 securities.
Beyond 10 securities, the gains tend to be smaller. Note that increasing the
number of issues tends to be less efficient at achieving diversification for the
highest-quality A+ issues. Apparently the companies comprising this group
are more homogeneous than the companies grouped under the other quality
codes.

These results show that, while some risks can be eliminated through
diversification, others cannot. Thus we are led to distinguish between a

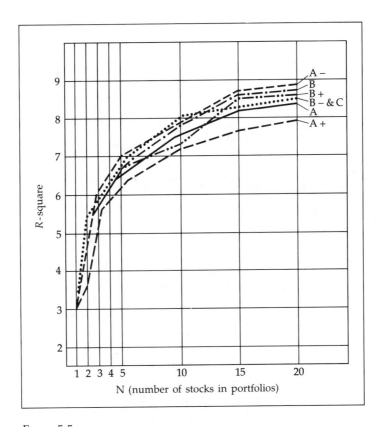

FIGURE 5-5
Correlation versus Number of Issues in Portfolio.
Source: Wayne H. Wagner and Sheila Lau, "The Effect of Diversification on Risks," *Financial Analysts Journal* (November–December 1971), Exhibit 2, p. 50.

security's "unsystematic" risk, which can be washed away by mixing the security with other securities in a diversified portfolio, and its "systematic" risk, which cannot be eliminated by diversification. This proposition is illustrated in Figure 5-6. It shows total portfolio risk declining as the number of holdings increases. Increasing diversification gradually tends to eliminate the unsystematic risk, leaving only systematic, i.e., market-related risk. The remaining variability results from the fact that the return on nearly every security depends to some degree on the overall performance of the market. Consequently, the return on a well-diversified portfolio is highly correlated with the market, and its variability or uncertainty is basically the uncertainty of the market as a whole. Investors are exposed to market uncertainty no matter how many stocks they hold.

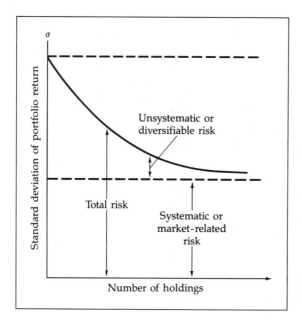

FIGURE 5-6
Systematic and
Unsystematic Risk

The Risk of Individual Securities

We have concluded that the systematic risk of an individual security is that portion of its total risk (standard deviation of return) that cannot be eliminated by combining it with other securities in a well-diversified portfolio. We now need a way of quantifying the systematic risk of a security and relating the systematic risk of a portfolio to that of its component securities. This can be accomplished by dividing security return into two parts: one perfectly correlated with and proportionate to the market return, and a second independent from (uncorrelated with) the market. The first component of return is usually referred to as *systematic*, the second as *unsystematic* or *diversifiable* return. Thus we have

$$\text{Security return} = \text{Systematic return} + \text{Unsystematic return} \qquad (4)$$

As the systematic return is proportional to the market return, it can be expressed as the symbol beta (β) times the market return, R_m. The proportionality factor beta is a *market sensitivity index*, indicating how sensitive the security return is to changes in the market level. (How to estimate beta for a security or portfolio will be discussed later.) The unsystematic return, which is independent of market returns, is usually represented by the symbol epsilon (ϵ'). Thus, the security return, R, may be expressed

$$R = \beta R_m + \epsilon'. \qquad (5)$$

For example, if a security has a β factor of 2.0, then a 10% market return will generate a 20% systematic return for the stock. The security return for the period would be the 20% plus the unsystematic component. The unsystematic component depends on factors unique to the company, such as labor difficulties, higher-than-expected sales, and so on.

The security returns model given by Equation (5) is usually written in such a way that the average value of the residual term, ϵ', is zero. This is accomplished by adding a factor, alpha (α), to the model to represent the average value of the unsystematic returns over time. That is, we set $\epsilon' = \alpha + \epsilon$ so that

$$R = \alpha + \beta R_m + \epsilon, \qquad (6)$$

where the average ϵ over time should tend to zero.

The model for security returns given by Equation (6) is usually referred to as the *market model*.[8] Graphically, the model can be depicted as a line fitted to a plot of security returns against rates of return on the market index. This is shown for a hypothetical security in Figure 5-7.

The beta factor can be thought of as the slope of the line. It gives the expected increase in security return for a 1% increase in market return. In Figure 5-7, the security has a beta of 1.0. Thus, a 10% market return will result, *on the average*, in a 10% security return.

The alpha factor is represented by the intercept of the line on the vertical security return axis. It is equal to the average value over time of the unsystematic returns (ϵ') on the stock. For most stocks, the alpha factor tends to be small and unstable.

Using this definition of security return given by the market model, the specification of systematic and unsystematic risk is straightforward—they are simply the standard deviations of the two return components.[9]

---

[8] It is also referred to as the single-index market model and the security characteristic line.

[9] The relationship between the risk components is given by

$$\sigma^2 = \beta^2\sigma_m^2 + \sigma_{\epsilon'}^2.$$

This follows directly from Equation (5) and the assumption of statistical independence of R_m and ϵ'. The R^2 term previously discussed is a ratio of systematic to total risk (both measured in terms of variance):

$$R^2 = \frac{\beta^2\sigma_m^2}{\sigma^2}$$

Note also that the R^2 is the square of the correlation coefficient between security and market returns.

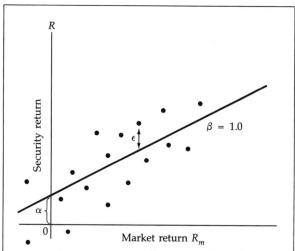

Beta (β), the market sensitivity index, is the slope of the line.
Alpha (α), the average of the residual returns, is the
intercept of the line on the security axis.
Epsilon (ϵ), the residual returns, are the perpendicular
distances of the points from the line.

FIGURE 5-7
The Market Model for
Security Returns

The systematic risk of a security is equal to β times the standard deviation of the market return:

$$\text{Systematic risk} = \beta\sigma_m \tag{7}$$

The unsystematic risk equals the standard deviation of the residual return factor ϵ:

$$\text{Unsystematic risk} = \sigma_\epsilon \tag{8}$$

Given measures of individual-security systematic risk, we can now compute the systematic risk of the portfolio. It is equal to the beta factor for the portfolio, β_p, times the risk of the market index, σ_m.

$$\text{Portfolio systematic risk} = \beta_p\sigma_m \tag{9}$$

The portfolio beta factor in turn can be shown to be simply an average of the individual security betas, weighted by the proportion of each security in the portfolio, or

$$\beta_p = X_1\beta_1 + X_2\beta_2 + \ldots + X_n\beta_n$$

or more concisely as

$$\beta_p = \sum_{i=1}^{n} X_i\beta_i \tag{10}$$

where X_i = the proportion of portfolio market value represented by security i.

   n = the number of securities.

Thus, the systematic risk of a portfolio is simply the market value-weighted average of the systematic risk of the individual securities. It follows that the β for a portfolio consisting of all stocks is 1. If a stock's β exceeds 1, it is above the average. If the portfolio is composed of an equal dollar investment in each stock (as was the case for the 100-security portfolio in Figure 5-2), the β_p is simply an unweighted average of the component security betas.

The unsystematic risk of the portfolio is also a function of the unsystematic security risks, but the form is more complex.[10] The important point is that with increasing diversification this risk approaches zero.

With these results for portfolio risk, it is useful to return to Figure 5-4. The figure shows the decline in portfolio risk with increasing diversification for each of the six quality groups. Note, however, that the portfolio standard deviations for each of the six groups decrease toward different limits because the average risks ($\tilde{\beta}$) of the groups differ.

Table 5-2 shows a comparison of the standard deviations for the 20-stock portfolios with the predicted lower limits based on average security systematic risks. The lower limit is equal to the average beta for the quality group ($\tilde{\beta}$) times the standard deviation of the market return (σ_m). The standard deviations in all cases are close to the predicted values. These results support the contention that portfolio systematic risk equals the average systematic risk of the component securities.

---

[10] Assuming the unsystematic returns (ϵ'_i) of securities to be uncorrelated (as is reasonably true in practice), the unsystematic portfolio risk is given by

$$\sigma^2(\epsilon'_p) = \sum_{i=1}^{n} X_i^2\sigma^2(\epsilon'_i),$$

where $\sigma^2(\epsilon'_i)$ is the unsystematic risk for stock i. Assume the portfolio is made up of equal investment in each security and $\bar{\sigma}^2(\epsilon')$ is the average value of the $\sigma^2(\epsilon'_i)$. Then, $X_i = 1/N$ and

$$\sigma^2(\epsilon'_p) = \frac{1}{N}\bar{\sigma}^2(\epsilon'),$$

which (assuming $\bar{\sigma}^2(\epsilon')$ is finite) obviously approaches zero as the number of issues in the portfolio increases.

TABLE 5-2	STANDARD DEVIATIONS OF 20-STOCK PORTFOLIOS AND PREDICTED LOWER LIMITS (JUNE 1960–MAY 1970)		

(1)	(2)	(3)	(4)
STOCK QUALITY GROUP	STANDARD DEVIATION OF 20-STOCK PORTFOLIOS ($\sigma_m \cdot \%$/MO.)	AVERAGE BETA VALUE FOR QUALITY GROUP ($\tilde{\beta}$)	LOWER LIMIT* ($\tilde{\beta} \cdot \sigma_m$, %/MO.)
A+	3.94	0.74	3.51
A	4.17	0.80	3.80
A−	4.52	0.89	4.22
B+	4.45	0.87	4.13
B	6.27	1.24	5.89
B− & C	6.32	1.23	5.84

*σ_m is 4.75% per month.

Source: Wayne H. Wagner and Sheila Lau, "The Effect of Diversification on Risk," *Financial Analysts Journal* (November–December 1971), p. 52, and Table C, p. 53.

To summarize the main results thus far, first, roughly 40% to 50% of total security risk can be eliminated by diversification. Second, the remaining systematic risk is equal to the security β times market risk. Third, portfolio systematic risk is a weighted average of security systematic risks.

The implications of these results are substantial. First, we would expect realized rates of return over substantial periods of time to be related to the systematic as opposed to the total risk of securities. As the unsystematic risk is relatively easily eliminated, we should not expect the market to offer investors a "risk premium" for bearing such risk. Second, because security systematic risk is equal to the security beta times σ_m (which is common to all securities), beta is useful as a *relative* risk measure. The β gives the systematic risk of a security (or portfolio) relative to the risk of the market index. Thus, it is often convenient to speak of systematic risk in relative terms (i.e., in terms of beta rather than beta times σ_m).

Estimating Beta

The beta of a security or portfolio can be estimated only using statistical analysis. More specifically, we use regression analysis on historical data to estimate the market model given by Equation (6). The estimated slope for the market model is the estimate of beta. A series of returns is computed according to Equation (1) over some time interval for some broad market index (such as the S&P 500 stock market index) and for the stock (or portfolio).[11] For example, monthly returns can be calculated for the past five years; thus, there would be 60 return observations for both the market index and the stock or portfolio. Or, weekly returns can be calculated for the past year. There is nothing in portfolio theory that indicates whether weekly, monthly, or even daily returns should be used. Nor does theory indicate any specific number of observations, except that statistical methodology requires that more observations will give a more reliable measure of beta.[12] Our purpose here is not to provide an explanation of the mechanics of calculating beta but to point out the practical problems in obtaining beta. (There are many econometric issues also, but we do not focus on these.)

There will be a difference in the calculated beta depending on: (1) the length of time over which a return is calculated (e.g., daily, weekly, monthly), (2) the number of observations used (e.g., three years of monthly returns or five years of monthly returns), (3) the specific time period used (e.g., January 1, 1985, to December 31, 1989, or January 1, 1983, to December 31, 1987), and (4) the market index selected (e.g., the S&P 500 stock market index or an index consisting of all stocks traded on exchanges weighted by their relative market value). Moreover, there is the question of the stability of beta over different time intervals—that is, does the beta of a stock or portfolio remain relatively unchanged over time, or does it change?[13]

The interesting question has to do with the economic determinants of the beta of a stock. The risk characteristics of a company should be reflected in its beta. Several empirical studies have attempted to identify these macroeconomic and microeconomic factors.[14]

---

[11] We discuss several broad market indexes in Chapter 8.

[12] This assumes that the economic determinants that affect the beta of a stock do not change over the measurement period.

[13] See Frank J. Fabozzi and Jack C. Francis, "Stability Tests for Alphas and Betas over Bull and Bear Markets," *Journal of Finance* (September 1977), pp. 1093–1099, and "Beta as a Random Coefficient," *Journal of Financial and Quantitative Analysis* (March 1978), pp. 101–116.

[14] See, for example, Frank J. Fabozzi and Jack C. Francis, "Industry Effects and the Determinants of Beta," *Quarterly Review of Economics and Business* (Autumn 1979), pp. 61–74; Frank J. Fabozzi, Teresa Garlicki, Arabinda Ghosh, and Peter Kislowski, "Market Power as a Determinant of Systematic Risk: Empirical Evidence," *Review of Business and Economic Research* (Spring 1986), pp. 61–70; and Frank J. Fabozzi and Jack C. Francis, "The Effects of Changing Macroeconomic Conditions on the Parameters of the Single-Index Market Model," *Journal of Financial and Quantitative Analysis* (June 1979), pp. 351–356.

THE CAPITAL ASSET PRICING MODEL

We have now developed two measures of risk: one is a measure of total risk (standard deviation), the other a relative index of systematic or non-diversifiable risk (beta). The beta measure would appear to be the more relevant for the pricing of securities. Returns expected by investors logically should be related to systematic as opposed to total risk. Securities with higher systematic risk should have higher expected returns.

The question of interest now is the form of the relationship between risk and return. In this section we describe a relationship called the *capital asset pricing model* (CAPM), which is based on elementary logic and simple economic principles. The basic postulate underlying finance theory is that assets with the same systematic risk should have the same expected rate of return; that is, the prices of assets in the capital markets should adjust until equivalent risk assets have identical expected returns. This principle is called the "law of one price."

To see the implications of this postulate, consider an investor who holds a risky portfolio with the same risk as the market portfolio (beta equal to 1.0).[15] What return should she expect? Logically, she should expect the same return as that of the market portfolio. Consider another investor who holds a riskless portfolio (beta equal to zero). In this case the investor should expect to earn the rate of return on riskless assets, such as Treasury bills.[16] The investor who takes no risk earns the riskless rate of return.

Now consider the case of an investor who holds a mixture of these two portfolios. Assume he invests a proportion X of his money in the risky portfolio and $(1 - X)$ in the riskless portfolio. What systematic risk does he bear, and what return should he expect? The risk of the composite portfolio is easily computed. Recall that the beta of a portfolio is simply a weighted average of the component security betas, where the weights are the portfolio proportions. Thus, the portfolio beta, β_p, is a weighted average of the beta of the market portfolio and that of the riskless portfolio. The market beta is 1.0, the beta of the risk-free rate is 0. Thus,

$$\beta_p = (1 - X) \times 0 + X \times 1$$
$$= X \tag{11}$$

Thus, β_p is equal to the fraction of the money invested in the risky portfolio.

---

[15] We use the term portfolio in a general sense, including the case where the investor holds only one security. Because portfolio return and (systematic) risk are simply weighted averages of security values, risk/return relationships that hold for securities must also be true for portfolios, and vice versa.

[16] Treasury bills are discussed in Chapter 13.

If 100% or less of the investor's funds are invested in the risky portfolio, the portfolio beta will be between 0 and 1. If the investor borrows at the risk-free rate and invests the proceeds in the risky portfolio, so that X is larger than 1 and $(1 - X)$ is negative, the portfolio beta will be greater than 1.

The expected return of the composite portfolio is also a weighted average of the expected returns on the two portfolios; that is,

$$E(R_p) = (1 - X) \times R_f + X \times E(R_m), \tag{12}$$

where $E(R_p)$ and $E(R_m)$ are the expected returns on the portfolio and the market index, and R_f is the risk-free rate. Now, from Equation (11) we know that X is equal to β_p. Substituting into Equation (12), we have

$$E(R_p) = (1 - \beta_p) \times R_f + \beta_p \times E(R_m),$$

or

$$E(R_p) = R_f + \beta_p \times [E(R_m) - R_f]. \tag{13}$$

Equation (13) is the capital asset pricing model. This extremely important theoretical result says that the expected return on a portfolio should exceed the riskless rate of return by an amount that is proportional to the portfolio beta. That is, the relationship between expected return and risk should be linear.

The model is often stated in *risk premium* form. Risk premiums or *excess returns* are obtained by subtracting the risk-free rate from the rate of return. The expected portfolio and market risk premiums—designated $E(r_p)$ and $E(r_m)$, respectively—are given by

$$E(r_p) = E(R_p) - R_f$$
$$E(r_m) = E(R_m) - R_f.$$

Substituting these risk premiums into Equation (13), we obtain

$$E(r_p) = \beta_p E(r_m). \tag{14}$$

In this form, the CAPM states that the expected risk premium for the investor's portfolio is equal to its beta value times the expected market risk premium. Or, equivalently stated, the expected risk premium should be equal to the quantity of risk (as measured by beta) and the market price of risk (as measured by the expected market risk premium).

We can illustrate the model by assuming that the short-term (risk-free) interest rate is 6% and the expected return on the market is 10%. The expected risk premium for holding the market portfolio is simply the difference between the 10% and the short-term interest rate of 6%, or 4%. Investors who hold the market portfolio expect to earn 10%, which is 4% greater than they could earn on a short-term market instrument for certain. In order to satisfy Equation (13), the expected return on securities or portfolios with different levels of risk must be as follows:

BETA	EXPECTED RETURN
0.0	6%
0.5	8
1.0	10
1.5	12
2.0	14

The predictions of the model are inherently sensible. For safe investments ($\beta = 0$), the model predicts that investors would expect to earn the risk-free rate of interest. For a risky investment, ($\beta > 0$), investors would expect a rate of excess return proportional to the market sensitivity (β) of the investment. Thus, stocks with lower-than-average market sensitivities would offer expected returns less than the expected market return. Stocks with above-average values of beta (such as most airline securities) would offer expected returns in excess of the market.

Underlying Assumptions

In our development of the CAPM we have implicitly made a number of assumptions that are required if the model is to be established on a rigorous basis. These assumptions involve investor behavior and conditions in the capital markets. The assumptions following are sufficient to allow a single derivation of the model.

1. The market is made up of risk-averse investors who measure risk in terms of standard deviation of portfolio return. This assumption provides a basis for the use of risk measures such as beta.

2. All investors have a common time horizon for investment decision making (e.g., one month, one year, and so on). This assumption allows us to measure investor expectations over some common interval, thus making comparisons meaningful.

3. All investors are assumed to have the same expectations about future security returns and risks. The only reason why they choose different portfolios is differences in systematic risk and in risk preferences.

Without this assumption, the analysis would become much more complicated.

4. Capital markets are perfect in the sense that all assets are completely divisible, there are no transactions costs or differential taxes, and borrowing and lending rates are equal to each other and the same for all investors. Without these conditions, frictional barriers would exist to the equilibrium conditions on which the model is based.

While these assumptions are sufficient to derive the model, it is not clear that all are necessary in this exact form. It may well be that several of the assumptions can be relaxed substantially without major change in the form of the model. A good deal of research has been conducted toward this end.

Tests of the Capital Asset Pricing Model

The CAPM is indeed a simple and elegant model, but these qualities do not in and of themselves guarantee that it will be useful in explaining observed risk/return patterns. Here we briefly review the empirical literature on attempts to verify the model.

The major difficulty in testing the CAPM is that the model is stated in terms of investors' expectations and not in terms of realized returns. To test the CAPM, it is necessary to convert the theoretical CAPM given by Equation (14) into a form that can be tested empirically. We will not go through this exercise here, but will simply provide the model that is typically tested.[17] Nor will we delve into the econometric problems associated with testing the CAPM, although we will discuss later an important theoretical issue that raises serious questions about the testability of the CAPM and therefore the empirical findings of researchers.

The empirical analogue of Equation (14) asserts that over the period of time analyzed (1) there is a linear relationship between the average risk premium return on the market and the average risk premium return on a stock or portfolio, and its slope is β, and (2) the linear relationship should pass through the origin. Moreover, according to the CAPM, beta is a complete measure of a stock's risk. Consequently, various alternative risk measures that might be proposed, the most common being the standard deviation of return, should not be significant contributors to the explanation of a stock's return. Recall that the standard deviation measures a stock's total risk, which includes both systematic and unsystematic components.

---

[17] The interested reader can find the procedure for developing the empirical model tested in Franco Modigliani and Gerald A. Pogue, "Introduction to Risk and Return: Concepts and Evidence: Part II," *Financial Analysts Journal* (May–June 1974), pp. 69–86.

The CAPM holds for both individual securities and portfolios. Therefore, the empirical tests can be based on either. Tests based on individual securities, however, are not the most efficient method of obtaining estimates of the magnitude of the risk/return trade-off for two reasons.

The first problem is called the "errors in variables bias"; it results from the fact that the beta of a stock typically is measured by correlating the stock's return over some sample of historical data. The slope of the resulting line (the regression coefficient) is the estimate of beta. It is subject to errors from various sources. These errors are random in their effect—that is, some stocks' betas are overestimated and some are underestimated. Nevertheless, when these estimated beta values are used in the test, the measurement errors tend to attenuate the relationship between average return and risk. By carefully grouping the securities into portfolios of securities with similar betas, much of this measurement error problem can be eliminated. The errors in individual stocks' betas cancel out so that the portfolio beta can be measured with much greater precision. This in turn means that tests based on portfolio returns will be more efficient than tests based on security returns.

The second problem relates to the obscuring effect of residual variation. Realized security returns have a large random component, which typically accounts for about 70% of the variation of return. (This is the diversifiable or unsystematic risk of the stock.) By grouping securities into portfolios, we can eliminate much of this noise and thereby get a much clearer view of the relationship between return and systematic risk.

It should be noted that grouping does not distort the underlying risk/return relationship. The relationship that exists for individual securities is exactly the same for portfolios of securities.

The major results of the empirical tests conducted in the early 1970s are summarized below:[18]

1. The evidence shows a significant positive relationship between realized returns and systematic risk as measured by beta. The average market risk premium estimated is usually less than predicted by the CAPM, however.

2. The relationship between risk and return appears to be linear. The studies give no evidence of significant curvature in the risk/return relationship.

---

[18] Some of the earlier studies are: Nancy Jacob, "The Measurement of Systematic Risk for Securities and Portfolios: Some Empirical Results," *Journal of Financial and Quantitative Analysis* (March 1971), pp. 815–834; Merton H. Miller and Myron S. Scholes, "Rates of Returns in Relation to Risk: A Reexamination of Recent Findings," and Fischer Black, Michael C. Jensen, and Myron S. Scholes, "The Capital Asset Pricing Model: Some Empirical Evidence," in Michael C. Jensen (ed.), *Studies in the Theory of Capital Markets* (New York: Praeger Books, 1972); Marshall E. Blume and Irwin Friend, "A New Look at the Capital Asset Pricing Model," *Journal of Finance* (March 1973), pp. 19–33; and Eugene F. Fama and James D. MacBeth, "Risk, Return and Equilibrium: Empirical Tests," Working Paper No. 7237, University of Chicago, Graduate School of Business, August 1972.

3. Tests that attempt to discriminate between the effects of systematic and unsystematic risk do not yield definitive results. Both kinds of risk appear to be positively related to security returns, but there is substantial support for the proposition that the relationship between return and unsystematic risk is at least partly spurious—that is, partly a reflection of statistical problems rather than the true nature of capital markets.

Obviously, we cannot claim that the CAPM is absolutely right. On the other hand, the early empirical tests do support the view that beta is a useful risk measure and that high-beta stocks tend to be priced so as to yield correspondingly high rates of return.

In 1977, however, Richard Roll wrote a paper criticizing the previously published tests of the CAPM.[19] Roll argued that while the CAPM is testable in principle, no correct test of the theory had yet been presented. He also argued that there was practically no possibility that a correct test would ever be accomplished in the future.

The reasoning behind Roll's assertions revolves around his contribution that there is only one potentially testable hypothesis associated with the CAPM, namely, that the true market portfolio is mean–variance efficient. Furthermore, because the true market portfolio must contain all worldwide assets, the value of most of which cannot be observed (e.g., human capital), the hypothesis is in all probability untestable.[20]

Since 1977 there have been a number of studies that purport either to support or reject the CAPM. These tests have attempted to examine implications of the CAPM other than the linearity of the risk/return relation as the basis of their methodology. Unfortunately, none provides a definitive test, and most are subject to substantial criticism, suffering from the same problem of identifying the "true" market portfolio. We mention two studies to provide a flavor of the post-Roll tests.

In 1980 Pao Cheng and Robert Grauer published the results of a test of the CAPM that they claimed were "free from the ambiguity imbedded in past

---

[19] Richard Roll, "A Critique of the Asset Pricing Theory: Part I. On the Past and Potential Testability of the Theory," *Journal of Financial Economics* (March 1977), pp. 129–176.

[20] The hypothesis tested in the traditional tests of the CAPM cited earlier, namely, that there is a linear relationship between average security returns and beta values, sheds no light on the question whatsoever. This follows because an approximately linear relation between risk and return would be achieved in tests involving large, well-diversified common stock portfolios, irrespective of whether securities were priced according to the CAPM or some totally different model. The result is tautological. The fact that a positive relationship between realized returns and betas is typically found simply indicates that the returns on the proxy indexes used for the true market portfolio were larger than the average return to the global minimum-variance portfolio.

tests."[21] Specifically, they made assumptions about the joint distribution of security returns so as to permit a test of the CAPM that circumvents the need to identify the "true" market portfolio. They then tested whether the predicted relationship holds among portfolio market values over various historical periods. The advantage of this approach is that the market portfolio is not required and betas do not have to be estimated. Unfortunately, the results of the Cheng and Grauer tests are inconclusive. Some results favor the CAPM; others reject it. The authors conclude that on balance their results provide evidence against the CAPM. Some have criticized these results on the basis that the assumptions are unwarranted, and, as the authors admit, their test is a joint test of the CAPM and the return distribution they assumed, rather than a pure test of the CAPM.

In 1982, Robert Stambaugh conducted a sensitivity analysis to determine whether changing the nature of the market proxy has a significant impact on the results of tests of the CAPM.[22] He expanded on the types of investments included in his proxy from stocks listed on the New York Stock Exchange to corporate and government bonds to real estate to durable goods such as house furnishings and automobiles. Results indicate that the nature of the conclusions is not materially affected as one expands the composition of the proxy for the market portfolio.

These results at first appear to be comforting until we realize that at the domestic level many investments, including human capital, are not included even in the broadest indexes examined. More importantly, the market portfolio—at least insofar as the public regards these markets as equivalent to the domestic one—should be internationally diversified, and the total invested capital of the United States is only a small fraction of invested capital worldwide. Moreover, many of these investments can be expected to exhibit a low degree of correlation with returns on investments in the United States. Stambaugh's results tell us only that when we move from using a market proxy that represents a very small fraction of the market portfolio to a proxy that represents a larger but still very small fraction, empirical results do not tend to change much.

THE MULTIFACTOR CAPM

The CAPM described above assumes that the only risk that an investor is concerned with is uncertainty about the future price of a security. Investors, however, usually are concerned with other risks that will affect their ability to

---

[21] Pao L. Cheng and Robert R. Grauer, "An Alternative Test of the Capital Asset Pricing Model," *American Economic Review* (September 1980), pp. 660–671.

[22] Robert F. Stambaugh, "On the Exclusion of Assets from Tests of the Two-Parameter Model: A Sensitivity Analysis," *Journal of Financial Economics* (November 1982), pp. 237–268.

consume goods and services in the future. Three examples would be the risks associated with future labor income, the future relative prices of consumer goods, and future investment opportunities.

Recognizing these other risks that investors face, Robert Merton has extended the CAPM to describe consumers deriving their optimal lifetime consumption when they face these "extra-market" sources of risk.[23] These extra-market sources of risk are also referred to as "factors," so the model derived by Merton is called a *multifactor CAPM* and is given below in risk-premium form:

$$E(r_p) = B_{pm} E(r_m) + B_{pF1} E(r_{F1}) + B_{pF2} E(r_{F2}) + \ldots + B_{pFK} E(r_{FK}) \qquad (15)$$

where K = number of factors or extra-market sources of risk,

$\quad B_{pFk}$ = the sensitivity of the portfolio to the k-th factor, and

$\quad E(r_{Fk})$ = the expected return of factor k minus the risk-free rate.

The total extra-market sources of risk are equal to

$$B_{pF1} E(r_{F1}) + B_{pF2} E(r_{F2}) + \ldots + B_{pFK} E(r_{FK}) \qquad (16)$$

Equation (15) says that investors want to be compensated for the risk associated with each source of extra-market risk, in addition to market risk. Note that if there are no extra-market sources of risk, Equation (15) reduces to the CAPM as given by Equation (14). In the case of the CAPM, investors hedge the uncertainty associated with future security prices through diversification by holding the market portfolio, which can be thought of as a mutual fund that invests in all securities based on their relative capitalizations. In the multifactor CAPM, besides investing in the market portfolio, investors will also allocate funds to something equivalent to a mutual fund that hedges a particular extra-market risk. While not all investors are concerned with the same sources of extra-market risk, those that are concerned with a specific extra-market risk will basically hedge them in the same way.

As individual securities are nothing more than portfolios consisting of only one security, Equation (15) must hold for each security, i. That is

---

[23] Robert C. Merton, "An Intertemporal Capital Asset Pricing Model," *Econometrica* (September 1973), pp. 867–888. A less technical version is published in "A Reexamination of the CAPM," in Irwin Friend and James Bicksler (eds.), *Risk and Return in Finance* (Cambridge, MA: Ballinger Publishing, 1976). Other papers on multifactor CAPMs are: John C. Cox, Jonathan E. Ingersoll, and Stephen A. Ross, "An Intertemporal Asset Pricing Model with Rational Expectations," *Econometrica* (March 1985), pp. 363–384, and Douglas T. Breeden, "An Intertemporal Asset Pricing Model with Stochastic Consumption and Investment Opportunities," *Journal of Financial Economics* (September 1979), pp. 265–296.

$$E(r_i) = B_{im} \, E(r_m) + B_{iF1} \, E(r_{F1}) + B_{iF2} \, E(r_{F2}) + \ldots + B_{iFK} \, E(r_{FK}) \qquad (17)$$

From an empirical perspective, it may be difficult to identify the relevant extra-market risks. Moreover, it is difficult to distinguish the multifactor CAPM empirically from the next risk and return model described.

ARBITRAGE PRICING THEORY MODEL

An alternative model to the CAPM and the multifactor CAPM was developed by Stephen Ross in 1976.[24] This model is based purely on arbitrage arguments, and hence is called the Arbitrage Pricing Theory (APT) model. It postulates that a security's expected return is influenced by a variety of factors, as opposed to just the single market index of the CAPM.

The APT model assumes that there are several factors that determine the rate of return on a security, not just one as in the case of the CAPM. To understand this, look back at Equation (5), which states that the return on a security is dependent on its market sensitivity index and an unsystematic return. The APT in contrast states that the return on a security is linearly related to H "factors." The APT does not specify what these factors are, but it is assumed that the relationship between security returns and the factors is linear.

For now, to illustrate the APT model, let's assume a simple world with a portfolio consisting of three securities in the presence of two factors. The notation is as follows:

$\tilde{R}_i$ = the random rate of return on security i ($i = 1,2,3$)
$E(R_i)$ = the expected return on security i ($i = 1,2,3$)
β_{ih} = the sensitivity of the i-th security to the h-th factor
$\tilde{F}_h$ = the h-th factor that is common to the returns of all three assets ($h = 1,2$)
$\tilde{e}_i$ = the unsystematic return for security i ($i = 1,2,3$)

The APT model asserts that the random rate of return on security i is given by the relationship:

---

[24] Stephen A. Ross, "The Arbitrage Theory of Capital Asset Pricing," *Journal of Economic Theory* (December 1976), pp. 343–362, and "Return, Risk and Arbitrage," in Friend and Bicksler (eds.), *Risk and Return in Finance*. Since the publication by Ross, there have been several studies that have refined the theory. See, for example, Gur Huberman, "A Simple Approach to Arbitrage Pricing Theory," *Journal of Economic Theory* (October 1982), pp. 183–191, and Jonathan E. Ingersoll, "Some Results in the Theory of Arbitrage Pricing," *Journal of Finance* (September 1984), pp. 1021–1039.

$$\tilde{R}_i = E(R_i) + \beta_{i1}\,\tilde{F}_1 + \beta_{i2}\,\tilde{F}_2 + \tilde{e}_i \tag{18}$$

For equilibrium to exist among these three assets, the following arbitrage condition must be satisfied: using no additional funds (wealth) and without increasing risk, it should not be possible, on average, to create a portfolio to increase return. In essence, this condition states that there is no "money machine" available in the market.

Illustration

Suppose that the market value of the investor's portfolio is initially $100,000, divided as follows: (1) $20,000 in security 1; (2) $30,000 in security 2; and (3) $50,000 in security 3. The investor then changes the initial portfolio as follows: (1) $35,000 in security 1; (2) $25,000 in security 2; and (3) $40,000 in security 3. If V_i = the *change* in the dollar amount invested in the i-th security as a percentage of the investor's wealth, the V_i's would be as follows:

$$V_1 = \frac{\$35,000 - \$20,000}{\$100,000} = 0.15$$

$$V_2 = \frac{\$25,000 - \$30,000}{\$100,000} = -0.05$$

$$V_3 = \frac{\$40,000 - \$50,000}{\$100,000} = -0.10$$

Note that the sum of the V_i's is equal to zero because no additional funds were invested. That is, rebalancing of the portfolio does not change the market value of the initial portfolio. Rebalancing does do two things. First, it changes the future return of the portfolio. Second, it changes the total risk of the portfolio, both the systematic risk associated with the two factors and the unsystematic risk. Let's consider the first consequence.

Mathematically, the *change* in the portfolio's future return ($\Delta\tilde{R}_p$) can be shown to be as follows:

$$\Delta\tilde{R}_p = [V_1\,E(R_1) + V_2\,E(R_2) + V_3\,E(R_3)] + [V_1\,\beta_{11} + V_2\,\beta_{21} + V_3\,\beta_{31}]\,\tilde{F}_1$$
$$+ [V_1\,\beta_{12} + V_2\,\beta_{22} + V_3\,\beta_{32}]\,\tilde{F}_2 + [V_1\,\tilde{e}_1 + V_2\,\tilde{e}_2 + V_3\,\tilde{e}_3] \tag{19}$$

Equation (19) indicates that the change in the portfolio return will have a component that depends on systematic as well as unsystematic risk. While in our example we assume only three securities, when there are a large number of securities, the unsystematic risk can be eliminated by diversification as explained earlier in this chapter. Thus, Equation (19) would reduce to:

$$\Delta \tilde{R}_p = [V_1\, E(R_1) + V_2\, E(R_2) + V_3\, E(R_3)] + [V_1\, \beta_{11} + V_2\, \beta_{21} + V_3\, \beta_{31}]\, \tilde{F}_1$$
$$+ [V_1\, \beta_{12} + V_2\, \beta_{22} + V_3\, \beta_{32}]\, \tilde{F}_2 \tag{20}$$

Now let's look at the systematic risk with respect to each factor. The *change* in the portfolio risk with respect to factor 1 is just the betas of each security multiplied by their respective V_i's. Consequently, the change in the portfolio's sensitivity to systematic risk from factor 1 is:

$$V_1\, \beta_{11} + V_2\, \beta_{21} + V_3\, \beta_{31} \tag{21}$$

For factor 2, it is:

$$V_1\, \beta_{12} + V_2\, \beta_{22} + V_3\, \beta_{32} \tag{22}$$

One of the conditions that is imposed for no arbitrage is that the change in systematic risk with respect to each factor will be zero. That is, Equations (21) and (22) should satisfy the following:

$$V_1\, \beta_{11} + V_2\, \beta_{21} + V_3\, \beta_{31} = 0 \tag{23}$$

$$V_1\, \beta_{12} + V_2\, \beta_{22} + V_3\, \beta_{32} = 0 \tag{24}$$

If Equations (23) and (24) are satisfied, then Equation (20) reduces to

$$\Delta E(R_p) = V_1\, E(R_1) + V_2\, E(R_2) + V_3\, E(R_3) \tag{25}$$

Now let's put all the conditions for no arbitrage together in terms of the equations above. As stated earlier, using no additional funds (wealth) and without increasing risk, it should not be possible, on average, to create a portfolio to increase return. By no additional funds (wealth), this means the no new funds condition: $V_1 + V_2 + V_3 = 0$.

The condition that there be no change in the portfolio's sensitivity to each systematic risk is set forth in Equations (23) and (24).

Finally, the expected additional portfolio return from reshuffling the portfolio must be zero. This can be expressed by setting Equation (25) equal to zero, the no additional portfolio return condition:

$$V_1\, E(R_1) + V_2\, E(R_2) + V_3\, E(R_3) = 0$$

Taken together, these equations, as well as the condition that there be a sufficiently large number of securities so that unsystematic risk can be eliminated, describe mathematically the conditions for equilibrium pricing.

These conditions can be solved mathematically, because the number of securities is greater than the number of factors, to determine the equilibrium value for the portfolio as well as the equilibrium value for each of the three securities. Ross has shown that the following risk and return relationship, in risk premium form, will result for each security i:

$$E(r_i) = \beta_{iF1} \, E(r_{F1}) + \beta_{iF2} \, E(r_{F2}) \tag{26}$$

where r_i = the excess return of security i over the risk-free rate,
    β_{iFj} = the sensitivity of security i to the j-th factor, and
    r_{Fj} = the excess return of the j-th systematic factor over the risk-free rate, which can be thought of as the price (or risk premium) for the j-th systematic risk.

Equation (26) can be generalized to the case where there are H factors as follows:

$$E(r_i) = \beta_{iF1} \, E(r_{F1}) + \beta_{iF2} \, E(r_{F2}) + \ldots + \beta_{iFH} \, E(r_{FH}) \tag{27}$$

Equation (27) is the APT model. It states that investors want to be compensated for all the factors that *systematically* affect the return of a security. The compensation is the sum of the product of the quantity of systematic risk accepted for factor i, which is measured by the beta of the security with respect to the factor, and how the financial market prices that factor's risk, which is measured by the difference between the expected return for the factor and the risk-free rate. As in the case of the two other risk and return models described earlier, an investor is not compensated for accepted unsystematic risk.

Contrast Equation (27) with the CAPM. If there is only one factor, Equation (27) reduces to Equation (14), and the one factor would be market risk. The CAPM is therefore a special case of the APT model. Now contrast Equation (27) with the multifactor CAPM given by Equation (15). They look similar. Both say that investors are compensated for accepting all systematic risk and no unsystematic risk. The multifactor CAPM states that one of these systematic risks is market risk, while the APT model does not.

Supporters of the APT model argue that it has several major advantages over the CAPM or the multifactor CAPM. First, it makes less restrictive assumptions about investor preferences toward risk and return. The CAPM theory assumes investors trade off between risk and return solely on the basis of the expected returns and standard deviations of prospective investments. The APT, on the other hand, simply requires that some rather unobtrusive bounds be placed on potential investor utility functions. Second, no assumptions are made about the distribution of security returns. Finally, as the APT does not rely on identifying the true market index, the theory is potentially testable.

Empirical Evidence

To date, attempts to test the APT model empirically in the stock market have been inconclusive. Indeed, because of inability to find a set of factors that consistently explain security returns, some question whether the APT is testable at all. The APT gives no direction as to the choice of the factors themselves or even how many factors might be required. Thus, the APT replaces the problem of the market portfolio in the CAPM with uncertainty over the choice and measurement of the underlying factors.

One study by Nai-fu Chen, Richard Roll, and Stephen Ross suggests four plausible economic factors:[25]

1. Unanticipated changes in industrial production
2. Unanticipated changes in the spread between the yield on low-grade and high-grade bonds
3. Unanticipated changes in interest rates and the shape of the yield curve[26]
4. Unanticipated changes in inflation

SUMMARY

This chapter explains the principles of portfolio theory, a theory that deals with the construction of optimal portfolios by rational risk-averse investors, and its implications for the returns on different assets, and hence security prices. One way to evaluate the risk of a portfolio is by estimating the extent to which future portfolio values are likely to deviate from expected portfolio return. This is measured by the variance of the portfolio's return and is called the total portfolio risk. Total portfolio risk can be decomposed into two types of risk: systematic risk and unsystematic risk.

Systematic risk, also called market risk, is the risk that affects all securities. The beta of any security or portfolio is the relative systematic risk of the asset and is measured statistically (using historical return data) by the

---

[25] Nai-fu Chen, Richard Roll, and Stephen A. Ross, "Economic Forces and the Stock Market: Testing the APT and Alternative Asset Pricing Theories," *Journal of Business* (July 1980), pp. 383–403.

[26] The yield curve is discussed in Chapter 12.

slope of the regression between the asset's and the market's returns. The regression line estimated is called the market model. Unsystematic risk is the risk that is unique to a company, and it can be eliminated by diversifying the portfolio. Thus, systematic risk and unsystematic risk are referred to as non-diversifiable and diversifiable risk, respectively.

The capital asset pricing model is an economic theory that attempts to provide a relationship between risk and return, or, equivalently, it is a model for the pricing of risky securities. The CAPM asserts that the only relevant risk that investors will require to be compensated for assuming is systematic risk, because that risk cannot be eliminated by diversification. Basically, CAPM says that the expected return of a security or a portfolio is equal to the rate on a risk-free security plus a risk premium. The risk premium in the CAPM is proportional to the security or the portfolio beta. More specifically, the risk premium is the product of the quantity of risk and the market price of risk, measured by the beta, and the difference between the expected market return and risk-free rate, respectively.

While there have been numerous empirical tests of the CAPM, Richard Roll has criticized these studies because of the difficulty of identifying the true market portfolio. None of the post-Roll tests has been able to accomplish this. And in line with Roll's criticism, such tests are not likely to appear soon.

This is not to say that the CAPM is defective on a theoretical level. The model follows logically from its assumptions, and it comes to a conclusion that is intuitively appealing. It makes sense that investors will price securities according to the contribution that each makes to the risk of their overall portfolios. Thirty years ago it was believed that the risk of an individual security could be measured on the basis of the standard deviation of its rate-of-return distribution without regard to its relationships with other securities. The insight provided by the CAPM represents a major step forward in our understanding of the way securities are priced in the marketplace. In fact, it may be possible that the CAPM is the true underlying structure for security prices, but researchers are simply having a difficult time proving it.

The CAPM assumes that investors are concerned with only one risk: the risk having to do with the future price of a security. However, there are other risks, such as the capacity of investors to consume goods and services in the future. Robert Merton has developed a multifactor CAPM that assumes investors face such extra-market sources of risk called factors. The expected return in the multifactor CAPM is the market risk, as in the case of the basic CAPM, plus a package of risk premiums. Each risk premium is the product of the beta of the security or portfolio with respect to the particular factor and the difference between the expected return for the factor less the risk-free rate.

The Arbitrage Pricing Theory model is developed purely on arbitrage arguments. It postulates that the expected return on a security or a portfolio is influenced by several factors. Proponents of the APT model cite its less restrictive assumptions as a feature that makes it more appealing than the CAPM or multifactor CAPM. Moreover, testing the APT model does not require identification of the "true" market portfolio. It does, however, require empirical determination of the factors because they are not specified by the theory. Consequently, the APT model replaces the problem of identifying the market portfolio in the CAPM with the problem of choosing and measuring the underlying factors. Attempts at identifying the factors empirically have not been conclusive.

All things considered, the CAPM, multifactor CAPM, and APT model all provide interesting conceptual insights into the issues of the pricing of risk and portfolio selection in securities markets. Neither can be said to dominate the others in terms of theoretical content or the simplicity of empirical testing. Only the future will decide which has the best claim to the ultimate truth. Indeed, on this question, all three pricing theories will probably make valuable contributions to the development of the next generation of equilibrium models.

QUESTIONS

1. Suppose the probability distribution for the one-period return of some asset is as follows:

RETURN	PROBABILITY
0.20	0.10
0.15	0.20
0.10	0.30
0.03	0.25
−0.06	0.15

   a. What is this asset's expected one-period return?

   b. What is this asset's variance and standard deviation for the one-period return?

2. "A portfolio's expected return and variance of return are simply the weighted average of the individual asset expected returns and variances." Do you agree with this statement?

3. In the January 25, 1991, issue of *The Value Line Investment Survey*, you note the following:

COMPANY	BETA (β)
IBM	0.95
Bally Manufacturing	1.40
Cigna Corp.	1.00
British Telecom	0.60

a. How do you interpret these betas?

b. Is it reasonable to assume that the expected return on British Telecom is less than that on IBM shares?

c. "Given that Cigna Corporation has a β of 1.00, one can mimic the performance of the stock market as a whole by buying only these shares." Do you agree with this statement?

d. Suppose you picked up *The Value Line Investment Survey* from ten years ago. Would you expect the β values for these companies to be exactly the same as given above? Why or why not?

4. Assume the following:

Expected market return = 15%

Risk-free rate = 7%

If a security's beta is 1.3, what is its expected return according to the CAPM?

5. Professor Harry Markowitz, corecipient of the 1990 Nobel Prize in Economics, wrote the following:

> A portfolio with sixty different railway securities, for example, would not be as well diversified as the same size portfolio with some railroad, some public utility, mining, various sort of manufacturing, etc.

Why is this true?

6. Following is an excerpt from an article, "Risk and Reward," in *The Economist* of October 20, 1990:

> Next question: is the CAPM supported by the facts? That is controversial, to put it mildly. It is a tribute to Mr. Sharpe [cowinner of the 1990 Nobel Prize in Economics] that his work, which dates from the early 1960s, is still argued over so heatedly. Attention has lately turned away from beta to more complicated ways of carving up risk. But the significance of CAPM for financial economics would be hard to exaggerate.

    a. Summarize Roll's argument on the problems inherent in empirically verifying the CAPM.

    b. What are some of the other "more complicated ways of carving up risk"?

7. **a.** What are the difficulties in practice of applying the arbitrage pricing theory model?

    b. Does Roll's criticism also apply to this pricing model?

    c. "In the CAPM investors should be compensated for accepting systematic risk; for the APT model, investors are rewarded for accepting both systematic risk and unsystematic risk." Do you agree with this statement?

CHAPTER

6

INTRODUCTION TO FINANCIAL FUTURES MARKETS

LEARNING OBJECTIVES

After reading this chapter you will understand:

- what a futures contract is.

- the basic economic function of a futures contract.

- the difference between futures and forward contracts.

- the role of the clearinghouse.

- the mark-to-market and margin requirements of a futures contract.

- the risk/return relationship of futures positions.

- how a futures contract is priced.

- why the actual futures price may differ from the theoretical futures price.

- the principles of hedging and the risks associated with hedging.

- the role of futures markets in the economy.

A futures contract is an agreement that requires a party to the agreement either to buy or sell *something* at a designated future date at a predetermined price. The basic economic function of futures markets is to provide an opportunity for market participants to hedge against the risk of adverse price movements.

Futures contracts are products created by exchanges. To create a particular futures contract, an exchange must obtain approval from the Commodity Futures Trading Commission (CFTC), a government regulatory agency. When applying to the CFTC for approval to create a futures contract, the exchange must demonstrate that there is an economic purpose for the contract. While many futures contracts are approved for trading, not all succeed if there is lack of investor interest.

Prior to 1972, only futures contracts involving traditional agricultural commodities (such as grain and livestock), imported foodstuffs (such as coffee, cocoa, and sugar), or industrial commodities were traded. Collectively, such futures contracts are known as *commodity futures*.

Futures contracts based on a financial instrument or a financial index are known as *financial futures*. Financial futures can be classified as (1) stock index futures, (2) interest rate futures, and (3) currency futures. The first financial futures contracts were currency futures contracts, which were introduced in 1972 by the International Monetary Market (IMM) of the Chicago Mercantile Exchange (the "Merc" or CME). In October 1975, the Chicago Board of Trade (CBT) pioneered trading in a futures contract based on a fixed-income instrument. In 1982, three futures contracts based on broadly-based common stock indexes made their debut.

As the value of a futures contract is derived from the value of the underlying instrument, they are commonly called *derivative instruments*. In the next chapter we will discuss another derivative instrument, an option contract.

In Chapters 10, 19, and 21, we'll take a closer look at stock index futures, interest rate futures, and currency futures, respectively.[1] Our purpose in this chapter is to provide an introduction to financial futures contracts, how they are priced, and how they can be used for hedging. More detailed strategies employing futures contracts will be discussed in later chapters.

MECHANICS OF FUTURES TRADING

A futures contract is a firm legal agreement between a buyer (seller) and an established exchange or its clearinghouse in which the buyer (seller) agrees to take (make) delivery of *something* at a specified price at the end of a designated

---

[1] In Chapter 22 we review futures on non-U.S. financial products, focusing in particular on Japanese stock index and government bond futures contracts.

period of time. The price at which the parties agree to transact in the future is called the *futures price*. The designated date at which the parties must transact is called the *settlement* or *delivery* date.

To illustrate, suppose there is a futures contract traded on an exchange where the something to be bought or sold is Asset XYZ, and the settlement is three months from now. Assume further that Bob buys this futures contract, and Sally sells this futures contract, and the price at which they agree to transact in the future is $100. Then $100 is the futures price. At the settlement date, Sally will deliver Asset XYZ to Bob. Bob will give Sally $100, the futures price.

Liquidating a Position

Most financial futures contracts have settlement dates in the months of March, June, September, or December. This means that at a predetermined time in the contract settlement month the contract stops trading, and a price is determined by the exchange for settlement of the contract. The contract with the closest settlement date is called the *nearby* futures contract. The *next* futures contract is the one that settles just after the nearby contract. The contract farthest away in time from settlement is called the *most distant* futures contract.

A party to a futures contract has two choices on liquidation of the position. First, the position can be liquidated prior to the settlement date. For this purpose, the party must take an offsetting position in the same contract. For the buyer of a futures contract, this means selling the same number of identical futures contracts; for the seller of a futures contract, this means buying the same number of identical futures contracts.

The alternative is to wait until the settlement date. At that time the party purchasing a futures contract accepts delivery of the underlying asset (financial instrument, currency, or commodity) at the agreed-upon price; the party that sells a futures contract liquidates the position by delivering the underlying asset at the agreed-upon price. For some futures contracts that we shall describe in later chapters in this book, settlement is made in cash only. Such contracts are referred to as *cash settlement contracts*.

The Role of the Clearinghouse

Associated with every futures exchange is a clearinghouse, which performs several functions. One of these functions is guaranteeing that the two parties to the transaction will perform. To see the importance of this function, consider potential problems in the futures transaction described earlier from the perspective of the two parties—Bob the buyer and Sally the seller. Each must be concerned with the other's ability to fulfill the obligation at the settlement date. Suppose that at the settlement date the price of Asset XYZ in the cash market is $70. Sally can buy Asset XYZ for $70 and deliver it to Bob who, in turn, must pay her $100. If Bob does not have the capacity to pay $100 or refuses to pay, however, Sally has lost the opportunity to realize a profit of $30. Suppose, instead, that the price of Asset XYZ in the cash market is $150 at the settlement date. In this case, Bob is ready and willing to accept delivery of Asset XYZ and pay the agreed-upon price of $100. If Sally does not have the ability or refuses to deliver Asset XYZ, Bob has lost the opportunity to realize a profit of $50.

The clearinghouse exists to meet this problem. When an investor takes a position in the futures market, the clearinghouse takes the opposite position and agrees to satisfy the terms set forth in the contract. Because of the clearinghouse, the investor need not worry about the financial strength and integrity of the party taking the opposite side of the contract. After initial execution of an order, the relationship between the two parties ends. The clearinghouse interposes itself as the buyer for every sale and the seller for every purchase. Thus investors are free to liquidate their positions without involving the other party in the original contract, and without worry that the other party may default. This is the reason why we define a futures contract as an agreement between a party and a clearinghouse associated with an exchange.

Besides its guarantee function, the clearinghouse makes it simple for parties to a futures contract to unwind their positions prior to the settlement date. Suppose that Bob wants to get out of his futures position. He will not have to seek out Sally and work out an agreement with her to terminate the original agreement. Instead, Bob can unwind his position by selling an identical futures contract. As far as the clearinghouse is concerned, its records will show that Bob has bought and sold an identical futures contract. At the settlement date, Sally will not deliver Asset XYZ to Bob but will be instructed by the clearinghouse to deliver to someone who bought and still has an open futures position. In the same way, if Sally wants to unwind her position prior to the settlement date, she can buy an identical futures contract.

Margin Requirements

When a position is first taken in a futures contract, the investor must deposit a minimum dollar amount per contract as specified by the exchange. This amount is called *initial margin* and is required as deposit for the contract.[2] The

---

[2] Individual brokerage firms are free to set margin requirements above the minimum established by the exchange.

initial margin may be in the form of an interest-bearing security such as a Treasury bill. As the price of the futures contract fluctuates, the value of the investor's equity in the position changes. At the end of each trading day, the exchange determines the settlement price for the futures contract. This price is used to *mark to market* the investor's position, so that any gain or loss from the position is reflected in the investor's equity account.

Maintenance margin is the minimum level (specified by the exchange) by which an investor's equity position may fall as a result of an unfavorable price movement before the investor is required to deposit additional margin. The additional margin deposited is called *variation margin,* and it is an amount necessary to bring the equity in the account back to its initial margin level. Unlike initial margin, variation margin must be in cash not interest-bearing instruments. Any excess margin in the account may be withdrawn by the investor. If a party to a futures contract who is required to deposit variation margin fails to do so within 24 hours, the futures position is closed out.

Although there are initial and maintenance margin requirements for buying securities on margin, the concept of margin differs for securities and futures. When securities are acquired on margin, the difference between the price of the security and the initial margin is borrowed from the broker. The security purchased serves as collateral for the loan, and the investor pays interest. For futures contracts, the initial margin, in effect, serves as "good faith" money, an indication that the investor will satisfy the obligation of the contract. Normally no money is borrowed by the investor.

We illustrate futures margin requirements and the mark-to-market procedure more fully in Chapter 10 when we discuss stock index futures.

Market Structure

All futures exchanges in the U.S. trade more than one futures contract. On the exchange floor, each futures contract is traded at a designated location in a polygonal or circular platform called a *pit.* The price of a futures contract is determined by open outcry of bids and offers in an auction market. Because of the large number of traders attempting to communicate to other traders the price and quantity that they wish to transact at, pit traders are often forced to communicate using a system of hand signals. There is no designated market maker in the futures market as there is on an exchange where common stock is traded.

Trading on the floor of the exchange is restricted to members of the exchange. A membership is said to be a *seat* on the exchange. The price of a seat is determined by supply and demand. Non-exchange members can lease a seat, which conveys to them the right to trade on an exchange. Floor traders include two types: *locals* and *floor brokers* (also called *pit brokers*). Locals buy and sell futures contracts for their own account, thereby risking their own capital. They are professional risk takers. Their presence in the futures market adds liquidity to the market and brings bid and offer prices closer together. Consequently, as we explain in Chapter 8, collectively they play the same effective role as a market maker. Most locals do not maintain an open position overnight. The number of locals and the amount of capital that they can commit to the market far exceeds that of the floor brokers.

Floor brokers, just like locals, buy and sell for their own account. They execute customer orders as well. These orders come through an authorized futures broker, called a *futures commissions merchant*, or in the form of orders requested by other floor traders. For trades that they execute on behalf of others, floor brokers receive a commission. While floor brokers can both execute orders for customers and trade for their own account, most of their trades involve the former. When floor brokers do trade for their own account, such trades must not conflict with the interests of customers for whom they are executing trades.

This system of trading in futures markets is not very different from what it was in the 1800s. Monitoring of this sort of system is difficult, which has led to allegations that floor traders profit at the expense of customers whose orders are to be executed.

Several approaches for improving the system of trading futures via electronic trading are at the experimental stage. One approach is a computerized automated system for executing routine trades. Another approach is to automate the entire competitive trading system that now takes place in the pit. The Chicago Mercantile Exchange is working with Reuters Holdings to develop such a system (called the Globex system) for trading of futures contracts globally when a futures exchange is closed. Outside the U.S., various forms of electronic trading of futures contracts have already been introduced.

Daily Price Limits

The exchange has the right to impose a limit on the daily price movement of a futures contract from the previous day's closing price. A daily price limit sets the minimum and maximum price at which the futures contract may trade that day. When a daily price limit is reached, trading does not stop but rather continues at a price that does not violate the minimum or maximum price.

The rationale offered for the imposition of daily price limits is that they provide stability to the market at times when new information may cause the futures price to exhibit extreme fluctuations. Those who support daily price limits argue that giving market participants time to digest or reassess such information when trading ceases when price limits would be violated gives them greater confidence in the market. Not all economists agree with this rationale. The question of the role of daily price limits and whether they are necessary remains the subject of extensive debate.

FUTURES VERSUS FORWARD CONTRACTS

A forward contract, just like a futures contract, is an agreement for the future delivery of *something* at a specified price at the end of a designated period of time. Futures contracts are standardized agreements as to the delivery date (or month) and quality of the deliverable, and are traded on organized exchanges. A forward contract differs in that it is usually non-standardized (that is, the terms of each contract are negotiated individually between buyer and seller), there is no clearinghouse, and secondary markets are often non-existent or extremely thin. Unlike a futures contract, which is an exchange-traded product, a forward contract is an over-the-counter instrument.

Although both futures and forward contracts set forth terms of delivery, futures contracts are not intended to be settled by delivery. In fact, generally less than 2% of outstanding contracts are settled by delivery. Forward contracts, in contrast, are intended for delivery.

Futures contracts are marked to market at the end of each trading day, while forward contracts are not. Consequently, futures contracts are subject to interim cash flows as additional margin may be required in the case of adverse price movements, or as cash is withdrawn in the case of favorable price movements. There are no interim cash flow effects with forward contracts because no variation margin is required.

Finally, the parties in a forward contract are exposed to credit risk because either party may default on the obligation. Credit risk is minimal in the case of futures contracts because the clearinghouse associated with the exchange guarantees the other side of the transaction.

Other than these differences, most of what we say about futures contracts applies equally to forward contracts.

RISK AND RETURN CHARACTERISTICS OF FUTURES CONTRACTS

When an investor takes a position in the market by buying a futures contract, the investor is said to be in a *long position* or to be *long futures*. If, instead, the investor's opening position is the sale of a futures contract, the investor is said to be in a *short position* or *short futures*.

The buyer of a futures contract will realize a profit if the futures price increases; the seller of a futures contract will realize a profit if the futures price decreases. For example, suppose one month after Bob and Sally take their positions in the futures contract, the futures price of Asset XYZ increases to $120. Bob, the buyer of the futures contract, could then sell the futures contract and realize a profit of $20. Effectively, at the settlement date he has agreed to buy Asset XYZ for $100 and agreed to sell Asset XYZ for $120. Sally, the seller of the futures contract, will realize a loss of $20.

If the futures price falls to $40 and Sally buys the contract, she realizes a profit of $60 because she agreed to sell Asset XYZ for $100 and now can buy it for $40. Bob would realize a loss of $60. Thus, if the futures price decreases, the buyer of the futures contract realizes a loss while the seller of a futures contract realizes a profit.

Leveraging Aspect of Futures

When a position is taken in a futures contract, the party need not put up the entire amount of the investment. Instead, only initial margin must be put up. Consequently, suppose Bob has $100 to invest in Asset XYZ because he believes its price will appreciate. If Asset XYZ is selling for $100, he can buy one unit of the asset. His payoff will then be based on the price action of one unit of Asset XYZ.

Suppose instead that the exchange where the futures contract for Asset XYZ is traded requires initial margin of $5. Then Bob can purchase 20 contracts with his $100 investment. (This example ignores the fact that Bob may need funds for variation margin.) His payoff will then depend on the price action of 20 units of Asset XYZ. Thus he can leverage the use of his funds. While the degree of leverage available in the futures market varies from contract to contract, the leverage attainable is considerably greater than in the cash market.

At first, the leverage available in the futures market may suggest that the market benefits only those who want to speculate on price movements. This is not true. As we shall see later in this chapter, futures markets can be used to reduce price risk. Without the leverage possible in futures transactions, the cost of reducing price risk using futures would be too high for many market participants.

PRICING OF FUTURES CONTRACTS

To understand what determines the futures price, consider once again the futures contract where the underlying instrument is Asset XYZ. The following assumptions will be made:

1. In the cash market Asset XYZ is selling for $100.

2. Asset XYZ pays the holder (with certainty) $12 per year in four quarterly payments of $3, and the next quarterly payment is exactly three months from now.

3. The futures contract requires delivery three months from now.

4. The current three-month interest rate at which funds can be loaned or borrowed is 8% per year.

What should the price of this futures contract be? That is, what should the futures price be? Suppose the price of the futures contract is $107. Consider this strategy:

Sell the futures contract at $107

Purchase Asset XYZ in the cash market for $100

Borrow $100 for three months at 8% per year

The borrowed funds are used to purchase Asset XYZ, resulting in no initial cash outlay for this strategy. At the end of three months, $3 will be received from holding Asset XYZ. Three months from now, Asset XYZ must be delivered to settle the futures contract, and the loan must be repaid. This strategy produces an outcome as follows:

1. FROM SETTLEMENT OF THE FUTURES CONTRACT

Proceeds from sale of Asset XYZ to settle the futures contract	= 107
Payment received from investing in Asset XYZ for 3 months	= 3
Total proceeds	= 110

2. FROM THE LOAN

Repayment of principal of loan	= 100
Interest on loan (2% for 3 months)	= 2
Total outlay	= 102
Profit	= 8

Notice that this strategy will guarantee a profit of $8. Moreover, this profit is generated with *no investment* outlay because the proceeds obtained to purchase the Asset XYZ were borrowed. The profit will be realized *regardless of what the futures price at the settlement date is*. The profit is a riskless arbitrage profit. Obviously, in a well-functioning market, arbitrageurs would sell the futures and buy Asset XYZ, forcing the futures price down and bidding up Asset XYZ's price so as to eliminate this profit.

Suppose instead that the futures price is $92 and not $107. Let's consider the following strategy:

> Buy the futures contract at $92
>
> Sell (short) Asset XYZ for $100
>
> Invest (lend) $100 for three months at 8% per year[3]

Once again, there is no initial cash outlay for the strategy. Three months from now, Asset XYZ must be purchased to settle the long position in the futures contract. Asset XYZ accepted for delivery will then be used to cover the short position (i.e., to cover the short sale of Asset XYZ in the cash market). By shorting Asset XYZ, the short seller must pay the lender of Asset XYZ the proceeds that the lender would have earned for the quarter. Therefore, $3 must be paid to the lender of Asset XYZ. The outcome in three months would be as follows:

1. FROM SETTLEMENT OF THE FUTURES CONTRACT

Price paid for purchase of Asset XYZ to settle the futures contract	= 92
Proceeds to lender of Asset XYZ in order to borrow the asset	= 3
Total outlay	= 95

2. FROM THE LOAN

Proceeds received from maturing of investment	= 100
Interest earned from the 3-month loan investment (2% for 3 months)	= 2
Total proceeds	= 102
Profit	= 7

---

[3] Technically, a short seller may not be entitled to the full use of the proceeds resulting from the sale. We'll discuss this later in this section.

The $7 profit from this strategy is a riskless arbitrage profit. It requires no initial cash outlay, and again a profit will be realized regardless of what the future price is at the settlement date.

Is there a futures price that will eliminate the riskless arbitrage profit? Yes, there is. There will be no arbitrage profit if the futures price is $99. Let's look at what would happen if the two previous strategies are followed, assuming a futures price of $99.

First, consider the strategy:

Sell the futures contract at $99

Purchase Asset XYZ for $100

Borrow $100 for three months at 8% per year

In three months the outcome will be as follows:

1. FROM SETTLEMENT OF THE FUTURES CONTRACT

Proceeds from sale of Asset XYZ to settle the futures contract	= 99
Payment received from investing in Asset XYZ for 3 months	= 3
Total proceeds	= 102

2. FROM THE LOAN

Repayment of the principal of loan	= 100
Interest (2% for 3 months)	= 2
Total outlay	= 102
Profit	= 0

There is no arbitrage profit with this strategy.
Next consider the strategy:

Buy the futures contract at $99

Sell (short) Asset XYZ for $100

Invest (lend) $100 for 3 months at 8% per year

The outcome in three months would be as follows:

1. FROM SETTLEMENT OF THE FUTURES CONTRACT

Price paid for purchase of Asset XYZ to settle futures contract	= 99
Proceeds to lender of Asset XYZ in order to borrow the asset	= 3
Total outlay	= 102

2. FROM THE LOAN

Proceeds received from maturing of investment	= 100
Interest earned from the 3-month loan investment (2% for 3 months)	= 2
Total proceeds	= 102
Profit	= 0

Thus, neither strategy results in an arbitrage profit. Hence, a futures price of $99 is the equilibrium price because any higher or lower futures price will permit riskless arbitrage profits.

Theoretical Futures Price Based on Arbitrage Model

According to the arbitrage arguments we have just presented, we see that the equilibrium futures price can be determined based on the following information:

1. the price of the asset in the cash market.
2. the cash yield earned on the asset until the settlement date. In our example, the cash yield on Asset XYZ is $3 on a $100 investment or 3% quarterly (12% annual cash yield).
3. the interest rate for borrowing and lending until the settlement date. The borrowing and lending rate is referred to as the *financing cost*. In our example, the financing cost is 2% for the three months.

Let:

r = financing cost (%)
y = cash yield (%)
P = cash market price ($)
F = futures price ($),

and consider the strategy:

Sell the futures contract at F
Purchase Asset XYZ for P
Borrow P until the settlement date at r

The outcome at the settlement date then is:

1. FROM SETTLEMENT OF THE FUTURES CONTRACT

Proceeds from sale of Asset XYZ to settle the futures contract	$= F$
Payment received from investing in Asset XYZ for 3 months	$= yP$
Total proceeds	$= F + yP$

2. FROM THE LOAN

Repayment of the principal of loan	$= P$
Interest on loan	$= rP$
Total outlay	$= P + rP$

The profit will equal:

Profit = Total proceeds − Total outlay

$\text{Profit} = F + yP - (P + rP)$

The equilibrium futures price is where the profit from this strategy is zero. Thus, to have equilibrium, the following must hold:

$$0 = F + yP - (P + rP)$$

Solving for the theoretical futures price, we have:

$$F = P + P\,(r - y)$$

Alternatively, consider the strategy:

Buy the futures contract at F
Sell (short) Asset XYZ for P
Invest (lend) P at r until the settlement date

The outcome at the settlement date would be:

1. FROM SETTLEMENT OF THE FUTURES CONTRACT

Price paid for purchase of Asset XYZ to settle futures contract	$= F$
Payment to lender of Asset XYZ in order to borrow the asset	$= yP$
Total outlay	$= F + yP$

2. FROM THE LOAN

Proceeds received from maturing of the loan investment	$= P$
Interest earned	$= rP$
Total proceeds	$= P + rP$

The profit will equal:

Profit = Total proceeds − Total outlay

Profit $= P + rP - (F + yP)$

Setting the profit equal to zero so that there will be no arbitrage profit and solving for the futures price, we would obtain the same equation for the futures price as derived earlier:

$$F = P + P (r - y)$$

Let's apply this equation to our previous example to determine the theoretical futures price. Here:

$r = 0.02$
$y = 0.03$
$P = \$100$

Then, the theoretical futures price is:

$F = \$100 - \$100 (0.03 - 0.02)$
$= \$100 - \$1 = \$99$

This agrees with the equilibrium futures price we demonstrated earlier.

The theoretical futures price may be at a premium to the cash market price (higher than the cash market price) or at a discount from the cash market price (lower than the cash market price) depending on P $(r - y)$. The term $r - y$, which reflects the difference between the cost of financing and the asset's cash yield, is called the *net financing cost*. The net financing cost is more commonly called the *cost of carry* or, simply, *carry*. *Positive carry* means that the yield earned is greater than the financing cost; *negative carry* means that the financing cost exceeds the yield earned. Then the following relationships hold:

CARRY	FUTURES PRICE
Positive ($y > r$)	will sell at a discount to cash price ($F < P$)
Negative ($y < r$)	will sell at a premium to cash price ($F > P$)
Zero ($r = y$)	will be equal to the cash price ($F = P$)

Price Convergence at the Delivery Date

At the delivery date, the futures price must be equal to the cash market price. Thus, as the delivery date approaches, the futures price will converge to the cash market price. This can be seen by looking at the equation for the theoretical futures price. As the delivery date approaches, the financing cost approaches zero, and the yield that can be earned by holding the investment approaches zero. Hence the cost of carry approaches zero, and the futures price will approach the cash market price.

A Closer Look at the Theoretical Futures Price

To derive the theoretical futures price using the arbitrage argument, we made several assumptions. When the assumptions are violated, there will be a divergence between the actual futures price and the theoretical futures price; that is, the difference between the two prices will differ from carry. The implications of this for pricing will be discussed in more detail when we focus on stock index futures in Chapter 10 and interest rate futures in Chapter 19. For the time being we shall look at reasons for the deviation of the actual futures price from the theoretical futures price that are common to all financial futures contracts.

1. Interim Cash Flows. No interim cash flows due to variation margin are assumed. In addition, any dividends or coupon interest payments are assumed to be paid at the delivery date rather than at an interim date. However, we know that interim cash flows can occur for both of these reasons. Because we assume no variation margin, the theoretical price for the contract is technically the theoretical price for a forward contract, not the theoretical price for a futures contract. This is because, unlike a futures contract, a forward contract is not marked to market at the end of each trading day, and therefore does not require variation margin.

2. Differences between Lending and Borrowing Rates.   In deriving the theoretical futures price it is assumed that the borrowing rate and lending rate are equal. Typically, however, the borrowing rate is greater than the lending rate. Letting

r_B = Borrowing rate

r_L = Lending rate

for the strategy:

Sell the futures contract at F

Purchase the asset for P

Borrow P until the settlement date at r_B

the futures price that would produce no arbitrage profit is:

$$F = P + P\,(r_B - y)$$

For the strategy:

Buy the futures contract at F

Sell (short) the asset for P

Invest (lend) P at r_L until the settlement date

the futures price that would produce no profit is:

$$F = P + P\,(r_L - y)$$

These two equations together provide boundaries between which the futures price will be in equilibrium. The first equation establishes the upper boundary, and the second equation the lower boundary. For example, assume that the borrowing rate is 8% per year, or 2% for three months, while the lending rate is 6% per year, or 1.5% for three months. According to the first equation, the upper boundary is:

$$F \text{ (upper boundary)} = \$100 + \$100\,(0.02 - 0.03) = \$99$$

The lower boundary according to the second equation is:

$$F \text{ (lower boundary)} = \$100 + \$100 \, (0.015 - 0.03) = \$98.50$$

Thus the equilibrium price must satisfy the condition $98.50 < F < 99$.

3. Transactions Costs. In determining the theoretical futures price, we have ignored transactions costs involved in establishing the positions. In actuality, there are transactions costs of entering into and closing the cash position as well as round-trip transactions costs for the futures contract that do affect the futures price. Transactions costs widen the boundaries for the futures price.

4. Proceeds from Short-Selling. In the strategy involving short-selling of Asset XYZ, it is assumed that the proceeds from the short sale are received and reinvested. In practice, for individual investors, the proceeds are not received, and, in fact, the individual investor is required to put up margin (securities margin not futures margin) to short-sell. For institutional investors, the asset may be borrowed, but there is a cost to borrowing. This cost of borrowing can be incorporated into the model by reducing the yield on the asset.

5. Deliverable Asset and Settlement Date Known. Our example assumes that (1) only one asset is deliverable, and (2) the settlement date occurs three months from now. In Chapter 19 where we discuss Treasury bond futures contracts, we will see that there are several Treasury bond issues that can be delivered to satisfy the futures contract. The choice of which Treasury bond issue to deliver is given to the short. Thus, the buyer of this futures contract does not know what the deliverable asset will be. Also, for the same futures contract, the short is also given the choice of when in the settlement month to deliver the Treasury bond issue. As a result, the buyer does not know the specific settlement date. These factors influence the futures price.

6. Deliverable Is a Basket of Securities. Some futures contracts involve not a single asset but a basket of assets or an index. Stock index futures, discussed in Chapter 10, and the municipal bond index futures contract, explained in Chapter 19, are examples. The problem in arbitraging these two futures contracts is that it is too expensive to buy or sell every asset included in the index. Instead, a portfolio containing a smaller number of assets may be constructed to "track" the index. The arbitrage, however, is no longer risk-free because there is the risk that the portfolio will not track the index exactly. All of this leads to higher transactions costs and uncertainty about the outcome of the arbitrage.

7. Differences in the Tax Treatment of Securities and Futures Contracts. The sale or exchange of a security results in a taxable transaction. The rules for taxing a futures position are different. The profit or loss on a futures contract position is taxed at the end of an investor's tax year. That is, even if a futures position is acquired and held, a taxable event is assumed to have occurred at the end of every tax year.

GENERAL PRINCIPLES OF HEDGING WITH FUTURES

The major function of futures markets is to transfer price risk from hedgers to speculators. That is, risk is transferred from those willing to pay to avoid risk to those wanting to assume the risk in the hope of gain. Hedging in this case is the employment of a futures transaction as a temporary substitute for a transaction to be made in the cash market. The hedge position locks in a value for the cash position. As long as cash and futures prices move together, any loss realized on one position (whether cash or futures) will be offset by a profit on the other position. When the profit and loss are equal, the hedge is called a *perfect* or *textbook hedge*. In a market where the futures contract is correctly priced, a perfect hedge should provide a return equal to the risk-free rate.

In practice, hedging is not that simple. The amount of the loss or profit on a hedge will be determined by the relationship between the cash price and the futures price when a hedge is placed and when it is lifted. The difference between the cash price and the futures price is called the *basis*. That is,

Basis = Cash price − Futures price

As we explained earlier, if a futures contract is priced according to its theoretical value, the difference between the cash price and the futures price should be equal to the cost of carry. The risk that the hedger takes is that the basis will change because the futures will be mispriced relative to the cash price. This is called *basis risk*. Therefore, *hedging involves the substitution of basis risk for price risk;* that is, the substitution of the risk that the basis will change for the risk that the cash price will change.

When a futures contract is used to hedge a position where either the portfolio or the individual financial instrument is not identical to the instrument underlying the futures, it is called *cross hedging*. Cross hedging is common in asset/liability and portfolio management because there are no futures contracts on specific common stock shares and bonds. Cross hedging introduces another risk—the risk that the price movement of the underlying instrument of the futures contract may not accurately track the price movement of the portfolio or financial instrument to be hedged. This is called *cross-hedging risk*. Therefore, the effectiveness of a cross hedge will be determined by:

1. The relationship between the cash price of the underlying instrument and its futures price when a hedge is placed and when it is lifted.

2. The relationship between the market (cash) value of the portfolio and the cash price of the instrument underlying the futures contract when the hedge is placed and when it is lifted.

A *short hedge* is used to protect against a decline in the future cash price of a financial instrument or portfolio. To execute a short hedge, the hedger sells a futures contract (agrees to make delivery). Consequently, a short hedge is also known as a *sell hedge*. By establishing a short hedge, the hedger has fixed the future cash price and transferred the price risk of ownership to the buyer of the futures contract.

A *long hedge* is undertaken to protect against an increase in the price of a financial instrument or portfolio to be purchased in the cash market at some future time. In a long hedge, the hedger buys a futures contract (agrees to accept delivery). A long hedge is also known as a *buy hedge*.

These points will be made clearer in the illustrations presented below.

Hedging Illustrations

We illustrate the principles of hedging and cross hedging using an agricultural commodity, corn, rather than a financial instrument or portfolio, because a corn futures contract is not as complicated as a stock index futures contract, an interest rate futures contract, or a currency futures contract. The principles we illustrate still are equally applicable to these futures contracts but it is easier to grasp the sense of the farm product example without involving financial contract nuances. In Chapter 10, we will illustrate hedging for a stock portfolio.

Suppose that a corn farmer expects to sell 30,000 bushels of corn three months from now. Assume further that the management of a food processing company plans to purchase 30,000 bushels of corn three months from now. Both the corn farmer and the management of the food processing company want to lock in a price today. That is, each wants to eliminate the price risk associated with corn three months from now. The cash or spot price for corn is currently $2.75 per bushel.

A corn futures contract is available with the following terms: (1) the settlement date for the contract is five months from now and (2) 5,000 bushels of corn must be delivered. Notice that the settlement date is two months after the parties expect to lift their hedge. The futures price for this futures contract is currently $3.20 per bushel.

As the corn farmer seeks to lock in the price of the corn to eliminate the risk of a decline in the price three months from now, he will place a short or sell hedge. That is, he will promise to make delivery of corn at the current futures price. The corn farmer will sell six futures contracts, because each contract calls for the delivery of 5,000 bushels of corn. Three months from now, the corn farmer will deliver his corn at the prevailing price in the spot market and buy the corn futures contract, which will then have two months to settlement, to offset his short position in that contract. The price at which the corn farmer will buy the corn futures contract depends on the futures contract price three months from now.

The management of the food processing company seeks to lock in the cost of corn to eliminate the risk of an increase in the price of corn three months from now. Consequently, management will place a buy or long hedge. That is, it will agree to accept delivery of corn at the futures price. Protection is sought against a price increase for 30,000 bushels of corn, so six contracts are bought. Three months from now, the food processing company will have to purchase corn in the spot market, paying the prevailing market price. To offset the long corn futures position which has two months remaining until settlement, the food processing company sells the contract at the then-prevailing futures price.

Let's look at what happens under various scenarios for the cash price and the futures price of corn three months from now when the hedge is lifted.

Suppose that, when the hedge is lifted, the cash price declines to $2.00 and the futures contract price declines to $2.45. Notice what has happened to the basis under this scenario. At the time the hedge was placed, the basis is −$.45 ($2.75 − $3.20). When the hedge is lifted, the basis is still −$.45 ($2.00 − $2.45).

The corn farmer, at the time the hedge was placed, wanted to lock in a price of $2.75 per bushel of corn, or $82,500 for 30,000 bushels. He sold six futures contracts at a price of $3.20 per bushel, or $96,000 for 30,000 bushels. When the hedge is lifted, the value of the farmer's corn is $60,000 ($2.00 × 30,000). The corn farmer realizes a decline in the cash market value of his corn of $22,500, but the futures price has declined to $2.45, so the cost to the corn farmer to liquidate his futures position is only $73,500 ($2.45 × 30,000). The corn farmer realizes a gain in the futures market of $22,500. The net result is that the gain in the futures market matches the loss in the cash market. Consequently, the corn farmer, by hedging, succeeds in ensuring a price per unit of $2.75, precisely equal to the initial price he had intended to realize for himself. This is an example of a perfect or textbook hedge.

Because there was a decline in the cash price, the food processing company would realize a gain in the cash market of $22,500 but would realize a loss in the futures market of the same amount. Therefore, this buy or long hedge is also a perfect or textbook hedge from the perspective of the food processing company, ensuring a cost per unit equal to the initial price of $2.75.

This scenario illustrates two important points. First, for both participants there was no overall gain or loss. The reason for this result is that we assume the basis did not change when the hedge was lifted. Thus, if the basis does not change, a perfect hedge will be achieved. Second, note that the management of the food processing company would have been better off if it had not hedged. The cost of corn would have been $22,500 less in the cash market three months later. This should not be interpreted as a sign of poor planning by management. Management is not in the business of speculating on the future price of corn. Hedging is a standard practice to insure the price to be paid at the delivery date, thus eliminating future price uncertainty.

Suppose that the cash price of corn when the hedge is lifted increases to $3.55, and that the futures price increases to $4.00. Notice that the basis is unchanged at −$.45. As long as the basis is unchanged, the cash and futures price we have assumed in this scenario will produce a perfect hedge.

The corn farmer will gain in the cash market because the value of 30,000 bushels of corn is $106,500 ($3.55 × 30,000). This represents a $24,000 gain, compared to the cash value at the time the hedge was placed. However, the corn farmer must liquidate his position in the futures market by buying six futures contracts at a total cost of $120,000, which is $24,000 more than when the contracts were sold. The loss in the futures market offsets the gain in the cash market, and we have a perfect hedge. The food processing company would realize a gain in the futures market of $24,000 but would have to pay $24,000 more in the cash market to acquire 30,000 bushels of corn.

Note that the management of the food processing company under this scenario saved $24,000 in the cost of corn by employing a hedge. The corn farmer, though, would have been better off if he had not used a hedging strategy and simply sold his product on the market three months later. Again, it must be emphasized that the corn farmer, just like the management of the food processing company, employed a hedge to protect against unforeseen adverse price changes in the cash market.

These scenarios assume that the basis does not change when the hedge is lifted. In the real world, the basis does, in fact, change between the time a hedge is placed and when it is lifted. Here is what happens when the basis changes.

Assume that the cash price of corn decreases to $2.00, just as in the first scenario; assume also that the futures price decreases to $2.70 rather than $2.45. The basis has now widened from −$.45 to −$.70 ($2.00 − $2.70). For the short (sell) hedge, the loss in the cash market of $22,500 is offset only partially by a $15,000 gain realized in the futures market. Consequently, the hedge results in an overall loss of $7,500.

There are two points to note here. First, if the corn farmer had not employed the hedge, the loss would have been $22,500, because the value of 30,000 bushels of corn is $60,000, compared to $82,500 three months earlier.

Although the hedge is not a perfect hedge because the basis widened, the loss of $7,500 is less than the loss of $22,500 if no hedge had been placed. This is what we meant earlier when we said that hedging substitutes basis risk for price risk. Second, the management of the food processing company faces the same problem from an opposite perspective. An unexpected gain for either participant results in an unexpected loss of equal dollar value for the other. That is, the participants face a "zero-sum game." Consequently, the food processing company would realize an overall gain of $7,500 from its long (buy) hedge. This gain represents a gain of $22,500 in the cash market and a realized loss of $15,000 in the futures market.

Cross Hedging Illustrations

Suppose that a zucchini farmer plans to sell 37,500 bushels of zucchini three months from now and that a food processing company plans to purchase the same amount of zucchini three months from now. Each party wants to hedge against price risk, but zucchini futures contracts are not traded. Both parties believe that there is a close price relationship between zucchini and corn. Specifically, both parties believe that the cash price of zucchini will be 80% of the cash price of corn. The cash price of zucchini is currently $2.20 per bushel, and the cash price of corn is currently $2.75 per bushel. The futures price of corn is currently $3.20 per bushel.

Let's examine various scenarios to see how effective the cross hedge will be. In each scenario, the difference between the cash price of corn and the futures price of corn at the time the cross hedge is placed and at the time it is lifted will be assumed to be unchanged at −$.45. We assume this so we may focus on the importance of the relationship between the two cash prices at the two times.

We must first determine how many corn futures contracts must be used in the cross hedge. The cash value of 37,500 bushels of zucchini at the cash price of $2.20 per bushel is $82,500. To protect a value of $82,500 using corn futures with a current cash price of $2.75, the price of 30,000 bushels of corn ($82,500/$2.75) must be hedged. Each corn futures contract involves 5,000 bushels, so six corn futures contracts are used.

Suppose that the cash prices of zucchini and corn decrease to $1.60 and $2.00 per bushel, respectively, and the futures price of corn decreases to $2.45 per bushel. The relationship between the cash price for zucchini and corn assumed when the cross hedge was placed holds at the time the cross hedge is lifted. That is, the cash price of zucchini is 80% of the cash price of corn. The basis for the cash price of corn and the futures price of corn is still −$.45 at the time the cross hedge is lifted.

The short cross hedge produces a gain in the futures market of $22,500 and an exactly offset loss in the cash market. The opposite occurs for the long cross hedge. There is neither overall gain nor loss from the cross hedge in this case. That is, we have a perfect cross hedge. The same would occur if we assume that the cash price of both commodities increases by the same percentage and the basis does not change.

Suppose that the cash prices of both commodities decrease, but the cash price of zucchini falls by a greater percentage than the cash price of corn. For example, suppose that the cash price of zucchini falls to $1.30 per bushel while the cash price of corn falls to $2.00 per bushel. The futures price of corn falls to $2.45 so that the basis is not changed. The cash price of zucchini at the time the cross hedge is lifted is 65% of the cash price of corn, rather than 80% as assumed when the cross hedge was constructed.

For the short cross hedge, the loss in the cash market exceeds the realized loss in the futures market by $11,200. For the long cross hedge, the opposite is true. There is an overall gain from the cross hedge of $11,200. Had the cash price of zucchini fallen by less than the decline in the cash price of corn, the short cross hedge would have produced an overall gain, while the long cross hedge would have generated an overall loss.

THE ROLE OF FUTURES IN FINANCIAL MARKETS

Without financial futures, investors would have only one trading location to alter portfolio positions when they get new information that is expected to influence the value of assets—the cash market. If economic news that is expected to impact the value of an asset adversely is received, investors can reduce their price risk exposure to that asset. The opposite is true if the new information is expected to impact the value of that asset favorably: an investor would increase price risk exposure to that asset. There are, of course, transactions costs associated with altering exposure to an asset—explicit costs (commissions), and hidden or execution costs (bid–ask spreads and market impact costs).[4]

Futures provide another market that investors can use to alter their risk exposure to an asset when new information is acquired. But which market—cash or futures—should the investor employ to alter a position *quickly* on the receipt of new information? The answer is simple: the one that is the more efficient to use to achieve the objective. The factors to consider are liquidity, transactions costs, taxes, and leverage advantages of the futures contract.

The market that investors feel is the one that is more efficient to use to achieve their investment objective should be the one where prices will be established that reflect the new economic information. That is, this will be the

---

[4] These are discussed in Chapter 8.

market where *price discovery* takes place. Price information is then transmitted to the other market. In many of the markets that we will discuss in this book, it is in the futures market that it is easier and less costly to alter a portfolio position. We give evidence for this when we discuss the specific contracts in later chapters. Therefore, it is the futures market that will be the market of choice and will serve as the price discovery market. It is in the futures market that investors send a collective message about how any new information is expected to impact the cash market.

How is this message sent to the cash market? Recall our discussion on determination of the futures price, where we showed that the futures price and the cash market price are tied together by the cost of carry. If the futures price deviates from the cash market price by more than the cost of carry, arbitrageurs (in attempting to obtain arbitrage profits) would pursue a strategy to bring them back into line. Arbitrage brings the cash market price into line with the futures price. It is the mechanism that assures that the cash market price will reflect the information that has been collected in the futures market.

Effect of Futures on Volatility of Underlying Asset

Some investors and the popular press consider that the introduction of a futures market for an asset will increase the price volatility of the asset in the cash market. This criticism of futures contracts is referred to as the "destabilization hypothesis."[5]

There are two variants of the destabilization hypothesis: (1) the liquidity variant, and (2) the populist variant. According to the liquidity variant, large transactions that are too difficult to accommodate in the cash market will be executed first in the futures markets because of better liquidity. The increased volatility that may occur in the futures contracts market is only temporary because volatility will return to its normal level once the liquidity problem is resolved. The implication is that there should be no long-term impact on the volatility of the underlying cash market asset.

The populist variant in contrast asserts that, as a result of speculative trading in derivative contracts, the cash market instrument does not reflect fundamental economic value. The implication here is that the asset price would better reflect economic value in the absence of a futures market.

Whether the introduction of futures markets destabilizes prices is an empirical question. We will look at the evidence for the stock market in

---

[5] Lawrence Harris, "S&P 500 Futures and Cash Stock Price Volatility," University of Southern California, unpublished paper, 1987.

Chapter 10, but for now, it is worth noting that the analysis of one researcher concludes that in general it would take a substantial number of "irrational" speculators to destabilize cash markets.[6]

Is Increased Asset Price Volatility Bad?

Whether or not the introduction of futures contracts increases cash market price volatility, we might ask whether greater volatility has negative effects on markets. At first glance, it might seem that volatility has adverse effects from the points of view of allocative efficiency and market participation.

Actually, it has been pointed out that this inference may not be justified if, say, the introduction of new markets lets prices respond more promptly to changes in fundamentals, and if the fundamentals themselves are subject to large shocks.[7] Thus the greater volatility resulting from an innovation may simply more faithfully reflect the actual variability of fundamental values. In this case, "more" asset volatility need not be bad but rather may be a manifestation of a well-functioning market. Of course, to say that more volatility need not be bad does not mean that it is good. Clearly, price volatility greater than what can be justified by relevant new information or fundamentals (or by standard asset pricing models) is undesirable. By definition, it makes prices inefficient. This is referred to as "excess volatility."[8]

No one has been able to test whether recent financial innovations have increased or decreased excess volatility. Moreover, as Edwards points out, "Too little volatility is equally bad, although this concept does not seem to have generated enough interest to have been given the label of 'deficient volatility.'"[9]

In any event, as Edwards notes in the case of stock index futures:

Investors are concerned about the present and future value of their investments (and wealth). Greater volatility leads to a perception of greater risk, which threatens investors' assets and wealth. When the

---

[6] Jerome L. Stein, "Real Effects of Futures Speculation: Rational Expectations and Diverse Opinions," working paper no. 88, Center for the Study of Futures Markets, Columbia University, 1984.

[7] Eugene F. Fama, "Perspectives on October 1987, or What Did We Learn from the Crash?" in Robert J. Barro et al. (eds.), *Black Monday and the Future of Financial Markets* (Homewood, IL: Dow Jones-Irwin, 1989), p. 72.

[8] Franklin R. Edwards, "Futures Trading and Cash Market Volatility: Stock Index and Interest Rate Futures," *The Journal of Futures Markets*, Vol. 8, No. 4 (1988), p. 423.

[9] Ibid.

stock market takes a sharp nose-dive, investors see the value of their assets rapidly dissipating. They are not consoled by being told that there is no social cost associated with this price change, only a redistribution of wealth. Even more fundamental, when asset prices exhibit significant volatility over very short periods of time (such as a day), investors "lose confidence in the market." They begin to see financial markets as the province of the speculator and the insider, not the rational.[10]

SUMMARY

This chapter has explained the basic features of financial futures markets. The traditional purpose of futures markets is to provide an important opportunity to hedge against the risk of adverse future price movements. Futures contracts are creations of exchanges, which require initial margin from parties. Each day positions are marked to market. Additional (variation) margin is required if the equity in the position falls below the maintenance margin. The clearinghouse guarantees that the parties to the futures contract will satisfy their obligations.

A forward contract differs in several important ways from a futures contract. In contrast to a futures contract, the parties to a forward contract are exposed to the risk that the other party to the contract will fail to perform. The positions of the parties are not marked to market, so there are no interim cash flows associated with a forward contract. Finally, unwinding a position in a forward contract may be difficult.

A buyer (seller) of a futures contract realizes a profit if the futures price increases (decreases). The buyer (seller) of a futures contract realizes a loss if the futures price decreases (increases). Because only initial margin is required when an investor takes a futures position, futures markets provide investors with substantial leverage for the money invested.

The theoretical futures price is determined by the cash market price and the cost of carry. At the delivery date, the futures price converges to the cash market price. There are reasons why the actual futures price will depart from the theoretical futures price. In practice, there is not one theoretical futures price but a band above and below it. The actual futures price tends to remain within the band through the operation of arbitrageurs.

The basis is the difference between the cash price and the futures price. The basis should equal the cost of carry. Basis risk occurs when the basis

---

[10] Franklin R. Edwards, "Does Futures Trading Increase Stock Price Volatility?" *Financial Analysts Journal* (January–February 1988), p. 64.

changes between the time a hedge is placed and the time it is lifted. Hedging eliminates price risk but substitutes basis risk. Cross hedging occurs when the underlying instrument of the futures contract is different from the financial instrument or portfolio to be hedged, and most hedging in financial markets involves cross hedging. The risk associated with cross hedging is that the financial instrument or portfolio to be hedged will not be tracked exactly by the instrument underlying the futures contract.

Investors can use the futures market or the cash market to react to economic news that is expected to change the value of an asset. Futures markets are the market of choice for altering asset positions and therefore represent the price discovery market, because of the lower transactions costs involved and the greater speed with which orders can be executed. The actions of arbitrageurs assure that price discovery in the futures markets will be transmitted to the cash market.

Critics of futures markets believe that they are the source of greater price volatility in the cash market for the underlying asset. Although this is an empirical question not fully discussed here, even if price volatility in the cash market were greater because of the introduction of futures markets, this does not necessarily mean that greater volatility is bad for the economy.

QUESTIONS

1. The chief financial officer of the corporation you work for recently told you that he had a strong preference to use forward contracts rather than futures contracts to hedge: "You can get contracts tailor-made to suit your needs." Comment on the CFO's statement. What other factors influence the decision to use futures or forward contracts?

2. You work for a conservative investment firm. You recently asked the firm's managing director for permission to open up a futures account so that you could trade financial futures as well as cash instruments. She replied, "Are you crazy? I might as well write you a check, wish you good luck, and put you on a bus to Atlantic City. The futures markets are nothing more than a respectable game of craps. Don't you think you're taking enough risk trading cash instruments?" How would you try to persuade the managing director to let you use futures?

3. Suppose there is a financial asset ABC, which is the underlying asset for a futures contract with settlement six months from now. You know the following about this financial asset and futures contract:

   1. In the cash market ABC is selling for $80.

2. ABC pays $8 per year in two semiannual payments of $4, and the next semiannual payment is due exactly six months from now.

3. The current six-month interest rate at which funds can be loaned or borrowed is 6%.

   a. What is the theoretical (or equilibrium) futures price?

   b. What action would you take if the futures price is $83?

   c. What action would you take if the futures price is $76?

   d. Suppose that ABC pays interest quarterly instead of semiannually. If you know that you can reinvest any funds you receive three months from now at 1% for three months, what would the theoretical futures price for six-month settlement be?

   e. Suppose that the borrowing rate and lending rate are not equal. Instead, suppose that the current six-month borrowing rate is 8% and the six-month lending rate is 6%. What is the boundary for the theoretical futures price?

4. You are a major producer of goat cheese. Concerned that the price of goat cheese might plummet, you are considering some kind of hedging strategy. Unfortunately, you discover that there are no exchange-traded futures on goat cheese. A business associate suggests a cross hedge with orange juice futures. Specifically, your business associate suggests a short hedge using orange juice futures.

   a. Before you commit to this hedging strategy, what other kinds of information would you like to know?

   b. Why is it likely that this hedge will not turn out to be a perfect (i.e., "textbook") hedge?

5. Discuss these three statements:

   a. "Of course the futures are more expensive than the cash price— there's positive carry."

   b. "Hedging with futures is substituting basis risk for price risk."

   c. "The futures market is where price discovery takes place."

CHAPTER

7

INTRODUCTION TO OPTION MARKETS

LEARNING OBJECTIVES

After reading this chapter you will understand:

- what an option contract is.
- the difference between a futures contract and an option contract.
- the risk/return characteristics of an option.
- the basic components of the option price.
- the factors that influence the option price.
- the fundamentals of option pricing models.
- the principles of the binomial option pricing model and how it is derived.
- the role of options in financial markets.

I n Chapter 6 we introduced our first derivative instrument, a futures contract. In this chapter we introduce a second derivative contract, an options contract. As we did in the previous chapter, we will not look at specific options contracts but instead focus on the general characteristics of the contract. We will discuss options on common stocks in Chapter 9, options on stock indexes in Chapter 10, options on bonds in Chapter 19, and options on currencies in Chapter 21.

In this chapter we discuss the differences between options and futures contracts and show how to determine the price of an option, based on arbitrage arguments. In later chapters we will illustrate how investors can use options to create payoffs that can better satisfy their investment objectives.

OPTION CONTRACT DEFINED

An option is a contract in which the writer of the option grants the buyer of the option the *right,* but not the obligation, to purchase from or sell to the writer something at a specified price within a specified period of time (or at a specified date). The writer, also referred to as the seller, grants this right to the buyer in exchange for a certain sum of money, which is called the *option price* or *option premium.* The price at which the asset may be bought or sold is called the *exercise* or *strike price.* The date after which an option is void is called the *expiration date.* Our focus in this book is on options where the "something" underlying the option is a financial instrument, financial index, or financial futures contract. We'll postpone our discussion of options on futures contracts (called futures options) until Chapter 19, however.

When an option grants the buyer the right to purchase the designated instrument from the writer (seller), it is referred to as a *call option,* or *call.* When the option buyer has the right to sell the designated instrument to the writer (seller), the option is called a *put option,* or *put.*

An option is also categorized according to when the option buyer may exercise the option. There are options that may be exercised at any time up to and including the expiration date. Such options are referred to as *American options.* There are options that may be exercised only at the expiration date. Options with this feature are called *European options.*

Let's use an illustration to demonstrate the fundamental option contract. Suppose that Jack buys a call option for $3 (the option price) with the following terms:

1. the underlying asset is one unit of Asset XYZ
2. the exercise price is $100

3. the expiration date is three months from now, and the option can be exercised any time up to and including the expiration date (that is, it is an American option)

At any time up to and including the expiration date, Jack can decide to buy from the writer (seller) of this option one unit of Asset XYZ, for which he will pay a price of $100. If it is not beneficial for Jack to exercise the option, he will not, and we'll explain shortly how he decides when it will be beneficial. Whether Jack exercises the option or not, the $3 he paid for the option will be kept by the option writer. If Jack buys a put option rather than a call option, then he would be able to sell Asset XYZ to the option writer for a price of $100.

The maximum amount that an option buyer can lose is the option price. The maximum profit that the option writer (seller) can realize is the option price. The option buyer has substantial upside return potential, while the option writer has substantial downside risk. We'll investigate the risk/reward relationship for option positions later in this chapter.

There are no margin requirements for the buyer of an option once the option price has been paid in full. Because the option price is the maximum amount that the investor can lose, no matter how adverse the price movement of the underlying asset, there is no need for margin. Because the writer (seller) of an option has agreed to accept all of the risk (and none of the reward) of the position in the underlying asset, the writer is generally required to put up the option price received as margin. In addition, as price changes occur that adversely affect the writer's position, the writer is required to deposit additional margin (with some exceptions) as the position is marked to market.

Exchange-Traded versus OTC Options

Options, like other financial instruments, may be traded either on an organized exchange or in the over-the-counter market. An exchange that wants to create an options contract must obtain approval from either the Commodities Futures Trading Commission or the Securities and Exchange Commission.[1] Exchange-traded options have three advantages. First, the exercise price and expiration date of the contract are standardized. Second, as in the case of futures contracts, the direct link between buyer and seller is severed after the order is executed because of the interchangeability of exchange-traded options. The clearinghouse associated with the exchange

---

[1] By an agreement between the CFTC and the SEC and pursuant to an act of Congress, options on futures are regulated by the former.

where the option trades performs the same function in the options market that it does in the futures market. Finally, the transactions costs are lower for exchange-traded options than for OTC options.

The higher cost of an OTC option reflects the cost of customizing the option for the many situations where an institutional investor needs to have a tailor-made option because the standardized exchange-traded option does not satisfy its investment objectives. As we explained in Chapters 2 and 3, investment banking firms and commercial banks act as principals as well as brokers in the OTC options market. While an OTC option is less liquid than an exchange-traded option, this is typically not of concern to an institutional investor—most institutional investors who use OTC options as part of an asset/liability strategy intend to hold them to expiration.

DIFFERENCES BETWEEN OPTIONS AND FUTURES CONTRACTS

Notice that unlike in a futures contract, one party to an option contract is not obligated to transact. Specifically, the option buyer has the *right* but not the obligation to transact. The option writer (seller) does have the obligation to perform. In the case of a futures contract, both buyer and seller are obligated to perform. Of course, a futures buyer does not pay the seller to accept the obligation, while an option buyer pays the seller an option price.

Consequently, the risk/reward characteristics of the two contracts are also different. In the case of a futures contract, the buyer of the contract realizes a dollar-for-dollar gain when the price of the futures contract increases and suffers a dollar-for-dollar loss when the price of the futures contract drops. The opposite occurs for the seller of a futures contract. Options do not provide this symmetric risk/reward relationship. The most that the buyer of an option can lose is the option price. While the buyer of an option retains all the potential benefits, the gain is always reduced by the amount of the option price. The maximum profit that the writer (seller) may realize is the option price; this is offset against substantial downside risk. This difference is extremely important because, as we shall see in subsequent chapters, investors can use futures to protect against symmetric risk and options to protect against asymmetric risk.

We'll return to the difference between options and futures for hedging at the end of the chapter.

RISK AND RETURN CHARACTERISTICS OF OPTIONS

Here we illustrate the risk and return characteristics of the four basic option positions—buying a call option (long a call option), selling a call option (short a call option), buying a put option (long a put option), and selling a put option (short a put option). The illustrations *assume that each option position is held to the expiration date and not exercised early.* Also, to simplify the illustrations, we ignore transactions costs.

Buying Call Options

Assume that there is a call option on Asset XYZ that expires in one month and has a strike price of $100. The option price is $3. Suppose that the current price of Asset XYZ is $100. What is the profit or loss for the investor who purchases this call option and holds it to the expiration date?

The profit and loss from the strategy will depend on the price of Asset XYZ at the expiration date. A number of outcomes are possible.

1. If the price of Asset XYZ at the expiration date is less than $100, then the investor will not exercise the option. It would be foolish to pay the option writer $100 when Asset XYZ can be purchased in the market at a lower price. In this case, the option buyer loses the entire option price of $3. Notice, however, that this is the maximum loss that the option buyer will realize regardless of how low Asset XYZ's price declines.

2. If Asset XYZ's price is equal to $100 at the expiration date, there is again no economic value in exercising the option. As in the case where the price is less than $100, the buyer of the call option will lose the entire option price, $3.

3. If Asset XYZ's price is more than $100 but less than $103 at the expiration date, the option buyer will exercise the option. By exercising, the option buyer can purchase Asset XYZ for $100 (the strike price) and sell it in the market for the higher price. Suppose, for example, that Asset XYZ's price is $102 at the expiration date. The buyer of the call option will realize a $2 gain by exercising the option. Of course, the cost of purchasing the call option was $3, so $1 is lost on this position. By failing to exercise the option, the investor loses $3 instead of only $1.

4. If Asset XYZ's price at the expiration date is equal to $103, the investor will exercise the option. In this case, the investor breaks even, realizing a gain of $3 that offsets the cost of the option, $3.

5. If Asset XYZ's price at the expiration date is more than $103, the investor will exercise the option and realize a profit. For example, if the price is $113, exercising the option will generate a profit on Asset XYZ of $13. Reducing this gain by the cost of the option ($3), the investor will realize a net profit from this position of $10.

Table 7-1 shows the profit and loss in tabular form for the buyer of the hypothetical call option, while Figure 7-1 graphically portrays the result.

TABLE 7-1   PROFIT/LOSS PROFILE FOR A LONG CALL POSITION

Assumptions:
  Option price = $3
  Strike price = $100
  Time to expiration = 1 month

PRICE OF ASSET XYZ AT EXPIRATION DATE	NET PROFIT/LOSS*
$150	$ 47
140	37
130	27
120	17
115	12
114	11
113	10
112	9
111	8
110	7
109	6
108	5
107	4
106	3
105	2
104	1
103	0
102	−1
101	−2
100	−3
99	−3
98	−3
97	−3
96	−3
95	−3
94	−3
93	−3
92	−3
91	−3
90	−3
89	−3
88	−3
87	−3
86	−3
85	−3
80	−3
70	−3
60	−3

*Price at expiration − $100 − $3
Maximum loss = −$3

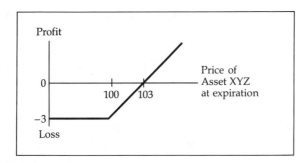

FIGURE 7-1
Profit/Loss Profile for a Long
Call Position

While the break-even point and the loss will depend on the option price and the strike price, the profile shown in Figure 7-1 will hold for all buyers of call options. The shape indicates that the maximum loss is the option price and that there is substantial upside potential.

It is worthwhile to compare the profit and loss profile of the call option buyer to taking a long position in one unit of Asset XYZ. The payoff from the position depends on Asset XYZ's price at the expiration date. Consider again the five price outcomes given above:

1. If Asset XYZ's price at the expiration date is less than $100, then the investor loses the entire option price of $3. In contrast, a long position in Asset XYZ will have one of three possible outcomes:

    a. if Asset XYZ's price is less than $100 but greater than $97, the loss on the long position in Asset XYZ will be less than $3.

    b. if Asset XYZ's price is $97, the loss on the long position in Asset XYZ will be $3.

    c. if Asset XYZ's price is less than $97, the loss on the long position in Asset XYZ will be greater than $3. For example, if the price at the expiration date is $80, the long position in Asset XYZ will result in a loss of $20.

2. If Asset XYZ's price is equal to $100, the buyer of the call option will realize a loss of $3 (option price). There will be no gain or loss on the long position in Asset XYZ.

3. If Asset XYZ's price is more than $100 but less than $103, the option buyer will realize a loss of less than $3, while the long position in Asset XYZ will realize a profit.

4. If the price of Asset XYZ at the expiration date is equal to $103, there will be no loss or gain from buying the call option. The long position in Asset XYZ, however, will produce a gain of $3.

5. If Asset XYZ's price at the expiration date is greater than $103, both the call option buyer and the long position in Asset XYZ will post a profit, but the profit for the buyer of the call option will be $3 less than that for the long position. If Asset XYZ's price is $113, for example, the profit from the call position is $10, while the profit from the long position in Asset XYZ is $13.

Table 7-2 compares the long call strategy and the long position in Asset XYZ. This comparison clearly demonstrates the way in which an option can change the risk/return profile for investors. An investor who takes a long position in Asset XYZ realizes a profit of $1 for every $1 increase in Asset XYZ's price. As Asset XYZ's price falls, however, the investor loses dollar-for-dollar. If the price drops by more than $3, the long position in Asset XYZ results in a loss of more than $3. The long call strategy, in contrast, limits the loss to only the option price of $3 but retains the upside potential, which will be $3 less than for the long position in Asset XYZ.

Which alternative is better, buying the call option or buying the asset? The answer depends on what the investor is attempting to achieve. This will become clearer in later chapters as we explain various strategies using either option positions or cash market positions.

We can also use this hypothetical call option to demonstrate the speculative appeal of options. Suppose an investor has strong expectations that Asset XYZ's price will rise in one month. At an option price of $3, the speculator can purchase 33.33 call options for each $100 invested. If Asset XYZ's price rises, the investor realizes the price appreciation associated with 33.33 units of Asset XYZ, while with the same $100, the investor could buy only one unit of Asset XYZ selling at $100, realizing the appreciation associated with one unit if Asset XYZ's price increases. Now, suppose that in one month the price of Asset XYZ rises to $120. The long call position will result in a profit of $566.50 [($20 × 33.33) − $100)] or a return of 566.5% on the $100 investment in the call option. The long position in Asset XYZ results in a profit of $20, for only a 20% return on $100.

It is this greater leverage that attracts investors to options when they wish to speculate on price movements. There are some drawbacks of leverage, however. Suppose that Asset XYZ's price is unchanged at $100 at the expiration date. The long call position results in this case in a loss of the entire investment of $100, while the long position in Asset XYZ produces neither a gain nor a loss.

Writing (Selling) Call Options

To illustrate the option seller's (writer's) position, we use the same call option we used to illustrate buying a call option. The profit and loss profile of the short call position (that is, the position of the call option writer) is the mirror

TABLE 7-2   COMPARISON OF LONG CALL POSITION AND LONG ASSET POSITION

Assumptions:
  Price of Asset XYZ = $100
  Option price = $3
  Strike price = $100
  Time to expiration = 1 month

PRICE OF ASSET XYZ AT EXPIRATION DATE	NET PROFIT/LOSS FOR	
	LONG CALL	LONG ASSET XYZ
$150	$47	$50
140	37	40
130	27	30
120	17	20
115	12	15
114	11	14
113	10	13
112	9	12
111	8	11
110	7	10
109	6	9
108	5	8
107	4	7
106	3	6
105	2	5
104	1	4
103	0	3
102	−1	2
101	−2	1
100	−3	0
99	−3	−1
98	−3	−2
97	−3	−3
96	−3	−4
95	−3	−5
94	−3	−6
93	−3	−7
92	−3	−8
91	−3	−9
90	−3	−10
89	−3	−11
88	−3	−12
87	−3	−13
86	−3	−14
85	−3	−15
80	−3	−20
70	−3	−30
60	−3	−40

image of the profit and loss profile of the long call position (the position of the call option buyer). That is, the profit of the short call position for any given price for Asset XYZ at the expiration date is the same as the loss of the long call position. Consequently, the maximum profit that the short call position can produce is the option price. The maximum loss is not limited because it is the highest price reached by Asset XYZ on or before the expiration date, less the option price; this price can be indefinitely high. This can be seen in Figure 7-2, which shows the profit/loss profile for a short call position.

Buying Put Options

To illustrate a put option purchase strategy, we assume a hypothetical put option on one unit of Asset XYZ with one month to maturity and a strike price of $100. Assume the put option is selling for $2. The current price of Asset XYZ is $100. The profit or loss for this position at the expiration date depends on the market price of Asset XYZ. The possible outcomes are:

1. If Asset XYZ's price is greater than $100, the buyer of the put option will not exercise it because exercising would mean selling Asset XYZ to the writer for a price that is less than the market price. A loss of $2 (the option price) will result in this case from buying the put option. Once again, the option price represents the maximum loss to which the buyer of the put option is exposed.

2. If the price of Asset XYZ at expiration is equal to $100, the put will not be exercised, leaving the put buyer with a loss equal to the option price of $2.

3. Any price for Asset XYZ that is less than $100 but greater than $98 will result in a loss; exercising the put option, however, limits the loss to less than the option price of $2. For example, suppose that the price is $99 at the expiration date. By exercising the option, the option buyer will realize a loss of $1. This is because the buyer of the put option can sell Asset XYZ, purchased in the market for $99, to the writer for $100, realizing a gain of $1. Deducting the $2 cost of the option results in a loss of $1.

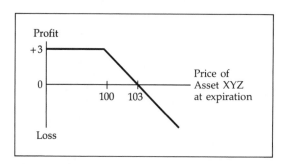

FIGURE 7-2
Profit/Loss Profile for a Short Call Position

4. At a $98 price for Asset XYZ at the expiration date, the put buyer will break even. The investor will realize a gain of $2 by selling Asset XYZ to the writer of the option for $100, offsetting the cost of the option ($2).

5. If Asset XYZ's price is below $98 at the expiration date, the long put position (the put buyer) will realize a profit. For example, suppose the price falls at expiration to $80. The long put position will produce a profit of $18: a gain of $20 for exercising the put option less the $2 option price.

The profit and loss profile for the long put position is shown in tabular form in the second column of Table 7-3 and in graphical form in Figure 7-3. As with all long option positions, the loss is limited to the option price. The profit potential, however, is substantial: the theoretical maximum profit is generated if Asset XYZ's price falls to zero. Contrast this profit potential with that of the buyer of a call option. The theoretical maximum profit for a call buyer cannot be determined beforehand because it depends on the highest price that can be reached by Asset XYZ before or at the option expiration date.

To see how an option alters the risk/return profile for an investor, we again compare it to a position in Asset XYZ. The long put position is compared to taking a short position in Asset XYZ because this is the position that would realize a profit if the price of the asset falls. Suppose an investor sells Asset XYZ short for $100. The short position in Asset XYZ would produce the following profit or loss compared with the long put position:

1. If Asset XYZ's price rises above $100, the long put option results in a loss of $2, but the short position in Asset XYZ realizes one of the following:
   a. if the price of Asset XYZ is less than $102, there will be a loss of less than $2.
   b. if the price of Asset XYZ is equal to $102, the loss will be $2, the same as the long put position.
   c. if the price of Asset XYZ is greater than $102, the loss will be greater than $2. For example, if the price is $125, the short position will realize a loss of $25, because the short-seller must now pay $125 for Asset XYZ that he sold short at $100.

2. If Asset XYZ's price at expiration is equal to $100, the long put position will realize a $2 loss, while there will be no profit or loss on the short position in Asset XYZ.

3. Any price for Asset XYZ that is less than $100 but greater than $98 will result in a loss of less than $2 for the long put position but a profit for the short position in Asset XYZ. For example, a price of $99 at the expiration date will result in a loss of $1 for the long put position but a profit of $1 for the short position.

TABLE 7-3 PROFIT/LOSS PROFILE FOR A LONG PUT POSITION AND COMPARISON WITH A SHORT ASSET POSITION

Assumptions:
  Price of Asset XYZ = $100
  Option price = $2
  Strike price = $100
  Time to expiration = 1 month

PRICE OF ASSET XYZ AT EXPIRATION DATE	NET PROFIT/LOSS FOR	
	LONG PUT*	SHORT ASSET XYZ†
$150	−$2	−$50
140	−2	−40
130	−2	−30
120	−2	−20
115	−2	−15
110	−2	−10
105	−2	− 5
100	−2	0
99	−1	1
98	0	2
97	1	3
96	2	4
95	3	5
94	4	6
93	5	7
92	6	8
91	7	9
90	8	10
89	9	11
88	10	12
87	11	13
86	12	14
85	13	15
84	14	16
83	15	17
82	16	18
81	17	19
80	18	20
75	23	25
70	28	30
65	33	35
60	38	40

*$100 − Price at expiration − $2
Maximum loss = −$2
†$100 − Price of Asset XYZ

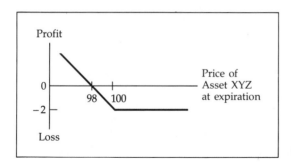

FIGURE 7-3
Profit/Loss Profile for a Long
Put Position

4. At a $98 price for Asset XYZ at the expiration date, the long put position will break even, but the short position in Asset XYZ will generate a $2 profit.

5. At a price below $98, both positions will generate a profit; however, the profit will always be $2 less for the long put position.

Table 7-3 gives this comparison of the profit and loss profile for the long put position and short position in Asset XYZ. While the investor who takes a short position in Asset XYZ faces all the downside risk as well as the upside potential, the long put position limits the downside risk to the option price while still maintaining upside potential (reduced only by an amount equal to the option price).

Writing (Selling) Put Options

The profit and loss profile for a short put option is the mirror image of the long put option. The maximum profit from this position is the option price. The theoretical maximum loss can be substantial should the price of the underlying asset fall; at the outside, if the price were to fall all the way to zero, the loss would be as large as the strike price less the option price. Figure 7-4 graphically depicts this profit and loss profile.

To summarize, buying calls or selling puts allows the investor to gain if the price of the underlying asset rises. Selling calls and buying puts allows the investor to gain if the price of the underlying asset falls.

Considering the Time Value of Money

Our illustrations of the four option positions do not address the time value of money. Specifically, the buyer of an option must pay the seller the option price at the time the option is purchased. Thus, the buyer must finance the purchase price of the option or, assuming the purchase price does not have to

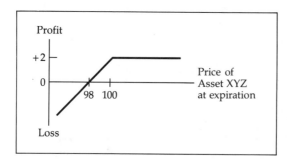

FIGURE 7-4
Profit/Loss Profile for a Short
Put Position

be borrowed, the buyer loses the income that can be earned by investing the amount of the option price until the option is sold or exercised. In contrast, assuming that the seller does not have to use the option price amount as margin for the short position or can use an interest-earning asset as security, the seller has the opportunity to earn income from the proceeds of the option sale.

The time value of money changes the profit/loss profile of the option positions we have discussed. The break-even price for the buyer and the seller of an option will not be the same as in our illustrations. The break-even price for the underlying asset at the expiration date is higher for the buyer of the option; for the seller, it is lower.

Our comparisons of the option position with positions in the underlying instrument also ignore the time value of money. We have not considered the fact that the underlying asset may generate interim cash flows (dividends in the case of common stock, interest in the case of bonds). The buyer of a call option is not entitled to any interim cash flows generated by the underlying asset. The buyer of the underlying asset, however, would receive any interim cash flows and would have the opportunity to reinvest them. A complete comparison of the position of the long call option position and the long position in the underlying asset must take into account the additional dollars from reinvesting any interim cash flows. Moreover, any effect on the price of the underlying asset as a result of the distribution of cash must be considered. This occurs, for example, when the underlying asset is common stock and, as a result of a dividend payment, the stock declines in price. For simplicity, however, we continue to ignore the time value of money in the discussion to follow.

PRICING OF OPTIONS

So far, in our illustrations we have simply picked an option price as a given. The next question we ask is: How is the price of an option determined in the market?

Basic Components of the Option Price

The option price is a reflection of the option's *intrinsic value* and any additional amount over its intrinsic value. The premium over intrinsic value is often referred to as the *time value* or *time premium*. While the former term is more common, we will use the term time premium to avoid confusion between the time value of money and the time value of the option.

Intrinsic Value.   The intrinsic value of an option is the economic value of the option if it is exercised immediately, except that if there is no positive economic value that will result from exercising immediately then the intrinsic value is zero.

The intrinsic value of a *call* option is the difference between the current price of the underlying asset and the strike price if positive, zero otherwise. For example, if the strike price for a call option is $100 and the current asset price is $105, the intrinsic value is $5. That is, an option buyer exercising the option and simultaneously selling the underlying asset would realize $105 from the sale of the asset, which would be covered by acquiring the asset from the option writer for $100, thereby netting a $5 gain.

When an option has intrinsic value, it is said to be "in the money." When the strike price of a call option exceeds the current asset price, the call option is said to be "out of the money"; it has no intrinsic value. An option for which the strike price is equal to the current asset price is said to be "at the money." Both at-the-money and out-of-the-money options have an intrinsic value of zero because it is not profitable to exercise the option. Our call option with a strike price of $100 would be: (1) in the money when the current asset price is greater than $100, (2) out of the money when the current asset price is less than $100, and (3) at the money when the current asset price is equal to $100.

For a put option, the intrinsic value is equal to the amount by which the current asset price is below the strike price. For example, if the strike price of a put option is $100 and the current asset price is $92, the intrinsic value is $8. That is, the buyer of the put option who exercises the put option and simultaneously sells the underlying asset will net $8 by exercising. The asset will be sold to the writer for $100 and purchased in the market for $92. For our put option with a strike price of $100, the option would be: (1) in the money when the asset price is less than $100, (2) out of the money when the current asset price exceeds the strike price, (3) at the money when the strike price is equal to the asset's price.

Time Premium.   The time premium of an option is the amount by which the option price exceeds its intrinsic value. The option buyer hopes that, at some time prior to expiration, changes in the market price of the underlying asset will increase the value of the rights conveyed by the option. For this prospect, the option buyer is willing to pay a premium above the intrinsic value. For example, if the price of a call option with a strike price of $100 is $9 when the current asset price is $105, the time premium of this option is $4 ($9 minus its intrinsic value of $5). Had the current asset price been $90 instead of $105, then the time premium of this option would be the entire $9 because the option has no intrinsic value. Clearly, other things equal, the time premium of an option will increase with the amount of time remaining to expiration.

There are two ways in which an option buyer may realize the value of a position taken in the option. First is to exercise the option. The second is by selling the call option for $9. In the first example above, selling the call is preferable because the exercise of an option will realize a gain of only $5—it will cause the immediate loss of any time premium. There are circumstances under which an option may be exercised prior to the expiration date; they depend on whether the total proceeds at the expiration date would be greater by holding the option or exercising and reinvesting any cash proceeds received until the expiration date.

Put–Call Parity Relationship

Is there a relationship between the price of a call option and the price of a put option on the same underlying instrument, with the same strike price and the same expiration date? There is. To see this relationship, which is commonly referred to as the *put–call parity relationship,* let's use an example.

In our previous illustrations we used a put and call option on the same underlying asset (Asset XYZ), with one month to expiration, and a strike price of $100. The price of the underlying asset was assumed to be $100. The call price and put price were assumed to be $3 and $2, respectively. Consider this strategy:

Buy Asset XYZ at a price of $100

Sell a call option at a price of $3

Buy a put option at a price of $2

This strategy involves:

Long Asset XYZ

Short the call option

Long the put option

Table 7-4 shows the profit and loss profile at the expiration date for this strategy. Notice that, no matter what Asset XYZ's price is at the expiration date, the strategy will produce a profit of $1 without anybody making any net

TABLE 7-4   PROFIT/LOSS PROFILE FOR A STRATEGY INVOLVING A LONG POSITION IN ASSET XYZ, SHORT CALL OPTION POSITION, AND LONG PUT OPTION POSITION

Assumptions:
   Price of Asset XYZ = $100
   Call option price = $3
   Put option price = $2
   Strike price = $100
   Time to expiration = 1 month

PRICE OF ASSET XYZ AT EXPIRATION DATE	PROFIT FROM ASSET XYZ*	PRICE RECEIVED FOR CALL	PRICE PAID FOR PUT	OVERALL PROFIT
$150	0	3	−2	1
140	0	3	−2	1
130	0	3	−2	1
120	0	3	−2	1
115	0	3	−2	1
110	0	3	−2	1
105	0	3	−2	1
100	0	3	−2	1
95	0	3	−2	1
90	0	3	−2	1
85	0	3	−2	1
80	0	3	−2	1
75	0	3	−2	1
70	0	3	−2	1
65	0	3	−2	1
60	0	3	−2	1

*There is no profit, because at a price above $100, Asset XYZ will be called from the investor at a price of $100, and at a price below $100, Asset XYZ will be put by the investor at a price of $100.

investment. Ignoring (1) the cost of financing the long position in Asset XYZ and the long put position, and (2) the return from investing the proceeds from the sale of the call, this situation cannot exist in an efficient market. In implementing the strategy to capture the $1 profit, the actions of market participants will have one or more of the consequences following that will tend to eliminate the $1 profit: (1) the price of Asset XYZ will increase, (2) the call option price will drop, and/or (3) the put option price will rise.

   In our example, assuming Asset XYZ's price does not change, this means that the call price and the put price must tend toward equality. This is true only when we ignore the time value of money (financing cost, opportunity cost, cash payments, and reinvestment income). Also, our illustration does not consider the possibility of early exercise of the options. Thus, we have been considering a put–call parity relationship for only European options.

It can be shown that the put–call parity relationship for an option where the underlying asset makes cash distributions is:

Put option price − Call option price = Present value of strike price + Present value of cash distribution − Price of underlying asset

This relationship is actually the put–call parity relationship for European options. It is approximately true for American options. If this relationship does not hold, arbitrage opportunities exist. That is, there will exist portfolios consisting of long and short positions in the asset and related options that will provide an extra return with (practical) certainty.

Factors that Influence the Option Price

There are six factors that influence the option price:

1. current price of the underlying asset
2. strike price
3. time to expiration of the option
4. expected price volatility of the underlying asset over the life of the option
5. short-term risk-free interest rate over the life of the option
6. anticipated cash payments on the underlying asset over the life of the option

The impact of each of these factors may depend on whether (1) the option is a call or a put, and (2) the option is an American option or a European option. A summary of the effect of each factor on put and call option prices is presented in Table 7-5.

Current Price of the Underlying Asset.   The option price will change as the price of the underlying asset changes. For a call option, as the price of the underlying asset increases (all other factors constant, the strike price in particular), the option price increases. The opposite holds for a put option: as the price of the underlying asset increases, the price of a put option decreases.

Strike Price.   The strike price is fixed for the life of the option. All other factors equal, the lower the strike price, the higher the price for a call option. For put options, the higher the exercise price, the higher the price.

	EFFECT OF AN INCREASE OF FACTOR ON	
FACTOR	CALL PRICE	PUT PRICE
Current price of underlying asset	increase	decrease
Strike price	decrease	increase
Time to expiration of option	increase	increase
Expected price volatility	increase	increase
Short-term interest rate	increase	decrease
Anticipated cash payments	decrease	increase

TABLE 7-5   SUMMARY OF FACTORS THAT AFFECT THE PRICE OF AN OPTION

Time to Expiration of the Option.   An option is a "wasting asset." That is, after the expiration date the option has no value. All other factors equal, the longer the time to expiration of the option, the greater the option price. This is because, as the time to expiration decreases, less time remains for the underlying asset's price to rise (for a call buyer) or fall (for a put buyer)—that is, to compensate the option buyer for any time premium paid—and therefore the probability of a favorable price movement decreases. Consequently, for American options, as the time remaining until expiration decreases, the option price approaches its intrinsic value.

Expected Price Volatility of the Underlying Asset Over the Life of the Option.   All other factors equal, the greater the expected volatility (as measured by the standard deviation or variance) of the price of the underlying asset, the more an investor would be willing to pay for the option, and the more an option writer would demand for it. This is because the greater the volatility, the greater the probability that the price of the underlying asset will move in favor of the option buyer at some time before expiration.

Notice that it is the standard deviation or variance, not the systematic risk as measured by beta,[2] that is relevant in the pricing of options.

Short-Term Risk-Free Interest Rate Over the Life of the Option.   Buying the underlying asset ties up one's money. Buying an option on the same quantity of the underlying asset makes the difference between the asset price and the option price available for investment at (at least) the risk-free rate. Consequently, all other factors constant, the higher the short-term risk-free interest

---

[2] Beta is explained in Chapter 5.

rate, the greater the cost of buying the underlying asset and carrying it to the expiration date of the call option. Hence, the higher the short-term risk-free interest rate, the more attractive the call option will be relative to the direct purchase of the underlying asset. As a result, the higher the short-term risk-free interest rate, the greater the price of a call option.

Anticipated Cash Payments on the Underlying Asset Over the Life of the Option.   Cash payments on the underlying asset tend to decrease the price of a call option because the cash payments make it more attractive to hold the underlying asset than to hold the option. For put options, cash payments on the underlying asset tend to increase their price.

Option Pricing Models

In the previous chapter, we illustrated that the theoretical price of a futures contract can be determined on the basis of arbitrage arguments. Theoretical boundary conditions for the price of an option also can be derived through arbitrage arguments. For example, using arbitrage arguments it can be shown that the minimum price for an American call option is its intrinsic value; that is,

Call option price $\geq$ Max (0, Price of asset $-$ Strike price)

This expression says that the call option price will be greater than or equal to the difference between the price of the underlying asset and the strike price (intrinsic value), or zero, whichever is higher.

The boundary conditions can be "tightened" by using arbitrage arguments coupled with certain assumptions about the cash distribution of the asset.[3] The extreme case is an option pricing model that uses a set of assumptions to derive a single theoretical price, rather than a range. As we shall see below, deriving a theoretical option price is much more complicated than deriving a theoretical futures price, because the option price depends on the expected price volatility of the underlying asset over the life of the option.

Several models have been developed to determine the theoretical value of an option. The most popular one was developed by Fischer Black and Myron Scholes in 1973 for valuing European call options.[4] Several modifications to their model have followed since then. We'll discuss the Black–Scholes model

[3] See John C. Cox and Mark Rubinstein, *Option Markets* (Englewood Cliffs, N.J.: Prentice-Hall, 1985), Chapter 4.

[4] Fischer Black and Myron Scholes, "The Pricing of Corporate Liabilities," *Journal of Political Economy* (May–June 1973), pp. 637–659.

and its assumptions in Chapter 9. For now, we use another pricing model called the *binomial option pricing model* to see how arbitrage arguments can be used to determine a fair value for a call option.[5]

Basically, the idea behind the arbitrage argument is that if the payoff from owning a call option can be replicated by (1) purchasing the asset underlying the call option, and (2) borrowing funds, the price of the option is then (at most) the cost of creating the replicating strategy.

Deriving the Binomial Option Pricing Model

To derive a one-period binomial option pricing model for a call option, we begin by constructing a portfolio consisting of: (1) a long position in a certain amount of the asset, and (2) a short call position in the underlying asset. The amount of the underlying asset purchased is such that the position will be hedged against any change in the price of the asset at the expiration date of the option. That is, the portfolio consisting of the long position in the asset and the short position in the call option will produce the risk-free interest rate. A portfolio constructed in this way is called a *hedged portfolio*.

To illustrate, assume that there is an asset that has a current market price of $80 and only two possible future values one year from now:

State	Price
1	$100
2	70

Assume further that there is a call option on this asset with a strike price of $80 (the same as the current market price) that expires in one year. Suppose an investor forms a hedged portfolio by acquiring 2/3 of a unit of the asset and selling one call option. The 2/3 of a unit of the asset is the so-called *hedge ratio* (how we derive the hedge ratio will be explained later). Let us consider the outcomes for this hedged portfolio corresponding to the two possible outcomes for the asset.

If the price of the asset one year from now is $100, the buyer of the call option will exercise it. This means that the investor will have to deliver one unit of the asset in exchange for the strike price, 80. As the investor has only one unit of the asset, she has to buy 1/3 at a cost of 33 1/3 (the market price

---

[5] John C. Cox, Stephen A. Ross, and Mark Rubinstein, "Option Pricing: A Simplified Approach," *Journal of Financial Economics* (September 1979), pp. 229–263; Richard J. Rendleman and Brit J. Bartter, "Two-State Option Pricing," *Journal of Finance* (December 1979), pp. 1093–1110; and William F. Sharpe, *Investments* (Englewood Cliffs, N.J.: Prentice-Hall, 1981), Chapter 16.

of 100 times 1/3). Consequently, the outcome will equal the strike price of 80 received, minus the 33 1/3 cost to acquire the 1/3 unit of the asset to deliver, plus whatever price the investor initially sold the call option for. That is, the outcome will be:

$$80 - 33 \ 1/3 + \text{Call option price} = 46 \ 2/3 + \text{Call option price.}$$

If, instead, the price of the asset one year from now is $70, the buyer of the call option will not exercise it. Consequently, the investor will own 2/3 of a unit of the asset. At the price of 70, the value of 2/3 of a unit is 46 2/3. The outcome in this case is then the value of the asset plus whatever price the investor received when she initially sold the call option. That is, the outcome will be:

$$46 \ 2/3 + \text{Call option price.}$$

It is apparent that, given the possible asset prices, the portfolio consisting of a short position in the call option and 2/3 of a unit of the asset will generate an outcome that hedges changes in the price of the asset; hence, the hedged portfolio is riskless. Furthermore, this will hold regardless of the price of the call, which affects only the magnitude of the outcome.

Deriving the Hedge Ratio.   To show how the hedge ratio can be calculated, we will use the following notation:

S = current asset price
u = 1 plus the percentage change in the asset's price if the price goes up in the next period
d = 1 plus the percentage change in the asset's price if the price goes down in the next period
r = a risk-free one-period interest rate (the risk-free rate until the expiration date)
C = current price of a call option
C_u = intrinsic value of the call option if the asset price goes up
C_d = intrinsic value of the call option if the asset price goes down
E = strike price of the call option
H = hedge ratio, that is, the amount of the asset purchased per call sold

In the first illustration we started with, u, d, and H are:

u = 1.250 ($100/$80)
d = 0.875 ($70/$80)
H = 2/3

State 1 in our illustration means that the asset's price goes up; State 2 means that the asset's price goes down.

The investment made in the hedged portfolio is equal to the cost of buying H amount of the asset minus the price received from selling the call option. Therefore, because

Amount invested in the asset $= HS$

then

Cost of the hedged portfolio $= HS - C$

The payoff of the hedged portfolio at the end of one period is equal to the value of the H amount of the asset purchased minus the call option price. The payoffs of the hedged portfolio for the two possible states are:

If the asset's price goes up: $uHS - C_u$
If the asset's price goes down: $dHS - C_d$

In our illustration, we have

If the asset's price goes up: $1.250\ H\ \$80 - C_u$ or $\$100\ H - C_u$
If the asset's price goes down: $0.875\ H\ \$80 - C_d$ or $\$70\ H - C_d$

Regardless of the state that occurs, we want the payoff of the hedged portfolio to be the same. That is, we want

$$uHS - C_u = dHS - C_d \qquad (1)$$

Solving Equation (1) for H we have

$$H = \frac{C_u - C_d}{(u - d)\ S} \qquad (2)$$

To determine the hedge ratio, H, we must know C_u and C_d. These two values are equal to the difference between the price of the asset and the strike price. Of course, the minimum value of the call option is zero. Mathematically, this can be expressed as follows:

If the asset's price goes up: $C_u = \text{Max}\ [0,\ (uS - E)]$
If the asset's price goes down: $C_d = \text{Max}\ [0,\ (dS - E)]$

As the strike price in our illustration is $80, uS is $100, and dS is $70. Then

If the asset's price goes up: $C_u = \text{Max } [0, (\$100 - \$80)] = \$20$
If the asset's price goes down: $C_d = \text{Max } [0, (\$70 - \$80)] = \$0$

For our illustration, we substitute the values of u, d, S, C_u, and C_d into Equation (2) to obtain the hedge ratio:

$$H = \frac{\$20 - \$0}{(1.25 - 0.875)\ \$80} = \frac{2}{3}$$

The value for H agrees with the amount of the asset purchased in our earlier illustration.

Now we can derive a formula for the call option price. Figure 7-5 diagrams the situation. The top left half of the figure shows the current price of the asset for the current period and at the expiration date. The lower left-hand portion of the figure does the same thing using the notation above. The upper right-hand side of the figure gives the current price of the call option and the

FIGURE 7-5
One-Period Option Pricing Model

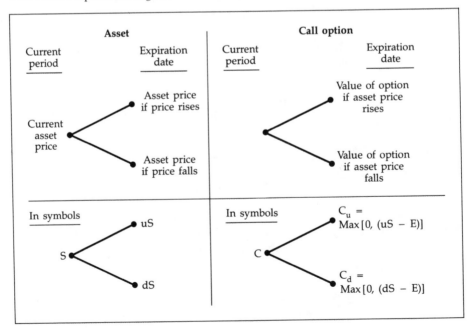

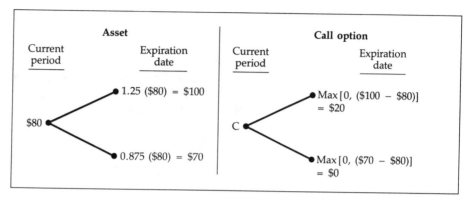

FIGURE 7-6
One-Period Option Pricing Model Illustration

value of the call option at the expiration date; the lower right-hand side does the same thing using our notation. Figure 7-6 uses the values in our illustration to construct the outcomes for the asset and the call option.

Deriving the Price of a Call Option. To derive the price of a call option we can rely on the basic principle that the hedged portfolio, being riskless, must have a return equal to the riskless rate. Given that the amount invested in the hedged portfolio is $HS - C$, the amount that should be generated one period from now is:

$$(1 + r) (HS - C) \tag{3}$$

We also know what the payoff will be for the hedged portfolio if the asset's price goes up or goes down. Because the payoff of the hedged portfolio will be the same whether the asset's price goes up or down, we can use the payoff if it goes up, which is

$$uHS - C_u$$

The payoff of the hedged portfolio given above should be the same as the amount to be generated by investing the initial cost of the portfolio given by Equation (3). Equating the two, we have:

$$(1 + r) (HS - C) = uHS - C_u \tag{4}$$

Substituting Equation (2) for H in Equation (4), and solving for the call option price, C, we find

$$C = \left(\frac{1 + r - d}{u - d}\right) \frac{C_u}{(1 + r)} + \left(\frac{u - 1 - r}{u - d}\right) \frac{C_d}{(1 + r)} \qquad (5)$$

Equation (5) is the formula for the one-period binomial option pricing model. We would have derived the same formula if we had used the payoff if the asset's price goes down.

Applying Equation (5) to our illustration where

$$u = 1.250$$
$$d = 0.875$$
$$r = 0.10$$
$$C_u = \$20$$
$$C_d = \$0$$

we get

$$C = \left(\frac{1 + 0.10 - 0.875}{1.25 - 0.875}\right) \frac{\$20}{1 + 0.10} + \left(\frac{1.25 - 1 - 0.10}{1.25 - 0.875}\right) \frac{\$0}{1 + 0.10}$$

$$= \$10.90$$

This value agrees with our first finding for the call option price.

This approach to pricing options may seem oversimplified, given that we assume only two possible future states for the underlying asset. In fact, we can extend the procedure by making the periods smaller and smaller, so we can calculate a fair value for the option. To illustrate these basic principles we extend the original illustration to a two-period model.

Extension to Two-Period Model.   The extension to two periods requires that we introduce more notation. To help understand the notation, look at Figure 7-7. The left panel of the figure shows, for the asset, the initial price, the price one period from now if the price goes up or goes down, and the price at the expiration date (two periods from now) if the price in the previous period goes up or goes down. The right panel of Figure 7-7 shows the value of the call option at the expiration date and the value one period prior to the expiration date.

The new notation has to do with the value of the call option at the expiration date. We now use two subscripts. Specifically, C_{uu} is the call value if the asset's price went up in both periods, C_{dd} is the call value if the asset's price went down in both periods, and C_{ud} (which is equal to C_{du}) is the call value if the asset's price went down in one period and up in one period.

We solve for the call option price, C, by starting at the expiration date to determine the value of C_u and C_d. This can be done by using Equation (5) because that equation gives the price of a one-period call option. Specifically,

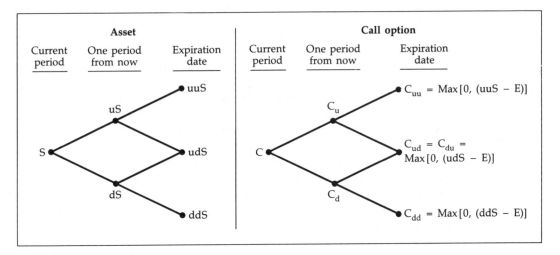

FIGURE 7-7
Two-Period Option Pricing Model

$$C_u = \left(\frac{1 + r - d}{u - d}\right)\frac{C_{uu}}{(1 + r)} + \left(\frac{u - 1 - r}{u - d}\right)\frac{C_{ud}}{(1 + r)} \tag{6}$$

and

$$C_d = \left(\frac{1 + r - d}{u - d}\right)\frac{C_{du}}{(1 + r)} + \left(\frac{u - 1 - r}{u - d}\right)\frac{C_{dd}}{(1 + r)} \tag{7}$$

Once C_u and C_d are known, we can solve for C using Equation (5).

To make this more concrete, let's use numbers. We will assume that the asset's price can go up by 11.8% per period or down by 6.46% per period. That is:

$$u = 1.118 \quad \text{and} \quad d = 0.9354$$

Then, as shown in the top left panel of Figure 7-8, the asset can have three possible prices at the end of two periods:

Price goes up both periods: $uuS = (1.118)\,(1.118)\,\$80 = \$100$
Price goes down both periods: $ddS = (0.9354)\,(0.9354)\,\$80 = \$70$
Price goes up one period and down the other:

$$udS = (1.118)\,(0.9354)\,\$80 = duS = (0.9354)\,(1.118)\,\$80 = \$83.66$$

Notice that the first two prices are the same as in the one-period illustration. By extending the length of time until expiration to two periods rather than one, and adjusting the change in the asset price accordingly, we now have three possible outcomes. If we increase the number of periods, the number of possible outcomes that the asset price may take on at the expiration date will increase. Consequently, what seemed like an unrealistic assumption about two possible outcomes for each period becomes more realistic with respect to the number of possible outcomes that the asset price may take at the expiration date.

Now we can use the values in the top right panel of Figure 7-8 to calculate C. The riskless interest rate for one period is now 4.88% because when compounded this rate will produce an interest rate of 10% from now to the expiration date (two periods from now). First, consider the calculation of C_u using Equation (6). From Figure 7-8 we see that

$$C_{uu} = \$20 \quad \text{and} \quad C_{ud} = \$3.66$$

therefore,

$$C_u = \left(\frac{1 + 0.0488 - 0.9354}{1.118 - 0.9354}\right) \frac{\$20}{1 + 0.0488}$$

$$+ \left(\frac{1.118 - 1 - 0.0488}{1.118 - 0.9354}\right) \frac{\$3.66}{1 + 0.0488} = \$13.1652$$

From Figure 7-8,

$$C_{dd} = \$0 \quad \text{and} \quad C_{du} = \$3.66$$

therefore,

$$C_d = \left(\frac{1 + 0.0488 - 0.9354}{1.118 - 0.9354}\right) \frac{\$3.66}{1 + 0.0488}$$

$$+ \left(\frac{1.118 - 1 - 0.0488}{1.118 - 0.9354}\right) \frac{\$0}{1 + 0.0488} = \$2.1672$$

We have inserted the values for C_u and C_d in the bottom panel of Figure 7-8 and can now calculate C by using Equation (5) as follows

$$C = \left(\frac{1 + 0.0488 - 0.9354}{1.118 - 0.9354}\right) \frac{\$13.1652}{1 + 0.0488}$$

$$+ \left(\frac{1.118 - 1 - 0.0488}{1.118 - 0.9354}\right) \frac{\$2.1672}{1 + 0.0488} = \$8.58$$

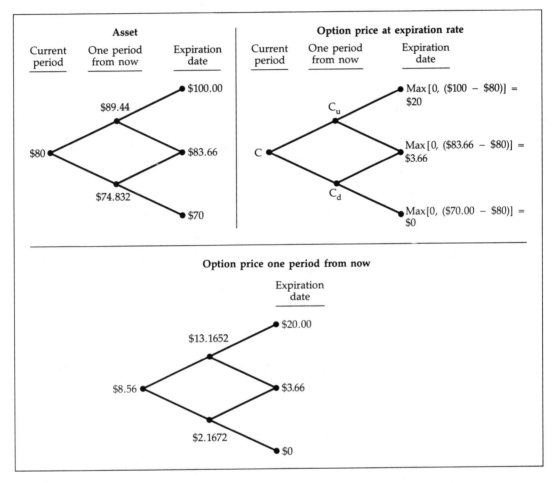

FIGURE 7-8
Two-Period Option Pricing Model Illustration

ECONOMIC ROLE OF THE OPTION MARKETS

In the previous chapter, we explained the important role that futures play in our financial markets: they allow investors to hedge the risks associated with adverse price movements. Hedging with futures lets a market participant lock in a price, and thereby eliminates price risk. In the process, however, the investor gives up the opportunity to benefit from a favorable price movement. In other words, hedging with futures involves trading off the benefits of a favorable price movement for protection against an adverse price movement.

Hedging with options has a variety of potential benefits, which we discuss in later chapters. For now, we provide an overview of how options can be used for hedging, and how the outcomes of hedging with options differ from those of hedging with futures. To see this, let's return to the initial illustration in this chapter where the underlying instrument for the option is Asset XYZ.

First let's consider an investor who owns Asset XYZ which is currently selling for $100 but expects to sell it one month from now. The investor's concern is that one month from now Asset XYZ's price may decline below $100. One alternative available to this investor is to sell Asset XYZ now. Suppose, however, the investor does not want to sell this asset now because either she expects that the price will rise in one month or there are some restrictions that prevent the sale of Asset XYZ now. Suppose also that an insurance company is aware of the situation faced by this investor and offers to sell her an insurance policy providing that, if at the end of one month Asset XYZ's price is less than $100, the insurance company makes up the difference between $100 and the market price. That is, if one month from now Asset XYZ's price is $80, the insurance company will pay the investor $20.

The insurance company naturally charges the investor a premium to write this policy. Let's suppose that the premium is $2. Holding aside the cost of the insurance policy, the payoff that this investor then faces is as follows. The minimum price for Asset XYZ that the investor is assured is $100 because if the price is less, the insurance company will make up the difference. If Asset XYZ's price is greater than $100, however, the investor will receive the higher price. Once we consider the premium of $2 to purchase this insurance premium, the investor is effectively assured a minimum price of $98 ($100 minus $2), but if the price is above $100 the investor realizes the benefits of a higher price (reduced always by the $2 for the insurance policy). By buying this insurance policy, the investor has purchased protection against an adverse price movement, while maintaining the opportunity to benefit from a favorable price movement reduced by the cost of the insurance policy.

Insurance companies don't offer such policies, but we have described a contract in this chapter that provides the same protection as this hypothetical insurance policy. Consider the put option on Asset XYZ with one month to expiration, a strike price of $100, and an option price of $2 that we used in our illustrations earlier in this chapter. The payoff is identical to the hypothetical insurance policy. The option price resembles the hypothetical insurance premium; this is the reason why the option price is referred to as the option premium. A put option can be used to hedge against a decline in the price of the underlying instrument.

This is quite a different payoff from a futures contract. Suppose that a futures contract with Asset XYZ as the underlying instrument is available with a futures price equal to $100 and a settlement date one month from now. By selling this futures contract, the investor would be agreeing to sell Asset XYZ for $100 one month from now. If Asset XYZ's price falls below $100, the investor is protected because she will receive $100 upon delivery of the asset to satisfy the futures contract. If Asset XYZ's price rises above $100, however, the investor will not realize the price appreciation because she must deliver the asset for an agreed-upon amount of $100. By selling the futures contract, the investor has locked in a price of $100, failing to realize a gain if the price rises but avoiding a loss if the price declines.

Call options, too, can be used to hedge. A call option can be used to protect against a rise in the price of the underlying instrument while maintaining the opportunity to benefit from a decline in the price of the underlying instrument. Suppose, for example, that an investor expects to receive $100 one month from now, and plans to use that money to purchase Asset XYZ, which is selling currently for $100. The risk that the investor faces is that Asset XYZ's price will rise above $100 one month from now. By purchasing the call option with a strike price of $100 and with an option price of $3 that we used earlier in this chapter, the investor has hedged the risk of a rise in the price of Asset XYZ.

The hedge outcome is as follows. If the price rises above $100 one month from now, the investor would exercise the call option and realize the difference between the market price of Asset XYZ and $100. Thus, holding aside the cost of the option, the investor is assuring a maximum price that she will have to pay for Asset XYZ of $100. Should the asset's price fall below $100, the call option expires worthless, but the investor benefits by being able to purchase Asset XYZ at a price less than $100. Once the $3 cost of the option is considered, the payoff is as follows. The maximum price that the investor will have to pay for Asset XYZ is $103 (the strike price plus the option price), but if the price of the asset declines below $100 the investor will benefit by the amount of the price decline less $3.

Compare this situation to a futures contract where Asset XYZ is the underlying instrument, settlement is in one month, and the futures price is $100. Suppose that the investor buys this futures contract. If one month from now the price of Asset XYZ rises above $100, the investor has contracted to buy the asset for $100, thereby eliminating the risk of a price rise; if the price falls below $100, however, the investor cannot benefit because she has contracted to pay $100 for the asset.

It should be clear now how hedging with options differs from hedging with futures. This difference cannot be overemphasized. Options and futures are not interchangeable instruments.

Is it possible to create the same hedging payoff that an option provides against an adverse price movement in a world in which there are no option contracts? It should be obvious from our illustrations of how to price an option that the same payoff can be accomplished synthetically with an appropriate position in the cash market instrument and by borrowing funds. So why do we need option contracts? The reason is that an option contract is a more *efficient* vehicle to create the hedged position.

While our focus has been on hedging price risk, options also allow investors an efficient way to expand the range of return characteristics available. That is, investors can use options to "mold" a return distribution for a portfolio to fit particular investment objectives.[6]

SUMMARY

In this chapter we have reviewed the fundamentals of options. An option grants the buyer of the option the right either to buy (in the case of a call option) or to sell (in the case of a put option) the underlying asset to the seller (writer) of the option at a stated price called the strike (exercise) price by a stated date called the expiration date. The price that the option buyer pays to the writer of the option is called the option price or option premium. An American option allows the option buyer to exercise the option at any time up to and including the expiration date; a European option may be exercised only at the expiration date.

The buyer of an option cannot realize a loss greater than the option price, and has all the upside potential. By contrast, the maximum gain that the writer (seller) of an option can realize is the option price; the writer is exposed to all the downside risk.

The option price consists of two components: the intrinsic value and the time premium. The intrinsic value is the economic value of the option if it is exercised immediately (except that if there is no positive economic value that will result from exercising immediately, then the intrinsic value is zero). The time premium is the amount by which the option price exceeds the intrinsic value. Six factors influence the option price: (1) the current price of the underlying asset, (2) the strike price of the option, (3) the time remaining to the expiration of the option, (4) the expected price volatility of the underlying asset, (5) the short-term risk-free interest rate over the life of the option, and (6) anticipated cash payments on the underlying asset.

---

[6] See Stephen A. Ross, "Options and Efficiency," *Quarterly Journal of Economics* (February 1976), pp. 75–89, and Fred Arditti and Kose John, "Spanning the State Space with Options," *Journal of Financial and Quantitative Analysis* (March 1980), pp. 1–9.

Arbitrage arguments can be used to place a lower boundary on the option price. There is also a relationship between the call option price, the put option price, and the price of the underlying asset known as the put–call parity relationship. The theoretical option price can be calculated using the binomial option pricing model, also based on arbitrage arguments.

QUESTIONS

1. "There's no real difference between options and futures. Both are hedging tools, and both are derivative products. It's just that with options you have to pay an option premium, while futures require no upfront payment except for a 'good faith' margin. I can't understand why anyone would use options." Do you agree with this statement?

2. You have just opened up the morning's newspaper to check the prices of *call* options on Asset ABC. It is now December, with the near contract maturing in one month's time. Asset ABC's price is currently trading at $50.

STRIKE	JAN.	MARCH	JUNE
$40	$11	$12	$11.50
50	6	7	8.50
60	7	8	9.00

Glancing at the figures, you note that two of these quotes seem to violate some of the rules you learned regarding options pricing.

a. What are these discrepancies?

b. How could you take advantage of the discrepancies? What is the minimum profit you would realize by arbitraging based on these discrepancies?

c. Suppose the price of the January 40 call were $9 rather than $11. The option would thus be selling for less than its intrinsic value. Why might it not be the case that an arbitrage profit were instantly available?

3. The payoff from a long position in a forward contract on the settlement date is the difference between the spot price of the underlying asset at the

maturity of the forward contract and the forward price. For example, if you are long a forward contract to purchase an asset at $100, your payoff at the settlement date would be as follows:

Spot Price	Forward Price	Payoff
80	100	−20
90	100	−10
100	100	0
110	100	10
120	100	20

A forward contract is equivalent to being long a call option and short a put option, with the strike price such that the price of the call is equal to the price of the put.

a. For the five spot prices above, demonstrate that being long a forward is equivalent to being long a call and short a put.

b. Why do you think that the strike price has to be set such that the price of the call is equal to the price of the put?

4. Indicate whether you agree or disagree with the statements following.

   a. "To determine the theoretical value of an option, we will need some measure of the volatility of the underlying asset. Because financial theorists tell us that the appropriate measure of risk is beta (i.e., systematic risk), then we should use this value."

   b. "It does not make sense that the price of a call option should rise in value if the price of the underlying asset falls."

5. For an asset that does not make cash distributions over the life of an option, it does not pay to exercise a call option prior to the expiration date. Why?

6. Consider two strategies:
   Strategy 1: Purchase one unit of Asset M currently selling for $103. A distribution of $10 is expected one year from now.
   Strategy 2: (a) Purchase a call option on Asset M with an expiration date one year from now and a strike price of $100; and (b) place sufficient funds in a 10% interest-bearing bank account sufficient to exercise the option at expiration ($100) and to pay the cash distribution that would be paid by Asset M ($10).

    a. What is the investment required under Strategy 2?

    b. What are the payoffs of Strategy 1 and Strategy 2, assuming that the price of Asset M one year from now is:

        (i) $120

        (ii)   103

        (iii) 100

        (iv)   80

    c. For the four prices of asset M one year from now, demonstrate that the following relationship holds:

    Call option price ≥ Max [0, (Price of underlying asset − Present value of strike price − Present value of cash distribution)]

7. The current price of Asset W is $25. There are no cash distributions expected for this asset for the next year. The one-year interest rate is 10%. The asset's price will be either $35 or $15 one year from now. What is the price of a European call option on Asset W with a strike price of zero that expires in one year's time?

8. **a.** Calculate the option value for a two-period European call option with the following terms:

    Current price of underlying asset = $100

    Strike price = $10

    One-period risk-free rate = 5%

    The stock price can either go up or down by 10% at the end of one period.

    b. Recalculate the value for the option when the stock price can move either up or down by 50% at the end of one period. Compare your answer with the calculated value in part (**a**). Why is the answer different from what you might have expected?

LEARNING OBJECTIVES

After reading this chapter you will understand:

- the reasons why the stock market has undergone significant structural changes since the 1960s.

- frictions that cause the stock market to depart from a perfect market.

- the various trading locations for stocks.

- trading mechanisms such as the types of orders, short-selling, and margin transactions.

- the role of a dealer as a market maker and the costs associated with market making.

- the key structural difference between a stock exchange and an over-the-counter market.

- what is meant by a fragmented market, and why stock markets in the 1960s and early 1970s were characterized as fragmented markets.

- the key elements of the proposed national market system.

- trading arrangements to accommodate institutional traders such as block trades and program trades.

- what the upstairs market is and its role in institutional trading.

- that transactions costs include commissions, fees, execution costs, and opportunity costs.

- the role played by stock market indicators and how those indicators are constructed.

- the various stock market indicators currently followed by market participants.

- what is meant by the pricing efficiency of a market.

- the different forms of pricing efficiency and the empirical evidence on pricing efficiency.

- the implications of pricing efficiency for a common stock strategy.

- what an indexing strategy is, and how such a strategy can be implemented.

- the reasons offered for the market crash of 1987.

Equity securities represent an ownership interest in a corporation. Holders of equity securities are entitled to the earnings of the corporation when those earnings are distributed in the form of dividends; they are also entitled to a prorata share of the remaining equity in case of liquidation. There are two types of equity securities: common stock and preferred stock. The key distinction between these two forms of equity securities is the degree to which they may participate in any distribution of earnings and capital and the priority given to each in the distribution of earnings. Typically, preferred stockholders are entitled to a fixed dividend that they receive before common stockholders may receive dividends. We refer therefore to preferred stock as a senior corporate security, in the sense that preferred stock interests are senior to the interests of common stockholders. We postpone an explanation of preferred stock to Chapter 15 where we discuss the market for senior corporate securities.

Our focus in this chapter is on the secondary market for common stock. It is in this market that the opinions of investors about the economic prospect of a company are expressed through the trades they execute. These trades together give the market consensus opinion about the price of the stock. In turn, the company's cost of common stock is determined. This market has undergone significant changes since the 1960s, reflecting primarily three interacting factors: (1) the *institutionalization* of the stock market as a result of a shift away from traditional small investors to large institutional investors, (2) changes in government regulation of the market, and (3) innovation, largely because of advances in computer technology.[1]

Evidence of institutionalization of the stock market can be seen from the ownership distribution of stocks and the share of trading by individuals (referred to as "retail" trading) and institutions (pension funds, insurance companies, investment companies, bank trusts, and foundations). In 1949, institutional ownership of New York Stock Exchange (NYSE)-listed stocks was 13%; in recent years, it has been almost 50%. Moreover, over 80% of the volume of trading on the NYSE is done by institutional investors.[2] This, of course, does not mean that individuals' ownership of stocks has diminished. Instead, institutions trade on behalf of individuals, who hold stock through the instruments of mutual funds, pension funds, and so forth. The institutionalization of this market has had important implications for the design of trading systems because the demands made by institutional investors are different from those made by traditional small investors.

Besides describing the arrangements to accommodate institutional investors in the secondary market for common stocks, this chapter reviews evidence on how efficiently common stocks are priced and the implications of efficiency for investment strategies. An important issue is whether stock price volatility has increased in recent years and, if so, what institutional characteristics have caused it. As the culprit that is alleged to have increased

---

[1] As we shall see in Chapter 22, these are the same factors that have led to the globalization of markets.

[2] Securities Industry Association, *Trends* (March 16, 1989).

stock price volatility is the introduction of stock index futures and stock index options, we'll postpone discussion of this question until we cover these contracts in Chapter 10. We conclude the chapter with a discussion of the reasons offered for the stock market crash of October 1987.

SECONDARY MARKETS

In this section, we will describe the various institutional arrangements for trading common stocks in the United States. While our discussion of the mechanisms is limited to common stock, the principles are applicable to other financial assets as well. We begin with an explanation of what is meant by a "perfect market" and the reasons why actual markets may not be perfect.

Perfect Markets

In general, a "perfect market" results when the number of buyers and sellers is sufficiently large, and all participants are small enough relative to the market so that no individual market agent can influence the commodity's price. Consequently, all buyers and sellers are price takers, and the market price is determined where there is equality of supply and demand. This condition is more likely to be satisfied if the commodity traded is fairly homogeneous (for example, corn or wheat). But there is more to a perfect market than market agents being price takers. It is also required that there are no transactions costs or impediments that interfere with the supply and demand of the commodity. Economists refer to these various costs and impediments as "frictions." The costs associated with frictions generally result in buyers paying more than in the absence of frictions and/or sellers receiving less.

In the case of financial markets, frictions would include:

- commissions charged by brokers
- bid–ask spreads charged by dealers
- order handling and clearance charges
- taxes (notably on capital gains) and government-imposed transfer fees
- costs of acquiring information about the financial asset
- trading restrictions, such as exchange-imposed restrictions on the size of a position in the financial asset that a buyer or seller may take
- restrictions on market makers and margin requirements
- halts to trading that may be imposed by regulators where the financial asset is traded.

Trading Locations

In the United States, secondary trading of common stock occurs in a number of trading locations: major national stock exchanges, regional stock exchanges, and the over-the-counter (OTC) market. In addition to these trading locations, independently-operated electronic trading systems are being developed.

In the U.S., stock prices on exchanges and in the OTC market are determined continuously throughout the trading day as buyers and sellers submit orders. For example, given order flow at 10 a.m., the market clearing price of a stock may be $70; at 11 a.m. of the same trading day, the market clearing price of the same stock, again based on order flows, may be $70.75. This type of market structure is called a *continuous market*.

In contrast is a *call market structure*. In a call market orders are batched for simultaneous execution at the same price. That is, at certain times in the trading day (or possibly more than once in a day), a market maker holds an auction for a stock. The auction may be an oral auction or a written auction. In either case, the price at which the market clears will be determined (so-called price fixing). The role of a market maker in a call market is that of an auctioneer. The market maker does not take a position in the stock, as a dealer does in a continuous market. While the call market structure for stocks does not now exist in the U.S., there are some European stock markets with this structure.[3]

Stock Exchanges.   Stock exchanges are formal organizations, approved and regulated by the Securities and Exchange Commission (SEC), that are made up of members that use the facilities to exchange certain common stocks.[4] Stocks that are traded on an exchange are said to be *listed stocks*. To be listed, a company must apply and satisfy requirements established by the exchange where listing is sought. Since August 1976, the listing of a common stock on more than one exchange has been permitted.

To have the right to trade securities on the floor of the exchange, firms or individuals must buy a "seat" on the exchange; that is, they must become a member of the exchange. The cost of a seat is market-determined. A member

---

[3] The auction for actively traded stocks in such markets is usually an oral auction; a written auction is used for less actively traded stocks. The German stock market has a market structure that combines a continuous market and a call market.

[4] Securities other than common stock are traded on exchanges. We shall discuss some of these products in the next chapter. Some exchanges trade derivative instruments, which we discuss in later chapters. While some bonds are traded on exchanges, the main market for such securities is the over-the-counter market.

firm may trade for its own account or on behalf of a customer. In the latter case it is acting as broker.

Each stock is traded at a specific location on the trading floor called a *post*. Firms that are members of an exchange and that are brokers trade stock on behalf of their customers. On an exchange the market maker role for a listed stock is performed by a *specialist*. A member firm may be designated as a specialist for the common stock of more than one company, but only one specialist is designated for the common stock of a given company. An important difference between exchanges and the OTC market is the market structure design with respect to a single market maker or multiple market makers. This is a critical institutional difference underlying some controversy associated with secondary trading on an exchange versus over-the-counter, and we discuss it later in this chapter.

The two major national stock exchanges are the New York Stock Exchange (NYSE), popularly referred to as the "Big Board," and the American Stock Exchange (ASE or AMEX). The NYSE is the largest exchange in the U.S. As of June 1991, about 2,300 companies were listed, with a total common stock market value of approximately $3.2 trillion. A highly controversial rule is the NYSE's Rule 390. This rule, applicable only to the NYSE, requires permission from the exchange for a member firm to execute a transaction of an NYSE-listed stock off the exchange.[5] In recent years the NYSE has faced considerable competition for certain types of orders from regional exchanges and the London Stock Exchange.

The AMEX is the second largest exchange, with 1,063 issues as of the end of 1990, and a total market value of $102 billion. Several other products that we will discuss in later chapters are also traded on this exchange.

There are five regional stock exchanges: Midwest, Pacific, Philadelphia, Boston, and Cincinnati. On these exchanges there are two kinds of stocks listed: (1) stocks of companies that could not qualify for listing (or do not wish to list) on one of the major national exchanges, and (2) stocks that are also listed on one of the major national exchanges. The latter are called "dually listed stocks." The motivation for dual listing is that a local brokerage firm that purchases a membership on a regional exchange can trade these stocks without having to purchase a considerably more expensive membership on the major national stock exchange where the stock is also listed. A local brokerage firm, of course, could use the services of a member of a major national stock exchange to execute an order, if it were willing to give up part of its commission.

The regional stock exchanges themselves compete with the NYSE for the

---

[5] Certain stocks listed on the NYSE are exempt from this rule.

execution of smaller trades such as those for 5,000 shares or less. Major national brokerage firms have in recent years routed such orders to regional exchanges because of the lower cost they charge for executing orders. As a result, in 1989, 25% of the trades in stocks listed on the NYSE were executed on one of the five regional stock exchanges. These trades were primarily for smaller orders, as evidenced by the fact that they represented only 12% of the trading volume of shares listed on the NYSE.

At one time stock exchanges fixed minimum commissions on transactions, according to the value and the volume of shares involved. The fixed commission structure did not allow the commission rate to decline as the number of shares in the order increased, thereby ignoring the economies of scale in executing transactions. For example, brokers incurred lower total costs in executing an order of 10,000 shares of one stock for one investor than in executing 100 orders for the same stock from 100 investors. The institutional investors who had come to dominate trading activity demanded larger order size, yet did not reap the benefits of the economies of scale in order execution that brokers did. Pressure from institutional investors led the SEC in April 1971 to permit negotiated commissions for that portion of trades with a market value in excess of $500,000; one year later, the market value that was negotiable was dropped to $300,000. By May 1975, fixed minimum commissions on stocks traded on an exchange were eliminated. Commissions are now fully negotiable between investors and their brokers.

Over-the-Counter Market.   The over-the-counter (OTC) market is the market for unlisted stocks. The National Association of Securities Dealers (NASD), a private organization, represents and regulates the dealers in the OTC market under the supervision of the SEC. The National Association of Securities Dealers Automatic Quotation (NASDAQ) system is an electronic quotation system that provides price quotations to market participants about the more actively traded issues in the OTC market. As of the end of 1990, there were about 3,800 common stocks included in the NASDAQ system with a total market value of $229 billion.

A stock may be both listed on an exchange and traded in the OTC market. The *third market* refers to the trading of such listed stocks in the OTC market.[6] Dealers in this market are not members of an exchange, and therefore were not required to charge the fixed minimum commissions once set by the exchange. The third market grew as institutional investors used it in the early

---

[6] The "first market" refers to the trading of listed stocks executed on the floor of the exchange. The "second market" refers to the execution of unlisted stock trades in the over-the-counter market.

1960s to avoid fixed minimum commissions. In 1989, about 5% of the trades and 3% of the trading volume of NYSE-listed stocks occurred in the third market.

Independent Electronic Trading Systems.   It is not always necessary for two transactors to use the services of a broker or a dealer to execute a transaction. The direct trading of stocks between two transactors without the use of a broker is called the *fourth market*. This market grew for the same reasons as the third market: the excessively high minimum commissions established by the exchanges. Its growth was limited initially by the availability of information on other institutions that wanted to trade.

Today, systems have been developed that allow institutional investors to *cross trades* (i.e., match buyers and sellers) via computer. The two major systems that handle large institution-to-institution trades are INSTINET and POSIT. The latter started in late 1980 and currently has 80 institutional money managers. POSIT, which stands for Portfolio System for Institutional Investors, is a trading system developed by BARRA and Jefferies & Co. POSIT is more than a simple order-matching system but rather matches the purchase and sale of portfolios in such a way so as to optimize the liquidity of the system.[7]

Trading Mechanics

Below we describe the key features involved in trading stocks. Later in the chapter, we'll discuss trading arrangements (block trades and program trades) that developed specifically for coping with the trading needs of institutional investors.

Types of Orders and Trading Priority Rules.   When an investor wants to buy or sell a share of common stock, the price and conditions under which the order is to be executed must be communicated to a broker. The simplest type of order is the *market order*, an order executed at the best price available in the market. The best price is assured by requiring that when more than one order on the same side of the market reaches the market at the same time, the order with the best price is given priority. Thus, buyers offering a higher price are given priority over those offering a lower price; sellers asking a lower price are given priority over those asking a higher price.

Another priority rule is needed to handle receipt of more than one order at the same price. Most often, the priority in executing such orders is based

---

[7] A description of the algorithm used to maximize the liquidity of POSIT is described in "An Inside Look at the POSIT Matching Algorithm," *POSITNEWS* (Summer/Fall 1990), p. 2.

on the time of arrival of the order—first orders in are the first orders executed—although there may be a rule that gives higher priority to certain types of market participants over other types of market participants who are seeking to transact at the same price. For example, on exchanges orders can be classified as either "public orders" or orders of those member firms dealing for their own account (both non-specialists and specialists). Exchange rules require that public orders be given priority over orders of member firms dealing for their own account.

The danger of a market order is that an adverse move may take place between the time the investor places the order and the time the order is executed. To avoid this danger, the investor can place a *limit order* that designates a price threshold for the execution of the trade. A *buy limit order* indicates that the stock may be purchased only at the designated price or lower. A *sell limit order* indicates that the stock may be sold at the designated price or higher. The danger of a limit order is that there is no guarantee that it will be executed at all. The designated price may simply not be obtainable. A limit order that is not executable at the time it reaches the market is recorded in a *limit order book*.

The limit order is a *conditional order:* it is executed only if the limit price or a better price can be obtained. Another type of conditional order is the *stop order*, which specifies that the order is not to be executed until the market moves to a designated price, at which time it becomes a market order. A *buy stop order* specifies that the order is not to be executed until the market rises to a designated price (i.e., trades at or above, or is bid at or above, the designated price). A *sell stop order* specifies that the order is not to be executed until the market price falls below a designated price (i.e., trades at or below, or is offered at or below, the designated price). A stop order is useful when an investor cannot watch the market constantly. Profits can be preserved or losses minimized on a stock position by allowing market movements to trigger a trade. In a sell (buy) stop order the designated price is less (greater) than the current market price of the stock. In a sell (buy) limit order, the designated price is greater (less) than the current market price of the stock.

There are two dangers associated with stop orders. Stock prices sometimes exhibit abrupt price changes, so the direction of a change in a stock price may be quite temporary, resulting in the premature trading of a stock. Also, once the designated price is reached, the stop order becomes a market order and is subject to the uncertainty of the execution price noted earlier for market orders.

A *stop-limit order*, a hybrid of a stop order and a limit order, is a stop order that designates a price limit. In contrast to the stop order, which becomes a market order if the stop is reached, the stop-limit order becomes a limit order if the stop is reached. The order can be used to cushion the market impact of a stop order. The investor may limit the possible execution price after the activation of the stop. As with a limit order, the limit price may never be reached after the order is activated, which therefore defeats one purpose of the stop order—to protect a profit or limit a loss.

An investor may also enter a *market if touched order*. This order becomes a market order if a designated price is reached. However, a market if touched order to buy becomes a market order if the market *falls* to a given price, while a stop order to buy becomes a market order if the market *rises* to a given price. Similarly, a market if touched order to sell becomes a market order if the market rises to a specified price, while the stop order to sell becomes a market order if the market falls to a given price. We can think of the stop order as an order designed to get out of an existing position at an acceptable price (without specifying the exact price), and the market if touched order as an order designed to get into a position at an acceptable price (also without specifying the exact price).

Orders may be placed to buy or sell at the open or the close of trading for the day. An *opening order* indicates a trade to be executed only in the opening range for the day, and a closing order indicates a trade is to be executed only within the closing range for the day.

An investor may enter orders that contain order cancellation provisions. A *fill or kill order* must be executed as soon as it reaches the trading floor or it is immediately cancelled. Orders may designate the time period for which the order is effective—a day, week, or month, or perhaps by a given time within the day. An *open order*, or *good till cancelled order*, is good until the order is specifically cancelled.

Orders are also classified by their size. One *round lot* is typically 100 shares of a stock. An *odd lot* is defined as less than a round lot. For example, an order of 75 shares of Digital Equipment Corporation (DEC) is an odd lot order. An order of 350 shares of DEC includes an odd lot portion of 50 shares. A *block trade* is defined on the NYSE as an order of 10,000 shares of a given stock or a total market value of $200,000 or more. We'll discuss block trades in more detail later in this chapter.

Automated Order Routing.   Both the major national stock exchanges and the regional stock exchanges have systems for routing orders of a specified size that are submitted by brokers via computer directly to the specialists' posts where the order can be executed. On the NYSE, this system is called the *SuperDOT* (Super Designated Order Turnaround) system. SuperDOT handled 128,000 orders per day in 1988. The AMEX's *Post Execution Reporting* system allows orders up to 2,000 shares to be routed directly to specialists. The regional stock exchanges have computerized systems for routing small orders to specialists. The *Small Order Execution* system of the NASDAQ routes and executes orders up to 1,000 shares of a given stock.

Short-Selling.   An investor who expects that the price of a stock will increase can benefit from buying the stock. However, suppose that an investor expects that the price of a stock will decline and wants to benefit should the price actually decline. What can the investor do? The investor can sell the stock without owning it. How can this happen? The investor can arrange to have her broker borrow the stock from someone else, and the borrowed stock can be delivered to satisfy her sale. This practice is referred to as *selling short*. The stock is purchased subsequently by the investor to return the stock to the party that lent the stock. In this way, the investor *covers* her short position.

Let's make this concrete with an illustration. Suppose Ms. Stokes believes that Wilson Cosmetics common stock is overpriced at $20 per share and wants to be in a position to benefit if her assessment is correct. Ms. Stokes calls her broker, Mr. Yats, indicating that she wants to sell 100 shares of Wilson Cosmetics. Mr. Yats will do two things: (1) sell 100 shares of Wilson Cosmetics on behalf of Ms. Stokes, and (2) arrange to borrow 100 shares of that stock. Suppose that Mr. Yats is able to sell the stock for $20 per share and arrange to borrow the stock from Mr. Jordan. The shares borrowed from Mr. Jordan will be delivered to the buyer of the 100 shares. The proceeds from the sale (ignoring commissions) will be $2,000. However, the proceeds will not be given to Ms. Stokes because she has not given her broker the 100 shares.

Now, let's suppose one week later the price of Wilson Cosmetics stock declines to $15 per share. Ms. Stokes may instruct her broker to *buy* 100 shares of Wilson Cosmetics. The cost of buying the shares (once again ignoring commissions) is $1,500. The shares purchased are then delivered to Mr. Jordan, who you may recall loaned 100 shares to Ms. Stokes. At this point, Ms. Stokes has sold 100 shares and bought 100 shares. So she no longer has any obligation to her broker or Mr. Jordan—she has covered her short position. She is entitled to the funds in her account that were generated by the selling and buying activity. She sold the stock for $2,000 and bought it for $1,500. Thus, she realizes a profit before commissions of $500. From this amount, commissions are subtracted.

Two more costs will reduce the profit further. First, a fee will be charged by the lender of the stock. Second, if there are any dividends paid by Wilson Cosmetics while the stock is borrowed, Ms. Stokes must compensate Mr. Jordan for the dividends he would have been entitled to.

If instead of falling, the price of Wilson Cosmetics stock rises, Ms. Stokes will realize a loss when she is forced to cover her short position. For example, if the price rises to $27, Ms. Stokes will lose $700, to which must be added commissions and the cost of borrowing the stock.

There are exchange-imposed restrictions as to when a short sale may be executed; they are intended to prevent investors from destabilizing the price of a stock when the market price is falling. These are the so-called *tick-test rules.* A short sale can be made only when either (1) the sale price of the particular stock is higher than the last trade price (referred to as an *uptick trade*), or (2) if there is no change in the last trade price of the particular stock, the previous trade price must be higher than the trade price that preceded it (referred to as a *zero uptick*). For example, if Ms. Stokes wanted to short Wilson Cosmetics at a price of $20, and the two previous trade prices were $20 1/8 and then $20, she could not do so at this time because of the uptick trade rule. If the previous trade prices were $19 7/8, $19 7/8, and then $20, she could short the stock at $20 because of the uptick trade rule. Suppose that the sequence of the last three trades is: $19 7/8, $20, and $20. Ms. Stokes could short the stock at $20 because of the zero uptick rule.

The ability of investors to sell short is an important mechanism in financial markets. In the absence of an effective short-selling mechanism, stock prices will tend to be biased toward the view of more optimistic investors.

Margin Transactions.   Investors can borrow cash to buy securities and use the securities themselves as collateral. For example, suppose Mr. Boxer has $10,000 to invest and is considering buying Wilson Cosmetics, which is currently selling for $20 per share. With his $10,000, Mr. Boxer can buy 500 shares. Suppose his broker can arrange for him to borrow an additional $10,000 so that Mr. Boxer can buy an additional 500 shares. Thus, with a $10,000 investment, he can purchase a total of 1,000 shares. The 1,000 shares will be used as collateral for the $10,000 borrowed, and Mr. Boxer will have to pay interest on the amount borrowed.

A transaction in which an investor borrows to buy additional shares using the shares themselves as collateral is called buying on margin. By borrowing funds, an investor creates financial leverage. Note that Mr. Boxer, for a $10,000 investment, realizes the consequences associated with a price change of 1,000 shares rather than 500 shares. He will benefit if the price rises but be worse off if the price falls (compared to borrowing no funds).

To illustrate, let's look at what happens if the price subsequently changes. If the price of Wilson Cosmetics rises to $29 per share, ignoring commissions and the cost of borrowing, Mr. Boxer will realize a profit of $9 per share on 1,000 shares, or $9,000. Had Mr. Boxer not borrowed $10,000 to buy the additional 500 shares, his profit would be only $4,500. Suppose, instead, the price of Wilson Cosmetics stock decreases to $13 per share. Then by borrowing so that he could buy 500 additional shares, he lost $7 per share on 1,000 shares instead of just $7 on 500 shares.

The funds borrowed to buy the additional stock will be provided by the broker, and the broker gets the money from a bank. The interest rate that banks charge brokers for such purposes is named the *call money rate* (also called the *broker loan rate*). The broker charges the investor the call money rate plus a service charge.

The broker is not free to lend as much as it wishes to the investor to buy securities. The Securities and Exchange Act of 1934 prohibits brokers from lending more than a specified percentage of the market value of the securities. The *initial margin requirement* is the proportion of the total market value of the securities that the investor must pay for in cash. The 1934 act gives the Board of Governors of the Federal Reserve the responsibility to set initial margin requirements, which it does under Regulations T and U. The Fed changes margin requirements as an instrument of economic policy. The initial margin requirement has been below 40% and is currently 50%, and the initial margin requirement varies for stocks and bonds.

The Fed also establishes a maintenance margin requirement. This is the minimum proportion of the equity in the investor's margin account to the total market value. If the investor's margin account falls below the minimum maintenance margin, the investor is required to put up additional cash. The investor receives a *margin call* from the broker specifying the additional cash to be put into the investor's margin account. If the investor fails to put up the additional cash, the securities are sold.

As we indicated in Chapter 6, investors who take positions in the futures market are also required to satisfy initial and maintenance margin requirements. Margin requirements for the purchase of securities are different in concept from those in futures markets. In a margin transaction involving securities, the initial margin requirement is equivalent to a down payment; the balance is borrowed funds for which interest is paid (the call rate plus a service charge). In the futures market, the initial margin requirement is effectively "good faith" money, indicating that the investor will satisfy the obligation of the futures contract. No money is borrowed by the investor.

The Role of the Dealer as Market Maker

Because of the imbalance of buy and sell orders that may reach the market at a given time, the price of a stock may change abruptly from one transaction to the next, in the absence of any intervention. For example, suppose that the market clearing price for ABC stock is $50 as determined by several recent trades, but a flow of buy orders without an accompanying supply of sell orders arrives in the market. This temporary imbalance could be sufficient to push the price of ABC stock to, say, $55. The cost of having to pay a price higher than $50 can be viewed as the price of "immediacy." By immediacy it is meant that buyers and sellers want to trade immediately rather than waiting for the arrival of sufficient orders on the other side of the trade so that the price is closer to the price of the last known transaction. In the absence of any intervention, this temporary imbalance would have a destabilizing effect on the stock price.

As we explained in Chapter 1, a broker is an entity that acts on behalf of an investor who wishes to execute orders. A broker is an agent of the investor; no position is taken by the broker in the financial asset that is the subject of the trade. In contrast, a dealer is an entity that stands ready and willing to buy a financial asset for its own account (i.e., add to an inventory of the financial asset) or sell from its own account (i.e., reduce the inventory of the financial asset). At a given time, dealers are willing to buy a financial asset at a price (the bid price) that is less than what they are willing to sell the same financial asset for (the ask price).

In the 1960s, two economists, George Stigler[8] and Harold Demsetz,[9] analyzed the role of dealers in securities markets. They viewed dealers as the suppliers of immediacy (i.e., the ability to trade promptly) to the market. The bid–ask spread can be viewed in turn as the price charged by dealers for supplying immediacy together with short-run price stability (i.e., continuity or smoothness) in the presence of short-term order imbalances. There are two other roles that dealers play: providing better price information to market participants, and, in certain market structures, providing the services of an auctioneer in bringing order and fairness to a market.[10]

The price stabilization role follows from our earlier example of what may happen to the price of a particular transaction in the absence of any intervention when there is a temporary imbalance of orders. By taking the opposite side of a trade when there are no other orders, the dealer prevents the price from materially diverging from the price at which a recent trade was consummated.

Investors are concerned not only with immediacy, but they also want to trade at prices that are reasonable, given prevailing conditions in the market. While dealers do not know with certainty the true price of a stock, they do have a privileged position in some market structures with respect not just to the flow of market orders but also to limit orders. The latter is particularly true in market structures where one or more dealers are entitled to keep the book of limit orders. Their privileged position allows them to be in a better position

---

[8] George Stigler, "Public Regulation of Securities Markets," *Journal of Business* (April 1964), pp. 117–134.

[9] Harold Demsetz, "The Cost of Transacting," *Quarterly Journal of Economics* (October 1968), pp. 35–36.

[10] For a more detailed discussion of these roles, see Robert A. Schwartz, *Equity Markets: Structure, Trading and Performance* (New York: Harper & Row, 1988), pp. 389–397.

to affect the quality of price information that they signal to market participants.

Finally, the dealer acts as an auctioneer in some market structures, thereby providing order and fairness in the operations of the market. For example, the specialist performs this function by organizing trading to make sure that the exchange rules for the priority of trading are followed, and by keeping a limit book.

What factors determine the price dealers should charge for the services they provide? Or equivalently, what factors determine the bid–ask spread? One of the most important is the order processing costs incurred by dealers. The costs of equipment necessary to do business and the administrative and operations staff are examples. The lower these costs, the narrower the bid–ask spread. With the reduced cost of computing and better-trained personnel, these costs have declined since the 1960s.

Dealers also have to be compensated for bearing risk. A dealer's position may involve carrying inventory of a stock (a long position) or selling a stock that is not in inventory (a short position). There are three types of risks associated with maintaining a long or short position in a given stock. First, there is the uncertainty about the future price of the stock. A dealer who has a net long position in the stock is concerned that the price will decline in the future; a dealer who is in a net short position is concerned that the price will rise. As the dealer does not hold a diversified portfolio, there is no way to eliminate unsystematic or unique risk.[11] Thus, the dealer is exposed to both systematic risk and unsystematic risk.[12]

The second type of risk has to do with the expected time it will take the dealer to unwind a position and its uncertainty. And this, in turn, depends primarily on the thickness of the market for the stock.[13] Finally, while a dealer may have access to better information about order flows than the general public, there are some trades where the dealer takes the risk of trading with someone who has better information.[14] This results in the better-informed trader obtaining a better price at the expense of the dealer. Consequently, a dealer in establishing the bid–ask spread for a trade will assess whether the trader might have better information. Some trades that we will discuss later

---

[11] For a demonstration of why unsystematic risk is relevant to dealers, see Thomas Ho and Hans Stoll, "Optimal Dealer Pricing Under Transaction and Return Uncertainty," *Journal of Financial Economics* (March 1981), pp. 47–74.

[12] These two types of risk are discussed in Chapter 5.

[13] Thickness is defined in Chapter 1.

[14] Walter Bagehot, "The Only Game in Town," *Financial Analysts Journal* (March–April 1971), pp. 12–14, 22.

can be viewed as "informationless trades." This means that the dealer knows or believes that a trade is being requested to accomplish an investment objective that is not motivated by the potential future price movement of the stock.

Role of Dealers in Exchange and OTC Markets.   There is an important structural difference between exchanges and the OTC market. On the exchanges there is only one market maker or dealer per stock, known as the specialist. The specialist keeps the limit order book. Designation of who will be a specialist for a stock is determined by the exchange, taking numerous factors into account. Because capital is necessary to perform as a market maker, one requirement is satisfaction of the minimum capital requirement. Currently, the minimum capital requirement is $1 million.[15] Prior to the October 1987 market crash, it was only $100,000. Specialists realize a profit only from those trades in which they are involved.

As there is only one specialist for a given stock, there is no competition from other market makers on the exchange. Does this mean that the specialist has a monopolistic position? Not necessarily, because specialists do face competition from several sources. The existence of public limit orders affects the bid–ask spread. There are brokers in the crowd who have public orders that compete with specialists. In the case of multiple-listed stocks there is competition from specialists on other exchanges where the stock is listed. For stocks that are exempt from Rule 390 (restricting member firms to execute trades on the exchange), there is competition from dealers in the OTC market (discussed below). Finally, as we discuss later in this chapter, when a block trade is involved, specialists compete with the "upstairs market."

In the OTC market, in contrast, there may be more than one dealer for a stock. For example, at the time of this writing, there are more than 50 dealers for MCI Corporation. The number of dealers depends on the volume of trading in a stock. If a stock is not actively traded, there may be no need for more than one or two dealers. As trading activity increases in a stock, there are no barriers preventing more entities from becoming a dealer in that stock, other than satisfaction of capital requirements. Competition from more dealers—or the threat of new dealers—forces bid–ask spreads to more competitive levels. Moreover, the capital-raising ability of more than one dealer is believed to be more beneficial to markets than that of a single specialist in performing the role of a market maker.

---

[15] There is also a position assumption capability requirement. At the present time, it is 15,000 shares.

The greater competition and greater potential capital arguments have been put forth by those citing the advantages of the OTC market. The exchanges, however, argue that the commitment of the dealers to provide a market in the OTC market is not the same obligation as that of the specialist on the exchange. On the NYSE, for example, Rule 104 sets forth the specialist's obligation to maintain fair and orderly markets. Failure to fulfill this obligation results in a loss of specialist status. In the aftermath of the October 1987 market crash ("Black Monday"), 11 stocks were taken away from member firms that had been specialists for those stocks because the NYSE's Market Surveillance Division interpreted their actions as failing to fulfill their responsibilities under Rule 104. A dealer in the OTC market is under no obligation to continue its market making activity during volatile and uncertain market conditions. This became most apparent during Black Monday, when some dealers stopped making markets.

To what extent do trades from public orders meet other public orders, which therefore do not need the specialist to take the other side of the trade? That is, to what extent do specialists perform the function of stabilizing markets? Information provided by the NYSE indicates that, in 1988, 77% of all shares traded were public orders meeting public orders. Only 9% of shares traded involved specialist activity. The balance of trading, 14%, was by non-specialist member firms dealing for their own accounts.[16] The 9% participation by specialists, however, may understate the importance of the role played by the specialist because the activity may have occurred under difficult market conditions.

The National Market System

In the 1960s and early 1970s, U.S. secondary markets for stocks became increasingly fragmented. By a "fragmented market" we mean one in which some orders for a given stock are handled differently from other orders.

Here are two examples of a fragmented stock market. First is the different handling of small orders versus large orders on the same exchange. Small orders typically are executed immediately without trying to work the order to obtain the best execution. Large orders are worked by the floor trader and, as explained later, in the case of block trades, are typically negotiated in the upstairs market.[17] A second example is stock that can be bought on several exchanges as well as in the over-the-counter market. An order to buy IBM

---

[16] James E. Shapiro, "The NYSE Trading System: Background and Issues," a paper presented at the NYSE Academic Seminar on May 5, 1989.

[17] Schwartz, *Equity Markets*, pp. 22–23.

stock, for example, could be executed on one of the exchanges where IBM is listed (i.e., on the specialist system) or in the third market using the multiple-dealer system. Thus, the treatment of the order differs, depending upon where it is ultimately executed.

The concern of public policy makers has been that investors were not receiving the best execution. That is, transactions were not necessarily being executed by a broker on behalf of a customer at the most favorable price available. Another concern with the increased fragmentation of the secondary market for stocks was a growing number of completed transactions in listed stocks that were not reported to the public. This is because transactions in the third market and on the regional exchanges were not immediately disclosed on the major national exchange ticker tapes where the stock was listed.

Congress asked the SEC to investigate the situation. The investigation produced the *Institutional Investor Study Report*, which the SEC presented to Congress in 1971, substantiating the concerns we noted above. Prior to the study, the SEC had favored competing but separate markets for stock trading. In its letter accompanying the report, however, the SEC reversed its position by endorsing the development of a "central market system," which would link the various secondary markets to assure that investors realized the best execution. Such a system would maximize the market making capacity for a stock by putting the specialist on an exchange in competition not only with specialists for the same stock on other exchanges, but also with dealers in the OTC market. In subsequent years, the SEC issued several statements concerning the problems of fragmentation and the means by which a central market system could be developed.[18]

As a result of increased concerns in the equity markets, Congress enacted the Securities Act of 1975. The most important provision of this legislation for us here is Section 11A(a) (2), which amended the Securities Exchange Act of 1934, directing the SEC to "facilitate the establishment of a national market system for securities. . . ." The SEC in its efforts to implement a national market system (previously referred to by the SEC as a "central market system") targeted six elements, described as follows by Posner:

1. a system for public reporting of completed transactions on a consolidated basis (consolidated tape),
2. a composite system for the collection and display of bid and asked quotations (composite quotation system),

---

[18] Securities and Exchange Commission, *Statement of the Future Structure of the Securities Market*, February 2, 1972, and *Policy Statement on the Structure of the Central Market System*, March 29, 1973.

3. systems for transmitting orders to buy and sell securities and reports of completed transactions from one market to another (market linkage systems),

4. elimination of restrictions on the ability of exchange members to effect over-the-counter transactions in listed securities (off-board trading rules),

5. nationwide protection of limit price orders, against inferior execution in another market, and

6. rules defining the securities that are qualified to be traded in the NMS.[19]

These six elements required either changes in technology or legislative initiative. A consolidated tape, a composite quotation system, a market linkage system, and a system for nationwide protection of limit price orders are examples of the former; elimination of off-board trading rules and securities to be included in a national market system are examples of the latter.

Overall, the general issue that the SEC faced was how to design the national market system. Should it be structured as an electronic linkage of existing exchange floors? Or should it be an electronic trading system that was not tied to any existing exchange?

After several pilot programs since the passage of the 1975 act,[20] the following is what has been implemented for listed stocks. The Intermarket Trading System (ITS), whose operations began in April 1978, was developed as an electronic system that displays the quotes posted on all the exchanges where a stock is listed, as well as in the OTC market, and provides for intermarket executions. A display system on trades on listed stocks in different market centers is provided by the *Consolidated Quotation System.*

TRADING ARRANGEMENTS FOR INSTITUTIONAL INVESTORS

As we noted earlier in this chapter, the trading practices of institutional investors had to be accommodated, with the increase in institutional trading. This has resulted in the evolution of special arrangements for the execution of

---

[19] N. S. Posner, "Restructuring the Stock Markets: A Critical Look at the SEC's National Market System," *New York University Law Review* (November–December 1981), p. 916.

[20] For a discussion of these pilot programs see William C. Melton, "Corporate Equities and the National Market System," Federal Reserve Bank of New York, *Quarterly Review* (Winter 1978–79), pp. 13–25.

certain types of orders commonly sought by institutional investors: (1) orders requiring the execution of a trade of a large number of shares of a given stock, and (2) orders requiring the execution of trades in a large number of different stocks at as near a time as possible. The former types of trades are called *block trades;* the latter are called *program trades.* An example of a block trade would be a mutual fund that seeks to buy 15,000 shares of IBM stock. An example of a program trade is a pension fund that seeks to buy shares of 200 *names* (by names we mean companies) at the end of a trading day.

The institutional arrangement that has evolved to accommodate these two types of institutional trades is development of a network of trading desks of the major investment banking firms and institutional investors that communicate with each other by means of electronic display systems and telephones. This network is referred to as the *upstairs market.* Participants in the upstairs market play a key role not only in providing liquidity to the market so that such institutional trades can be executed, but also because through arbitrage activities that help to integrate the fragmented stock market.

Block Trades

Block trades are defined as trades of 10,000 shares or more of a given stock, or trades of shares with a market value of $200,000 or more.[21] In 1961, there were about nine block trades per day, which accounted for about 3% of trading volume; in recent years, by contrast, there have been about 3,000 block trades per day accounting for almost half the trading volume.[22]

As executing large numbers of block orders places strains on the specialist system, special procedures have been developed to handle them. An institutional customer contacts its salesperson at a brokerage firm, indicating that it wishes to place a block order. The salesperson then gives the order to the brokerage firm's block execution department.[23] Notice that the salesperson does not submit the order to be executed to the exchange where the stock might be traded or, in the case of an unlisted stock, try to execute the order on the NASDAQ system. The sales traders in the block execution department then contact other institutions in the hope of finding one or more institutions that would be willing to take the other side of the order. That is, they use the

---

[21] *New York Stock Exchange Guide* (CCH) Rule 127.10, sec. 2127.10.

[22] U.S. Congress, Office of Technology Assessment, *Electronic Bulls & Bears: U.S. Securities Markets & Information Technology,* OTA-CIT-469 (Washington, DC: U.S. Government Printing Office, September 1990), p. 8.

[23] Before a firm can do block trading, it must obtain permission from both the SEC and the exchanges.

upstairs market in their search to fill the block trade order. If this can be accomplished, the execution of the order is complete.

If, on the other hand, the sales traders cannot find enough institutions to take the entire block (e.g., if the block trade order is for 40,000 shares of IBM, but only 25,000 can be crossed with other institutions), then the balance of the block trade order is given to the firm's market maker. The market maker must then make a decision as to how to handle the balance of the block trade order. There are two choices: (1) the brokerage firm can take a position in the stock, or (2) the unfilled order can be executed by using the services of competing market makers. Remember that in the former case the brokerage firm is committing its own capital.

Program Trades

Program trades involve the buying and/or selling of a large number of names *simultaneously*. Such trades are also called *basket trades*, because effectively a "basket" of stocks is being traded. Some obvious examples of why an institutional investor may want to use a program trade are deployment into the stock market of new cash, implementation of a decision to move funds invested from the bond market to the stock market (or vice versa), rebalancing the composition of a stock portfolio because of a change in investment strategy, or liquidation of a stock portfolio of a pension fund money manager whose services a plan sponsor has terminated.

There are other reasons that an institutional investor may have a need to execute a program trade that will become apparent later in this chapter when we discuss an investment strategy called indexing. Another use, which we explain when we discuss stock index futures contracts in Chapter 10, is to arbitrage any price discrepancies between the stock market and the stock index futures market. This strategy is called *index arbitrage*. Unfortunately, the popular press tends to use the terms program trading and index arbitrage interchangeably, which is incorrect. One is an investment strategy (index arbitrage), and the other is an institutional trading arrangement (program trading). It is true that a program trade will be employed to implement an index arbitrage. Another confusion is that because computers are used to execute a program trade, the popular press has wrongly characterized program trading as "computerized trading."

There are several commission arrangements available to an institution for a program trade. Each has numerous variants. Considerations in selecting one (besides commission costs) are the risk of failing to realize the best execution price, and the risk that the brokerage firms to be solicited about executing the program trade will use their knowledge of the program trade to benefit from the anticipated price movement that might result (i.e., they will "frontrun" the transaction).

A program trade executed on an *agency basis* involves the selection of a brokerage firm solely on the basis of commission bids (cents per share) submitted by various brokerage firms. The brokerage firm selected uses its best efforts as an agent of the institution to obtain the best price. The disadvantage of the agency basis arrangement for a program trade is that, while commissions may be the lowest, the execution price may not be the best because of market impact costs (discussed in the next section) and the potential frontrunning by the brokerage firms that were solicited to submit a commission bid.

In an *agency incentive* arrangement, a benchmark portfolio value is established for the portfolio that is the subject of the program trade. The price for each name in the program trade is determined as either the price at the end of the previous day or the average price of the previous day. If the brokerage firm can execute the trade on the next trading day such that a better-than-benchmark portfolio value results (i.e., a higher value in the case of a program trade involving selling, or a lower value in the case of a program trade involving buying), then the brokerage firm receives a specified commission plus some predetermined additional compensation.

What if the brokerage firm does not achieve the benchmark portfolio value? Here is where the variants come into play. One arrangement may call for the brokerage firm to receive just an agreed-upon commission. Other arrangements may involve sharing the risk of not realizing the benchmark portfolio value with the brokerage firm. That is, if the brokerage firm falls short of the benchmark portfolio value, it must absorb a portion of the shortfall. In these risk-sharing arrangements, the brokerage firm is risking its own capital. The greater the risk-sharing the brokerage firm must accept, the higher the commission it will charge.

One problem that remains is the possibility of frontrunning. If brokerage firms know that an institution will execute a program trade with the prices as determined the previous day, they can take advantage of the knowledge. To minimize the possibility of frontrunning, other types of program trade arrangements have been used. They call for a brokerage firm to be given not specific names and quantities, but only enough information about key portfolio parameters to allow several brokerage firms to bid on the entire portfolio. The winning bidder is then selected and given the details of the portfolio. This increases the risk to the brokerage firm of successfully executing the program trade, but the brokerage firm can use the derivative products in Chapter 10 to protect itself if the characteristics of the portfolio in the program trade are similar to the general market.

Brokerage firms can execute the trade in the upstairs market or send orders electronically to exchange floors or the NASDAQ system through the automated order routing systems such as the NYSE SuperDOT System.

TRANSACTIONS COSTS[24]

In an investment era where one-half of one percentage point can make a difference when a money manager is compared against a performance benchmark, an important aspect of the investment process is the cost of implementing an investment strategy. Transactions costs are more than merely brokerage commissions. Transactions costs consist of *commissions, fees, execution costs,* and *opportunity costs.*

Commissions are the fees paid to brokers to trade securities. Since May 1975 commissions have been fully negotiable. According to a survey by Greenwich Associates, the trend of average commissions in cents per share has declined from $0.136 in 1977 to $0.087 in 1989.[25] Included in the category of fees are custodial fees and transfer fees. Custodial fees are the fees charged by an institution that holds securities in safekeeping for an investor.

Execution costs represent the difference between the execution price of a security and the price that would have existed in the absence of the trade. Execution costs can be further decomposed into *market* (or *price*) *impact* and *market timing* costs. Market impact cost is the result of the bid–ask spread and a price concession extracted by dealers to mitigate their risk that an investor's demand for liquidity is information-motivated.[26] Market timing cost arises when an adverse price movement of the stock during the time of the transaction can be attributed in part to other activity in the stock and is not the result of a particular transaction. Execution costs then are related to both the demand for liquidity and the trading activity on the trade date.

There is a distinction between *information-motivated trades* and *information-less trades.*[27] Information-motivated trading occurs when investors believe they possess pertinent information not currently reflected in the stock's price. This style of trading tends to increase price impact because it emphasizes the speed of execution, or because the market maker believes a desired trade is driven by information and increases the bid–ask spread to provide some protection. It can involve the sale of one stock in favor of another. Informationless trades are the result of either a reallocation of wealth or implementation of an investment strategy that utilizes only existing information. An example of the former is a pension fund's decision to invest cash in

---

[24] The discussion in this section draws from Bruce M. Collins and Frank J. Fabozzi, "A Methodology for Measuring Transactions Costs," *Financial Analysts Journal* (March–April 1991), pp. 27–36.

[25] "Getting Down to Business," Greenwich Associates, Greenwich, CT, 1990.

[26] By a price concession we mean the investor will have to pay a higher price when buying and a lower price when selling.

[27] L. Cuneo and W. Wagner, "Reducing the Cost of Stock Trading," *Financial Analysts Journal* (November–December 1975), pp. 835–843.

the stock market. Other examples of informationless trades include portfolio rebalances, investment of new money, or liquidations. In these circumstances, the demand for liquidity alone should not lead the market maker to demand the significant price concessions associated with new information.

The problem with measuring execution costs is that the true measure, which is the difference between the price of the stock in the absence of the investor's trade and the execution price, is not observable. Furthermore, the execution prices are dependent on supply and demand conditions at the margin. Thus, the execution price may be influenced by competitive traders who demand immediate execution, or other investors with similar motives for trading. This means that the execution price realized by an investor is the consequence of the structure of the market mechanism, the demand for liquidity by the marginal investor, and the competitive forces of investors with similar motivations for trading.

The cost of not transacting represents an opportunity cost.[28] Opportunity costs may arise when a desired trade fails to be executed. This component of costs represents the difference in performance between an investor's desired investment and the same investor's actual investment after adjusting for execution costs, commissions, and fees.

Opportunity costs have been characterized as the hidden cost of trading, and it has been suggested that the shortfall in performance of many actively managed portfolios is the consequence of failing to execute all desired trades.[29] Measurement of opportunity costs is subject to the same problems as measurement of execution costs. The true measure of opportunity cost depends on knowing what the performance of a stock would have been if all desired trades had been executed at the desired time across an investment horizon. As these are the desired trades that the investor could not execute, the benchmark is inherently unobservable.[30]

STOCK MARKET INDICATORS

Stock market indicators have come to perform a variety of functions, from serving as benchmarks for evaluating the performance of professional money managers to answering the question "How did the market do today?" Thus,

---

[28] For discussion of opportunity cost, within the context of costs defined as the implementation shortfall of an investment strategy, see André F. Perold, "The Implementation Shortfall: Paper versus Reality," *Journal of Portfolio Management* (Summer 1988), pp. 4–9.

[29] See J. L. Treynor, "What Does it Take to Win the Trading Game?" *Financial Analysts Journal* (January–February 1981), pp. 55–60, for a discussion of the consequences of high opportunity costs.

[30] Methodologies have been proposed to estimate execution costs and opportunity costs. See, for example, Collins and Fabozzi, "A Methodology for Measuring Transactions Costs."

stock market indicators (indexes or averages) have become a part of everyday life. Even though many of the stock market indicators are used interchangeably, each measures a different facet of the "stock market."[31]

The most commonly quoted stock market indicator is the Dow Jones Industrial Average. Other stock market indicators cited in the financial press are the Standard & Poor's 500 Composite, the New York Stock Exchange Composite Index, the American Stock Exchange Market Value Index, the NASDAQ Composite Index, and the Value Line Composite Index.[32] Yet, there are a myriad of other stock market indicators such as the Wilshire stock indexes and the Russell stock indexes, which are followed primarily by institutional money managers.

In general, market indicators rise and fall in unison. There are, however, important differences in the magnitude of these moves. To understand the reasons for these differences, it is necessary to understand how indicators are constructed. Three factors differentiate stock market indicators: the universe of stocks represented by the indicator, the relative weights assigned to the stocks, and the method of averaging used.

A stock market indicator can include all publicly traded stocks or a sample of publicly traded stocks. No stock market indicator currently available is based on all publicly traded stocks, however. Breadth of coverage is different for each market indicator.

The stocks included in a stock market indicator must be combined in certain proportions to construct the index or average. Each stock, therefore, must be assigned some relative weight. One of three approaches is used to assign relative weights to the stock market indicators: (1) weighting by the market value of the company (i.e., market capitalization, which is the price of the stock times the number of shares outstanding), (2) weighting by the price of the company's stock, and (3) weighting each company equally regardless of its market value or price.

Given the stocks that will be used to create the sample and the relative weighting to be assigned to each stock, it is then necessary to average the individual components. Two methods of averaging are possible: arithmetic and geometric. An arithmetic mean is basically a simple average of the component stocks, calculated by summing the components after weighting

---

[31] For a discussion of the implications of a stock market indicator for investment management, see: Joanne M. Hill, Frank J. Fabozzi, and Jonathan C. Jankus, "Stock Market Indicators," Chapter 7 in Frank J. Fabozzi and Gregory M. Kipnis (eds.), *The Handbook of Stock Index Futures and Options* (Homewood, IL: Dow Jones-Irwin, 1989); and Bruce M. Collins and David C. Cushing, "A Guide to Equity Index Fund Management," in Frank J. Fabozzi (ed.), *Managing Institutional Assets* (New York: Harper & Row, 1990).

[32] In Chapter 22 we discuss non-U.S. stock market indicators and international stock market indicators.

them (if appropriate) and dividing by the sum of the weights. A geometric average involves multiplication of the components, after which the product is raised to the power of 1 divided by the number of components. All properly constructed stock market indicators are constructed using arithmetic averaging.[33]

Stock market indicators can be classified into three groups: (1) those produced by stock exchanges based on all stocks traded on the exchange, (2) those produced by organizations that subjectively select the stocks to be included in the index, and (3) those where stock selection is based on an objective measure, such as the market capitalization of the company. In the first group we have the New York Stock Exchange Composite Index and the American Stock Exchange Market Value Index, which reflect the market value of all stocks traded on the respective stock exchange. While it is not an exchange, the NASDAQ Composite Index falls into this category.

The three most popular stock market indicators that fall into the second group are the Dow Jones Industrial Average (DJIA), the Standard & Poor's (S&P) 500, and the Value Line Composite Average (VLCA). The DJIA is constructed from 30 of the largest blue-chip industrial companies traded on the NYSE. The companies included in the average are those selected by Dow Jones & Company, publisher of *The Wall Street Journal*. The composition of the average changes over time as companies are dropped because of merger or bankruptcy, or because of a low level of trading activity, or because a company not in the average becomes very prominent. When a company is replaced by another company, the average is readjusted in such a way as to provide comparability with earlier values.

The S&P 500 represents selected samples of stocks chosen from the two major national stock exchanges and the over-the-counter market. The stocks in the index at any given time are determined by a committee of Standard & Poor's Corporation, which may occasionally add or delete individual or entire industry groups. The aim of the committee is to capture present overall stock market conditions representing a very broad range of economic indicators. The VLCA, produced by Arnold Bernhard & Co., covers a broad range of widely held and actively traded NYSE, AMEX, and OTC issues selected by Value Line.

In the third group we have the Wilshire Indexes produced by Wilshire Associates (Santa Monica, California) and Russell Indexes produced by the Frank Russell Company (Tacoma, Washington), a consultant to pension funds and other institutional investors. The criterion for inclusion in each of these indexes is solely market capitalization. The most comprehensive is the

---

[33] Prior to 1988, the Value Line Composite Index was constructed using geometric averaging. Value Line still gives the geometric average for this index in their reports.

Wilshire 5000, which actually includes almost 6,000 companies. (At the outset it included 5,000 stocks.) The Wilshire 4500 includes all the stocks in the Wilshire 5000 except for those in the S&P 500. Thus, the Wilshire 4500 includes companies with smaller market capitalizations than the Wilshire 5000. The motivation for creating a stock market indicator that reflects a sector of the stock market with smaller market capitalization will be evident later when we discuss market anomalies.[34] The Russell 3000 encompasses the 3,000 largest companies ranked by market capitalization, while the Russell 1000 includes the largest 1,000 market capitalization companies. The Russell 2000 includes the bottom two-thirds of the companies in the Russell 3000, so it too represents a small capitalization market index.

Besides the stock market indicators cited above, there are indexes developed by exchanges that are the underlying index for the stock index options and futures traded on these exchanges. The Standard & Poor's 100 and the Major Market Index (MMI) are two examples. We'll discuss these further in Chapter 10 when we cover stock index options and futures contracts.

With the exception of the DJIA, VLCA, and MMI, the preeminent stock market indicators are market value-weighted. The DJIA is a price-weighted index, with the index adjusted for stock splits and stock dividends. The VLCA and MMI are equally-weighted indexes.

PRICING EFFICIENCY AND IMPLICATIONS FOR PORTFOLIO STRATEGIES

The term *efficient capital market* has been used in several contexts to describe the operating characteristics of a capital market. There is a distinction, however, between an *operationally* (or *internally*) efficient market and a *pricing* (or *externally*) efficient capital market.[35]

In an operationally efficient market, investors can obtain transaction services as cheaply as possible, given the costs associated with furnishing those services. In the equity markets, for example, since the elimination of fixed minimum commissions in May 1975, the commission structure has moved closer to the competitive level dictated by the intrinsic cost of providing brokerage services. As for the dealer spread, the movement toward a national market system should tighten those spreads.

---

[34] For a comparison of the various small market capitalization indexes, see Bruce M. Collins and Frank J. Fabozzi, "Considerations in Selecting a Small Capitalization Benchmark," *Financial Analysts Journal* (January–February 1990), pp. 40–46.

[35] Richard R. West, "Two Kinds of Market Efficiency," *Financial Analysts Journal* (November–December 1975), pp. 30–34.

Pricing efficiency refers to a market where prices at all times fully reflect all available information that is relevant to the valuation of securities. When a market is price-efficient, strategies pursued to outperform a broad-based stock market index will not *consistently* produce superior returns after adjusting for (1) risk and (2) transactions costs.

As we explained in Chapter 5, there are various measures of risk. Within the context of the capital asset pricing model, risk is measured by beta, which is a proxy measure for the systematic risk of a portfolio. In the arbitrage pricing model, there is more than one measure of systematic risk. As for transactions costs, we have explained that they should be interpreted to include more than merely commissions and fees.

Empirical Tests of Pricing Efficiency

There have been numerous studies of the pricing efficiency of the stock market. While it is not our intent in this chapter to provide a comprehensive review of these studies, we can summarize their basic findings and the implications for investment strategies.[36]

In his seminal review article on pricing efficiency, Eugene Fama points out that in order to test whether the stock market is price-efficient, two definitions are necessary. First, it is necessary to define what is meant that prices "fully reflect" information. Second, the "relevant" set of information that is assumed to be "fully reflected" in prices must be defined.[37]

Fama, as well as others, defines "fully reflects" in terms of the expected return from holding a stock. As we discuss in Chapter 5, the expected return over some holding period is equal to expected dividends plus the expected price change all divided by the initial price. The price formation process defined by Fama and others is that the expected return one period from now is a stochastic (i.e., random) variable that already takes into account the "relevant" information set.[38]

Tests of pricing efficiency then investigate whether it is possible to generate *abnormal returns*. An abnormal return is defined as the difference between the actual return and the expected return from an investment strategy. The expected return used in empirical tests is one generated from

---

[36] For a detailed review of these studies, see Chapters 3–5 in Diana R. Harrington, Frank J. Fabozzi, and H. Russell Fogler, *The New Stock Market* (Chicago: Probus Publishing, 1990).

[37] Eugene F. Fama, "Efficient Capital Markets: A Review of Theory and Empirical Work," *Journal of Finance* (May 7, 1970), pp. 383–417.

[38] If it is assumed that investors will not invest in a stock unless its *expected* return is greater than zero, then the price formation process is called a *submartingale process*.

some pricing model. The most common models used in empirical tests are the capital asset pricing model (an equilibrium model) or the market model, which we discussed in Chapter 5. Consequently, expected return considers the risk associated with the investment. More specifically, it considers systematic risk as proxied by beta. Calculation of the actual return takes transactions costs from commissions and fees into account. Execution and opportunity costs are typically not considered in these studies.

To summarize, the abnormal return is calculated as follows:

Abnormal return = Actual return (net of transactions costs)
  − Expected return (from some pricing model)

This abnormal return is then tested to determine if it is statistically different from zero. If it is, it is not sufficient to conclude that the investment strategy that produced the positive abnormal return can outperform the market in the future and therefore there is a pricing inefficiency.[39] The empirical test depends critically on the expected return calculated from an assumed pricing model. If this model is misspecified because it either fails to consider the appropriate measure of risk (for example, if the arbitrage pricing model is the appropriate equilibrium pricing model) or the market risk parameter beta is not estimated properly, then the results are questionable.

As for definition of the "relevant" information set, Fama classified the pricing efficiency of the stock market into three forms: (1) weak form, (2) semistrong form, and (3) strong form.[40] The distinction between these forms lies in the relevant information that is believed to be taken into consideration in the price of the security at all times. *Weak efficiency* means that the price of the security reflects the past price and trading history of the security. *Semistrong efficiency* means that the price of the security fully reflects all public information (which, of course, includes but is not limited to historical price and trading patterns). *Strong efficiency* exists in a market where the price of a security reflects all information, whether or not it is publicly available.

Tests of Weak Form Pricing Efficiency.   The preponderance of empirical evidence is that the common stock market is efficient in the weak form. These tests explore whether historical price movements can be used to project future prices in such a way as to produce positive abnormal returns. The implications are that investors who follow a strategy of selecting stocks on the

---

[39] If a statistically significant negative abnormal return is found, an investment strategy involving shorting stock would be pursued.

[40] Fama, "Efficient Capital Markets: A Review of Theory and Empirical Work," op. cit.

basis of price patterns or trading volume—such investors are referred to as *technical analysts* or *chartists*—should not expect to do better than the market. In fact, they may fare worse because of higher transactions costs associated with frequent buying and selling of stocks.

Tests of Semistrong Form Pricing Efficiency. Evidence on semistrong pricing efficiency is mixed. There are studies suggesting that investors who select stocks on the basis of fundamental security analysis (i.e., analyzing financial statements, the quality of management, and the economic environment of a company) will not outperform the market. The reason is simply that there are many analysts undertaking basically the same sort of analysis, with the same publicly available data, so that the price of the stock reflects all the relevant factors that determine value.

While some studies question the usefulness of fundamental security analysis, a good number of other studies suggest that there are pockets of pricing inefficiency in the stock market. That is, there are some investment strategies that have historically produced statistically significant positive abnormal returns. These market anomalies are referred to as the *small-firm effect*, the *low price–earnings ratio effect*, the *neglected firm effect*, and various *calendar effects*.

The small-firm effect emerges in several studies that have shown that portfolios of small firms (in terms of total market capitalization) have outperformed the stock market (consisting of both large and small firms).[41] Because of these findings, there has been increased interest in stock market indicators that monitor small capitalization firms.

The low price–earnings ratio effect is based on studies showing that portfolios consisting of stocks with a low price–earnings ratio have outperformed portfolios consisting of stocks with a high price–earnings ratio.[42] However, another study finds that, after adjusting for transactions costs necessary to rebalance a portfolio as prices and earnings change over time, the superior performance of portfolios of low price–earnings ratio stocks no longer holds.[43] An explanation for the presumably superior performance is that stocks trade at low price–earnings ratios because they are temporarily

[41] Marc R. Reinganum, "Misspecification of Capital Asset Pricing: Empirical Anomalies Based on Earnings Yields and Market Values," *Journal of Financial Economics* (March 1981), pp. 19–46; and Rolf W. Banz, "The Relationship Between Return and Market Value of Stocks," *Journal of Financial Economics* (March 1981), pp. 103–126.

[42] Sanjoy Basu, "Investment Performance of Common Stocks in Relation to their Price–Earnings Ratios: A Test of the Efficient Market Hypothesis," *Journal of Finance* (June 1977), pp. 663–682.

[43] Haim Levy and Zvi Lerman, "Testing P/E Ratio Filters with Stochastic Dominance," *Journal of Portfolio Management* (Winter 1985), pp. 31–40.

out of favor with market participants. As fads do change, companies not currently in vogue will rebound at some indeterminate time in the future.[44]

Not all firms receive the same degree of attention from security analysts, and one school of thought is that firms that are neglected by security analysts will outperform firms that are the subject of considerable attention. One study has found that an investment strategy based on changes in the level of attention devoted by security analysts to different stocks may lead to positive abnormal returns.[45] This market anomaly is referred to as the neglected firm effect.

While some empirical work focuses on selected firms according to some criterion such as market capitalization, price–earnings ratio, or degree of analysts' attention, studies on calendar effects look at the best time to implement strategies. Examples of anomalies are the January effect, month-of-the-year effect, day-of-the-week effect, and the holiday effect. It seems from the empirical evidence that there are times when the implementation of a strategy will, on average, provide a superior performance relative to other calendar time periods.

One of the difficulties with all of these pricing efficiency studies is that the factors that are believed to give rise to market anomalies are interrelated. For example, small firms may be those that are not given much attention by security analysts and that trade at low price–earnings ratio. Current research has attempted to disentangle these effects.[46]

Aside from the various effects reviewed above, some authors[47] claim that the pricing of equities is not rational because the variability of stock prices, particularly that of broad indices, is too large to be consistent with rational prices (while it is consistent with the presence of "bubbles" which we discuss in the next section).

Other authors have called attention to periods of irrational over- or under-valuation of the market as a whole. In particular, Modigliani and Cohn[48]

---

[44] David Dreman, *Contrarian Investment Strategy: The Psychology of Stock Market Success* (New York: Random House, 1979).

[45] Avner Arbel and Paul Strebel, "Pay Attention to Neglected Firms," *Journal of Portfolio Management* (Winter 1983), pp. 37–42.

[46] See Bruce I. Jacobs and Kenneth N. Levy, "Stock Market Complexity and Investment Opportunity," in Fabozzi, *Managing Institutional Assets*, op. cit.

[47] Robert J. Shiller, "Do Stock Prices Move Too Much to Be Justified by Subsequent Changes in Dividends?" *American Economic Review* 71 (1981), pp. 421–435, and "The Probability of Gross Violations of a Present Value Variance Inequality," *Journal of Political Economy* 96 (1988), pp. 1089–1092.

[48] Franco Modigliani and Richard A. Cohn, "Inflation, Rational Valuation and the Market," *Financial Analysts Journal* (March/April 1979), pp. 24–44.

provide some evidence that the stock market was undervalued during the inflation of the 1970s because of the markets' inability to value equity correctly in the presence of significant inflation.

Testing of Strong Form Pricing Efficiency.   Empirical tests of strong form pricing efficiency fall into two groups: (1) studies of the performance of professional money managers, and (2) studies of the activities of "insiders" (individuals who are either company directors, major officers, or major stockholders). Studying the performance of professional money managers to test the strong form of pricing efficiency has been based on the belief that professional managers have access to better information than the general public. Whether this is true is moot, because the empirical evidence suggests professional managers have not been able to outperform the market consistently. In contrast, evidence based on the activities of insiders has generally revealed that insiders consistently outperform the stock market.[49] Consequently, strong form pricing efficiency—where the relevant information set includes non-public information—is not supported with respect to insider trading activity.

Implications for Investing in Common Stock

Common stock investment strategies can be classified into two general categories: active strategies and passive strategies. Active strategies are those that attempt to outperform the market by one or more of the following: timing the selection of transactions, such as in the case of technical analysis, identifying undervalued or overvalued stocks using fundamental security analysis, or selecting stocks according to one of the market anomalies. Obviously, the decision to pursue an active strategy must be based on the belief that there is some type of gain from such costly efforts; for there to be a gain, pricing inefficiencies must exist. The particular strategy chosen depends on why the investor believes this is the case.

If investors believe that the market is efficient with respect to pricing stocks, then they should accept the implication that attempts to outperform the market cannot be successful systematically, except by luck. This does not mean that investors should shun the stock market, but rather that they should pursue a passive strategy, which is one that does not attempt to outperform the market. Is there an optimal investment strategy for someone who holds this belief in the pricing efficiency of the stock market? Indeed there is. Its theoretical basis is modern portfolio theory and capital market theory that we

---

[49] Researchers obtain information about the activities of insiders from reports they are required to file with the SEC. These reports are available to the public six weeks after filing.

discussed in Chapter 5. According to modern portfolio theory, the "market" portfolio offers the highest level of return per unit of risk in a market that is price-efficient. A portfolio of financial assets with characteristics similar to those of a portfolio consisting of the entire market (i.e., the market portfolio) will capture the pricing efficiency of the market.

But how can such a passive strategy be implemented? More specifically, what is meant by a "market" portfolio, and how should that portfolio be constructed? In theory, the market portfolio consists of *all* financial assets, not just common stock. The reason is that investors compare all investment opportunities, not just stock, when committing their capital. Thus, the principles of investing we accept are based on *capital* market theory, not *stock* market theory. When the theory has been followed by those investing in the stock market, the market portfolio has been defined as consisting of a large universe of common stocks. But how much of each common stock should be purchased when constructing the market portfolio? Theory states that the chosen portfolio should be an appropriate fraction of the market portfolio; hence the weighting of each stock in the market portfolio should be based on its relative market capitalization. Thus, if the aggregate market capitalization of all stocks included in the market portfolio is $T and the market capitalization of one of these stocks is $A, then the fraction of this stock that should be held in the market portfolio is $A/$T.

The passive strategy that we have just described is called *indexing*. Because pension fund sponsors increasingly believe that money managers have been unable to outperform the stock market, the amount of funds managed using an indexing strategy has increased since the 1980s. However, index funds are still a relatively small fraction of institutional stock investments. The stock market index whose performance the passive money manager attempts to replicate is called the *bogey*. There are currently several mutual funds with the investment objective to create an indexed portfolio to match some bogey, the most common being the S&P 500.

There are several methodologies for constructing an indexed portfolio.[50] The first is to buy each and every stock in the bogey. Another is to construct an indexed portfolio consisting of a sample of all the stocks in the bogey that is constructed in such a way as to minimize the risk of failing to replicate the performance of the bogey. This risk is referred to as *mistracking* or *tracking error*. An indexed portfolio with less than the complete set of stocks in the bogey typically is constructed using mathematical optimization techniques. A third technique involves investing the whole portfolio in Treasury bills and

---

[50] For a discussion of these techniques, see Bruce M. Collins, "Index Fund Investment Management," Chapter 10 in Frank J. Fabozzi (ed.), *Portfolio and Investment Strategies* (Chicago: Probus Publishing, 1989).

buying a stock index futures contract (whose underlying stock index is the bogey) for an amount equal to the value of the portfolio. (Stock index futures are discussed in Chapter 10. For the present it is necessary only to understand that if stock index futures are priced based on their theoretical price, then a package of a long position in stock index futures and Treasury bills will produce the same return as holding the stocks in the bogey. Moreover, this can be done without incurring the transactions costs associated with buying the stocks in the bogey.)

When an indexing strategy is followed, it is critical that any new cash coming into the portfolio be invested in such a way within the indexed portfolio as to leave the relative proportion of each stock unchanged. For example, suppose that the bogey for an index strategy is the S&P 500, and the indexed portfolio is constructed using all 500 stocks. Suppose further that $10 million of additional funds are received and must be invested in the same portfolio. Then the money manager must invest the $10 million in all 500 stocks, with an amount in each stock based on its relative market capitalization. Moreover, all stocks must be purchased at as close to one time as possible. Similarly, $10 million to be withdrawn from the portfolio would require selling a proportionate amount of each stock as close in time as possible. Both objectives are accomplished via program trading.

Before leaving the topic of indexing, it is worthwhile to note that there are strategies referred to as *enhanced indexing*. The objective of such strategies is to create a portfolio that is essentially an indexed portfolio but in which the money manager makes small bets by tilting the portfolio to a sector of the stock market that is believed will outperform the bogey or employs mispriced stock index futures. The difference between this strategy and pure active strategies depends on the size of the bets that the manager is placing—that is, the extent to which the portfolio created is expected to depart from the bogey. In the case of enhanced indexing, the deviation is small; in active strategies, the portfolio constructed may have little resemblance to a bogey.

THE MARKET CRASH OF 1987

The largest single-day decline in the history of the stock market occurred on Monday, October 19, 1987. On this day, popularly referred to as "Black Monday," the DJIA declined by 23%. Other countries besides the U.S. also saw a precipitous drop in their stock markets.

The aftermath saw several studies commissioned by the U.S. government, regulators, and exchanges to assess the causes of the crash and offer recommendations guarding against a reoccurrence. The four government-related studies include: (1) a presidential task force commission study, popularly known as the Brady Report,[51] (2) the General Accounting Office (GAO) study,[52] (3) the SEC study,[53] and (4) the Commodity Futures Trading Commission study.[54] There were studies in addition by the New York Stock Exchange (popularly referred to as the Katzenbach Report),[55] and the Chicago Mercantile Exchange (popularly referred to as the Miller Report).[56]

Explanations for Black Monday that these various studies offer include: (1) presence or absence of institutional arrangements, (2) overvaluation of stock prices prior to the crash, and (3) overreaction to economic news. While an analysis of these explanations for Black Monday is beyond the scope of this chapter, we can note that a study by several well-respected university-affiliated researchers sponsored by The Mid-America Institute (MAI) for Public Policy Research seems to help us eliminate some misconceptions about the causes. The MAI task force study also evaluates some of the recommendations made by the commissioned studies. Such an evaluation is needed because, as Alan Meltzer, one of the contributors to the Mid-America Institute-sponsored study, notes:[57]

> A striking but generally disregarded feature of the recommendations made is that, often, no claim is made and no evidence offered that the events of October would have been different if the recommended changes had been in effect. Indeed, in some reports, there is little relation between the problems described and some of the solutions proposed.

Institutional Arrangements

The six commissioned studies focus on institutional characteristics of the market such as (1) the presence of a specialist, (2) the existence of computer-directed trading, (3) the nature of price limits, (4) continuous

---

[51] Brady Report, *Presidential Task Force on Market Mechanisms*.

[52] U.S. Congress, General Accounting Office, *Preliminary Observations on the October 1987 Crash*, 1988.

[53] Securities and Exchange Commission, *The October 1987 Market Break*, A Report by the Division of Market Regulation, 1988.

[54] Commodity Futures Trading Commission, *Final Report on Stock Index Futures and Cash Market Activity During October 1987*, Divisions of Economic Analysis and Trading and Markets, 1988.

[55] Nicholas Katzenbach, *An Overview of Program Trading and its Impact on Current Market Practices*, December 21, 1987.

[56] *The Final and Preliminary Reports of the CME Committee of Inquiry*, 1988.

[57] Alan H. Meltzer, "Overview," in Robert J. Barro et al. (eds.), *Black Monday and the Future of Financial Markets* (Homewood, IL: Dow Jones–Irwin, 1989).

versus call auctions, (5) the level of margin requirements, and (6) the existence of derivative instruments (futures and options).

Roll has since looked at the institutional arrangements in 23 countries with major stock markets.[58] He estimates a regression relating the change in the decline in a country's stock market to the presence or absence of ten institutional arrangements. His regression results do not provide support for the position that institutional arrangements can be used to explain the decline in stock prices in the 23 stock markets studied.

In Chapter 10, we'll focus on derivative instruments—stock index futures and stock index options—and additional empirical evidence challenging whether their existence may have caused the market crash, as many contend.

Overvaluation of Stock Prices prior to Black Monday

Another argument is that the decline in stock prices in the U.S. was a result of a permanent return to fundamental values from which the market had progressively departed during the frenzied rise of the previous year or so. Support for this explanation for the cause of the crash has been documented by the Brady report, Bernstein and Bernstein,[59] and Fama.[60] As Bernstein and Bernstein state:

> careful studies of stock selection techniques published by Goldman Sachs & Co. and Zacks Investment Research during the summer of 1987 demonstrated that, for at least a year, sheer price momentum had been the only functioning model for selected stocks: The stocks that moved were the stocks that were moving. Valuation parameters of all kinds had been left far behind in the dust, a common complaint among managers all during 1987.[61]

This formulation is consistent with a more specific explanation of the episode, namely, that it represented the bursting of a speculative bubble that had been developing throughout the year, carrying market prices well above fundamentals. The sharp decline brought the market back to values more nearly consistent with the fundamentals.

---

[58] Richard Roll, "The International Crash of October 1987," *Black Monday and the Future of Financial Markets*, op. cit.

[59] Peter L. Bernstein and Barbara S. Bernstein, "Where the Postcrash Studies Went Wrong," *Institutional Investor* (April 1988), pp. 173–177.

[60] Eugene F. Fama, "Perspectives on October 1987, or What Did We Learn From the Crash?" in *Black Monday and the Future of Financial Markets*, op. cit.

[61] Bernstein and Bernstein, op. cit., p. 175.

A bubble essentially occurs when prices rise progressively above fundamental values, and overvaluation continues to be supported by the continuing rise in prices along with expectations of further rises. Of course, holders can enjoy an attractive return only as long as the price rises exponentially, so the price itself must get farther and farther away from its fundamental value to provide remuneration for risk. As the rate of price increases slows down, this contributes to reducing the belief among market participants that the explosive process can continue, which makes continuation of the bubble more precarious. With the path becoming more and more unstable, almost any news can cause the bubble to burst; when it does, prices must go all the way back to the rationally warranted level (or even lower, initially—so-called overshooting).

The main difficulty with the bubble explanation is that, while it seems appealing, at least compared with other explanations offered, it is hard to support statistically. However, recently Roll has reported an ingenious test that provides evidence in support of the bubble hypothesis. He argues that bubbles should be characterized by serial dependence (autocorrelation) in the returns. Relying on data from stock markets of 23 countries including nearly all the major markets, he is able to provide convincing evidence of such dependence for the precrash period from the beginning of January to August 1987.[62] At the same time, he acknowledges the need for further tests to check for the possibility of a statistical pitfall that could bias the test.

Overreaction to Economic News

Some market observers suggest that the crash is attributable to an overreaction to some economic news. Several candidates for such economic news include concern about the negative impact of the merchandise trade news, additional increases in interest rates, proposed tax legislation, and news over the preceding weekend about a further decline in the value of the dollar expressed by Treasury Secretary Baker. This argument, however, lacks support because the decline was not temporary.

Is There a Conclusion?

It is worth noting that even though more than 60 years have passed since the October 29, 1929, market crash (the largest at that time), no consensus has been reached as to the reason for that decline. It should come as no surprise that there is no consensus explaining Black Monday after only a few years of investigation.

---

[62] Roll, "The International Crash of October 1987," op. cit.

SUMMARY

Common stock represents an ownership interest in a corporation. Secondary trading of common stock occurs in one or more of the following trading locations: two major national stock exchanges (the NYSE and AMEX), five regional stock exchanges, and the OTC market (NASDAQ system). Independent electronic trading systems such as INSTINET and POSIT permit institution-to-institution trading without the use of a broker.

The secondary market has undergone significant changes since the 1960s. The major participants are now institutional investors rather than small (retail) investors. Elimination of fixed commissions and the government's mandate to develop a national market system to reduce the fragmentation of the stock market have fostered increased competition among market makers on the exchanges and in the over-the-counter-market. Advances in computer technology have ushered in developments for linking the various market locations and systems for institution-to-institution direct trading.

Dealers provide three functions in markets: (1) opportunity for investors to trade immediately rather than waiting for the arrival of sufficient orders on the other side of the trade (i.e., "immediacy"), while at the same time maintaining short-run price stability ("continuity"), (2) better price information to market participants, and (3) in certain market structures, the services of an auctioneer in bringing order and fairness to a market. An important structural difference between exchanges and the OTC market is that on exchanges there is only one market maker or dealer per stock, the specialist, while there is no restriction on the number of dealers in the OTC market.

To accommodate the trading needs of institutional investors who tend to place orders of larger sizes and with a large number of names, special arrangements have evolved. Block trades are trades of 10,000 shares or more of a given stock or trades with a market value of $200,000 or more. Program trades, or basket trades, involve the buying and/or selling of a large number of names simultaneously. The institutional arrangement that has evolved to accommodate these needs is the upstairs market, which is a network of trading desks of the major investment banking firms and institutional investors that communicate with each other by means of electronic display systems and telephones.

Transactions costs include commissions, fees, execution costs, and opportunity costs. Execution costs represent the difference between the execution price of a security and the price that would have existed in the absence of the trade, and arise out of the demand for immediate execution through both the demand for liquidity and the trading activity on the trade date. Opportunity costs arise when a desired trade fails to be executed.

Stock market indicators can be classified into three groups: (1) those produced by stock exchanges and that include all stocks traded on the exchange, such as the New York Stock Exchange Composite Index, the American Stock Exchange Market Value Index, and the NASDAQ Composite Index; (2) those in which a committee subjectively selects the stocks to be included in the index, such as the Dow Jones Industrial Average, the Standard & Poor's 500, and the Value Line Composite Average; and (3) those in which the stocks selected are based solely on market capitalization, such as the Wilshire indexes (Wilshire 5000 and Wilshire 4500) and the Russell indexes (Russell 3000, Russell 2000, and Russell 1000).

A market is price-efficient if at all times prices fully reflect all available information that is relevant to the valuation of securities. In such a market, strategies pursued to outperform a broad-based stock market index will not consistently produce superior returns after adjusting for risk and transactions costs. Superior performance is measured in terms of abnormal returns, which is the difference between expected returns and actual returns. There are three forms of pricing efficiency according to what is hypothesized to be the relevant information set: (1) weak form, (2) semistrong form, and (3) strong form.

Most of the empirical evidence appears to suggest that markets are efficient in the weak form. The evidence on the semistrong form is mixed, as pockets of inefficiency have been observed. These market anomalies include the small-firm effect, the low price–earnings ratio effect, the neglected firm effect, and various calendar effects. Empirical tests of strong form pricing efficiency reveal two sets of results: (1) studies of the performance of professional money managers suggest that they have not outperformed the market, and (2) analysis of the activity of insiders generally finds that they consistently outperform the market.

Active strategies are pursued by investors who believe that markets are sufficiently mispriced that it is possible to capitalize on strategies that are designed to exploit the perceived inefficiency. The optimal strategy to pursue when the stock market is perceived to be price-efficient is indexing, because it allows the investor to capture the efficiency of the market.

Black Monday, October 19, 1987, saw the largest single decline in the stock market. Despite several studies, there is no universally accepted conclusion as to the reasons for the crash, although we support the view that it represented the bursting of a speculative bubble.

QUESTIONS

1. This quotation is from an interview with William Donaldson, Chairman of the New York Stock Exchange, that appeared in *The New York Times* of January 30, 1990:

Sure it's possible to beat the market. . . . By investing for the long term with an individual selection of stocks, it's quite possible to beat the market.

My concern is that by simply buying an index, investors are not channeling their capital into the best investments, and that has long-term negative implications for the cost of capital in this country. The risk of indexing and treating all companies the same is to give in to a very mediocre goal.

a. What is meant by "beating the market"?

b. What can you infer about Donaldson's views on pricing efficiency from his comment?

c. Assuming he is correct, why do you think so few professional stock pickers have been able to "beat the market"?

2. This quotation is from the same interview with William Donaldson:

There's a need to understand the advantages of an auction market versus a dealer market. The auction market allows a buyer and a seller to get together and agree on a price and the dealer is not involved at all. That's opposed to a dealer market where the house is on both sides of the trade and the dealer makes the spread rather than having the spread shared by the buyer and the seller. . . .

One of the things we're coming to the forefront on now is the whole idea of what makes a good market. I think the best market is where you have the maximum number of people coming together in a single location and bidding against each other. . . . That is far superior to what we are getting now, which is a fractionalization of the market. Traders on machines, trades in the closet, trades in many areas where buyers and sellers don't have the opportunity to meet.

Discuss Donaldson's opinion. In your answer be sure to address the pros and cons of the different trading locations and practices addressed in the chapter.

3. Following is a quotation from "The Taxonomy of Trading Strategies" by Wayne H. Wagner that appears in *Trading Strategies and Execution Costs* published by The Institute of Chartered Financial Analysts in 1988. (The publication is the product of a conference held in New York City on December 3, 1987.)

The NYSE is not the only operating market; there are ancillary markets that provide trading facilities beyond what is available on the Exchange floor. This suggests that some needs are not well served by the process as it occurs on the Exchange. Examples of how the NYSE is augmented by other trading facilities include the supporting specialists (particularly on the regional exchange); the upstairs brokers . . . ; the third market, the fourth market, and crossing networks; and the informal floor accommodations. All of these structures are intended to accommodate trading. Without these facilities, the NYSE as it exists today probably could not exist. . . .

a. What is meant by: (i) the upstairs brokers, (ii) the third market, (iii) the fourth market, and (iv) crossing networks?

b. How would you complete the last sentence in the quotation by Wagner?

4. The following statements are taken from Greta E. Marshall's article "Execution Costs: The Plan Sponsor's View," which appears in *Trading Strategies and Execution Costs:*

a. "There are three components of trading costs. First there are direct costs which may be measured—commissions. Second, there are indirect—or market impact—costs. Finally, there are the undefined costs of not trading." What are market impact costs, and what do you think the "undefined costs of not trading" represent?

b. "Market impact, unlike broker commissions, is difficult to identify and measure." Why is market impact cost difficult to measure?

5. Why should an investor who believes that the market is efficient pursue an indexing strategy?

6. a. What is a program trade?

b. What are the various types of commission arrangements for executing a program trade and the advantages and disadvantages of each?

7. What is an "informationless trade," and who would execute such a trade?

8. In every issue of *The Wall Street Journal*, information appears on the performance (measured in terms of total return) for mutual funds with the same stated objective. The top 15 performers and the bottom 10 performers are shown. This information is called the "Mutual Fund Scorecard." In the Monday, February 4, 1991, issue, the following ranking was reported for several of the top performers based on the 12-month period ending January 31, 1991, for mutual funds with capital appreciation as their objective:

FUND	12-MONTH TOTAL RETURN
Seligman Capital	20.77%
M-S Mainstay: Cap. Appre.	20.11
Janus Twenty Fund	20.09
Piper Jaffray: Sector	19.64
ABT Inv: Emerging Growth	19.13

a. On the basis of the figures reported above, can you determine if these mutual funds beat the market?

b. Should the total return figures reported above be used to provide a relative performance ranking?

LEARNING OBJECTIVES

After reading this chapter you will understand:

- the basic features of stock options.

- how stock options can change the risk/return profile of a stock portfolio.

- the different stock option strategies that institutional investors use.

- the empirical evidence on whether there is a stock option strategy that consistently beats other strategies.

- the intuition behind the Black–Scholes option pricing model and its limitations.

- evidence on the pricing efficiency of the stock options market.

- products with option-like features: warrants and primes and scores.

C hapter 7 was an introduction to options contracts. In this chapter, we will look at options on individual common stocks (or, simply, stock options). We will discuss strategies that institutional investors use, and we introduce a popular model used to determine the theoretical price of a stock option, the Black–Scholes option pricing model. We also discuss two option-related products, warrants and primes/scores.

While the most important use of options is to alter return distributions to satisfy particular investment objectives, investors also have tried to use the options market to generate abnormal returns.[1] We review the evidence on stock option strategies, focusing on two critical empirical questions. First, is there, as often suggested in promotional literature, an option strategy that outperforms other option and stock strategies? Second, is the market for stock options efficient?

EXCHANGE-TRADED OPTIONS

Options were traded only in the over-the-counter market until 1973. In 1973, the Securities and Exchange Commission (SEC) authorized the establishment of a "pilot" program for the trading of options on organized exchanges. On February 1, 1973, the Chicago Board Options Exchange (CBOE) was granted permission by the SEC to register as a national securities exchange so that the CBOE could be used to "test the market" for the trading of listed options on common stock. Trading on call options on common stock began on the CBOE in April 1973. Since 1973, the SEC has granted permission to other exchanges to trade options: the American Stock Exchange in 1974, the Philadelphia Exchange in 1975, the Pacific and the Midwest Stock Exchanges in 1976, and the New York Stock Exchange in 1982. SEC permission to trade put options on common stocks on organized exchanges was not granted until March 1977.

The SEC did not grant permission to trade options without extensive investigation. Public hearings were held in February of 1974 to address several questions concerning options: (1) did they serve a useful economic role, (2) are they in the public interest, and (3) what impact would listed options have on the trading habits of the investing public. The evidence presented at the hearings supported the view that listed option trading would benefit the financial markets and the economy.

The SEC was concerned about the listing of options on the same common stock on more than one exchange, so it recommended that (1) options terms and conditions be standardized, (2) a common clearing system be established,

---

[1] Abnormal returns are defined in Chapter 8.

and (3) a common tape for recording transactions in listed options be developed. The SEC approved the creation of a national clearing system for options, the Options Clearing Corporation (OCC), established jointly at the time by the CBOE and the American Stock Exchange. Since its establishment in 1974, the OCC issues, guarantees, registers, clears, and settles all transactions involving listed options on all exchanges.

As the listed options market grew, evidence of manipulative practices and fraudulent and deceptive selling practices was found. In July 1977 the SEC imposed a moratorium on the listing of additional options until it could study the matter further. The *Options Study* began in October 1977 to "determine whether standardized options trading is occurring in a manner and in an environment which is consistent with fair and orderly markets, the public interest, the protection of investors, and other objectives of the Act."[2] The study addresses what, if any, steps the SEC should take to protect investors from abusive practices. Among its key recommendations were procedures to improve market surveillance in order to detect manipulative practices and policies that the exchanges and brokerage firms should implement to improve the caliber of brokers selling options and prevent abusive selling practices. The SEC worked with several groups to implement its recommendations.

In March 1980, the SEC was satisfied that the major regulatory deficiency it cited in the *Options Study* had been adequately addressed, and it lifted the moratorium on expansion of the listed options markets and granted permission to list options on the other financial products discussed in the next chapter and Chapters 19 and 21. While the ending of the moratorium did allow the four exchanges that were approved for trading options to list options on more companies, the SEC did not allow the multiple listing of options. That is, the SEC did not allow the listing of an option on the same underlying common stock on more than one exchange. Instead, the SEC worked out a mechanism for allocating options on stocks among the four exchanges. These rules on multiple listing were subsequently changed. Effective January 1990, any exchange could list any new stock and ten stocks from other exchanges. Effective January 1991, any exchange can list options on any stock eligible for option trading.

Exchange-traded stock options are for 100 shares of the designated common stock. While most underlying stocks are those of listed companies, stock options on a number of over-the-counter stocks are also available.

The Options Clearing Corporation has established standard strike price guidelines for listed options. For stocks with a price above $100, strike prices are set at $10 intervals; for stocks with a price below $100 and above $30, strike prices are set at $5 intervals; and for stocks priced between $10 and $30 the

---

[2] Securities Exchange Act Release No. 14056 (October 17, 1977).

interval is $2.50. While the strike price is not changed because of cash dividends paid to common stockholders, for exchange-traded options the strike price is adjusted for stock splits, stock dividends, reorganization, and other recapitalizations.

All exchange-traded stock options in the U.S. may be exercised any time before the expiration date; that is, they are American options. They expire at 11:59 p.m. Eastern Standard Time on the Saturday following the third Friday of the expiration month. To exercise an expiring option, exchange rules provide that the owner of the option instruct his or her broker to do so no later than 5:30 p.m. Eastern time on the business day immediately preceding the expiration date. Notices to exercise a non-expiring option (i.e., on a date other than the expiration date) must be made between 10 a.m. and 8:00 p.m. Eastern Standard Time. When a non-expiring option is exercised, the OCC assigns it the next day to someone who has written the option; assignment is on a random basis.

Options are designated by the name of the underlying common stock, the expiration month, the strike price, and the type of option (put or call). Thus, an IBM call option with a strike price of 115 and expiring in October is referred to as the "IBM October 115 call."

STOCK OPTION PRICING MODELS

In our Chapter 7 introduction to option pricing, we explained the factors that influence the price of an option and that a lower boundary for the option price can be determined based only on arbitrage arguments. We also set forth the basic principle behind an option pricing model. Here we provide more detailed discussion of option pricing models.

Black–Scholes Option Pricing Model

Arbitrage conditions provide boundaries for option prices, but to identify investment opportunities and construct portfolios to satisfy their investment objectives, investors want an exact price for an option. By imposing certain assumptions (to be discussed later) and using arbitrage arguments, Black and Scholes developed the formula given below to compute the fair (or theoretical) price of a European call option on a non-dividend-paying stock:[3]

$$C = SN(d_1) - Xe^{-rt} N(d_2)$$

---

[3] Fischer Black and Myron Scholes, "The Pricing of Options and Corporate Liabilities," *Journal of Political Economy* 81 (May 1973), pp. 637–654.

where $d_1 = \dfrac{\ln\,(S/X)\,+\,(r\,+\,0.5s^2)t}{s\sqrt{t}}$

$d_2 = d_1 - s\sqrt{t}$

C = call option price

S = current stock price

X = exercise price

r = short-term risk-free interest rate

e = 2.718 (natural antilog of 1)

t = time remaining to the expiration date (measured as a fraction of a year)

s = standard deviation of the stock price

$N(.)$ = the cumulative probability density. The value for $N(.)$ is obtained from a normal distribution function that is tabulated in most statistics textbooks.

Notice that five of the factors that we said in Chapter 7 influence the price of an option are included in the formula. (The sixth factor, anticipated cash dividends, is not included because the model is for a non-dividend-paying stock.) In the Black–Scholes model, the direction of the influence of each of these factors is the same as stated in Chapter 7. Four of the factors—strike price, stock price, time to expiration, and risk-free interest rate—are easily observed. The standard deviation of the stock price must be estimated.

The option price derived from the Black–Scholes option pricing model is "fair" in the sense that if any other price existed, it would be possible to earn riskless arbitrage profits by taking an offsetting position in the underlying stock. That is, if the price of the call option in the market is higher than that derived from the Black–Scholes option pricing model, an investor could sell the call option and buy a certain number of shares in the underlying stock.[4] If the reverse is true, that is, the market price of the call option is less than the "fair" price derived from the model, the investor could buy the call option and sell short a certain number of shares in the underlying stock. This process of hedging by taking a position in the underlying stock allows the investor to lock in the riskless arbitrage profit. The number of shares necessary to hedge the position changes as the factors that affect the option price change, so the hedged position must be changed constantly.

Figures 9-1 and 9-2 provide illustrations to demonstrate calculation of the

---

[4] The number of shares will not necessarily be equal to the number of shares underlying the call option. The reason is that the change in the value of the call price generally will be less than the change in the stock price. In the Black–Scholes model, the number of shares is given by the function $N(d_1)$.

FIGURE 9-1
First Illustration of Black–Scholes Option Pricing Model

Call option:
    Strike price = \$45
    Time remaining to expiration = 183 days

Current stock price = \$47
Expected price volatility = standard deviation = 25%
Risk-free rate = 6%

Therefore:

    $S = 47$
    $X = 45$
    $t = 0.5$ (183 days/365, rounded)
    $s = 0.25$
    $r = 0.06$

The call option price (C) is found as follows:

$$C = SN(d_1) - Xe^{-rt} N(d_2)$$

$$d_1 = \frac{\ln{(S/X)} + (r + 0.5\ s^2)t}{s\sqrt{t}}$$

Substituting:

$$d_1 = \frac{\ln{(47/45)} + (0.06 + 0.5\ [0.25]^2)\ 0.5}{0.25\ \sqrt{0.5}}$$

$$= 0.61722$$

$$d_2 = d_1 - s\sqrt{t}$$

Substituting:

$$d_2 = 0.61722 - 0.25\ \sqrt{0.5}$$

$$= 0.440443$$

From a normal distribution table:

    $N(0.617) = 0.7324$ and $N(0.440) = 0.6700$

Then:

$$C = 47\ (0.7324) - 45\ (e^{-(0.06)(0.5)})\ (0.67)$$

$$= \$5.74$$

FIGURE 9-2
Second Illustration of Black–Scholes Option Pricing Model

Call option:
  Strike price = $45
  Time remaining to expiration = 183 days

Current stock price = $47
Expected price volatility = standard deviation = 40%
Risk-free rate = 6%

All the values except the expected price volatility are the same as in Figure 9-1.

Therefore:

  $S = 47$
  $X = 45$
  $t = 0.5$ (183 days/365, rounded)
  $s = 0.40$
  $r = 0.06$

Then:

$$d_1 = \frac{\ln (S/X) + (r + 0.5\ s^2)t}{s\sqrt{t}}$$

Substituting:

$$d_1 = \frac{\ln (47/45) + (0.06 + 0.5\ [0.40]^2)\ 0.5}{0.40\ \sqrt{0.5}}$$

$$= 0.471941$$

$$d_2 = d_1 - s\sqrt{t}$$

Substituting:

$$d_2 = 0.471941 - 0.40\ \sqrt{0.5}$$

$$= 0.189098$$

From a normal distribution table:

  $N(0.472) = 0.6808$ and $N(0.189) = 0.5753$

Then:

$$C = 47\ (0.6808) - 45\ (e^{-(0.06)(0.5)})\ (0.5753)$$

$$= \$7.37$$

fair value of a call option using the Black–Scholes option pricing model.[5] The two illustrations differ only in the assumption made about the volatility (variance) of the price of the underlying stock. Notice that with the higher assumed volatility, the price of the call option is greater. The higher the expected price volatility of the underlying stock price, the higher the price of a call option.

Table 9-1 shows the option value as calculated from the Black–Scholes option pricing model for different assumptions concerning (1) the standard deviation, (2) the risk-free rate, and (3) the time remaining to expiration. Notice that: (1) the lower (higher) the volatility, the lower (higher) the option price; (2) the lower (higher) the risk-free rate, the lower (higher) the option price; and (3) the shorter (longer) the time remaining to expiration, the lower (higher) the option price. All of this agrees with what we stated in Chapter 7 as to the effect of a change in one of the factors on the price of a call option.

We have focused our attention on call options. How do we value put options? Recall from Chapter 7 that the put–call parity relationship indicates the relationship among the price of the common stock, the call option price, and the put option price. If we can calculate the fair value of a call option, the fair value of a put with the same strike price and expiration on the same stock can be calculated from the put–call parity relationship.

Assumptions Underlying the Black–Scholes Model and Extensions

The Black–Scholes model is based on several restrictive assumptions. These assumptions were necessary to develop the hedge to realize riskless arbitrage profits if the market price of the call option deviates from the price obtained from the model. Let's look at these assumptions, along with extensions of the basic model.

The Option Is a European Option. The Black–Scholes model assumes that the call option is a European call option. Because the Black–Scholes model is on a non-dividend-paying stock, early exercise of an option will not be economic because by selling rather than exercising the call option, the option holder can recoup the time value. The binomial option pricing model, also known as the Cox–Rubinstein–Ross model, can easily handle American call

---

[5] The call option values calculated in Figures 9-1 and 9-2 are off slightly because approximate values are used for the cumulative normal distribution table. The exact option values are $5.70 when the standard deviation is 25% and $7.43 when the standard deviation is 40%.

| TABLE 9-1 | COMPARISON OF BLACK–SCHOLES CALL OPTION PRICE VARYING ONE FACTOR AT A TIME |

BASE CASE

Call option:
    Strike price = $45
    Time remaining to expiration = 183 days
Current stock price = $47
Expected price volatility = standard deviation = 25%
Risk-free rate = 10%

HOLDING ALL FACTORS CONSTANT EXCEPT EXPECTED PRICE VOLATILITY

EXPECTED PRICE VOLATILITY	CALL OPTION PRICE
15%	4.69
20	5.17
25 (base case)	5.74
30	6.26
35	6.84
40	7.37

HOLDING ALL FACTORS CONSTANT EXCEPT THE RISK-FREE RATE

RISK-FREE INTEREST RATE	CALL OPTION PRICE
7%	5.27
8	5.41
9	5.50
10 (base case)	5.74
11	5.84
12	5.99
13	6.13

HOLDING ALL FACTORS CONSTANT EXCEPT TIME REMAINING TO EXPIRATION

TIME REMAINING TO EXPIRATION	CALL OPTION PRICE
30 days	2.85
60	3.52
91	4.15
183 (base case)	5.74
273	6.99

options.[6] (See Chapter 7 for the basic principle of this model.) The fair value of the option in the case of a binomial option pricing model cannot be given by a formula but requires an iterative process.

Variance of the Stock Price.   The Black–Scholes model assumes that the variance of the stock price is (1) constant over the life of the option, and (2) known with certainty. If (1) does not hold, an option pricing model can be developed that allows the variance to change. The violation of (2), however, is more serious. As the Black–Scholes model depends on the riskless hedge argument, and, in turn, the variance must be known to construct the proper hedge, if the variance is not known, the hedge will not be riskless.

Stochastic Process Generating Stock Prices.   To derive an option pricing model, an assumption is needed about the way stock prices move. The Black–Scholes model is based on the assumption that stock prices are generated by one kind of stochastic (random) process called a *diffusion process*. In a diffusion process, the stock price can take on any positive value, but when it moves from one price to another, it must take on all values in between. That is, the stock price does not jump from one stock price to another, skipping over interim prices. An alternative assumption is that stock prices follow a *jump process;* that is, prices are not continuous and smooth but do jump from one price across intervening values to the next. Merton[7] and Cox and Ross[8] have developed option pricing models assuming a jump process, which is more realistic.

Risk-Free Interest Rate.   In deriving the Black–Scholes model two assumptions were made about the risk-free interest rate. First, it was assumed that the interest rates for borrowing and lending were the same. Second, it was assumed that the interest rate was constant and known over the life of the option. The first assumption is unlikely to hold because borrowing rates are higher than lending rates. The effect on the Black–Scholes model is that the option price will be bounded between the call price derived from the model using the two interest rates. The model can handle the second assumption by

---

[6] John C. Cox, Stephen A. Ross, and Mark Rubinstein, "Option Pricing: A Simplified Approach," *Journal of Financial Economics,* 7, 1979, pp. 229–263.

[7] Robert Merton, "The Theory of Rational Option Pricing," *Bell Journal of Economics and Management Science,* 4 (Spring 1973), pp. 141–183.

[8] John C. Cox and Stephen A. Ross, "The Valuation of Options for Alternative Stochastic Processes," *Journal of Financial Economics* 3 (March 1976), pp. 145–166.

replacing the risk-free rate over the life of the option by the geometric average of the period returns expected over the life of the option.[9]

Dividends.   The original Black–Scholes model is for a non-dividend-paying stock. In the case of a dividend-paying stock, it may be advantageous for the holder of the call option to exercise the option early. To understand why, suppose that a stock pays a dividend such that, if the call option is exercised, dividends would be received prior to the option's expiration date. If the dividends plus the accrued interest earned from investing the dividends from the time they are received until the expiration date are greater than the time premium of the option, then it would be optimal to exercise the option.[10] In the case where dividends are not known with certainty, it will not be possible to develop a model using the riskless arbitrage argument.

In the case of known dividends, a shortcut to adjust the Black–Scholes model is to reduce the stock price by the present value of the dividends. Black has suggested an approximation technique to value a call option for a dividend-paying stock.[11] A more accurate model for pricing call options in the case of known dividends has been developed by Roll,[12] Geske,[13] and Whaley.[14]

Taxes and Transactions Costs.   The Black–Scholes model ignores taxes and transactions costs. The model can be modified to account for taxes, but the problem is that there is not one unique tax rate. Transactions costs include both commissions and the bid–ask spreads for the stock and the option, as well as other costs associated with trading options.

---

[9] Returns on short-term Treasury bills cannot be known with certainty over the *long* term; only the *expected* return is known, and there is a variance around it. The effects of variable interest rates are considered in Merton, ''The Theory of Rational Option Pricing,'' op. cit.

[10] Recall from Chapter 7 that the time premium is the excess of the option price over its intrinsic value.

[11] See Fischer Black, ''Fact and Fantasy in the Use of Options,'' *Financial Analysts Journal* (July–August 1975), pp. 36–41, 61–72. The approach requires that the investor at the time of purchase of the call option and for every subsequent period specify the exact date the option will be exercised.

[12] Richard Roll, ''An Analytic Formula for Unprotected American Call Options on Stocks with Known Dividends,'' *Journal of Financial Economics* (November 1977), pp. 251–258.

[13] Robert Geske, ''A Note on an Analytical Formula for Unprotected American Call Options on Stocks with Known Dividends,'' *Journal of Financial Economics* (December 1979), pp. 375–380, and Robert Geske, ''Comment on Whaley's Note,'' *Journal of Financial Economics* (June 1981), pp. 213–215.

[14] Robert Whaley, ''On the Valuation of American Call Options on Stocks with Known Dividends,'' *Journal of Financial Economics* (June 1981), pp. 207–211.

OPTION STRATEGIES

Naked Strategies

There are four basic option strategies: (1) long call strategy (buying call options), (2) short call strategy (selling or writing call options), (3) long put strategy (buying put options), and (4) short put strategy (selling or writing put options). We illustrated the risk–reward characteristics of these four strategies in Chapter 7; they are usually referred to as positions. By themselves these positions are called *naked* strategies because they do not involve an offsetting or risk-reducing position in another option or the underlying common stock.

The profit and loss from each strategy depends on the price of the underlying asset, in our case common stock, at the expiration date (on the assumption that the option is not exercised or sold earlier). The most that the option buyer can lose with each strategy is the option price. At the same time, the option buyer preserves the benefits of a favorable price movement of the underlying asset (a price increase for a call option and a price decline for a put option) reduced by the option price. By contrast, the maximum profit that the option writer can realize is the option price, while remaining exposed to all the risks associated with an unfavorable price movement.

The long call strategy (buying call options) is the most straightforward option strategy for taking advantage of an anticipated increase in the stock price, while at the same time limiting the maximum loss to the option price. The speculative appeal of call options is that they provide an investor with the opportunity to capture the price action of more shares of common stock for a given number of dollars available for investment. An investor who believes that the price of some common stock will decrease or change very little can, if the expectation is correct, realize income by writing (selling) a call option (following a short call strategy). The profit and loss of the option writer is the mirror image of the option buyer's.

The most straightforward option strategy for benefiting from an expected decrease in the price of some common stock, while avoiding the unfavorable consequences should the price rise, is to follow a long put strategy (buying put options). The short put strategy (selling put options) is employed if the investor expects that the price of a stock will increase or stay the same. The maximum profit from this strategy is the option price. The maximum loss for the short put strategy will occur if the price of the stock declines to zero at or before the expiration date.

Individual investors and institutional investors use at least two other naked option strategies: (1) the long call/paper buying strategy, and (2) the cash-secured put writing strategy.

Long Call/Paper Buying Strategy.   This naked strategy involves allocating a portion of a portfolio's funds to purchase a call option and investing the balance of the funds in a risk-free or low-risk money market instrument[15] such as Treasury bills or commercial paper.[16] This strategy is less risky than allocating all the portfolio's funds to stocks. The long call option allows the investor to participate in any stock price increase. The funds invested in the risk-free or low-risk money market instrument provide a cushion against any stock price decline.

Cash-Secured Put Writing Strategy.   If an investor wants to purchase a stock at a price less than the prevailing market price, one way is to place a limit buy order—of course, the result may be that the order never gets placed.[17] Alternatively, the investor can use the options market to accomplish effectively the same thing: write a put option with a strike price near the desired price. Sufficient funds are then placed in escrow to satisfy the investor's obligation if the buyer of the put option exercises the option.

Covered (Hedge) Strategies

In contrast to naked option strategies, *covered or hedge strategies* involve a position in an option and a position in the underlying stock. The aim is for one position to help offset any unfavorable price movement in the other position. The two popular covered or hedge strategies that we discuss and for which we give empirical evidence later in this chapter are: (1) the covered call writing strategy, and (2) the protective put buying strategy.

Covered Call Writing Strategy.   A covered call writing strategy involves writing a call option on stocks in the portfolio. That is, the investor takes a short position in a call option and a long position in the underlying stock. If the price of the stock declines, there will be a loss on the long stock position. However, the income generated from the sale of the call option will either (1) fully offset, (2) partially offset, or (3) more than offset the loss in the long stock position so as to generate a profit.

To illustrate, suppose that a money manager holds 100 shares of XYZ Corporation and that the current price of a share is $100. The total value of the

---

[15] Money market instruments are the subject of Chapter 13.

[16] While this strategy involves investing in some risk-free or low-risk money market instrument, it does not involve a long or short position in the stock. For this reason, it is still classified as a naked option strategy.

[17] Limit buy orders are explained in the previous chapter.

portfolio is $10,000. Also suppose that a call option on 100 shares of XYZ with a $100 strike price that expires in three months can be sold for $700. (The option is at the money because the strike price is equal to the current price of the stock.) If the money manager has decided to hold the 100 shares and write one call option (each call option is for 100 shares of the underlying stock), the profit or loss for this strategy will depend on the price of XYZ stock at the expiration date. One of the following outcomes will occur:

1. If the price of XYZ stock is greater than $100, the call option buyer will exercise the option and pay the option writer $100 per share. The 100 shares in the portfolio are exchanged for $10,000. The value of the portfolio at the expiration date is then $10,700 ($10,000 received from the option buyer exercising the option plus $700 received from writing the call option). In fact, more than $10,700 will be in the portfolio if the $700 is invested when it is received. At a minimum, though, the profit from this strategy if the price of XYZ stock is greater than $100 is $700, the option price. If the price of XYZ stock rises above $107, however, there will also be an opportunity loss equal to the excess of the value of the stock over $10,700.

2. If the price of XYZ stock is equal to $100 at the expiration date, the call option buyer will not exercise the option. The value of the portfolio will still be at least $10,700: 100 shares of XYZ with a market value of $100 per share and the proceeds of $700 received from writing the call option.

3. If the price of XYZ stock is less than $100 but greater than $93, there will be a profit but it will be less than $700. For example, suppose that the price of the stock is $96. The long stock position will have a value of $9,600 while the short call position will have a value of $700. The portfolio value is therefore $10,300, resulting in a profit of $300.

4. At a price of $93, the long stock position will have a value of $9,300 and the short call position will have a value of $700, resulting in no profit or loss, as the portfolio value is $10,000.

5. Should the price of XYZ stock be less than $93 at expiration, the portfolio will realize a loss. For example, suppose that the price of the stock at expiration is $88. The portfolio value will be $9,500: the long stock position will be worth $8,800 and the short call position will have produced $700. Hence, there is a loss of $500. The worst case is if the price of XYZ stock declines to zero. This would result in a portfolio value of $700 and a loss of $9,300.

The profit and loss profile for this covered call writing strategy is graphically portrayed in Figure 9-3. There are two important points to note in this illustration. First, this strategy has allowed the investor to reduce the

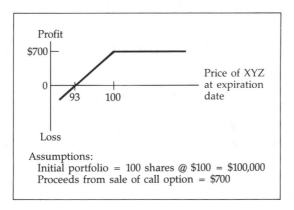

Profit

$700

0

93   100

Loss

Price of XYZ
at expiration
date

Assumptions:
Initial portfolio = 100 shares @ $100 = $100,000
Proceeds from sale of call option = $700

FIGURE 9-3
Profit/Loss Profile for a
Covered Call Writing Position

downside risk for the portfolio. In this example, for the at-the-money call option, the risk is reduced by an amount equal to the option price. In exchange for this reduction of downside risk, the investor has agreed to cap the potential profit. For the at-the-money option used in our illustration, the maximum profit is the option price.

The second point can be seen by comparing Figure 7-4 (page 200) with Figure 9-3. Notice that the shape of the two profit and loss profiles is the same. That is, the covered call writing strategy has the same profit and loss profile as a naked short put strategy. Indeed, in our example, the covered call writing strategy has the same profit and loss outcome as writing a put on 100 shares of XYZ stock with a strike price of $100 and three months to expiration (provided the price of the call and put options are the same). This is not an accident. As we explained in Chapter 7, portfolios with equivalent payoffs can be constructed with different positions in options and the underlying instrument. A covered call writing position is equivalent to a long position in the stock and a short call position, and a long position in a stock and a short position in a call will have a similar payoff to a short put position.

Protective Put Buying Strategy.   An investor may want to protect the value of a stock held in the portfolio against the risk of a decline in market value. A way of doing this with options is to buy a put option on that stock. By doing so, the investor is guaranteed the strike price of the put option less the cost of the option. Should the stock price rise rather than decline, the investor is able to participate in the price increase, with the profit reduced by the cost of the option. This strategy is called a *protective put buying strategy;* it involves a long put position (buying a put option) and a long position in the underlying stock that is held in the portfolio.

As an illustration, suppose that a money manager has 100 shares of XYZ stock in a portfolio and that the current market value of the stock is $100 per share (a portfolio value of $10,000). Assume further that a two-month put option selling for $500 can be purchased on 100 shares of XYZ stock with a strike price of $100. Two months from now at the expiration date the profit or loss can be summarized as follows:

1. If the price of XYZ stock is greater than $105, the investor will realize a profit from this strategy. For example, if the price is $112, the long stock position will have a value of $11,200. The cost of purchasing the put option was $500, so the value of the portfolio is $10,700, for a profit of $700.

2. If the price of XYZ stock is equal to $105, no profit or loss will be realized from this strategy.

3. There will be a loss if the price of XYZ stock is less than $105 but at least $100. For example, a price of $102 will result in a loss for this strategy of $300: a gain in the long stock position of $200 but a loss of $500 to acquire the long put position.

4. In none of the previous outcomes will the investor exercise the put option, but if the price of XYZ stock is below $100 per share, the option will be exercised. At any price below $100 per share, the investor will be assured of receiving $100 per share for the 100 shares of stock. In this case, the value of the portfolio will be $10,000 minus the cost of the option ($500), resulting in a loss of $500.

The graphical presentation of the profit and loss profile for this protective put buying strategy is shown in Figure 9-4. By implementing this strategy, the money manager has effectively assured a price of $95 per share. He has maintained all the upside potential, reduced only by the cost of the put option.

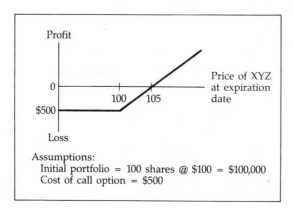

Figure 9-4
Profit/Loss Profile for a
Protective Put Buying Position

There are a wide variety of other strategies that combine two or more options on the same underlying stock. These include spread strategies (vertical spreads, horizontal spreads, diagonal spreads, and butterfly spreads) and combination strategies (the most popular of which is the straddle strategy). These strategies are discussed elsewhere in books on options strategies.

Is There a Superior Options Strategy?

The development of the options market brought with it a number of myths about strategies that were alleged to generate consistently superior returns over purchasing stocks. For example, the popular literature and advertising by the options industry has recommended that individual and institutional investors follow a covered call strategy that could be expected to generate "extra return" from the income received by selling (writing) a call option on stocks held in their portfolio. The proliferation of this popular literature and misleading advertisements led Fischer Black to write: "For every fact about options, there is a fantasy—a reason given for trading or not trading in options that doesn't make sense when examined carefully."[18]

Is there indeed an options strategy that has consistently outperformed a simple strategy of buying common stocks? Here we will examine the empirical evidence on this issue.

Call Option Strategies.   There have been several studies that have empirically examined whether there are call option strategies that might provide superior risk-adjusted returns. The first major study was by Merton, Scholes, and Gladstein (MSG hereafter).[19] Using simulation analysis, they examined the risk and return patterns of the covered call writing and long call/paper buying strategies discussed earlier.[20] These strategies are examined not for a single stock option position but for portfolios of option positions.

The simulation analysis is based on two samples of underlying stocks: (1) the 136 stocks on which listed options were available as of December 1975, and (2) the 30 stocks included in the Dow Jones Industrial Average (DJIA). The time period over which the simulations were performed was July 1, 1963,

---

[18] Black, "Fact and Fantasy in the Use of Options," *op. cit.*, p. 36.

[19] Robert C. Merton, Myron S. Scholes, and Matthew L. Gladstein, "The Return and Risk of Alternative Call Option Portfolio Investment Strategies," *Journal of Business*, Vol. 51, No. 2, 1978, pp. 183–243.

[20] For a critique of the simulation approach and an alternative approach to testing performance of various option strategies, see Gary L. Gastineau, *The Options Manual* (New York: McGraw-Hill, 1988, Third Edition).

through December 31, 1975, an interval of 12.5 years. This time interval encompassed a variety of market environments (bull and bear markets, high and low volatility). The simulations were performed using six-month holding periods. For the two call option strategies investigated, the option prices used in the simulations were calculated from the Black–Scholes model adjusted for dividends. That is, the prices are theoretical prices not actual (observed) prices.[21] Transactions costs and taxes were ignored in all simulations.

The findings do not support the claims of those who preach that a covered call strategy can generate "extra return" for investors. As for the long call/paper buying strategy, there are instances where this strategy clearly outperformed the long stock strategy, as the average return was higher and the risk was lower. Consequently, for the period investigated and according to the assumptions employed, the MSG study suggests that it may have been possible to earn superior returns from a long call/paper buying strategy.[22]

While there have been no other comprehensive studies of the long call/paper buying strategy, there have been other studies of covered call writing strategies because this is the strategy most widely used by most institutional investors. Pounds studied the eight-year period 1969 to 1976 for a sample of 43 stocks with listed call options.[23] Theoretical rather than actual prices again are used, but in this study commissions are considered.

Pounds finds that at-the-money and in-the-money covered call option strategies outperformed the long stock position.[24] Does this mean that a covered call strategy is superior to a long stock strategy? As Pounds points out, it is not possible to make this inference because the market did not rise during his study period. Consequently, a flat or declining market would favor a covered call writing strategy. When he investigated subperiods when the market increased within his eight-year study period, he found that the long stock portfolio outperformed all the covered call option strategies.

Is there a superior covered call option strategy according to Pounds's results? He argues that the out-of-the-money covered call strategy gives the best results and the in-the-money covered call strategy the worst results because there is a substantial reduction in risk. While this may be true for the

---

[21] For part of their study, MSG use actual rather than theoretical prices; results did not differ significantly.

[22] MSG do suggest several possible explanations for the superior performance of the long call/paper buying strategy.

[23] Henry M. Pounds, "Covered Call Options Writing: Strategies and Results," *Journal of Portfolio Management* (Winter 1978), pp. 31–42.

[24] The average return was greater and the standard deviation lower. The out-of-the-money call option had a slightly lower average return but a substantially lower standard deviation.

entire period, for subperiods writing out-of-the-money call options resulted in better performance only when stock prices did not rise. Otherwise, the in-the-money covered call writing strategy performed better.

Yates and Kopprasch also investigated the covered call writing strategy, but using actual call option prices for the July 1973–July 1980 period.[25] They constructed an index, Institutional Option Writers Index (IOWI), that institutions could use to measure their option-writing performance. The underlying portfolio for the index was constructed by using all stocks with listed CBOE call options in the January, April, July, and October expiration cycle. Commissions were not considered.

The results of this study lend support to the position that the covered call writing strategy would have outperformed the S&P 500 and the underlying portfolio over the entire time period. While it is expected that the covered call strategy would have outperformed the long stock strategies during down markets, results indicate that the IOWI also performed well in up markets. These results, as well as others reported by Yates and Kopprasch, are at variance with those of MSG and Pounds.

Put Option Strategies.   In a follow-up study to their call option strategies, Merton, Scholes, and Gladstein investigate the risk/return patterns of two put option strategies: (1) uncovered (or "naked") put option writing, and (2) protective put option buying strategies.[26] The simulation period for the second study was the 14-year period from July 1, 1963, through June 30, 1977. The same two stock samples used in their previous study were investigated. As theory would predict, they found that (1) compared to the fully covered call writing strategy, the uncovered put writing is more conservative, and (2) both option strategies are more conservative than a long stock position. The average return for all the option strategies they report was less than that of the long stock position.

The second put option strategy simulated by MSG was the protective put strategy. In the case of protective put strategies, the standard deviation and range of returns were lower than for the long stock position. The higher the exercise price for the put option, the lower the volatility. The reduction in risk comes at the expense of a lower average return.

---

[25] James W. Yates and Robert W. Kopprasch, "Writing Covered Call Options: Profits and Risks," *Journal of Portfolio Management* (Fall 1978), pp. 74–79.

[26] Robert C. Merton, Myron S. Scholes, and Matthew L. Gladstein, "The Return and Risk of Alternative Put Option Portfolio Investment Strategies," *Journal of Business,* Vol. 55, No. 1, 1982, pp. 1–55.

Summary of Findings.   With the exception of the Yates and Kopprasch study, none of the studies cited indicates that there is a superior option strategy. The empirical evidence suggests that option strategies have investment characteristics that are consistent with the familiar trade-off between risk and return: the higher the expected return, the more the expected risk as measured by return volatility. The relative risk characteristics of the strategies described by the simulations are consistent with those that would be expected from the risk/return characteristics of the portfolio. This view is best summarized by MSG in their conclusion to the first study:

> The specific *levels* of the returns generated, however, are strongly dependent on the actual experience of the underlying stocks during the simulation period. To avoid the creation of new myths about option strategies, the reader is warned not to infer from our findings that any one of the strategies is superior to the others for all investors. *Indeed, if options and their underlying stocks are correctly priced, then there is no single best strategy for all investors.*[27]

The last sentence is particularly noteworthy. In a market that prices options fairly, there should be no options strategy that is superior. We turn next to the question of whether options are fairly priced.

PRICING EFFICIENCY OF THE STOCK OPTIONS MARKET

A market is said to be efficient if investors cannot earn abnormal returns after accounting for risk and transactions costs. In Chapter 8 we discussed the problems associated with testing for the pricing efficiency of the stock market. Here we focus on tests of the pricing efficiency of the market for stock options.

A problem encountered by researchers in this area is that tests require information on the price of two instruments at the exact same time—the stock price and the option price. When prices are available on both assets at the same time, the data are said to be synchronous. In empirical tests, prices used may be non-synchronous because of data availability limitations. That is, the stock price used in a study may be the closing price for the day, while the

---

[27] Merton, Scholes, and Gladstein, "The Return and Risk of Alternative Call Option Portfolio Investment Strategies," p. 184.

option price may be the price at the beginning of the same trading day. An empirical study that finds abnormal trading profits using non-synchronous data does not necessarily indicate that the options market is inefficient.

Beyond the problem of non-synchronous data, there is the problem of determining the fair price of an option to be used in the empirical tests. Thus, researchers must rely on some option pricing model, which makes the findings only as good as the option pricing model employed.

Tests of market efficiency fall into two categories. The first category is tests using no option pricing model. Instead, violations of boundary conditions or violations of put–call parity are examined to determine if abnormal trading profits are possible. The second set of tests employ various option pricing models to assess whether mispriced options can be identified and exploited using the riskless hedge strategy.

Tests Not Based on an Option Pricing Model

Boundary conditions for the price of an option can be determined. Violations of boundary conditions may permit an investor to earn abnormal profits. Also, there is a relationship between put and call prices that must hold. Violations of the put–call parity relationship may permit an investor to earn a return in excess of the riskless interest rate.

There are two studies that have examined pricing efficiency in the U.S. stock options market using boundary conditions for call option prices. A finding that a boundary condition is violated is not sufficient to argue that the market is inefficient. It is also necessary to test whether profits can be generated from trading strategies based on any violations.

The first is a study by Galai based on daily closing prices of options traded on the Chicago Board Options Exchange between April and October 1973, the first six months of the operation of this exchange.[28] The empirical test was for the lower boundary for a call option of a dividend-paying stock. Galai does find violations of the lower boundary condition. Arbitrage trading based on these violations could have generated small profits. A study by Bhattacharya using transactions data for options traded on the CBOE finds that, when transactions costs are accounted for, profits resulting from arbitrage trading when boundary violations occurred disappear.[29]

---

[28] Dan Galai, "Tests of Market Efficiency and the Chicago Board Options Exchange," *Journal of Business* 50 (1970), pp. 167–197.

[29] Mihtu Bhattacharya, "Transactions Data Tests of Efficiency of the Chicago Board Options Exchange," *Journal of Financial Economics*, 12 (August 1983), pp. 161–165.

If the put–call parity relationship is violated, it is possible for investors to create a riskless hedge to produce a return in excess of the riskless interest rate. There have been two studies of market efficiency based on violations of the put–call parity relationship for *listed* options.[30]

Klemkosky and Resnick examined 606 riskless hedges for 15 companies having both put and call options listed on the Chicago Board Options Exchange, American Stock Exchange, and Philadelphia Stock Exchange between July 1977 and June 1978.[31] Of the 606 hedges examined, 540 were riskless hedges in that conditions were such that there would be no rational early exercise of the call option. Of these riskless hedges, 306 were unprofitable *ex post*, while 234 where profitable *ex post*. After considering transactions costs of $20 for a member firm to obtain a round lot position in a hedge, only 147 turned out profitable. The authors conclude: "The empirical results of the models tests are consistent with put–call parity theory and thus support this aspect of efficiency for the registered options markets. The small degree of inefficiency detected appears to be the result of overpriced calls."[32]

In a follow-up study, Klemkosky and Resnick further investigate the hedges that produced profitable returns.[33] Specifically, they constructed hedges 5 and 15 minutes after a hedge was initially identified as having an *ex ante* return greater than $20. The purpose was to test the relationship on an *ex ante* basis by employing the *ex post* results as information from which to construct the hedge. They find that (1) *ex ante* profitability was less than the *ex post* profitability, and (2) the prices adjust rapidly enough to eliminate most if not all of the abnormal profit.

Tests Based on Option Pricing Models

Tests of market efficiency based on an option pricing model involve two steps. First, a model is used to identify under- or overvalued options. There are two approaches to identifying a mispriced option. Rather than computing a theoretical option price for comparison to the market price, an implied volatility can be calculated. How is this done? Recall from our discussion of

---

[30] There have been two studies on over-the-counter options investigating put–call parity: Hans Stoll, "The Relationship between Put and Call Option Prices," *Journal of Finance* (December 1969), pp. 801–824, and J. Gould and Dan Galai, "Transactions Costs and the Relationship between Put and Call Prices," *Journal of Financial Economics* (July 1974), pp. 105–130.

[31] Robert C. Klemkosky and Bruce G. Resnick, "Put–Call Parity and Market Efficiency," *Journal of Finance* (December 1979), pp. 1141–1155.

[32] Klemkosky and Resnick, ibid., p. 1154.

[33] Robert C. Klemkosky and Bruce G. Resnick, "An Ex Ante Analysis of Put–Call Parity," *Journal of Financial Economics*, 8 (1980), pp. 363–378.

the factors that determine the price of an option that, with the exception of expected price volatility, the other factors are known, and of course the market price of the option can be observed. The volatility consistent with the observations and the option pricing model can be calculated. This is called the *implied volatility*. The other approach to identifying a mispriced option calls for comparing the implied volatility to the historical volatility. An option is assumed to be overvalued (undervalued) if the implied volatility is greater (less) than historical volatility (assuming true volatility is constant).

The second step is to create a hedged position to exploit any option that is identified as mispriced and determine if it is sufficiently mispriced to produce a return greater than the risk-free rate. (Remember that the position created is a hedged portfolio, which means its return should be a risk-free rate.)

The first study examining market efficiency using an option pricing model is that performed by Black and Scholes.[34] Using the option pricing model they developed, they could not reject the hypothesis that the market is efficient. Galai, however, did detect evidence of market inefficiency.[35] Stronger evidence of market inefficiency was found by Trippi[36] and Chiras and Manaster,[37] using implied volatility. Both studies found there were trading strategies that could produce abnormally high returns.

A criticism of the Trippi and Chiras and Manaster studies is that these researchers failed to take transactions costs into consideration. In the options market, transactions costs include: (1) floor trading and clearing costs, (2) any state transfer tax that might be imposed, (3) SEC transactions fee, (4) margin requirements, (5) net capital charges, and (6) bid-ask spreads. The magnitude of these costs needs to be considered in empirical studies that investigate market efficiency. These costs vary for market makers, arbitrageurs, and individuals in the options markets, so the market may be efficient for one type of market participant but not another.

Phillips and Smith have examined these transactions costs and then adjusted the Trippi and Chiras and Manaster studies to account for them.[38]

---

[34] Fischer and Black and Myron Scholes, "The Valuation of Option Contracts and a Test of Market Efficiency," *Journal of Finance* (May 1972), pp. 399–417.

[35] Dan Galai, "Empirical Tests of Boundary Conditions for CBOE Options," *Journal of Financial Economics* 6 (1978), pp. 187–211.

[36] Robert Trippi, "A Test of Option Market Efficiency Using a Random-Walk Valuation Model," *Journal of Economics and Business* 29 (1977), pp. 93–98.

[37] Donald Chiras and Steven Manaster, "The Information Content of Option Prices and a Test of Market Efficiency," *Journal of Financial Economics* 6 (1978), pp. 213–234.

[38] Susan M. Phillips and Clifford W. Smith, "Trading Costs for Listed Options: Implications for Market Efficiency," *Journal of Financial Economics* 8 (1980), pp. 179–201.

After making the adjustment, they find that abnormally high returns were eliminated. Thus, the hypothesis that the option market is efficient is supported.

Finally, Blomeyer and Klemkosky used transaction-by-transaction option and price data (thereby overcoming the problem of non-synchronous data) and two option pricing models to calculate implied volatility to test the efficiency of the market.[39] Unlike Trippi and Chiras and Manaster, Blomeyer and Klemkosky considered transactions costs as suggested by Phillips and Smith. In the absence of transactions costs, they found abnormal returns; after considering transactions costs, abnormal returns were eliminated.

All these empirical studies are based on either historical volatility or implied volatility. An investor who consistently does a better job of estimating volatility than other market participants can realize abnormal returns in the option markets.

RELATED PRODUCTS

Some exchange-traded products have option features: warrants and primes and scores.

Warrants

A warrant is a contract that gives the holder of the warrant the right but not the obligation to buy a designated number of shares of a stock at a specified price before a set date. Consequently, a warrant is nothing more than a call option. As a warrant can be exercised at any time up to and including the expiration date of the warrant, it is an American call option.

There are several differences between the exchange-traded call options on common stocks that we have described in this chapter and warrants, however. First, the expiration date for an exchange-traded call option is much shorter than that for a warrant at the time of issuance. There are some warrants, for example, that have no expiration date; these are called perpetual warrants. Second, and most important, the issuer of a warrant is the company itself. That is, unlike exchange-traded options, which allow entities other than the issuer of the common stock to write a call option, the option writer in the case of a warrant is the company itself. Consequently, when a warrant is exercised, the number of shares of stock outstanding will increase accordingly. This will tend to result in a dilution of earnings. The fact that the

---

[39] Edward C. Blomeyer and Robert C. Klemkosky, "Tests of Market Efficiency for American Call Options," in *Option Pricing*, Menachem Brenner (ed.) (Lexington, MA: D.C. Heath, 1983), pp. 101–121.

exercise of a warrant dilutes earnings means that a model used to price warrants must take this into account. There are several warrant pricing models that do just that.[40]

When initially issued, a warrant is part of another type of security. Warrants are typically attached to a bond or preferred stock. Usually warrants may be detached from the host security that they were attached to and then be traded separately. There are warrants that trade in all the trading locations described in the previous chapter: the major national exchanges, regional exchanges, and the over-the-counter market.

Primes and Scores

The return on a stock has two components: dividend income and capital appreciation. Primes and scores separate the cash flow components of certain stocks into these two components. Specifically, a *prime* entitles the holder of the security to receive (1) the dividends of the underlying stock, and (2) the market value of the stock at a specified future date up to a preset amount, called the termination value. The term "prime" stands for "prescribed right to income." A *score* entitles the instrument holder to all the appreciation above the termination value. Usually, the termination value is 20% to 25% above the current stock price. The term "score" stands for "special claim on residual income."

We can see why these instruments have option-like features. The buyer of a call option is entitled to all appreciation of a stock above the strike price. In the case of a score, the termination value is the effective strike price. The score holder is entitled to any amount above that and nothing if the price at some future date is below that amount. Consequently, a score has the payoff profile of a call option.

Recall that a covered call writing strategy that we described in this chapter is one where the writer owns the underlying stock but has sold a call option against that stock. If the price rises above the call's strike price, the covered call writer forgoes the opportunity to benefit from any price appreciation above the strike price. The covered call writer is entitled to any dividends from the underlying stock until the expiration date. The prime has the same payoff. The holder of a prime forgoes the opportunity to benefit from a rise in

---

[40] See George M. Constantides, "Warrant Exercise and Bond Conversion," *Journal of Financial Economics* (September 1984), pp. 371–398; David C. Emanuel, "Warrant Valuation and Exercise Strategy," *Journal of Financial Economics* (August 1983), pp. 211–235; Dan Galai and Meir Schneller, "The Pricing of Warrants and the Value of the Firm," *Journal of Finance* (December 1978), pp. 1333–1342; and Eduardo S. Schwartz, "The Valuation of Warrants: Implementing a New Approach," *Journal of Financial Economics* (January 1977), pp. 79–93.

the price of the underlying stock above the termination value but is entitled to all the dividends.

Primes and scores on individual stocks are not issued originally as securities. Instead, a trust is created in which the stock of a specific company is placed. The trust then issues a prime and a score for each share of stock placed in the trust. The trust has a maturity of five years, with its size restricted to no more than 5% of the total number of shares of the outstanding stock of the company. At the end of five years, the trust is terminated, and the prime and score holders receive the agreed-upon amount. At any time during a trading day, a combination of one unit of a prime and one unit of a score may be redeemed from the trust for one share of the underlying stock. There is no charge for the redemption.

In an efficient market, a package of a prime and a score should sell for the same price as the underlying stock after adjusting for transactions costs. Yet Jarrow and O'Hara have reported that primes and scores were mispriced relative to the underlying stock.[41] More specifically, they find that a package of primes and scores often exceed the price of the underlying stock by a considerable amount. They explain the discrepancy as arising from market imperfections with respect to short-selling and transactions costs.

At the time of this writing there are 25 trusts that have been created by Americus Shareowners Service Corporation, which created the first trust in 1938. These trusts are called Americus Trusts. The prime and score created are then traded separately on the American Stock Exchange. All 25 outstanding trusts mature some time in 1992. While probably no new Americus Trusts will be created in the future because of adverse tax circumstances,[42] the study of primes and scores is of interest to financial economists because they represent an attempt to split up cash flows from a security. While the splitting up of cash flows from bonds has been common in the bond and mortgage-backed securities markets, as we will see in later chapters, it has not been pursued aggressively in the equities market.

A recent failed attempt to split cash flows occurred in December 1988 when four companies (American Express, Dow Chemical, Pfizer, and Sara Lee) announced that they would exchange one share of their common stock for a package of securities consisting of a bond, a preferred stock, and a warrant. The package of securities was referred to as "unbundled stock units." The three securities effectively would have split the cash flow into

---

[41] Robert A. Jarrow and Maureen O'Hara, "Primes and Scores: An Essay on Market Imperfections," *Journal of Finance* (December 1989), pp. 1263–1287.

[42] Specifically, in 1986 the IRS ruled that the income realized by the trust from holding the underlying stock is taxable. This reduces the distribution to the holders of the primes and scores by the amount of taxes paid by the trust.

three components: a stream of current common stock dividends, a stream of incremental common stock dividends, and capital appreciation.[43] The unbundled stock units concept is similar to the primes and scores. In this example, however, the unbundled stock units would have split the cash flow three ways rather than into two components. Other differences between primes and scores and unbundled stock units are: (1) the former are created by an entity other than the company issuing the stock, while the latter would have been issued by the company itself, and (2) the Americus Trust has a maturity of 5 years, while the maturity of the proposed securities included in unbundled stock units would have been 30 years.

The key point of these examples is that any attempt to split cash flows from a share of common stock results in at least one component that is an instrument with an option-like feature.

SUMMARY

Stock options permit investors to mold the shape of the return distribution to meet investment objectives better. Among the strategies that institutional investors use to control portfolio risk are basic naked option strategies, covered call writing, and protective put buying. The empirical evidence reviewed in this chapter suggests that there is no options strategy that dominates any other.

In 1973, Black and Scholes introduced a model that could be used to price a European call option on a non-dividend-paying stock. Subsequent researchers have modified and extended the Black-Scholes model.

The empirical evidence on the pricing efficiency of the stock options market suggests that, after considering transactions costs, the market appears to be efficient. An investor who wishes to use this market should do so for its original purpose: to shape return distributions so that they are more consistent with investment objectives. It does seem, however, that astute investors can earn abnormal returns in an efficient market if they can predict volatility better than the market can.

There are several products that resemble options on common stock. Warrants are effectively long-term call options where the writer of the option is the company itself. The pricing of a warrant must take into consideration the potential dilution effect on earnings. A prime and a score are products created by a trust where the return from holding a stock is divided into two components: the dividend stream and capital appreciation. A score has the

---

[43] For a further discussion of unbundled stock units, see John D. Finnerty and Victor M. Borun, "An Analysis of Unbundled Stock Units," *Global Finance Journal* (Fall 1989), pp. 47–70.

payoff characteristics of a call option, a prime that of a covered call writing strategy. While primes and scores will probably no longer be issued, they do reflect an attempt to partition cash flows from common stock ownership. Future attempts to do so will also result in the creation of products with option-like features.

QUESTIONS

1. Overheard at a party:

   > You have to be foolish not to sell a call option on stock you own. You don't really lose anything because if the stock is called, you own it and just have to give it up. In return, you receive fee income that you get to keep no matter what the buyer of the call option does. This is a no-lose proposition in my opinion.

   a. What type of strategy is this person suggesting?

   b. Is this view of call options correct?

2. a. Assuming the values below for a European call option, calculate the theoretical option price using the Black–Scholes model:

   Strike price = $100

   Current stock price = $100

   Dividend = $0

   Risk-free rate = 8%

   Expected price volatility = 20%

   Time to expiration = 91 days

   b. What is the intrinsic value and time premium for this call option?

3. For the call option in the previous question, what would be the theoretical option price, intrinsic value, and time premium if:

   a. The current stock price is $55 instead of $100?

   b. The current stock price is $150 instead of $100?

4. You are meeting with a pension plan sponsor who has asked you for advice on several investment policy guidelines that it has formulated for its money managers. One of the guidelines involves the use of options for hedging:

Protective put buying and covered call writing strategies are recognized by the investment community as means for hedging a stock position. The former will not be permitted by any of our fund managers because it involves a cost that may not be recouped if the put option is not exercised. We will permit covered call writing because there is no cost generated to protect the portfolio.

What advice would you give the plan sponsor concerning this investment policy guideline?

5. Suppose an investor wants to follow a protective put buying strategy for a stock she owns that has a market price of $60. She is told that there are three 180-day put options available on that stock with strike prices of $56, $58, and $60.

   a. Which put option will give her the greatest price protection?

   b. Which put option will be the most expensive?

6. "As a warrant is nothing more than a European call option, the Black–Scholes option pricing model can be used to value it." Do you agree with this statement?

LEARNING OBJECTIVES

After reading this chapter you will understand:

- the investment features of stock index options and futures.

- institutional strategies that employ stock index options and futures.

- why stock index futures prices may diverge from their theoretical price.

- the empirical evidence on the pricing efficiency of the stock index options and futures market.

- the role of stock index options and futures in the financial market.

- the role, if any, that these contracts may have played in the stock market crash of October 19, 1987.

I n the previous chapter we covered options on individual stocks. In this chapter we will discuss stock index options and futures contracts. The underlying instrument for these contracts, referred to as index derivative products, is a stock index. Since the inception of the stock index futures and stock index options markets, trading volume in these contracts has grown rapidly.

For each contract, we discuss (1) its basic characteristics, (2) how it can be employed by institutional investors, and (3) empirical evidence on market efficiency. As we have reviewed the pricing of futures and options in previous chapters, our focus here will be on the pricing nuances associated with index derivative products. (Index derivative products on Japanese stock indexes traded in the U.S. and non-U.S. stock indexes traded outside the U.S. are discussed in Chapter 22.) We also look at the empirical evidence on the role of stock index futures and options in the U.S. financial market and the role these contracts played in the October 19, 1987, stock market crash.

STOCK INDEX OPTIONS

In March 1983, trading in an option whose underlying instrument was a stock index, the S&P 100 (originally called the CBOE 100), began on the Chicago Board Options Exchange. It was followed by options trading on the American Stock Exchange on an index designed by that exchange called the Major Market Index (MMI).[1] The total put–and–call volume for all broad- and narrow-based index options was approximately 74 million contracts in 1989. In the same year, the total volume of option contracts traded on all exchanges was approximately 227 million. Thus, in 1989 the total put–and–call volume for all broad- and narrow-based index options represented about one-third of the total volume of option contracts traded on all exchanges.[2]

As in the case of options on individual stocks, stock index options are regulated by the Securities and Exchange Commission.

Basic Features of Stock Index Options

Figure 10-1 lists the major stock index options traded in the U.S. and summarizes the key features of these contracts. In addition to the contracts shown in Figure 10-1, which are based on broad-based indexes, there are

---

[1] The index includes 20 stocks and was constructed to be similar to the Dow Jones Industrial Average.

[2] Total put–and–call volume for all index products reached a peak of 138 million in 1986, the year prior to the October 1987 crash. In that year, this volume was almost one-half the total volume of option contracts traded on all exchanges.

FIGURE 10-1
Summary of Major Stock Index Option Contracts Traded in the U.S. (as of June 1991)

CONTRACT	EXCHANGE	EXERCISE PROVISION	CONTRACT MONTHS	POSITION LIMITS
S&P 100 Index	CBOE	American	4 consecutive mos.	25,000 contracts
S&P 500 Index	CBOE	European	Mar., June, Sept., Dec.	25,000 contracts
NYSE Index	NYSE	American	3 consecutive mos.	45,000 contracts
Major Market Index	AMEX	European	3 consecutive mos.	17,000 contracts
Institutional Index	AMEX	European	Mar., June, Sept., Dec.	25,000 contracts

Features common to all contracts:
1. The contract value is the index value × the multiple. The multiple for each contract is $100.
2. All contracts settle in cash.
3. The expiration day is the Saturday after the third Friday of the expiration month.

options traded on narrow-based indexes. These include the Computer Technology Index and the Oil Index, both traded on the AMEX, and the Utilities Index, traded on the Philadelphia Stock Exchange.

The level of trading volume for each contract differs. A useful statistic measuring the liquidity of a contract is the number of contracts that have been entered into but not yet liquidated. This figure is called the contract's *open interest*. An open interest figure is reported for all listed contracts. For example, on November 1, 1990 the open interest for the call and put options on the S&P 100 was 411,463 contracts and 387,592 contracts, respectively; in contrast, open interest on the Computer Technology index was 273 contracts for the call options and 94 contracts for the put options. The most successful stock index futures contract has been the S&P 100 contract traded on the CBOE.

Unlike stock options, where a stock can be delivered if the option is exercised, it is complicated, to say the least, to settle a stock index option by delivering all the stocks that comprise the index. Instead, stock index options are *cash settlement contacts*. This means that, if the option is exercised, the option writer pays cash to the option buyer. There is no delivery of any stock.

The value of a stock index option contract is equal to the index value multiplied by $100. The $100 is referred to as the *multiple* for the contract. That is,

Dollar value of a stock index option contract = Index value × $100

For example, if the cash index value for the S&P 100 is 300, then the dollar value of the S&P 500 contract is:

$$300 \times \$100 = \$30,000$$

A one-point movement in the index value, say, from 300 to 301, is therefore equal to $100.

The option price is found by multiplying the quoted option price by $100. For example, if the quoted option price is 4 1/4, then the dollar price is $425 (4.25 times $100).

The strike index is converted into a dollar value by multiplying the strike index by the multiple for the contract. For example, if the strike index is 290, the dollar value is $29,000 (290 × $100). If, for example, an investor purchases a call option on the S&P 100 with a strike index of 290, and exercises the option when the index value is 300, then the investor has the right to purchase the index for $29,000 when the market value of the index is $30,000. Upon exercise, the buyer of the call option would receive $1,000 from the option writer.

Exercise provisions for stock index options come in both the American and European variety. The S&P 100 and the NYSE index options are American options. The S&P 500, the Major Market, and the Institutional index options are European options. Institutional investors find European options attractive because they need not fear that a short position they take in an option in order to accomplish an investment objective will be exercised early. Options expire on the Saturday following the third Friday of the contract month.

There are also options on stock index futures. These options are not as widely used as options on stock indexes. Options on futures contracts are the contracts of choice in the interest rate options market so we will postpone our discussion of options on futures until Chapter 19.

Pricing Efficiency of the Stock Index Options Markets

Empirical tests of the pricing of index options are subject to the same problems as stock options discussed in the previous chapter. Moreover, there is the added problem of estimating the amount and timing of dividends for the stocks in the index.

Two studies have examined the pricing efficiency of the stock index options market. Evnine and Rudd looked at the S&P 100 and Major Market Index (MMI) options.[3] Their data base consisted of prices from a real-time

---

[3] Jeremy Evnine and Andrew Rudd, "Index Options: The Early Evidence," *Journal of Finance* (July 1985), pp. 743–756.

pricing service for the period between June 26 and August 30, 1984. For each trading day prices for every hour were included, for a total of 1,798 observations. For every hour, the information in the data base contained essentially the same information that would be displayed on screens on the exchange floor. There was still the problem that the last option trade recorded for the hour was not synchronized with the last value recorded for the index. The index option prices included bid–ask prices, so part of the cost of transacting was considered in the analysis.

Chance investigated the S&P 100 index options for the period January 3, through April 27, 1984, using a data base supplied by a regional brokerage and investment banking firm.[4] The final daily bid and ask quotes and their update times were included in his data base. The prices were market makers' quotes as the market closed and the final index level. As the prices are quotes rather than the closing transaction price, the problem of non-synchronicity of the option and the index is not present. While there are problems in updating both the option quotes and the index, Chance argues that all quotes reflect transactions that could have been executed.

As we explained in Chapter 7, arbitrage arguments can be used to put a lower boundary on the price of a call option. Evnine and Rudd tested for violations of the lower boundary; that is, instances where the ask price of the call was below the difference between the value of the cash index and the strike price. They found 30 instances when the lower boundary for the call option on the S&P 100 was violated, 11 instances for the MMI. Evnine and Rudd report that there were occasions that the size of the violation became so large that even "upstairs traders" would have been capable of taking advantage of these violations.[5]

A possible explanation for the large size of these violations, as Evnine and Rudd note, is that during the week when these violations were observed (August 1 to August 6), there was a dramatic rise in the market. Consequently, the value of the cash index was being updated faster than the bid–ask prices, possibly causing the observed violations.

Both Evnine and Rudd and Chance test for violations of the put–call parity relationship. The Evnine and Rudd results suggest that if stock index options are treated as European, significant profit opportunities are possible. The violations suggest that the S&P 100 index call options were underpriced (which means that the puts were overpriced). The reverse is true for the MMI options. Even if the options are considered American options, these results

---

[4] Don M. Chance, "Parity Tests of Index Options," *Advances in Futures and Options Research* 2 (1987), pp. 47–64.

[5] As explained in Chapter 8, block trades (that is, trades of 10,000 shares or more) typically are negotiated between traders and institutional investors using a network that links them together. This market is referred to as the upstairs market.

suggest that there were profit opportunities. When Chance tested the put–call parity relationship, he finds a significant number of violations in the 1,690 portfolios examined.

Why do we observe these violations? The reason is more than likely attributable to the difficulty of arbitraging between the index option market and the cash market. Two problems in arbitraging are the difficulty and expense of creating a portfolio to replicate the performance of the cash market index and estimating dividends for the stocks in the index. We'll elaborate on this further when we discuss stock index futures later in this chapter.

Portfolio Strategies with Stock Index Options

In the previous chapter, we explained how stock options can be used to take advantage of the anticipated price movement of individual stocks. Alternatively, they can be used to protect current or anticipated positions in individual stocks. For example, an investor can protect against a decline in the price of a stock held in her portfolio by buying a put option on that stock. By doing so, the investor is guaranteed a minimum price equal to the strike price minus the option price. Also, if an investor anticipated buying a stock in the future but fears that the stock price will rise making it more expensive to buy the stock, she can buy a call option on the stock. By pursuing this strategy, the investor has guaranteed that the maximum price that will be paid in the future is the strike price plus the option price.

Now consider an institutional investor that holds a portfolio consisting of a large number of stock issues. To protect against an adverse price movement, the institutional investor would have to buy a put option on every stock issue in the portfolio, which would be quite costly. By taking an appropriate position in a suitable stock index option, an institutional investor with a diversified portfolio can protect against adverse price movements.[6] For example, suppose that an institutional investor holding a diversified portfolio of common stock that is highly correlated with the S&P 100 is concerned that the stock market will decline in value over the next three months. Suppose that a three-month put option on the S&P 100 is available. Because the put option buyer gains when the price of the underlying stock index declines, if an institutional investor purchases this put option (i.e., follows a protective buying put strategy) rather than liquidating the portfolio, adverse movements in the value of the portfolio due to a decline in the stock market will be offset (in whole or in part) by the gain in the put option.

---

[6] The appropriate number of stock index options to buy depends on the beta of the portfolio with respect to the underlying stock. The procedure for calculating the appropriate position in a stock index option is beyond the scope of this chapter.

When stock options or stock index options are used to protect an existing or anticipated position, the investor need not exercise the option if there is a favorable price movement. This is an important characteristic of options compared to futures in attempting to protect a position. An institutional investor can obtain downside protection using options at a cost equal to the option price, but preserve upside potential (reduced by the option price).

STOCK INDEX FUTURES MARKET

Chapter 6 covers the fundamental characteristics of futures contracts. A futures contract is a firm legal agreement between a buyer and an established exchange or its clearing house in which the buyer agrees to take delivery of *something* at a specified price at a designated time (called the *settlement date*). On the other side of the contract is a seller who agrees to deliver the "something." A stock index futures contract is a futures contract where the underlying "something" is a stock index.

In 1982, three futures contracts on broadly based common stock indexes made their debut: the Standard & Poor's 500 futures contract traded on the International Monetary Market of the Chicago Mercantile Exchange, the New York Stock Exchange Composite futures contract traded on the New York Futures Exchange, and the Value Line Average traded on the Kansas City Board of Trade. Since then broad-based and specialized stock index futures contracts have been introduced. Figure 10-2 shows the currently traded major stock index futures contracts. The most actively traded contract is the S&P 500 futures contract.

Stock index futures contracts are regulated by the Commodity Futures Trading Commission, although in recent years there have been proposals to shift regulatory authority to the SEC.

Basic Features of Stock Index Futures

The dollar value of a stock index futures contract is the product of the index value and the contract's multiple; that is,

Dollar value of a stock index futures contract = Index value × Multiple

The multiple is indicated in Figure 10-2. For all contracts except the Major Market index, the multiple is $500. For the Major Market index it is $250. To illustrate, if the cash index value for the S&P 500 is 310, the dollar value of a stock index futures contract is:

$310 \times \$500 = \$155,000$

FIGURE 10-2
Summary of Major Stock Index Futures Contracts Traded in the U.S.
(as of June 1991)

| Contract | Exchange | Multiple | Initial Margin | | Last Trading Day in Delivery |
			Speculator	Hedger	
S&P 500 Index	CBOE	$500	$22,000	$9,000	Thurs. prior to 3rd Friday
NYSE Index	NYSE	500	9,000	4,000	Thurs. prior to 3rd Friday
Major Market Index	AMEX	250	21,000	7,500	3rd Friday
Value Line Maxi Index	KCBT	500	7,000	5,000	3rd Friday

Features common to all contracts:
1. The contract value is the index value × the multiple.
2. All contracts settle in cash.
3. The contract months are March, June, September and December. With the exception of the Major Market Index, three months trade at one time. For the Major Market Index the contract months are the 3 near months and the next month in the cycle.
4. Initial margin requirements are subject to change by the exchange.

If an investor buys an S&P 500 futures contract at 310 and sells it at 330, the investor realizes a profit of 20 times $500, or $10,000. If the futures contract is sold instead for 260, the investor will realize a loss of 50 times $500, or $25,000.

As in the case of stock index options, stock index futures contracts are cash settlement contracts. This means that at the settlement date, cash will be exchanged to settle the contract. For example, if an investor buys an S&P 500 futures contract at 310 and the settlement index is 350, settlement would be as follows. The investor has agreed to buy the S&P 500 for 310 times $500, or $155,000. The S&P 500 value at the settlement date is 350 times $500, or $175,000. The seller of this futures contract must pay the investor $20,000 ($175,000 − $155,000). Had the index at the settlement date been 240 instead of $350, the value of the S&P 500 would be $120,000 (240 × $500). The investor must pay the seller of the contract $35,000 ($155,000 − $120,000).

The minimum price fluctuation or "tick" for all stock index futures contracts is 0.05. The dollar value of a tick is found by multiplying 0.05 by the contract's multiple. For stock index futures contracts with a multiple of $500, the dollar value of a tick is $25 (0.05 × $500).

As we explain in Chapter 6, there are margin requirements (initial, maintenance, and variation) for futures contracts. Margin requirements are revised periodically to reflect the change in the index and other economic conditions, and current information is available from the exchange where the contract is traded or a brokerage firm. As of June 1991, for traders classified as speculators, the S&P 500 futures contract's initial and maintenance requirements are $22,000 and $8,000, respectively. If the cash value for the index is 290 (roughly the index on October 31, 1990), the dollar value of the contract is $145,000. The initial margin is therefore about 15% of the contract value. For a speculator who purchases *stock* on margin, however, the initial margin requirement is 50% of the stock position, and the maintenance margin requirement is 25%.[7] The lower margin requirements for stock index futures contracts give a speculator greater leverage in the futures market compared to the stock market.

Margin requirements for traders classified as hedgers are lower. For the S&P 500 futures contract, the initial margin requirement is $8,000 instead of $22,000. The maintenance margin is the same ($8,000).

Illustration of Margin Requirements

As explained in Chapter 6, futures positions are marked to market at the end of each trading day. An illustration will demonstrate the mechanics of margin requirements and the mark-to-market procedure.[8]

1. A hedger purchases 193 S&P 500 futures contracts on April 14, 1988. The actual closing settlement price for the contract on that day was 259.
2. The closing settlement prices for the nine trading days following April 14, 1988, are shown in the second column of Table 10-1.
3. The initial and maintenance margin requirements at that time were $10,000 per contract for hedgers.

The dollar value of each S&P 500 futures contract when the settlement index was 259 was $129,500. As the hedger purchased 193 contracts, the total dollar value of the contracts was $24,993,500. The third column of Table 10-1 shows the dollar value for each of the nine trading days following April 14, 1988. The initial margin requirement is $1,930,000 for the 193 contracts; maintenance margin is $193,000 for the 193 contracts. The last column in Table 10-1 shows the variation margin for the nine trading days following April 14,

---

[7] As explained in Chapter 6, margin is a different concept in futures transactions and cash market transactions. For futures, margin is essentially a performance bond. For cash market instruments, margin is a down payment with the balance borrowed from a broker.

[8] This illustration is taken from Bruce M. Collins and Frank J. Fabozzi, "Mechanics of Trading Stock Index Futures," Chapter 5 in Frank J. Fabozzi and Gregory M. Kipnis (eds.), *The Handbook of Stock Index Futures and Options* (Homewood, IL: Dow Jones-Irwin, 1989).

TABLE 10-1 ILLUSTRATION OF MARGIN REQUIREMENTS AND MARKING TO MARKET

Day 1 is August 14,1988
Initial margin per S&P 500 contract = $10,000*
Initial margin for 193 S&P 500 contracts = $1,930,000 (193 × $10,000)
Maintenance margin per S&P 500 contract = $10,000*
Maintenance margin for 193 S&P 500 contracts = $1,930,000

Day	Settlement Price	Value for 193 Contracts	Equity in Account	Variation Margin
1	259.00	$24,993,500	$1,930,000	—
2	258.60	24,954,900	1,891,400	$ (38,600)
3	259.25	25,017,625	1,992,725	62,725
4	257.30	24,829,450	1,804,550	(188,175)
5	257.90	24,887,350	1,987,900	57,900
6	256.20	24,723,300	1,823,850	(164,050)
7	261.85	25,268,525	2,475,225	545,225
8	263.85	25,461,525	2,668,225	193,000
9	264.80	24,553,200	2,759,900	91,675
10	264.00	25,476,000	2,682,700	(77,200)

* Margin requirements at the time.

1988. A negative number (i.e., a number in parentheses) means that there will be a margin call; a positive number means that funds can be withdrawn.

On Day 1, the hedger must put up initial margin of $1,930,000, which may be in the form of a Treasury bill. Once the equity in the account falls below the maintenance margin (which in the case of a hedger is the same as the initial margin of $1,930,000), additional margin (variation margin) will be required. This must be in cash (Treasury bills are not acceptable to satisfy variation margin) and must be supplied in 24 hours.

On Day 2 of our illustration, the settlement price falls to 258.60, reducing the value of the 193 contracts to $24,954,900. The decrease in the contract value is subtracted from the equity in the account. This is what is meant by marking to market. The equity therefore declines to $1,891,400. As the equity on Day 2 is below the maintenance margin of $1,930,000, there will be a margin call of $38,600 ($1,930,000 minus $1,891,400).

When the equity in the account exceeds the maintenance margin, the hedger can withdraw the excess. On Day 3, for example, the settlement price for the index was 259.25, increasing the value of the contracts to $25,017,625. The resulting equity in the account was $1,992,725, $62,725 greater than the maintenance margin requirement. The hedger can withdraw the $62,725.

This example surely shows that anyone using the stock index futures market to pursue some strategy must have sufficient funds to satisfy margin calls.

The commissions paid on stock index futures transactions, like commissions on common stock transactions, are fully negotiable. Round-trip commissions for individual investors range from $40 to $100 per contract at full-service brokerage firms, lower than that at discount brokerage firms. For institutional investors, the typical commission per contract is under $25. Assuming a round-trip commission of $50 per contract, the cost of transacting is typically less than 0.1% of the contract value. A round-trip commission for a portfolio consisting of the underlying stocks by contrast would be about 1% of the value of the stocks. The lower transactions costs in the stock index futures market have made it more attractive for institutional investors to implement positions in that market over the cash market.

Pricing of Stock Index Futures

In Chapter 6, we demonstrated that arbitrage arguments can be used to determine the theoretical futures price. In the case of stock index futures, we need the information following:

1. the value of the cash (spot) market index.
2. the dividend yield on the stocks in the index that would be earned until the settlement date.
3. the interest rate for borrowing and lending until the settlement date. The borrowing and lending rate is referred to as the *financing cost.*

The theoretical futures price that will prevent arbitrage profits can be shown to be equal to:

Futures price = Cash market price + Cash market price (Financing cost − Dividend yield)

where "Financing cost" is the cost of financing a position until the settlement date of the futures contract, and "Dividend yield" is the dividends over the same period. Moreover, it is assumed that dividends are received only at the settlement date. The difference between the financing cost and the dividend yield is called the *net financing cost* because it adjusts the financing cost for the yield earned. The net financing cost is more commonly called the *cost of carry* or, simply, *carry. Positive carry* means that the yield earned is greater than the financing cost; *negative carry* means that the financing cost exceeds the yield earned.

This equation for the theoretical futures price indicates that it may sell at a premium to the cash market price (higher than the cash market price) or at a discount from the cash market price (lower than the cash market price), depending on the financing cost and the dividend yield.

Recall from Chapter 6 that to derive the theoretical futures price using the arbitrage argument, also called the *cost of carry model*, several assumptions must be made. When these assumptions do not hold, there will be a divergence between the actual futures price and the theoretical futures price. We discussed several of these assumptions for futures contracts in general in Chapter 6. Here we highlight the assumptions that are unique to stock index futures:

1. No interim cash flows from dividend payments are assumed in deriving the pricing model. We know that interim cash flows do occur, and incorporating interim dividend payments into the pricing model is not difficult. The problem is that the value of the dividend payments at the settlement date will depend on the interest rate at which the dividend payments can be reinvested. The lower the dividend, and the closer the dividend payments to the settlement date of the futures contract, the less important the reinvestment income is in determining the futures price.

2. In determining the cost of carry, both the financing cost and the dividend yield must be known. While the financing cost may be known, the dividend rate and the pattern of dividend payments are not known with certainty. They must be projected from the historical dividend payments of firms in the index.

3. For the arbitrage to work when the futures price is below its theoretical value, the investor must be able to use the proceeds from selling the cash index short. In practice, for individual investors, the proceeds are not received, and, in fact, the individual investor is required to put up margin (securities margin, not futures margin) to short-sell. For institutional investors, the securities may be borrowed, but there is a cost to borrowing them.

4. In the case of a short sale of the stocks in the index, all stocks must be sold simultaneously. The stock exchange rule for the short-selling of stock may prevent the arbitrage strategy from bringing the actual futures price in line with the theoretical futures price. The short-selling rule for stocks specifies that a short sale can be made only at a price that is higher than the previous trade (referred to as an up-tick), or at a price that is equal to the previous trade but higher than the last trade at a different price (referred to as a zero-tick). If the arbitrage requires selling the stocks in the index simultaneously, and the last transaction for some of the stocks is not an up-tick, the stocks cannot be shorted simultaneously.

5. Another difficulty in arbitraging the cash and futures market is that it is too expensive to buy or sell every stock included in the index. Instead, a portfolio containing a smaller number of stocks may be constructed to "track" the index. The arbitrage, however, is no longer risk-free because we have introduced risk that the portfolio will not track the index exactly. This is referred to as *tracking error risk*.

6. The basic arbitrage model ignores not only taxes but also the differences between the tax treatment of cash market transactions and futures transactions.

Violation of the assumptions made in developing the cost of carry pricing model means that there will be discrepancies between the actual price and the theoretical futures price. Basically, there will be boundaries around which the futures price can trade that will not permit arbitrage profits. Researchers have derived upper and lower bounds for the theoretical futures prices that take into consideration several of the factors discussed above.[9]

Pricing Efficiency of the Stock Index Futures Market

Using theoretical futures prices and their bounds, several studies have examined the pricing efficiency of the stock index futures market. The first study to examine this issue empirically was by Cornell and French.[10] They compare actual futures prices to theoretical futures prices for the S&P 500 futures contract and the NYSE futures contract on the first days of trading of June, July, August, and September 1982. In all but two of the cases they examine, the theoretical (predicted) futures price was higher than the actual futures price. The discrepancy they find was attributable to the difference in the tax treatment of futures and cash market transactions.

After deriving upper and lower bounds for the theoretical futures price, Modest and Sundaresan examine the June 1982 S&P futures contract from April 21, 1982, to June 16, 1982, and the December 1982 S&P 500 futures contracts from April 21, 1982, to September 15, 1982, to determine if the actual futures prices were outside the bounds.[11] Recall from our discussion of the theoretical futures price that the futures pricing model assumes that

---

[9] David M. Modest and Mahadevan Sundaresan, "The Relationship between Spot and Futures Prices in Stock Index Futures: Some Preliminary Evidence," *Journal of Futures Markets* (Spring 1983), pp. 15–42.

[10] Bradford Cornell and Kenneth R. French, "Taxes and the Pricing of Stock Index Futures," *Journal of Finance* (June 1983), pp. 675–694.

[11] Modest and Sundaresan, "The Relationship between Spot and Futures Prices in Stock Index Futures: Some Preliminary Evidence," op. cit.

short-sellers have the use of the proceeds from selling the cash index short. Three sets of theoretical bounds are tested by Modest and Sundaresan assuming: (1) no use of the proceeds by short-sellers, (2) use of half the proceeds by short-sellers, and (3) use of all the proceeds by short-sellers. Recall also that the theoretical futures price is dependent on the expected dividend yield. Modest and Sundaresan construct theoretical bounds with and without adjusting for dividends. Thus, a total of six theoretical bounds were constructed for the two S&P 500 futures contracts investigated— theoretical bounds were constructed with and without dividend adjustments for each assumption about how much of the proceeds short-sellers of the cash index would have the use of.

Modest and Sundaresan find that the actual futures prices for both futures contracts were within the theoretical bounds constructed when the investor has no use of the proceeds from short-selling the cash index when dividends are considered. Thus, under these conditions, no arbitrage profits were possible. While there were sporadic instances where the theoretical bounds were violated, under realistic assumptions they find few opportunities to generate arbitrage profits (i.e., few violations of the theoretical bounds) even at the inception of stock index futures trading.

While the Cornell and French and Modest and Sundaresan studies examined pricing efficiency when the contracts started trading, Peters looks at whether the stock index futures market became more efficient over time.[12] He examines market efficiency for the S&P 500 futures contract and the NYSE futures contract from the September 1982 contract to the December 1983 contract to determine if the actual prices moved closer to the theoretical prices. Results show that the market has become more efficient in pricing futures, a finding that he attributes to better estimation of the dividend stream for each index contract.

Collins tests the pricing efficiency of the futures market by examining whether an investment strategy of buying the cash market index and selling the futures could have generated an abnormal return.[13] In an efficient market, the return on this strategy should be approximately equal to the return on a Treasury security with a maturity equal to the maturity of the futures contract. An abnormal return occurs if the return realized from this strategy exceeds the yield on a comparable maturity Treasury security. Selected S&P 500

---

[12] Ed Peters, "The Growing Efficiency of Index-Futures Markets," *Journal of Portfolio Management* (Summer 1985), pp. 52–56.

[13] Bruce M. Collins, "An Empirical Analysis of Stock Index Futures Prices," unpublished doctoral dissertation, Fordham University 1987.

futures contracts were examined beginning with the December 1982 contract and extending to the September 1985 contract. Transactions costs were considered. His results suggest that, while there were instances of pricing inefficiency, the market has become more efficient. Other statistical tests performed by Collins lead to the same conclusion.

Portfolio Strategies with Stock Index Futures

There are seven investment strategies for which institutional investors can use stock index futures:

- speculating on the movement of the stock market
- controlling the risk of a stock portfolio (altering beta)
- hedging against adverse stock price movements
- constructing indexed portfolios
- index arbitrage
- creating portfolio insurance
- asset allocation

Speculating on the Movement of the Stock Market.   Prior to development of stock index futures, an investor who wanted to speculate on the future course of stock prices had to buy or short individual stocks. Now, the stock index can be bought or sold in the futures market. But making speculation easier for investors is not the main function of stock index futures contracts. The other strategies discussed below show how institutional investors can effectively use stock index futures to meet investment objectives.

Controlling the Risk of a Stock Portfolio.   An institution that wishes to alter its exposure to the market can do so by revising the portfolio's beta. This can be done by rebalancing the portfolio with stocks that will produce the target beta, but there are transactions costs associated with rebalancing a portfolio. Because of the leverage embedded in futures, institutions can use stock index futures to achieve a target beta at a considerably lower cost. Buying stock index futures will increase a portfolio's beta, and selling will reduce it.

Hedging against Adverse Stock Price Movements.   Hedging is a special case of controlling a stock portfolio's exposure to adverse price changes. In a hedge, the objective is to alter a current or anticipated stock portfolio position so that its beta is zero. A portfolio with a beta of zero should generate a risk-free interest rate. This is consistent with the capital asset pricing model discussed in Chapter 5, and also consistent with our discussion of futures contracts in Chapter 6.

Remember that using stock index futures to hedge locks in a price, although the hedger cannot then benefit from a favorable movement in the portfolio's value. With stock index options, the hedger has downside protection but retains the upside potential reduced by the cost of the option.

An illustration will show how stock index futures can be used to hedge the risk of a portfolio against an adverse price movement.[14] Suppose that a portfolio manager owned all the stocks in the Dow Jones Industrial Average on July 1, 1986. The market value of the portfolio held was $1 million. Also assume that the portfolio manager wanted to hedge the position against a decline in stock prices from July 1, 1986, to August 31, 1986, using the September 1986 S&P 500 futures contract. As the S&P 500 futures September contract is used here to hedge a portfolio of Dow Jones Industrials to August 31, this is a cross hedge, as explained in Chapter 6.

The first step in the hedge is to determine whether to buy or sell the futures contract. Because the portfolio manager wants to protect against a decline in the portfolio's value, he will sell stock index futures contracts. The second step is to determine the appropriate number of contracts to sell. While computation is beyond the scope of this chapter, it can be demonstrated that for our illustration six is the approximate number of contracts to sell to obtain the same market risk exposure with the futures as with the portfolio of Dow Jones Industrial stocks.

Table 10-2 summarizes the actual outcome of this hedge, assuming that it is lifted on August 31, 1986. The hedge resulted in a loss of $11,100. And assuming commissions of $20 per contract, commissions for 6 futures contracts would have been $120, for an overall loss of $11,220. The reason for the loss was the adverse change in the basis (which is the difference between the cash price and futures price), as shown in the last column of the lower panel of Table 10-2. Had the hedge not been employed, however, the loss would have been $73,500, the loss in the cash market. This is what we meant in Chapter 6 when we said that hedging substitutes basis risk for price risk.

This hedge is called a short or sell hedge. A long or buy hedge can be used in anticipation of the purchase of stocks at some future date. In this case, stock index futures contracts are purchased. For example, shortly after stock index futures began trading, Westinghouse Electric Corporation's pension fund bought 400 stock index contracts between July 29 and August 11, 1982.[15]

---

[14] This illustration is adapted from Frank J. Fabozzi and Edgar E. Peters, "Hedging with Stock Index Futures," Chapter 13 in *The Handbook of Stock Index Futures and Options*, op. cit.

[15] "Stock Futures Used in Rally," *Pension & Investment Age*, October 25, 1982, pp. 1, 52.

TABLE 10-2   HEDGING A $1 MILLION DOW JONES INDUSTRIAL INDEX FUND USING S&P 500 FUTURES

SITUATION

Own $1 million worth of Dow Jones Industrial stocks on 7/1/86.
Need to hedge against an adverse market move.
Hedge is lifted 8/31/86.

FACTS

	7/1/86	8/31/86
Value of portfolio	$1,000,000	$927,500
Cash price of S&P 500	252.04	234.91
Price of 9/86 S&P futures	253.95	233.15

OUTCOME

CASH MARKET	FUTURES MARKET	BASIS
7/1/86—Time hedge is placed Own $1,000,000 portfolio	Sell 6 9/86 S&P 500 futures contracts at 253.95	−1.91
8/31/86—Time hedge is lifted Own $927,500 portfolio	Buy 6 9/86 S&P 500 futures contracts at 233.15	+1.76
Loss in cash market = $73,500 Overall loss = $11,100	Gain in futures market = $62,400	

The reason cited by a company source for purchasing these contracts, which were worth over $20 million, was that the company was not "ready to buy individual stocks in such a short period of time." A company source stated that stock index futures gave the pension fund "a quick way of putting money into the market," and one "much cheaper" than if the fund had purchased stock in the cash market. This Westinghouse hedging strategy can be viewed as a long hedge.

Two examples of how investment banking firms can use stock index futures to hedge their activities were reported shortly after stock index futures began trading. In June 1982, International Harvester traded its stock portfolio to Goldman Sachs in exchange for a bond portfolio.[16] As recipient of the stock portfolio, Goldman Sachs was exposed to market risk. To protect itself against a decline in the value of the stock portfolio, Goldman Sachs placed a short hedge on a "significant" portion of the stock portfolio, using all three stock index futures trading at the time to implement the hedge. Salomon Brothers used stock index futures to protect itself against a decline in stock prices in a transaction involving $400 million of stock. In that transaction, the New York City Pension Fund switched $400 million of funds that were being managed by Alliance Capital to Bankers Trust so that the latter could manage the funds using an indexing approach. Salomon Brothers guaranteed prices at which the city and Bankers Trust could purchase or sell the stocks in the portfolio being transferred. To do this, Salomon Brothers used options on individual stocks to protect certain stock prices, but also used stock index futures to protect itself against broad market movements that would decrease the value of the stocks in the portfolio.

Constructing Indexed Portfolios.   As we explained in Chapter 8, an increasing number of institutional equity funds are indexed to some broad-based stock market index. There are management fees and transactions costs associated with creating a portfolio to replicate a stock index that has been targeted to be matched. The higher these costs, the greater the divergence between the performance of the indexed portfolio and the target index. Moreover, because a fund manager creating an indexed portfolio will not purchase all the stocks that comprise the index, the indexed portfolio is exposed to tracking error risk. Instead of using the cash market to construct an indexed portfolio, the manager can use stock index futures. In fact, of the 60 or so largest pension funds that are indexed, about one-third use stock index futures in managing the fund.

Let's illustrate why stock index funds can be used to create an indexed portfolio. If stock index futures are priced according to their theoretical value, a portfolio consisting of a long position in stock index futures and Treasury bills will produce the same portfolio return as that of the underlying cash index. To see this, suppose that an index fund manager wished to index a $9 million portfolio using the S&P 500 as the target index. Also assume the following:

1. The S&P 500 is currently 300.

2. The S&P 500 futures index with six months to settlement is currently selling for 303.

---

[16] Kimberly Blanton, "Index Futures Contracts Hedge Big Block Trades," *Pension & Investments Age*, July 19, 1982, pp. 1, 38.

3. The expected dividend yield for the S&P 500 for the next six months is 2%.

4. Six-month Treasury bills are currently yielding 3%.

The theoretical futures price is 303.[17]

Consider two strategies that the index fund manager may choose to pursue:

Strategy 1: Purchase $9 million of stocks in such a way as to replicate the performance of the S&P 500.

Strategy 2: Buy 60 S&P 500 futures contracts with a settlement six months from now at 303, and invest $9 million in six-month Treasury bills.[18]

How will the two strategies perform under various scenarios for the S&P 500 value when the contract settles six months from now? Let's investigate three scenarios: the S&P 500 increases to 330, remains unchanged at 300, and declines to 270. At settlement, the futures price converges to the value of the index. Tables 10-3 through 10-5 show the value of the portfolio for both strategies for each of the three scenarios. As can be seen, for a given scenario the performance of the two strategies is identical.

This result should not be surprising because a futures contract can be replicated by selling the instrument underlying the futures contract and buying Treasury bills. In the case of indexing, we are replicating the underlying instrument by buying the futures contract and investing in Treasury bills.

Therefore, if stock index futures contracts are properly priced, index fund managers can use stock index futures to create an index fund. Suppose instead that the futures price is less than the theoretical futures price (i.e., the futures contracts are cheap). If that situation occurs, the index fund manager can enhance the indexed portfolio's return by buying the futures and buying Treasury bills. That is, the return on the futures/Treasury bill portfolio will be greater than that on the underlying index when the position is held to the settlement date.

---

[17] The theoretical futures price is found using the formula presented earlier:

Cash market price + Cash market price (Financing cost − Dividend yield)

The financing cost is 3% and the dividend yield is 2%. Therefore,

$$300 + 300 \,(0.03 - 0.02) = 303$$

[18] There are two points to note here. First, this illustration ignores margin requirements. The Treasury bills can be used for initial margin. Second, 60 contracts are selected in this strategy because with the current market index at 300 and a multiple of $500, the cash value of 60 contracts is $9 million.

TABLE 10-3   COMPARISON OF PORTFOLIO VALUE FROM PURCHASING STOCKS TO REPLICATE AN INDEX AND A FUTURES/TREASURY BILL STRATEGY WHEN THERE IS NO MISPRICING AND MARKET INCREASES

Assumptions

1. Amount to be invested = $9 million
2. Current value of S&P 500 = 300
3. Value of the S&P 500 at settlement (six months later) = 330
4. Current value of S&P futures contract = 303
5. Expected dividend yield = 2%
6. Yield on Treasury bills = 3%

STRATEGY 1: DIRECT PURCHASE OF STOCKS

Increase in value of index	= 330/300 − 1 = 0.10
Market value of portfolio that mirrors the index 1.10 × $9,000,000	= $ 9,900,000
Dividends 0.02 × $9,000,000	= $ 180,000
Value of portfolio	= $10,080,000
Dollar return	= $ 1,080,000

STRATEGY 2: FUTURES/T-BILL PORTFOLIO

Number of S&P 500 contracts to be purchased = 60

Gain from sale of one contract	
Purchased for	303
Sold for	330
Gain per contract	27
Gain for 60 contracts 60 × $500 × 27	= $ 810,000
Value of Treasury Bills $9,000,000 × 1.03	= $ 9,270,000
Value of portfolio	= $10,080,000
Dollar return	= $ 1,080,000

To see this, suppose that in our previous illustration the current futures price is 301 instead of 303, so that the futures contract is cheap (undervalued). Table 10-6 shows that for all three scenarios the value of the portfolio is $60,000 greater by buying the futures contract and Treasury bills rather than buying the stocks directly.

TABLE 10-4 COMPARISON OF PORTFOLIO VALUE FROM PURCHASING STOCKS TO REPLICATE AN INDEX AND A FUTURES/TREASURY BILL STRATEGY WHEN THERE IS NO MISPRICING AND MARKET DOES NOT CHANGE

Assumptions

1. Amount to be invested = $9 million
2. Current value of S&P 500 = 300
3. Value of the S&P 500 at settlement (six months later) = 300
4. Current value of S&P futures contract = 303
5. Expected dividend yield = 2%
6. Yield on Treasury bills = 3%

STRATEGY 1: DIRECT PURCHASE OF STOCKS

Change in value of index	$= 300/300 - 1 = 0$
Market value of portfolio that mirrors the index 1.00 × $9,000,000	= $9,000,000
Dividends 0.02 × $9,000,000	= $ 180,000
Value of portfolio	= $9,180,000
Dollar return	= $ 180,000

STRATEGY 2: FUTURES/T-BILL PORTFOLIO

Number of S&P 500 contracts to be purchased = 60	
Loss from sale of one contract	
Purchased for	303
Sold for	300
Loss per contract	3
Loss for 60 contracts 60 × $500 × 3	= $ (90,000)
Value of Treasury Bills $9,000,000 × 1.03	= $9,270,000
Value of portfolio	= $9,180,000
Dollar return	= $ 180,000

Alternatively, if the futures contract is expensive based on its theoretical price, an index fund manager who owns stock index futures and Treasury bills will swap that portfolio for the stocks in the index. An index manager who swaps between the futures/Treasury bills portfolio and a stock portfolio based on the value of the futures contract relative to the cash market index is attempting to enhance the portfolio's return. This strategy, referred to as a

TABLE 10-5   COMPARISON OF PORTFOLIO VALUE FROM PURCHASING STOCKS TO REPLICATE AN INDEX AND A FUTURES/TREASURY BILL STRATEGY WHEN THERE IS NO MISPRICING AND MARKET DECLINES

Assumptions

1. Amount to be invested = $9 million
2. Current value of S&P 500 = 300
3. Value of the S&P 500 at settlement (six months later) = 270
4. Current value of S&P futures contract = 303
5. Expected dividend yield = 2%
6. Yield on Treasury bills = 3%

STRATEGY 1: DIRECT PURCHASE OF STOCKS

Decrease in value of index	= 270/300 − 1 = −0.10
Market value of portfolio that mirrors the index	
0.90 × $9,000,000	= $8,100,000
Dividends	
0.02 × $9,000,000	= $ 180,000
Value of portfolio	= $8,280,000
Dollar return	= $ (720,000)

STRATEGY 2: FUTURES/T-BILL PORTFOLIO

Number of S&P 500 contracts to be purchased = 60	
Loss from sale of one contract	
Purchased for	303
Sold for	270
Loss per contract	33
Loss for 60 contracts	
60 × $500 × 33	= $ (990,000)
Value of Treasury Bills	
$9,000,000 × 1.03	= $9,270,000
Value of portfolio	= $8,280,000
Dollar return	= $ (720,000)

TABLE 10-6	ENHANCEMENT OF PORTFOLIO RETURN FOR A FUTURES/TREASURY BILL PORTFOLIO WHEN FUTURES CONTRACT IS UNDERPRICED

Assumptions

1. Amount to be invested = $9 million
2. Current value of S&P 500 = 300
3. Current value of S&P 500 futures contract = 301
4. Expected dividend yield = 2%
5. Yield on Treasury bills = 3%
6. Theoretical price of futures contract = 303

If value of index at settlement is 330

Value of portfolio for Strategy 1 (direct purchase of stocks)
   (from Table 10-3) = $10,080,000

Value of portfolio for Strategy 2 (futures/T-bill portfolio)
   Gain per contract = 330 − 301 = 29

Gain for 60 contracts = 60 × $500 × 29 =	$ 870,000
Value of Treasury bills	$ 9,270,000
Value of portfolio	$10,140,000

If value of index at settlement is 300

Value of portfolio for Strategy 1 (direct purchase of stocks)
   (from Table 10-4) = $9,180,000

Value of portfolio for Strategy 2 (futures/T-bill portfolio)
   Loss per contract = 300 − 301 = 1

Loss for 60 contracts = 60 × $500 × 1 =	$ (30,000)
Value of Treasury bills	$9,270,000
Value of portfolio	$9,240,000

If value of index at settlement is 270

Value of portfolio for Strategy 1 (direct purchase of stocks)
   (from Table 10-5) = $8,280,000

Value of portfolio for Strategy 2 (futures/T-bill portfolio)
   Loss per contract = 270 − 301 = 31

Loss for 60 contracts = 60 × $500 × 31 =	$ (930,000)
Value of Treasury bills	$9,270,000
Value of portfolio	$8,340,000

stock replacement strategy, is one of several strategies used to attempt to enhance the return of an indexed portfolio.[19]

Index Arbitrage. Opportunities to enhance returns as a result of the mispricing of the futures contract are not restricted to index fund management. Money managers and arbitrageurs monitor the cash and futures market to see when the differences between the theoretical futures price and actual futures price are sufficient so that an arbitrage profit can be attained: selling the futures index if it is expensive and buying stocks, or buying the futures index if it is cheap and selling the stocks. Program trading is used to execute the buy and sell orders.[20]

Creating Portfolio Insurance. In Chapter 7, we explained how a put option can protect the value of an asset. At the expiration date of the put option, the minimum value for the asset will be the strike price minus the cost of the put option. Put options on stock indexes can do the same for a diversified portfolio of stocks.

Alternatively, an institutional investor can create a put option synthetically by using either (1) stock index futures, or (2) stocks and a riskless asset. Allocation of the portfolio's funds to stock index futures or between stocks and a riskless asset is adjusted as market conditions change.[21] A strategy that seeks to insure the value of a portfolio using a synthetic put option strategy is called *dynamic hedging.*

Given that put options on stock indexes are available to portfolio managers, why should they bother with dynamic hedging? There are four reasons. First, the size of the market for options on stock indexes is not as large as that for stock index futures and therefore may not easily accommodate a large portfolio insurance program without moving the price of the option substantially. Second, exchanges impose position limits on the amount of contracts that an investor can have a position in.[22] In the case of institutions that want to protect large equity portfolios, position limits may effectively prevent them from using exchange-traded index options to protect their portfolio.

---

[19] For a further discussion of this strategy, see Bruce M. Collins, "Index Fund Investment Management," Chapter 10 in Frank J. Fabozzi (ed.), *Portfolio and Investment Management* (Chicago: Probus Publishing, 1989).

[20] Program trading is discussed in Chapter 8.

[21] For a more detailed explanation of this strategy, see Mark Rubinstein and Hayne Leland, "Replicating Options with Positions in Stock and Cash," *Financial Analysts Journal* (July–August 1981), pp. 63–72, or Hayne Leland, "Portfolio Insurance," Chapter 12 in *The Handbook of Stock Index Futures and Options,* op. cit.

[22] Regulators will grant approval for contract trading only if the exchange imposes a position limit, because it is believed such a limit will stabilize the option price.

Third, existing exchange-traded index options contracts are of shorter maturity than the period over which some investors sought protection. Finally, the cost of a put option may be higher than the transactions costs associated with dynamic hedging. Yet while the cost of a put option is known (and is determined by expected price volatility), the cost of creating portfolio insurance by using stock index futures or stocks will be determined by actual price volatility in the market. The greater the actual price volatility in the market, the more rebalancing of the portfolio is necessary, and the higher the cost of creating portfolio insurance.

How does dynamic hedging work using stocks and a riskless asset? Recall that the buyer of a put option establishes a floor for the value of an asset but retains the opportunity to benefit if the asset's price rises. A dynamic hedging strategy seeks to reproduce the payoff of a long put option position by changing the allocation of the portfolio's funds between the risky asset and a riskless asset. In this case, the risky asset is the equity portfolio, and the riskless asset may be a money market instrument such as Treasury bills. When stock prices decline, the investor must reduce the exposure to the stock market and increase the holding of the riskless asset. Placing more funds in the riskless asset will help to insure the floor value for the portfolio. Thus, when stock prices decline, a commensurate amount of stocks are sold and the proceeds invested in a riskless asset such as Treasury bills. When stock prices rise, a commensurate amount of stocks are purchased with the proceeds obtained from selling a portion of the riskless asset. This action increases the exposure of the portfolio to the equity market so that the investor can capture the benefits of a rising market. Fewer funds need be placed in the riskless asset, because the likelihood of achieving the floor value for the portfolio declines in a rising equity market. To execute the orders to buy or sell stocks, program trading is used.

Instead of implementing dynamic hedging by changing the allocation of the portfolio between stocks and a riskless asset, stock index futures can be used. When stock prices decline, stock index futures are sold. This is equivalent to selling stocks and investing the funds in a riskless asset. When stock prices rise, stock index futures are purchased, which is equivalent to buying stocks and reducing the portfolio's allocation to a riskless asset.[23]

Asset Allocation. The decision on how to divide funds across the major asset classes (for example, equities, bonds, foreign securities, real estate) is referred to as the asset allocation decision. Futures and options can be used to implement an asset allocation decision more effectively than transacting in the cash markets.

---

[23] Determination of the amount of stock to buy or sell is based on an option pricing model.

For example, suppose that a pension fund sponsor with assets of $1 billion has allocated $300 million to the bond market and $700 million to the stock market. Suppose further that the sponsor has decided to alter that bond/stock mix to $600 million in bonds and $400 million in stock. Liquidation of $300 million in stock will involve significant transactions costs—both commissions and execution (market impact) costs.[24] Moreover, the external money managers who are managing the stock portfolios will face disruption as funds are withdrawn by the sponsor. Rather than liquidating the stock portfolio immediately, the sponsor can sell an appropriate number of stock index futures contracts. This effectively decreases the exposure of the pension fund to the stock market. To increase the fund's exposure to the bond market, the sponsor can buy interest rate futures contracts.[25]

Stock index options and options on bonds also can be used to implement an asset allocation strategy.[26]

STOCK INDEX CONTRACTS, STOCK PRICE VOLATILITY, AND BLACK MONDAY

A great deal of debate surrounds the introduction of stock index options and futures. In this section, we'll discuss the arguments at issue and review the empirical evidence. The first question is whether the introduction of stock index futures and options trading, and strategies employing these contracts, adds value to our financial markets, or whether index futures and options just provide a form of legalized gambling for market participants. The second controversy is whether stock price volatility has increased as a result of futures and options trading. Finally, we'll focus on the extent to which the existence of these contracts may have contributed to the October 1987 market crash, popularly known as *Black Monday*.

Are Derivative Index Markets Beneficial to the Financial Markets?

In the absence of stock index futures and options markets, investors have only one market in which to alter portfolio positions when new information is received—the cash market. If there is economic news that investors expect

---

[24] These costs are described in Chapter 8.

[25] These contracts are explained in Chapter 19.

[26] For a further discussion, see Ravi E. Dattatreya and Bruce M. Collins, "Asset Allocation Using Futures and Options," in Frank J. Fabozzi (ed.), *Managing Institutional Assets* (NY: Harper & Row, 1990).

might impact the cash flow of all stocks adversely, they can reduce their equity exposure by selling stocks. The opposite is true if investors expect the new information to increase the cash flow of all stocks: in that case, an investor would increase the equity exposure of the portfolio. There are, of course, transactions costs associated with altering equity risk exposure— explicit costs (commissions), and hidden or execution costs (bid–ask spreads and market impact costs).

Stock index futures provide another market that institutional investors can use to alter equity risk exposure when new information is acquired. But which market—cash or futures—should the investor employ to alter a position *quickly* upon receipt of new information? As we explained in Chapter 6, it will be the one that is the more efficient to use to achieve the objective. The factors to consider are commissions, bid–ask spreads, market impact costs (hence the importance of market liquidity), and the leverage offered.

The market that investors feel is the one that is more efficient to use to achieve their investment objective will be the one where price discovery takes place. Price information will then be transmitted to the other market. So, for example, if the futures market is the market of choice, it will serve as the price discovery market. That is, it will be the market where investors send their collective message about how any new information is expected to impact the cash market. Then, there must be a mechanism for transmitting that message to the cash market. That mechanism is index arbitrage.

A comparison of transactions costs indicates that they are substantially lower in the stock index futures market. Typically, transactions costs in this market are between 5% to 10% of transactions costs in the cash market. For example, the firm of Morgan Stanley estimates that the transactions costs associated with trading a $120 million portfolio of stocks would be about $161,000 compared to only $10,000 using S&P 500 stock index futures. The corresponding execution costs (market impact costs), according to Morgan Stanley, would be $520,000 for the portfolio of stocks and $20,000 for stock index futures.[27]

The speed at which orders can be executed also gives the advantage to the futures market. It has been estimated that to sell a block of stock at a reasonable price would take about two to three minutes, while a futures transaction can be accomplished in 30 seconds or less.[28] The advantage is also on the side of the futures market when it comes to the amount of money that must be put up in a transaction (i.e., leverage). As we explained earlier,

---

[27] "Program Trading" (Morgan Stanley, October 8, 1987).

[28] Thomas Byrne, "Program Trading—A Trader's Perspective," *Commodities Law Letter*, Vol. VI, Nos. 9 and 10, p. 9.

margin requirements for transactions in the stock market are considerably higher than in the stock index futures market. Thus, a study by the SEC's Division of Market Regulation concludes:

> [Institutions can] sell portions of their equity positions in a faster, less expensive manner by using index futures than by selling directly on stock exchanges. . . .
>
> Futures are used instead of stocks because of the increased speed and reduced transaction costs entailed in trading a single product in the futures market. . . .
>
> As a result of the futures market's liquidity, investors can execute large transactions with much smaller market effects than is possible in the separate stocks.

Which market is the one that investors have selected to employ to alter their risk exposure? Merrick found that, prior to 1985, the cash market dominated the price discovery process, relative to the stock index futures market.[29] Since 1985, however, the S&P 500 futures market has played the dominant price discovery role. This reversal of the dominant market was not an accident. It followed the pattern of trading volume. When trading volume in the futures market surpassed that on the cash market, the futures market dominated.

How does the existence of competing markets with the attributes that we described above affect the stock market? In her testimony before Congress on July 23, 1987, Susan Phillips, then the Chairperson of the Commodity Futures Trading Commission, stated that: "The depth and liquidity of the futures markets facilitate the absorption of new fundamental information quickly, thus improving the efficiency of the stock markets . . ."[30]

Is it possible for the futures market to take on a life of its own, so that the futures price does not reflect the economic value of the underlying instrument? It could be, if there were not a mechanism to bring futures prices and cash market prices in line. This mechanism is index arbitrage, which we described earlier.

Critics of stock index futures point to program trading, index arbitrage, and dynamic hedging (portfolio insurance) when there is a substantial decline in the cash market and/or increased stock price volatility. As we explained in Chapter 8, program trading is a technique for trading lists of stocks as close

---

[29] John J. Merrick, Jr., "Price Discovery in the Stock Market," Federal Reserve Bank of Philadelphia Working Paper No. 87-4, March 1987.

[30] Testimony before the Subcommittee on Telecommunications and Finance, Committee on Energy and Commerce, U.S. House of Representatives, July 23, 1987, p. 1.

in time as possible. It is not, as is often stated in the popular press, a trading strategy. Program trades typically are implemented electronically using the automated order execution facilities of the exchanges (e.g., the Super DOT (Designated Order Turnaround) of the New York Stock Exchange) that allow orders to be transmitted simultaneously to the appropriate specialist post.

Why is it important for an institution to execute a list of orders as close in time as possible? There are several investment strategies that depend on this: indexing, index arbitrage, and portfolio insurance. The question is whether any of these strategies that rely on program trading and stock index futures are disruptive to the stock market.

Indexing. Indexing, as we explained in Chapter 8, is not a strategy that attempts to trade on information. Indexing is a strategy that theory tells us investors should employ in an efficient market in order to capture the efficiency embodied in the market. Yet the theory tells us nothing about how to implement the strategy. To manage an indexed portfolio, a money manager first constructs an initial portfolio that it is hoped will replicate the performance of the market. The money manager must rebalance the portfolio, however, as new monies are added to or withdrawn from an indexed portfolio. Program trading is used so that all stocks in the portfolio can be sold or purchased by simultaneous order at the closing prices, so that the performance of the indexed portfolio will do a good job tracking the index. Therefore, indexing should not be a disruptive market force.

Index Arbitrage. As we just explained, there must be a mechanism to transmit the message about investor expectations from the price discovery market to the other market. Only if the cost of carry is zero will the futures price and the cash price be the same. Otherwise, the futures price will differ from the cash price by an amount equal to the cost of carry. Because of transactions costs and other factors, there are boundaries around the theoretical futures price limiting generation of arbitrage profits if the futures price trades within the bounds. In an attempt to capture arbitrage profits, those who follow an index arbitrage are simply tying the futures and cash markets together. This link prevents futures contracts from taking on a life of their own, and thereby allows hedgers to use stock index futures to carry out strategies to protect portfolio values at a fair price.

What happens if the futures price is outside the boundaries? An investor can generate arbitrage profits by selling the more expensive instrument and buying the cheaper instrument, driving the price of the expensive one down and driving the price of the cheaper one up until the futures price is within the theoretical boundaries.

Suppose that the cash market is cheap relative to the futures market. An investor will borrow funds and buy the stocks and simultaneously sell the futures contract. At the expiration of the contract, the stock will be sold in order to provide cash to cover the loan. The investor will liquidate the stock position by submitting market-on-close sell orders at the expiration of the futures contract.[31] If, in contrast, the futures price is cheap relative to the stocks, the investor will buy the futures and sell the stock. At the settlement date, the investor must cover the short sale of the stock and therefore must buy the stock. The short position would be covered by submitting market-on-close orders to buy the stocks.

What might happen on the settlement date when the stock portfolio in an index arbitrage must be liquidated in the case of a long stock position and stocks purchased in the case of a short position? There will certainly be an increase in orders but what will happen to stock prices? It depends on the composition of the orders. If they are balanced between arbitrageurs who have created long positions and short positions, then we should not expect any significant price movement. If orders are not balanced, the action should result in a significant change in prices. Thus, it is possible that stock price volatility will increase at settlement dates. We'll look at the empirical evidence later.

Critics of index arbitrage argue that arbitrageurs consider only the relationship between cash and futures and the cost of transacting rather than make decisions based on the economic value of the underlying market. The response to these critics is that there must be a movement in at least one of the markets for arbitrage trading to be profitable. As long as non-arbitrageurs are pricing in at least one of the markets according to economic information, price changes capture assessments of this information. Arbitrage then irons out the inconsistency between the markets.

We can also see the importance of program trading in this strategy. An index arbitrage strategy requires program trading to implement the buy or sell orders so that trades will occur as close in time as possible. Without program trading, the theoretical bands for the futures price would be much greater.

Dynamic Hedging. Recall that dynamic hedging (portfolio insurance) involves buying stocks or futures when the market is rising and selling when the market is falling. The concern with this strategy that is expressed by the SEC Division of Market Regulation and other critics is that it may have a "cascade" effect when stock prices decline. To understand this argument, consider what would happen if stock prices decline and dynamic hedging is

---

[31] A market-on-close order is a market order executed on the day it was entered at the official closing of the market.

employed using stocks and a riskless asset. The strategy requires that stocks be sold. But if there are many institutional investors following a dynamic strategy, this will mean a substantial number of stocks will be sold, causing further decline in stock prices. In turn, more stocks must be sold, leading to more decline in stock prices.

The same would happen if stock index futures are used to implement a dynamic hedging program. Their sales in the futures market would depress futures. What would arbitrageurs do? They would take offsetting positions in futures (by buying futures) and in stocks (by selling stocks). This action, it is argued, would lower cash prices further, and cause portfolio insurers to sell futures, resulting in a spiraling effect.

Proponents of dynamic hedging argue that the cascade effect is unlikely. At some point, value-oriented investors would step in when stocks are priced below their value based on economic fundamentals. However, Grossman (in a paper published several months before Black Monday) presented theoretical arguments that suggest that the imbalance of buyers and sellers of portfolio insurance could change stock market volatility. Specifically, if the demand for portfolio insurance exceeds the amount that market participants are willing to supply of portfolio insurance (that is, the amount of put options that market participants are willing to sell), volatility will increase; it would decrease if supply exceeded demand.[32]

SEC Study of the September 11–12, 1986, Market Decline.   We do have some evidence about index-related strategies during periods of sharp market declines. The Dow Jones Industrial Average dropped 86.61 points (a 4.61% decline) on September 11, 1986. The next day it dropped by another 34.17 points (1.91%). The Division of Market Regulation of the SEC investigated this two-day decline in stock prices to determine the role index-related strategies may have played. It concluded that:

> The magnitude of the September decline was a result of changes in investors' perception of fundamental economic conditions, rather than artificial forces arising from index-related strategies.[33]

---

[32] Sanford J. Grossman, "An Analysis of the Implications for Stock and Futures Price Volatility of Program Trading and Dynamic Hedging Strategies," presented at the Conference on the Impact of Stock Index Futures Trading at the Center for the Study of Futures Markets, Columbia University, June 8, 1987. The paper was subsequently published in the July 1988 issue of the *Journal of Business*. A less technical version of this paper is "Insurance Seen and Unseen: The Impact of Markets," *Journal of Portfolio Management* (Summer 1988), pp. 5–8.

[33] Securities and Exchange Commission, Division of Market Regulation, "The Role of Index-Related Trading in the Market Decline on September 11 and 12, 1986," March 1987.

The SEC further states that

> Index-related futures trading was instrumental in the rapid transmission of these changed investor perceptions to individual stock prices, and may have condensed the time period in which the decline occurred.

The SEC study also was concerned with (1) the "cascade" effect resulting from the implementation of portfolio insurance strategies, and (2) potential manipulative uses employing stock index futures. The SEC did not find either present on September 11 and 12. Moreover, with respect to the "cascade effect," the SEC study concludes that there were sufficient economic forces to counteract it. As for potential manipulation, the SEC study notes that manipulation would be too costly and more risky than other potential manipulation targets.

The SEC concludes that:

> Analysis of this particular market decline does not provide an independent basis to conclude that radical regulatory or structural changes are necessary at this time. . . . However, close monitoring should be maintained.

The SEC study therefore exonerates index-related strategies.

What Has Been the Effect on Stock Price Volatility?

The view held by some investors and the popular press is that stock index futures and options, program trading, and index-related strategies (index arbitrage and dynamic hedging) have resulted in an increase in the volatility of stock prices. This criticism of futures contracts is not confined to stock index futures, but as we explained in Chapter 6, it has been leveled at all futures contracts. In that same chapter we also questioned whether greater price volatility for a market was necessarily bad.

Several studies have empirically investigated the effect of the introduction of futures trading, and the effect of index-related strategies on stock price volatility. The difficulty in carrying out the empirical tests is determining what the volatility of the cash market price would have been in the absence of futures trading. A simple comparison of price volatility before and after the introduction of futures trading, while informative, is not sufficient. The pitfall of this approach is that there are other factors that will influence volatility—the variability of economic information that affects stock price volatility. Thus, an increase in price volatility may be due to an increase in the variability of economic information that affects stock market prices. Or, failure to observe an increase in price volatility may be due to a decrease in the variability of economic information, masking any increase in price volatility. Thus studies must control for the other factors that impact stock price volatility.

Studies have examined interday (i.e., day-to-day) price volatility[34] and intraday price volatility[35] using a wide range of measures of price volatility. A fair conclusion of all of these studies is that the introduction of stock index options and futures and index-related strategies has not increased stock price volatility except, possibly, during periods when stock index futures and options expire.

Did Stock Index Contracts Cause Black Monday?

On Monday, October 19, 1987 ("Black Monday"), the DJIA declined by 23%, the largest single-day decline in its history. The decline was not unique to the U.S. Every major stock market in the world suffered a decline in local currency units.

In response to the crash, six studies were commissioned in the U.S. to assess the cause of the crash and make recommendations on reducing the likelihood of another crash. Studies were commissioned by (1) then-President Reagan (Presidential Task Force on Market Mechanisms, popularly known as the Brady Report), (2) the General Accounting Office, (3) the Securities and Exchange Commission, (4) the New York Stock Exchange, (5) the Chicago Mercantile Exchange, and (6) the Commodity Futures Exchange.

According to the popular press and many market observers, no study was needed. The culprits were well-known—market participants who employed index-related strategies. For example, *The Wall Street Journal* the day following the crash reported: "In a nightmarish fulfillment of some traders' and academicians' worst fears, the five year old index futures for the first time plunged into a panicky, unlimited free-fall, fostering a sense of crisis

---

[34] Studies that have looked at the impact of the introduction of stock index futures on interday price volatility are: Carolyn D. Davis and Alice P. White, "Stock Market Volatility," Staff Study, Board of Governors of the Federal Reserve System, August 1987; John J. Merrick, Jr., "Volume Determination in Stock and Stock Index Futures Markets: An Analysis of Volume and Volatility Effects," *The Journal of Futures Markets* (October 1987), pp. 483–496; Lawrence Harris, "S&P 500 Cash Stock Price Volatilities," *Journal of Finance* (December 1989), pp. 1155–1576; and Franklin R. Edwards, "Does Futures Trading Increase Stock Price Volatility?" *Financial Analysts Journal* (January–February 1988), pp. 63–69.

[35] Studies of intraday price volatility include: Laszlo Birinyi, Jr., and H. Nicholas Hanson, "Market Volatility: An Updated Study" (Salomon Brothers, July 1986), and Hans R. Stoll and Robert E. Whaley, "Expiration Day Effects of Index Options and Futures," *Financial Analysts Journal* (March–April 1987), pp. 16–28.

throughout U.S. capital markets."[36] The evidence that has accumulated since, however, does not confirm that index-related trading was the culprit. We review the evidence below. (Other possible causes for the crash are discussed in Chapter 8.)

Index-Related Trading and the Crash. Program trading was severely limited on October 19 and the morning of October 20 because the unavailability of the NYSE Designated Order Turnaround (DOT) system made it difficult to execute trades. Suspension of the DOT system, however, gave the impression that it was program trading that caused the chaotic market. The actual motivation for suspension was the fear that the specialist system could not execute all the program trades.

Index arbitrage traders could not operate in the chaotic market environment even before suspension of the DOT system. At the outset on October 19, index arbitrageurs could not transact in the cash market because many of the major issues in the S&P 500 did not open for trading until 11 a.m. or later. It was difficult to execute the program trades necessary to implement an index arbitrage strategy in the futures market, with prices too volatile and bid–ask spreads too wide. Further in the day, the execution of an index arbitrage strategy became even more difficult. Delays in reporting trades in the cash market meant that identifying profitable arbitrage opportunities between the cash and futures market could not be done. Delays in executing orders in the cash market, particularly after suspension of the DOT system, meant that even if a profitable arbitrage could be identified there would be no assurance that one could execute at the prices used to identify the arbitrage opportunity. Thus, index arbitrage was not the culprit. It may be argued, on the contrary, that the impediments to index arbitraging made matters worse because this reduced demand in the stock index futures market.

Dynamic Hedging (Portfolio Insurance) and the Crash. Recall that Grossman argued that an imbalance between the demand for portfolio insurance and the supply of portfolio insurance will alter the volatility of the market. When the demand exceeds supply, volatility will increase, causing a dramatic decline in prices when the market is declining. It is interesting to note that on the morning of October 19, 1987, several options exchanges did begin trading in long-term index options that were designed to satisfy the needs of the portfolio insurance market.[37] A supply of long-term put index options—that is, actual exchange-traded put options—it is argued, could have satisfied the

---

[36] Scott McMurray and Robert L. Rose, "Chicago's 'Shadow Markets' Led Free Fall in a Plunge that Began Right at Opening," *The Wall Street Journal* (October 20, 1987), p. 28.

[37] Gary L. Gastineau, "Eliminating Option Position Limits: A Key Structural Reform" (New York: Salomon Brothers Inc, August 30, 1988), p. 3.

demand from portfolio insurers. Two things probably prevented that from happening. First, the new exchange-traded contracts did not have sufficient time to develop so that market participants could be comfortable with using them. Second, even if market participants did want to use these new contracts, as we explained earlier in this chapter, there were position limits imposed on investors by the exchange that may have prevented them from doing so. In discussing Black Monday, SEC Commissioner Joseph A. Grundfest in an article published in mid-1989 wrote:

> Had all investors involved in portfolio insurance found it possible, and desirable, to satisfy their demand for "insurance" by buying puts instead of relying on dynamic hedges, the market would have had more information about the intensity of investor concern about a downside move. Under those circumstances, there's reason to believe that prices might not have fallen as low on the downside had the market simply been better informed of investors' own concerns. Thus, to the extent position limits on index options forced investors away from the options market and into secret dynamic hedging strategies, the government's position limit restrictions may have unwittingly exacerbated the market's decline.[38]

Thus, the culprit might not be dynamic hedging/portfolio insurance but, instead (1) the inability to develop a long-term exchange-traded index option market, and (2) government imposition of a regulatory feature—position limits—that impeded the use of the exchange-traded market. But whether or not one is willing to accept this hypothesis, it should be understood that it is entirely untested and has therefore no empirical underpinning.

Index Trading Volume and the Crash. By looking at trading volume statistics, Hill provides some additional evidence on the size of the role that the stock index futures market played on October 19 and 20.[39] On Monday, S&P 500 futures trading volume was 162,022 contracts, approximately 1.5 times the average daily number of contracts traded in the previous week. In contrast, trading volume on the NYSE was 2.7 times greater than the average daily number of shares traded in the previous week (604 million versus 224 million shares). Based on normal levels of S&P 500 futures trading to NYSE stock trading, approximately 250,000 to 300,000 contracts would have been traded. Thus, actual futures trading was considerably below normal trading

---

[38] Joseph A. Grundfest, "Perestroika on Wall Street: The Future of Securities Trading," *Financial Executive* (May–June 1989), p. 25.

[39] Joanne M. Hill, "Program Trading, Portfolio Insurance, and the Stock Market Crash" (Kidder, Peabody, January 1988), pp. 27–28.

according to the number of shares traded. This low level of futures trading continued on Tuesday, with NYSE trading remaining at 600 million shares, and futures trading volume down to 126,462 contracts.

Stock index options and futures were introduced in the early 1980s. The underlying stock market index may be a broad-based index or a narrow-based index. The dollar value of a contract is determined by the product of the index value and the contract's multiple. Unlike options on individual common stock, stock index products are cash settlement contracts. That is, the contracts are settled in cash at the expiration or settlement date.

Stock index options can be used to bet on the movement of stock prices (speculating) or to protect a portfolio position against an adverse price movement (hedging). In addition, the following index-related strategies can be employed by institutional investors: controlling market risk exposure, constructing an index fund, enhancing returns via index arbitrage, dynamic hedging, and implementing an asset allocation decision. Dynamic hedging is related to replicating a put option with stocks or stock index futures.

Studies of the efficiency of the stock index options market suggest that mispricing was present when these contracts began trading. The reason may be that it is difficult to arbitrage an option where the underlying instrument is an index. More recent studies suggest that although stock index futures were occasionally mispriced when trading commenced in 1983, they are now fairly priced.

Critics of stock index contracts believe that index-related trading has increased stock price volatility and is responsible for Black Monday. A closer examination suggests that the stock index futures market provides a less expensive and more speedy transaction market for investors to alter their exposure to economic information expected to impact stock prices. The stock index futures market has become the price discovery market.

The evidence cited in this chapter suggests that index-related trading has not increased stock market price volatility. Nor was it responsible for Black Monday.

1.   Two years ago Osaka became the first Japanese exchange to come out with a financial future—a stock-index future known as the Osaka 50. It was only a modest success, mainly because it had to be delivered in shares rather than cash.

This claim comes from the September 1989 issue of *Institutional Investor*. Why is cash settlement preferred for stock index futures?

2. On March 7, 1991, open interest for the S&P 500 June '91 futures contract was 70,278. Open interest for the December '91 contract was 357. What is open interest, and why would the open interest figures for the June and December contracts be of interest to a portfolio manager considering using stock index futures?

3. You notice that the S&P 500 Index is 380. The dividend yield for the stocks comprising the index is 4%. The interest rate for 12 months is 12%. The S&P 500 futures contract for settlement in 12 months' time is currently selling at 412.

    a. Is there an arbitrage opportunity? If so, how would you take advantage of it?

    b. What considerations would you want to address before executing this trade?

4. Donald Singleton is an investment banker for a regional firm. One of his clients, Dolby Manufacturing, Inc., is a private company that will be making an initial public offering of 20 million shares of common stock. Mr. Singleton's firm will buy the issue at $10 per share. He has suggested to the managing director of the firm, John Wilson, that the firm should hedge the position using stock index futures contracts. What should Mr. Wilson's response be?

5. In the August 18, 1989, issue of *The Wall Street Journal* there appeared an article entitled "Program Trading Spreads From Just Wall Street Firms." Following are two quotations from that article:

    > Brokerage firms in the business, which tiptoed back into program trading after the post-crash furor died down, argue that such strategies as stock-index arbitrage—rapid trading between stock index futures and stocks to capture fleeting price differences—link two related markets and thus benefit both.

    The second quotation in the article is from a senior vice president at Twenty-First Securities Corp.

    > Program trading is a product that is here, links markets, and it is not going to disappear. It is a function of the computerization of Wall Street.

    Do you agree with these statements?

6. The idea sounds almost un-American. Instead of using your smarts to pick stocks that will reach the sky, you put money in a fund that merely tracks a broad market index. But that is precisely what institutional investors are doing. . . . Indexing is a new force in the stock market. . . . But the impact of index-funds reaches far beyond stock prices.

   This quotation is from the June 8, 1987, issue of *Business Week*. Discuss how indexing may have contributed to the growth of the stock index derivatives markets.

7. The proliferation of futures and options markets has created new opportunities for international investors. It is now possible to change investment exposure from one country to another through the use of derivative instruments, augmented by a limited number of individual securities. Asset allocation in most major markets is now feasible using futures and options.

   Discuss this quotation from the December 1988 issue of *Euromoney* and the reasons for using derivative rather than cash instruments to facilitate asset allocation decisions.

8. Consider the testimony following given by Alan Greenspan, Chairman of the Board of Governors of the Federal Reserve, before a subcommittee in the U.S. Senate:

   In a more fundamental sense, we believe it is counterproductive to lay blame on one sector, in this case the market for stock index derivatives, for increasing occurrence of wide and rapid price swings in equity markets. . . . Rather, the volatility we observe reflects more basic changes in economic and financial processes prompted by technological advances and the increasing concentration of assets in institutional portfolios.

   a. Do you agree with Mr. Greenspan's view?

   b. Do you think that stock index derivatives were responsible for increased volatility and the October 1987 crash?

THEORY OF INTEREST RATE DETERMINATION AND BOND VALUATION : I

LEARNING OBJECTIVES

After reading this chapter you will understand:

- the role of individual preference in choosing current and future consumption in the determination of interest rates.

- the role of loan and production opportunities in the determination of interest rates.

- the factors that determine the real rate of interest in an economy.

- the relationship between the real rate of interest and the nominal rate of interest and inflation (Fisher's Law).

- the cash flow characteristics of a bond.

- how the price of a bond is determined.

- why the yield to maturity is used as a measure of a bond's return.

- the importance of the reinvestment rate in realizing the yield to maturity.
- why the price of a bond changes.

$\mathbf{I}$n this chapter we develop the theory of interest rate determination. We then apply this theory in this chapter and the next to the valuation of bonds. The various types of bonds are the subject of later chapters.

THEORY OF INTEREST RATE DETERMINATION

Interest rates are a measure of the price paid by a "borrower" (or "debtor") to a "lender" (or "creditor") for the use of resources during some time interval. The sum transferred from the lender to the borrower is referred to as the *principal* and the price paid for the use is usually expressed as a percentage of the principal per unit of time (mostly per year).

It is common in the bond market to refer to differences or changes in interest rates in terms of *basis points*. A basis point is equal to 0.0001, or 0.01%, and 100 basis points represent 1% of change. So, for example, the difference between 10% and 11% is said to be 100 basis points. If the interest rate increases from 10% to 10.35%, it is said to have increased by 35 basis points.

The transfer from savers to investors occurs through a variety of instruments, and the price paid may differ between one sort of instrument and another. Indeed, one finds at any one time a bewildering array of rates offered on different instruments. The spread between the lowest and the highest rate in the market might run as high as 1500 basis points (15 percentage points).

In this section we focus on the one interest rate that can be said to provide the anchor for other rates, namely, the short-term, riskless, real rate. All other rates differ from it by "maturity" differentials and by "risk premiums." By the *real rate* we mean the rate that would prevail in the economy if price levels remain constant, and are expected to be constant indefinitely.

To understand what determines the basic rate we must inquire why some people might decide not to consume all their current resources (i.e., to save), and why some others would want to invest. It should be noted that those desirous to borrow might want to use the proceeds either to make further loans (i.e., acquire financial assets) or to invest (i.e., acquire income-yielding physical assets such as plant, equipment, and residential structures). In this section we abstract from financial intermediaries and assume that all loans, directly or indirectly, end up being transferred to an investor.

Description of Preferences between Current and Future Consumption

Saving reflects primarily the choice between current consumption and future consumption. To understand that choice, as all consumer choices, we need to consider two fundamental concepts: *taste* or *preference*, and *opportunity*.

Consider first the representation of preferences. Suppose that our consumer is to choose among a variety of "baskets" (or "bundles"), where each basket consists of a certain quantity of current consumption and a certain quantity of future consumption. Tastes or preferences can then be described fully by a complete preference ranking of all the relevant baskets. Given that the amount of current and future consumption can vary by any small dose, some choices among the possible baskets will be ranked equally; that is, the consumer will be indifferent as to certain choices among baskets.

This consideration makes it possible to obtain a very effective representation of preference, as shown in Figure 11-1. The figure measures current consumption, C_1, along the horizontal axis, and future consumption, C_2, along the vertical. Hence any point in the diagram represents a commodity basket, such as H. There will be some other point, say, H^*, representing an indifferent choice to H; more generally, there will be a curve going from H to H^* and beyond, consisting of baskets indifferent to both H and H^*. Such a curve is called an *indifference curve*. We have labeled the indifference curve in Figure 11-1 as u.

Note that through every point in the diagram there will go an indifference curve, although they cannot intersect, for that would imply that a given basket is ranked both higher and lower than another—a clear inconsistency. The indifference curve u has been drawn falling from left to right; this is because both consumption now and later can be taken to be desirable. As basket H in Figure 11-1 includes more *current* consumption than basket H^*, in order for it to be indifferent from basket H^*, basket H must have less *future* consumption, C_2. The reason the curve is drawn convex to the origin is the

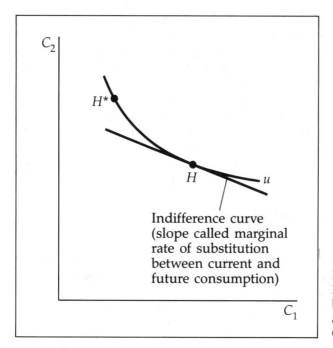

Indifference curve
(slope called marginal
rate of substitution
between current and
future consumption)

FIGURE 11-1
Indifference Curve
between Current
and Future
Consumption

assumption that, as the consumer gives up successive equal amounts of current consumption, it will take growing quantities of future consumption to make up for the loss of an additional unit. This assumption appears reasonable, although complete justification of it is beyond the scope of this chapter.

At any point on an indifference curve, such as H, we can draw a tangent to the curve. The slope of the tangent has been called by Irving Fisher, the father of the theory of interest rates, the *marginal rate of time preference*.[1] It measures how much additional consumption next period is needed to compensate the consumer for the loss of a unit of consumption now. That is, the slope of the tangent measures the *marginal rate of substitution between current and future consumption*. We might conjecture that a particular person would be impatient to consume now rather than later, and therefore that it would take more than one unit tomorrow to induce such a person to give up the enjoyment of one unit today. In other words, the marginal rate of time preference, or the slope of the indifference curve, would be larger than one.

---

[1] Irving Fisher, *The Theory of Interest Rates* (New York: Macmillan, 1930).

It is for this reason that Fisher proposed labeling the excess of the slope over unity a "measure of impatience."

It turns out, however, that this conjecture about the slope is wrong. It is easy to verify that the slope of the indifference curve changes as we move along it, and therefore that it is most unlikely to be everywhere more than unity. On the left side of the diagram where today's endowment is small, the slope can be counted on to be larger than unity. As we move to the right, and the current endowment grows larger relative to the future one, though, the slope must become smaller than one, meaning that the consumer may very well be willing to give up a unit of today's abundant supply for less than one unit to add to tomorrow's scarce supply. This is an important insight behind understanding why interest rates can in principle be negative.

Loan Market

To understand the saving behavior, we need to look at how preferences interact with opportunities. Let us consider first a case where the opportunities or baskets among which the person can choose are defined by: (1) an initial endowment of the commodity now and later, and (2) by a loan market where individuals are free to exchange this initial or current endowment for a different one by lending or borrowing at a fixed exchange rate of $R = 1 + r$ units of the commodity in the next period (i.e., the future in our illustration) per unit of the commodity lent in the current period. R is the gross return (principal plus interest) and r the net return or interest rate. For example, if a unit of current consumption is loaned at 5%, then r is 0.05 and R is 1.05.

We can represent this opportunity locus in Figure 11-2 by means of the negatively sloped straight line mm going through the endowment basket, point B (with current endowment Y_1 and future endowment Y_2). We refer to the opportunity locus in the loan market as the *market line*. It slopes down, because to get more C_1 you must reduce C_2. It is a straight line, because, at any point on it, by giving up one unit of the current consumption we can get the same additional amount, R, of future consumption. And it goes through B, because if there were no lending, so that current consumption were equal to the current endowment, Y_1, future consumption would have to equal the future endowment, Y_2. Thus, the opportunity locus must include point B.

Now let us add to the diagram a family of indifference curves, as shown in Figure 11-3. There will be one curve in the diagram that is tangent to the market line, such as curve u_4 at point D. The consumption basket corresponding to point D can be shown to be the preferred one among all those available, given the market line, hence it will be the chosen basket.

To see this, suppose the consumer started by considering point H on indifference curve u_2, where current consumption is greater than at D. Suppose next he considered giving up some current consumption in favor of

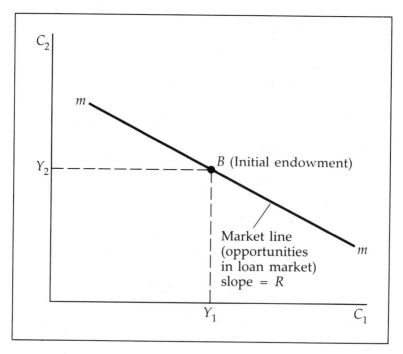

FIGURE 11-2
Representation of Opportunity Locus in the Loan Market (the Market Line)

more future consumption along his market opportunity line. He would first reach point F and would find it a preferable choice, being on a higher indifference curve, u_3. Continuing, he would reach point D on u_4, offering yet higher utility. But beyond D he immediately starts reaching lower and lower utility curves, such as curves u_2 and u_3. We see that the point of tangency of the market line with an indifference curve provides the best of all feasible choices.

Recalling that the slope of an indifference curve at any point measures the marginal rate of substitution between current and future consumption, we see that at the chosen point the marginal rate of substitution is equal to the market rate R (or the marginal rate of impatience equal to r). It is an important property of a perfect market that, because everybody is confronted with the same market rate r, everybody at the chosen point must exhibit the same degree of impatience. In particular, if r is positive, as it generally is in our type of economy, everybody will be "impatient"; that is, they will be willing to give up a unit of current consumption to lend more only if they can get $1 + r$ units later, with $r > 0$, because that opportunity is offered by the market.

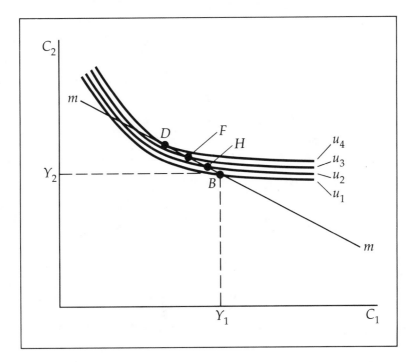

FIGURE 11-3
Family of Indifference Curves and the Market Line

So far we have taken the market rate r as a given. But what does in fact determine r in this simple economy? The answer, of course, is demand and supply. For any given R, each person will decide how much to consume now and how much to save or dissave (the difference between the current endowment and consumption). In this simple economy, saving or dissaving is the same as lending or borrowing. By summing up the *net* lending of each participant, for each R, we obtain a supply curve for loans, such as is graphed in Figure 11-4. We have drawn it as initially rising from left to right, on the commonly held assumption that net lending will rise as R rises. For sufficiently low R, net lending is shown as negative because borrowing would exceed lending. Suppose at first there is no investment. Then market equilibrium requires that *net* lending be zero. It therefore occurs at point E where the curve cuts the horizontal axis. (Note that we have drawn the net lending curve as declining in the rightmost section. We discuss the reason for this later.)

R will reflect two major forces, namely, the time preferences of participants and their endowments. More impatience will tend to make for a

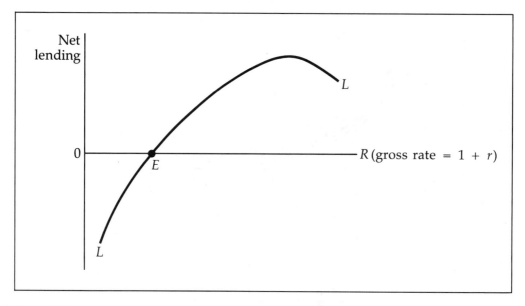

FIGURE 11-4
Supply Curve for Loans

smaller supply of loans (saving) at any given R and to lower the supply curve in Figure 11-4, thereby shifting E to the right. A large endowment of the current commodity relative to the future will make people more eager to lend, raise the curve, and thus reduce R. If this situation is sufficiently prevailing, E may be pushed to the left to the point where it is less than unity and therefore r is negative! This may seem paradoxical, but it is important to understand that there is no opportunity of transferring resources to the future through investment (or money, which is disregarded) outside of lending and borrowing.

Carryover Through Investment

It is instructive to enlarge the model to allow for the possibilities of investments—a productive process through which, by using current resources as an input, we can obtain an output of future commodities. An investment opportunity locus might look something like the curve *tt* of Figure 11-5, which is referred to as the *transformation curve* or the *production function*. It rises from left to right on the assumption that, the more is invested, the more will be the resulting future output. It is convex from below on the

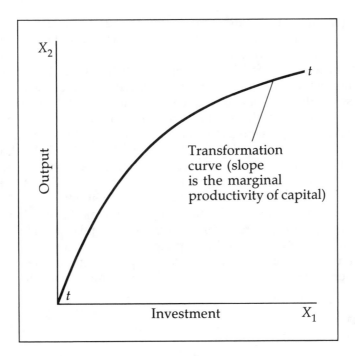

FIGURE 11-5
Representation of Opportunity Locus from Investment (Transformation Curve or
Production Function)

customary assumption of decreasing returns to scale (although increasing
returns are possible in some regions without changing the argument). The
slope of the transformation curve measures the *marginal productivity of capital*.

The consumer now has several decisions to make: how much to invest,
how much to lend (or borrow), and how much to consume now and later. But
only two of these are independent: indeed because current resources are
given, once the person has decided how much to consume and invest, net
lending will be determined uniquely by income minus the two other
expenditures. Similarly, net borrowing and investment, together with the
future endowment, uniquely fix future consumption.

Consider first the decision as to how much to invest. As the consumer's
"income," or what she has available to spend on consumption now and later,
is limited by the sum of her endowment and any profits she may derive from
her production opportunity, a necessary condition to achieve the best feasible
consumption is to insure for herself as large a profit as possible. To see how
this result can be achieved, look again at Figure 11-5. Recall that profit at any

output (or input) is the difference between the output produced with the input (or investment) and the cost of the input. The output for any investment is given by the curve *tt* in Figure 11-5.

What about the cost? Let us suppose initially that the owner of the firm has to borrow the entire amount that is needed to finance the investment. In that case clearly the cost of any given investment will be what is to be repaid next period, namely, the amount borrowed times the gross market rate *R*. This cost can be represented in Figure 11-5 by a straight line going through the origin with a slope, *R*, as shown in Figure 11-6 by the line *MM*. Profit for any output, then, is the difference between the curve *tt* and the line *MM*. This is illustrated in Figure 11-6 for an assumed investment of X_1^*. We refer to the line *MM* in the figure as the "cost line." As it represents the cost of borrowing, however, it has the same slope as the market line in Figure 11-2.

As the consumer increases investment from an investment of zero (i.e., at the origin), we can see from the graph that profits will initially rise (provided there are profits at all). The *additional* profit attributable to increased investment gets smaller and smaller, though, until a point in the figure is

FIGURE 11-6
Measuring the Profit from Investing

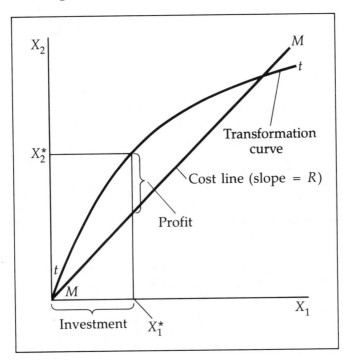

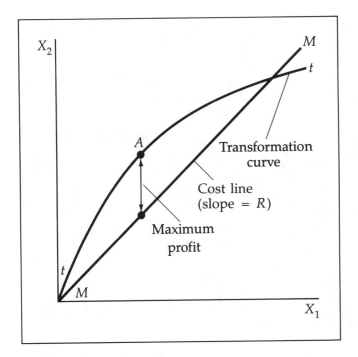

FIGURE 11-7
Profit Maximization Point

reached at which there is no more incremental profit. This point is shown as *A* in Figure 11-7. If the consumer continues to expand investment still farther, the profit (as measured by the vertical distance between the cost line *MM* and the transformation curve *tt*) becomes smaller and smaller. Point *A* has one distinguishing characteristic, which is that at this point the curve *tt* has precisely the same slope *R* as the cost curve *MM*. This is shown in Figure 11-8, where we have drawn through *A* a line *mm* with the same slope as *R* (and hence parallel to *MM*). This line is seen to be tangent to *tt* at *A*.

Because the slope of *tt* represents the marginal productivity of capital, we can conclude that the optimum rate of investment for the firm is where the marginal productivity of capital equals the market gross rate *R* or, equivalently, where the additional output that can be obtained from an additional unit of input is just equal to the cost of borrowing that additional unit of input (and the amount obtained by further increases in investment is less than the cost of borrowing).

We can now proceed to examine the consumption decision and its interaction with the investment decision. To this end, we first show how the transformation curve, curve *tt* in Figure 11-5, would be represented if

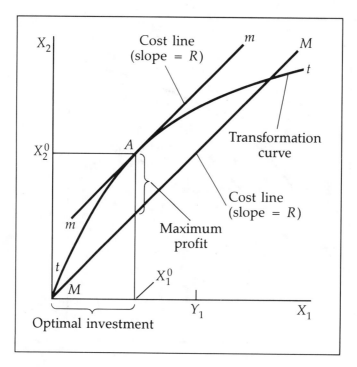

FIGURE 11-8
Profit Maximization and the Cost Line

graphed on the earlier Figures 11-1 through 11-3. This is what we have done in Figure 11-9. We obtain the transformation curve (production function), curve tt, in Figure 11-9 by rotating the curve tt in Figure 11-5 180 degrees and shifting the origin to point B, which represents the initial endowment as in Figure 11-2. The resulting curve is the locus of all achievable baskets of the current and future commodity that are available to the person through a combination of the initial endowment with the transformation opportunity.

The amount invested is shown in Figure 11-9 along the horizontal axis by the difference between the current endowment Y_1 and the point on the horizontal axis corresponding to any point on the transformation curve. This is illustrated in Figure 11-10. At point W in that figure, the corresponding value on the horizontal axis is I^W and the amount of the investment is the difference between Y_1 and I^W. Future consumption corresponding to the point W on the transformation curve is C_2^W, which consists of the future endowment Y_2 plus the profit from the investment as measured by the difference between C_2^W and Y_2.

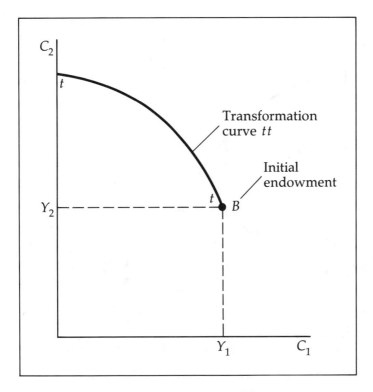

FIGURE 11-9
Transformation Curve Imposed on Current and Future Consumption Graph

Suppose for a moment that there were no market for exchanging C_1 with C_2. Then the curve tt in Figure 11-10 would represent the household opportunity locus. The person's best choice, the basket (C_1, C_2), would then be found at a point of tangency of that curve with an indifference curve. But in a market economy the budget constraint does not come from the initial endowment B in Figure 11-2, or by the initial endowment enlarged by the transformation function as in Figure 11-9, but instead from the endowment plus the profit that can be earned through the production and sale of C_2. It follows that to maximize satisfaction the agent should, to begin with, maximize the profits obtained from the transformation activity. This will yield a new budget equation which will include the best choice of the basket (C_1, C_2).

This can be shown graphically in Figure 11-11. Here point A on the transformation function tt is such that the slope there is equal to the slope of the market line mm. We know that this point, which corresponds to point A

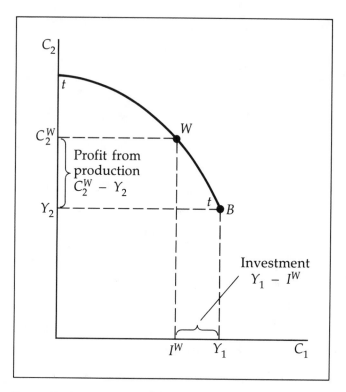

FIGURE 11-10
Measuring Investment and Profit from Investment

in Figure 11-8, represents the amount of investment — $(Y_1 - X_1^0)$ — and output (X_2^0) which maximize profits. Through point A there goes a new budget line mm (again tangent to tt at A) which represents the outcome of adding maximum profits to the endowment. The utility maximizing basket will then be at a point of tangency of this profit-augmented budget line with an indifference curve, such as point C^0.

A most important property resulting from the existence of a perfect loan market, together with a transformation, is that it separates the current consumption decision from current income by opening the possibility to saving and dissaving through transformation and net lending. Similarly, it frees the investment from the saving decision, as the person can bridge the gap between saving and investment through lending and borrowing. In the specific case of Figure 11-11, we find that the chosen consumption C_1^0 is less than the initial endowment Y_1, so the person saves an amount shown in the figure. But that is not sufficient to finance an optimal investment that is equal

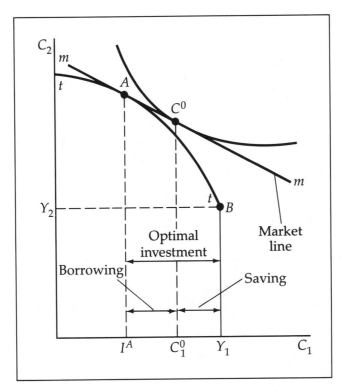

FIGURE 11-11
Optimal Investment and Borrowing Decisions

to the distance between Y_1 and I^A of the chosen production. Hence, the difference $(C_1^0 - I^A)$ is made up by borrowing, as indicated in the figure.

This illustrates how a rational person can both save and borrow. There are many other combinations that we can work out by varying the position of the chosen points A and C^0 relative to each other and to the endowment basket B. If A falls between C^0 and B, the person will end up saving more than she needs for her investment, and thus she will save, invest, and lend. If on the other hand C^0 falls to the right of B, the person will dissave, but she can invest at the same time by borrowing the sum of her investment and dissaving.

Incidentally, it should be apparent by now that we can drop our initial assumption that the investment is financed entirely by borrowing, for should it be financed by the owner's own saving, the cost to the investor of the funds would still be R per unit, which is the amount of interest that would have to be forgone in order to shift funds from making loans in the market to financing the investment (the opportunity cost).

Market Equilibrium

So far we have discussed how a person responds in terms of saving, investment, and borrowing to a given market R. But what determines R itself? The answer, once again, is demand and supply; that is, the price must be such as to clear the market. In the situation we have described there are two markets to clear. The first market for loans R must be such that gross lending equals gross borrowing, or, equivalently, that net borrowing is zero. The second market is that for the current commodity: there are two sources of demand for it, namely, consumption and investment, and R must be such that aggregate consumption (C) plus aggregate investment (I) must equal the given endowment (Y). Thus

$$C + I = Y, \text{ or equivalently, } I = Y - C = S \tag{1}$$

So, R must be such that the demand for investment equals the economy's net saving, denoted by S. But how can R clear two markets at the same time? It is well-known that one variable cannot satisfy two equations at the same time—unless one is redundant in the sense that the two have an identical solution. Indeed it happens that the two market clearing conditions are redundant. To see this, recall that the decisions of each individual must satisfy a "budget constraint"; that is, a person's net lending must equal the excess of her saving over her investment. If we sum up this constraint over the entire market we get

$$L = S - I \tag{2}$$

where L is net lending. It is apparent that if an interest rate clears the commodity market as given by Equation (1) by making $S = I$, then that same rate will make $L = 0$, or clear the loan market. Thus we can conclude that the equilibrium R must equate the supply of saving and the demand for investment or, equivalently, the demand for and supply of loanable funds. If we want to graph the mechanism determining R, it will be more enlightening to use the commodity market, i.e., the condition saving = investment.

Equilibrium in this market is represented graphically in Figure 11-12, where the rising curve is the supply of saving, analogous to LL in Figure 11-4. The investment function is drawn to decline uniformly with R. The justification for this choice can be found in Figure 11-8: we have shown that the investment chosen is at the point where the transformation curve has slope R. If R rises to R_1, the investment must shift to a point where the slope is R_1; because R_1 is larger than R, the transformation curve at R_1 must be steeper. But given the convexity of the transformation curve, this can occur

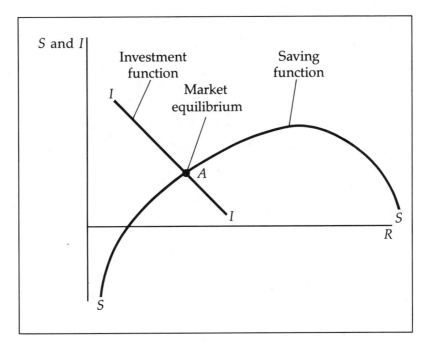

FIGURE 11-12
Market Equilibrium

only if investment is to the left of the initial level, i.e., smaller. The market clearing interest rate is then at the intersection of the saving and investment function, where the two are equal.

It is also apparent from Figure 11-12 that as long as the intersection occurs in a region where the saving rises with R, the market clearing interest rate will be higher, the higher the investment function. As can be seen in Figure 11-13, a shift of the investment function up and to the right (meaning more demand for investment at any given R) will raise the interest rate, and result in increased saving and investment. Similarly, an increased propensity to save, a shift of the saving curve up and to the left as shown in Figure 11-14, will reduce the interest rate and result in saving and investment, although by less than the shift, because the lower R will have a depressing effect on saving.

The basic conclusion is that the interest rate reflects the complex set of forces that control the demand for investment and the supply of saving. These are discussed extensively elsewhere, and we do not examine them here except for setting out a representative catalog of relevant factors: the rate of growth of population and productivity; fiscal policy, including incentives to

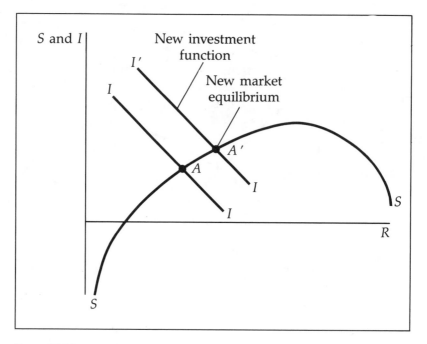

FIGURE 11-13
Change in *I, S,* and *R* if Investment Function Increases

save and invest; demographic variables; the role of bequests; the nature of technological progress; and the openness of international capital markets.

By way of illustrating how some of these forces work out, we discuss briefly the effect of fiscal investment incentives on saving, investment, and interest rates. This is a subject much discussed in recent years. If such incentives are effective, they will shift the *II* curve upward and to the right. If the initial intersection is at point *A* in Figure 11-12, the effect will certainly be that of raising interest rates (see Figure 11-3); but how nearly will it succeed in achieving the intended purpose of increasing investment? In the end, investment can rise only if and as far as savings rise; and the rise in saving depends on the extent to which saving responds to the higher rate. If the response is strong, there will be a relatively large rise in saving and investment, while the rise in interest rates will be contained. But in the opposite case the incentives will mostly increase interest rates and have little effect on investment.

To complete the picture, we consider also the case where the two curves intersect at a point like *G'* in Figure 11-15, where saving decreases in response

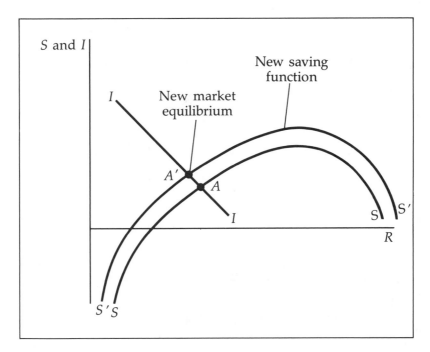

FIGURE 11-14
Change in *I*, *S*, and *R* if Saving Function Increases

to higher interest rates. Is such a response conceivable? If people get paid more for saving, could they possibly respond by saving less? The answer is that this is entirely possible; indeed, according to one school of thought, it is very likely. The reason is simple. Suppose that initially you own a portfolio of loans. An increasing R will have two effects influencing your response. First, future consumption is cheaper in terms of current consumption, which should encourage you to consume more later and save more now. But there is a second effect. As long as you are a creditor, a higher interest rate will make you richer and push you toward consuming more now *and* later. It is entirely possible that the second effect may predominate. In this case the supply of saving will decline with higher R, as shown by the terminal portion of the SS curve in Figure 11-15. If the intersection is in that region, the result of incentives can be quite perverse, as we can see if we shift the II curve up to the right from *I'I'* to *I"I"* and the equilibrium point from *G'* to *G"*. The effect is again to increase R, but now that increase will *reduce saving* and *hence investment.*

In other words, the fiscal incentive has the opposite effect from the intended one. The situation is made worse if the incentives are financed not

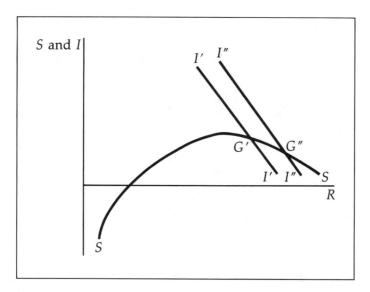

FIGURE 11-15
Possibility of Saving Decreasing in Response to Higher Interest Rate

by new taxes but by increased deficit, which reduces investment further by cutting net national saving directly and through a higher interest rate. Some think that these considerations may go some of the way to explain the catastrophic decline of saving during the heyday of Reaganomics. To be sure, net investment did not decline much, but that was because of the huge borrowing from non–U.S. savers made attractive by the high domestic interest rates, which has had the effect of making the country permanently poorer.

Efficiency Properties of Markets

The equilibrium achieved with the intermediation of the loan markets has an important property from the point of view of the efficiency of the economy in producing and allocating resources, a property that economists refer to as "Pareto optimality." Instinctively we think of economic efficiency as implying the absence, or minimization, of waste. Pareto optimality makes that notion precise and conceptually operational: an allocation is Pareto optimal if it is not possible to reallocate the goods (inputs and outputs) in such a way that *some* will be better off while *nobody will lose.*

It is clear that if an allocation is not Pareto optimal there must be some slack or waste; conversely, if there is slack, the allocation cannot be Pareto optimal. "Pareto optimality" in our simplified economy is assured by profit maximization, plus the fact that, at market equilibrium, both the marginal productivity of capital and the marginal rate of time preference equals R for every firm and for every consumer. This means that there is no way of increasing output by reshuffling inputs among firms; the additional output by those who would gain inputs will be offset precisely by the output lost by those losing inputs. By similar reasoning, we can infer that no welfare gain can come from reshuffling the given output among consumers.

While this is an important logical result, it turns out we cannot make too much of it in respect to existing free market economies. First, the result presupposes a perfectly competitive market, which free competition may fail to assure because of restrictive practices. Second, it ignores transactions costs, information costs, and the consequences of incomplete information. Third, there is the whole problem of externalities or effects—negative or positive— that production may have on people other than the buyer of the product. Finally, society may value things other than efficiency, such as the distribution of welfare; there may therefore be some non-Pareto optimal solution, trading efficiency for some other property. All these considerations are incentives to make markets more perfect and allow valuing externalities through the price mechanism.

Real and Nominal Interest Rates: Fisher's Law

The interest rate we have talked about so far is the *real* rate, which would prevail in the absence of inflation. This rate measures the amount of the commodity next period that can be exchanged for one unit of the commodity now. This generally differs from the *nominal* rate, which measures the amount of money to be repaid next period per unit borrowed now. The two rates are connected by a simple relation that is known as Fisher's Law. It rests on the principle that an exchange of *money* now for *money* later must imply the same rate of exchange between the *commodity* now and later, as implied by the real rate.

Suppose the real rate is $1 + r$; then by delivering one unit of the commodity now, we can obtain $(1 + r)$ units next period. But we could, alternatively, sell the commodity now at the spot price, say, p_1, and invest the proceeds in a loan at the nominal rate $(1 + i)$, obtaining $p_1 (1 + i)$ units of money next period.

How many units of the next-period commodity does that represent? To find the answer, clearly we must divide by the second-period price of the commodity, say p_2. Thus the second-period quantity is $p_1 (1 + i)/(p_2)$. This quantity must equal the real rate $(1 + r)$. Thus,

$$(1 + r) = \frac{1 + i}{1 + \dot{p}} \tag{3}$$

where the denominator follows from the fact that

$$\frac{p_1}{p_2} = \frac{1}{p_2/p_1} = \frac{1}{1 + [(p_2 - p_1)/p_1]}$$

and

$(p_2 - p_1)/p_1 = \dot{p}$ = the percentage rise in the price level over the period of the loan

Equation (3) can be restated in the form

$$(1 + i) = (1 + r)(1 + \dot{p})$$

This means that the nominal gross rate is the product of the gross real rate and one plus the rate of inflation. The equation above, in turn, implies

$$i = r + \dot{p} + r\dot{p}$$

For the more common values of r and $\dot{p}$, the product of r and $\dot{p}$ is small enough to be neglected, and the equation above can be written as

$$i \approx r + \dot{p}$$

or

$$r \approx i - \dot{p} \tag{4}$$

Equation (4) is the formula commonly used to compute the ex post real rate of interest, which cannot be observed directly in the market. It is equally common to measure the anticipated or ex ante real rate of interest by replacing $\dot{p}$ by anticipated inflation. The ex ante rate will differ from the ex post rate as a result of errors of expectation. It should be clear that the real rate so computed is not necessarily the same as the rate that would clear markets in the economy without inflation, because as a result of market imperfections, including taxation and possibly inflation illusion, inflation can alter the real rate. For instance, in the early phase of unanticipated inflation, the real rate typically falls. In other words, the real rate, besides reflecting fundamental forces such as saving and productivity, may be affected also by other forces, among which is inflation, especially in the short run.

BASIC PRINCIPLES OF BOND VALUATION

In the previous section we have focused on determinants of the one-period rate on debt instruments. We now relax the simplifying assumption that there are just two periods, the present and the future, and accept that the future may include a long sequence of periods and therefore that debt contracts may have varying maturities. In Chapters 14 to 16 we deal with the class of nominal instruments called *bonds*, where the stream of payments consists of a constant amount paid periodically (the *coupon payment*) and a terminal payment at maturity consisting of the last coupon payment and a lump sum or balloon payment called the *maturity value* or *par value* or *face value*. The balloon payment is usually close to the amount received by the borrower at issue, and therefore it is frequently referred to as repayment of principal.[2] This class of investments consists of bonds issued by the U.S. Treasury, federally sponsored agencies, corporations, municipalities, and foreign borrowers.

As the valuation of, and the return from, debt instruments depends on interest rates, we focus here on the determinants of this variable. While participants and observers of financial markets do refer to the "interest rate" in the economy, in reality, there is not one interest rate but many. We will show that the difference between rates quoted at the same date reflects a number of characteristics of the instrument, such as its term or maturity (the date at which the last payment is due), its risk of insolvency, its lack of liquidity, differences in tax treatment, and options embedded in the security that grant an option either to the bondholder or to the issuer.

So far what we have presented is the determinants of short-term interest rates. Our specific concern here is with longer-term rates and the valuation of bonds. We will concentrate first on one special case, namely, bonds that are (1) free of risk of default of the issuer, (2) enjoy no advantage from taxes, and (3) contain no embedded options (i.e., are not "callable," "putable," or "convertible"). Federal government debt, the subject of Chapter 14, is an example of this kind of obligation.[3] The rate earned on federal government debt instruments is usually characterized as the "riskless" rate. By riskless we mean that there is no risk that the U.S. government will default on its obligation to pay interest and repay principal. Our discussion initially assumes existence of perfect markets and that future interest rates are expected with certainty.[4]

---

[2] There are also bonds that have no maturity or maturity payment, and thus pay the coupon forever. These instruments, called perpetuals or consoles, do not exist in the U.S. financial system, but do exist in other markets, particularly the United Kingdom.

[3] Federal government bond returns actually do have a minor tax advantage because they are exempt from state and local taxes.

[4] A precise definition of perfect markets is provided in Chapter 8.

A useful way of understanding the valuation of longer-term instruments and how it relates to interest rates is to make use of the principle that, in perfect markets, all riskless instruments must have the same short-term return, and it must coincide with the riskless short-term rate for that period. This condition may be expected to be enforced through arbitrage. The one-period rate of return from, say, an instrument with maturity n and paying the stream $(a_1, \ldots, a_n)$, consists of the cash payment, a_1, plus the capital gain, or the difference between the next period price and the current price of the security, expressed as a percentage of initial value.

Let us denote by ${}_nP_j$ the price j periods $(j < n)$ from the present of an instrument maturing n periods later; the capital gain for the current period is ${}_{n-1}P_1 - {}_nP_0$. Hence the condition that the one-period return from holding the asset be equal to the short-term rate for the forthcoming period, denoted by r_1, can be written as

$$\frac{a_1 + ({}_{n-1}P_1 - {}_nP_0)}{{}_nP_0} = r_1 \tag{5}$$

Solving for ${}_nP_0$,

$$_nP_0 = \frac{a_1 + {}_{n-1}P_1}{1 + r_1} \tag{6}$$

The reason why the right-hand side of Equation (6) must be the equilibrium price of the n-period asset is that, as can be verified, if the current price, ${}_nP_0$, were larger than the right-hand side of Equation (6), then the one-period return of the instrument, given by Equation (5), would be smaller than the return r_1 obtainable by investing in the one-period instrument. As a result, no one would want to hold it, causing its price to drop. Similarly, if ${}_nP_0$ is smaller than the right-hand side of Equation (6), this yield for the instrument would be larger than r_1, and everyone would want to hold it.

Next we observe that ${}_{n-1}P_1$ must satisfy an equation like Equation (6), or

$$_{n-1}P_1 = \frac{a_2 + {}_{n-2}P_2}{1 + r_2}$$

Substituting this equation into Equation (6), we get

$$_nP_0 = \frac{a_1}{(1 + r_1)} + \frac{a_2 + {}_{n-2}P_2}{(1 + r_1)(1 + r_2)}$$

Repeating the same substitution recursively, up to the maturity of the instrument, we find

$$_nP_0 = \frac{a_1}{(1 + r_1)} + \frac{a_2}{(1 + r_1)(1 + r_2)} +$$

$$\frac{a_3}{(1 + r_1)(1 + r_2)(1 + r_3)} + \cdots +$$

$$\frac{a_n}{(1 + r_1)(1 + r_2)(1 + r_3)\cdots(1 + r_n)} \qquad (7)$$

Each term on the right-hand side will be recognized as the "present" or "discounted" value of the payments at each successive time. Thus the price of a debt instrument must equal the sum of the stream of the discounted payments that the debtor is required to make until maturity.

If the debt instrument is a bond, the cash flow $(a_1 \ldots a_n)$ can be written as $(C, C, \ldots, C + M)$, where C is the coupon payment and M the face or maturity value.

Let's illustrate the principles to this point. Suppose that an investor purchases a four-period debt instrument with these payments promised by the borrower:

YEAR	INTEREST PAYMENT	PRINCIPAL REPAYMENT	CASH FLOW
1	$100	0	$ 100
2	120	0	120
3	140	0	140
4	150	$1,000	1,150

In terms of our notation:

$a_1 = \$100 \qquad a_2 = \$120 \qquad a_3 = \$140 \qquad a_4 = \$1,150$

Assume that the one-period rates for the next four years are as follows:

$r_1 = 0.07 \qquad r_2 = 0.08 \qquad r_3 = 0.09 \qquad r_4 = 0.10$

The current value or price of this debt instrument today, denoted $_4P_0$, using Equation (7) is then

$$_4P_0 = \frac{100}{(1.07)} + \frac{120}{(1.07)(1.08)} + \frac{140}{(1.07)(1.08)(1.09)} +$$

$$\frac{1,150}{(1.07)(1.08)(1.09)(1.10)}$$

$$= \$1,138.43$$

Return from a Bond: Yield to Maturity Measure

Next we must consider how to construct a measure that will permit us to compare the rate of return of instruments having different payout streams (cash flows) and different maturities. For one-period instruments, the measure is clear; it is provided by the left-hand side of Equation (5). But that approach cannot be generalized readily to long-term assets. For instance, for an instrument with a cash flow (a_1, a_2), the measure $(a_1 + a_2)/P_0$ would not be a useful measure of yield. In the first place, if we seek a measure that can be used to compare instruments of different maturities, it must measure return per unit of time. And second, the proposed measure ignores the timing of receipts, thus failing to reflect the time value of money.

The widely accepted solution to this problem is provided by a measure known as the "yield to maturity." It is defined as that interest rate that makes the present value of the cash flow equal to the market value (price) of the instrument. Thus for the debt instrument in Equation (7), the yield to maturity is the interest rate y that satisfies the equation

$$_nP_0 = \frac{a_1}{(1 + y)} + \frac{a_2}{(1 + y)^2} + \frac{a_3}{(1 + y)^3} + \cdots + \frac{a_n}{(1 + y)^n} \tag{8}$$

which must generally be found by trial and error.

In the case where the instrument is a bond, and omitting the subscript before and after P, Equation (8) can be rewritten as

$$P = \frac{C}{(1 + y)} + \frac{C}{(1 + y)^2} + \frac{C}{(1 + y)^3} + \cdots + \frac{C + M}{(1 + y)^n} \tag{9}$$

After dividing both sides of Equation (9) by M, to obtain the price per dollar of maturity value, and factoring C, we obtain

$$\frac{P}{M} = \frac{C}{M} \sum_{t=1}^{n} \frac{1}{(1 + y)^t} + \frac{1}{(1 + y)^n} \tag{10}$$

Recognizing that the summation on the right-hand side of Equation (10) is the sum of a geometric progression,[5] we can rewrite Equation (10) as:

---

[5] That is,

$$\sum_{t=1}^{n} \frac{1}{(1 + k)^t} = \frac{1 - (1 + k)^{-n}}{k}$$

$$\frac{P}{M} = \frac{C}{M} \left[\frac{1 - (1 + y)^{-n}}{y} \right] + \frac{1}{(1 + y)^n} \tag{11}$$

The yield to maturity is the solution to Equation (11) for y, the yield of an n-period bond. In Equation (11) P/M is the so-called *par value relation*, usually expressed as a percentage. If it is equal to one, the bond sells "at par"; if it is larger than one, it sells at a "premium"; and if it is less than one, it sells at a "discount." C/M is the so-called coupon rate expressed as a ratio.

So far we have not specified the unit of time for measuring the frequencies with which interest is computed and the coupons are paid. Interest rates (and maturity) customarily are quoted per year (e.g., 7% per year), and we shall follow this convention; this means that in Equation (11) above it is implicitly assumed that the coupon rate is C per year and paid once a year. In fact, in the U.S. almost all bonds pay interest twice a year. Each coupon payment therefore amounts to $C/2$, which must be discounted twice a year at half the annual yield or $y/2$. As a result, Equation (11) is changed to

$$\frac{P}{M} = \frac{C}{2M} \left[\frac{1 - (1 + y/2)^{-2n}}{y/2} \right] + \frac{1}{(1 + y/2)^{2n}} \tag{12}$$

and the annual yield to maturity is the solution to Equation (12) for $y/2$, multiplied by two.

To illustrate calculation of the yield to maturity of a bond with semiannual coupon payments, consider a 7%, 20-year bond with a maturity or par value of $100, and selling for 74.26%, or 74.26 cents per $1 of par value. The cash flow for this bond per dollar of par value is (1) 40 six-month payments of $0.035, and (2) $1 received in 40 six-month periods from now. The present value at various semiannual interest rates ($y/2$) is:

Interest rate ($y/2$):	3.5%	4.0%	4.5%	5.0%	5.5%	6.0%	6.5%
Present value (P/M):	1.0000	0.9010	0.8160	0.7426	0.6791	0.6238	0.5756

When a 5.0% semiannual interest rate is used, the present value of the cash flows is equal to 0.7426 per $1 of par value, which is the price of the bond. Hence, 5.0% is the semiannual yield to maturity.

The annual yield to maturity should, strictly speaking, be found by compounding 5.0% for one year. That is, it should be 10.25.[6] But the accepted

---

[6] The return at the end of the year is:

$$(1.050)^2 - 1 = 1.1025 - 1 = 0.1025$$

convention in the market is to double $y/2$, the semiannual yield to maturity. Thus, the yield to maturity for the bond above is 10% (two times 5.0%). The yield to maturity computed using this convention—doubling the semiannual yield—is called the *bond equivalent yield* or *coupon equivalent yield*.

Reasons Why a Bond's Price Will Change

One can infer from Equation (11) or Equation (12) that the value of a bond depends on three things: (1) its coupon, (2) its maturity, and (3) interest rates. Hence the price of a bond can change over time for any one of the following reasons.

1. *A change in the level of interest rates in the economy.* For example, if interest rates in the economy increase because of Fed policy, the price of a bond will decrease; if interest rates fall, the price of a bond will rise.

2. *A change in the price of a bond selling at a price other than par as it moves toward maturity without any change in the required yield.* Over time the price of a discount bond rises if interest rates do not change; the price of a premium bond declines over time if interest rates do not change.

3. *For a non-Treasury security, a change in the required yield because of a change in the yield spread between non-Treasury and Treasury securities.* If the Treasury rate does not change, but the yield spread between Treasuries and non-Treasury securities changes (narrows or widens), the price of non-Treasury securities will change.

4. *A change in the perceived credit quality of the issuer.* Assuming interest rates in the economy and yield spreads between non-Treasuries and Treasuries do not change, the price of non-Treasuries will increase if the issuer's perceived credit quality has improved; the price will drop if perceived credit quality deteriorates.

What Determines the Premium–Par Yield

As noted earlier, in general, Equation (11) or Equation (12) cannot be solved explicitly for y (for $n > 2$). They must be solved by trial and error as illustrated, with one important exception.

It is apparent from Equation (11) that the par value, P/M, increases as the coupon rate, C/M, increases. Now consider a bond whose coupon rate is such that the corresponding value of P/M is one, that is, the bond sells at par. Then Equation (11) becomes

$$1 = \frac{C}{M}\left[\frac{1 - (1 + y)^{-n}}{y}\right] + \frac{1}{(1 + y)^n} \tag{13}$$

Equation (13) can be solved explicitly for y; the solution is $y = C/M$. In other words, if a bond sells at par, its yield to maturity is the same as its coupon rate; for example, if a 7.75%, 20-year bond sells at par, its yield to maturity is 7.75%. This means that, for a bond to be issued at par, the coupon rate offered must be the same as the market-required yield for that maturity. The coupon rate of an n-period bond selling at par may be labeled the *n-period par yield*.

It can also be verified from Equation (13) that if the coupon rate on a bond is less than the required yield to maturity, or par yield, the bond will sell at a discount; the converse is true for a bond with a coupon above par yield. The explanation for this relation is self-evident: if the cash payment per period—namely, the coupon—is below the required yield per period, the difference must be made up by an increase in price, or capital gain, over the life of the instrument. But this requires that the price of the bond be lower than its maturity value. In the U.S., bonds (other than zero-coupon issues) customarily are issued with a yield to maturity as to insure that the issue sells at close to par.[7]

Reinvestment of Cash Flow and Yield

The yield to maturity takes into account the coupon income and any capital gain or loss that the investor will realize by *holding the bond to maturity*. The measure has its shortcomings, however. We might think that if we acquire for P a bond of maturity m and yield y, then at maturity we can count on obtaining a terminal value equal to $P(1 + y)^n$. This inference is not justified. By multiplying both sides of Equation (9) by $(1 + y)^n$, we obtain

$$P(1 + y)^n = C(1 + y)^{n-1} + C(1 + y)^{n-2} + C(1 + y)^{n-3} + C + M$$

For the terminal value to be $P(1 + y)^n$, each of the coupon payments must be reinvested until maturity at an interest rate equal to the yield to maturity. If the coupon payment is semiannual, then each semiannual payment must be reinvested at the yield y.

An illustration demonstrates this point. Consider a 7%, 20-year bond that makes semiannual coupon payments of $3.50, and selling for $74.26 per $100 face value. As we demonstrated earlier, the yield to maturity for this bond is equal to 10%. If an investor can invest $74.26 in a certificate of deposit that pays 5% every six months for 20 years, or 10% per year (on a bond equivalent

---

[7] This custom has been reinforced by tax laws discouraging tax arbitrage by the substitution of low coupon payments for capital gains from a low issue price, which occurred at a time when coupon income was taxed at a higher rate than capital gains. These are the "original issue discount" rules included in the tax law.

basis), at the end of 20 years (40 six-month periods), the $74.26 investment will have grown to $522.79. That is, $74.26 $(1.05)^{40}$ = $522.79. The terminal value represents a return of the amount invested of $74.26 with interest earned over the 40 years of $448.53 ($522.79 minus $74.26).

Let's look at what the investor will receive by investing in the bond. There will be 40 semiannual interest payments of $3.50, which will total $140. When the bond matures, the investor will receive $100. Thus, the total dollars that the investor will receive is $240 if the bond is held to maturity. But this is $282.79 less than the terminal value of $522.79 necessary to produce a yield of 10% on a bond equivalent basis ($522.79 minus $240). How is this deficiency supposed to be made up? If the investor reinvests the coupon payments at a semiannual interest rate of 5% (or a 10% annual rate on a bond equivalent basis), then the interest earned on the coupon payments will be $282.79. Consequently, of the return on investment of $448.53 needed to generate a dollar return that gives a yield of 10%, about 63% ($282.79 divided by $448.53) must be generated by reinvesting the coupon payments.

Clearly, as the equation and the example illustrate, the investor will realize the yield to maturity that is calculated at the time of purchase only if (1) all the coupon payments can be reinvested at the yield to maturity, and (2) the bond is held to maturity. With respect to the first assumption, the risk that an investor faces is that future interest rates at which the coupon can be reinvested will be less than the yield to maturity at the time the bond is purchased. This risk is referred to as *reinvestment risk*. And if the bond is not held to maturity, it may have to be sold for less than its purchase price, resulting in a return that is less than the yield to maturity. The risk that a bond will have to be sold at a loss is referred to as *interest rate risk* or *price risk*.

Our focus in this section has been on coupon-bearing bonds. In the special case of a debt instrument that produces only one cash flow, the maturity value, the yield to maturity does measure the rate at which the initial investment rises. We can see this if we substitute zero for the coupon payments in the last equation. Bonds that do not make coupon payments are called *zero-coupon bonds*. The advantage of these bonds is that they do not expose the investor to reinvestment risk. At the same time, they deprive the investor of the opportunity to reinvest the coupon at a rate higher than y.

SUMMARY

In this first of two chapters on the theory of interest rate determination and bond valuation we have presented the theory of interest rates. We showed how consumers' choices between current and future consumption affect saving, relying on two fundamental concepts: taste or preference, and opportunity (in the loan market and production market). An important property that results from the existence of a perfect loan market, together with production opportunities, is that it separates the current consumption decision from current income by creating the possibility to save or dissave through production and net lending. Our conclusion is that the equilibrium interest rate reflects a complex set of forces that control the demand for investment and the supply of savings.

The market equilibrium achieved with the intermediation of the loan markets has an important property with respect to the efficiency of the economy in producing and allocating resources. It will not be possible to reallocate resources in such a way that some will be better off while nobody will be worse off. Economists refer to this as Pareto optimality.

The real rate of interest is the interest rate that would prevail in the absence of inflation. It can be shown that the nominal rate of interest is approximately equal to the real rate of interest plus anticipated inflation, a relationship referred to as Fisher's Law.

The theory of interest rate determination, which was cast in terms of a two-period model (today and tomorrow), can be extended to deal with the basic determinants of the value of long-term bonds. We do this by making use of the principle that, in perfect markets, all riskless instruments must have the same short-term return, which must coincide with the riskless short-term rate for that period.

The cash flow from a bond consists of periodic coupon payments (semiannual payments in the U.S.) and the repayment of the principal (called the maturity value or par value or face value). The value of a bond is the present value of the cash flow it provides until maturity. The yield to maturity measure is used as an index to compare the rate of return of instruments having different cash flows and different maturities. As the yield to maturity assumes that the investor will hold the bond to the maturity date, and that all cash flows can be reinvested at the calculated yield to maturity, it has limited value in determining the relative value of two bonds with different maturities over some investment horizon. The risk that cash flows will have to be reinvested at an interest rate lower than the calculated yield to maturity is called reinvestment risk. The risk that a bond will have to be sold at a price less than the purchase price is called interest rate risk, or price risk.

A bond's price will change over time for several reasons. First, the level of interest rates in the economy may change. Second, a bond selling at a price above par will decrease in price as its maturity date approaches if interest rates in the economy do not change; the price of a bond selling below par will decline if interest rates in the economy do not change. For non-U.S. Treasury securities there are two additional reasons why a bond's price may change: a change in the yield spread between Treasury and non-Treasury securities, or a change in the perceived credit quality of the issuer.

In the next chapter we continue study of the theory of the determinants of bond prices and long-term interest rates, focusing on the relationship between interest rates on bonds of the same issuer (the U.S. government) but with different maturities.

QUESTIONS

1. **a.** Why is the indifference curve between current and future consumption convex to the origin?
   b. What is meant by the marginal rate of time preference?
   c. What is meant by the marginal productivity of capital?
   d. How is the equilibrium market rate determined?

2. **a.** What is meant by the real rate of interest?
   b. What is meant by the nominal rate of interest?
   c. According to Fisher's Law, what is the relationship between the real rate and the nominal rate?
   d. What is the difficulty of measuring an economy's real rate of interest?

3. Determine the value of the following risk-free debt instrument, which promises to make the respective payments when the appropriate one-period annual rates are as shown in the last column:

YEAR	CASH PAYMENT	APPROPRIATE ANNUAL RATE
1	$15,000	8.0%
2	17,000	8.5
3	20,000	9.0
4	21,000	9.5

4. **a.** What is meant by the "yield to maturity" of a bond?
   b. What is meant by the yield to maturity calculated on a bond equivalent basis?

5. **a.** Show the cash flows for the four bonds below, each of which has a par value of $1,000 and pays interest semiannually:

BOND	COUPON RATE	NO. OF YEARS TO MATURITY	PRICE
W	7%	5	$884.20
X	8	7	948.90
Y	9	4	967.70
Z	0	10	456.39

b. Calculate the yield to maturity for the four bonds.

6. A portfolio manager is considering buying two bonds. Bond A matures in three years and has a coupon rate of 10% payable semiannually. Bond B, of the same credit quality, matures in 10 years and has a coupon rate of 12% payable semiannually. Both bonds are priced at par.

   a. Suppose the portfolio manager plans to hold the bond that is purchased for three years. Which would be the best bond for the portfolio manager to purchase?

   b. Suppose the portfolio manager plans to hold the bond that is purchased for six years instead of three years. In this case, which would be the best bond for the portfolio manager to purchase?

   c. Suppose that the portfolio manager is managing the assets of a life insurance company that has issued a five-year guaranteed investment contract (GIC). The interest rate that the life insurance company has agreed to pay is 9% on a semiannual basis. Which of the two bonds should the portfolio manager purchase to assure that the GIC payments will be satisfied and that a profit will be generated by the life insurance company?

7. Suppose you purchased a debt obligation three years ago at its par value of $100,000. The market price of this debt obligation today is $90,000. What are some of the reasons why the price of this debt obligation could have declined since you purchased it three years ago?

LEARNING OBJECTIVES

After reading this chapter you will understand:

- what is meant by the term structure of interest rates.

- what the yield curve is.

- the different shapes that the term structure can take.

- what is meant by a spot rate and a spot rate curve.

- how a spot rate curve can be determined from coupon instruments.

- what is meant by an implicit forward rate and how it can be calculated.

- how long-term rates are related to the current short-term rate and short-term forward rates.

- the different theories about the determinants of the shape of the term structure: pure expectations theory, the liquidity theory, the preferred habitat theory, and the market segmentation theory.

- the risks associated with investing in bonds when interest rates change.

- that the price/yield curve of an option-free bond is convex.

- that the two characteristics of a bond that affect its price volatility are its coupon and its maturity.

- what duration is and how it is calculated.

- the limitations of duration as a measure of price volatility of a bond when interest rates change.

- what the convexity measure of a bond is and how it is related to bond price volatility.

- how duration is used by institutional investors and dealers.

I n this chapter, we extend the theories and principles of the last chapter to the relationship between the yield on a bond and its maturity. This relationship is referred to as the *term structure of interest rates*. We also explain the various theories about the determinants of the term structure of interest rates. We conclude the chapter with the characteristics of a bond that affect its price volatility.

THE TERM STRUCTURE OF INTEREST RATES

In Table 12-1 we show the yield to maturity, coupon, and price for a series of hypothetical Treasury securities varying in maturities from half-a-year to 10 years. The behavior of the yield to maturity as the term to maturity increases is referred to as the *term structure of interest rates,* or simply *term structure*. The graphical depiction of the term structure is called the *yield curve*. Figure 12-1 shows four hypothetical yield curves.

TABLE 12-1	MATURITY AND YIELD TO MATURITY FOR 20 HYPOTHETICAL TREASURY SECURITIES		
MATURITY	COUPON	YIELD TO MATURITY	PRICE
0.50	0.0000	0.0800	96.15
1.00	0.0000	0.0830	92.19
1.50	0.0850	0.0890	99.45
2.00	0.0900	0.0920	99.64
2.50	0.1100	0.0940	103.49
3.00	0.0950	0.0970	99.49
3.50	0.1000	0.1000	100.00
4.00	0.1000	0.1040	98.72
4.50	0.1150	0.1060	103.16
5.00	0.0875	0.1080	92.24
5.50	0.1050	0.1090	98.38
6.00	0.1100	0.1120	99.14
6.50	0.0850	0.1140	86.94
7.00	0.0825	0.1160	84.24
7.50	0.1100	0.1180	96.09
8.00	0.0650	0.1190	72.62
8.50	0.0875	0.1200	82.97
9.00	0.1300	0.1220	104.30
9.50	0.1150	0.1240	95.06
10.00	0.1250	0.1250	100.00

A term structure such as the one reported in Table 12-1 and those shown in Figure 12-1, which are constructed from a collection of Treasury securities across the maturity spectrum, does not provide a satisfactory measure of the relation between required yield and maturity. The reason as we shall see is that different securities with the same maturity can have different yields, depending on the coupon rate (and hence the price of the bond relative to its par value—what we called the par value relation in the previous chapter) and the path of changing short-term interest rates between the current time period t and its maturity n periods from now.

Yield on Zero-Coupon Bonds: Spot Rates

The way to resolve the difficulty created by the non-uniqueness of the yield-maturity relation consists in identifying the n-period yield at date t, with the yield of a particular n-period bond, namely a "zero-coupon bond."

Recall that a zero-coupon bond is one that pays no coupons but only a terminal payment M at maturity n. We can use Equation (7) from Chapter 11 to infer the par value relation of an n-period zero-coupon bond. That is:

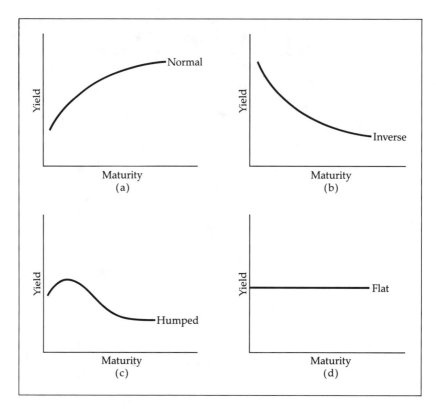

FIGURE 12-1
Four Hypothetical Yield Curves

$$_nP_0 = \frac{a_1}{(1 + r_1)} + \frac{a_2}{(1 + r_1)(1 + r_2)} +$$

$$\frac{a_3}{(1 + r_1)(1 + r_2)(1 + r_3)} + \cdots +$$

$$\frac{a_n}{(1 + r_1)(1 + r_2)(1 + r_3) \cdots (1 + r_n)}$$

where $_nP_0$ = price of an n-period instrument today
a_t = cash flow at time t
r_t = the one-period riskless rate t periods from now

Throughout this chapter, we shall also refer to the one-period rate, r_t, as the *short-term rate*, or simply, *short rate*. In addition, we use the following terminology interchangeably:

$$r_1 = \text{current one-period rate or current short-term rate}$$
$$r_2, \cdots, r_n = \text{future one-period rate or future short-term rate}$$

For an n-period instrument with only one terminal cash flow, the equation above reduces to:

$$_nP_0 = \frac{a_n}{(1 + r_1)(1 + r_2)(1 + r_3) \cdots (1 + r_n)}$$

Substituting the maturity value, M, for the cash flow a_n, we get

$$_nP_0 = \frac{M}{(1 + r_1)(1 + r_2)(1 + r_3) \cdots (1 + r_n)}$$

Dividing both sides of this equation by M, we get the par value relation of an n-period zero-coupon bond:

$$\frac{_nP_0}{M} = \frac{1}{(1 + r_1)(1 + r_2)(1 + r_3) \cdots (1 + r_n)} \tag{1}$$

Therefore, the par value relation of an n-period zero-coupon bond depends on (1) the current short-term rate, and (2) the set of all future short-term rates.

Now let's look at what Equation (9) from Chapter 11 tells us about the yield to maturity of an n-period zero-coupon bond. Equation (9) is:

$$P = \frac{C}{(1 + y)} + \frac{C}{(1 + y)^2} + \frac{C}{(1 + y)^3} + \cdots + \frac{C + M}{(1 + y)^n}$$

where P = price
$\quad\quad C$ = the bond's coupon payment
$\quad\quad y$ = yield to maturity

We can rewrite this equation for an n-period zero-coupon instrument using different notation. First, substitute $_nP_0$ for P. Second, denote by y_n the yield to maturity for an n-period instrument, and substitute it for y. We also refer to this yield as the *long-term rate*, or simply as the *long rate*. Third, because the instrument of interest to us is a zero-coupon bond, substitute zero for C. The equation becomes:

$$_nP_0 = \frac{M}{(1 + y_n)^n}$$

Dividing both sides by M, we get

$$\frac{_nP_0}{M} = \frac{1}{(1 + y_n)^n}$$ (2)

The yield to maturity on an n-period zero-coupon bond is the value of y_n satisfying Equation (2).

Equating the right-hand side of Equation (1) and Equation (2), we find that

$$\frac{1}{(1 + r_1)(1 + r_2)(1 + r_3) \cdots (1 + r_n)} = \frac{1}{(1 + y_n)^n}$$

or

$$y_n = [(1 + r_1)(1 + r_2) \cdots (1 + r_n)]^{1/n} - 1$$ (3)

Here $(1 + r_j)$ is the so-called *compounding factor* for period j, the reciprocal of the *discount factor* $1/(1 + r_j)$.

Equation (3) can be made more transparent by transposing 1 to the left side. The left-hand side then becomes $(1 + y_n)$, the n-period compounding factor, while the expression on the right-hand side can be recognized as an average of the n one-period compounding factors over the life of the bond, namely, the *geometric* average.

As long as interest rates are small relative to unity, as they normally are, then the right-hand side of Equation (3) (that is, the geometric mean of the compounding factors minus one) can be well-approximated by a simple arithmetic average,[1] so that Equation (3) simplifies to

$$y_n \approx \frac{1}{n} \sum_{t=1}^{n} r_t$$ (4)

It is this approximation that justifies thinking of the long rate as the simple average of all short rates. Thus if the current one-period rate (r_1) is 7%, and the one-period rate starting one period from now (r_2) is 5%, then the two-period yield (y_2) is roughly 6%. Precisely, it is

---

[1] To see this, add 1 to both sides of Equation (3), and take the logarithm of each side. Recall that, provided y and r are small compared with unity, then

$$\log [(1 + y_n)] \approx y_n$$

$$\text{and } \log [(1 + r_j)] \approx r_j$$

$$[(1.07)\ (1.05)]^{1/2} - 1 = 0.0599, \text{ or } 5.99\%$$

The advantage of defining the long-term rate (y_n) at any time as the yield to maturity (or simply, yield) of a zero-coupon bond, is that, as can be seen from Equation (4), we obtain a measure that depends only on the behavior of the short-term rates. It is therefore unique for any given maturity, while the yield of n-period coupon instruments generally varies with the coupon.[2] This measure of the n-period yield (or n-period interest rate) also is frequently referred to as the n-period *spot rate*. The term structure of interest rates can then be defined as the relation between y_n and n. We note that a non-zero-coupon bond—provided it is not callable—can be regarded as a sum of n zero-coupon bonds, $n - 1$ corresponding to the coupon payments C, and one corresponding to the last payment for the amount $C + M$.

In general the spot rates for longer maturities are not quoted directly in the normal financial sources. For zero-coupon issues of any given maturity, however, the long-term or spot rate for that maturity is simply the yield of that instrument. As will be seen in Chapter 14, government securities dealers have created zero-coupon Treasury securities—although only since 1982—by the process of "stripping" Treasury bonds of their coupon and selling both coupon and principal separately.

There are two problems with using the observed yields on zero-coupon bonds, or on stripped Treasury securities, to construct the term structure of interest rates. First, the liquidity of the stripped Treasury market is not as great as that of the Treasury coupon market. Thus, the observed yields on stripped Treasuries reflect a premium for limited marketability. Second, there are maturity sectors of the stripped Treasury securities market that attract specific investors who may be willing to trade off yield in exchange for an attractive feature associated with that particular maturity sector, thereby distorting the term structure relationship. For example, certain foreign governments, unlike domestic taxable entities, may grant investors preferential tax treatment on zero-coupon Treasuries. As a result, these foreign investors invest heavily in long-maturity stripped Treasury securities, driving down yields in that maturity sector.

---

[2] Before zero-coupon bonds were offered in the bond market, the n-period long-term rate was frequently defined as the "par yield" or coupon rate on an n-period bond selling at par, which also coincides with its yield as explained in the previous chapter. This definition of the long rate again has the desirable property that it does not vary from bond to bond depending on its coupon. The main drawback of this definition is that the long rate turns out to be related to short-term rates in a much more complex fashion; in particular, the resulting measure of the long rate is found to depend on the specific path sequence followed by the short-term rate, while the measure we have adopted is independent of the sequence—it makes no difference if short rates are first low and then high, or vice versa [see Equation (4)].

In the absence of usable zero-coupon bonds, it is possible to derive the family of spot rates from the price and coupon of coupon bonds, although the procedure is somewhat laborious.

Derivation of Spot Rates from Coupon Bonds

We can illustrate this derivation procedure by using the hypothetical price and maturity for the 20 Treasury securities shown in Table 12-1.

The basic principle is that the value of a Treasury coupon security should be equal to the value of a package of zero-coupon Treasury securities. Consider first the six-month Treasury security in Table 12-1. As will be explained in Chapter 13, this security is a Treasury bill and is a zero-coupon instrument; hence, its yield of 8% is equal to the six-month spot rate. Similarly, for the one-year Treasury, also a Treasury bill, the yield of 8.3% is the one-year spot rate. Given these two spot rates, we can compute the spot rate for a 1.5-year zero-coupon Treasury. The value or price of a 1.5-year zero-coupon Treasury should equal the present value of the three cash flows from the 1.5-year coupon Treasury, where the yield used for discounting is the spot rate corresponding to the cash flow. Using $100 as the par value, the cash flow for the 1.5-year coupon Treasury is:

0.5 years	$0.085 \times \$100 \times 0.5$	$= \$\ \ 4.25$
1.0 years	$0.085 \times \$100 \times 0.5$	$= \$\ \ 4.25$
1.5 years	$0.085 \times \$100 \times 0.5 + 100$	$= \$104.25$

The present value of the cash flow is then:

$$\frac{4.25}{(1 + y_1)^1} + \frac{4.25}{(1 + y_2)^2} + \frac{104.25}{(1 + y_3)^3}$$

where y_1 = one-half the six-month theoretical spot rate
$\quad\quad\ y_2$ = one-half the one-year theoretical spot rate
$\quad\quad\ y_3$ = one-half the 1.5-year theoretical spot rate

In our example: $y_1 = 8.0\%/2 = 0.04$ and $y_2 = 8.3\% = 0.0415$. The unknown is y_3.

Taking the present value of the 1.5-year coupon Treasury security and equating it to its price

$$99.45 = \frac{4.25}{(1.0400)^1} + \frac{4.25}{(1.0415)^2} + \frac{104.25}{(1 + y_3)^3}$$

Solving for the theoretical 1.5-year spot rate y_3

	YIELD TO	THEORETICAL
MATURITY	MATURITY	SPOT RATE
0.50	0.0800	0.08000
1.00	0.0830	0.08300
1.50	0.0890	0.08930
2.00	0.0920	0.09247
2.50	0.0940	0.09468
3.00	0.0970	0.09787
3.50	0.1000	0.10129
4.00	0.1040	0.10592
4.50	0.1060	0.10850
5.00	0.1080	0.11021
5.50	0.1090	0.11175
6.00	0.1120	0.11584
6.50	0.1140	0.11744
7.00	0.1160	0.11991
7.50	0.1180	0.12405
8.00	0.1190	0.12278
8.50	0.1200	0.12546
9.00	0.1220	0.13152
9.50	0.1240	0.13377
10.00	0.1250	0.13623

TABLE 12-2   THEORETICAL SPOT RATES

$$99.45 = 4.08654 + 3.91805 + \frac{104.25}{(1 + y_3)^3}$$

$$91.44541 = \frac{104.25}{(1 + y_3)^3}$$

$$(1 + y_3)^3 = 1.140024$$

$$y_3 = 0.04465, \text{ or a bond equivalent yield of } 8.93\%$$

One can follow this approach sequentially to derive the two-year rate from the calculated values of y_1, y_2, y_3, the half-year-, one-year-, and 1.5-year rates, and the price and coupon of the bond with a maturity of two years; and so on for the remaining 16 half-yearly rates. The spot rates thus obtained are shown in Table 12-2. They represent the term structure of interest rates for maturities up to ten years, at the particular time to which the bond price quotations refer.

Column 2 of Table 12-2 reproduces the calculated yield to maturity for the coupon issue listed in Table 12-1. A comparison of this column with the last column giving the yield to maturity of a zero-coupon bond is instructive, for it confirms that bonds of the same maturity may have different yields to maturity, contrary to a view still widely held, that the yield of bonds depends only on their maturity. While the two columns do not depart widely, they do differ after the third year, and by the ninth year the zero-coupon yield is nearly 100 basis points, or 10% higher than that of the same maturity with a coupon of 13% and selling at a premium.

This discrepancy reflects the fact that the zero-coupon yield is independent of the path of interest rates, while the yield of coupon bonds is not. This can be seen from Equation (4). For example, consider a five-period long-term rate (y_5), which depends on the current short-term rate r_1 and four future short-term rates (r_2, r_3, r_4, and r_5). Consider the following four possible paths for the five short-term rates:

	r_1	r_2	r_3	r_4	r_5
Path 1	4%	5%	6%	7%	8%
Path 2	8	7	6	5	4
Path 3	6	4	5	8	7
Path 4	5	8	3	7	6

Notice that we have assumed different paths of short rates of 4%, 5%, 6%, 7%, and 8%. For each path, the five-period long-rate will be the same, namely, the arithmetic average of 6%. Yet the yield to maturity will be different even though the coupon rate is assumed identical (but different from zero). Indeed, one can verify that for a given coupon rate and spot rate y_n, the value of the bond will be higher when the path of interest rates is rising. Basically, this is because lower initial rates will enhance the present value of earlier coupon payments. But, with a given path of coupon and principal payments, higher prices must mean a higher yield. Conversely, a declining path of interest rates will imply a lower yield.

The technique demonstrating how the theoretical spot rate curve can be constructed from observed yields, although useful, is more complex in practice. First, there may be more than one Treasury issue with the same maturity and coupon selling at different yields.[3] Second, there is not a current Treasury issue for every possible maturity, so a continuous spot rate curve

---

[3] A procedure for computing the theoretical spot rate curve by using Treasuries with different coupons but the same maturity is explained in John Caks, "The Coupon Effect on Yield to Maturity," *Journal of Finance* (March 1977), pp. 103–105.

cannot be constructed using the procedure we just illustrated. Several methodologies have been suggested to estimate the term structure statistically.[4]

Implicit Forward Rates

We must next draw attention to the fact that, while r_1 in Equation (7) of Chapter 11 is the actual current rate for a one-period loan beginning today, r_2 is *not* the actual market short rate for a one-period loan beginning in Period 2. Indeed, that rate will be established only at the beginning of Period 2. What is true instead is that in entering a contract currently for a two- or more-period instrument at the current spot rate, the contracting parties are making an implicit *forward* contract to lend and borrow in later periods at a "forward rate" that is fixed now.

We will denote the forward rate by $_mf_t$ where the left subscript refers to the length of the contract to which the rate applies and the right subscript to the time at which the contract begins. For example, $_{10}f_4$ is interpreted as the rate that applies on a 10-period contract beginning at the start of Period 4. The forward rate $_1f_4$ is interpreted as the rate that applies on a one-period contract beginning at the start of Period 4. When we refer to the *short-term forward rates* in this chapter, we mean the one-period forward rates. That is, $_1f_2$, $_1f_3$, $_1f_4$, . . . , $_1f_n$. Figure 12-2 provides a graphical illustration of forward rates.

This "implicit" forward rate can be deduced from the consideration following: under the current assumption of certainty, what can be obtained at maturity from a contract with maturity m must be the same as what can be obtained from an $m - 1$-period contract followed by a one-period contract at the forward rate for the last period. Thus, if you invest $1 in a two-period investment at the spot two-period rate (y_2), at the end of the second period you will have $(1 + y_2)^2$. As a one-period contract would have yielded $(1 + y_1)$,

---

[4] The objective in empirical estimation of the term structure is to fit a spot rate curve that (1) fits the data sufficiently well, and (2) is a sufficiently smooth function. See, for example, Willard R. Carleton and Ian Cooper, "Estimation and Uses of the Term Structure of Interest Rates," *Journal of Finance* (September 1976), pp. 1067–1083; J. Huston McCulloch, "Measuring the Term Structure of Interest Rates," *Journal of Business* (January 1971), pp. 19–31; J. Huston McCulloch, "The Tax Adjusted Yield Curve," *Journal of Finance* (June 1975), pp. 811–830; Oldrich A. Vasicek and H. Gifford Fong, "Term Structure Modeling Using Exponential Splines," *Journal of Finance* (May 1982), pp. 339–348; and Ronald Kahn, "Estimating the U.S. Treasury Term Structure of Interest Rates," Chapter 9 in Frank J. Fabozzi (ed.), *The Handbook of Treasury and Agency Securities* (Chicago: Probus Publishing, 1990). For a comprehensive review of methodologies for estimating the term structure, see Richard McEnally and James V. Jordan, "The Term Structure of Interest Rates," in Frank J. Fabozzi (ed.), *The Handbook of Fixed Income Securities* (Homewood, IL: BusinessOne-Irwin, Third Edition, 1990).

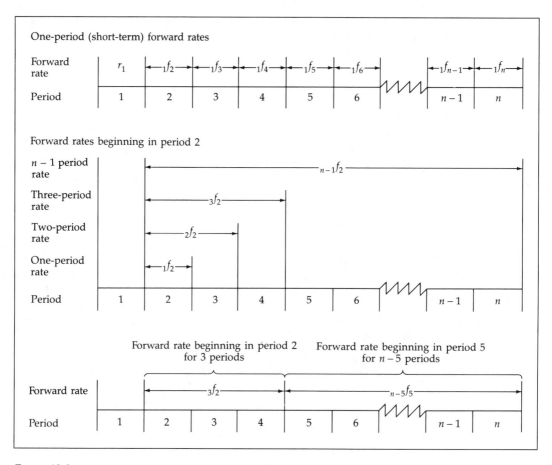

FIGURE 12-2
Graphical Illustration of Forward Rates

the rate you are getting for the second-period investment (i.e., an investment beginning at Period 2), $_1f_2$, must satisfy the condition

$$(1 + y_2)^2 = (1 + y_1)(1 + {}_1f_2)$$

or

$${}_1f_2 = \frac{(1 + y_2)^2}{(1 + y_1)} - 1$$

Because the one-period spot rate (y_1) is the same as the short rate (r_1), we can rewrite the equation above as:

$$_1f_2 = \frac{(1 + y_2)^2}{(1 + r_1)} - 1$$

This forward rate must be distinguished from the actual rate that will hold in the coming Period 2, namely, r_2.

Similarly, we can obtain the forward one-period rate, $_1f_m$, for a one-period contract, beginning at any period m, making use of the spot rates y_m and y_{m-1} and the relation

$$_1f_m = \frac{(1 + y_m)^m}{(1 + y_{m-1})^{m-1}} - 1 \tag{5}$$

The term structure contains implicit information not only about short-term forward rates (i.e., the one-period forward rates) but also about the forward rates for various maturities. This information can be retrieved using the same basic method: that the m-period return should be the same no matter what sequence of instruments is used. To illustrate, suppose we want to infer the forward three-period rate beginning in Period 2; that is, we want to know $_3f_2$. We know that

$$1 + _3f_2 = [(1 + _1f_3) (1 + _1f_4) (1 + _1f_5)]^{1/3}$$

or

$$(1 + _3f_2)^3 = (1 + _1f_3) (1 + _1f_4) (1 + _1f_5)$$

We also know that

$$(1 + y_5)^5 = (1 + y_1) (1 + _1f_2) (1 + _1f_3) (1 + _1f_4) (1 + _1f_5)$$

and

$$(1 + y_2)^2 = (1 + y_1) (1 + _1f_2)$$

Therefore,

$$\frac{(1 + y_5)^5}{(1 + y_2)^2} = (1 + _1f_3) (1 + _1f_4) (1 + _1f_5) = (1 + _3f_2)^3$$

or

$$_3f_2 = \frac{(1 + y_5)^{5/3}}{(1 + y_2)^{2/3}} - 1$$

Similarly, the six-period forward rate beginning in Period 4 would be given by

$$_6f_4 = \frac{(1 + y_{10})^{10/6}}{(1 + y_4)^{4/6}} - 1$$

In general, the formula for the forward rate is

$$_mf_j = \left[\frac{(1 + y_{m+j})^{m+j}}{(1 + y_j)^j} \right]^{1/m} - 1$$

Figure 12-3 is a graphic representation of short-term rates, forward rates, and spot rates.

Why should anyone care about forward rates? There are in fact very good reasons for doing so, for knowledge of the forward rates implicit in the current long-term rate is relevant in formulating an investment as well as a borrowing policy. To illustrate, suppose an investor wants to invest for two periods; the current short rate (y_1 or r_1) is 7%, the two-period rate y_2 is 6%. Using the formulas we have developed, the investor finds that by buying a two-period security he is making a forward contract *to lend* in Period 2 at the rate of 5%. If the investor believes that the second-period rate will turn out to be higher than 5%, it will be to his advantage to lend initially on a one-period contract, then at the end of the first period to reinvest interest and principal in the one-period contract available for the second period. Similarly, for a borrower, a sequence of short-term borrowings will be preferable to a two-period borrowing, if she believes that the second-period market rate will be lower than 5%.

DETERMINANTS OF THE SHAPE OF THE TERM STRUCTURE

If we plot the term structure—the yield to maturity, or the spot rate, at successive maturities against maturity—what is it likely to look like? Figure 12-1 shows four shapes that have been observed historically. Panel A shows an upward-sloping yield curve; that is, yield rises steadily as maturity increases. This shape is commonly referred to as a "normal" or "positive" yield curve. Panel B shows a downward-sloping or "inverted" yield curve,

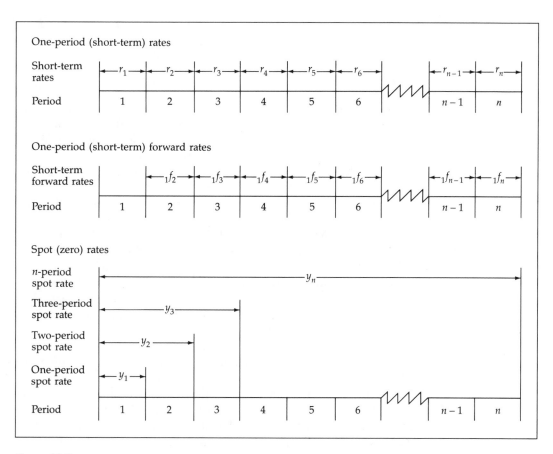

FIGURE 12-3
Graphical Illustration of Short-Term Rates, Forward Rates, and Spot Rates

where yields decline as maturity increases. Panel C shows a "humped" yield curve. Finally, panel D shows a "flat" yield curve.

Two major theories have evolved to account for these observed shapes of the yield curve: the expectations theory and the market segmentation theory.

There are several forms of the expectations theory—the pure expectations theory, the liquidity theory, and the preferred habitat theory. All share in common a hypothesis about the behavior of short-term forward rates and also assume that the forward rates negotiated in current long-term contracts are closely related to the market's expectations about future short-term rates. They differ, however, on whether other factors also affect forward rates, and how. The pure expectations theory postulates that no other systematic factors affect forward rates; the liquidity theory and the preferred habitat theory assert that there are other factors. Accordingly, the last two forms of the expectations theory are sometimes referred to as *biased expectations theories.*

The Pure Expectations Theory

According to the pure expectations theory, the forward rates exclusively represent expected future rates. Thus, the entire term structure at a given time reflects the market's current expectations of the family of future short-term rates. Under this view, a rising term structure, as in Panel A of Figure 12-1, must indicate that the market expects short-term rates to rise throughout the relevant future. Indeed, recalling that the spot rate is an average of all forward rates, a rising path of forward rates implies a rising term structure. Similarly, a flat term structure reflects an expectation that future short-term rates will be pretty much constant, while a falling structure must reflect an expectation that future short rates will decline steadily.

We can illustrate the above by considering how an expectation of a rising short-term future rate would affect the behavior of various market participants so as to result in a rising yield curve. Assume initially a flat term structure, and suppose that economic news subsequently leads market participants to expect interest rates to rise.

1. Those market participants interested in a long-term investment would not want to buy long-term bonds because they would expect the yield structure to rise sooner or later, resulting in a price decline for the bonds and a capital loss on the long-term bonds purchased. They would want to invest instead in short-term debt obligations until the rise in yield had occurred, permitting them to reinvest their funds at the higher yield.

2. Speculators expecting rising rates would anticipate a decline in the price of long-term bonds and therefore would want to sell or short them. (Should interest rates rise as expected, the price of longer-term bonds will fall. As the speculator sold these bonds short and can then purchase them at a lower price to cover the short sale, a profit will be earned.) The proceeds received from the shorting of longer-term bonds will be invested in short-term debt obligations.

3. Borrowers wishing to acquire long-term funds would be pulled toward borrowing in the long end of the market now in the expectation that borrowing at a later time would be more expensive.

All these responses would tend to lower the net demand (partly by increasing the supply) for long-maturity bonds, and increase demand for short-term debt obligations. Clearing of the market would require raising long-term yields in relation to short-term yields; that is, tilting the term structure upward until it is consistent with expectations of future interest rates. By analogous reasoning, an unexpected event leading to the expectation of lower future rates will result in the yield curve sloping down.

Unfortunately the pure expectations theory suffers from one shortcoming, which is quite serious, at least qualitatively. It neglects the risks inherent in investing (or borrowing) in bonds and like instruments. If forward rates were perfect predictors of future interest rates, then the future prices of bonds would be known with certainty. The returns over any investment period (or the cost of borrowing for any required period of financing) would be certain and independent of the maturity of the instrument initially acquired (or sold) and of the time at which the investor needed to liquidate his instrument (or the borrower to refinance her debt). But with uncertainty about future interest rates and hence about future prices of bonds, these instruments become risky investments, with the risk depending on the maturity of the instrument and the intended liquidation time.

Therefore, before we turn to a discussion of the other theories of the term structure of interest rates, we will set forth the risks associated from investing in bonds.

Risks from Investing in Bonds.   To understand the nature of these risks, consider an investor who wants to invest for the current period only, needing his principal at the end of the period. For convenience of exposition we assume that the only available investments are zero-coupon bonds. Even so, the investor faces a menu of possible investments. He can buy not only a one-period instrument, and be repaid by the issuer at the beginning of the next period, but also any bond with longer maturity, and sell it at the beginning of the next period.

How does the choice between these alternatives affect the outcome? If he buys a one-period instrument, the price per dollar of maturity value is $_1P_0 = 1/(1 + r_1)$, so his return per dollar from a one-period instrument, R_1, will be

$$R_1 = \frac{1 - {_1P_0}}{{_1P_0}} = 1 + r_1 - 1 = r_1$$

with certainty. Suppose instead he buys a two-period instrument, which will pay \$1 at the end of the second period, with the intention of liquidating at the beginning of the next period. The current price of this instrument, which may be denoted by $_2P_0$ (the current price of a two-period instrument, or equivalently a bond that matures at the end of two periods), will be given by:

$$_2P_0 = \frac{1}{(1 + y_2)^2} = \frac{1}{(1 + r_1)(1 + {_1f_2})}$$

where y_2 is the two-period rate and $_1f_2$ is the forward rate for Period 2.

But the realization price at the beginning of Period 2 (or equivalently at the end of Period 1) cannot currently be known with certainty because it is the price at that time of one dollar to be paid at the beginning of Period 3. That price will eventually be $1/(1 + r_2)$, but r_2 will not be known with certainty until next period when the market for one-period loans beginning next period has been cleared. Hence, as seen at the beginning of Period 1, when the investment decision is being made, that rate can be estimated only with uncertainty—it is a "stochastic" or "random" variable. We will denote it by $\tilde{r}_2$, where the tilde serves to remind us of the stochastic nature of the variable: $\tilde{r}_2$ stands for the set of values that r_2 might finally take. Hence, the price that will be received for the instrument next period can be written as

$$_1\tilde{P}_1 = \frac{1}{(1 + \tilde{r}_2)}$$

$_1\tilde{P}_1$ is also a stochastic variable because it takes a different value for different values of $\tilde{r}_2$.

As there are, by assumption, no coupon payments, the one-period return from the two-period investment, $\tilde{R}_2$, is the difference between the selling price, $_1\tilde{P}_1$, and the purchase price, $_2P_0$, divided by the purchase price, or

$$\tilde{R}_2 = \frac{_1\tilde{P}_1 - _2P_0}{_2P_0} \tag{6}$$

Equation (6) can be rewritten as:

$$\tilde{R}_2 = r_1 + \frac{_1\tilde{P}_1 - _1P_1}{_1P_1}(1 + r_1) = r_1 + \frac{1 + r_1}{1 + \tilde{r}_2}(_1f_2 - \tilde{r}_2) \tag{7}$$

If there were no errors of expectation, i.e., $_1f_2$ was a correct forecast of r_2, then the holding-period yield from the two-period investment is the same as from a one-period investment. But otherwise the two investment strategies will produce different outcomes. In particular, if the forward rate is below the actual rate r_2, then the one-period holding yield will be smaller than that of the one-period investment, as the two-period instrument will prove to have been overpriced. Because $(1 + r_1)/(1 + r_2)$ generally can be expected to be close to unity, Equation (7) suggests that if the forward rate were lower than the actual rate r_2 by, say, 100 basis points, then the holding yield from the two-period investment would turn out roughly 100 basis points lower.

Suppose next that an investor had chosen to acquire a much longer instrument, say m periods. The price she would pay currently per dollar of maturity value is the discounted value of a dollar m periods from now, or

$$_mP_0 = \frac{1}{(1 + r_1)(1 + {}_{m-1}f_2)^{m-1}}$$

where $_{m-1}f_2$ is the forward rate for the $m - 1$-period instrument beginning next period (Period 2).

The price the investor would receive upon the sale of the m-period instrument at the beginning of next period is

$$_{m-1}\tilde{P}_1 = (1 + {}_{m-1}\tilde{y}_2)^{m-1}$$

where $_{m-1}\tilde{y}_2$ is the anticipated value of $_{m-1}y_2$, the $m - 1$-period spot rate that will be established in the market next period.

It follows that the one-period holding yield from an m-period instrument is

$$\tilde{R}_m = \frac{_{m-1}\tilde{P}_1 - {}_mP_0}{_mP_0} \tag{8}$$

or,

$$\tilde{R}_m = r_1 + \frac{_{m-1}\tilde{P}_1 - {}_{m-1}P_1}{_{m-1}P_1}(1 + r_1) \tag{9}$$

Equation (9) is entirely analogous to the first equality in Equation (7). However, when we express the capital gain term in terms of interest rates we find

$$\frac{_{m-1}\tilde{P}_1 - {}_{m-1}P_1}{_{m-1}P_1} = \left(\frac{1 + {}_{m-1}f_2}{1 + {}_{m-1}\tilde{y}_2}\right)^{m-1} - 1$$

This expression can be approximated by[5]

$$(m - 1)\frac{1 + r_1}{1 + {}_{m-1}\tilde{y}_2}({}_{m-1}f_2 - {}_{m-1}\tilde{y}_2)$$

provided the difference between the forward rate and the actual rate is not too large. Substituting into Equation (9) we obtain

$$\tilde{R}_m = r_1 + (m - 1)\frac{1 + r_1}{1 + {}_{m-1}\tilde{y}_2}({}_{m-1}f_2 - {}_{m-1}\tilde{y}_2) \tag{10}$$

---

[5] This approximation is obtained by differentiating $\tilde{R}_m$ with respect to $_{m-1}\tilde{y}_2$.

Comparison of Equation (10) with Equation (7) shows that as long as $(1 + r_1) \approx (1 + r_2) \approx (1 + {_m}y_2)$, as we should expect, the one-period holding yield of a longer maturity investment tends to be riskier than for a shorter maturity investment because the effect of the error term on the m-period holding yield is magnified by a factor of $m - 1$. Thus a shortfall of the forward rate by 1 percentage point below the realization would result in a shortfall in the holding yield by $(m - 1)$ percentage points, if the investment is an m-period investment, compared with a shortfall of only one percentage point with a two-period investment.

The reason why the response of the holding-period yield, R, to errors in rates for a long maturity tends to be larger than the error in a short-term rate is that the percentage change of price in response to a change in the long rate is $(m - 1)$ times larger. At the same time, it must be recognized that long-term rates tend to be less variable than short-term rates, basically because they represent an average of many short rates.

In summary, the one-period holding yield is uncertain for any instrument except a one-period instrument, and, at least for zero-coupon bonds, the uncertainty or risk of the return rises with maturity at a linear rate (at least for small expectational errors). Later in this chapter we will demonstrate the role of maturity in determining the percentage variability in the price of any bond, not just zero-coupon ones. We will also demonstrate that the coupon rate also influences future price variability, and how a measure called *duration* can be used to capture the influence of both maturity and coupon rate on price volatility.

The Liquidity Theory

We have explained that the drawback of the pure expectations theory is that it does not consider the risks associated with investing in bonds. Yet, we have just established that there is uncertainty in the one-period yield of holding a bond and that it increases systematically with the maturity of the bond.

Given this observation, and the reasonable consideration that investors typically do not like uncertainty, J.R. Hicks[6] has hypothesized that to induce investors to hold longer-term maturities they must be offered a long-term rate higher than the average of expected future rates by a risk premium that is larger, the longer the term to maturity. Put differently, the forward rates should reflect both interest rate expectations and a "liquidity" premium (really a risk premium).

---

[6] John R. Hicks, *Value and Capital* (London: Oxford University Press, 1946), second ed., pp. 141–145.

According to this theory, which is called the *liquidity theory of the term structure*, the implicit forward rates will not be an unbiased estimate of the market's expectations of future interest rates because they embody a liquidity premium. An upward-sloping yield curve may reflect expectations that future interest rates either (1) will rise, or (2) will be flat or even fall, but with a liquidity premium increasing fast enough with maturity so as to produce an upward-sloping yield curve.

The Preferred Habitat Theory

Another theory originally formulated by Modigliani and Sutch[7] also adopts the view that the term structure reflects the expectation of the future path of interest rates as well as a risk premium, but rejects the assertion that the risk premium must rise uniformly with maturity. The latter conclusion could be accepted if all investors intend to liquidate their investment at the shortest possible date while all borrowers are anxious to borrow long, an assumption that can be rejected for a number of reasons.

In the first place, it is obvious that many investors wish to carry resources forward for appreciable periods of time—e.g., to buy a house, or to provide for retirement. Such investors are concerned with the amount available at the appropriate time, and not the path by which that goal is reached. Hence risk aversion dictates that they should *not* buy a short-term instrument but rather an instrument with a maturity matching the period for which they wish to invest. If these investors buy a shorter instrument they will bear reinvestment risk, i.e., the risk of a fall in the interest rates available for reinvesting proceeds of the shorter instrument. Investors can avoid that risk only by "locking in" the current long rate, through a long-term contract. Similarly, if they buy an instrument with maturity longer than the time they wish to invest for, they will bear the risk of a loss in the price of the asset (price risk) when liquidating it before its maturity, because of a rise in interest rates. Entirely analogous considerations apply to borrowers; prudence and safety call for borrowing for a maturity matching the length of time for which funds are required.

In the second place, a lot of the demand for and supply of securities these days comes from financial intermediaries, which have portfolios of dated assets and dated liabilities. Any such institution should have no interest or concern with the volatility of any particular asset or liability in its portfolio. It should be concerned only with the price sensitivity of net assets, which can

---

[7] Franco Modigliani and Richard Sutch, "Innovations in Interest Rate Policy," *American Economic Review* (May 1966), pp. 178–197.

be inferred from the duration of the whole portfolio (a measure of price volatility that we discuss more fully later). Portfolio duration is simply the average duration of all assets and liabilities weighted by shares of each asset or liability in the portfolio—with liabilities having negative duration. Under this condition, the preferred duration of the assets will average not around zero but rather around the duration of the liabilities.

To illustrate this preference for maturity sectors, consider a life insurance company that has issued a five-year guaranteed investment contract.[8] The insurance company will not want to invest in six-month instruments because of the associated reinvestment risk. As another example, assume a thrift has borrowed funds at a fixed rate for one year from the issuance of a one-year certificate of deposit. The thrift is exposed to price (or interest rate) risk if the borrowed funds are invested in a bond with 20 years to maturity. For either of these institutions there is a risk of shifting out of their preferred maturity sector.

The *preferred habitat theory* asserts that, to the extent that the demand and supply of funds in a given maturity range does not match, some lenders and borrowers will be induced to shift to maturities showing the opposite imbalances, but they will need to be compensated by an appropriate risk premium whose magnitude will reflect the extent of risk aversion.

Thus, the shape of the yield curve is determined by both expectations of future interest rates and a risk premium, positive or negative, to induce market participants to shift out of their preferred habitat. Clearly, according to this theory, yield curves sloping up, down, flat, or humped are all possible.

Market Segmentation Theory

The market segmentation theory also recognizes that investors have preferred habitats dictated by saving and investment flows, and that the major reason for the shape of the yield curve lies in asset/liability management constraints (either regulatory or self-imposed) and/or creditors (borrowers) restricting their lending (financing) to specific maturity sectors.[9] The market segmentation theory differs from the preferred habitat theory in that it assumes that neither investors nor borrowers are willing to shift from one maturity sector to another to take advantage of opportunities arising from differences between expectations and forward rates.

Thus, for this theory the shape of the yield curve is determined by supply of and demand for securities within each maturity sector. This formulation

---

[8] See Chapter 4 for a discussion of guaranteed investment contracts.

[9] This theory was suggested in J.M. Culbertson, "The Term Structure of Interest Rates," *Quarterly Journal of Economics* (November 1957), pp. 489–504.

seems untenable because it presupposes the prevalence of absolute risk aversion, while the evidence does not support that proposition. Thus market participants must be expected to shift away from their habitat when there are sufficiently large discrepancies between market and expected rates, insuring that the differences between them will not grow too large, which leads back to the preferred habitat model.

BOND PRICE VOLATILITY

We have explained that holding-period yields are affected by uncertainty about the future price of a bond, which is due to the stochastic nature of future interest rates. When interest rates rise, the price of a bond will fall. Maturity is one of the characteristics of a bond that we said will determine the responsiveness of a bond's price to a change in yields. In this section, we demonstrate this with hypothetical bonds. We will also show (1) other characteristics that influence a bond's price volatility, and (2) how to measure a bond's price volatility.

Review of Price/Yield Relationship

As explained in Chapter 11, a fundamental characteristic of an option-free bond (that is, a bond that is not callable, putable, or convertible) is that its price changes in the opposite direction from the change in yield. This behavior follows from the fact that the price of a bond is equal to the present value of its expected cash flow.

Table 12-3 illustrates this property for four hypothetical bonds: (1) a 9% coupon bond with 5 years to maturity, (2) a 9% coupon bond with 20 years to maturity, (3) a 5% coupon bond with 5 years to maturity, and (4) a 5% coupon bond with 20 years to maturity.

The graph of the price/yield relationship for any of these bonds would exhibit the shape shown in Figure 12-4. Notice that the relationship is not linear (that is, it is not a straight line). The shape of the price/yield relationship for any option-free bond is referred to as *convex*. Keep in mind that the price/yield relationship that we have discussed is appropriate only at a given point in the life of the bond.

Price Volatility Properties

Although the prices of all (option-free) bonds move in the opposite direction of the change in yields, neither dollar price changes nor percentage price changes are the same for all bonds. For our four hypothetical bonds, this can be seen in Table 12-4. The top panel of the table shows the dollar price change and the bottom panel the percentage price change for various changes in the yield assuming that initially all four bonds are priced to yield 9%.

TABLE 12-3   PRICE/YIELD RELATIONSHIP FOR FOUR HYPOTHETICAL BONDS

	PRICE AT GIVEN YIELD AND COUPON/MATURITY*			
YIELD	9%/5 YR	9%/20 YR	5%/5 YR	5%/20 YR
6.00%	112.7953	134.6722	95.7349	88.4426
7.00	108.3166	121.3551	91.6834	78.6449
8.00	104.0554	109.8964	87.8337	70.3108
8.50	102.0027	104.7693	85.9809	66.6148
8.90	100.3966	100.9267	84.5322	63.8593
8.99	100.0396	100.0921	84.2102	63.2626
9.00	100.0000	100.0000	84.1746	63.1968
9.01	99.9604	99.9081	84.1389	63.1311
9.10	99.6053	99.0865	83.8187	62.5445
9.50	98.0459	95.5592	82.4132	60.0332
10.00	96.1391	91.4205	80.6957	57.1023
11.00	92.4624	83.9539	77.3871	51.8616
12.00	88.9599	77.4306	74.2397	47.3380

*Par = 100.

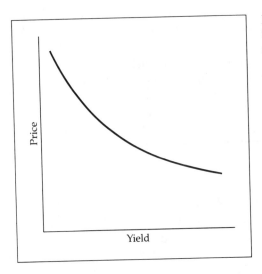

FIGURE 12-4
Shape of Price/Yield Relationship for
an Option-Free Bond

TABLE 12-4   INSTANTANEOUS DOLLAR AND PERCENTAGE PRICE CHANGES FOR FOUR HYPOTHETICAL BONDS

Four hypothetical bonds, priced initially to yield 9%:

9% coupon,   5 years to maturity, price = 100.0000
9% coupon, 20 years to maturity, price = 100.0000
5% coupon,   5 years to maturity, price =   84.1746
5% coupon, 20 years to maturity, price =   63.1968

| YIELD | CHANGE IN YIELD | COUPON/MATURITY | | | |
CHANGES FROM 9% TO	(BASIS POINTS)	9%/5 YR	9%/20 YR	5%/5 YR	5%/20 YR
		DOLLAR PRICE CHANGE PER $100 PAR			
6.00%	−300	12.7953	34.6722	11.5603	25.2458
7.00	−200	8.3166	21.3551	7.5088	15.4481
8.00	−100	4.0554	9.8964	3.6591	7.1140
8.50	− 50	2.0027	4.7693	1.8063	3.4180
8.90	− 10	0.3966	0.9267	0.3576	0.6625
8.99	− 1	0.0396	0.0921	0.0356	0.0658
9.01	1	− 0.3960	− 0.0919	− 0.0357	− 0.0657
9.10	10	− 0.3947	− 0.9135	− 0.3559	− 0.6523
9.50	50	− 1.9541	− 4.4408	− 1.7614	− 3.1636
10.00	100	− 3.8609	− 8.5795	− 3.4789	− 6.0945
11.00	200	− 7.5376	−16.0461	− 6.7875	−11.3352
12.00	300	−11.0401	−22.5694	− 9.9349	−15.8588
		PERCENTAGE PRICE CHANGE			
6.00	−300	12.80	34.67	13.73	39.95
7.00	−200	8.32	21.36	9.92	24.44
8.00	−100	4.06	9.90	4.35	11.26
8.50	− 50	2.00	4.77	2.15	5.41
8.90	− 10	0.40	0.93	0.42	1.05
8.99	− 1	0.04	0.09	0.04	0.10
9.01	1	− 0.04	− 0.09	− 0.04	− 0.10
9.10	10	− 0.40	− 0.91	− 0.42	− 1.03
9.50	50	− 1.95	− 4.44	− 2.09	− 5.01
10.00	100	− 3.86	− 8.58	− 4.13	− 9.64
11.00	200	− 7.54	−16.05	− 8.06	−17.94
12.00	300	−11.04	−22.57	−11.89	−25.09

Note from Table 12-4 that for a given bond the absolute dollar price change and the absolute percentage price change are not the same for an equal increase and decrease in the yield, except for very small changes in the yield. Even for a small change in yield, the absolute dollar price change is less symmetric than the absolute percentage price change. In general, the dollar price increase and the percentage price increase when the yield declines are greater than the dollar price decrease and percentage price decrease when the yield increases.

These two observations—that the absolute and percentage price change are not equal for all bonds, and that the absolute and percentage price change are asymmetric for equal changes in yield—are due to the characteristics of bonds that determine the shape of the price/yield relationship depicted in Figure 12-4. Later in this section we'll provide an explanation for the second observation. First we look at the particular characteristics of a bond that affect its price volatility.

Characteristics of a Bond that Affect Price Volatility

There are two characteristics of a bond that are the primary determinants of its price volatility: coupon and term to maturity.

First, let's look at price volatility in terms of *percentage* price change for a change in yields. For a given term to maturity and initial market yield, percentage price volatility is greater the lower the coupon rate. This property can be seen by comparing the 9% and 5% coupon bonds with the same maturity (lower panel of Table 12-4). The second characteristic of a bond that affects its price volatility is its term to maturity. For a given coupon rate and initial yield, the longer the term to maturity, the greater the price volatility, in terms of percentage price change.[10] This can be seen in the lower panel of Table 12-4 by comparing the 5-year bonds to the 20-year bonds with the same coupon.

Do the same properties hold if volatility is measured in terms of dollar price change rather than percentage price change? The upper panel of Table 12-4 demonstrates that, holding all other factors constant, the dollar price change is greater, the longer the term to maturity. However, the first characteristic concerning the effect of the coupon rate does not hold when volatility is measured in terms of dollar price change instead of percentage price change. In terms of dollar price change, for a given maturity and initial market yield, the lower the coupon rate, the smaller the dollar price change.

---

[10] There are exceptions for certain deep-discount, long-term *coupon* bonds.

Measure of Price Volatility: Duration

Participants in the bond market need to have a way to measure a bond's price volatility in order to measure interest rate risk and to implement portfolio and hedging strategies. The price sensitivity of a bond to a change in yield, y, can be measured by taking the derivative of bond price to a change in yield and then normalizing by the price of the bond. The price of a bond is given by Equation (9) from Chapter 11, repeated below:

$$P = \frac{C}{(1 + y)} + \frac{C}{(1 + y)^2} + \frac{C}{(1 + y)^3} + \cdots + \frac{C + M}{(1 + y)^n} \tag{11}$$

Taking the first derivative of Equation (11) with respect to yield, y, and dividing both sides by P, we get

$$\frac{dP}{dy} \frac{1}{P} = - \frac{1}{(1 + y)} D \tag{12}$$

where

$$D = \frac{\dfrac{(1)C}{(1 + y)} + \dfrac{(2)C}{(1 + y)^2} + \dfrac{(3)C}{(1 + y)^3} + \cdots + \dfrac{(n)(C + M)}{(1 + y)^n}}{P} \tag{13}$$

Equation (13) is called the *Macaulay duration* of a bond. It is named in honor of Frederick Macaulay who used this measure in a study published in 1938.[11] Duration is a weighted-average term to maturity of the components of a bond's cash flows, in which the time of receipt of each payment is weighted by the present value of that payment. The denominator is the sum of the weights, which is precisely the price of the bond. What makes Macaulay duration a valuable indicator is that, as can be seen from Equation (12), it is related to the responsiveness of a bond's price to changes in yield. The larger the Macaulay duration, the greater the price sensitivity of a bond to a change in yield.

---

[11] Frederick R. Macaulay, *Some Theoretical Problems Suggested by the Movement of Interest Rates, Bond Yields, and Stock Prices in the U.S. Since 1856* (New York: National Bureau of Economic Research, 1938). Hicks uses the same measure in his study of the properties of cash flows that make the ratio of their values invariant with respect to changes in interest. He called his measure *average maturity*. (See Hicks, *Value and Capital*, op. cit.) In a study of the impact of a rise in interest rates on the banking system, Samuelson uses a similar concept, which he calls the *average time period* of the cash flow. (See Paul A. Samuelson, "The Effects of Interest Rate Increases on the Banking System," *American Economic Review* (March 1945), pp. 16–27.)

Equation (13) is the formula for a bond that pays interest annually. As the bonds we are discussing pay interest semiannually, the formula for Macaulay duration must be adjusted to use a semiannual rather than annual yield and a semiannual interest payment. The number of periods used also should be double the number of years. These adjustments are made in the illustrations throughout this chapter.

Table 12-5 shows how Macaulay duration is calculated for the hypothetical 9%, five-year bond selling at 100 to yield 9%. Notice that we made adjustments to C, y, and n because we assume that the bond pays interest semiannually. We also divide the Macaulay duration measure given by Equation (13) by 2 to convert a measure given in semiannual periods to an annual measure. The Macaulay duration for the four bonds in Table 12-3 is given below, assuming a yield to maturity of 9% for each:

COUPON	MATURITY	MACAULAY DURATION
9%	5 years	4.13 years
9	20	9.61
5	5	4.43
5	20	10.87

There are two characteristics that affect the Macaulay duration of a bond, and therefore its price volatility. First, the Macaulay duration for a coupon bond is less than its maturity. For a zero-coupon bond, the Macaulay duration is equal to its maturity.[12] Therefore, for bonds with the same maturity and selling at the same yield, the lower the coupon rate, the greater a bond's Macaulay duration and volatility. Second, for two bonds with the same

---

[12] This can be seen by substituting zero for the coupon payments in Equation (13) to obtain

$$D = \frac{\dfrac{(1)0}{(1 + y)} + \dfrac{(2)0}{(1 + y)^2} + \dfrac{(3)0}{(1 + y)^3} + \cdots + \dfrac{(n)(0 + M)}{(1 + y)^n}}{P}$$

so,

$$D = \frac{\dfrac{nM}{(1 + y)^n}}{P}$$

But because $M/(1 + y)^n$ is just the price of the bond,

$$D = \frac{nP}{P} = n$$

TABLE 12-5   CALCULATION OF MACAULAY DURATION FOR A 9%, 5-YEAR BOND SELLING AT PAR

Formula for Macaulay duration:

$$\frac{\dfrac{(1)C}{(1 + y)} + \dfrac{(2)C}{(1 + y)^2} + \dfrac{(3)C}{(1 + y)^3} + \cdots + \dfrac{(n)(C + M)}{(1 + y)^n}}{P}$$

Information about bond per $100 par:
   annual coupon = 0.09 × $100 = $9.00
   yield to maturity = 0.09
   number of years to maturity = 5 years
   price = P = 100

Values for Macaulay duration adjusting for semiannual payments:
   C = $9.00/2 = $4.5
   y = 0.09/2 = 0.045
   n = 5 × 2 = 10

t	C	$\dfrac{C}{(1.045)^t}$	$t \times \dfrac{C}{(1.045)^t}$
1	$ 4.5	4.306220	4.30622
2	4.5	4.120785	8.24156
3	4.5	3.943335	11.83000
4	4.5	3.773526	15.09410
5	4.5	3.611030	18.05514
6	4.5	3.455531	20.73318
7	4.5	3.306728	23.14709
8	4.5	3.164333	25.31466
9	4.5	3.028070	27.25262
10	104.5	67.290443	672.90442
Total		100.000000	826.87899

$$\frac{(1)C}{(1 + y)} + \frac{(2)C}{(1 + y)^2} + \frac{(3)C}{(1 + y)^3} + \cdots + \frac{(m)(C + M)}{(1 + y)^m} = 826.87899$$

Macaulay duration in six-month periods = $\dfrac{826.87899}{100}$ = 8.27

Macaulay duration in years = $\dfrac{8.27}{2}$ = 4.13

coupon rate and selling at the same yield, the longer the maturity, the larger the Macaulay duration and price sensitivity.[13] These properties are consistent with our earlier observations with respect to Table 12-4.

From Equation (12) we have

$$\frac{dP}{P} = -\frac{1}{(1 + y)} D \ (dy) \tag{14}$$

Equation (14) shows how to calculate the percentage change in a bond's price for a given change in yield (dy). Bond market participants commonly combine the first two terms on the right-hand side of Equation (14) and refer to this measure as the *modified duration* of a bond. That is,

$$\text{Modified duration} = \frac{\text{Macaulay duration}}{(1 + y)}$$

Substituting for modified duration into Equation (14), and substituting yield change for dy, we obtain

$$\text{Percentage price change} = -\text{Modified duration} \times \text{Yield change} \tag{15}$$

To illustrate the relationship, consider the 5%, 20-year bond selling at 63.1968 to yield 9%. As the annual yield is 9%, y is 4.5%. The Macaulay duration for this bond is 10.87 years. Modified duration is 10.40 as shown below:

$$\text{Modified duration} = \frac{10.87}{1.045} = 10.40$$

Suppose yields increase instantaneously from 9.00% to 9.10%. The yield change is +0.10 (9.10 − 9.00). Then

$$-10.40 \times (+0.10) = -1.04\%$$

Notice from the lower panel of Table 12-4 that the actual percentage price change is −1.03%. Similarly, if yields decrease instantaneously from 9.00% to 8.90% (a 10 basis point decrease), the formula indicates that the percentage change in price would be +1.04%. From the lower panel of Table 12-4, the actual percentage price change would be +1.05%. This example illustrates

---

[13] This property does not necessarily hold for long-maturity deep-discount coupon bonds.

that for small changes in yield, duration provides a good approximation of the percentage price change.

Instead of a small change in yield, let's assume that yields increase by 200 basis points, from 9% to 11% (a yield change of +2.00). The percentage change in price estimated using duration would be:

$$-10.40 \times (+2.00) = -20.80\%$$

How good is this approximation? As can be seen from the lower panel of Table 12-4, the actual percentage change in price is only −17.94%. Moreover, if the yield decreases by 200 basis points, from 9% to 7%, the approximate percentage price change based on duration would be +20.80%, compared to an actual percentage price change of +24.44%. Not only is the approximation off, but we also can see that duration estimates a symmetric percentage change in price, which, as we pointed out earlier, is not a property of the price/yield relationship for an option-free bond.

Notice that the estimated new price based on duration in both instances where the yield changes by 200 basis points would be less than the actual price change. For example, for a decline in yield of 200 basis points, the estimated percentage price decline is more than the actual percentage price decline. Similarly, for the same decline in yield, the estimated percentage price rise is less than the actual percentage price rise.

A useful interpretation of modified duration can be obtained by substituting 100 basis points into Equation (15). The percentage price change would then be:

$$-\text{Modified duration} \times (+1.00) = -\text{Modified duration}$$

Thus, *modified duration can be interpreted as the percentage price change for a 100 basis point change in yields.*

We're now ready to tie together the price/yield relationship and several of the properties of bond price volatility that we discussed earlier. Recall the shape of the price/yield relationship, as shown in Figure 12-4. We referred to that shape as convex. In Figure 12-5, a line is drawn tangent to the price/yield relationship at yield y^*. The tangent shows the rate of change of price with respect to a change in interest rates at that point (yield level). The tangent is closely related to the modified duration (which tells us about the rate of percentage price changes).[14] The steeper the tangent line, the greater the modified duration; the flatter the tangent line, the lower the modified

---

[14] Technically, for the tangent line to be equal to modified duration, the axes in Figures 12-4 and 12-5 must be scaled in logarithms.

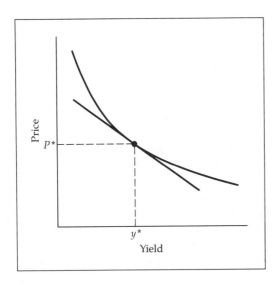

FIGURE 12-5
Tangent to Price/Yield Relationship

duration. Thus, for a given starting price, the tangent line and the modified duration can be used interchangeably, and can be thought of as one and the same method of estimating the rate of price changes. Below we simply use the term "duration" to refer to modified duration.

Notice what happens to duration (steepness of the tangent line) as yield changes: as yield increases (decreases), duration decreases (increases). This property holds for all option-free bonds.

If we draw a vertical line from any yield (on the horizontal axis), the distance between the horizontal axis and the tangent line represents the price approximated by using duration starting with the initial yield y^*. The approximation will always understate the actual price. This agrees with our illustration earlier of the relationship between duration and the approximate price change.

For small changes in yield, the tangent line and duration do a good job in estimating the actual price, but the farther the distance from the initial yield, y^*, the worse the approximation. It should be apparent that the accuracy of the approximation depends on the convexity (bowedness) of the price/yield relationship.

Curvature and Convexity

Mathematically, duration is a first approximation of the price/yield relationship. That is, duration attempts to estimate a convex relationship with a straight line (the tangent line).

A fundamental property of calculus is that a mathematical function can be approximated by a Taylor series. The more terms of a Taylor series used, the better the approximation. For example, the first two terms of a Taylor series for the price function given by Equation (11) would be

$$\frac{dP}{P} = \frac{dP}{dy}\frac{1}{P}\ dy + \frac{1}{2}\frac{d^2P}{dy^2}\frac{1}{P}\ dy^2 \tag{16}$$

The fact that duration is the first term of the Taylor series can be seen by comparing the first term on the right-hand side of Equation (16) with Equation (14). The second term of the Taylor series requires the calculation of the second derivative of the price function, Equation (11). The second derivative of Equation (11) normalized by price (i.e., divided by price) is

$$\frac{d^2P}{dy^2}\frac{1}{P} = \frac{\dfrac{(1)(2)C}{(1+y)} + \dfrac{(2)(3)C}{(1+y)^2} + \dfrac{(3)(4)C}{(1+y)^3} + \cdots + \dfrac{(n)(n+1)(C+M)}{(1+y)^n}}{(1+y)^2 P} \tag{17}$$

The measure in Equation (17) when divided by 2 is referred to popularly as the convexity of a bond. That is,

$$\text{Convexity} = \frac{1}{2}\frac{d^2P}{dy^2}\frac{1}{P} \tag{18}$$

This is an unfortunate misuse of terminology because it suggests that the convexity measure conveys the curvature of the convex shape of the price/yield relationship for a bond. It does not. It is simply an approximation of the curvature.

Table 12-6 sets forth the calculations for the convexity of the 9%, five-year bond selling at 100 to yield 9%. Once again, notice that C, y, and n are adjusted as we discussed earlier. Also note that we divide the convexity measure as given by Equation (18) by 2 in order to convert convexity measured in semiannual periods into convexity measured in years.

The second term on the right-hand side of Equation (16) is the incremental percentage change in price due to convexity. From Equation (18), it can be expressed as

$$\text{Percentage change in price due to correction for convexity} = \\ \text{Convexity} \times (\text{Change in yield})^2 \tag{19}$$

For example, convexity for the 5% coupon bond maturing in 20 years is 80.43. Then the approximate percentage price change due solely to correction for convexity if the yield increases from 9% to 11% (+2.00 yield change) is:

$$80.43 \times (+0.02)^2 = 3.22\%$$

If the yield decreases from 9% to 7% (−2.00 yield change), the approximate percentage price change due solely to convexity would also be 3.22%.

TABLE 12-6   CALCULATION OF CONVEXITY FOR A 9%, 5-YEAR BOND SELLING AT PAR

Formula for convexity:

$$\frac{\dfrac{(1)(2)C}{(1+y)} + \dfrac{(2)(3)C}{(1+y)^2} + \dfrac{(3)(4)C}{(1+y)^3} + \cdots + \dfrac{(n)(n+1)(C+M)}{(1+y)^n}}{2(1+y)^2 P}$$

Information about bond per $100 par:
   annual coupon = 0.09 × $100 = $9.00
   yield to maturity = 0.09
   number of years to maturity = 5 years
   price = P = 100

Values for convexity adjusting for semiannual payments:
   C = $9.00/2 = $4.5
   y = 0.09/2 = 0.045
   n = 5 × 2 = 10

t	C	$\dfrac{C}{(1.045)^t}$	$t(t+1)\dfrac{C}{(1.045)^t}$
1	$ 4.5	4.306220	8.6124
2	4.5	4.120785	24.7242
3	4.5	3.943335	47.3196
4	4.5	3.773526	75.4700
5	4.5	3.611030	108.3300
6	4.5	3.455531	145.1310
7	4.5	3.306728	185.1752
8	4.5	3.164333	227.8296
9	4.5	3.028070	272.5290
10	104.5	67.290443	7,401.9440
Total		100.000000	8,497.0650

$$\frac{(1)(2)C}{(1+y)} + \frac{(2)(3)C}{(1+y)^2} + \frac{(3)(4)C}{(1+y)^3} + \cdots + \frac{(n)(n+1)(C+M)}{(1+y)^n} = 8{,}497.0650$$

$$\text{Convexity in six-month periods} = \frac{8{,}497.0650}{2(1.045)^2\,100} = 38.90$$

$$\text{Convexity in years} = \frac{38.90}{2} = 19.45$$

The approximate total percentage price change based on both duration and convexity is found by simply adding the two estimates. For example, if yields change from 9% to 11%, we have an approximate percentage price change due to:

Duration   = −20.80%
Convexity Correction = + 3.22
                                    _____
Total   = −17.58%

From Table 12-4, the actual percentage price change would be −17.94%.

For a decrease of 200 basis points, from 9% to 7%, we have an approximate percentage price change due to:

Duration   = +20.80%
Convexity Correction = + 3.22
                                    _____
Total   = +24.02%

The actual percentage price change would be +24.44%.

Consequently, for large yield movements, a better approximation for bond price movements when interest rates change is obtained by using both duration and convexity.

What is convexity measuring? Convexity is measuring the rate of change of dollar duration as yields change. For all option-free bonds, modified and dollar duration increases as yields decline. This is a positive attribute of any option-free bond, because as yields decline, price appreciation accelerates. When yields increase, the duration for all option-free bonds will decrease. Once again, this is a positive attribute, because as yields decline, this feature will decelerate the price depreciation. This is the reason why we observed that the absolute and percentage price change is greater when yields decline compared to when they increase by the same number of basis points. Thus, an option-free bond is said to have *positive convexity*.

One final but important note. *Duration and convexity are measures of price volatility assuming the yield curve is initially flat and that if there are any yield shifts they are parallel ones.* That is, the Treasury yields of all maturities change by the same number of basis points. To see where we assume this, look back at the price function we analyzed for changes in yield [Equation (11)]. Each cash flow is discounted at the same yield. If the yield curve does not shift in a parallel fashion, duration and convexity will not do as good a job of approximating the percentage price change of a bond.

Use of Duration in Institutional Investment Strategies

Despite the limitations of duration as a measure of bond price volatility, it is used by most portfolio managers and dealers. Dealers use duration to estimate the interest rate risk exposure of their bond inventory and to hedge that exposure. Portfolio managers also use it to quantify their interest rate exposure and will adjust portfolio duration to capitalize on anticipated changes in interest rates. For example, if interest rates are expected to decline, and therefore bond prices rise, a portfolio manager will increase the portfolio's duration. The portfolio's duration will be shortened if interest rates are expected to fall. Hedging is a special case where the portfolio duration is adjusted to zero; that is, there is no interest rate risk exposure.

Another popular strategy that relies on duration is *immunization*, which is used by life insurance companies and pension funds. To illustrate, suppose a life insurance company has guaranteed a policyholder a 10% return for five years. That is, it has issued a five-year guaranteed interest contract (GIC).[15] Ignoring the fact that the life insurance company wants to earn a return higher than 10% so that it can realize a profit, the target return is then 10%. If the life insurance company purchases a five-year Treasury security with a yield to maturity of 10%, won't that assure that the 10% target return will be realized?

Not so. The reason is that while there will be no uncertainty about the proceeds to be received at the end of five years because the maturity value will be received, the reinvestment income is unknown. If the life insurance company must reinvest the coupon payments at an interest rate lower than 10% because interest rates have dropped, the target return will not be achieved. That is, the life insurance company is exposed to reinvestment risk.

Suppose, instead, that the life insurance company can purchase a 10-year Treasury security with a 10% yield to maturity. Will this assure that the 10% target return will be achieved? Once again, the answer is no. In this case, the company is exposed not only to reinvestment risk, but also to interest rate risk because the securities must be sold prior to maturity. If interest rates rise, the securities must be sold at a loss.

Is there a strategy that this life insurance company can pursue to make it highly likely that the target return will be achieved? There is. To understand the strategy, focus on the two types of risks faced by the life insurance company in this example—interest rate risk and reinvestment risk. Interest rate risk is the risk that interest rates will rise. Reinvestment risk is the risk

---

[15] GICs are discussed in Chapter 4.

that interest rates will fall. What we have then, is a "good news/bad news" situation when interest rates change. Specifically, when interest rates rise, the securities will be sold at a loss at the end of five years (the bad news), but there will be more income generated from reinvesting the coupon payments at the higher interest rate (the good news). Should interest rates fall rather than rise, the securities will be sold at a higher price at the end of the investment horizon (the good news), but the reinvestment income will be less (the bad news).

The answer is therefore: create a portfolio of securities where a loss in one component of the return (price loss or reinvestment income loss) is off-set by a gain in the other. But how does a portfolio manager go about constructing such a portfolio? Under certain conditions, a portfolio constructed such that its Macaulay duration is equal to the investment horizon will realize the target return at a minimum. In our example, this means that the life insurance company should construct a portfolio with a Macaulay duration equal to five years (the investment horizon). This strategy is called immunization, because it attempts to immunize the portfolio against any change in interest rates.[16]

Our explanation of an immunization strategy focuses on immunizing a portfolio that seeks to satisfy a liability at the end of some time period (five years in the case of our GIC illustration). Immunization strategies are also used by both life insurance companies and pension funds to immunize against adverse interest rate changes in seeking to satisfy multiple-period liabilities (annuities in the case of life insurance companies and scheduled pension benefit payments in the case of pension funds). In such cases, two conditions must be satisfied. First, the portfolio must be constructed so that the duration of the assets is equal to the Macaulay duration of the liabilities.[17] Second, the convexity of the assets must be greater than the convexity of the liabilities.[18]

---

[16] The theory of immunization was first set forth in F.M. Reddington, "Review of the Principle of Life Office Valuations," *Journal of the Institute of Actuaries* (1952), pp. 286–340. For an explanation of the different types of immunization strategies see Peter C. Christensen, Frank J. Fabozzi, and Anthony LoFaso, "Bond Immunization: An Asset Liability Strategy Optimization," Chapter 42 in Frank J. Fabozzi (ed.), *The Handbook of Fixed Income Securities*, (Homewood, IL: BusinessOne-Irwin, Third Edition, 1991).

[17] Remember that liabilities are simply negative cash flows. Consequently, a duration and convexity can be calculated for a liability stream.

[18] The derivation of these conditions is beyond the scope of this chapter. The interested reader is referred to: H. Gifford Fong and Oldrich Vasicek, "A Risk Minimizing Strategy for Portfolio Immunization," *Journal of Finance* (June 1984), pp. 1541–1546.

SUMMARY

The term structure of interest rates shows the relation between the yield on bonds that differ by maturity. The term structure is often depicted graphically by the yield curve, which shows the relation between coupon bonds and their corresponding maturity. While the yield to maturity of a bond with maturity n is a measure of the n-period interest rate, it is not a satisfactory measure because different one-period bonds may have different yields. To insure uniqueness, we define the n-period long rate as the yield of an n-period zero-coupon bond, also known as the n-period spot rate. One plus the spot rate is a (geometric) average of all the future short-term compounding factors (one plus the short rate) spanning the interval from the time the bond is acquired to maturity. Spot rates can be readily computed from the price of zero-coupon bonds if they are traded and there are no biases in the observed zero-coupon yields. Otherwise, spot rates can be derived from the price and yields of coupon bonds.

The future rates whose average determines the spot rates are not known at the present time as they will be established in each future period. From the current spot rates, we can calculate the path of future interest rates or forward rates that are implicit in the family of spot rates. Forward rates can be computed for any future short period or for a stretch of periods. One plus the n-period forward rate is equal to the geometric average of the forward one-period compounding factor.

Several answers have been proposed for what determines the forward rates and the term structure, the relation between the forward rate at successive maturity and the maturity itself. The pure expectations theory hypothesizes that the one-period forward rates simply represent the market's expectations of future market rates. The long-term spot rate, being an average of the short-term forward rates until maturity, would itself be fully explained by the market expectations of future short rates. The term structure might then be rising, falling, or flat, according to whether the market expects rising, falling, or unchanged short-term rates. But this formulation fails to recognize that future short- and long-term rates may differ from the corresponding forward rates because of expectations error, and that these errors may be the sources of substantial risk when investors buy bonds whose maturity is different from the time for which they plan to hold the bond.

The fact that there is short-term risk in long lending and that it seems to increase with maturity has given rise to an alternative "liquidity" theory of the term structure, according to which forward rates are the sum of expected future rates and a risk premium that increases for more and more distant future rates and, hence, rises with the maturity of a bond.

This formulation has shortcomings because it presupposes that all lenders want to lend short and all borrowers want to borrow long. If so, long borrowers would have to offer lenders a premium, rising with maturity, to accept the risk of going long. But in reality we know that both lenders and borrowers have quite varied maturity preferences. Each agent can eliminate risk, not by borrowing or lending short, but by lending (or borrowing) for a period coinciding with their preferred habitat. But at the same time agents would presumably be willing to depart from their preferred habitat by the inducement of a risk premium.

Accordingly, the third version of the expectations theory—namely, the preferred habitat theory—suggests, like the liquidity theory, that forward rates are the sum of a component reflecting expected future rates and a risk premium. But the premium will not rise continuously with maturity but will materialize in any maturity neighborhood where supply exceeds demand. A negative premium or discount would be expected if supply exceeds demand.

One final formulation is the market segmentation theory. In common with the preferred habitat theory, it recognizes that participants in the bond market have maturity preferences. But it postulates that these preferences are absolute and cannot be overcome by the expectation of a higher return from a different maturity, no matter how large. Thus each maturity is a separate market; the interest rate in the market is determined by the given demand and supply, and is totally unrelated to expectations of future rates. This formulation is of doubtful use because it implies highly irrational, implausible, and counterfactual behavior.

Finally, we explore the sensitivity of bond prices to changes in interest rates. A graph of the relationship between price and yield for any option-free bond would have a convex shape. Not all bonds change by the same percentage or dollar amount if interest rates change. Two characteristics of a bond that affect its price volatility and therefore its interest rate risk exposure are maturity and coupon rate. For a given yield and coupon rate, the longer the maturity, the greater the price volatility. While there are exceptions, for a given yield and maturity, price volatility is greater, the lower the coupon rate.

A measure of price volatility that relates coupon and maturity is Macaulay duration, defined as the average time to maturity of the cash flow that is found by weighting the time of receipt of a cash flow by the present value of that cash flow. The modified duration of a bond is the approximate percentage price change of a bond for a 100 basis point change in interest rates. Dollar duration measures the dollar price change when interest rates change. Convexity is another measure of price volatility to be used in conjunction with modified duration to improve the estimate for price volatility for large changes in interest rates. The convexity measure of a bond shows the rate of change of the dollar duration of a bond as interest rates change.

Institutional investors adjust the duration of a portfolio to increase (decrease) their interest rate risk exposure if interest rates are expected to fall (rise). A strategy called immunization is used by institutional investors to protect a portfolio against an adverse change in interest rates. Basically this strategy seeks to offset interest rate risk and reinvestment risk.

QUESTIONS

1. You are a pension fund consultant. At various times you have heard comments on interest rates from one of your clients. How would you respond to each comment?

   a. "The yield curve is upward-sloping today. This suggests that the market consensus is that interest rates are expected to increase in the future."

   b. "I can't make any sense out of today's term structure. For short-term yields (up to three years) the spot rates increase with maturity; for maturities greater than three years but less than eight years, the spot rates decline with maturity; and for maturities greater than eight years the spot rates are virtually the same for each maturity. There is simply no theory that explains a term structure with this shape."

   c. "When I want to determine the market's consensus of future interest rates, I calculate the implicit forward rates."

2. You observe the yield curve below for Treasury securities (all yields are shown on a bond equivalent basis):

Year	Yield to Maturity	Spot Rate
0.5	5.25%	5.25%
1.0	5.50	5.50
1.5	5.75	5.76
2.0	6.00	?
2.5	6.25	?
3.0	6.50	?
3.5	6.75	?
4.0	7.00	?
4.5	7.25	?
5.0	7.50	?
5.5	7.75	7.97
6.0	8.00	8.27
6.5	8.25	8.59
7.0	8.50	8.92
7.5	8.75	9.25
8.0	9.00	9.61
8.5	9.25	9.97
9.0	9.50	10.36
9.5	9.75	10.77
10.0	10.00	11.20

All the securities maturing from 1.5 years on are selling at par. The 0.5-year and 1-year securities are zero-coupon instruments.

a. Calculate the missing spot rates.

b. As all the securities maturing from 1.5 years on are trading at par, the yield curve in our example is called the "par yield curve." When the yield curve is upward-sloping, what is the relationship between the par yield curve and the spot rate curve?

c. What should the price of a six-year Treasury security be?

d. What is the implicit six-month forward rate starting in the sixth year?

3. You observe the following yield curve for Treasury securities (all yields are shown on a bond equivalent basis):

YEAR	YIELD TO MATURITY	SPOT RATE
0.5	10.00%	10.00%
1.0	9.75	9.75
1.5	9.50	9.48
2.0	9.25	9.22
2.5	9.00	8.95
3.0	8.75	8.68
3.5	8.50	8.41
4.0	8.25	8.14
4.5	8.00	7.86
5.0	7.75	7.58
5.5	7.50	7.30
6.0	7.25	7.02
6.5	7.00	6.74
7.0	6.75	6.18
7.5	6.50	5.90
8.0	6.25	5.62
8.5	6.00	5.35
9.0	5.75	5.07
9.5	5.50	?
10.0	5.25	?

All the securities maturing from 1.5 years on are selling at par. The 0.5-year and 1-year securities are zero-coupon instruments.

a. Calculate the missing spot rates.

b. When the yield curve is downward-sloping, what is the relationship between the par yield curve and the spot rate curve?

c. What should the price of a four-year Treasury security be?

4. Can you tell from the information below which of the following three bonds will have the greatest price volatility, assuming each is trading to offer the same yield to maturity?

BOND	COUPON RATE	MATURITY
X	8%	9 years
Y	10	11
Z	11	12

5. Calculate the requested measures for bonds A and B (assume each bond pays interest semiannually):

	A	B
Coupon	8%	9%
Yield to maturity	8%	8%
Maturity (in years)	2	5
Par	100.00	100.00
Price	100.000	104.055

a. Macaulay duration

b. modified duration

c. convexity

6. For bonds A and B in the previous question:

a. Calculate the actual price of the bonds for a 100-basis point increase in interest rates.

b. Using duration, estimate the price of the bonds for a 100-basis point increase in interest rates.

c. Using both duration and convexity, estimate the price of the bonds for a 100-basis point increase in interest rates.

d. Comment on the accuracy of your results in (b) and (c), and state why one approximation is closer to the actual price than the other.

e. Without working through calculations, indicate whether the duration of the two bonds would be higher or lower if the yield to maturity is 10% rather than 8%.

7. State why you would agree or disagree with the following statement: "As the duration of a zero-coupon bond is equal to its maturity, the responsiveness of a zero-coupon bond to interest rate changes is the same regardless of the level of interest rates."

8. The November 26, 1990, issue of *Bondweek* includes an article, "Van Kampen Merritt Shortens." The article begins as follows:

> Peter Hegel, first v.p. at Van Kampen Merritt Investment Advisory, is shortening his $3 billion portfolio from 110% of his normal duration of 6 1/2 years to 103–105% because he thinks that in the short run the bond rally is near an end.

Explain Hegel's strategy and the use of the duration measure in this context.

CHAPTER

13

MONEY MARKET INSTRUMENTS

LEARNING OBJECTIVES

After reading this chapter you will understand:

- what the money market is.
- the kinds of instruments traded in the money market.
- what a Treasury bill is.
- the auction process for Treasury bills.
- what commercial paper is and who the major issuers are.
- the difference between directly placed and dealer-placed commercial paper.
- what a bankers acceptance is and how it is created.
- what a certificate of deposit is and the different types of certificates of deposit.
- what a repurchase agreement is and how it can be used to finance a security position.

- the factors that influence the interest rate on repurchase agreements.
- what the federal funds market is.

In this chapter and the next five we turn our attention to debt securities—instruments that obligate the debtor to make a contractually fixed series of payments, generally in nominal dollars, up to some terminal date called the "maturity date." This chapter focuses on debt instruments that at the time of issuance have a maturity of one year or less. These instruments are referred to as *money market instruments*, and the market they trade in is called the *money market*. In Chapters 14 through 18 we deal with debt instruments with longer-term maturities.

The assets traded in the money market include Treasury bills, commercial paper, medium-term notes, bankers acceptances, short-term federal agency securities, short-term municipal obligations, certificates of deposit, repurchase agreements, floating-rate instruments, and federal funds. Short-term federal agency securities and municipal securities are discussed in Chapters 14 and 16, respectively; medium-term notes are reserved for Chapter 15. Medium-term notes are corporate debt instruments with maturities ranging from 9 months to 30 years.

TREASURY BILLS

Treasury securities are issued by the U.S. Treasury and backed by the full faith and credit of the U.S. government. As a result, market participants perceive Treasury securities to carry no risk of default.

The U.S. Treasury issues three types of securities—bills, notes, and bonds. At issuance, bills have a maturity of one year or less, notes more than two years but less than 10 years to maturity, and bonds 10 years or more to maturity. In the next chapter we cover Treasury securities in greater detail, but here we limit our discussion of Treasury securities to bills because they fall into the category of money market instruments—that is, instruments with one year or less to maturity. For reasons to be explained, Treasury bills are the most liquid assets in the U.S.

A Treasury bill is a discount security. Such securities do not make periodic interest payments. The security holder receives interest instead at the maturity date, when the amount received at the maturity date (called the *face value, maturity value,* or *par value*) is larger than the purchase price. For example, suppose an investor purchases a six-month Treasury bill that has a face value of $100,000 for $96,000. By holding the bill until the maturity date, the investor will receive $100,000; the difference of $4,000 between the proceeds received at maturity and the amount paid to purchase the bill represents the interest. Treasury bills are only one example of a number of money market instruments that are discount securities.

As of December 31, 1990, the amount of Treasury bills outstanding was $527 billion.

Bid and Offer Quotes on Treasury Bills

Bids and offers on Treasury bills are quoted in a special way. Unlike bonds that pay coupon interest, Treasury bill values are quoted on a bank discount basis, not on a price basis. The yield on a bank discount basis is computed as follows:

$$Y_D = \frac{D}{F} \times \frac{360}{t}$$

where Y_D = annualized yield on a bank discount basis (expressed as a decimal)

D = dollar discount, which is equal to the difference between the face value and the price

F = face value

t = number of days remaining to maturity

As an example, a Treasury bill with 100 days to maturity, a face value of $100,000, and selling for $97,569 would be quoted at 8.75% on a bank discount basis:

$D = \$100,000 - \$97,569$

$\quad = \$2,431$

Therefore:

$$Y_D = \frac{\$2,431}{\$100,000} \times \frac{360}{100}$$

$$= 8.75\%$$

Given the yield on a bank discount basis, the price of a Treasury bill is found by first solving the formula for Y_D for the dollar discount (D), as follows:

$$D = Y_D \times F \times \frac{t}{360}$$

The price is then:

$$\text{Price} = F - D$$

or, equivalently

$$\text{Price} = F \left(1 - Y_D \frac{t}{360}\right)$$

For the 100-day Treasury bill with a face value of $100,000, if the yield on a bank discount basis is quoted as 8.75%, D is equal to:

$$D = 0.0875 \times \$100,000 \times \frac{100}{360}$$

$$= \$2,431$$

Therefore:

$$\text{Price} = \$100,000 - \$2,431$$

$$= \$97,569$$

The quoted yield on a bank discount basis is not a meaningful measure of the return from holding a Treasury bill for two reasons. First, the measure is based on a face value investment rather than on the actual dollar amount invested. Second, the yield is annualized according to a 360-day rather than 365-day year, making it difficult to compare Treasury-bill yields with Treasury notes and bonds, which pay interest on a 365-day basis. The use of 360 days for a year is a money market convention for some money market instruments, however. Despite its shortcomings as a measure of return, this is the method dealers have adopted to quote Treasury bills. Many dealer quote sheets and some reporting services provide two other yield measures that attempt to make the quoted yield comparable to that for a coupon bond and other money market instruments.

The measure that seeks to make the Treasury bill quote comparable to Treasury notes and bonds is called the bond equivalent yield, which we explained in Chapter 11. The *CD equivalent yield* (also called the *money market equivalent yield*) makes the quoted yield on a Treasury bill more comparable to yield quotations on other money market instruments that pay interest on a 360-day basis. It does this by taking into consideration the price of the Treasury bill rather than its face value. The formula for the CD equivalent yield is:

$$\text{CD equivalent yield} = \frac{360 \; Y_D}{360 - t \; (Y_D)}$$

As an illustration, consider once again the hypothetical 100-day Treasury bill with a face value of $100,000, selling for $97,569, and offering a yield on a bank discount basis of 8.75%. The CD equivalent yield is:

$$= \frac{360 \; (0.0875)}{360 - 100 \; (0.0875)}$$

$$= 8.97\%$$

The Primary Market for Treasury Bills

Treasury securities typically are issued on an auction basis according to regular cycles for securities of specific maturities. Three-month and six-month Treasury bills are auctioned every Monday. The amounts to be auctioned are ordinarily announced the previous Tuesday afternoon. The one-year (52-week bill) Treasury bills are auctioned in the third week of every month, with announcement on the preceding Friday. When the Treasury is temporarily short of cash, it issues *cash management bills.* The maturities of cash management bills coincide with the length of time that the Treasury anticipates the shortfall of funds.

Figure 13-1 shows the announcement of a Treasury auction for a 52-week (364-day) Treasury bill. The results of this auction are shown in Figure 13-2.

The auction for Treasury bills and Treasury coupon securities is conducted on a yield basis. Competitive bids for Treasury bills must be submitted on a bank discount basis, as we have explained. Non-competitive tenders may also be submitted for up to a $1 million face amount. Such tenders are based only on quantity, not yield. The price paid by non-competitive bidders is the average price determined by the competitive bidders. Figure 13-3 is a reproduction of a tender form for a Treasury bill.

FOR RELEASE AT 12:00 NOON   June 23, 1989

TREASURY'S 52-WEEK BILL OFFERING

The Department of the Treasury, by this public notice, invites
tenders for approximately $9,000   million of 364-day Treasury bills
to be dated · July 6, 1989,   and to mature July 5, 1990
(CUSIP No. 912794 UM 4). This issue will result in a paydown for
the Treasury of about $ 225   million, as the maturing 52-week bill
is outstanding in the amount of $9,234   million. Tenders will be
received at Federal Reserve Banks and Branches and at the Bureau
of the Public Debt, Washington, D. C. 20239, prior to 1:00 p.m.,
Eastern Daylight Saving time, Thursday, June 29, 1989.

The bills will be issued on a discount basis under competitive
and noncompetitive bidding, and at maturity their par amount will
be payable without interest. This series of bills will be issued
entirely in book-entry form in a minimum amount of $10,000 and in
any higher $5,000 multiple, on the records either of the Federal
Reserve Banks and Branches, or of the Department of the Treasury.

The bills will be issued for cash and in exchange for
Treasury bills maturing July 6, 1989.   In addition to the
maturing 52-week bills, there are $14,792 million of maturing bills
which were originally issued as 13-week and 26-week bills. The disposition of this latter amount will be announced next week. Federal
Reserve Banks currently hold $2,525 million as agents for foreign
and international monetary authorities, and $ 7,655 million for their
own account. These amounts represent the combined holdings of such
accounts for the three issues of maturing bills. Tenders from Federal Reserve Banks for their own account and as agents for foreign
and international monetary authorities will be accepted at the
weighted average bank discount rate of accepted competitive tenders.
Additional amounts of the bills may be issued to Federal Reserve
Banks, as agents for foreign and international monetary authorities,
to the extent that the aggregate amount of tenders for such accounts
exceeds the aggregate amount of maturing bills held by them. For
purposes of determining such additional amounts, foreign and international monetary authorities are considered to hold $292   million
of the original 52-week issue. Tenders for bills to be maintained
on the book-entry records of the Department of the Treasury should
be submitted on Form PD 5176-3.

FIGURE 13-1
Announcement of a Treasury Bill Offering

TREASURY'S 13-, 26-, AND 52-WEEK BILL OFFERINGS, Page 2

Each tender must state the par amount of bills bid for,
which must be a minimum of $10,000. Tenders over $10,000 must
be in multiples of $5,000. Competitive tenders must also show
the yield desired, expressed on a bank discount rate basis with
two decimals, e.g., 7.15%. Fractions may not be used. A single
bidder, as defined in Treasury's single bidder guidelines, shall
not submit noncompetitive tenders totaling more than $1,000,000.

Banking institutions and dealers who make primary markets
in Government securities and report daily to the Federal Reserve
Bank of New York their positions in and borrowings on such securities may submit tenders for account of customers, if the names
of the customers and the amount for each customer are furnished.
Others are only permitted to submit tenders for their own account.
Each tender must state the amount of any net long position in the
bills being offered if such position is in excess of $200 million.
This information should reflect positions held as of one-half hour
prior to the closing time for receipt of tenders on the day of the
auction. Such positions would include bills acquired through "when
issued" trading, and futures and forward transactions as well as
holdings of outstanding bills with the same maturity date as the
new offering, e.g., bills with three months to maturity previously
offered as six-month bills. Dealers, who make primary markets in
Government securities and report daily to the Federal Reserve Bank
of New York their positions in and borrowings on such securities,
when submitting tenders for customers, must submit a separate tender
for each customer whose net long position in the bill being offered
exceeds $200 million.

A noncompetitive bidder may not have entered into an agreement,
nor make an agreement to purchase or sell or otherwise dispose of
any noncompetitive awards of this issue being auctioned prior to
the designated closing time for receipt of tenders.

Payment for the full par amount of the bills applied for
must accompany all tenders submitted for bills to be maintained on
the book-entry records of the Department of the Treasury. A cash
adjustment will be made on all accepted tenders for the difference
between the par payment submitted and the actual issue price as
determined in the auction.

No deposit need accompany tenders from incorporated banks
and trust companies and from responsible and recognized dealers
in investment securities for bills to be maintained on the book-
entry records of Federal Reserve Banks and Branches. A deposit of
2 percent of the par amount of the bills applied for must accompany
tenders for such bills from others, unless an express guaranty of
payment by an incorporated bank or trust company accompanies the
tenders.

10/87

FIGURE 13-1   (cont.)

TREASURY'S 13-, 26-, AND 52-WEEK BILL OFFERINGS, Page 3

Public announcement will be made by the Department of the
Treasury of the amount and yield range of accepted bids. Competitive bidders will be advised of the acceptance or rejection of
their tenders. The Secretary of the Treasury expressly reserves
the right to accept or reject any or all tenders, in whole or in
part, and the Secretary's action shall be final. Subject to these
reservations, noncompetitive tenders for each issue for $1,000,000
or less without stated yield from any one bidder will be accepted
in full at the weighted average bank discount rate (in two decimals)
of accepted competitive bids for the respective issues. The calculation of purchase prices for accepted bids will be carried to
three decimal places on the basis of price per hundred, e.g.,
99.923, and the determinations of the Secretary of the Treasury
shall be final.

Settlement for accepted tenders for bills to be maintained
on the book-entry records of Federal Reserve Banks and Branches
must be made or completed at the Federal Reserve Bank or Branch
on the issue date, in cash or other immediately-available funds
or in Treasury bills maturing on that date. Cash adjustments
will be made for differences between the par value of the maturing
bills accepted in exchange and the issue price of the new bills.
In addition, Treasury Tax and Loan Note Option Depositaries may
make payment for allotments of bills for their own accounts and
for account of customers by credit to their Treasury Tax and Loan
Note Accounts on the settlement date.

If a bill is purchased at issue, and is held to maturity,
the amount of discount is reportable as ordinary income on the
Federal income tax return of the owner for the year in which
the bill matures. Accrual-basis taxpayers, banks, and other
persons designated in section 1281 of the Internal Revenue Code
must include in income the portion of the discount for the period
during the taxable year such holder held the bill. If the bill
is sold or otherwise disposed of before maturity, any gain in
excess of the basis is treated as ordinary income.

Department of the Treasury Circulars, Public Debt Series -
Nos. 26-76, 27-76, and 2-86, as applicable, Treasury's single
bidder guidelines, and this notice prescribe the terms of these
Treasury bills and govern the conditions of their issue. Copies
of the circulars, guidelines, and tender forms may be obtained
from any Federal Reserve Bank or Branch, or from the Bureau of
the Public Debt.

10/87

FIGURE 13-1   (cont.)

FOR IMMEDIATE RELEASE   June 29, 1989

RESULTS OF TREASURY'S 52-WEEK BILL AUCTION

Tenders for $9,003 million of 52-week bills to be issued
July 6, 1989,   and to mature July 5, 1990,   were accepted
today. The details are as follows:

RANGE OF ACCEPTED COMPETITIVE BIDS:

	Discount Rate	Investment Rate (Equivalent Coupon-Issue Yield)	Price
Low -	7.55%	8.12%	92.366
High -	7.62%	8.20%	92.295
Average -	7.58%	8.16%	92.336

Tenders at the high discount rate were allotted 79%.

TENDERS RECEIVED AND ACCEPTED
(In Thousands)

Location	Received	Accepted
Boston	$ 23,215	$ 23,215
New York	19,263,425	8,268,925
Philadelphia	16,065	16,065
Cleveland	25,670	25,670
Richmond	24,625	24,625
Atlanta	15,645	15,645
Chicago	1,034,035	146,935
St. Louis	22,490	19,490
Minneapolis	13,530	13,530
Kansas City	34,720	34,720
Dallas	8,870	8,870
San Francisco	986,450	159,450
Treasury	245,685	245,685
TOTALS	$21,714,425	$9,002,825
Type		
Competitive	$18,272,935	$5,561,335
Noncompetitive	641,490	641,490
Subtotal, Public	$18,914,425	$6,202,825
Federal Reserve	2,800,000	2,800,000
Foreign Official Institutions	-0-	-0-
TOTALS	$21,714,425	$9,002,825

7.56 - 92.356   7.57 - 92.346   7.59 - 92.326
7.60 - 92.316   7.61 - 92.305

FIGURE 13-2
Results of Treasury Auction

The auction results are determined by first deducting the total non-competitive tenders and non-public purchases (such as purchases by the Federal Reserve itself) from the total securities being auctioned. The remainder is the amount to be awarded to the competitive bidders. The lowest-yield (i.e., highest price) bidders are awarded securities at their bid price. Successively higher-yielding bidders are awarded securities at their bid price until the total amount offered (less non-competitive tenders) is awarded. The highest yield accepted by the Treasury is referred to as the "stop yield," and bidders at that price are awarded a percentage of their total tender offer. The difference between the average yield of all the bids accepted by the Treasury and the stop is called the "tail."

The auction result for the 364-day Treasury bill offering on June 23, 1989 (the announcement shown in Figure 13-1), was as follows:

Total issue	=	$9.00 billion
Less non-competitive bids	=	0.64
Less Federal Reserve	=	2.80
Left for competitive bidders	=	$5.56 billion

Total competitive bids might have been received as follows:

AMOUNT (IN BILLIONS)	BID
$0.20	7.55% (lowest yield/highest price)
0.26	7.56
0.33	7.57
0.57	7.58 (average yield/average price)
0.79	7.59
0.96	7.60
1.25	7.61
1.52	7.62 (stop or largest yield/stop or lowest price)

The Treasury would allocate bills to competitive bidders from the low-yield bid to the high-yield bid until $5.56 billion is distributed. Those who bid 7.55% to 7.61% will be awarded the entire amount for which they bid. The total that would be awarded to these bidders is $4.36 billion, leaving $1.2 billion to be awarded, less than the $1.52 billion bid at 7.62%. Each of the bidders at 7.62% would be awarded 79% ($1.2/$1.52) of the amount they bid. For example, if a financial institution bid for $100 million at 7.62%, it would be awarded $79 million. The results of the auction would show 7.55% high,

IMPORTANT — This is a standard form. Its terms are subject to change at any time by the Treasury. This tender will be construed as a bid to purchase the securities for which the Treasury has outstanding an invitation for tenders. (See reverse side for further instructions.)

TENDER FOR 12-MONTH BOOK-ENTRY TREASURY BILLS
(For Use in Subscribing Through a Financial Institution)
Do Not Use This Form for Direct Subscriptions to the Treasury

TO FEDERAL RESERVE BANK OF NEW YORK   Dated at ....
   Fiscal Agent of the United States
   New York, N.Y. 10045   .... , 19......

Pursuant and subject to the provisions of Treasury Department Circulars No. 26-76 and No. 27-76, Public Debt Series, and to the provisions of the public notice issued by the Treasury Department inviting tenders for the current offering of 12-month Treasury bills, the undersigned hereby offers to purchase such currently offered Treasury bills in the amount indicated below, and agrees to make payment therefor at your Bank on or before the issue date in accordance with the provisions of the official offering circular.

COMPETITIVE TENDER	*Do not fill in both Competitive and Noncompetitive tenders on one form*	NONCOMPETITIVE TENDER

$............................ (maturity value) or any lesser amount that may be awarded.

Rate: .... (Bank Discount Basis)
(Rate must be expressed in two decimal places, for example, 7.15 percent. See reverse side of form for additional explanation.)

$............................ (maturity value)
(Not to exceed $1,000,000 for one bidder through all sources)
at the average of accepted competitive bids.
A noncompetitive bidder may not have entered into an agreement, or may not make an agreement with respect to the purchase or sale or other disposition of any noncompetitive awards of this issue in this auction prior to the designated closing time for receipt of tenders.

Certification by Competitive Bidders: The Bidder's ☐   Customer's ☐   net long position in these bills (including bills acquired through "when issued" trading, and futures and forward transactions, as well as holdings of outstanding bills with the same maturity date as the new offering) as of 12:30 p.m. Eastern time on the day of this auction, was —

☐ Not in excess of $200 million.
☐ In excess of $200 million, amounting to $ .... million.

Subject to allotment, please issue and accept payment for the bills as indicated below:

Safekeeping or Delivery Instructions *(No changes will be accepted)*	Payment Instructions

Book-Entry—
☐1. Hold in safekeeping at FRBNY (for member bank only) in-
  ☐ Investment Account (4)
  ☐ General Account (5)
  ☐ Trust Account (6)
☐2. Hold as collateral for Treasury Tax and Loan Note Account*(7)
☐3. Wire to ....(8)
(Exact Receiving Bank Wire Address/Account)
	Payment will be made as follows:
	☐ By charge to our reserve account
	☐ By check in *immediately available funds*
	☐ By surrender of eligible maturing securities
	☐ By charge to my correspondent bank
	
	....
	(Name of Correspondent)

*The undersigned certifies that the alloted securities will be owned solely by the undersigned.

Insert this tender in envelope marked "Tender for Treasury Securities"	Name of Subscriber (Please Print or Type)
	Address
	City State Zip Code
	Phone (Include Area Code) Signature of Subscriber or Authorized Signature
	Title of Authorized Signer

(Banking institutions submitting tenders for customer account must list customers' names on lines below or on an attached rider)

....
(Name of customer)   (Name of customer)

                                                                        (OVER)

FIGURE 13-3
Tender Form for a Treasury Bill Offering

INSTRUCTIONS:

1. No tender for less than $10,000 will be considered, and each tender must be for a multiple of $5,000 (maturity value).

2. Only banking institutions and dealers who make primary markets in Government securities and report daily to this Bank their positions with respect to Government securities and borrowings thereon, may submit tenders for customer account; in doing so, they may consolidate competitive tenders *at the same rate* (except that a separate tender must be submitted for each customer whose net long position in the bill being offered exceeds $200 million) and may consolidate noncompetitive tenders, provided a list is attached showing the name of each bidder and the amount bid for his account. Others will not be permitted to submit tenders except for their own account.

3. If the person making the tender is a corporation, the tender should be signed by an officer of the corporation authorized to make the tender, and the signing of the tender by an officer of the corporation will be construed as a representation that such officer has been so authorized. If the tender is made by a partnership, it should be signed by a member of the firm, who should sign in the form ".................................., a copartnership by ...., a member of the firm".

4. Tenders will be received without deposit from incorporated banks and trust companies and from responsible and recognized dealers in investment securities. Tenders from others must be accompanied by payment of 2 percent of the face amount of Treasury bills applied for, unless the tenders are accompanied by an express guaranty of payment by an incorporated bank or trust company. All checks must be drawn to the order of the Federal Reserve Bank of New York; and personal checks must be certified. Checks endorsed to this Bank will not be accepted.

5. The Bank Discount Basis is the difference between the dollar price of a Treasury bill and the maturity value for a given number of days based on a 360-day year. (The investment return or annualized bond-equivalent yield on a Treasury bill is at a higher rate than the bank discount basis.)

6. If the language of this tender is changed in any respect, which, in the opinion of the Secretary of the Treasury, is material, the tender may be disregarded.

FIGURE 13-3   *(cont.)*

7.58% average and 7.62% the stop yield, with 79% awarded at the stop. Bidders higher in yield than 7.62% "missed" or were "shut out." This auction would have a tail of 0.04 (7.62 minus 7.58).

COMMERCIAL PAPER

A corporation that needs long-term funds can raise those funds in either the equity market or the corporate bond market. A municipality or state government that needs long-term funds can obtain those funds by issuing bonds in the municipal bond market, as we explain in Chapter 16. If any of these entities needs short-term funds, they might attempt to acquire those funds by bank borrowing. For example, a manufacturing firm that needs $20 million to purchase inventory, with proceeds from the sale of that inventory expected in three months, may obtain a three-month bank loan. A state government that needs to meet a $50 million payroll to be covered in one month by tax proceeds may seek a one-month bank loan.

An alternative to bank borrowing for large corporations (non-financial and financial) and municipalities with strong credit ratings is commercial paper. Commercial paper is short-term unsecured promissory notes issued in the open market as an obligation of the issuing entity.

While the commercial paper market once was limited to entities with strong credit ratings, in recent years some lower-credit-rated corporations have issued commercial paper by obtaining credit enhancements or other collateral to allow them to enter the market as issuers.[1] Issuers of commercial paper are not restricted to U.S. corporations. Foreign corporations and sovereign entities also issue commercial paper.

While the original purpose of commercial paper was to provide short-term funds for seasonal and working capital needs, it has been issued for other purposes in recent years, frequently for "bridge financing." For example, suppose that a corporation needs long-term funds to build a plant or acquire equipment. Rather than raising long-term funds immediately, the issuer may elect to postpone the offering until more favorable capital market conditions prevail. The funds raised by issuing commercial paper are used until longer-term securities are sold. Commercial paper has been used as bridge financing to finance corporate takeovers.[2]

The maturity of commercial paper is typically less than 270 days; the most common maturity range is 30 to 50 days or less.[3] There are reasons for this. First, the Securities Act of 1933 requires that securities be registered with the SEC. Special provisions in the 1933 act exempt commercial paper from registration so long as the maturity does not exceed 270 days. To avoid the costs associated with registering issues with the SEC, issuers rarely issue commercial paper with maturities exceeding 270 days. To pay off holders of maturing paper, issuers generally issue new commercial paper. Another consideration in determining the maturity is whether the paper would be eligible collateral by a bank if it wanted to borrow from the Federal Reserve Bank's discount window. In order to be eligible, the maturity of the paper may not exceed 90 days. Since eligible paper trades at a lower cost than paper that is not eligible, issuers prefer to issue paper whose maturity does not exceed 90 days.

---

[1] Some lower-rated companies have issued commercial paper without credit enhancements or collateral. Such issues are popularly referred to as *high-yield commercial paper*. We discuss the market for debt instruments of lower-rated issuers in Chapter 15.

[2] Commercial paper also has been used as an integral part of an interest rate swap transaction. We discuss interest rate swaps in Chapter 20.

[3] *Money Market Instruments* (New York: Merrill Lynch Money Markets Inc., 1989), p. 16.

The risk that the investor faces is that the borrower will be unable to issue new paper at maturity. As a safeguard against this, commercial paper typically is backed by unused bank credit lines. As we explain in Chapter 15, the companies that rate the risk that an issuer will default on a debt obligation also rate commercial paper.

The commercial paper market has grown from $124 billion in December 1980 to $508 billion in October 1989. Since 1988, the size of the commercial paper market has exceeded that of the Treasury bill market.

Investors in commercial paper are institutional investors. Money market mutual funds purchase roughly one-third of all the commercial paper issued. Pension funds, commercial bank trust departments, state and local governments, and non-financial corporations seeking short-term investments purchase the balance. The minimum round-lot transaction is $100,000. Some issuers will sell commercial paper in denominations of $25,000.

Issuers of Commercial Paper

As of 1988, there were 1,350 entities issuing commercial paper.[4] Corporate issuers of commercial paper can be divided into financial companies and non-financial companies. Of the $508 billion of commercial paper outstanding as of October 1989, $387 billion was issued by financial companies.

There are three types of financial companies: captive finance companies, bank-related finance companies, and independent finance companies. Captive finance companies are subsidiaries of equipment manufacturing companies. Their primary purpose is to secure financing for the customers of the parent company. The three major U.S. automobile manufacturers, for example, have captive finance companies: General Motors Acceptance Corporation (GMAC), Ford Credit, and Chrysler Financial. GMAC is by far the largest issuer of commercial paper in the U.S. Bank holding companies may have a finance company subsidiary that provides loans to individuals and businesses to acquire a wide range of products. Independent finance companies are those that are not subsidiaries of equipment manufacturing firms or bank holding companies.

While the typical issuers of commercial paper are those with high credit ratings, smaller and less well-known companies with lower credit ratings have been able to issue paper in recent years. They have been able to do so by means of credit support from a firm with a high credit rating (such paper is called *credit-supported commercial paper*) or by collateralizing the issue with high-quality assets (such paper is called *asset-backed commercial paper*). An

---

[4] *Handbook of Securities of the United States Government and Agencies* (New York: First Boston Corporation, 1988), p. 140.

example of credit-supported commercial paper is an issue supported by a letter of credit. The terms of such a letter of credit specify that the bank issuing it guarantees that the bank will pay off the paper when it comes due, if the issuer fails to. Banks charge a fee for letters of credit. From the issuer's perspective, the fee enables it to enter the commercial paper market and obtain funding at a lower cost than bank borrowing. Paper issued with this credit enhancement is referred to as *LOC paper*. The credit enhancement may also take the form of a surety bond from an insurance company.[5]

Directly Placed versus Dealer-Placed Paper

Commercial paper is classified as either direct paper or dealer paper. Direct paper is sold by the issuing firm directly to investors without using a securities dealer as an intermediary. A large majority of the issuers of direct paper are financial companies. Because they require a continuous source of funds in order to provide loans to customers, they find it cost-effective to establish a sales force to sell their commercial paper directly to investors. Directly placed paper represents about $210 billion of the $389 billion issued by financial companies.

In the case of dealer-placed commercial paper, the issuer uses the services of a securities firm to sell its paper. Commercial paper sold in this way is referred to as "dealer paper." Roughly 60% of the commercial paper outstanding at the end of 1989 was dealer paper. Competitive pressures have forced dramatic reductions in the underwriting fees charged by dealer firms.[6]

Historically, the dealer market has been dominated by large investment banking firms because commercial banks were prohibited from underwriting commercial paper by the Glass–Steagall Act. In June 1987, however, the Fed granted subsidiaries of bank holding companies permission to underwrite commercial paper.[7] While investment banking firms still dominate the dealer market, commercial banks are making inroads.[8] This seems natural because for the most part the funds raised in the commercial paper market represent those previously raised via short-term bank loans. Banks obviously seek the

---

[5] A surety bond is a policy written by an insurance company to protect another party against loss or violation of a contract.

[6] The lower underwriting fees brought about by competitive pressure forced Salomon Brothers in October 1987 to eliminate its commercial paper operations.

[7] Bankers Trust first attempted to underwrite commercial paper in 1978.

[8] At the end of 1989, the four largest commercial paper dealers were Merrill Lynch, Goldman Sachs, Shearson Lehman Hutton, and First Boston. The three largest commercial banks that underwrite commercial paper are Bankers Trust, Citicorp, and Morgan Guaranty.

income associated with commercial paper underwriting in order to recoup part of the lost interest income from borrowers who use the commercial paper market to replace short-term bank loans.

The Secondary Market

Despite the fact that the commercial paper market is larger than markets for other money market instruments, secondary trading activity is much smaller. The typical investor in commercial paper is an entity that plans to hold it until maturity, given that an investor can purchase commercial paper with the specific maturity desired. Should an investor's economic circumstances change so that there is a need to sell the paper, it can be sold back to the dealer or, in the case of directly placed paper, the issuer will repurchase it.

Yields on Commercial Paper

Commercial paper, like T-bills, is a discount instrument. That is, it is sold at a price that is less than its maturity value. The difference between the maturity value and the price paid is the interest earned by the investor, although there is some commercial paper that is issued as an interest-bearing instrument. For commercial paper, a year is treated as having 360 days.

The yield offered on commercial paper tracks that of other money market instruments. The commercial paper rate is higher than that on Treasury bills for three reasons. First, the investor in commercial paper is exposed to credit risk. Second, interest earned from investing in Treasury bills is exempt from state and local income taxes. As a result, commercial paper has to offer a higher yield to offset this tax advantage. Finally, commercial paper is less liquid than Treasury bills. The liquidity premium demanded is probably small, however, because investors typically follow a buy-and-hold strategy with commercial paper and so are less concerned with liquidity. The rate on commercial paper is higher by a few basis points than the rate on certificates of deposit, which we discuss later in this chapter. The higher yield available on commercial paper is attributable to the poorer liquidity relative to certificates of deposit.

BANKERS ACCEPTANCES

Simply put, a bankers acceptance is a vehicle created to facilitate commercial trade transactions. The instrument is called a bankers acceptance because a bank accepts the ultimate responsibility to repay a loan to its holder. The use of bankers acceptances to finance a commercial transaction is referred to as "acceptance financing."

The transactions in which bankers acceptances are created include (1) the importing of goods into the U.S., (2) the exporting of goods from the U.S. to foreign entities, (3) the storing and shipping of goods between two foreign countries where neither the importer nor the exporter is a U.S. firm,[9] and (4) the storing and shipping of goods between two entities in the U.S.

As of October 1989, the dollar amount of bankers acceptances outstanding was $63 billion.[10] Of this amount, $16 billion was created in transactions involving the importing of goods into the U.S. and $14 billion in the exporting of goods from the U.S. The balance, $33 billion, mostly covers transactions involving the storing and shipping of goods between two foreign countries. Little use is made of acceptance financing by two parties within the U.S. Unlike the commercial paper market, the bankers acceptance market has been shrinking since 1984, when it reached a peak of $78 billion.

Bankers acceptances are sold on a discounted basis just as Treasury bills and commercial paper. The major investors in bankers acceptances are money market mutual funds and municipal entities.

Illustration of the Creation of a Bankers Acceptance

The best way to explain the creation of a bankers acceptance is by an illustration.

Several entities are involved in our transaction:

- Car Imports Corporation of America ("Car Imports"), a firm in New Jersey that sells automobiles
- West Germany Autos Inc. ("WGA"), a manufacturer of automobiles in Germany
- Hoboken Bank of New Jersey ("Hoboken Bank"), a commercial bank in Hoboken, New Jersey
- West Berlin National Bank ("Berlin Bank"), a bank in Germany
- High-Caliber Money Market Fund, a mutual fund in the U.S. that invests in money market instruments

Car Imports and WGA are considering a commercial transaction. Car Imports wants to import 15 cars manufactured by WGA. WGA is concerned with the ability of Car Imports to make payment on the 15 cars when they are received.

Acceptance financing is suggested as a means for facilitating the transaction. Car Imports offers $300,000 for the 15 cars. The terms of the sale

---

[9] Bankers acceptances created from these transactions are called *third country acceptances.*

[10] *Federal Reserve Bulletin,* February 1990.

stipulate payment to be made to WGA 60 days after it ships the 15 cars to Car Imports. WGA determines whether it is willing to accept the $300,000. In considering the offering price, WGA must calculate the present value of the $300,000, because it will not be receiving payment until 60 days after shipment. Suppose that WGA agrees to these terms.

Car Imports arranges with its bank, Hoboken Bank, to issue a letter of credit. The letter of credit indicates that Hoboken Bank will make good on the payment of $300,000 that Car Imports must make to WGA 60 days after shipment. The letter of credit, or time draft, will be sent by Hoboken Bank to WGA's bank, Berlin Bank. Upon receipt of the letter of credit, Berlin Bank will notify WGA, who will then ship the 15 cars. After the cars are shipped, WGA presents the shipping documents to Berlin Bank and receives the present value of $300,000. WGA is now out of the picture.

Berlin Bank presents the time draft and the shipping documents to Hoboken Bank. The latter will then stamp "accepted" on the time draft. By doing so, the Hoboken Bank has created a bankers acceptance. This means that Hoboken Bank agrees to pay the holder of the bankers acceptance $300,000 at the maturity date. Car Imports will receive the shipping documents so that it can procure the 15 cars once it signs a note or some other type of financing arrangement with Hoboken Bank.

At this point, the holder of the bankers acceptance is the Berlin Bank. It has two choices. It can continue to hold the bankers acceptance as an investment in its loan portfolio, or it can request that the Hoboken Bank make a payment of the present value of $300,000. Let's assume that Berlin Bank requests payment of the present value of $300,000.

Now the holder of the bankers acceptance is the Hoboken Bank. It has two choices: retain the bankers acceptance as an investment as part of its loan portfolio or sell it to an investor. Suppose that Hoboken Bank chooses the latter, and that High-Caliber Money Market Fund is seeking a high-quality investment with the same maturity as that of the bankers acceptance. The Hoboken Bank sells the bankers acceptance to the money market fund at the present value of $300,000. Rather than sell the instrument directly to an investor, Hoboken Bank could sell it to a dealer who would then resell it to an investor such as a money market fund. In either case, at the maturity date, the money market fund presents the bankers acceptance to Hoboken Bank, receiving $300,000, which the bank in turn recovers from Car Imports.

Accepting Banks

The banks that create bankers acceptances (that is, accepting banks) can be classified into four groups. First are the money center banks—banks that raise most of their funds from the domestic and international money markets and rely less on depositors for funds. The major money center banks that issue bankers acceptances are Bankers Trust, Bank of America, Chase

Manhattan, Citibank, and Morgan Guaranty. They maintain their own sales forces to sell bankers acceptances rather than using the services of a dealer.

The second group of accepting banks are some of the larger regional banks such as Harris Trust and Pittsburgh National Bank. A regional bank is one that relies primarily on deposits for its funding and makes less use of the money markets to obtain funds. The larger regional banks will maintain their own sales forces to sell the bankers acceptances they create but will use dealers to unload those they cannot sell.

Japanese banks are the third group of accepting banks. Japanese banks are classified as one of the following: city banks, local banks, long-term credit banks, trust banks, and mutual banks.[11] City banks are the most powerful depository institutions in Japan, with the 13 city banks holding approximately 20% of all deposits in Japan. Japanese city banks are now the major issuers of bankers acceptances. In April 1988, for example, there was approximately $32 billion of Japanese bankers acceptances outstanding, close to half of the total at that time.[12] Because they do not have the sales force to distribute the bankers acceptances they create directly to investors, Japanese accepting banks use the services of dealers.

The fourth group of accepting banks are Yankee banks. These are foreign banks with U.S. branches. Included in this group are non-Japanese branches of foreign banks.[13] The amount of bankers acceptances issued by Yankee banks is small. For example, First Boston Corporation estimates that in April 1988 the amount of foreign bankers acceptances outstanding (Japanese and Yankee) was $35 billion, and Japanese bankers acceptances outstanding represented $32 billion of that amount. Therefore, Yankee bankers acceptances outstanding totaled only $3 billion.

Credit Risk.   Investing in bankers acceptances exposes the investor to credit risk. This is the risk that neither the borrower nor the accepting bank will be able to pay the principal due at the maturity date.

Eligible Bankers Acceptance.   An accepting bank that has decided to retain a bankers acceptance in its portfolio may be able to use it as collateral for a loan at the discount window of the Federal Reserve. The reason we say "may" is that bankers acceptances must meet certain eligibility requirements established by the Federal Reserve. One requirement for eligibility is maturity, which with a few exceptions cannot exceed six months. While the other requirements for eligibility are too detailed to review here, the basic

---

[11] For a discussion of these different institutions, see Chapter 22.

[12] *Handbook of Securities of the United States Government and Agencies*, p. 130. The largest issuer of Japanese bankers acceptances is Dai-Ichi Kangyo Bank.

[13] Allgemaine, Crédit Lyonnais, and Deutsche Bank are examples.

principle is simple.[14] The bankers acceptance should be financing a self-liquidating commercial transaction.

Eligibility is also important because the Federal Reserve imposes a reserve requirement on funds raised via bankers acceptances that are ineligible. Bankers acceptances sold by an accepting bank are potential liabilities of the bank, but no reserve requirements are imposed for eligible bankers acceptances. Consequently, most bankers acceptances satisfy the various eligibility criteria. Finally, the Federal Reserve also imposes a limit on the amount of eligible bankers acceptances that may be issued by a bank.[15]

Rates Banks Charge on Bankers Acceptances.   To calculate the rate to be charged the customer for issuing a bankers acceptance, the bank determines the rate for which it can sell its bankers acceptance in the open market. To this rate it adds a commission. It is here that competition from Japanese banks has significantly affected the bankers acceptance business. Japanese banks have been willing to accept lower commissions than U.S. banks. For a high-credit-rated customer, for example, a commercial bank may charge 25 to 30 basis points, while a Japanese bank may charge 10 to 15 basis points.[16] In the case of ineligible bankers acceptances, a bank will add an amount to offset the cost of the reserve requirements imposed.

Dealers

We mentioned that banks may sell their bankers acceptances directly to investors, or may sell all or part to dealers. When the bankers acceptance market was growing in the early 1980s, there were over 25 dealers. By 1989, the decline in the amount of bankers acceptances issued drove many one-time major dealers such as Salomon Brothers out of the business. Today, the major dealer is Merrill Lynch. Lehman Brothers is another dealer in bankers acceptances. The other key dealers are commercial banks such as Bankers Trust and Morgan Guaranty.

LARGE-DENOMINATION NEGOTIABLE CDs

A certificate of deposit (CD) is a certificate issued by a bank or thrift that indicates a specified sum of money has been deposited at the issuing depository institution. CDs are issued by banks and thrifts to raise funds for financing their business activities. A CD bears a maturity date and a specified

---

[14] The eligibility requirements are described in Jean M. Hahr and William C. Melton, "Bankers' Acceptances," *Quarterly Review,* Federal Reserve Bank of New York, Summer 1981.

[15] It may not exceed 150% of a bank's capital and surplus.

[16] Marcia Stigum, *The Money Market* (Homewood, IL: Dow Jones-Irwin, 1990), p. 1007.

interest rate, and can be issued in any denomination. CDs issued by banks are insured by the Federal Deposit Insurance Corporation but only for amounts up to $100,000. As for maturity, there is no limit on the maximum, but by Federal Reserve regulations CDs cannot have a maturity of less than seven days.

A CD may be non-negotiable or negotiable. In the former case, the initial depositor must wait until the maturity date of the CD to obtain the funds. If the depositor chooses to withdraw funds prior to the maturity date, an early withdrawal penalty is imposed. In contrast, a negotiable CD allows the initial depositor (or any subsequent owner of the CD) to sell the CD in the open market prior to the maturity date.

Negotiable CDs were introduced in the early sixties. At that time the interest rate banks could pay on various types of deposits was subject to ceilings administered by the Federal Reserve (except for demand deposits defined as deposits of less than one month that by law could pay no interest). For complex historical reasons, these ceiling rates started very low, rose with maturity, and remained below market rates up to some fairly long maturity. Before introduction of the negotiable CD, those with money to invest for, say, one month had no incentive to deposit it with a bank for they would get a below-market rate, unless they were prepared to tie up their capital for a much longer period of time. When negotiable CDs came along, they could buy a three-month or longer negotiable CD yielding a market interest rate, and recoup all or more than the investment (depending on market conditions) by selling it in the market.

This innovation was critical in helping banks to increase the amount of funds raised in the money market, a position that had languished in the earlier postwar period. It also motivated competition among banks, ushering in a new era. There are now two types of negotiable CDs. The first is the large-denomination CD, usually issued in denominations of $1 million or more. These are the negotiable CDs whose history we described above.

In 1982, Merrill Lynch entered the retail CD business by opening up a primary and secondary market in small-denomination (less than $100,000) CDs. While it made the CDs of its numerous banking and savings institution clients available to retail customers, Merrill Lynch also began to give these customers the negotiability enjoyed by institutional investors by standing ready to buy back the CDs prior to maturity. Today, several retail-oriented brokerage firms offer CDs that are salable in a secondary market. These are the second type of negotiable CD. Our focus in this chapter, though, is on the large-denomination negotiable CD and we refer to them simply as CDs throughout the chapter.

The largest group of CD investors is investment companies, and money market funds make up the bulk of them. Far behind are banks and bank trust departments, followed by municipal entities and corporations.

CD Issuers

CDs can be classified into four types, based on the issuing bank. First are CDs issued by domestic banks. Second are CDs that are denominated in U.S. dollars but are issued outside of the U.S. These CDs are called *Eurodollar CDs* or *Euro CDs*. A third type of CD is the *Yankee CD*, which is a CD denominated in U.S. dollars and issued by a foreign bank with a branch in the U.S. Finally, *thrift CDs* are those issued by savings and loan associations and savings banks.

Money center banks and large regional banks are the primary issuers of domestic CDs. Most CDs are issued with a maturity of less than one year. Those issued with a maturity greater than one year are called *term CDs*.

Unlike Treasury bills, commercial paper, and bankers acceptances, yields on domestic CDs are quoted on an interest-bearing basis. CDs with a maturity of one year or less pay interest at maturity. For purposes of calculating interest, a year is treated as having 360 days. Term CDs issued in the U.S. normally pay interest semiannually, again with a year taken to have 360 days.

A floating-rate CD (FRCD) is one whose coupon interest rate changes periodically in accordance with a predetermined formula that indicates the spread (or margin) above some index at which the coupon will reset periodically. There are FRCDs that reset the coupon daily, weekly, monthly, quarterly, or semiannually. Typically FRCDs have maturities from 18 months to 5 years.

Euro CDs are U.S. dollar-denominated CDs issued primarily in London by U.S., Canadian, European, and Japanese banks. Branches of large U.S. banks once were the major issuers of Euro CDs. In 1982, of the $93 billion Euro CDs issued, $50 billion were issued by branches of U.S. banks.[17] Since 1982, however, the share of Euro CDs issued by branches of U.S. banks has declined, and Japanese banks have become the major issuers of Euro CDs.

Yields on CDs

The yields posted on CDs vary depending on three factors: (1) the credit rating of the issuing bank, (2) the maturity of the CD, and (3) the supply and demand for CDs. With respect to the third factor, banks and thrifts issue CDs as part of their liability management strategy, so the supply of CDs will be driven by the demand for bank loans and the cost of alternative sources of capital to fund these loans. Moreover, bank loan demand will depend on the

---

[17] As reported in *Quarterly Bulletin* published by the Bank of England.

cost of alternative funding sources such as commercial paper. When loan demand is weak, CD rates decline. When demand is strong, the rates rise. The effect of maturity depends on the shape of the yield curve.

Credit risk has become more of an issue. At one time domestic CDs issued by money center banks traded on a no-name basis. Recent financial crises in the banking industry, however, have caused investors to take a closer look at issuing banks. Prime CDs (those issued by high-rated domestic banks) trade at a lower yield than non-prime CDs (those issued by lower-rated domestic banks). Because of the unfamiliarity investors have with foreign banks, generally Yankee CDs trade at a higher yield than domestic CDs.

Euro CDs offer a higher yield than domestic CDs. There are three reasons for this. First, there are reserve requirements imposed by the Federal Reserve on CDs issued by U.S. banks in the U.S. that do not apply to issuers of Euro CDs. The reserve requirement effectively raises the cost of funds to the issuing bank because it cannot invest all the proceeds it receives from the issuance of a CD, and the amount that must be kept as reserves will not earn a return for the bank. Because it will earn less on funds raised by selling domestic CDs, the domestic issuing bank will pay less on its domestic CD than a Euro CD. Second, the bank issuing the CD must pay an insurance premium to the FDIC, which again raises the cost of funds. Finally, Euro CDs are dollar obligations that are payable by an entity operating under a foreign jurisdiction, exposing the holders to a risk (referred to as sovereign risk) that their claim may not be enforced by the foreign jurisdiction. As a result, a portion of the spread between the yield offered on Euro CDs and domestic CD reflects what can be termed a sovereign risk premium. This premium varies with the degree of confidence in the international banking system.

CD yields are higher than yields on Treasury securities of the same maturity. The spread is due mainly to the credit risk that a CD investor is exposed to and the fact that CDs offer less liquidity. The spread due to credit risk will vary with both economic conditions and confidence in the banking system, increasing when there is a flight to quality or when there is a crisis in the banking system.

At one time, there were more than 30 dealers who made markets in CDs. The presence of that many dealers provided good liquidity to the market. Today, fewer dealers are interested in making markets in CDs, and the market can be characterized as an illiquid one.

REPURCHASE AGREEMENTS

A repurchase agreement is the sale of a security with a commitment by the seller to buy the security back from the purchaser at a specified price at a designated future date. Basically, a repurchase agreement is a collateralized loan, where the collateral is a security. The agreement is best explained with an illustration.

Suppose a government securities dealer has purchased $10 million of a particular Treasury security. Where does the dealer obtain the funds to finance that position? Of course, the dealer can finance the position with its own funds or by borrowing from a bank. Typically, however, the dealer uses the repurchase agreement or "repo" market to obtain financing. In the repo market the dealer can use the $10 million of the Treasury security as collateral for a loan. The term of the loan and the interest rate that the dealer agrees to pay (called the "repo rate") are specified. When the term of the loan is one day, it is called an *overnight repo;* a loan for more than one day is called a *term repo.*

The transaction is referred to as a repurchase agreement because it calls for the sale of the security and its repurchase at a future date. Both the sale price and the purchase price are specified in the agreement. The difference between the purchase (repurchase) price and the sale price is the dollar interest cost of the loan.[18]

Back to the dealer who needs to finance $10 million of a Treasury security that it purchased and plans to hold overnight. Suppose that a customer of the dealer has excess funds of $10 million. (The customer might be a municipality with tax receipts that it has just collected, and no immediate need to disburse the funds.) The dealer would agree to deliver ("sell") $10 million of the Treasury security to the customer for an amount determined by the repo rate and buy ("repurchase") the same Treasury security from the customer for $10 million the next day. Suppose that the overnight repo rate is 6.5%. Then, as will be explained below, the dealer would agree to deliver the Treasury securities for $9,998,194 and repurchase the same securities for $10 million the next day. The $1,806 difference between the "sale" price of $9,998,194 and the repurchase price of $10 million is the dollar interest on the financing. From the customer's perspective, the agreement is called a *reverse* repo.

The formula following is used to calculate the dollar interest on a repo transaction:

$$\text{Dollar interest} = (\text{Dollar principal}) \times (\text{Repo rate}) \times \left(\frac{\text{Repo term}}{360}\right)$$

Notice that the interest is computed on a 360-day basis. In our example,

---

[18] For a more detailed description of the mechanics of repurchase agreements, see Oskar H. Rogg, "Repurchase Agreements," Chapter 8 in Frank J. Fabozzi (ed.), *The Handbook of Treasury and Agency Securities* (Chicago: Probus Publishing, 1990).

at a repo rate of 6.5% and a repo term of one day (overnight), the dollar interest is $1,806 as we show below:

$$= \$10,000,000 \times 0.065 \times \frac{1}{360}$$

$$= \$1,806$$

The advantage to the dealer of using the repo market for borrowing on a short-term basis is that the rate is less than the cost of bank financing. We'll explain why later in this section. From the customer's perspective, the repo market offers an attractive yield on a short-term secured transaction that is highly liquid.

While the example illustrates financing a dealer's long position in the repo market, dealers can also use the market to cover a short position. For example, suppose a government dealer sold $10 million of Treasury securities two weeks ago and must now cover the position—that is, deliver the securities. The dealer can do a reverse repo (agree to buy the securities and sell them back). Of course, the dealer eventually would have to buy the Treasury security in the market in order to cover its short position.

There is a good deal of Wall Street jargon describing repo transactions. To understand it, remember that one party is lending money and accepting security as collateral for the loan; the other party is borrowing money and giving collateral to borrow money. When someone lends securities in order to receive cash (i.e., borrow money), that party is said to be "reversing out" securities. A party that lends money with the security as collateral is said to be "reversing in" securities. The expressions "to repo securities" and "to do repo" are also used. The former means that someone is going to finance securities using the security as collateral; the latter means that the party is going to invest in a repo. Finally, the expressions "selling collateral" and "buying collateral" are used to describe a party financing a security with a repo on the one hand, and lending on the basis of collateral, on the other.

The collateral in a repo is not limited to government securities. Money market instruments, federal agency securities (the subject of the next chapter), and mortgage-backed securities (the subject of Chapter 18) are also used.

No official statistics are available on the size of the repo market. One informed source, however, estimates that the term repo market conservatively represents $100 to $150 billion.[19]

---

[19] Stigum, *The Money Market*, p. 575.

Credit Risks

Despite the fact that there may be high-quality collateral underlying a repo transaction, both parties to the transaction are exposed to credit risk. The failure of a few small government securities dealer firms involving repo transactions in the 1980s has made market participants more cautious about the creditworthiness of the counterparty to a repo.[20]

Why does credit risk occur in a repo transaction? Consider our initial example where the dealer used $10 million of government securities as collateral to borrow. If the dealer cannot repurchase the government securities, the customer may keep the collateral; if interest rates on government securities have increased subsequent to the repo transaction, however, the market value of the government securities will decline, and the customer will own securities with a market value less than the amount it loaned to the dealer. If the market value of the security rises instead, the dealer firm will be concerned with the return of the collateral, which then has a market value higher than the loan.

Repos are now more carefully structured to reduce credit risk exposure. The amount loaned is less than the market value of the security used as collateral, which provides the lender with some cushion should the market value of the security decline. The amount by which the market value of the security used as collateral exceeds the value of the loan is called "margin."[21] The amount of margin is generally between 1% and 3%. For borrowers of lower creditworthiness and/or when less liquid securities are used as collateral, the margin can be 10% or more.

Another practice to limit credit risk is to mark the collateral to market on a regular basis. Recall that the practice of marking to market, which we first discussed when we explained futures contracts in Chapter 6, means recording the value of a position at its market value. When market value changes by a certain percentage, the repo position is adjusted accordingly. Suppose that a dealer firm has borrowed $20 million using collateral with a market value of $20.4 million. The margin is 2%. Suppose further that the market value of the collateral drops to $20.1 million. A repo agreement can specify either (1) a margin call, or (2) repricing of the repo. In the case of a margin call, the dealer firm is required to put up additional collateral with a market value of $300,000 in order to bring the margin up to $400,000. If repricing is agreed upon, the principal amount of the repo will be changed

---

[20] Failed firms include Drysdale Government Securities, Lion Capital, RTD Securities, Inc., Belvill Bressler & Schulman, Inc., and ESM Government Securities, Inc.

[21] Margin is also referred to as the "haircut."

from $20 million to $19.7 million (the market value of $20.1 million divided by 1.02). The dealer would then send the customer $300,000.

One concern in structuring a repo is delivery of the collateral to the lender. The most obvious procedure is for the borrower to deliver the collateral to the lender. At the end of the repo term, the lender returns the collateral to the borrower in exchange for the principal and interest payment. This procedure may be too costly, though, particularly for short-term repos, because of the costs associated with delivering the collateral. The cost of delivery would be factored into the transaction by a lower repo rate offered by the borrower. The risk of the lender not taking possession of the collateral is that the borrower may sell the security or use the same security as collateral for a repo with another party.

As an alternative to delivering the collateral, the lender may agree to allow the borrower to hold the security in a segregated customer account. Of course, the lender still faces the risk that the borrower uses the collateral fraudulently by offering it as collateral for another repo transaction.

Another method is for the borrower to deliver the collateral to the lender's custodial account at the borrower's clearing bank. The custodian then has possession of the collateral that it holds on behalf of the lender. This practice reduces the cost of delivery because it is merely a transfer within the borrower's clearing bank. If, for example, a dealer enters into an overnight repo with Customer A, the next day the collateral is transferred back to the dealer. The dealer can then enter into a repo with Customer B for, say, five days without having to redeliver the collateral. The clearing bank simply establishes a custodian account for Customer B and holds the collateral in that account.

Participants in the Market

Because it is used by dealer firms (investment banking firms and money center banks acting as dealers) to finance positions and cover short positions, the repo market has evolved into one of the largest sectors of the money market. Financial and non-financial firms participate in the market as both sellers and buyers, depending on the circumstances they face. Thrifts and commercial banks are typically *net sellers* of collateral (i.e., net borrowers of funds); money market funds, bank trust departments, municipalities, and corporations are typically *net buyers* of collateral (i.e., providers of funds).

While a dealer firm uses the repo market as the primary means for financing its inventory and covering short positions, it will also use the repo market to run a matched book where it takes on repos and reverse repos with the same maturity. The firm will do so to capture the spread at which it enters into the repo and reverse repo agreement. For example, suppose that a dealer firm enters into a term repo of 10 days with a money market fund and a reverse repo rate with a thrift for 10 days in which the collateral is identical. This means that the dealer firm is borrowing funds from the money market fund and lending money to the thrift. If the rate on the repo is 7.5% and the rate on the reverse repo is 7.55%, the dealer firm is borrowing at 7.5% and lending at 7.55%, locking in a spread of 0.05% (five basis points).

Another participant is the repo broker. To understand the role of the repo broker, suppose that a dealer firm has shorted $50 million of a security. It will then survey its regular customers to determine if it can borrow via a reverse repo the security it shorted. Suppose that it cannot find a customer willing to do a repo transaction (repo from the customer's point of view, reverse repo from the dealer's). At that point, the dealer firm will use the services of a repo broker. When the collateral is difficult to acquire, it is said to be a "hot" or "special" issue.

The Fed and the Repo Market.   The Federal Reserve influences short-term interest rates through its open market operations—that is, by the outright purchase or sale of government securities. This is not the common practice followed by the Fed, however. It uses the repo market instead to implement monetary policy by purchasing or selling collateral. By buying collateral (i.e., lending funds), the Fed injects money into the financial markets, thereby exerting downward pressure on short-term interest rates. When the Fed buys collateral for its own account, this is called a *system repo*. The Fed also buys collateral on behalf of foreign central banks in repo transactions that are referred to as *customer repos*. It is primarily through system repos that the Fed attempts to influence short-term rates. By selling securities for its own account, the Fed drains money from the financial markets, thereby exerting upward pressure on short-term interest rates. This transaction is called a *matched sale.*

Note the language that is used to describe the transactions of the Fed in the repo market. When the Fed lends funds based on collateral, we call it a system or customer *repo*, not a reverse repo. Borrowing funds using collateral is called a *matched sale*, not a repo. The jargon is confusing, which is why we used the terms of "buying collateral" and "selling collateral" to describe what parties in the market are doing.

Determinants of the Repo Rate

There is no one repo rate; rates vary from transaction to transaction depending on several factors.

Quality.   The higher the credit quality and liquidity of the collateral, the lower the repo rate.

Term of the Repo.   The effect of the term of the repo on the rate depends on the shape of the yield curve.

Delivery Requirement.   As noted earlier, if delivery of the collateral to the lender is required, the repo rate will be lower. If the collateral can be deposited with the bank of the borrower, a higher repo rate is paid.

Availability of Collateral.   The more difficult it is to obtain the collateral, the lower the repo rate. To understand why this is so, remember that the borrower (or equivalently the seller of the collateral) has a security that is a hot or special issue. The party that needs the collateral will be willing to lend funds at a lower repo rate in order to obtain the collateral.

While the factors above determine the repo rate on a particular transaction, the federal funds rate discussed below determines the general level of repo rates. The repo rate will be a rate below the federal funds rate. The reason is that a repo involves collateralized borrowing, while a federal funds transaction is unsecured borrowing.

FEDERAL FUNDS

The last market we discuss in this chapter is the federal funds market. The rate determined in this market is the major factor that influences the rate paid on all the other money market instruments described in this chapter.

As we explained in Chapter 2, depository institutions (commercial banks and thrifts) are required to maintain reserves. The reserves are deposits at their district Federal Reserve Bank, which are called federal funds. The level of the reserves that a bank must maintain is based on its average daily deposits over the previous 14 days. Of all depository institutions, commercial banks are by far the largest holders of federal funds.

No interest is earned on federal funds. Consequently, a depository institution that maintains federal funds in excess of the amount required incurs an opportunity cost—the loss of interest income that could be earned on the excess reserves. At the same time, there are depository institutions whose federal funds are less than the amount required. Typically, smaller banks have excess reserves, while money center banks find themselves short of reserves and must make up the shortfall. Banks maintain federal funds desks whose managers are responsible for the bank's federal funds position.

One way that banks with less than the required reserves can bring reserves to the required level is to enter into a repo with a non-bank customer. An alternative is for the bank to borrow federal funds from a bank that has excess reserves. The market in which federal funds are bought (borrowed) by banks that need these funds and sold (lent) by banks that have excess federal funds is called the federal funds market. The equilibrium interest rate, which is determined by the supply and demand for federal funds, is the federal funds rate.

The federal funds rate and the repo rate are tied together because both are a means for a bank to borrow. The federal funds rate is higher because the lending of federal funds is done on an unsecured basis; this differs from the repo, in which the lender has a security as collateral. The spread between the two rates varies depending on market conditions; typically the spread is around 25 basis points.

While the term of most federal funds transactions is overnight, there are longer-term transactions that range from one week to six months. Trading typically takes place directly between the buyer and seller—usually between a large bank and one of its correspondent banks. Some federal funds transactions require the use of a broker.

SUMMARY

Money market instruments are debt obligations that at issuance have a maturity of one year or less. Treasury securities with a maturity of one year or less when they are issued are called Treasury bills. Interest is not paid periodically, but Treasury bills are issued at a discount from their face value. The interest the investor earns is the difference between the face value received at the maturity date and the price paid to purchase the Treasury bill. Bids and offers on Treasury bills are quoted on a bank discount basis. Treasury bills are auctioned on a regularly scheduled cycle.

Commercial paper is a short-term unsecured promissory note issued in the open market that represents the obligation of the issuing entity. It is sold on a discount basis. To avoid SEC registration, the maturity of commercial paper is less than 270 days. Generally, commercial paper maturity is less than 90 days so that it will qualify as eligible collateral for the bank to borrow from the Federal Reserve Bank's discount window. Financial and non-financial corporations issue commercial paper, with the majority issued by the former. Until recent years, the commercial paper market was limited to entities with strong credit ratings, but lately lower-rated issuers have used credit enhancements to enter the market. Direct paper is sold by the issuing firm directly to investors without using a securities dealer as an intermediary; with dealer-placed commercial paper, the issuer uses the services of a securities firm to sell its paper. There is little liquidity in the commercial paper market.

A bankers acceptance is a vehicle created to facilitate commercial trade transactions, particularly international transactions. They are called bankers acceptances because a bank accepts the responsibility to repay a loan to the holder of the vehicle created in a commercial transaction in case the debtor fails to perform. Bankers acceptances are sold on a discounted basis as are Treasury bills and commercial paper. The four types of accepting banks are money center banks, larger regional banks, Japanese banks, and Yankee banks. Japanese banks are the major issuers of bankers acceptances.

Certificates of deposit are issued by banks and thrifts to raise funds for financing their business activities. Unlike other bank deposits, these are negotiable in the secondary market. CDs can be classified into four types: domestic CDs, Eurodollar CDs (or Euro CDs), Yankee CDs, and thrift CDs. Japanese banks have now become major issuers of Euro CDs. Unlike Treasury bills, commercial paper, and bankers acceptances, yields on domestic CDs are quoted on an interest-bearing basis. A floating-rate CD is one whose coupon interest rate changes periodically in accordance with a predetermined formula.

A repurchase agreement is a lending transaction in which the borrower uses a security as collateral for the borrowing. The transaction is referred to as a repurchase agreement because it specifies the sale of a security and its subsequent repurchase at a future date. The difference between the purchase (repurchase) price and the sale price is the dollar interest cost of the loan. An overnight repo is for one day; a loan for more than one day is called a term repo. The collateral in a repo may be a Treasury security, money market instrument, federal agency security, or mortgage-backed security. The parties to a repo are exposed to credit risk, limited by margin and mark-to-market practices included in a repo agreement. Dealers use the repo market to finance positions and cover short positions, and to run a matched book so that they can earn spread income. The Fed uses the repo market to implement monetary policy. Factors that determine the repo rate are the federal funds rate, the quality of the collateral, the term of the repo, the delivery requirement, and the availability of the collateral.

The federal funds market is the market where depository institutions borrow (buy) and sell (lend) federal funds. The federal funds rate, which is the rate at which all money market interest rates are anchored, is determined in this market. The federal funds rate is higher than the repo rate because borrowing done in the federal funds market is unsecured borrowing.

QUESTIONS

1. Suppose that the price of a Treasury bill with 90 days to maturity and a $1 million face value is $980,000.

   a. What is the yield on a bank discount basis?

   b. Why is the yield on a bank discount basis not a meaningful measure of the return from holding a Treasury bill?

2. The bid and ask yields for a Treasury bill maturing on January 16, 1992 were quoted by a dealer as 5.91% and 5.89%, respectively. Shouldn't the bid yield be less than the ask yield, because the bid yield indicates how much the dealer is willing to pay, and the ask yield is what the dealer is willing to sell the Treasury bill for?

3. In a Treasury auction, as the dollar amount of non-competitive bids submitted increases, what happens to the average yield bid?

4. a. Why is commercial paper an alternative to short-term bank borrowing for a corporation?

   b. What is the difference between directly placed paper and dealer-placed paper?

   c. What does the yield spread between commercial paper and Treasury bills of the same maturity reflect?

5. a. The banks that create bankers acceptances can be classified into four groups. Name them.

   b. Why is the "eligibility" of a bankers acceptance important?

   c. How does a bank determine the rate it will charge its customer for issuing a bankers acceptance?

6. What are the four types of negotiable CDs?

7. a. How can a repurchase agreement be used by a dealer firm to finance a long position in a Treasury security?

   b. One party in a repo transaction is said to "buy collateral," the other party to "sell collateral." Why?

   c. Why would the lender of funds in a repo transaction be exposed to credit risk?

   d. When there is a shortage of a specific security for a repo transaction, will the repo rate increase or decrease?

8. **a.** What is a system repo?

    b. What is a customer repo?

9. **a.** What is the federal funds market?

    b. Which rate should be higher: the overnight repo rate, or the overnight federal funds rate?

LEARNING OBJECTIVES

After reading this chapter you will understand:

- the importance of the Treasury market.

- the different types of the securities issued by the Treasury.

- how Treasury securities are quoted in the secondary market.

- the zero-coupon Treasury securities market.

- arbitrage profit potential from stripping Treasury securities.

- the difference between federally sponsored agency securities and federally related institutions.

- what affects the yield spread between federally sponsored agency securities and Treasury securities.

- functions of the federally sponsored agencies that issue securities.

I n this chapter and the four to follow we discuss the long-term debt market. The size of this market and its composition as of December 31, 1989, are summarized in Table 14-1. Of the $8.6 trillion long-term debt market, the largest component by far is the mortgage market, which we discuss in Chapter 17. The mortgage-backed securities sector (securities where the underlying collateral is a pool of residential or commercial real estate mortgages), the subject of Chapter 18, is the fastest growing sector of the long-term debt market. The second largest sector is the market for U.S. Treasury securities, while the smallest sector shown in Table 14-1 is the U.S. government agency securities market.[1]

The corporate bond sector includes bonds issued by U.S. corporations and non-U.S. entities that issue bonds in the U.S. The former market is discussed in Chapter 15; the latter market, called the Yankee bond market, is the subject of Chapter 22. The municipal sector is the "tax-exempt" sector where state and local governments raise funds.

TREASURY SECURITIES

U.S. Treasury securities are backed by the full faith and credit of the United States government. Consequently, market participants view them as having no *credit* risk. Interest rates on Treasury securities are the benchmark interest rates throughout the U.S. economy as well as in international capital markets. Market participants talk of interest rates on non-Treasury securities as trading above (or below) a particular Treasury security.

Two factors account for the prominent role of U.S. Treasury securities: volume (in terms of dollars outstanding) and liquidity. The Department of the Treasury is the largest single issuer of debt in the world, with Treasury securities accounting for $1.9 trillion (represented by over 180 different Treasury note and bond issues and 30 Treasury bill issues). The entire U.S. corporate bond market accounts by contrast for about $1.4 trillion and over 10,000 issues; the U.S. municipal bond market similarly accounts for about $802 billion, with more than 70,000 separate issuers and millions of individual issues.

The large volume of total debt and the large size of any single issue have contributed to making the Treasury market the most active and hence the

---

[1] As we explain in Chapter 18, a majority of the securities backed by a pool of mortgages are guaranteed by a federally sponsored agency of the U.S. government. These securities are classified as part of the mortgage-backed securities market rather than as U.S. government agency securities.

TABLE 14-1	COMPOSITION OF THE U.S. BOND MARKET AS OF DECEMBER 31, 1990 (DOLLARS IN BILLIONS; BASED ON PAR VALUE)		
U.S. Treasury Securities		$2,210	(25.4%)
U.S. Agencies Securities (excluding agency pass-through securities)		309	(3.6%)
Corporate Bonds		1,506	(17.3%)
Domestic	1,387		
Yankee	119		
Municipal Securities		852	(9.8%)
Mortgages—Nonsecuritized (1-4 multifamily, farm commercial)		2,783	(32.0%)
Mortgage-backed Securities		1,029	(11.9%)
Total U.S. Bond Market*		$8,599	

*Excludes asset-backed securities.

Source: This table is prepared from data supplied by Salomon Brothers Inc.

most liquid market in the world. The spread between bid and ask prices is considerably narrower than in other sectors of the bond market, and most issues can be purchased easily. Many issues in the corporate and municipal markets are illiquid by contrast, and cannot be traded readily.

There are two categories of government securities—discount and coupon securities. The fundamental difference between the two types lies in the form of the stream of payments that the holder receives, which is reflected in turn in the prices at which the securities are issued. Coupon securities pay interest every six months, plus principal at maturity. Discount securities pay only a contractually fixed amount at maturity, called *maturity value* or *face value*. Discount instruments are issued below maturity value, and return to the investor the difference between issue and maturity price.

Current Treasury practice is to issue all securities with maturities of one year or less as discount securities. These securities are called Treasury *bills;* we discussed them in Chapter 13 in our treatment of money market instruments. All securities with maturities of two years or longer are issued as coupon securities. Treasury coupon securities issued with original maturities between 2 and 10 years are called *notes;* those with original maturities greater than 10 years are called *bonds*. While there is therefore a distinction between Treasury notes and bonds, in this chapter we refer to both as simply bonds.

When the issuer of a bond has the right but not the obligation (i.e., an option) to retire the issue prior to the maturity date, the issue is said to be "callable." The issuer will benefit from exercising this option if interest rates decline below the coupon rate of the issue. Indeed, in this case the issuer can retire the bond issue and replace it with another issue at a lower coupon rate. The privilege of the issuer to call the issue is a disadvantage to the bondholders for they can reinvest what they receive only at a lower interest rate (see Chapter 11). Although Treasury notes are not callable, many outstanding Treasury bond issues are callable within five years of maturity. Treasury bonds issued since February 1985 are not callable.

Treasury securities are available in book-entry form at the Federal Reserve Bank. This means that the investor receives only a receipt as evidence of ownership instead of an engraved certificate. An advantage of book-entry is ease in transferring ownership of the security. Treasury bills come only in book-entry form, and Treasury coupon securities issued after January 1, 1983, are required to be in book-entry form.

Interest income from Treasury securities is subject to federal income taxes but is exempt from state and local income taxes.

The Primary Market

Treasury securities typically are issued on an auction basis with regular cycles for securities of specific maturities. As we explained in the previous chapter, three-month and six-month Treasury bills are auctioned every Monday, and one-year Treasury bills are auctioned on the third week of every month.

The Treasury regularly issues coupon securities with maturities of 2, 3, 5, 7, 10, and 30 years.[2] Table 14-2 summarizes the months that Treasury coupon securities are issued. Two- and 5-year notes are auctioned each month. At the beginning of the second month of each calendar quarter (February, May, August, and November), the Treasury conducts its regular refunding operations. At this time, it auctions 3-year, 10-year, and 30-year Treasury securities. The Treasury announces on the Wednesday of the month preceding: (1) the amount that will be auctioned, (2) what portion of that amount is to replace maturing Treasury debt, (3) what portion of that amount is to raise new funds, and (4) the estimated cash needs for the balance of the quarter and how it plans to obtain the funds. During the second half of each calendar quarter, the Treasury conducts its "mini-refunding" and issues 7-year Treasury notes.

---

[2] Prior to April 1986, the Treasury issued 20-year bonds. The most recent change in the Treasury auction cycle occurred during December 1990, when the Treasury discontinued the quarterly auction of the 4-year Treasury note and began a monthly auction of the 5-year Treasury note, which had previously been auctioned quarterly.

| | TABLE 14-2   TREASURY COUPON SECURITIES AUCTIONED BY MONTH |

	NUMBER OF YEARS TO MATURITY					
MONTH	2	3	5	7	10	30
January	x		x			
February	x	x	x		x	x
March	x		x	x		
April	x		x			
May	x	x	x		x	x
June	x		x	x		
July	x		x			
August	x	x	x		x	x
September	x		x	x		
October	x		x			
November	x	x	x		x	x
December	x		x	x		

x = auctioned in month indicated.

The auction for Treasury coupon securities, like that for Treasury bills, is conducted on a yield basis.[3] Competitive and non-competitive bids may be submitted. Figure 14-1 shows the announcement of an auction for Treasury notes.

Any firm can deal in government securities, but in implementing its open market operations, the Federal Reserve will deal directly only with dealers that it designates as *primary* or *recognized* dealers. Basically, the Federal Reserve wants to be sure that firms requesting status as primary dealers have adequate capital relative to positions assumed in Treasury securities and do a reasonable amount of volume in Treasury securities (at least 1% of Treasury market activity).

When a firm requests status as a primary dealer, the Federal Reserve requests first that the applying firm informally report its positions and trading

---

[3] Prior to 1974, the Treasury set the coupon before the auction, and auctions were on a price basis. But this type of auction permitted prices significantly greater or less than par. Since 1974, however, auctions have been on a yield basis and coupons set after the auction.

volume. If these are acceptable to the Federal Reserve, it gives the firm status as a *reporting dealer*. This means that the firm will be put on the Federal Reserve's regular reporting list. After the firm serves for some time as a reporting dealer, the Federal Reserve will make it a primary dealer if it is convinced that the firm will continue to meet the criteria established.

The auction process relies on the participation of the primary government securities dealers. Primary dealers are expected to participate in every auction and typically bid for about 3% of every issue that is auctioned. They subsequently redistribute the issue, whether at a profit or a loss, to both non-primary dealers and institutional investors. Primary dealers are also expected to maintain a certain level of trading activity in the secondary market.

Table 14-3 lists the primary government dealers as of January 1991.

FIGURE 14-1
Announcement of a Treasury Note Offering

```
FOR RELEASE AT 4:00 P.M.           CONTACT:   Office of Financing
April 5, 1989                                 202/376-4350


     TREASURY TO AUCTION $7,000 MILLION OF 7-YEAR NOTES

     The Department of the Treasury will auction $7,000 million
of 7-year notes to refund $3,238 million of 7-year notes maturing
April 15, 1989, and to raise about $3,750 million new cash.  The
public holds $3,238 million of the maturing 7-year notes, including
$650 million currently held by Federal Reserve Banks as agents for
foreign and international monetary authorities.

     The $7,000 million is being offered to the public, and any
amounts tendered by Federal Reserve Banks as agents for foreign
and international monetary authorities will be added to that
amount.  Tenders for such accounts will be accepted at the
average price of accepted competitive tenders.

     In addition to the public holdings, Federal Reserve Banks for
their own accounts hold $110 million of the maturing securities
that may be refunded by issuing additional amounts of the new
notes at the average price of accepted competitive tenders.

     Details about the new security are given in the attached
highlights of the offering and in the official offering circular.

                              oOo


Attachment
```

```
                   HIGHLIGHTS OF TREASURY
                   OFFERING TO THE PUBLIC
                      OF 7-YEAR NOTES
                TO BE ISSUED APRIL 17, 1989


                                              April 5, 1989

Amount Offered:
To the public .................. $7,000 million

Description of Security:
Term and type of security ....... 7-year notes
Series and CUSIP designation .... F-1996
                                  (CUSIP No. 912827 XK 3)
Maturity date ................... April 15, 1996'
Interest rate ................... To be determined based on
                                  the average of accepted bids
Investment yield ................ To be determined at auction
Premium or discount ............. To be determined after auction
Interest payment dates .......... October 15 and April 15
Minimum denomination available .. $1,000

Terms of Sale:
Method of sale .................. Yield auction
Competitive tenders ............. Must be expressed as an
                                  annual yield, with two
                                  decimals, e.g., 7.10%
Noncompetitive tenders .......... Accepted in full at the aver-
                                  age price up to $1,000,000
Accrued interest
payable by investor ............. None

Payment Terms:
Payment by non-
institutional investors ......... Full payment to be
                                  submitted with tender
Payment through Treasury Tax
and Loan (TT&L) Note Accounts ... Acceptable for TT&L Note
                                  Option Depositaries
Deposit guarantee by
designated institutions ......... Acceptable

Key Dates:
Receipt of tenders .............. Wednesday, April 12, 1989,
                                  prior to 1:00 p.m., EDST
Settlement (final payment
due from institutions):
  a) funds immediately
     available to the Treasury .. Monday, April 17, 1989
  b) readily-collectible check .. Thursday, April 13, 1989
```

FIGURE 14-1   *(cont.)*

TABLE 14-3   PRIMARY GOVERNMENT SECURITIES DEALERS

Bank of America NT & SA	Greenwich Capital Markets, Inc.
Barclays de Zoete Wedd Securities Inc.	Harris Government Securities Inc.
Bear, Stearns & Co., Inc.	Kidder, Peabody & Co., Incorporated
BT Securities Corporation	Aubrey G. Lanston & Co., Inc.
Carroll McEntee & McGinley Incorporated	Lehman Government Securities, Inc.
Chase Securities, Inc.	Manufacturers Hanover Securities
Chemical Securities, Inc.	Corporation
Citicorp Securities Markets, Inc.	Merrill Lynch Government Securities Inc.
Continental Bank, National Association	J.P. Morgan Securities, Inc.
CRT Government Securities, Ltd.	Morgan Stanley & Co. Incorporated
Daiwa Securities America Inc.	The Nikko Securities Co. International, Inc.
Dean Witter Reynolds Inc.	Nomura Securities International, Inc.
Deutsche Bank Government Securities, Inc.	Paine Webber Incorporated
Dillon, Read & Co. Inc.	Prudential-Bache Securities, Inc.
Discount Corporation of New York	Salomon Brothers Inc.
Donaldson, Lufkin & Jenrette Securities	Sanwa-BGK Securities Co., L.P.
Corporation	Smith Barney, Harris Upham & Co., Inc.
The First Boston Corporation	SBC Government Securities Inc.
First Chicago Capital Markets, Inc.	UBS Securities Inc.
Fuji Securities Inc.	S.G. Warburg & Co., Inc.
Goldman, Sachs & Co.	Yamaichi International (America), Inc.

Source: Market Reports Division, Federal Reserve Bank of New York, January 17, 1991.

The Secondary Market

The secondary market for Treasury securities is an over-the-counter market where a group of U.S. government securities dealers provide continuous bids and offers on specific outstanding Treasuries.[4] The secondary market is the most liquid financial market in the world.

---

[4] Some trading of Treasury coupon securities does occur on the New York Stock Exchange, but the volume of these exchange-traded transactions is very small when compared to over-the-counter transactions.

In the secondary market, the most recently auctioned Treasury issues for each maturity are referred to as "on the run" or "current coupon" issues. Issues auctioned prior to the current coupon issues typically are referred to as "off the run" issues; they are not as liquid as on the run issues. That is, the bid–ask spread is larger for off the run issues relative to on the run issues.

Dealer profits are generated from one or more of three sources: (1) the bid–ask spread, (2) appreciation in the securities held in inventory or depreciation in the securities sold short, and (3) the difference between the interest earned on the securities held in inventory and the cost of financing that inventory. The last source of profits is referred to as *carry* and depends on the shape of the yield curve. Dealers obtain funds to finance inventory position using the repo market, which we described in Chapter 13.

Another component of the Treasury secondary market is the "when-issued market," or "wi market," where Treasury securities are traded prior to the time they are issued by the Treasury. When-issued trading for both Treasury bills and Treasury coupon issues extends from the day the auction is announced until the issue day. All deliveries on when-issued trades occur on the issue day of the Treasury security traded.

Government Brokers.   Treasury dealers trade with the investing public and with other dealer firms. When they trade with each other, it is through intermediaries known as government brokers. Dealers leave firm bids and offers with brokers who display the highest bid and lowest offer in a computer network tied to each trading desk and displayed on a monitor. The dealer responding to a bid or offer by "hitting" or "taking" pays a commission to the broker. The size and prices of these transactions are visible to all dealers at once.

Treasury dealers use brokers because of the speed and efficiency with which trades can be accomplished. Brokers never trade for their own account, and they keep the names of the dealers involved in trades confidential. Five major brokers handle about 50% of the daily trading volume. They include Fundamental Brokers, Inc.; RMJ Securities Corp.; Garban Ltd.; Cantor, Fitzgerald Securities Corp.; and Chapdelaine & Company Government Securities, Inc. These five firms service the primary government dealers and a dozen or so other large government dealers aspiring to be primary dealers.

The quotes provided on the government dealer screens represent prices in the "inside" or "interdealer" market, and the primary dealers have resisted attempts to allow the general public to have access to them. Only one government broker, Cantor, Fitzgerald Securities Corp., disseminates prices to non-primary dealers. In 1989, when RMJ Securities offered to disseminate quotes to some large institutional investors, pressure from the primary dealers persuaded the broker to withdraw its offer.

Bid and Offer Quotes on Treasury Securities.   As we explained in Chapter 13, Treasury bill bids and offers are computed in a special way, on a bank discount basis (in basis points) not on a price basis. Treasury coupon securities are quoted differently. They trade on a dollar price basis in price units of 1/32 of 1% of par (par is taken to be $100). For example, a quote of 92-14 refers to a price of 92 and 14/32. On the basis of $100,000 par value, a change in price of 1% equates to $1,000, and 1/32 equates to $31.25. A *plus* sign following the number of 32nds means that a 64th is added to the price. For example, 92-14+ refers to a price of 92 and 29/64 or 92.453125% of par value.

On quote sheets and screens, the price quote is followed by some "yield to maturity" measure. Yield quotes can be based on the Street or the Treasury method. The difference between the two yield measures is the procedure used to discount the first coupon payment when it is not exactly six months away.[5] This occurs for two reasons. First, for certain securities, the first coupon payment may be more or less than six months away. This situation is referred to as an "odd" or "irregular" first coupon payment. When the first coupon payment is more than six months away, it is said to have a long first coupon.[6] When the first coupon payment is less than six months from the

---

[5] The difference between the Street and Treasury practices for computing yield is the procedure for discounting over a long first coupon period and over a fractional six-month period. The Treasury method (also called the "Fed" method) assumes simple interest over the period from the valuation date to the next coupon payment. The Street method (also called the Securities Industry Association or "SIA" method) assumes compound interest over the period from the valuation date to the next coupon payment. For example, suppose that the next coupon payment is X days from the valuation date (or previous coupon date), and W is the number of days between the issuance date (or previous coupon date) and the first coupon date (or next coupon date). Letting K denote the ratio of X to W, the discounting of a coupon payment, $C/2$, for both methods for a semiannual yield to maturity, y, is

simple interest over period (Treasury method)

$$\frac{C/2}{(1 + Ky)}$$

compound interest over period (Street method):

$$\frac{C/2}{(1 + y)^K}$$

[6] The five-year Treasury note issued prior to January 1991 was an example of a Treasury security usually issued as a long first coupon security. The first coupon payment for the five-year Treasury note was approximately eight months after the issuance date.

date of issuance, the Treasury security is said to have a short first coupon.[7] The second circumstance when the first coupon payment may come in less than six months is when a security is purchased between coupon dates. From a practical point of view, once a security is issued and traded in the secondary market, investors and traders use the Street method.

Accrued Interest and Invoice Price. When an investor purchases a bond between coupon payments, if the issuer is not in default, the investor must compensate the seller of the bond for the coupon interest earned from the time of the last coupon payment to the settlement date of the bond. This amount is called *accrued interest,* computed as follows:

$$\frac{C}{2} \times \frac{\text{Number of days from last coupon payment to settlement date}}{\text{Number of days in coupon period}}$$

Market conventions determine the number of days in a coupon period and the number of days from the last coupon payment to the settlement date. For a Treasury coupon security, both are equal to the actual number of days. (This is referred to as "actual over actual" basis.)[8] The accrued interest for a Treasury coupon security is therefore determined as follows:

$$\frac{C}{2} \times \frac{\text{Actual number of days from last coupon payment to settlement date}}{\text{Actual number of days in coupon period}}$$

The *invoice price* is the total proceeds that the buyer of the bond pays the seller. The invoice price is equal to the price agreed upon by the buyer and the seller plus accrued interest.

Completed Transactions and Public Quotation System. In Chapter 8 we discussed movement in the stock market toward a consolidated tape for reporting trades on exchanges and the over-the-counter market and a

---

[7] The Treasury issues a security with a short first coupon when the auction date is the fifteenth or the end of the month, but that day falls on a weekend or holiday. In such cases, the Treasury issues the security on the next business day, but pays the first coupon on the fifteenth or at the end of the month six months later. Thus, the first coupon payment is less than six months away.

[8] For corporate and municipal bonds, the day count convention is "30/360" which means a year is treated as having 360 days and a month as having 30 days. Therefore, the number of days in a coupon period is 180.

composite quotation system for the collection and display of bid and ask quotations. In the Treasury market, however, despite the fact that trading activity is concentrated in the over-the-counter market, and that daily trading volume exceeds $100 billion, reporting of trades does not exist. Nor is there a display of bid and ask quotations that provides *reliable* price quotes at which the *general public* can transact. Such quotations do exist, as we explained earlier, in the interdealer market on government broker screens.

An example will show how the price of a specific government security can vary among dealers at a given time. Portfolio managers of a large institutional investor telephoned five major government dealers to obtain a price quote for the 10.75% coupon Treasury maturing on August 15, 2005.[9] The five quotes were:

DEALER	BID PRICE	ASK PRICE
A	128-2	128-6
B	128-3	128-5
C	128-4	128-8
D	128-5	128-9
E	128-6	128-8

Recall that the number after the hyphen indicates the number of 32nds of 1%. Consequently, the difference between the highest and lowest price that this Treasury issue could be sold for is 4/32, or 1/8 of 1% (the difference between the bid prices of dealer A and dealer E). The difference between the lowest and highest ask price if this issue were to be purchased is also 4/32 (dealer D's ask price minus dealer B's ask price). In dollar terms, for a transaction involving $10 million, the difference between the best and the worst transaction price would be $12,500, a significant price difference in what is the most active and liquid bond market in the world. Also notice how the bid–ask spread differs from dealer to dealer, from 2/32 for two of the dealers to 4/32 for the other three.

This example highlights shortcomings of not only the U.S. Treasury market, but all the bond markets that we discuss: lack of both a reporting system for completed transactions and a quotation system. Two passages

---

[9] Sharmin Mossavar-Rahmani, "Understanding and Evaluating Index Fund Management," in Frank J. Fabozzi and T. Dessa Garlicki (eds.), *Advances in Bond Analysis and Portfolio Strategies* (Chicago: Probus Publishing, 1987), p. 438.

from a recent General Accounting Office study of the securities market seem to indicate that the bond market will come under increasing Congressional scrutiny:

> The bond market is increasingly important to both corporate and government financing, but the operation of these markets is not well known to policy makers. *A policy-oriented assessment of the changes underway in bond markets may be far overdue.*

And,

> A near monopoly on provision of bond market quotations by one vendor has persisted for years, largely because of the absence of regulation in this field. Since the size and importance of this market is increasing, there may be important but hidden policy questions here that should be explored. *No substantial policy studies of bond markets have been conducted for use by Congress, and one may be much needed.*[10]

Stripped Treasury Securities

Product Development.   The Treasury does not issue zero-coupon notes or bonds. In August 1982, however, both Merrill Lynch and Salomon Brothers created synthetic zero-coupon Treasury receipts. Merrill Lynch marketed its Treasury receipts as "Treasury Income Growth Receipts" (TIGRs), Salomon Brothers marketed its as "Certificates of Accrual on Treasury Securities" (CATS). The procedure was to purchase Treasury bonds and deposit them in a bank custody account. The firms then issued receipts representing an ownership interest in each coupon payment on the underlying Treasury bond in the account and a receipt on the underlying Treasury bond's maturity value. This process of separating each coupon payment, as well as the principal (called the *corpus*), to sell securities against them is referred to as "coupon stripping." Although the receipts created from the coupon stripping process are not issued by the U.S. Treasury, the underlying bond deposited in the bank custody account is a debt obligation of the U.S. Treasury, so the cash flow from the underlying security is certain.

To illustrate the process, suppose $100 million of a Treasury bond with a 20-year maturity and a coupon rate of 10% is purchased to create zero-coupon Treasury securities. The cash flow from this Treasury bond is 40 semiannual

---

[10] GAO, *Securities Markets in the Electronics Age*, Chapter 1, in manuscript, pp. 8 and 32.

payments of $5 million each ($100 million times 0.10 divided by 2) *and* the repayment of principal (corpus) of $100 million 20 years from now. This Treasury bond is deposited in a bank custody account. Receipts are then issued, each with a different single payment claim on the bank custody account. As there are 41 different payments to be made by the Treasury, a receipt representing a single payment claim on each payment is issued, which is effectively a zero-coupon bond. The amount of the maturity value for a receipt on a particular payment, whether coupon or corpus, depends on the amount of the payment to be made by the Treasury on the underlying Treasury bond. In our example, 40 coupon receipts each have a maturity value of $5 million, and one receipt, the corpus, has a maturity value of $100 million. The maturity dates for the receipts coincide with the corresponding payment dates by the Treasury.

Other investment banking firms followed suit by creating their own receipts.[11] They all are referred to as *trademark* zero-coupon Treasury securities because they are associated with a particular firm.[12] Receipts of one firm were rarely traded by competing dealers, so the secondary market was not liquid for any one trademark. Moreover, the investor was exposed to the risk—as small as it may be—that the custodian bank may go bankrupt.

To broaden the market and improve liquidity of these receipts, a group of primary dealers in the government market agreed to issue generic receipts that would not be directly associated with any of the participating dealers. These generic receipts are referred to as "Treasury Receipts" (TRs). Rather than representing a share of the trust as the trademarks do, TRs represent ownership of a Treasury security. A common problem with both trademark and generic receipts was that settlement required physical delivery, which is often cumbersome and inefficient.

Prior to June 1982, the Treasury was not a supporter of coupon stripping. In fact, a strongly worded letter from the Federal Reserve Bank of New York to primary government dealers stated, "in our view trading in Treasury securities stripped of coupons, or trading in the detached coupons themselves, is not a desirable market practice and should be discouraged."[13] The Treasury's objection was that taxpayers were able to undertake transactions

---

[11] Lehman Brothers offered "Lehman Investment Opportunities Notes" (LIONs); E.F. Hutton offered "Treasury Bond Receipts" (TBRs); and Dean Witter Reynolds offered "Easy Growth Treasury Receipts" (ETRs). There were also GATORs, COUGARs, and—you'll like this one—DOGS (Dibs on Government Securities).

[12] They are also called "animal products" for obvious reasons.

[13] See Thomas J. Kluber and Thomas Stauffacher, "Zero Coupon Treasury Securities," Chapter 11 in Frank J. Fabozzi (ed.), *The Handbook of Treasuries* (Chicago: Probus Publishing, 1986).

involving stripped Treasuries that could reduce their tax liability. In June 1982, the Treasury withdrew its objections to coupon stripping when provisions of the Tax Equity and Fiscal Responsibility Act of 1982 eliminated such tax abuses.

Although the Treasury benefited indirectly from coupon stripping through a heightened demand for its securities, in February 1985 it announced its Separate Trading of Registered Interest and Principal of Securities (STRIPS) program to facilitate the stripping of designated Treasury securities. Specifically, all new Treasury bonds and all new Treasury notes with maturities of 10 years and longer are eligible.[14] The zero-coupon Treasury securities created under the STRIPS program are direct obligations of the U.S. government. Moreover, the securities clear through the Federal Reserve's book entry system.[15] Creation of the STRIPS program ended the origination of trademarks and generic receipts. By December 1988, 65% of the zero-coupon Treasury market consisted of those created under the STRIPS program. About 14% were TRs, and the balance were trademarks (with CATS and TIGRs having the "lion's" share of 8% and 13%, respectively).[16]

Arbitrage Profits from Coupon Stripping. The profit potential for a government dealer who strips a Treasury security lies in arbitrage resulting from the mispricing of the security. To understand how this mispricing arises, recall from Chapter 12 that the price of a bond should equal the present value of its cash flows, where each cash flow is discounted at the appropriate *spot rate*. Discounting at a single yield figure such as the yield to maturity will result in mispricing, and may permit arbitrage profits. The potential profit depends on the actual yields on Treasury securities and the theoretical spot rate curve.

To see the dealer's profit potential from coupon stripping, we'll use the 20 hypothetical Treasury securities given in Table 12-1 in Chapter 12 (page 369). The longest maturity bond given in that table is the 10-year, 12.5% coupon bond selling at par and therefore with a yield to maturity of 12.5%. Suppose that a government dealer buys the issue at par and strips it, expecting to sell the zero-coupon Treasury securities at the yields to maturity indicated in Table 12-1 for the corresponding maturity.

---

[14] By December 1988, 23% of those securities eligible for stripping under the STRIPS program were stripped.

[15] In 1987, the Treasury permitted the conversion of stripped coupons into book-entry form under its Coupons Under Book-Entry Safekeeping (CUBES) program.

[16] Monte Shapiro and Carol E. Johnson, "Overview of Government Zero Market and Investment Strategies," Chapter 5 in Frank J. Fabozzi (ed.), *The Handbook of Treasury and Agency Securities* (Chicago: Probus Publishing, 1990).

		PRESENT VALUE	YIELD TO	PRESENT VALUE
MATURITY	CASH FLOW	AT 12.5%	MATURITY	AT YIELD TO MATURITY
0.50	6.25	5.8824	0.0800	6.0096
1.00	6.25	5.5363	0.0830	5.7618
1.50	6.25	5.2107	0.0890	5.4847
2.00	6.25	4.0942	0.0920	5.2210
2.50	6.25	4.6157	0.0940	4.9676
3.00	6.25	4.3442	0.0970	4.7040
3.50	6.25	4.0886	0.1000	4.4418
4.00	6.25	3.8481	0.1040	4.1663
4.50	6.25	3.6218	0.1060	3.9267
5.00	6.25	3.4087	0.1080	3.6938
5.50	6.25	3.2082	0.1090	3.4863
6.00	6.25	3.0195	0.1120	3.2502
6.50	6.25	2.8419	0.1140	3.0402
7.00	6.25	2.6747	0.1160	2.8384
7.50	6.25	2.5174	0.1180	2.6451
8.00	6.25	2.3693	0.1190	2.4789
8.50	6.25	2.2299	0.1200	2.3210
9.00	6.25	2.0987	0.1220	2.1528
9.50	6.25	1.9753	0.1240	1.9930
10.00	106.25	31.6046	0.1250	31.6046
Total		100.0000		104.1880

Table 14-4 shows the price that would be received for each zero-coupon Treasury security created. The price for each is just the present value of the cash flow from the stripped Treasury discounted at the yield to maturity corresponding to the maturity of the security (from Table 12-1). The total proceeds received from selling the zero-coupon Treasury securities created would be $104.1880 per $100 of par value of the Treasury issue purchased by the dealer. This would result in an arbitrage profit of $4.1880 per $100 of the 10-year, 12.5% coupon Treasury security purchased.

To understand why the government dealer has the opportunity to realize this profit, look at the third column of Table 14-4, which shows how much the government dealer paid for each cash flow by buying the entire package of cash flows (i.e., by buying the bond). For example, consider the $6.25 coupon payment in 4 years. By buying the 10-year Treasury bond priced to yield 12.5%, the dealer effectively pays a price based on 12.5% (6.25% semiannual) for that coupon payment, or, equivalently, $3.8481. Under the assumptions of this illustration, however, investors were willing to accept a lower yield to maturity, 10.4% (5.2% semiannual), to purchase a zero-coupon Treasury security with 4 years to maturity. Thus investors were willing to pay $4.1663. On this one coupon payment, the government dealer realizes a profit equal to the difference between $4.1663 and $3.8481 (or $0.3182). From all the cash flows, the total profit is $4.1880. In this instance, coupon stripping shows that the sum of the parts is greater than the whole.

Suppose that, instead of the observed yield to maturity from Table 12-1, the yields that investors want are the same as the theoretical spot rates that are shown in Table 12-2. If we use these spot rates to discount the cash flows, the total proceeds from the sale of the zero-coupon Treasury securities would be equal to $100, making coupon stripping uneconomic.

Reconstituting a Bond.   In our illustration of coupon stripping, the price of the Treasury security is less than its theoretical price. Suppose instead that the Treasury security is greater than its theoretical price. In such cases, investors can purchase in the market a package of zero-coupon Treasury securities such that the cash flow of the package of securities replicates the cash flow of the mispriced coupon Treasury security. By doing so, the investor will realize a yield higher than the yield on the coupon Treasury security. For example, suppose that the market price of the 10-year Treasury security we used in our illustration (Table 14-4) is $106. By buying the 20 zero-coupon bonds shown in Table 14-4 with a maturity value identical to the cash flow shown in the second column, the investor is effectively purchasing a 10-year Treasury coupon security at a cost of $104.1880 instead of $106.

It is the process of coupon stripping and reconstituting that will prevent the actual spot rate curve observed on zero-coupon Treasuries from departing significantly from the theoretical spot rate curve. As more stripping and reconstituting occurs, forces of demand and supply will cause rates to return to their theoretical spot rate levels. This is, in fact, what has happened in the Treasury market.

FEDERAL AGENCY SECURITIES

The federal agency securities market can be divided into two sectors—the federally sponsored agency securities market and the federally related institution securities market. Federally sponsored agencies, also called *government sponsored entities*, are privately owned, publicly chartered entities. They were created by Congress to reduce the cost of capital for certain borrowing sectors of the economy deemed to be important enough to warrant assistance. The entities in these privileged sectors include farmers, homeowners, and students. Federally sponsored agencies issue securities directly in the marketplace. The market for these securities, while smaller than that of Treasury securities, has in recent years become an active and important sector of the bond market.

Federally related institutions are entities that are arms of the federal government that do not issue securities directly in the marketplace (although they did prior to 1973). Instead, they obtain all or part of their financing by borrowing from the Federal Financing Bank, an entity created in 1973. The relatively small size of these issues made the borrowing cost for individual issues significantly greater than that of Treasury securities. Creation of the Federal Financing Bank was intended to consolidate and reduce the borrowing cost of federally related institutions.

Federally related institutions include: the Export–Import Bank of the United States, the Commodity Credit Corporation, the Farmers Housing Administration, the General Services Administration, the Government National Mortgage Association, the Maritime Administration, the Private Export Funding Corporation, the Rural Electrification Administration, the Rural Telephone Bank, the Small Business Administration, the Tennessee Valley Authority, and the Washington Metropolitan Area Transit Authority. All federally related institutions are exempt from SEC registration. With the exception of securities of the Private Export Funding Corporation and the Tennessee Valley Authority, the securities are backed by the full faith and credit of the United States government. As of November 1989, the amount of federally related institution debt outstanding was $36.9 billion.[17]

Federally Sponsored Agency Securities

There are eight federally sponsored agencies. The *Federal Farm Credit Bank System* is responsible for the credit market in the agricultural sector of the economy. The *Farm Credit Financial Association Corporation* was created in 1987 to address problems in the existing Farm Credit System. Three federally sponsored agencies—*Federal Home Loan Bank, Federal Home Loan Mortgage Corporation*, and *Federal National Mortgage Association*—are responsible for providing credit to the mortgage and housing sectors. The *Student Loan Marketing Association* provides funds to support higher education. The *Financing Corporation* was created in 1987 to recapitalize the Federal Savings and Loan Insurance Corporation. Because of continuing difficulties in the savings and loan association industry, the *Resolution Trust Corporation* was created in 1989 to liquidate or bail out insolvent institutions.

---

[17] *Federal Reserve Bulletin*, March 1990.

The federally sponsored agencies issue two types of securities: discount notes and bonds. Discount notes are short-term obligations, with maturities ranging from overnight to 360 days. Bonds are sold with maturities greater than 2 years.

With the exception of the securities issued by the Farm Credit Financial Assistance Corporation, federal agency securities are not backed by the full faith and credit of the U.S. government, as is the case with Treasury securities. Consequently, investors purchasing a federally sponsored agency security are exposed to credit risk. The yield spread between these securities and Treasury securities of comparable maturity reflects differences in perceived credit risk and liquidity. The spread attributable to credit risk reflects financial problems faced by the issuing federally sponsored agency and the likelihood that the federal government will allow the credit agency to default on its outstanding obligations.

Two examples will illustrate this point. In late 1981 and early 1982, the net income of the Federal National Mortgage Association weakened, causing analysts to report that the securities of this credit agency carried greater risk than previously perceived. As a result, the yield spread over Treasuries on its debt rose from 91 basis points (on average) in 1981 to as high as 150 basis points.[18] In subsequent years, the Federal National Mortgage Association's net income improved, and its yield spread to Treasuries narrowed. As another example, in 1985 the yield spread on securities of the Farm Credit Bank System rose substantially above those on comparable maturity Treasuries because of the agency's financial difficulties. The spread between 1985 and 1986 varied with the prospects of Congressional approval of a bailout measure for the system.

The price quotation convention for federally sponsored agency securities is the same as that for Treasury securities. That is, the bid and ask price quotations are expressed as a percentage of par plus fractional 32nds of a point.

Below we provide a brief description of six of the eight federally sponsored agencies. The two agencies not discussed here—Federal Home Loan Mortgage Corporation and Federal National Mortgage Association—are covered in Chapter 18.

Federal Farm Credit Bank System.   The purpose of the Federal Farm Credit Bank System (FFCBS) is to facilitate adequate, dependable credit and related services to the agricultural sector of the economy. The Farm Credit System consists of three entities: the Federal Land Banks, Federal Intermediate Credit Banks, and Banks for Cooperatives. Before 1979, each entity issued securities

---

[18] Michael J. Moran, "The Federally Sponsored Credit Agencies: An Overview," *Federal Reserve Bulletin* (June 1986), p. 380.

in its own name. Starting in 1979, they began to issue debt on a consolidated basis as "joint and several obligations" of the FFCBS. All financing for the FFCBS is arranged through the Federal Farm Credit Banks Funding Corporation, which issues consolidated obligations through a selling group consisting of approximately 150 members. For discount notes, the selling group consists of only four dealers.

Farm Credit Financial Assistance Corporation. In the 1980s, the FFCBS faced financial difficulties because of defaults on loans made to farmers occasioned largely by high interest rates in the late 1970s and early 1980s and depressed prices on agricultural products. To recapitalize the Federal Farm Credit Bank System, in 1987 Congress created the Farm Credit Financial Assistance Corporation (FACO). This federally sponsored agency is authorized to issue debt to assist the FFCBS. FACO bonds, unlike the debt of other federally sponsored government agencies, are backed by the Treasury.

Federal Home Loan Bank System. The Federal Home Loan Bank System (FHLBS) consists of the 12 district Federal Home Loan Banks (which are instrumentalities of the U.S. government) and their member banks. An independent federal agency, the Federal Home Loan Bank Board, was originally responsible for regulating all federally chartered savings and loan associations and savings banks, as well as state-chartered institutions insured by the Federal Savings and Loan Insurance Corporation. These responsibilities have been curtailed since 1989. The major source of debt funding for the Federal Home Loan Banks is the issuance of consolidated debt obligations. These obligations are joint and several obligations of the 12 Federal Home Loan Banks.

Financing Corporation. The deposits of savings and loans were once insured by the Federal Savings and Loan Insurance Corporation (FSLIC), overseen by the Federal Home Loan Bank Board. When difficulties encountered in the savings and loan industry raised concerns about FSLIC's ability to meet its responsibility to insure deposits, Congress passed the Competitive Equality and Banking Act in 1987. This legislation included provisions to recapitalize FSLIC and establish a new federally government sponsored agency, the Financing Corporation (FICO), to issue debt in order to provide funding for FICO.

FICO is capitalized by the non-voting stock purchased by the 12 regional Federal Home Loan Banks. FICO issued its first bonds in September 30, 1987—a 30-year non-callable $500 million issue. The issue was priced 90 basis points over the 30-year Treasury security at the time. The principal of these bonds is backed by zero-coupon Treasury securities. The legislation permits

FICO to issue up to $10.825 billion but not more than $3.75 billion in any one year. FICO is legislated to be dismantled in 2026, or after all securities have matured, whichever comes sooner.

Resolution Trust Corporation.   The 1987 legislation that created FICO did not go far enough to resolve the problems facing the beleaguered savings and loan industry. In 1989, Congress passed more comprehensive legislation, the Financial Institutions Reform, Recovery and Enforcement Act (FIRREA). This legislation has three key elements. First, it transfers supervision of savings and loans to a newly created Office of Thrift Supervision. Second, it shifts the FSLIC insurance function to a Savings Association Insurance Fund, placed under the supervision of the Federal Deposit Insurance Corporation. Third, it establishes the Resolution Trust Corporation (RTC) as a federally sponsored agency charged with the responsibility of liquidating or bailing out insolvent savings and loan institutions. RTC is to obtain its funding from the Resolution Funding Corporation (REFCORP), which is authorized to issue up to $40 billion of long-term bonds. The principal of this debt is backed by zero-coupon Treasury bonds. REFCORP has issued both 30-year and 40-year bonds.[19]

Student Loan Marketing Association.   Popularly known as "Sallie Mae," the Student Loan Marketing Association provides liquidity for private lenders participating in the Federal Guaranteed Student Loan Program, the Health Education Assistance Loan Program, and the PLUS loan program (a program that provides loans to the parents of undergraduate students). Sallie Mae is permitted to purchase and offer investors participation in student loans. Sallie Mae issues unsecured debt obligations in the form of discount notes. In January 1982, Sallie Mae first issued floating-rate securities based on the bond equivalent yield on 91-day Treasury bills. Sallie Mae also has long-term fixed-rate securities and zero-coupon bonds outstanding.

Future Regulation of Federally Sponsored Agencies

The U.S. bailout of the savings and loan industry raised increasing concerns in Congress over the potential cost of bailing out federally sponsored agencies. The Financial Institutions Reform, Recovery and Enforcement Act of 1989 mandated the General Accounting Office (GAO) and the Secretary of

---

[19] The 40-year bonds represent the first offering of such a government or government agency bond since the Treasury issued 40-year bonds in the 1950s. The auction for the $5 billion, 40-year bond offering in January 1990 was not a successful undertaking.

the Treasury to study the issues and prepare reports for Congress. Specifically, both the GAO and the Treasury were to investigate whether each federally sponsored agency maintained appropriate capital levels, given the risks associated with their activities. In addition, the Treasury was to assess the impact of the activities of federally sponsored agencies on federal borrowing.

The GAO and the Treasury were directed to prepare two reports, an interim report published in August 1990 and a final report due in May 1991. Our discussion of the results is based on the Treasury and GAO interim reports because the final reports had not been issued at this writing.

The Treasury interim report recommends that a federally sponsored agency be required to maintain a triple-A credit rating from two nationally recognized rating companies. (We discuss rating companies in the next chapter.) The rating must be achieved in the absence of government sponsorship (i.e., as a standalone private entity). Failure to obtain such a credit rating would result in the loss of sponsorship by the federal government. The GAO interim report puts forth two possible forms of regulation. One is the same as that recommended by the Treasury. The alternative is to require federally sponsored agencies to maintain a specified level of risk-weighted capital similar to the risk-weighted capital requirements for commercial banks that we described in Chapter 2. At the time of this writing, Congress has not settled upon the form of regulation, if any, to implement.

SUMMARY

The U.S. Treasury market is closely watched by all participants in the financial markets because interest rates on Treasury securities are the benchmark interest rates throughout the world. The Treasury issues three types of securities: bills, notes, and bonds. Treasury bills have a maturity of one year or less, are sold at a discount from par, and do not make periodic interest payments. Treasury notes and bonds are coupon securities. Treasury securities are issued on a competitive bid auction basis, according to a regular auction cycle. The auction process relies on the participation of the primary government securities dealers, with which the Federal Reserve deals directly. The secondary market for Treasury securities is an over-the-counter market, where dealers trade with the general investing public and with other dealers. In the secondary market, Treasury bills are quoted on a bank discount basis; Treasury coupon securities are quoted on a price basis. Treasury dealers finance their position in the repo market.

While the Treasury does not issue zero-coupon Treasury securities, government dealers have created these instruments synthetically by a process called coupon stripping. Zero-coupon Treasury securities include trademarks, Treasury receipts, and STRIPS. Creation of the first two types of zero-coupon Treasury securities has ceased; STRIPS now dominate the market. The advantage of zero-coupon Treasury securities is that they eliminate reinvestment risk. The motivation for government dealers to create these securities is the arbitrage opportunities available.

Federally sponsored agency securities and federally related institution securities comprise the federal agency securities market. The former are privately owned, publicly chartered entities created to reduce the cost of borrowing for certain sectors of the economy. Federally related institutions are arms of the federal government whose debt is guaranteed by the U.S. government. While federally sponsored agencies issue their own securities, federally related institutions obtain all or part of their financing by borrowing from the Federal Financing Bank. The yield spread between securities issued by federally sponsored agencies and Treasury securities of comparable maturity depends on the agency's perceived credit risk and liquidity. Congress is considering future regulation of federally sponsored agencies.

QUESTIONS

1. **a.** The following is from the February 1991 monthly report published by Blackstone Financial Management:

    On February 1, 1991, the Federal Reserve lowered the discount rate from 6.5% to 6.0% and moved the fed funds target rate from 6.75% to 6.25%. The aggressive easing of monetary policy prompted a significant steepening of the yield curve. Two-year Treasury notes fell 41 basis points to 6.82% while Treasury bonds declined only 16 basis points.

    Explain how the "aggressive easing of monetary policy" resulted in "a steepening of the yield curve."

    b. In the March 1991 monthly report, the following appeared:

    The further perception that the Federal Reserve had largely concluded it [sic] aggressive easing of monetary policy, along with a sell-off of short and intermediate Treasuries by Middle Eastern accounts to raise cash to finance war costs, produced a flatter yield curve. . . .

    Explain why the yield curve became flatter as a result of the actions described above.

c. Also in the March 1991 monthly report was the following:

> The Treasury also brought $34.5 billion in new securities to the market in February as part of the normal quarterly refunding. . . . the auctions went slightly better than expected given the significant size and the uncertainties surrounding the duration of the war. The 3-year was issued at a 6.98% average yield, the 10-year at a 7.85% average yield, and the 30-year at a 7.98% average yield. All bids were accepted at the average yield or better (i.e., with no tail), indicating ample demand for the securities.

What is meant by the average yield and the tail? Why does the absence of a tail indicate ample demand for the Treasuries auctioned?

2. a. Why has coupon stripping resulted in pricing of Treasuries based on theoretical spot rates?

b. If the actual price of a Treasury is less than its theoretical price based on spot rates, how can a market participant take advantage of this situation?

3. When stripped Treasury securities were first created, callable 30-year Treasury bonds were being issued by the Treasury. Such issues could be called by the Treasury five years before the maturity date. Why would the presence of a call feature make it difficult to strip a Treasury security?

4. Define each of the following:

a. An on the run issue

b. An off the run issue

c. The when-issued market

d. A primary dealer

e. A reporting dealer

5. Why do government dealers use government brokers?

6. a. What is the difference between a federally sponsored agency security and a federally related institution?

b. Are federally sponsored agency securities backed by the full faith and credit of the U.S. government?

7. In the February 1991 monthly report of Blackstone Financial Management is the quotation:

> The Resolution Funding Corporation (REFCORP) issued $4.95 billion 30-year bonds and $2 billion 40-year bonds in January. . . . Since the

auction, the 30-year REFCORP issue has tightened 4 basis points to a 25 basis point spread while other agency issues of similar maturities widened 3 to 4 basis points.

In the March 1991 monthly issue, the following appeared:

Within the agency sector, most issues tightened 2 to 5 basis points to their respective Treasury maturities, with the exception of 30-year REFCORP. These issues widened by 2 basis points. . . .

a. What is the Resolution Funding Corporation?

b. What happened to investors' perceptions of the credit risk of REFCORP between January and February?

CHAPTER 15

CORPORATE SENIOR SECURITIES MARKET

LEARNING OBJECTIVES

After reading this chapter you will understand:

- the key provisions of a corporate bond issue.

- the risks associated with investing in corporate bonds.

- call risk and the basic principle underlying the valuation of callable corporate bonds.

- why bonds with special features are issued.

- the high-yield or "junk" bond sector of the corporate bond market.

- the purposes for which proceeds are used by junk bond issuers.

- bond structures that have been used in the junk bond market.

- medium-term notes and the reasons behind their use.

- the difference between preferred stock, corporate debt, and common stock.

471

- the difference between the three types of preferred stock: fixed-rate, adjustable-rate, and auction and remarketed preferred stock.

I n this chapter, we focus on corporate senior securities. These are securities that have priority over common stock in the case of bankruptcy. They include bonds, medium-term notes, and preferred stock. One sector of the corporate bond market that has mushroomed in recent years and has been the subject of considerable discussion is the high-yield or junk bond market. We'll take a look at this specific market sector as well, examining the issuers, the investors, and various bond structures.

The corporate bonds discussed in this chapter are issued by domestic firms in the U.S. bond market and denominated in U.S. dollars. In Chapter 22 international capital markets will be discussed. There we look at bonds issued by foreign corporations in the U.S. bond market. This market is called the *Yankee bond market,* and the bonds are denominated in both U.S. dollars and foreign currencies.

CORPORATE BONDS

As the name indicates, corporate bonds are issued by corporations. The average size of an issue in 1988 was $162.4 million.[1] As of year end 1990, there were $1.4 trillion of domestic corporate bonds outstanding, with more than 80% issued by non-financial corporations. The largest investor group is life insurance companies, which own about 30% of corporate bonds, followed by pension funds, public and private, which own about 24%. The relative

---

[1] *Moody's Bond Survey,* 1988.

amount of corporate bonds held by other investor groups is: households (12%), foreign investors (13%), depository institutions (10%), non-life insurance companies (6%), and mutual funds and securities brokers and dealers (5%).[2]

Classification of Corporate Bonds

Corporate bonds are classified by the type of issuer. The four general classifications used by bond information services are: (1) utilities, (2) transportations, (3) industrials, and (4) banks and finance companies. Finer breakdowns are often made to create more homogeneous groupings. For example, utilities are subdivided into electric power companies, gas distribution companies, water companies, and communication companies. Transportations are divided further into airlines, railroads, and trucking companies. Industrials are the catchall class, and the most heterogeneous of the groupings with respect to investment characteristics. Industrials include all kinds of manufacturing, merchandising, and service companies.

Tables 15-1a and 15-1b show the public financing by issuer classification from 1973 to 1988. Notice the percentage decline of utilities (communications, electrics, and gas and water) since 1980—from 36.5% of all new issues in 1973 to 10.9% in 1988. Over the 16-year period, industrials raised the largest amount of public debt, followed by financial institutions and then utilities.

Terms of a Corporate Bond Issue

The essential features of a corporate bond are relatively simple. The corporate issuer promises to pay a specified percentage of par value on designated dates (the coupon payments) and to repay par or principal value of the bond at maturity. Failure to pay either the principal or interest when due constitutes legal default, and investors can go to court to enforce the contract. Bondholders, as creditors, have a prior legal claim over common and preferred stockholders as to both income and assets of the corporation for the principal and interest due them.

The promises of corporate bond issuers and the rights of investors who buy them are set forth in great detail in contracts called *bond indentures*. If bondholders were handed the complete indenture they would have trouble understanding the language and even greater difficulty in determining from time to time whether the corporate issuer were keeping all the promises made. These problems are solved for the most part by bringing in a corporate

---

[2] Estimated from various issues of *Flow Accounts, Financial Assets and Liabilities*, Board of Governors of the Federal Reserve System, Washington, D.C.

TABLE 15-1A PUBLIC FINANCING IN THE TAXABLE BOND MARKETS BY ISSUER CLASSIFICATION, 1973–1988* (NON-CONVERTIBLE BOND OFFERINGS—PAR VALUE [IN MILLIONS])

	TOTAL	COMMU- NICA- TIONS	ELEC- TRICS	GAS AND WATER	INDUS- TRIALS	FINANCE	BANKS AND THRIFTS	TRANS- PORTA- TION	INTER- NATIONAL
1988	$ 98,867	$ 638	$ 7,653	$ 2,512	$ 45,104	$ 22,949	$13,616	$ 2,480	$ 3,915
1987	104,634	2,495	12,283	2,848	42,056	24,329	13,945	1,593	5,085
1986	142,562	10,231	21,893	2,825	60,364	22,837	15,644	3,750	5,018
1985	80,118	3,210	6,354	1,566	32,161	19,817	9,638	1,427	5,945
1984	48,890	830	5,000	825	19,510	10,223	8,255	1,247	3,000
1983	35,697	1,965	5,400	1,470	9,391	5,927	6,758	896	3,890
1982	44,168	720	7,170	1,665	14,281	8,373	5,217	1,062	5,680
1981	40,655	3,820	6,425	1,640	12,729	7,175	1,975	1,316	5,575
1980	36,695	5,975	6,418	1,000	12,257	5,310	2,025	1,445	2,265
1979	24,941	3,700	4,760	555	6,114	3,236	2,200	991	3,385
1978	20,799	2,880	4,708	170	3,287	4,140	630	734	4,250
1977	25,929	2,625	5,306	302	4,472	5,723	1,520	873	5,108
1976	30,165	2,200	5,012	1,058	7,635	5,510	1,185	1,270	6,295
1975	34,918	3,035	6,932	1,319	14,100	2,538	920	967	5,107
1974	26,663	3,396	7,642	752	7,853	2,125	2,325	920	1,650
1973	13,315	3,149	4,757	449	1,235	1,923	555	522	725
Total	$809,016	$50,869	$117,713	$20,956	$292,549	$152,135	$86,408	$21,493	$66,893

*Excludes convertible bonds, non-underwritten offerings such as those sold on a best-efforts basis, medium-term notes, debt issued in exchange for stock or other debt, and structured transactions such as asset-based financings.

Source: Derived from *Moody's Bond Survey,* various issues.

trustee as a third party to the contract. The indenture is made out to the corporate trustee as a representative of the interests of bondholders; that is, a trustee acts in a fiduciary capacity for investors who own the bond issue. A corporate trustee is a bond or trust company with a corporate trust department whose officers are experts in performing the functions of a trustee.

Most corporate bonds are *term bonds;* that is, they run for a term of years, then become due and payable. Term bonds are often referred to as "bullet-maturity" bonds. Any amount of the liability that has not been paid off prior to maturity must be paid off at that time. The term may be long or short. Generally, obligations due in under 10 years from the date of issue are called *notes,* or *medium-term notes.* Most corporate borrowings take the form of

TABLE 15-1B PUBLIC FINANCING IN THE TAXABLE BOND MARKETS BY ISSUER CLASSIFICATION, 1973–1988* (NON-CONVERTIBLE BOND OFFERINGS — PERCENTAGE DISTRIBUTION)

	COMMU-NICA-TIONS	ELEC-TRICS	GAS AND WATER	INDUS-TRIALS	FINANCE	BANKS AND THRIFTS	TRANS-PORTA-TION	INTER-NATIONAL
1988	0.65	7.74	2.54	45.62	23.21	13.77	2.51	3.96
1987	2.38	11.74	2.72	40.19	23.25	13.33	1.52	4.86
1986	7.18	15.36	1.98	42.34	16.02	10.97	2.63	3.52
1985	4.01	7.93	1.95	40.14	24.73	12.03	1.78	7.42
1984	1.70	10.23	1.69	39.91	20.91	16.88	2.55	6.14
1983	5.50	15.13	4.12	26.31	16.60	18.93	2.51	10.90
1982	1.63	16.23	3.77	32.33	18.96	11.81	2.40	12.86
1981	9.40	15.80	4.03	31.31	17.65	4.86	3.24	13.71
1980	16.28	17.49	2.73	33.40	14.47	5.52	3.94	6.17
1979	14.83	19.08	2.23	24.51	12.97	8.82	3.97	13.57
1978	13.85	22.63	0.82	15.80	19.90	3.03	3.53	20.43
1977	10.12	20.46	1.16	17.25	22.07	5.86	3.37	19.70
1976	7.29	16.61	3.51	25.31	18.27	3.93	4.21	20.87
1975	8.69	19.85	3.78	40.38	7.27	2.63	2.77	14.63
1974	12.74	28.66	2.82	29.45	7.97	8.72	3.45	6.19
1973	23.65	35.72	3.37	9.27	14.44	4.17	3.92	5.44
Average 1973–1988	6.29	14.55	2.59	36.16	18.80	10.68	2.66	8.27

*Excludes convertible bonds, non-underwritten offerings such as those sold on a best-efforts basis, medium-term notes, debt issued in exchange for stock or other debt, and structured transactions such as asset-based financings.

Source: Derived from Moody's Bond Survey, various issues.

bonds due in 20 to 30 years. Term bonds may be retired by payment at final maturity or retired prior to maturity if provided for in the indenture. Some corporate bond issues are arranged so that specified principal amounts become due on specified dates. Such issues are called serial bonds. Equipment trust certificates (discussed later) are structured as serial bonds.

Security for Bonds.   Either real property (using a mortgage) or personal property may be pledged to offer security beyond the issuer's general credit standing. A mortgage bond grants the bondholders a lien against the pledged assets, that is, a legal right to sell the mortgaged property to satisfy unpaid obligations to the bondholders. In practice, foreclosure and sale of mortgaged property is unusual. Usually in the case of default a financial reorganization of the issuer provides for settlement of the debt to bondholders. The mortgage lien is important, though, because it gives the mortgage bondholders a strong bargaining position relative to other creditors in determining the terms of any reorganization.

Some companies do not own fixed assets or other real property, and so have nothing on which they can give a mortgage lien to secure bondholders. Instead, they own securities of other companies; they are holding companies, and the other companies are subsidiaries. To satisfy the desire of bondholders for security, they will pledge stocks, notes, bonds or whatever other kind of obligations they own. These assets are termed *collateral* (or personal property); bonds secured by such assets are called *collateral trust bonds.*

Many years ago the railway companies developed a way of financing purchase of cars and locomotives (*rolling stock*) in a way that enabled them to borrow at just about the lowest rates in the corporate bond market. Railway rolling stock has for a long time been seen as excellent security for debt. The equipment is sufficiently standardized that it can be used by one railroad as well as another. It can be readily moved from the tracks of one railroad to another's, and there is generally a good market for lease or sale of cars and locomotives. The railroads have taken advantage of these characteristics of rolling stock by developing a legal arrangement for giving investors a legal claim on it that is different from, and generally superior to, a mortgage lien. The legal arrangement vests legal title to railway equipment in a trustee.

The procedure works like this. A railway company orders some cars and locomotives from a manufacturer. The manufacturer then transfers legal title to the equipment to a trustee, who in turn leases it to the railroad, and at the same time sells *equipment trust certificates* to obtain the funds to pay the manufacturer. The trustee collects lease payments from the railroad and uses the money to pay interest and principal on the certificates. The principal is therefore paid off on specified dates. Although the railway companies developed the equipment trust arrangement, it has been used since by companies engaged in providing other kinds of transportation. For example, trucking companies finance the purchase of huge fleets of trucks in the same manner; airlines use this kind of financing to purchase transport planes; and international oil companies use it to buy huge tankers.

Debenture bonds are debt securities not secured by a specific pledge of property, but that does not mean that they have no claim on property of issuers or on their earnings. Debenture bondholders have the claim of general creditors on all assets of the issuer not pledged specifically to secure other debt. And they have a claim on pledged assets even to the extent that these assets have more value than necessary to satisfy secured creditors. *Subordinated debenture bonds* rank after secured debt, after debenture bonds, and often after some general creditors in their claim on assets and earnings.

The type of security issued determines the cost to the corporation. For a given corporation, mortgage bonds will cost less than debenture bonds, and debenture bonds will cost less than subordinated debenture bonds.

Guaranteed bonds are obligations guaranteed by another entity. The safety of a guaranteed bond depends upon the guarantor's financial capability, as well as the financial capability of the issuer. The terms of the guarantee may call for the guarantor to guarantee the payment of interest and/or repayment of the principal.

It is important to recognize that the superior legal status of any debt security will not prevent bondholders from suffering financial loss when the issuer's ability to generate cash flow adequate to pay its obligations is seriously eroded.

Provisions for Paying Off Bonds. Most corporate issues have a call provision allowing the issuer an option to buy back all or part of the issue prior to maturity. Some issues specify that the issuer must retire a predetermined amount of the issue periodically. Various types of corporate call provisions are discussed below.[3]

1. *Call and Refund Provisions:* An important question in negotiating the terms of a new bond issue is whether the issuer shall have the right to redeem the *entire amount* of bonds outstanding on a date before maturity. Issuers generally want this right because they recognize that at some time in the future the general level of interest rates may fall sufficiently below the issue's coupon rate that redeeming the issue and replacing it with another issue with a lower coupon rate would be attractive. This right is a disadvantage to the bondholder.

The usual practice is a provision that denies the issuer the right to redeem bonds during the first 5 to 10 years following the date of issue with proceeds received from issuing lower-cost debt obligations ranking equal or superior to the debt to be redeemed. This type of redemption is called *refunding*. While most long-term issues include these refunding restrictions, they may be callable immediately, in whole or in part, if the source of funds comes from other than lower-interest cost money. Cash flow from operations, proceeds from a common stock sale, or funds from the sale of property are examples of such sources.

Investors often confuse refunding protection with call protection. Call protection is much more absolute, in that bonds cannot be redeemed *for any reason*. Refunding restrictions provide protection only against the one type of redemption mentioned above. Failure to recognize this difference has resulted in unnecessary losses for some investors.

---

[3] For a more detailed explanation of corporate call provisions, see Richard S. Wilson and Frank J. Fabozzi, *The New Corporate Bond Market* (Chicago, IL: Probus Publishing, 1990).

Long-term industrial issues generally have 10 years of refunding protection but are then immediately callable. Electric utilities most often have 5 years of refunding protection, although during times of high interest rates issues with 10 years of refunding protection have been sold. Long-term debt of the former members of the Bell Telephone System have 5 years of call protection.

Many short- to intermediate-term bonds and notes are not callable for the first three to seven years (in some cases, they are not callable for the life of the issue). Thereafter, the issue may be called for any reason.

As a rule, corporate bonds are callable at a premium above par. Generally, the level of the premium declines as the bond approaches maturity, often reaching par a number of years after issuance. The initial amount of the premium may be as much as one year's coupon interest or as little as coupon interest for half a year. When less than the entire issue is called, the specific bonds to be called are selected randomly or on a pro rata basis. When bonds are selected randomly, the serial number of the certificates is published in *The Wall Street Journal* and major metropolitan dailies.

2. *Sinking Fund Provision:*   Corporate bond indentures may require the issuer to retire a specified portion of an issue each year. This is referred to as a *sinking fund* requirement. This kind of provision for repayment of corporate debt may be designed to liquidate all of a bond issue by the maturity date, or it may be arranged to pay only a part of the total by the end of the term. If only a part is paid, the remainder is called a *balloon maturity*. The purpose of the sinking fund provision is to reduce credit risk.

Generally, the issuer may satisfy the sinking fund requirement by either (1) making a cash payment of the face amount of the bonds to be retired to the corporate trustee, who then calls the bonds for redemption using a lottery, or (2) delivering to the trustee bonds purchased in the open market that have a total face value equal to the amount that must be retired. If the bonds are retired using the first method, interest payments stop at the redemption date.

Usually, the periodic payments required for sinking fund purposes will be the same for each period. A few indentures might permit variable periodic payments, where payments change according to certain prescribed conditions set forth in the indenture. Many corporate bond indentures include a provision that grants the issuer the option to retire double the amount stipulated for sinking fund retirement. This is referred to as the *doubling option*.

Usually, the sinking fund call price is the par value if the bonds were originally sold at par. When issued at a price in excess of par, the call price generally starts at the issuance price and scales down to par as the issue approaches maturity.

Industrial issues almost always include sinking fund provisions. Finance companies almost always do not. The inclusion or absence of a sinking fund provision in public utility bonds depends on the type of public utility.

Credit Ratings

Professional money managers use various techniques to analyze information on companies and bond issues in order to estimate the ability of the issuer to live up to its future contractual obligations.[4] This activity is known as *credit analysis.*

Some large institutional investors and most investment banking firms have their own credit analysis departments. Few individual investors and institutional bond investors, though, do their own analysis. Instead, they rely primarily on commercial rating companies that perform credit analysis and issue their conclusions in the form of ratings. The five commercial rating companies are (1) Moody's Investors Service, (2) Standard & Poor's, (3) Duff and Phelps, (4) McCarthy, Crisanti & Maffei, and (5) Fitch Investors Service.

The two most widely used systems of bond ratings are those of Moody's and Standard & Poor's. In both systems the term *high grade* means low credit risk, or conversely, high probability of future payments. The highest-grade bonds are designated by Moody's by the letters Aaa, and by Standard & Poor's by AAA. The next highest grade is Aa or AA; for the third grade both rating agencies use A. The next three grades are Baa or BBB, Ba or BB, and B, respectively. There are also C grades. Standard & Poor's uses plus or minus signs to provide a narrower credit quality breakdown within each class, and Moody's uses 1, 2, or 3 for the same purpose. Bonds rated triple A (AAA or Aaa) are said to be *prime;* double A (AA or Aa) are of *high quality;* single A issues are called *upper medium grade,* and triple B are *medium grade.* These four categories are referred to as *investment grade.* Lower-rated bonds are said to have speculative elements or be *distinctly speculative.* They are also known as *high yield* or *junk bonds.*

Table 15-2 summarizes sixteen years of annual corporate public financing by Moody's ratings. Notice the dramatic decline of new issues rated Aaa, from a high of 42.6% in 1977 to only 11.89% in 1988. In fact, each year prior to 1982 a little more than half the issues had either Aaa or Aa ratings. By 1988, only about 25% were rated Aaa or Aa at the time of issuance and the proportion of issues rated Ba and lower had increased dramatically.

---

[4] For an in-depth discussion of credit analysis, see Jane Tripp Howe, "Credit Analysis for Corporate Bonds," Chapter 17 in Frank J. Fabozzi (ed.), *The Handbook of Fixed Income Securities* (Homewood, IL: Business One-Irwin, 1991).

TABLE 15-2   PUBLIC FINANCING IN THE TAXABLE BOND MARKETS BY ISSUER CLASSIFICATION, 1973–1988   (NON-CONVERTIBLE BOND OFFERINGS—PAR VALUE [IN MILLIONS])

	TOTAL	Aaa	% OF TOTAL	Aa	% OF TOTAL	A	% OF TOTAL	Baa	% OF TOTAL	Ba and Lower*	% OF TOTAL
1988	$ 98,868	$ 11,758	11.89	$ 13,501	13.66	$ 32,494	32.87	$14,639	14.81	$ 26,476	26.78
1987	104,634	10,587	10.12	21,860	20.89	30,521	29.17	16,475	15.75	25,191	24.07
1986	142,562	12,253	8.59	37,943	26.62	40,159	28.17	21,866	15.34	30,341	21.28
1985	80,118	9,016	11.25	16,539	20.64	27,953	34.99	9,772	12.20	16,838	21.02
1984	48,890	2,350	4.81	13,730	28.08	15,117	30.92	4,145	8.48	13,548	27.71
1983	35,697	3,920	10.98	11,110	31.12	9,030	25.30	5,125	14.36	6,512	18.24
1982	44,168	6,072	13.75	14,659	33.19	15,340	34.73	4,274	9.68	3,823	8.65
1981	40,655	11,835	29.11	9,980	24.55	12,662	31.15	4,085	10.05	2,093	5.14
1980	36,695	10,109	27.55	10,721	29.22	11,900	32.43	2,540	6.92	1,425	3.88
1979	24,941	10,400	41.70	5,712	22.90	5,780	23.17	1,744	6.99	1,305	5.24
1978	20,799	7,967	38.30	5,646	27.15	4,415	21.23	1,618	7.78	1,153	5.54
1977	25,929	11,046	42.60	5,239	20.21	5,033	19.41	2,093	8.07	2,518	9.71
1976	30,165	9,907	32.84	8,786	29.13	8,039	26.65	3,023	10.02	410	1.36
1975	34,918	11,348	32.50	8,932	25.58	12,011	34.40	2,482	7.11	145	0.41
1974	26,663	7,420	27.83	8,510	31.92	7,500	28.13	1,933	7.25	1,300	4.87
1973	13,315	4,046	30.39	3,225	24.22	4,052	30.43	519	3.90	1,473	11.06
Total	$809,016	$140,033	17.31	$196,093	24.24	$242,006	29.91	$96,333	11.91	$134,552	16.63

*Ba and lower category includes non-rated issues.

Source: Richard S. Wilson and Frank J. Fabozzi, *The New Corporate Bond Market* (Chicago: Probus Publishing, 1990), Table 1-3c. Derived from *Moody's Bond Survey,* various issues.

Risks Associated with Investing in Corporate Bonds

The risks associated with investing in corporate bonds are (1) interest rate risk, (2) reinvestment risk, (3) purchasing power risk or inflation risk, (4) credit risk, (5) call risk, (6) marketability risk, and (7) event risk. We discussed the first three risks in Chapter 11. The last four are discussed below.

Credit Risk.   Unlike Treasury securities, corporate bonds expose the investor to credit risk—the risk that the issuer will default on its obligations. At any given time the yield offered in the market for a corporate bond varies according to market perception of the uncertainty of future payment of interest and principal: yield then depends on the bond's perceived quality or credit rating. To compensate for greater credit risk, lower quality-rated issues must offer higher yields than issues with higher ratings. The yield spread

TABLE 15-3	AVERAGE PROMISED YIELDS ON CORPORATE BONDS BY QUALITY RATING: 1976–1989*			
YEAR	Aaa	Aa	A	Baa
1976	8.43%	8.75%	9.09%	9.75%
1977	8.02	8.24	8.49	8.97
1978	8.73	8.92	9.20	9.49
1979	9.63	9.94	10.20	10.69
1980	11.94	12.50	12.89	13.67
1981	14.17	14.75	15.29	16.04
1982	13.79	14.41	15.43	16.11
1983	12.04	12.42	13.10	13.55
1984	12.71	13.26	13.74	14.19
1985	11.37	11.82	12.28	12.72
1986	9.02	9.47	9.95	10.39
1987	9.38	9.68	9.99	10.58
1988	9.71	9.94	10.23	10.83
1989	9.26	9.46	9.74	10.18

*The annual yields are the average of the monthly averages as reported in *Moody's Bond Record*.

between two issues that are identical in all respects except for quality is referred to as a *quality spread* or *credit spread*.

Both Moody's and Standard & Poor's periodically publish average yields at market prices on a number of long-term corporate bond issues grouped by ratings. These average yields by category always show the lowest yields on triple-A rated bonds, somewhat higher yields on double-A rated bonds, then still higher yields on single-A rated bonds. There is a relatively large differential between the average yield on single-A and triple-B bonds. Table 15-3 presents the average promised yields from 1976 to 1989 as reported by Moody's for its top four quality ratings.

The quality spread between corporate bond issues of different quality and between corporate bonds and Treasury securities varies over the business cycle. Specifically, quality spreads between lower- and higher-quality bonds tend to widen when the economy is in a recession or economic downturn but narrow during periods of economic prosperity. Narrowing of the spread between high-grade and lower-grade credit issues in good times occurs because there is reduced likelihood of default even in the case of lower-rated issues. Investors then attempt to increase yield by selling higher-rated issues and placing those funds in lower-rated issues. When investors anticipate a poorer economic climate, there is often a "flight to quality" as investors pursue more conservative credit risk exposure by selling lower-quality and purchasing higher-quality issues. This widens the spread between high-grade and lower-grade credit issues.

Call Risk.   We have noted that corporate bonds are typically callable or redeemable. Whether the issuer has the choice to retire all or part of an issue prior to maturity or is required to do so, the bondholder faces a risk that the issue will be called away at a disadvantageous time. This risk is referred to as *call risk* or *timing risk.*

The disadvantage of call provisions has to do with a change in interest rates. If and when interest rates decline relative to the coupon rate to a point where call becomes advantageous to the issuer, the market value of the bond will not rise as much as that of similar issues of the same quality. The price will be "compressed" toward the call price, eventually coinciding with it when the call is announced. This creates an asymmetric risk for the holder, who suffers the full burden of any rise in interest through a fall in price but does not reap the benefit of higher price through lower interest rates.

This situation is depicted in Figure 15-1. The solid line shows the price/yield curve for a non-callable bond. The broken line shows how the price/yield relationship of a callable bond changes when the market interest rate declines below the coupon interest rate of the issue. This characteristic of a bond is referred to as "price compression," or, more popularly, as "negative convexity."

From the investor's perspective, the borrower's right to call a bond is nothing more than a call option that bondholders grant the issuer. It can be valued using an option pricing framework.[5] More specifically, we can recast the price of a callable bond into its component parts: a package of a non-callable bond and a call option sold to the issuer. That is:

Price of a callable bond = Price of a non-callable bond − Price of a call option

We subtract the price of a call option from the price of a non-callable bond because the bondholder has sold a call option to the corporation, which reduces the callable bond's price. (This is depicted in Figure 15-1 by the vertical distance between the price/yield curve for the non-callable bond and the callable bond.) The theoretical price of a non-callable bond can be determined by calculating the value of the call option using one of the option pricing models discussed in Chapter 19 and observing the price of the callable bond in the market.

---

[5] See Chapter 13 in Wilson and Fabozzi, *The New Corporate Bond Market.*

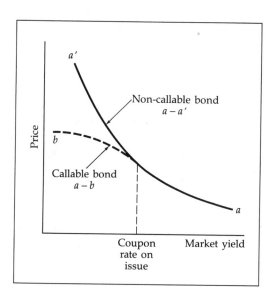

FIGURE 15-1
Price/Yield Curve for a Callable
Corporate Bond

Recall that some indentures have a sinking fund provision with a doubling option. The doubling option effectively reduces the bondholder's call protection because falling interest rates may make it advantageous for the issuer to exercise the option at the special sinking fund call price to retire a substantial portion of the high-cost outstanding issue. Thus, while the purpose of the sinking fund provision is to reduce credit risk by requiring the issuer to pay off the majority of the issue prior to the stated maturity date, the mandatory call provision also increases call risk.

Marketability Risk.   Any bond that is quoted continuously by a dealer is a marketable bond; there is a market for it. But investors who seek to implement trading and portfolio strategies want to know much more than that; they want to know how good the market is. Differences in the quality of markets for different corporate bond issues give a way to look at this.

The principal basis for grading the marketability of securities is the size of the spread between dealers' bid and offer prices. A narrow spread—say, one-quarter to one-half of 1%—indicates a very marketable issue. A wide spread—such as 2% or 3%—means low marketability. The principal determinant of the size of the spread is the volume of trading in an issue (i.e., the "thickness" of the market). This stems from the fact that a high frequency of arrival of new orders reduces the market maker's cost of holding inventories and mitigates the risk of unfavorable price movements while inventories are being held. The number of dealers moreover is more or less proportionate to the volume of trading. If there is a lot of business in a bond issue, a lot of dealers seek the business. A large volume of trading and a large number of dealers make a highly competitive market where bid–ask spreads are pressed downward.

Event Risk.   Occasionally the ability of an issuer to make interest and principal payments changes seriously and unexpectedly because of (1) a natural or industrial accident or some regulatory change, or (2) a takeover or corporate restructuring. These risks are referred to generically as *event risk.* Examples of the first type of event risk would be a change in the accounting treatment of loan losses for commercial banks or cancellation of nuclear plants by public utilities.

A good example of the second type of event risk is the 1988 takeover of RJR Nabisco for $25 billion through a financing technique known as a *leveraged buyout* (LBO). The new company took on a substantial amount of debt incurred to finance the acquisition of the firm.[6] In the case of RJR Nabisco, the debt and equity after the leveraged buyout were $29.9 and $1.2 billion, respectively. Because the corporation must service a larger amount of debt, its bond quality rating was reduced; RJR Nabisco's quality rating as assigned by Moody's dropped from A1 to B3. To see how much more investors demanded because of the company's new capital structure with a greater proportion of debt, look at Figure 15-2. The figure shows the impact of the initial LBO bid announcement on yield spreads for RJR Nabisco's debt. The yield spread to a benchmark Treasury increased from about 100 basis points to 350 basis points.

Event risk can have spillover effects on other firms. A nuclear accident, for example, will affect all utilities producing nuclear power. And in the case of takeovers, consider once again the RJR Nabisco LBO. An LBO of $25 billion was considered impractical prior to the RJR Nabisco LBO, but the RJR transaction showed that size was not an obstacle, and other large firms previously thought to be unlikely candidates for an LBO became fair game. To see the spillover effect, look at Figure 15-3, which shows how event risk fears caused yield spreads to widen for three large firms.

Term Structure of Credit Spreads

In Chapter 12 we discussed the term structure of interest rates for Treasury securities. Theoretical Treasury spot rates reflect the appropriate interest rate for a zero-coupon bond with no credit risk. When there is credit or default risk

---

[6] For a discussion of event risk associated with takeovers, see N.R. Vijayarghavan and Randy Snook, ''Takeover Event Risk and Corporate Bond Portfolio Management,'' in Frank J. Fabozzi (ed.), *Advances and Innovations in Bond and Mortgage Markets* (Chicago: Probus Publishing, 1989).

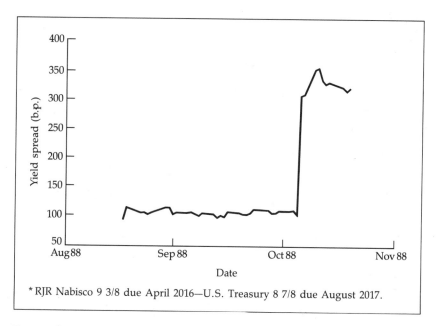

* RJR Nabisco 9 3/8 due April 2016—U.S. Treasury 8 7/8 due August 2017.

FIGURE 15-2

RJR Nabisco—Impact of the Initial LBO Bid Announcement on Yield Spreads.
Source: N. R. Vijayarghavan and Randy Snook, "Takeover Event Risk and Corporate Bond Portfolio Management," in Frank J. Fabozzi (ed.), *Advances and Innovations in Bond and Mortgage Markets* (Chicago: Probus Publishing, 1989), p. 55.

associated with the cash flow of a bond, as there is in the case of corporate bonds, a credit spread must be added to the risk-free spot rate. The question is: Should a constant credit spread be added to every risk-free spot rate, regardless of maturity, or should the credit spread differ depending on maturity? That is, if the spot rate for a 2-year Treasury security is 8% and for a 30-year Treasury security 9%, should the same credit spread be added to 8% and 9%, or should the credit spread added to 8% be different from that added to 9%?

In considering the proper approach to employ, we need to address the changing probability of default. If the probability of default per unit of time of a corporate bond is assumed to increase the farther into the future that the cash flow is to be received, adding a constant spread to each risk-free spot rate will undervalue the relatively less risky cash flows to be received in the near term and overvalue the relatively more risky cash flows to be received in the more distant future. There is no theory, however, that the probability of default increases over time in all economic environments.

One way to determine the relationship between the credit spread and

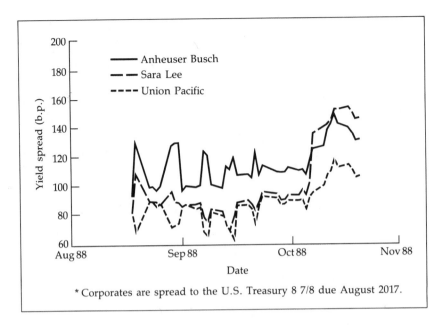

FIGURE 15-3
Anheuser Busch, Sara Lee and Union Pacific—Event Risk Fears and Widening Yield Spreads.
Source: N. R. Vijayarghavan and Randy Snook, "Takeover Event Risk and Corporate Bond Portfolio Management," in Frank J. Fabozzi (ed.), *Advances and Innovations in Bond and Mortgage Markets* (Chicago: Probus Publishing, 1989), p. 56.

maturity is to look at the yields on non-callable zero-coupon corporate bonds. Unfortunately, there are few such bonds traded, particularly at the long end of the term structure. Even where such bonds are observed, their yields also reflect a liquidity risk premium.

Litterman and Iben have developed a methodology for inferring the term structure of credit risk spreads from the prices of traded corporate bonds.[7] While a discussion of their methodology is beyond the scope of this chapter, their empirical results are worth noting. They find that the term structure of credit spreads in the corporate market is generally upward-sloping. This means that the market perceives higher probabilities of default in the more distant future.

---

[7] The original study is Robert Litterman and Thomas Iben, "Corporate Bond Valuation and the Term Structure of Credit Spreads," Financial Strategy Group, Goldman Sachs & Co., November 1988. An updated version was published with the same title in the Spring 1991 issue of the *Journal of Portfolio Management*.

Bonds with Special Features

Prior to the 1970s, the securities issued in the U.S. bond market had a simple structure. They had a fixed coupon rate and a fixed maturity date. The only option available to the issuer was the right to call all or part of the issue prior to the stated maturity date. The historically high interest rates that prevailed in the United States in the late 1970s and early 1980s, however, and the volatile interest rates since the 1970s ushered in new structures or increased use of special features that made issues more attractive to both borrowers and investors.

Convertible and Exchangeable Bonds. The conversion provision in a corporate bond issue grants the bondholder the right to convert the bond to a predetermined number of shares of common stock of the issuer. A convertible bond is therefore a corporate bond with a call option to buy the common stock of the issuer. Exchangeable bonds grant the bondholder the right to exchange the bonds for the common stock of a firm *other* than the issuer of the bond. For example, Dart & Kraft has an outstanding bond issue that is exchangeable for the common stock of Minnesota Mining and Manufacturing. (Dart & Kraft obtained the 3M common stock in exchange for the sale of Riker Laboratories.) Some Ford Motor Credit bonds are exchangeable for the common stock of the parent company, Ford Motor Company. A few issues are exchangeable into more than one security. General Cinema, for example, has an outstanding issue that is convertible into the common stock of R.J. Reynolds and Sea-Land Corporation.

The number of shares of common stock that the bondholder will receive from exercising the call option of a convertible bond or exchangeable bond is called the *conversion ratio*. The conversion privilege may be permitted for all or only some portion of the bond's life, and the conversion ratio may decline over time. It is always adjusted proportionately for stock splits and stock dividends.

Convertible issues are callable by the issuer. This is a valuable feature for the issuer, since an important reason for using convertibles is when a firm seeking to raise additional capital would prefer to raise equity funds but deems the current market price of its stock too undervalued so that selling stock would dilute the equity of current stockholders. So it issues a convertible setting the conversion ratio on the basis of a price it regards as acceptable. Once the market price reaches the conversion point the firm wants to see the conversion occur in view of the risk that the price may decline again. It has therefore an interest in forcing conversion, even though this is not in the interest of the owners of the security as its price is likely to be adversely affected by the call.

The price of a convertible bond should reflect the value of the embedded options. The two embedded options are (1) the call option on the stock that the investor has effectively purchased, and (2) the call option on the convertible bond that the investor has effectively sold to the corporate issuer.[8] That is, the convertible bondholder is in a long call position with respect to the common stock and in a short call position with respect to the bond issue.

Corporate takeovers add another risk to investing in convertible bonds. If an issuer is acquired by another company or by its own management (as in the case of a management-led leveraged buyout), the stock price may not appreciate sufficiently for the holders of the convertible bond to benefit from the conversion feature. As the stock of the acquired company may no longer trade after a takeover, the investor can be left with a bond that pays a lower coupon rate than comparable risk corporate bonds.

Issues of Debt with Warrants.   A bond may be issued with warrants attached as part of the offer. A warrant grants the holder the right to purchase a designated security at a specified price. Therefore, as we explained in Chapter 9, a warrant is simply a call option that permits the holder to purchase the common stock of the issuer of the debt or the common stock of a firm other than the issuer's. Alternatively, the warrant may grant the holder the right to purchase a debt obligation of the issuer. Warrants generally can be detached from the bond and sold separately. The typical warrant can be exercised with cash or by exchanging the debt at par. In the case of convertible and exchangeable bonds, only the bond may be used to exercise the option.

The warrant may permit the bondholder to buy common stock of the issuer, as does a convertible bond. The embedded call option in the convertible bond, however, cannot be sold separately from the bond, while a warrant can be. Thus, the holder of a bond and a warrant has a long position in the corporate bond of the issuer and a long position in a call option on the common stock of the issuer. The same is true of a unit of debt with warrants to buy common stock of a firm other than the issuer. The holder of a bond and a warrant in this case has a long position in the corporate bond of the issuer and a long position in a call option on the common stock of some other firm.

---

[8] A number of articles present models for valuing convertible bonds using an options approach: Michael Brennan and Eduardo Schwartz, "Convertible Bonds: Valuation and Optimal Strategies for Call and Conversion," *Journal of Finance* (December 1977), pp. 1699–1715; Jonathan Ingersoll, "A Contingent-Claims Valuation of Convertible Securities," *Journal of Financial Economics* (May 1977), pp. 289–322; Michael Brennan and Eduardo Schwartz, "Analyzing Convertible Bonds," *Journal of Financial and Quantitative Analysis* (November 1980), pp. 907–929; and George M. Constantinides, "Warrant Exercise and Bond Conversion in Competitive Markets," *Journal of Financial Economics* (September 1984), pp. 371–398.

Putable Bonds.   A putable bond grants the bondholder the right to sell the bond back to the issuer at par value on designated dates. The advantage to the bondholder is that, if interest rates rise after the issue date, thereby reducing the value of the bond, the bondholder can put the bond to the issuer for par. Thus, a putable corporate bond is a package composed of a non-putable corporate bond plus a long put option on the corporate bond. This will insure that the bond will stay close to par, somewhat like instruments earning a short-term floating rate, except that the non-putable bond also provides protection against deterioration in credit rating.

Zero-Coupon Bonds.   The first public offering of zero-coupon corporate bonds was by J.C. Penney Company, Inc., in April 1982.[9] Recall from Chapter 14 that the yield to maturity of a corporate bond when it is purchased indicates the accumulated terminal return the investor will realize if all coupon payments are reinvested at a rate equal to the yield to maturity. But the investor's actual return if a coupon corporate bond is held to maturity depends on the rate at which the coupon payments can be reinvested. That is, the investor faces reinvestment risk. We illustrated this risk in Chapter 11.

   In the case of a zero-coupon corporate bond, there are no coupon payments to reinvest, or all coupons are reinvested automatically by the issuer at the yield to maturity. So the investor faces no reinvestment risk—holding a zero-coupon bond to maturity results in a return equal to the yield to maturity at the time of purchase.

Floating-Rate Securities.   The coupon interest on floating-rate securities is reset periodically according to some predetermined benchmark. For example, the coupon rate may be reset every six months at a rate equal to a spread of 50 basis points over the six-month Treasury bill rate.

   Floating-rate securities are attractive to some institutional investors because they allow purchase of an asset with an income stream that closely matches the floating nature of some of their liabilities. In theory, a floating-rate security with frequent resets should trade at par if market participants think that the appropriate spread off the benchmark since the time of issuance has not changed. For example, suppose that a single-A-rated floating-rate security is issued with a coupon that resets every three months to 40 basis points over the three-month Treasury bill rate. If the perceived credit quality of this issuer, and hence the spread required by the market has

---

[9] A private offering of zero-coupon bonds was made by PepsiCo prior to this offering. As we explained in Chapter 3, new innovative structures often appear in the private placement market before they appear in public offerings.

remained constant, the issue should sell at par, as the interest it pays coincides with that demanded. If, on the other hand, it deteriorates, so that the market at the reset date wants 55 basis points over the three-month Treasury bill for this bond, the price of the issue will sell below par. The opposite could occur if the credit quality improves and the market is willing to accept a lower spread.

Some investors look at certain floating-rate instruments as a passive substitute for short-term holdings, particularly that part of a short-term portfolio that is maintained more or less consistently at certain minimum levels. Thus, floating-rate securities save on the costs of constant rollover of short-term securities as they reach maturity.

Why do corporations issue floating-rate securities? Closer matching of their income flows from floating-rate assets with floating-rate liabilities can be of major importance, especially with lenders such as banks, thrifts, and finance companies. Issuers can fix or lock in a spread between the cost of borrowed funds and the rate at which they are lent out. Another reason might be to avoid uncertainties associated with what could be an unreceptive market at some future date. The issuer can tap a new source for intermediate- to long-term funds at short-term rates, thereby making fewer trips to the marketplace and avoiding related issuance costs. Also, in the presence of inflation, a floating-rate security (rolled over if needed) may have a lower interest cost than a fixed-rate long-term security. The reason is that, with inflation, the long rate may incorporate a substantial premium against the uncertainty of future inflation and interest rates. Finally, as we shall see in Chapter 19, an issuer may find that it can issue a floating-rate security and change the payments from a floating-rate payment to a fixed-rate payment using an interest rate swap agreement. The issuer might choose this approach if the cost of the issue of a floating-rate security and then an interest rate swap will be less than the issuance of a fixed-rate security.

There may be other salient features to a floating-rate issue. For example, many floating-rate issues include a put option. Some issues are exchangeable into fixed-rate securities, either automatically at a certain date (often five years after issuance) or at the option of the issuer. A few issues are convertible into the common stock of the issuer. Some floating-rate issues have a ceiling or maximum interest rate on the coupon rate; some have a floor or minimum interest rate on the coupon rate.

Secondary Market

There are really two secondary corporate bond markets: the exchange market (the New York and American Stock Exchanges) and the over-the-counter (OTC) market. The great bulk of trading volume takes place in the OTC market, which is the market used by institutional investors and professional money managers.

As of 1987, there were 885 issuers and 3,346 corporate bond issues listed on the New York Stock Exchange (NYSE). The par value of all bonds listed on the NYSE was $1.65 billion. In 1986, the NYSE achieved an historical high average daily trading volume of $41.7 million. In 1987, average daily trading volume declined to $38.4 million. Compare this to average daily trading volume in the OTC market: $14.59 billion in 1986, $14.89 billion in 1987, and $13.18 billion in 1988.

The corporate bond market is subject to the same problems with respect to the public reporting of completed transactions and public information on reliable bid and ask prices as the Treasury securities market is.

Market convention for determining the number of days in a corporate bond coupon period and the number of days from the last coupon payment to settlement date differs from that for a Treasury coupon security. While a calendar year has 365 days (366 days in the case of a leap year), corporate bond interest is computed as if the year were 360 days. Each month in a corporate bond year is 30 days whether it is February, April, or August. A 12% coupon corporate bond pays $120 per year per $1,000 par value, accruing interest at $10 per month or $0.33333 per day. The accrued interest on a 12% corporate bond for three months is $30; for three months and 25 days, $38.33, and so forth. The corporate calendar is referred to as "30/360."

HIGH-YIELD SECTOR OF THE CORPORATE BOND MARKET

As we have noted, *high-yield bonds,* commonly called *junk bonds,* are issues with quality ratings below triple B. Bond issues in this sector of the market may have been rated investment grade at the time of issuance and have been downgraded subsequently to non-investment grade, or they may have been rated non-investment grade at the time of issuance. Bonds in the former category are commonly referred to as "fallen angels." Three examples of fallen angels are ITT World Communications, Interco, and RJR Nabisco. Downgrading of the last two issues came after the leveraged buyout that took the companies private and substantially increased their debt/equity ratios.

The modern high-yield market began in the later half of the 1970s.[10] The high-yield market grew from approximately $15 billion at year-end 1976 to approximately $205 billion by year-end 1989. Due to the market's dramatic successes (such as the $1.5 billion leveraged buyout [LBO] of Metromedia by John Kluge in 1984 and Kolberg Kravis Roberts & Company's 1986 LBO of

---

[10] The evolution of the high yield market since the early 1900s is described in J. Thomas Madden and Joseph Balestrino, "Evolution of the High-Yield Market," Chapter 2 in Frank J. Fabozzi (ed.), *The New High-Yield Debt Market* (NY: Harper & Row, 1991).

Beatrice, a company with many well-known brand names), the media began to report stories helping to bring to a peak investors' appetites. The market's early growth was dominated by a single investment bank, Drexel Burnham Lambert, and it was not until the mid-1980s that this firm began to experience serious competition from other investment banks, namely Merrill Lynch, Morgan Stanley, and First Boston.[11]

The Role of High-Yield Bonds in Corporate Finance

The introduction of original-issue high-yield bonds has been a very important financial innovation with wide impact throughout the financial system. There was a common view that high default risk bonds would not be attractive to the investing public, at least at interest rates that would be acceptable to the borrower. The view rested on the skewed nature of the outcomes offered by the instrument: The maximum return that an investor may obtain is capped by the coupon and face value, but the loss could be as large as the principal invested. It was the merit of Drexel Burnham Lambert, and particularly of Michael Milken of that firm, to disprove that view as evidenced by the explosive growth of that market.

Before development of the high-yield market, U.S. corporations that could not issue securities in the public debt market would borrow from commercial banks or finance companies on a short-term to intermediate-term basis or would be shut off from credit. With the advent of the high-yield bond structure, financing shifted from commercial banks to the public market. John Paulus, Chief Economist at Morgan Stanley, has estimated that about two-thirds of the $90 to $100 billion of the high-yield bonds issued represent simply a replacement of commercial bank borrowing.[12] He concludes that high-yield bonds are "no more a threat to the stability of the financial system than that bank debt itself was."

In essence, the high-yield bond market shifts the risk from commercial banks to the investing public in general. There are several advantages to such a shift. First, when commercial banks lend to high credit risk borrowers, that risk is accepted indirectly by all U.S. citizens, who may not wish to accept the risk. The reason is that commercial bank liabilities are backed by the Federal Deposit Insurance Company. If high credit risk corporations default on their loans, causing an FDIC bailout, all taxpayers eventually may have to pay. The liabilities of other investors (excluding thrifts that have invested in high yield bonds) are not backed by the U.S. government (and therefore U.S. citizens).

---

[11] Drexel Burnham Lambert underwrote more than 45% of new high-yield issues.

[12] As of November 1986 in a speech at a conference sponsored by *Citizens for a Sound Economy*.

The risks of this investing are accepted by the specific investor group willing to accept them.

The second advantage is that commercial bank loans are typically short-term floating-rate loans, which make debt financing less attractive to corporations. High-yield bond issues give corporations the opportunity to issue long-term, fixed-rate debt. Third, commercial banks set interest rates based on their credit analysis. When high-yield bonds are traded in a public market, the investing public establishes the interest rate.

Finally, the high-yield market opens the possibility of credit for some firms that previously had no means to it.

To see the potential for further growth in the high-yield bond market, consider the number of potential issuers. In 1989 Drexel Burnham Lambert estimated that there were about 23,000 companies in the U.S. with $35 million or more in revenue. Of this number, only 1,800 have sold bonds to the public: 800 are investment-grade issuers, and 1,000 are non-investment-grade issuers. This leaves more than 21,000 companies that have not issued public bonds, of whom DBL estimated that 95% would be non-investment-grade issuers.[13] Even if only a small proportion of these corporations issued bonds in the high-yield market, there would be a substantial growth in the market.

The high-yield sector represents about 25% of the total corporate bond market. Manufacturing firms represent the largest category of issuers, followed by firms in the finance, insurance, and real estate industries. The overall quality of new nonconvertible issues in this market sector has declined since 1982.

Corporate bond issuers use the proceeds from a bond sale for a number of purposes. These include working capital, expansion of facilities, refinancing of outstanding debt, and financing takeovers (mergers and acquisitions). In the case of non-investment-grade bonds, it is the use of the proceeds to finance takeovers (particularly hostile takeovers) that has aroused some public concern over the excessive use of debt by U.S. corporations.[14]

Several studies have examined how high-yield bond proceeds are actually being used. The United States General Accounting Office (GAO) reviewed a randomly selected sample of 124 high-yield bond issues from a universe of 333 issues offered in the 18-month period beginning January 1, 1986, categorized by reasons the issuer cited in its prospectus. One-half of the 124 firms stated that proceeds were to be used for one of the following reasons: (1) acquisition, (2) merger, (3) future acquisition, or (4) retirement of debt from

---

[13] *1989 High Yield Market Report: Financing America's Future*, p. 7.

[14] A hostile takeover is one in which the targeted firm's management resists the merger or acquisition.

previous mergers and acquisitions.[15] Further evidence is provided by First Boston, which found that the percentage of proceeds of new issues of junk bonds used for either leveraged buyouts, acquisition refinancing, or recapitalizations was about 48% in the first half of 1988. In the first half of 1989, however, there was a substantial rise in proceeds used for one of these three purposes to 80%.[16] Finally, a study by Paulus and Waite of Morgan Stanley found that, for the years 1987 to 1989, the annual proceeds raised were devoted to financing the market for corporate control—primarily leveraged buyouts. Prior to 1987, only about 15% of the proceeds were used for that purpose.[17]

Do U.S. corporations have excess debt? The empirical evidence does not suggest that the current debt level is high from an historical perspective. According to the Federal Reserve Board, which examined the debt-to-capital ratio from 1970 to 1988 for non-financial U.S. corporations, the ratio actually is lower now than in the 1970s.

The Board also looked at the interest coverage of non-financial corporations from 1970 to 1988—that is, the ratio of funds available to service debt to the interest cost. This ratio provides a measure of the ability of an issuer to meet its debt obligations. The higher the ratio, the less the burden for the issuer of the debt obligation, and the lower the risk of default. The coverage ratio has been lower in the 1980s than in the 1970s, indicating some increase in the debt burden relative to the 1970s, but the difference is neither large nor rising. Other studies have shown that the amount of debt used by U.S. corporations is far less than that used in Japan and Europe.[18]

Historical Performance of High-Yield Bonds

The *promised* yields offered on high-yield bonds have been substantial. For example, the yield spread over Treasury bonds between 1980 and 1989 ranged from 300 to 650 basis points, at least according to the Drexel Burnham Lambert 100 Bond Index. In late 1989 and 1990, a turbulent time for the high-yield sector, the yield spread increased to 700 to 800 basis points. Is this spread justified by a higher potential default rate? This intriguing question has been extensively investigated.

---

[15] United States General Accounting Office, "Issuers, Purchasers, and Purposes of High Yield, Non-Investment Grade Bonds" (February 1988), p. 31.

[16] "2nd Quarter Review," High Yield Research, First Boston Corporation, July 1989.

[17] John D. Paulus and Stephen R. Waite, "High Yield Bonds, Corporate Control, and Innovation," Chapter 1 in Fabozzi (ed.), *The New High-Yield Debt Market*.

[18] See, for example, Alan J. Auerbach, "Leveraged Buyouts: Corporate Debt and the Role of Tax Policy," Testimony before the Committee on Finance, U.S. Senate, January 25, 1989.

Most of the research on the high-yield bond sector focuses on default rates.[19] From an investment perspective, default rates by themselves are not of paramount significance: it is perfectly possible for a portfolio of high-yield bonds to suffer defaults and to outperform Treasuries at the same time, provided the yield spread of the portfolio is sufficiently high to offset the losses from default. Furthermore, because holders of defaulted bonds typically recover at least 30% of the face amount of their investment, the default *loss* rate is substantially lower than the default rate.[20] Therefore, focusing exclusively on default rates merely highlights the worst possible outcome that a diversified portfolio of high-yield bonds would suffer, assuming all defaulted bonds would be totally worthless. Assessing the potential rewards from investing in this market sector requires understanding not only default and default loss rates, but also total returns offered over various investment horizons.

First, let's look at what research has found for the default rate experience of low-quality corporate bonds. In their 1987 study, Altman and Nammacher found that the annual default rate for low-rated corporate debt was 2.15%, a figure that Altman has updated since to 2.40%. Drexel Burnham Lambert's (DBL) estimates have also shown default rates of about 2.40% per year. Asquith, Mullins, and Wolff, however, found that nearly one out of every

---

[19] See, for example, Edward I. Altman, "Measuring Corporate Bond Mortality and Performance," *Journal of Finance* (September 1989), pp. 909–922; Edward I. Altman, "Research Update: Mortality Rates and Losses, Bond Rating Drift," unpublished study prepared for a workshop sponsored by Merrill Lynch Merchant Banking Group, High Yield Sales and Trading, 1989; Edward I. Altman and Scott A. Nammacher, *Investing in Junk Bonds* (New York: John Wiley, 1987); Paul Asquith, David W. Mullins, Jr., and Eric D. Wolff, "Original Issue High Yield Bonds: Aging Analysis of Defaults, Exchanges, and Calls," *Journal of Finance* (September 1989), pp. 923–952; Marshall Blume and Donald Keim, "Risk and Return Characteristics of Lower-Grade Bonds 1977–1987," Working Paper (8-89), Rodney L. White Center for Financial Research, Wharton School, University of Pennsylvania, 1989; Marshall Blume and Donald Keim, "Realized Returns and Defaults on Lower-Grade Bonds," Rodney L. White Center for Financial Research, Wharton School, University of Pennsylvania, 1989; Bond Investors Association, "Bond Investors Association Issues Definitive Corporate Default Statistics," press release dated August 15, 1989; Gregory T. Hradsky and Robert D. Long, "High Yield Default Losses and the Return Performance of Bankrupt Debt," *Financial Analysts Journal* (July–August 1989), pp. 38–49; "Historical Default Rates of Corporate Bond Issuers 1970–1988," Moody's Special Report, July 1989 (New York: Moody's Investors Service); "High-Yield Bond Default Rates," *Standard & Poor's Creditweek*, August 7, 1989, pp. 21–23; David Wyss, Christopher Probyn, and Robert de Angelis, "The Impact of Recession on High-Yield Bonds," DRI-McGraw-Hill (Washington, D.C.: Alliance for Capital Access, 1989); and the 1984–1989 issues of *High Yield Market Report: Financing America's Futures* (New York and Beverly Hills: Drexel Burnham Lambert, Incorporated).

[20] For instance, a default rate of 5% and an average recovery rate of 30% imply a default loss rate of only 3.5% (70% of 5%).

three junk bonds defaults. The large discrepancy arises because the research-ers use three different definitions of "default rate"; even if applied to the same universe of bonds (which they are not), all three results could be valid simultaneously.[21]

Altman and Nammacher define the default rate as the par value of all high-yield bonds that defaulted in a given calendar year, divided by the total par value outstanding during the year. Their estimates (2.15% and 2.40%) are simple averages of the annual default rates over a number of years. DBL takes the cumulative dollar value of all defaulted high-yield bonds, divides by the cumulative dollar value of all high-yield issuance, and further divides by the weighted average number of years outstanding to obtain an average *annual* default rate. Asquith, Mullins, and Wolff use a *cumulative* default statistic. For all bonds issued in a given year, the default rate is the total par value of defaulted issues as of the date of their study, divided by the total par amount originally issued to obtain a cumulative default rate. Their result (that about one in three high-yield bonds default) is not normalized by the number of years outstanding.

While all three measures are useful indicators of bond default propensity, they are not directly comparable. Even when restated on an annualized basis, they do not all measure the same quantity. The default statistics from all studies, however, are surprisingly similar once cumulative rates have been annualized. A majority of studies place the *annual* default rates for all original issue high-yield bonds between 3% and 4%.[22]

But, as we indicated earlier, default rates do not tell us how the securities in this market sector have performed. While there have been a number of studies on total returns, the findings have not been uniform, as the periods and the bonds studied differ substantially among researchers. Furthermore, each study employs different assumptions about a broad range of important factors, including reinvestment rates, treatment of defaults, and accrued interest. Recent studies by Cheung, Bencivenga, and Fabozzi,[23] Blume, Keim, and Patel,[24] and Cornell and Green[25] provide empirical evidence on the

---

[21] As a parallel, we know that the mortality rate in the United States is currently less than 1% per year, but we also know that 100% of all humans (eventually) die.

[22] The Altman and Nammacher and Hradsky and Long studies cite significantly lower default rates, but they employ a definition of default rate that ignores the effect of aging on the propensity to default.

[23] Rayner Cheung, Joseph C. Bencivenga, and Frank J. Fabozzi, "Original Issue High-Yield Bonds: Historical Return and Default Experiences 1977–1989," Working Paper, January 1991.

[24] Marshall E. Blume, Donald B. Keim, and Sandeep A. Patel, "Returns and Volatility of Low-Grade Bonds 1977–1989," *Journal of Finance* (March 1991), pp. 49–74.

[25] Bradford Cornell and K. Green, "The Investment Performance of Low-Grade Bond Funds," *Journal of Finance* (March 1991), pp. 29–48.

performance of the high-yield bond market. The first two studies examine original-issue high-yield bonds. Both find that from 1977 (the start of the modern high-yield bond market) to December 31, 1989, the actual return on original-issue high yield bonds was greater than that on Treasuries and high-grade corporate bonds, but less than that on common stock. As a result, both studies conclude that there is no evidence that this sector of the bond market is systematically mispriced.

Cornell and Green do not look at individual bonds. Instead, for the period 1977 to 1989, they investigated the performance of mutual funds specializing in high-yield bonds. There are several drawbacks to this approach. First, there is an implicit assumption that the high-yield market is efficient so that fund managers cannot systematically find undervalued bonds. Second, fund managers are given the discretion to not fully allocate their funds to the high-yield market. To the extent that mutual fund managers pursue an active asset allocation strategy between the money market and long-term debt markets, performance will be misleading because it encompasses the timing ability of managers. The third disadvantage is that mutual fund managers are not restricted to original issue high-yield bonds (i.e., they can invest in fallen angels). Finally, there are management fees, administrative fees, and custodial fees that reduce returns. Despite these drawbacks, the Cornell and Green approach provides useful information about this sector of the bond market. They conclude that high-yield bonds are fairly priced relative to high-grade bonds after adjusting for risk.

Consequently, none of the studies seem to suggest that investing in the high-yield market offers exceptional value. Rather, long-run returns are in line with what capital market theory would suggest: in the long-run, high-yield bonds have outperformed both high grade corporate bonds and Treasuries but have been outperformed by common stock. Therefore, any claim of superior performance by high-yield bonds must be taken with the greatest caution.

High-Yield Bond Structures

There are several problems with generalizing the performance results we have discussed to today's high-yield bond market.[26] The one we want to call attention to here is that all the bonds in the earlier years investigated by studies cited had conventional structures; that is, the bonds paid a fixed coupon rate and were term bonds. Today, however, there are more complex bond structures in the junk bond area, particularly for bonds issued for LBO

---

[26] These problems are set forth in Laurie S. Goodman, "High-Yield Default Rates: Is There Cause for Concern?" *Journal of Portfolio Management* (Winter 1990), pp. 54–59.

financing and recapitalizations producing higher debt. The structures we describe below have features that are more attractive to issuers.

In an LBO or a recapitalization, the heavy interest payment burden that the corporation assumes places severe cash flow constraints on the firm. To reduce this burden, firms involved in LBOs and recapitalizations have issued bonds with deferred coupon structures that permit the issuer to avoid using cash to make interest payments for a period of three to seven years. There are three types of deferred coupon structures: (1) deferred-interest bonds, (2) step-up bonds, and (3) payment-in-kind bonds.

Deferred-interest bonds are the most common type of deferred coupon structure. These bonds sell at a deep discount and do not pay interest for an initial period, typically from three to seven years.[27] *Step-up bonds* do pay coupon interest, but the coupon rate is low for an initial period and then increases ("steps up") to a higher coupon rate. Finally, *payment-in-kind* (*PIK*) *bonds* give the issuer an option to pay cash at a coupon payment date or give the bondholder a similar bond (i.e., a bond with the same coupon rate and a par value equal to the amount of the coupon payment that would have been paid). The period during which the issuer can make this choice varies from five to ten years.[28]

In October 1987, a junk bond came to market with a structure allowing the issuer to reset the coupon rate so that the bond will trade at a predetermined price.[29] The coupon rate may reset annually or even more frequently, or reset only one time over the life of the bond. Generally, the coupon rate at reset time will be the average of rates suggested by two investment banking firms. The new rate will then reflect: (1) the level of interest rates at the reset date, and (2) the credit spread the market wants on the issue at the reset date. This structure is called an *extendable reset.*

Notice the difference between an extendable reset bond and a floating-rate issue as described earlier. In a floating-rate issue, the coupon rate resets according to a fixed spread over some benchmark, with the spread specified in the indenture. The amount of the spread reflects market conditions at the time the issue is offered. The coupon rate on an extendable reset bond by contrast is reset based on market conditions (as suggested by several investment banking firms) at the time of the reset date. Moreover, the new

---

[27] Because no interest is paid for the initial period, these bonds are sometimes referred to as *zero-coupon bonds.*

[28] For a further discussion of PIK bonds, see Laurie S. Goodman and Alan H. Cohen, "Payment-in-Kind Debentures: An Innovation," *Journal of Portfolio Management* (Winter 1989), pp. 9–19.

[29] Most of the bonds have a coupon reset formula that requires the issuer to reset the coupon so that the bond will trade at a price of $101.

coupon rate reflects the new level of interest rates and the new spread that investors seek.

The advantage to issuers of extendable reset bonds is again that they can be assured of a long-term source of funds based on short-term rates. For investors, the advantage of these bonds is that the coupon rate will reset to the market rate—both the level of interest rates and the credit spread, in principle keeping the issue at par. In fact, experience with reset bonds has not been favorable during the recent period of difficulties in the high-yield bond market. The sudden substantial increase in default risk has meant that the rise in the rate needed to keep the issue at par was so large that it would have insured the bankruptcy of the firm. As a result, the rise in the coupon rate has been insufficient to keep the issue at the stipulated price.

Finally, there are high-yield structures collateralized by a pool of high-yield corporate bonds and with multiple classes of bondholders. These are called *collateralized bond obligations*. The bond structure in this case is similar to the collateralized mortgage obligations and asset-backed obligations to be discussed in Chapter 18.[30]

Investors in High-Yield Bonds

A GAO study interviewed investment banking firms to estimate what percentage certain investor classes held of all high-yield bonds in 1987. The results are as follows:[31]

Mutual funds, money managers	32%
Insurance companies	30
Pension funds	10
Individuals	10
Savings and loans	7
Foreign investors	3
Corporations	3
Securities dealers	1
Other	4
Total	100%

These estimates come from Drexel Burnham Lambert, the largest underwriter of high-yield bonds at the time. Salomon Brothers, another underwriter of high-yield bonds, indicated that 33% to 50% of the bonds were

---

[30] For a detailed explanation of collateralized bond obligations, see Robert Gerber, "Collateralized Bond Obligations," Chapter 6 in Fabozzi (ed.), *The New High-Yield Debt Market*.

[31] "Issuers, Purchasers, and Purposes of High Yield, Non-Investment Grade Bonds," p. 20.

held by mutual funds, about 10% to 20% were held by insurance companies, with the balance owned by individuals, pension funds, savings and loan associations, and foreign investors.

Regardless of the data source, mutual funds that specialize in high-yield bonds represent the largest group of investors, and there has been considerable growth in this sector. There were 23 high-yield bond mutual funds as of December 31, 1981, with total assets of $3.1 billion. By September 30, 1987, the number of mutual funds had increased to 72, representing total assets of $30.2 billion.[32] By 1988 the number of mutual funds had risen further to 86.[33]

As of December 31, 1986, life insurance companies were estimated to hold $33.4 billion, and property and casualty insurance companies $3.9 billion, of high-yield bonds. This would have represented approximately 3.5% and 0.9% of the assets of life insurance and property and casualty insurance companies, respectively.[34] The Department of Labor estimates pension fund assets to total about $1.4 trillion. Pension funds may invest perhaps 10% in high-yield bonds, implying holdings of roughly $14 billion. Commercial banks that are federally insured are discouraged by regulation from investing in high-yield bonds. While federally insured thrifts have not been permitted to invest in high-yield bonds since August 4, 1989, and must rid themselves of existing holdings by August 4, 1994, the amount that thrifts held almost doubled from $5.7 billion in June 1985 to $11.1 billion in September 1987. Of the 149 thrifts that held high-yield bonds as of September 1987, 10 held almost 78% ($8.7 billion) of the total.[35]

MEDIUM-TERM NOTES

A medium-term note is a corporate debt instrument, with the unique characteristic that notes are offered continuously to investors by an agent of the issuer. Investors can select from several maturity bands: 9 months to 1 year, more than 1 year to 18 months, more than 18 months to 2 years, and so on up to 30 years. Medium-term notes are registered with the Securities and Exchange Commission under Rule 415 (the shelf registration rule). Registering under Rule 415 gives the issuer the maximum flexibility for issuing securities on a continuous basis.

---

[32] Ibid., p. 20. The data were provided to the GAO by Lipper Analytical Services.

[33] Cornell and Green, "The Investment Performance of Low-Grade Bond Funds."

[34] Ibid., p. 20. The data were provided by the National Association of Insurance Commissioners, a group that represents state insurance commissioners.

[35] As reported in Federal Home Loan Bank Board thrift financial reports.

The yield offered on a medium-term note depends on (1) the particular maturity selected by the investor, (2) the Treasury yield curve at the time of offering, and (3) the credit risk premium demanded by the market, which depends on maturity. In other words, the medium-term note will be priced at a spread to the Treasury yield curve at the time of the offering. Medium-term notes typically are issued at par.

According to estimates reported by Merrill Lynch, investment companies are by far the largest institutional investors in medium-term notes. As of December 1989, of the more than 7,000 investors in medium-term notes, 46% were investment companies.[36] The second largest investor group is banks and bank trust departments (21%), followed by insurance companies (12%).

The medium-term note was pioneered by Merrill Lynch in 1981 to fill the funding gap between commercial paper and long-term bonds.[37] The first medium-term note issuer was Ford Motor Credit company. By 1983, GMAC and Chrysler Financial used Merrill Lynch as an agent to issue medium-term notes. Subsequent growth of the domestic medium-term note market and its importance as a funding source can be seen by comparing it to the amount of domestic public debt issued.[38] In 1982, when the first full-year medium-term notes were sold, $3.8 billion was offered, less than 10% of the $36.8 billion of domestic public debt issued. In sharp contrast, by 1989 the amount of domestic medium-term notes issued exceeded the issuance of domestic public debt: $118.4 billion versus $108.7 billion. In that year, 24.1% or $28.5 billion of the medium-term notes issued had maturities from nine months to two years; 50.1%, or $59.3 billion, had maturities between two and five years. Thus, in 1989 alone $87.8 billion (74.2%) of the medium-term notes issued had maturities between nine months and five years.[39]

As of December 31, 1989, the amount of medium-term notes outstanding was $339 billion. Of this amount, $261 billion was underwritten by Merrill Lynch.[40] Issuers in the market include finance companies, banks or bank holding companies, industrial companies, thrifts, utilities, and sovereign or

---

[36] The source of these data is a description of issuers included in "Money Market Instruments" (New York: Merrill Lynch, 1989).

[37] Actually, GMAC first used medium-term notes in 1972 to fund automobile loans with maturities of five years and less. The medium-term notes were issued directly to investors without the use of an agent.

[38] This includes non-convertible, dollar-denominated debt, excluding junk bonds, mortgage-backed securities, and asset-backed securities. The information was obtained from IDD Information Services.

[39] "Money Market Instruments."

[40] Ibid.

government agencies. As of December 1989, finance companies offered the largest number of programs, followed by banks or bank holding companies, and then industrials.[41]

The typical issuer of medium-term notes has a high quality rating. The system used by commercial rating companies to rate medium-term notes issued by corporations is the same as that used for corporate bonds. Usually the rating matches the bond rating of the corporate issue with the same seniority level. Consequently, unsecured medium-term notes usually carry the same rating as the corporate issuer's unsecured bonds; secured medium-term notes typically carry the same rating as the corporate issuer's secured bonds. While at one time restricted to high-rated issuers, the medium-term note market has been opened up to lower-rated issuers through use of credit enhancements such as letters of credit or guarantees, or by collateralizing the issue with high-quality assets.

Merrill Lynch's offerings provide a good example of the types of medium-term note programs available. As of February 1990, Merrill Lynch offered the following options: (1) fixed-rate MTNs, (2) floating-rate MTNs, (3) credit-supported MTNs, (4) collateralized MTNs, (5) amortizing notes, and (6) multicurrency MTNs.[42]

Fixed-rate MTNs pay interest semiannually, on a 30/360 day basis, just as other corporate bonds. The yield offered is some spread over a comparable-maturity Treasury security.

Floating-rate MTNs can be selected with monthly, quarterly, or semiannual reset periods. There are a wide variety of indexes that the investor can select from: LIBOR, commercial paper composite rate, Treasury bills, or prime rate. The spread that is added to or subtracted from the index selected will depend on the issuer's credit rating.

Credit-supported MTNs are backed by either an irrevocable letter of credit or some other guarantee, with the rating depending on the rating of the entity furnishing the credit support. Medium-term note issuers such as thrifts have issued MTNs collateralized by mortgage-backed securities.[43] Despite the lower credit rating of thrifts, overcollateralization has resulted in these issues receiving the highest credit rating.

Amortized notes offer an investor equal periodic dollar payments over the life of the issue. The payments include both principal and interest, and are

---

[41] Ibid.

[42] The information about these programs is given in "Medium-Term Notes: An Investment Opportunity" (NY: Merrill Lynch Money Markets, Inc.) and "Money Market Instruments."

[43] Mortgage-backed securities are discussed in Chapter 18.

structured so that the note is fully repaid when the final payment is made. Thus, an amortized note has a structure similar to a mortgage loan.[44] Amortized notes typically are unsecured corporate obligations. An advantage of this form of medium-term note is that the credit risk exposure of the investor declines as each payment is made by the issuer.

Multicurrency MTNs are non-dollar-denominated securities, with more than 10 foreign currencies to choose from. The investor will be paid in U.S. dollars, however, based on the exchange rate prevailing at the time of payment. A designated exchange rate agent converts interest and principal payments from the foreign currency into U.S. dollars.

PREFERRED STOCK

Preferred stock is a class of stock, not a debt instrument, but it shares characteristics of both common stock and debt. Like the holder of common stock, the preferred stockholder is entitled to dividends. Unlike those on common stock, however, dividends are a specified percentage of par or face value.[45] The percentage is called the dividend rate; it need not be fixed, but may float over the life of the issue.

Failure to make preferred stock dividend payments cannot force the issuer into bankruptcy. Should the issuer not make the preferred stock dividend payment, usually made quarterly, one of two things can happen, depending on the terms of the issue. The dividend payment can accrue until it is fully paid. Preferred stock with this feature is called cumulative preferred stock. If a dividend payment is missed and the securityholder must forgo the payment, the preferred stock is said to be non-cumulative preferred stock. Failure to make dividend payments may result in imposition of certain restrictions on management. For example, if dividend payments are in arrears, preferred stockholders might be granted voting rights.

Unlike debt, payments made to preferred stockholders are treated as a distribution of earnings. This means that they are not tax-deductible to the corporation under the current tax code. Interest payments are tax-deductible, not dividend payments. While this raises the after-tax cost of funds if a corporation issues preferred stock rather than borrowing, there is a factor that reduces the cost differential: a provision in the tax code exempts 70% of

---

[44] See Chapter 17.

[45] Almost all preferred stock limits the securityholder to the specified amount. Historically, there have been issues entitling the preferred stockholder to participate in earnings distribution beyond the specified amount (based on some formula). Preferred stock with this feature is referred to as non-participating preferred stock.

qualified dividends from federal income taxation if the recipient is a qualified corporation. For example, if Corporation A owns the preferred stock of Corporation B, for each $100 of dividends received by A, only $30 will be taxed at A's marginal tax rate. The purpose of this provision is to mitigate the effect of double taxation of corporate earnings. There are two implications of this tax treatment of preferred stock dividends. First, the major buyers of preferred stock are corporations seeking tax-advantaged investments. Second, the cost of preferred stock issuance is lower than it would be in the absence of the tax provision because the tax benefits are passed through to the issuer by the willingness of buyers to accept a lower dividend rate.

Preferred stock has some important similarities with debt, particularly in the case of cumulative preferred stock: (1) the returns to preferred stockholders promised by the issuer are fixed, and (2) preferred stockholders have priority over common stockholders with respect to dividend payments and distribution of assets in the case of bankruptcy. (The position of noncumulative preferred stock is considerably weaker.) It is because of this second feature that preferred stock is called a senior security. It is senior to common stock. On a balance sheet, preferred stock is classified as equity.

Almost all preferred stock has a sinking fund provision, and some preferred stock is convertible into common stock. Preferred stock may be issued without a maturity date. This is called *perpetual preferred stock*.

As we have noted, the estimated size of the domestic corporate bond market is $1.4 trillion. In contrast, as of 1988 the 1,370 preferred stock issues outstanding had a par value of only $57 billion, based on Federal Reserve Board estimates. The amount of medium-term notes issued in 1989 alone was more than double the amount of preferred stock outstanding. For the period 1982 to 1988, $45 billion of preferred stock was issued, as can be seen from Table 15-4.[46] In 1988, the average issue size was $71 million compared to $162 million for corporate bonds.

Historically, utilities have been the major issuers of preferred stock, accounting for more than half of each year's issuance. Since 1985, major issuers have become financially oriented companies—finance companies, banks, thrifts, and insurance companies. In 1985 and 1987, for example, only 10% of preferred stock issued was utility stock.

The same five commercial companies that assign ratings to corporate bond issues also rate preferred stock issues.

---

[46] Richard S. Wilson, "Nonconvertible Preferred Stock," Chapter 16 in *The Handbook of Fixed Income Securities*.

TABLE 15-4 PREFERRED STOCK FINANCING VOLUME BY ISSUER TYPE (1982–1988)								
TYPE AND NO. OF ISSUE	TOTAL (IN MILLIONS)	1988	1987	1986	1985	1984	1983	1982
Fixed dividend	$11,726.47	$1,122.50	$2,896.50	$2,259.63	$1,066.60	$ 463.00	$1,609.50	$2,308.74
No. of issues	199	18	41	36	10	11	33	50
Adjustable rate	$13,354.90	$ 457.46	$ 991.06	$ 513.00	$1,561.34	$2,632.89	$4,375.94	$2,823.21
No. of issues	147	5	8	10	19	33	48	24
Auction market	$16,761.50	$3,510.50	$3,344.50	$5,559.50	$3,797.00	$ 550.00	—	—
No. of issues	236	58	48	69	54	7	—	—
Remarketed	$ 3,345.00	$2,010.00	$ 990.00	$ 220.00	$ 125.00	—	—	—
No. of issues	40	19	15	4	2	—	—	—
Total volume	$45,187.87	$7,100.46	$8,222.06	$8,552.13	$6,549.94	$3,645.89	$5,985.44	$5,131.95
Total issues	622	100	112	119	85	51	81	74

Types of Preferred Stock

There are three types of preferred stock: (1) fixed-rate preferred stock, (2) adjustable-rate preferred stock, and (3) auction and remarketed preferred stock. Table 15-4 shows the issuance of each type of preferred stock for the years 1982–1988. Before 1982, all publicly issued preferred stock was fixed-rate preferred stock. In May of 1982, the first adjustable-rate preferred stock issue was sold in the public market.[47]

Adjustable-Rate Preferred Stock.   The dividend rate on an adjustable-rate preferred stock (ARPS) is fixed quarterly and based on a predetermined spread from the highest of three points on the Treasury yield curve. The predetermined spread is called the *dividend reset spread*. The three points on the yield curve (called the benchmark rate) to which the dividend reset spread is either added or subtracted is the highest of: (1) the three-month Treasury bill rate, (2) the two-year constant maturity rate, or (3) a 10-year or 30-year constant maturity rate.[48] The motivation for linking the dividend rate to the highest of the three points on the Treasury yield curve is to provide the investor with protection against unfavorable shifts in the yield curve.

Most ARPS are perpetual, with a floor and ceiling imposed on the dividend rate of most issues. Because most ARPS are not putable, however, ARPS can trade below par if after issuance the spread demanded by the market to reflect the issuer's credit risk is greater than the dividend reset spread.

As can be seen in Table 15-4, for the years 1983 and 1984 the volume and number of issues of ARPS exceeded that of fixed-rate preferred stock. The major issuers of ARPS have been bank holding companies. For example, of the 105 ARPS issued in 1982–1984, for a total par value of $9.8 billion, 49 were issued by bank holding companies, with a total par value of about $4.9 billion.[49] There are two reasons that bank holding companies have become major issuers of ARPS. First, floating-rate obligations provide a better liability match, given the floating-rate nature of their assets. Second, bank holding companies are seeking to strengthen their capital positions, and regulators permit bank holding companies to count perpetual preferred stock as part of

---

[47] Private placement of ARPS occurred as early as 1978—once again illustrating how an innovation is first developed in this market. For historical background on the development of the ARPS market, see Richard S. Wilson, "Adjustable Rate Preferred Stocks," Chapter 3 in Frank J. Fabozzi (ed.), *Floating Rate Instruments: Characteristics, Valuation and Portfolio Strategies* (Chicago: Probus Publishing, 1986).

[48] The Treasury constant maturity rate is reported in the Federal Reserve Report H.15(519). It is based on the closing market bid yields on actively traded Treasury securities.

[49] Wilson, op. cit, Table 13-1.

their primary capital. Issuing ARPS provides not only a better asset/liability match, but also permits bank holding companies to improve primary capital without having to issue common stock.

Auction and Remarketed Preferred Stock.   The popularity of ARPS declined when instruments began to trade below their par value—because the dividend reset rate is determined at the time of issuance, not by market forces. In 1984, a new type of preferred stock, auction preferred stock (APS), was designed to overcome this problem, particularly for corporate treasurers who sought tax-advantaged short-term instruments to invest excess funds.[50] The dividend rate on APS is set periodically, as with ARPS, but the dividend rate is established through an auction process.[51] Participants in the auction consist of current holders and potential buyers. The dividend rate that participants are willing to accept reflects current market conditions.

In the case of remarketed preferred stock (RP), the dividend rate is determined periodically by a remarketing agent who resets the dividend rate so that any preferred stock can be tendered at par and be resold (remarketed) at the original offering price. An investor has the choice of dividend resets every seven days or every 49 days.

The success of these two financial innovations—APS and RP—is clear in Table 15-4. Since 1985, APS and RP have become the dominant type of preferred stock issued. In 1988, for example, 77% of the issues were either APS or RP.

SUMMARY

Corporate bonds are debt obligating a corporation to pay periodic interest with full repayment at maturity. The promises of the corporate bond issuer and the rights of the investors are set forth in the bond indenture. Provisions to be specified include call and sinking fund provisions, as well as limitations on further debt and on management powers.

Security for bonds may be real or personal property. A mortgage bond grants the bondholders a lien against the pledged assets. Collateral trust bonds are secured by securities owned by the issuer. Debenture bonds are not secured by a specific pledge of property; bondholders have the claim of

---

[50] Each investment bank developed its own trademark name for APS. The instrument developed by Shearson Lehman/American Express was called Money Market Preferred (MMP). Salomon Brothers called it Dutch Auction Rate Transferable Securities (DARTS).

[51] The auction process is described in Richard S. Wilson, "Money Market Preferred Stock," Chapter 4 in *Floating Rate Instruments,* pp. 85–88.

general creditors on all assets of the issuer not pledged specifically to secure other debt. Subordinated debenture bonds are issues that rank after secured debt, after debenture bonds, and often after some general creditors in their claim on assets and earnings.

The risks associated with investing in corporate bonds are interest rate risk, reinvestment risk, purchasing power risk, credit risk, call risk, marketability risk, and event risk. Credit risk can be gauged by the quality rating assigned by the commercial rating agencies. Call risk is a disadvantage to bondholders because it exposes the holder to (1) uncertainty about the timing of cash flows, (2) reinvestment risk, and (3) price compression. Event risk refers to the possibility of an event that leads investors to doubt the ability of an issuer to make interest and principal payments. Event risk can occur because of a natural or industrial accident, or a takeover or corporate restructuring.

Special corporate bond features include convertible and exchangeable bonds, units of debt with warrants, putable bonds, zero-coupon bonds, and floating-rate securities.

Junk bonds or high-yield bonds are issues with quality ratings below triple-B. Several studies have demonstrated that a diversified portfolio of high-yield bonds historically would have generated returns greater than Treasury securities and investment-grade corporate bonds but less than common stock. Recent years have seen introduction of several complex bond structures in the junk bond area, particularly bonds issued for LBO financing and recapitalizations producing higher levels of debt to equity. These include deferred-coupon bonds (deferred-interest bonds, step-up bonds, and payment-in-kind bonds) and extendable reset bonds. The high-yield bond market has permitted the shifting of corporate borrowing from commercial banks to the public bond market.

While corporate bond trading takes place both on exchanges and in the OTC market, the real market is the OTC market. Trading volume in this market swamps that of exchange trading.

Medium-term notes are corporate debt obligations offered on a continuous basis. The maturities range from nine months to 30 years and have provided a financing alternative with maturities between those of commercial paper and long-term bonds. By 1989 the amount of domestic medium-term notes issued exceeded the issuance of domestic publicly issued corporate debt.

Preferred stock as a class of stock shares characteristics of both common stock and debt. Because a special provision in the tax code allows taxation of only a portion of dividends when they are received by a corporation, the major buyers of preferred stock are corporations. There are three types of preferred stock besides the traditional fixed-rate preferred stock. *Adjustable-*

rate preferred stock pays dividends according to a predetermined spread over the highest of three points on the Treasury yield curve. *Auction preferred stock* is designed to overcome the fact that ARPS can trade below par value; its dividend rate resets periodically based on the results of an auction. The dividend rate of *remarketed preferred stock* is reset periodically by a remarketing agent so that any preferred stock tendered can be resold (remarketed) at the original offering price.

QUESTIONS

1. **a.** What are the disadvantages of investing in a callable bond?
   b. What is the advantage to the issuer of issuing a callable bond?
   c. What is the difference between a non-callable bond and a non-refundable bond?

2. "A sinking fund provision in a bond issue benefits the investor." Do you agree with this statement?

3. What is the difference between a convertible bond and an exchangeable bond?

4. **a.** "A floating-rate note will always trade in the market at par value." Do you agree with this statement?
   b. "A floating-rate note and an extendable reset bond both have coupon rates readjusted periodically. Therefore, they are basically the same instrument." Do you agree with this statement?

5. A Merrill Lynch note structure called a Liquid Yield Option Note (LYON) has the following characteristics:
   - it is a zero-coupon instrument
   - it is convertible into the common stock of the issuer
   - it is putable
   - it is callable
   - it is a subordinated note
   a. Describe all the embedded options granted to the corporation that issues a LYON.
   b. Describe all the embedded options granted to the investor who purchases a LYON.

    c. The conversion ratio is fixed for the entire life of the note. If investors wish to convert to the shares of the issuer, they must exchange the LYON for the note. As a result, the conversion price increases over time. Why?

    d. What is a meant by a subordinated note?

6.   **a.** What is a payment-in-kind bond?

    b. An investor who purchases a payment-in-kind bond will find that increased interest rate volatility will have an adverse economic impact. If interest rates rise substantially, there will be an adverse consequence. So too will a substantial decline in interest rates have adverse consequences. Why?

7.   **a.** Why are corporate treasurers the main buyers of preferred stock?

    b. What was the reason for the popularity of auction and remarketed preferred stock?

LEARNING OBJECTIVES

After reading this chapter you will understand:

- who buys municipal securities and why the securities are attractive investments to these buyers.

- the types of municipal securities and why they are issued.

- the risks unique to investors in municipal securities.

- the primary and secondary markets for municipal securities.

- the yield relationship between municipal securities and taxable bonds.

- the yield relationship between municipal securities within the municipal market.

- the degree of regulation of the municipal securities market.

I n this chapter we discuss municipal securities and the market in which they trade. Municipal bonds are securities issued by state and local governments and by their creations, such as "authorities" and special districts. There are both tax-exempt and taxable municipal bonds. Interest on tax-exempt municipal bonds is exempt from federal income taxation. The large majority of municipal bonds outstanding are tax-exempt. Interest may or may not be taxable at the state and local level. Municipal securities come in a variety of types, with different redemption features, credit risks, and liquidity.

Municipal securities are issued for various purposes. Short-term notes typically are sold in anticipation of the receipt of funds from taxes or proceeds from the sale of a bond issue, for example. The proceeds from the sale of short-term notes permit the issuing municipality to cover seasonal and temporary imbalances between outlays for expenditures and tax inflows. Municipalities issue long-term bonds as the principal means for financing both (1) long-term capital projects such as the construction of schools, bridges, roads, and airports, and (2) long-term budget deficits that arise from current operations.

INVESTORS IN MUNICIPAL SECURITIES

As the single most important advantage of municipal securities to investors is the exemption of interest income from federal taxation, the investor groups that have purchased these securities are those who benefit the most from this exemption. The three categories of investors dominating the municipal securities market are households (retail investors), commercial banks, and property and casualty insurance companies. Although these three groups have dominated the market since the mid-1950s, their relative participation has shifted. It is the tax code that influences the relative demand for municipal securities. The two most recent pieces of legislations that have influenced the demand for municipal securities are the Tax Reform Act of 1986 and the Tax Act of 1990.[1]

Households (Retail Investors)

Retail investor participation in the municipal securities market has fluctuated considerably since 1972. With some interruptions, retail investor market share had been trending downward, but in 1981 the trend was reversed, and

---

[1] For a detailed discussion of the implications of the 1986 tax act on investor demand, see Appendix A of Sylvan G. Feldstein and Frank J. Fabozzi, *Dow Jones-Irwin Guide to Municipal Bonds* (Homewood, IL: Dow Jones-Irwin, 1987).

individual investors are now the largest holders of municipal securities. Individual investors may purchase municipal securities directly or through mutual funds and unit trusts.[2]

The Tax Reform Act of 1986 has two provisions that, on balance, make municipal securities more attractive to individual investors. On the one hand, the maximum marginal tax rate for individuals was reduced from 50% prior to the tax revision to 28% by 1988. In addition, investors were required to include certain tax-exempt municipal interest income as tax preference items that would be subject to an alternative minimum tax. Both the reduction in maximum marginal tax rates and the potential taxation of municipal interest income under the alternative minimum tax reduced the value of the tax exemption feature. At the same time, however, the Tax Reform Act of 1986 eliminated or reduced the attractiveness of other investment vehicles that individual investors were using to shelter investment income from taxation.

The 1990 Tax Act served to increase the attractiveness of municipal securities by raising the maximum marginal tax rate to 33%. In fact, the effective tax rate is higher than 33% because of various limitations placed on deductions that households may take.

Commercial Banks

In the 1960s several studies of the investment behavior of banks indicated that their demand for municipal securities can best be described as a "residual demand."[3] After commercial banks have met their reserve obligations, remaining funds are placed either in loans or income-producing taxable and tax-exempt securities. If loan demand is sufficiently strong, banks may sell portions of their municipal holdings to satisfy customer demand. Conversely, when loan demand is weak, banks will tend to increase their purchase of municipal securities.

While both taxable and non-taxable securities can be purchased, historically the after-tax yield on municipal securities has been more attractive. While individual investors are not entitled to deduct any interest cost that they incur to purchase municipal securities,[4] commercial banks (before the Tax Reform Act of 1986) were entitled to deduct 80% of the interest cost of

---

[2] Unit trusts are explained in Chapter 4.

[3] Donald R. Hodgman, *Commercial Bank Loan and Investment Policy* (Urbana, IL: University of Illinois Bureau of Economic and Business Research, 1963), pp. 38–40; and Stephen M. Goldfeld, *Commercial Bank Behavior and Economic Activity* (New York: Elsevier-North Holland Publishing, 1966).

[4] Specifically, the Internal Revenue Code specifies that interest paid or accrued on "indebtedness incurred or continued to purchase or carry obligations, the interest on which is wholly exempt from taxes," is not tax-deductible.

funds used to purchase municipal bonds. The 1986 Tax Act repealed this special exemption for banks for securities purchased after August 7, 1986. As a result, the demand for municipal securities by banks has declined dramatically.

Commercial banks hold the obligations of state and local governments for a variety of reasons besides shielding income from federal taxation. Most state and local governments mandate that public deposits at a bank be collateralized. Although Treasury or federal agency securities can serve as collateral, in fact the use of municipal securities is favored. Obligations of state and local governments may also be used as collateral when commercial banks borrow at the discount window of the Federal Reserve. Furthermore, banks frequently serve as underwriters or market makers of municipal securities, and these functions require maintaining inventories of these securities.

Property and Casualty Insurance Companies

Purchases of municipal securities by property and casualty companies are primarily a function of their underwriting profits and investment income. Company profitability depends primarily upon the difference between revenues generated from insurance premiums and investment income and the cost of claims filed, and claims on property and casualty companies are difficult to anticipate. Varying court awards for liability suits, the effect of inflation upon replacement and repair costs, and the unpredictability of weather are the chief factors that affect the level of claims experienced. Premiums for various types of insurance also are subject to competitive pressures and to approval from state insurance commissioners.

As can be expected then, the profitability of property and casualty companies is cyclical. Normally, intense price competition follows highly profitable years. During these high-income periods, property and casualty companies typically step up their purchases of municipal securities in order to shield income from income taxes. Lower rate increases for premiums are usually granted by state insurance commissioners during this time. Underwriting losses traditionally begin to exact a toll, as premium and investment income fails to keep pace with claims settlement costs. As underwriting losses mount, property and casualty insurance companies curtail their investment in municipal securities. The profitability cycle is completed when they win rate increases from state commissioners after sustaining continued underwriting losses.

The 1986 Tax Act includes several provisions that reduced, but did not eliminate, the demand for municipal securities by property and casualty insurance companies.[5]

---

[5] For an explanation of these provisions, see Feldstein and Fabozzi, *Dow Jones-Irwin Guide to Municipal Bonds*, p. 220.

TYPES AND FEATURES OF MUNICIPAL SECURITIES

There are basically two different types of municipal bond security structures: general obligation bonds and revenue bonds. There are also securities that share characteristics of both general obligation and revenue bonds.

General Obligation Bonds

General obligation bonds are debt instruments issued by states, counties, special districts, cities, towns, and school districts. Usually, a general obligation bond is secured by the issuer's unlimited taxing power.[6] For smaller governmental entities such as school districts and towns, the only available unlimited taxing power is on property. For larger general obligation bond issuers such as states and big cities, tax revenue sources are more diverse, and may include corporate and individual income taxes, sales taxes, and property taxes. The security pledges for these larger issuers, such as states, are sometimes referred to as being *full faith and credit obligations.*

Additionally, certain general obligation bonds are secured not only by the issuer's general taxing powers to create revenues accumulated in a general fund, but also by certain identified fees, grants, and special charges, which provide additional revenues from outside the general fund. Such bonds are known as *double-barreled* in security because of the dual nature of the revenue sources.

Revenue Bonds

The second basic type of security structure is found in a revenue bond. Such bonds are issued for either project or enterprise financings where the bond issuers pledge to the bondholders the revenues generated by the operating projects financed. In 1970, only 33.5%, or $5.96 billion of the total amount of municipal bonds issued in that year, were revenue bonds; in 1989, 65.6%, or $68.58 billion, of all municipals issued were revenue bonds.[7] Following are examples of revenue bonds.[8]

---

[6] Not all general obligation bonds are secured by unlimited taxing powers. Some are backed by taxes that are limited as to revenue sources and maximum property-tax millage amounts. Such bonds are known as *limited-tax general obligation bonds.*

[7] These data are derived from the Merrill Lynch Fixed Income Strategy Report, First Quarter 1990, p. 22.

[8] The descriptions are taken from Sylvan G. Feldstein and Frank J. Fabozzi, "Municipal Bonds," Chapter 12 in *The Handbook of Fixed Income Securities* (Homewood, IL: Dow Jones-Irwin, 1987), pp. 292–294.

Airport Revenue Bonds.   The revenues securing these bonds usually come from either traffic-generated sources—such as landing fees, concession fees, and airline fueling fees—or lease revenues from one or more airlines for the use of a specific facility such as a terminal or hangar.

College and University Revenue Bonds.   The revenues securing these bonds usually include dormitory room rental fees, tuition payments, and sometimes the general assets of the college or university as well.

Hospital Revenue Bonds.   The security for hospital revenue bonds usually depends on federal and state reimbursement programs (such as Medicaid and Medicare), third-party commercial payers (such as Blue Cross, HMOs, and private insurance), and individual patient payments.

Single-Family Mortgage Revenue Bonds.   These bonds are usually secured by the mortgages and loan repayments on single-family homes. Security features vary but can include Federal Housing Administration (FHA), Veterans Administration (VA), or private mortgage insurance.[9]

Multifamily Revenue Bonds.   These revenue bonds are usually issued for multifamily housing projects for senior citizens and low-income families. Some housing revenue bonds are secured by mortgages that are federally insured; others receive federal government operating subsidies or interest-cost subsidies; still others receive only local property tax reductions as subsidies.

Industrial Revenue Bonds.   Generally, industrial revenue bonds are issued by state and local governments on behalf of individual corporations and businesses. The security for these bonds usually depends on the economic soundness of the particular corporation or business involved.

Public Power Revenue Bonds.   These bonds are secured by revenues to be produced from electrical operating plants. Some bonds are for a single issuer, who constructs and operates power plants and then sells the electricity. Other public power revenue bonds are issued by groups of public and private investor-owned utilities for the joint financing of the construction of one or more power plants.

Resource Recovery Revenue Bonds.   A resource recovery facility converts refuse (solid waste) into commercially saleable energy, recoverable products,

---

[9] Mortgage insurance is discussed in Chapter 17.

and a residue to be landfilled. The major revenues securing these bonds usually are (1) fees paid by those who deliver the waste to the facility for disposal, (2) revenues from steam, electricity, or refuse-derived fuel sold to either an electric power company or another energy user, and (3) revenues from the sale of recoverable materials such as aluminum and steel scrap.

Seaport Revenue Bonds.   The security for these bonds can include specific lease agreements with the benefiting companies, or pledged marine terminal and cargo tonnage fees.

Sports Complex and Convention Center Revenue Bonds.   These bonds usually receive revenues from sporting or convention events held at the facilities and, in some instances, from earmarked outside revenues such as local motel and hotel room taxes.

Student Loan Revenue Bonds.   Student loan repayments under student loan revenue bond programs are sometimes 100% guaranteed either directly by the federal government or by a state guaranty agency.

Toll Road and Gas Tax Revenue Bonds.   There are generally two types of highway revenue bonds. Bond proceeds of the first type are used to build such specific revenue-producing facilities as toll roads, bridges, and tunnels. For these pure enterprise-type revenue bonds, the pledged revenues usually are the monies collected through tolls. The second type of highway revenue bond is one where bondholders are paid by earmarked revenues outside of toll collections, such as gasoline taxes, automobile registration payments, and driver's license fees.

Water Revenue Bonds.   Water revenue bonds are issued to finance the construction of water treatment plants, pumping stations, collection facilities, and distribution systems. Revenues usually come from connection fees and charges paid by the users of the water systems.

Hybrid and Special Bond Securities

Some municipal bonds that have the basic characteristics of general obligation bonds and revenue bonds have more issue-specific structures as well. Five examples are insured bonds, letter of credit-backed bonds, moral obligation bonds, refunded bonds, and "troubled city" bailout bonds.

Insured bonds are backed by insurance policies written by commercial insurance companies, as well as by the credit of the municipal issuer. Municipal bond insurance is a contractual commitment by an insurance company to pay the bondholder any bond principal and/or coupon interest that is due on a stated maturity date but that has not been paid by the bond issuer. Once issued, this municipal bond insurance usually extends for the term of the bond issue, and it cannot be cancelled by the insurance company.

Municipal bond insurance has been available since 1971. By 1990, approximately 25% of all new municipal issues were insured. Some of the largest and financially strongest insurance companies in the U.S. have been participants in this industry, as well as smaller monoline (single line) insurance companies. The monoline companies following are major municipal bond insurers as of 1990: AMBAC Indemnity Corporation, Capital Guaranty Insurance Company, Financial Guaranty Insurance Corporation, and Municipal Bond Investors Assurance. In general, although insured municipal bonds sell at yields lower than they would without the insurance, they tend to have yields substantially higher than triple-A-rated non-insured municipal bonds.

Some municipal bonds are backed by a commercial bank letter of credit besides being secured by the issuer's cash flow revenues. A moral obligation bond is a security structure for state-issued bonds legally authorizing but not requiring the state legislature to make an appropriation out of general state tax revenues.

Refunded bonds (also called prefunded bonds) are bonds that originally may have been issued as general obligation or revenue bonds but that are now secured by an "escrow fund" consisting entirely of direct U.S. government obligations that are sufficient for paying the bondholders. There are three reasons why a municipal issuer may refund an issue by creating an escrow fund. First, many refunded issues were originally issued as revenue bonds. Included in revenue issues are restrictive-bond covenants. The municipality may wish to eliminate these restrictions. The creation of an escrow fund to pay the bondholders legally eliminates any restrictive-bond covenants. Second, some issues are refunded in order to alter the maturity schedule of the obligation. Finally, when interest rates have declined after a municipal security has been issued, there is a tax arbitrage opportunity available to the issuer by paying existing bondholders a lower interest rate and using the proceeds to create a portfolio of U.S. government securities paying a higher interest rate.[10] Most refunded bonds are structured to be

---

[10] Since the interest rate that a municipality must pay on borrowed funds is less than the interest rate paid by the U.S. government, in the absence of any restrictions in the tax code, a municipal issuer can realize a tax arbitrage. This can be done by issuing a bond and immediately investing the proceeds in a U.S. government security. There are tax rules that prevent such arbitrage. Should a municipal issuer violate the tax-arbitrage rules, the issue will be ruled to be taxable. However, if subsequent to the issuance of a bond, interest rates decline so that the issuer will find it advantageous to call the bond, the establishment of the escrow fund will not violate the tax-arbitrage rules.

called at the first call date. When the objective is to eliminate restrictive-bond covenants, refunded bonds are structured to meet the maturity schedule of the original bond issue. Because refunded bonds are collateralized by U.S. government obligations, they are among the safest of all municipal obligations if the escrow is properly structured.[11]

"Troubled city" bailout bonds are structured to appear as pure revenue bonds, but in essence they are not. Revenues come from general-purpose taxes and revenues that otherwise would have gone to the state's or the city's general fund. These bond structures were created to bail out underlying general obligation bond issuers from severe budget deficits. Examples are the New York State Municipal Assistance Corporation of the City of New York Bonds (MAC) and the State of Illinois Chicago School Finance Authority Bonds.

Municipal Notes

Municipal securities issued for periods ranging not beyond three years are considered to be short-term in nature. These include tax anticipation notes (TANs), revenue anticipation notes (RANs), grant anticipation notes (GANs), bond anticipation notes (BANs), and tax-exempt commercial paper.

TANs, RANs, GANs, and BANs are temporary borrowings by states, local governments, and special jurisdictions. Usually, notes are issued for a period of 12 months, although it is not uncommon for notes to be issued for periods as short as three months and for as long as three years. TANs and RANs (also known as TRANs) are issued in anticipation of the collection of taxes or other expected revenues. These are borrowings to even out irregular flows into the treasuries of the issuing entity. BANs are issued in anticipation of the sale of long-term bonds.

Tax-exempt commercial paper is issued for periods ranging from 30 to 270 days. Generally tax-exempt commercial paper has backstop commercial bank agreements, which can include an irrevocable letter of credit, a revolving credit agreement, or a line of credit.

Redemption Features

Municipal bonds are issued with one of two debt retirement structures or a combination of both. Either a bond has a *serial* maturity structure or a *term* maturity structure. A serial maturity structure requires a portion of the debt obligation to be retired each year. A term maturity structure provides for the

---

[11] For a further discussion of refunded bonds, see Chapter 5 in Feldstein and Fabozzi, *Dow Jones-Irwin Guide to Municipal Bonds.*

debt obligation to be repaid on a final date. Usually term bonds have maturities ranging from 20 to 40 years and retirement schedules (sinking fund provisions) that begin 5 to 10 years before the final term maturity.

Municipal bonds may be called prior to the stated maturity date, either according to a mandatory sinking fund or at the option of the issuer.

Special Investment Features

In the previous chapter, we described zero-coupon bonds, floating-rate bonds, and putable bonds in the corporate bond market. In the municipal market there are securities with these features.

In the municipal bond market there are two types of zero-coupon bonds. One type is issued at a very deep discount and matures at par. The difference between the par value and the purchase price represents a predetermined compound yield. These zero-coupon bonds are similar to those issued in the taxable bond market for Treasuries and corporates. The second type is called a "municipal multiplier," or "compound interest bond." This is a bond issued at par that has interest payments. The interest payments are not distributed to the holder of the bond until maturity, but the issuer agrees to reinvest the undistributed interest payments at the bond's yield to maturity when it was issued. For example, suppose that a 10%, 10-year coupon bond with a par value of $5,000 is sold at par to yield 10%. Every six months, the maturity value of this bond is increased by 5% of the maturity value of the previous six months. At the end of 10 years, the maturity value of the bond will be equal to $13,266.[12] In the case of a 10-year zero bond priced to yield 10%, the bond would have a maturity value of $5,000 but sell for $1,884 when issued.[13]

CREDIT RATINGS

While municipal bonds have long been considered second in safety only to U.S. Treasury securities, today there are new concerns about the credit risks of municipal securities.[14]

---

[12] This is found by computing the future value of $5,000 20 periods from now using a 5% interest rate. That is,

$$\$5,000 \times (1.05)^{20} = \$13,266$$

[13] This is found by computing the present value of $5,000 20 periods from now using a 5% interest rate. That is,

$$\$5,000 \times \frac{1}{(1.05)^{20}} = \$1,884$$

[14] For a history of defaults of municipal bonds, see Chapter 2 in Feldstein and Fabozzi, *The Dow Jones-Irwin Guide to Municipal Bonds.*

The first concern came out of the New York City billion-dollar financial crisis in 1975. On February 25, 1975, the state of New York's Urban Development Corporation defaulted on a $100 million note issue that was the obligation of New York City; many market participants had been convinced that the state of New York would not allow the issue to default. Although New York City was able later to obtain a $140 million revolving credit from banks to cure the default, lenders became concerned that the city would face difficulties in repaying its accumulated debt, which stood at $14 billion on March 31, 1975.[15] This financial crisis sent a loud and clear warning to market participants in general—regardless of supposedly ironclad protection for the bondholder, when issuers such as large cities have severe financial difficulties, the financial stakes of public employee unions, vendors, and community groups may be dominant forces in balancing budgets. This reality was reinforced by the federal bankruptcy law taking effect in October 1979, which makes it easier for the issuer of a municipal security to go into bankruptcy.

The second reason for concern about municipal securities credit risk is the proliferation in this market of innovative financing techniques to secure new bond issues. In addition to the established general obligation bonds and revenue bonds, there are now more non-voter-approved, innovative, and legally untested security mechanisms. These innovative financing mechanisms include "moral obligation" bonds and commercial bank-backed letters of credit bonds, to name a few. What distinguishes these newer bonds from the more traditional general obligation and revenue bonds is that there is no history of court decisions or other case law that firmly establishes the rights of the bondholders and the obligations of the issuers. It is not possible to determine in advance the probable legal outcome if the newer financing mechanisms were to be challenged in court. This is illustrated most dramatically by the bonds of the Washington Public Power Supply System (WPPSS) where bondholder rights to certain revenues were not upheld by the highest court in the state of Washington.

As with corporate bonds, many institutional investors in the municipal bond market rely on their own in-house municipal credit analysts for determining the creditworthiness of a municipal issue; other investors rely on commercial credit ratings. The two leading commercial rating companies are Moody's and Standard & Poor's, and the assigned rating system is essentially the same as that used for corporate bonds.

---

[15] *Securities and Exchange Commission Staff Report on Transactions in Securities of the City of New York* (Washington, D.C.: U.S. Government Printing Office, 1977), p. 2. The reasons for the New York City financial crisis are documented in Donna E. Shalala and Carol Bellamy, "A State Saves a City: The New York Case," *Duke Law Journal* (January 1976), pp. 1119–1126.

In evaluating general obligation bonds, the commercial rating companies assess information in four basic categories.[16] The first category includes information on the issuer's debt structure to determine the overall debt burden. The second category relates to the issuer's ability and political discipline to maintain sound budgetary policy. The focus of attention here usually is on the issuer's general operating funds and whether it has maintained at least balanced budgets over three to five years. The third category involves determining the specific local taxes and intergovernmental revenues available to the issuer, as well as obtaining historical information both on tax collection rates, which are important when looking at property tax levies, and on the dependence of local budgets on specific revenue sources. The fourth and last category of information necessary to the credit analysis is an assessment of the issuer's overall socioeconomic environment. The determinations that have to be made here include trends of local employment distribution and composition, population growth, real estate property valuation, and personal income, among other economic factors.

While there are numerous security structures for revenue bonds, the underlying principle in rating is whether the project being financed will generate sufficient cash flow to satisfy the obligations due bondholders.[17] A natural question to ask is: How good are the ratings? Of the municipal securities that were rated by a commercial rating company in 1929 and plunged into default in 1932, 78% had been rated double-A or better, and 48% had been rated triple-A. Since then the ability of rating agencies to assess the creditworthiness of municipal securities has evolved to a level of general industry acceptance and respectability. In most instances, ratings adequately describe the financial condition of the issuers and identify the credit risk factors. A small but significant number of recent instances still have caused market participants to reexamine their reliance on the opinions of the rating agencies. One example is the bonds of the Washington Public Power Supply System mentioned above. The two major commercial rating companies gave their highest ratings to these bonds in the early 1980s. While these high-quality ratings were in effect, WPPSS sold over $8 billion in long-term bonds. By 1986 over $2 billion of these bonds were in default.

---

[16] Although there are many similarities in how Moody's and Standard & Poor's approach the credit rating of general obligation bonds, there are differences in their approaches as well. For a discussion of these differences, see Feldstein and Fabozzi, ''Municipal Bonds,'' pp. 304–309.

[17] A comprehensive discussion of the analysis of various revenue bond structures is found in: Sylvan G. Feldstein, Frank J. Fabozzi, and Irving M. Pollack (eds.), *The Municipal Bond Handbook: Volume II* (Homewood, IL: Dow Jones-Irwin, 1983); and Feldstein and Fabozzi, *Dow Jones-Irwin Guide to Municipal Bonds.*

RISKS ASSOCIATED WITH INVESTING IN MUNICIPAL SECURITIES

The investor in municipal securities is exposed to the same risks affecting corporate bonds plus an additional one that may be labeled *tax risk*. There are two types of tax risk to which tax-exempt municipal securities buyers are exposed. The first is the risk that the federal income tax rate will be reduced. The higher the marginal tax rate, the greater the value of the tax exemption feature. As the marginal tax rate declines, the price of a tax-exempt municipal security will decline. When in 1986 there were tax proposals to reduce marginal tax rates, tax-exempt municipal bonds began trading at lower prices.

The second type of tax risk is that a municipal bond issued as a tax-exempt issue may be eventually declared by the Internal Revenue Service to be taxable. This may occur because many municipal revenue bonds have elaborate security structures that could be subject to future adverse congressional action and IRS interpretation. A loss of the tax exemption feature will cause the municipal bond to decline in value in order to provide a yield comparable to similar taxable bonds. As an example, in June of 1980, the Battery Park City Authority sold $97.315 million in notes, which at the time of issuance legal counsel advised were exempt from federal income taxation. In November of 1980, however, the IRS held that interest on these notes was not exempt. The issue was not settled until September 1981, when the Authority and the IRS signed a formal agreement resolving the matter so as to make the interest on the notes tax-exempt.

THE PRIMARY MARKET

A substantial number of municipal obligations are brought to market each week. A state or local government can market its new issue by offering bonds publicly to the investing community or by placing them privately with a small group of investors. When a public offering is selected, the issue usually is underwritten by investment bankers and/or municipal bond departments of commercial banks. Public offerings may be marketed by either competitive bidding or direct negotiations with underwriters. When an issue is marketed via competitive bidding, the issue is awarded to the bidder submitting the best bid.

Most states mandate that general obligation issues be marketed through competitive bidding, but generally this is not required for revenue bonds. Usually state and local governments require a competitive sale to be announced in a recognized financial publication, such as *The Bond Buyer*, which is a trade publication for the municipal bond industry. *The Bond Buyer* also provides information on upcoming competitive sales and most negotiated sales, as well as the results of previous weeks.

An *official statement* describing the issue and the issuer is prepared for new offerings.

THE SECONDARY MARKET

Municipal bonds are traded in the over-the-counter market supported by hundreds of municipal bond dealers across the country. Markets are maintained on smaller issuers (referred to as "local credits") by regional brokerage firms, local banks, and by some of the larger Wall Street firms. Larger issuers (referred to as "general names") are supported by the larger brokerage firms and banks, many of whom have investment banking relationships with these issuers. There are brokers who serve as intermediaries in the sale of large blocks of municipal bonds among dealers and large institutional investors. In addition to these brokers and the daily offerings sent out over *The Bond Buyer's* "munifacts" teletype system, many dealers advertise their municipal bond offering for the retail market in what is known as *The Blue List.* This is a 100-plus-page booklet published every weekday by the Standard & Poor's Corporation that gives municipal securities offerings and prices.

In the municipal bond markets, an odd lot of bonds is $25,000 or less in par value for retail investors. For institutions, anything below $100,000 in par value is considered an odd lot. Dealer spreads depend on several factors. For the retail investor, the spread can range from as low as one-quarter of one point ($12.50 per $5,000 par value) on large blocks of actively traded bonds to four points ($200 per $5,000 of par value) for odd lot sales of an inactive issue. For institutional investors, the dealer spread rarely exceeds one-half of one point ($25 per $5,000 of par value).

The convention for both corporate and Treasury bonds is to quote prices as a percentage of par value with 100 equal to par. Municipal bonds, however, generally are traded and quoted in terms of yield (yield to maturity or yield to call). The price of the bond in this case is called a *basis price.* The exception is certain long-maturity revenue bonds. A bond traded and quoted in dollar prices (actually, as a percentage of par value) is called a *dollar bond.*

YIELDS ON MUNICIPAL BONDS

Because of the tax-exempt feature of municipal bonds, the yield on municipal bonds is less than that on Treasuries with the same maturity. The ratio of municipal yields to Treasury yields varies over time. The ratio has increased recently because of the decrease in the marginal tax rate since the 1986 Tax Act, making the tax-exemption feature less attractive to investors.

A common yield measure used to compare the yield on a tax-exempt municipal bond with a comparable taxable bond is the equivalent taxable yield. The equivalent taxable yield is computed as follows:

$$\text{Equivalent taxable yield} = \frac{\text{Tax-exempt yield}}{(1 - \text{Marginal tax rate})}$$

For example, suppose an investor in the 33% marginal tax bracket is considering the acquisition of a tax-exempt municipal bond that offers a yield of 8%. The equivalent taxable yield is 11.94%, as shown below:

$$\text{Equivalent taxable yield} = \frac{0.08}{(1 - 0.33)} = 0.1194, \text{ or } 11.94\%$$

When computing the equivalent taxable yield, the traditionally computed yield to maturity is not the tax-exempt yield if the issue is selling at a discount because only the coupon interest is exempt from federal income taxes. Instead, the yield to maturity after an assumed tax rate on the capital gain is computed and used in the numerator of the formula above.[18]

Yield spreads within the municipal bond market are attributable to several reasons: (1) differences between credit ratings, (2) differences between in-state and general market, and (3) differences between maturities.

Our statement in the previous chapter about quality spreads between credit ratings for corporate bonds over the interest rate cycle is true for municipal bonds: quality spreads widen during recessionary periods, but narrow during periods of economic prosperity. Another factor that can cause changes in the quality spread is a temporary oversupply of issues within a market sector. For example, a substantial new-issue volume of high-grade state general obligation bonds may tend to decrease the spread between high-grade and lower-grade revenue bonds. In a weak market environment, it is easier for high-grade municipal bonds to come to market than weaker ones. Therefore, it is not uncommon for high grades to flood weak markets, while at the same time there is a relative scarcity of medium- and lower-grade municipal bond issues.

Bonds of municipal issuers located in certain states yield considerably less than issues of identical credit quality that come from other states that trade in the "general market." One reason for this is that states often exempt interest

---

[18] The yield to maturity after an assumed tax on the capital gain is calculated in the same manner as the traditional yield to maturity as explained in Chapter 11. Instead of using the maturity value in computing the yield, the net proceeds after an assumed tax rate on the capital gain are used.

from in-state issues from state and local personal income taxes, while interest from out-of-state issues is generally not exempt. Consequently, in states with high income taxes such as New York and California, strong investor demand for in-state issues will reduce their yields relative to bonds of issuers located in states where state and local income taxes are not important considerations (for example, Illinois and Florida).

In the Treasury and corporate bond markets, it is not unusual to find at different times all four shapes for the yield curve described in Chapter 12. In the municipal bond market, long-term bonds typically offer higher yields than short- and intermediate-term bonds; that is, the municipal yield curve is typically normal or upward-sloping.

REGULATION OF THE MUNICIPAL SECURITIES MARKET[19]

Congress has specifically exempted municipal securities from both the registration requirements of the Securities Act of 1933 and the periodic reporting requirements of the Securities Exchange Act of 1934. Antifraud provisions apply nevertheless to offerings of or dealings in municipal securities.

The reasons for the exemption afforded municipal securities appear to relate to (1) a desire for governmental comity, (2) the absence of recurrent abuses in transactions involving municipal securities, (3) the greater level of sophistication of investors in this segment of the securities markets (that is, institutional investors once dominated the market), and (4) the fact that there were few defaults by municipal issuers. Consequently, between enactment of federal securities acts in the early 1930s and the early 1970s, the municipal securities market was relatively free from federal regulation.

In the early 1970s, however, circumstances changed. As incomes rose, individuals participated in the municipal securities market to a much greater extent, and public concern over selling practices occurred with greater frequency. Moreover, the financial problems of some municipal issuers, notably New York City, made market participants aware that municipal issuers have the potential to experience severe financial difficulties approaching bankruptcy levels.

Congress passed the Securities Act Amendment of 1975 to broaden federal regulation in the municipals market. This legislation brought brokers

---

[19] The discussion in this section is drawn from Thomas F. Mitchell, "Disclosure and the Municipal Bond Industry," Chapter 40, and Nancy H. Wojtas, "The SEC and Investor Safeguards," Chapter 42 in Frank J. Fabozzi, Sylvan G. Feldstein, Irving M. Pollack, and Frank Zarb (eds.), *The Municipal Bond Handbook: Volume I* (Homewood, IL: Dow Jones-Irwin, 1983).

and dealers in the municipal securities market, including banks that underwrite and trade municipal securities, under the regulatory umbrella of the Securities Exchange Act of 1934. The legislation mandates also that the SEC establish a 15-member Municipal Securities Rulemaking Board (MSRB) as an independent, self-regulatory agency, whose primary responsibility is to develop rules governing the activities of banks, brokers, and dealers in municipal securities. Rules adopted by the MSRB must be approved by the SEC. The MSRB has no enforcement or inspection authority. That authority is vested with the SEC, the National Association of Securities Dealers, and certain regulatory banking agencies such as the Federal Reserve Bank.

The Securities Act Amendment of 1975 does not require municipal issuers to comply with the registration requirement of the 1933 act or the periodic reporting requirement of the 1934 act, despite several legislative proposals to mandate financial disclosure. Even in the absence of federal legislation dealing with the regulation of financial disclosure, however, underwriters began insisting upon greater disclosure as it became apparent that the SEC was exercising stricter application of the antifraud provisions. Moreover, underwriters recognized the need for improved disclosure to sell municipal securities to an investing public that has become much more concerned about the credit risk of municipal issuers.

On June 28, 1989, the SEC formally approved the first bond disclosure rule, effective January 1, 1990. While the disclosure rule has several exemptions, in general it applies to new issue municipal securities offerings of $1 million or more.

SUMMARY

Municipal securities are issued by state and local governments and their authorities, with the coupon interest on most issues being exempt from federal income taxes. The primary investors in these securities are households (which includes mutual funds), commercial banks, and property and casualty insurance companies. Changes in the tax law have had an effect on the relative attractiveness of municipal securities for these three groups of investors.

The two basic security structures are general obligation bonds and revenue bonds. The former are secured by the issuer's generally taxing power. Revenue bonds are used to finance specific projects and are dependent on revenues from those projects to satisfy the obligations. There are also hybrid securities that have certain characteristics of both general obligation and revenue bonds, and some securities that have unique structures.

Municipal notes are issued for shorter periods (one to three years) than municipal bonds. Municipal bonds may be retired with a serial maturity structure, a term maturity structure, or a combination of both. As in the case of corporate bonds, there are zero-coupon bonds and floating-rate bonds. Investing in municipal securities exposes investors to the same qualitative risks as investing in corporate bonds, with the additional risk that a change in the tax law may affect the price of municipal securities adversely. Because of the tax-exempt feature, yields on municipal securities are lower than those on comparably rated taxable securities. Within the municipal bond market, there are quality spreads and maturity spread. Moreover, there are yield spreads related to differences between in-state issues and general market issues.

QUESTIONS

1. If Congress changes the tax law so as to increase marginal tax rates, what will happen to the price of municipal bonds?

2. Why would a property and casualty insurance company shift its allocation of funds from taxable fixed-income securities to tax-exempt fixed-income securities?

3. **a.** What is the difference between a general obligation bond and a revenue bond?

   b. Which type of bond would an investor analyze using an approach similar to that for analyzing a corporate bond?

4. What is the tax risk associated with investing in a municipal bond?

5. "An insured municipal bond is safer than an uninsured municipal bond." Do you agree with this statement?

6. What is a refunded bond?

CHAPTER

17

THE MORTGAGE MARKET

LEARNING OBJECTIVES

After reading this chapter you will understand:

- what a mortgage is.

- who the major originators of mortgages are.

- the mortgage origination process.

- the risks associated with the mortgage origination process and the embedded options in the transaction.

- the traditional fixed-rate, level-payment, fully amortized mortgage instrument, and its cash flow characteristics.

- deficiencies of the traditional mortgage: mismatch and tilt problems.

- alternative mortgage instruments, their cash flow characteristics, and how they correct for the deficiencies of the traditional mortgage instrument.

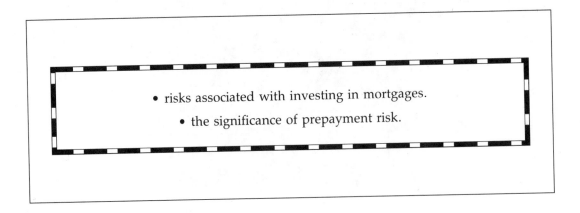

- risks associated with investing in mortgages.
- the significance of prepayment risk.

$\top$his chapter covers the mortgage market. We look at the market participants (mortgage originators and investors) and the risks they face. We also review the various types of mortgage instruments. These include level-payment fixed-rate mortgages, graduated-payment mortgages, adjustable-rate mortgages, price-level-adjusted mortgages, and a few other forms. Our discussion of mortgage origination and the types of mortgages highlights the options embedded in the mortgage instrument or in the transaction in the case of mortgage originations. In the next chapter, we discuss the development of the current secondary mortgage market.

WHAT IS A MORTGAGE?

By definition, a mortgage is a pledge of property to secure payment of a debt. Typically, property refers to real estate, which is often in the form of a house; the debt is the loan given to the buyer of the house by a lender. Thus, a mortgage might be a pledge of a house to secure payment of a loan. If a homeowner (the *mortgagor*) fails to pay the lender (the *mortgagee*), the lender has the right to foreclose the loan and seize the property in order to ensure that it is repaid.

When the loan is based on the credit of the borrower and on the collateral for the mortgage, the mortgage is said to be a *conventional mortgage*. The lender also may take out mortgage insurance to provide a guarantee for the fulfillment of the borrower's obligations.[1] There are two forms of mortgage insurance guaranteed by the U.S. government if the borrower can qualify: Federal Housing Administration (FHA) and Veteran's Administration (VA) insurance. There are also private mortgage insurers such as Mortgage Guaranty Insurance Company (owned by Northwestern Mutual) and PMI Mortgage Insurance Company (owned by Sears, Roebuck). The cost of mortgage insurance is paid to the guarantor by the mortgage originator but passed along to the borrower in the form of higher mortgage payments.

The types of real estate properties that can be mortgaged are divided into two broad categories: residential and non-residential properties. The former category includes houses, condominiums, cooperatives, and apartments. Residential real estate can be subdivided into single-family (one- to four-family) structures and multifamily structures (apartment buildings in which more than four families reside). Non-residential property includes commercial and farm properties.

MORTGAGE ORIGINATION

The original lender is called the *mortgage originator*. The principal originators of residential mortgage loans are thrifts, commercial banks, and mortgage bankers. Other private mortgage originators are life insurance companies and, to a much lesser extent, pension funds. Table 17-1 shows mortgage origination by type of residential property.

Mortgage originators may generate income from mortgage activity in one or more ways. First, they typically charge an origination fee. This fee is expressed in terms of *points,* where each point represents 1% of the borrowed funds. For example, an origination fee of two points on a $100,000 mortgage loan is $2,000. In addition, they may charge application fees and certain processing fees. The second source of revenue is the profit that might be generated from selling a mortgage at a higher price than it originally cost. This profit is called *secondary market profit.* Of course, if mortgage rates rise, an originator will realize a loss when the mortgages are sold in the secondary market.

While technically the sources of revenue attributable to the origination function are origination fees and secondary marketing profits, there are two other potential sources. First, mortgage originators may service the mortgages they originate, for which they obtain a *servicing fee.* Servicing of the

---

[1] There is also mortgage insurance that may be obtained by the borrower in the form of life insurance.

TABLE 17-1   ORIGINATIONS OF RESIDENTIAL MORTGAGE LOANS   (MILLIONS OF DOLLARS)

	THRIFTS	COMMERCIAL BANKS	MORTGAGE BANKERS	LIFE INSURANCE COMPANIES	PENSION FUNDS	FEDERAL CREDIT AGENCIES	STATE AND LOCAL CREDIT AGENCIES	TOTAL
			CONVENTIONAL 1-4 FAMILY					
1986	201,839	100,922	52,502	3,196	104	2,676	887	362,126
1987	200,022	112,380	57,578	2,726	23	2,890	557	376,176
1988	182,717	95,815	52,282	2,995	50	2,858	1,041	337,759
1989	151,362	117,335	33,730	997	186	2,694	882	307,186
			CONVENTIONAL MULTIFAMILY					
1986	22,439	7,133	4,267	3,723	19	1,625	1,922	41,128
1987	22,318	8,291	1,046	3,547	27	1,120	1,912	38,261
1988	20,259	6,899	2,525	3,732	103	1,153	527	35,198
1989	13,299	7,654	4,294	2,786	35	1,194	935	30,197
			FHA/VA 1-4 FAMILY					
1986	5,342	7,691	79,126	618	0	0	151	92,928
1987	8,758	12,171	52,515	483	0	0	167	74,094
1988	6,154	6,048	33,025	336	0	0	245	45,807
1989	6,314	5,858	31,876	446	19	0	327	44,840
			FHA MULTIFAMILY					
1986	330	43	2,905	0	0	114	5,348	8,740
1987	285	9	1,363	0	0	0	5,175	6,831
1988	292	21	2,001	0	13	2	631	2,960
1989	170	15	149	0	13	0	601	948
			TOTAL RESIDENTIAL ORIGINATIONS					
1986	229,950	115,789	138,800	7,537	123	4,415	8,308	504,922
1987	231,383	132,851	112,502	6,756	50	4,010	7,811	494,363
1988	209,422	108,783	89,833	7,063	166	4,013	2,444	421,724
1989	171,145	130,862	70,049	4,229	253	3,888	2,745	383,171

W. Criss Peters, a research assistant in Freddie Mac's department of financial research, prepared the data for these tables. Reprinted from *Secondary Mortgage Markets*, Summer 1991, by permission of Freddie Mac. All rights reserved.

Source: The U.S. Department of Housing and Urban Development, Survey of Mortgage Lending Activity.

mortgage involves collecting monthly payments from mortgagors and forwarding proceeds to owners of the loan, sending payment notices to mortgagors, reminding mortgagors when payments are overdue, maintaining records of mortgage balances, furnishing tax information to mortgagors, administering an escrow account for real estate taxes and insurance purposes, and, if necessary, initiating foreclosure proceedings. The servicing fee is a fixed percentage of the outstanding mortgage balance, typically 1/4% (25 basis points) to 1/2% (50 basis points) per year. The mortgage originator may sell the servicing of the mortgage to another party who would then receive the servicing fee. Second, the mortgage originator may hold the mortgage in its investment portfolio.

Regulatory and tax considerations have encouraged thrifts to invest in mortgages, and, until quite recently, they tried to keep mortgages in their portfolios. Lately, however, both because they have become more conscious of the problem of matching maturities and because the tax benefits have been reduced by the 1986 Tax Act, thrifts have tended to sell a good portion of what they originate and to become increasingly dependent on the fees generated from originating and servicing mortgages.

Mortgage bankers do not invest in mortgages. Instead, they derive their income from the origination fees. Commercial banks derive their income from all three sources, but there are no regulatory benefits to them from investing in mortgages or mortgage-backed securities.

The Mortgage Origination Process

A potential homeowner who wants to borrow funds to purchase a home will apply for a loan from one of the mortgage originators. The applicant completes an application form, which provides financial information about the applicant, and pays an application fee; then the mortgage originator performs a credit evaluation of the applicant. The two primary factors in determining whether the funds will be lent are the (1) payment-to-income (PTI) ratio, and (2) the loan-to-value (LTV) ratio. The former ratio is the ratio of monthly payments to monthly income and is a measure of the ability of the applicant to make monthly payments (both mortgage and real estate tax payments). The lower this ratio, the greater the likelihood that the applicant will be able to meet the required payments.[2]

The difference between the purchase price of the property and the amount borrowed is the borrower's down payment. The LTV is the ratio of

---

[2] Some applicants will request a loan and request that no credit check be performed. If the lender is satisfied that the collateral will be sufficient, the loan may be granted. A lower LTV will be required, and a higher mortgage rate will be charged.

the amount of the loan to the market (or assessed) value of the property. The lower this ratio, the greater the protection the lender has if the applicant defaults on the payments and the lender must repossess and sell the property. For example, if an applicant wants to borrow $150,000 on property with an assessed value of $200,000, the LTV is 75%. Suppose the applicant subsequently defaults on the mortgage. The lender can then repossess the property and sell it to recover the amount owed. But the amount that will be received by the lender depends on the market value of the property. In our example, even if conditions in the housing market are weak, the lender will still be able to recover the proceeds lent if the value of the property declines by $50,000. Suppose instead that the applicant wanted to borrow $180,000 for the same property. The LTV would then be 90%. If the lender had to sell the property because the applicant defaults, there is less protection for the lender.

If the lender decides to lend the funds, it sends a commitment letter to the applicant. This letter commits the lender to provide funds to the applicant. The length of time of the commitment varies between 30 and 60 days. At the time of the commitment letter, the lender will require that the applicant pay a commitment fee. It is important to understand that the commitment letter obligates the lender—not the applicant—to perform. The commitment fee that the applicant pays is lost if the applicant decides not to purchase the property or uses an alternative source of funds to purchase the property. Thus the commitment letter states that for a fee the applicant has the right but not the obligation to require the lender to provide funds at a certain interest rate and on certain terms. The cost of the commitment letter is the commitment fee, which applicants lose if they do not require the lender to lend the funds. Does this sound like an option? That's exactly what it is. A commitment letter is an option sold by the lender and purchased by the applicant.

At the time the application is submitted for approval, the mortgage originator will give the applicant a choice among the various types of mortgages to be discussed later in this chapter. Basically, the choice is between a fixed-rate mortgage or an adjustable-rate mortgage. In the case of a fixed-rate mortgage, the lender typically gives the applicant a choice of when the interest rate on the mortgage will be determined. The three choices may be: (1) at the time the loan application is submitted, (2) at the time a commitment letter is issued to the borrower, or (3) at the closing date (the date that the property is purchased). Looking at this choice as an option, note that if the applicant chooses to have the rate set at the application date, the applicant has purchased an option on the mortgage rate for a price equal to the application fee. The length of this option is equal to the time between the date the application is submitted and the commitment date. Once the commitment letter is sent out and accepted by the applicant by paying the commitment fee, the cost of the option becomes the commitment fee. It is important to understand these options because, as we explain below, they expose the mortgage originator to certain risks. A mortgage originator must protect itself against these risks.

Mortgage originators can either (1) hold the mortgage in their portfolio, (2) sell the mortgage to an investor that wishes to hold the mortgage in its portfolio or that will place the mortgage in a pool of mortgages to be used as collateral for the issuance of a security, or (3) use the mortgage themselves as collateral for the issuance of a security. When a mortgage is used as collateral for the issuance of a security, the mortgage is said to be *securitized*. (We discuss the process of securitizing mortgages further in Chapter 18.)

When a mortgage originator intends to sell the mortgage, it will obtain a commitment from the potential investor (buyer). Two federally-sponsored credit agencies and several private companies buy mortgages. As these agencies and private companies pool these mortgages and sell them to investors, they are called *conduits*.

The two agencies, the Federal Home Loan Mortgage Corporation and the Federal National Mortgage Association, purchase only *conforming* mortgages—that is, one that meets the agency underwriting standards to be included in a pool of mortgages underlying a security that they guarantee. Three underwriting standards established by these agencies in order to qualify as a conforming mortgage are (1) a maximum PTI, (2) a maximum LTV, and (3) a maximum loan amount. If an applicant does not satisfy the underwriting standards, the mortgage is called a *non-conforming mortgage*.[3] The mortgages acquired by the agency may be held as an investment in their portfolio or securitized.

Examples of private conduits are Citimae, Inc. (a subsidiary of Citicorp), Bear Stearns Mortgage Capital Corporation, Residential Funding Corporation (a subsidiary of Salomon Brothers), FBS Mortgage Corporation (a subsidiary of First Boston), and Sears Mortgage Securities Corporation. Private conduits typically securitize the mortgages purchased rather than hold them as an investment. Both conforming and non-conforming mortgages are purchased. Non-conforming mortgages do not necessarily have greater credit risk. For example, an individual with an annual income of $500,000 may apply for a mortgage loan of $200,000 on real estate that she wants to purchase for $1 million. This would be a non-conforming mortgage because the amount of the mortgage exceeds the limit currently established for a conforming mortgage, yet the individual's income can easily accommodate the monthly mortgage payments. Moreover, the lender's risk exposure is minimal, as it has lent $200,000 backed by collateral of $1 million.

---

[3] Loans that exceed the maximum loan amount and therefore do not qualify as conforming mortgages are called *jumbo* loans.

The mortgage rate that the originator will set on the loan will depend on the mortgage rate required by the investor who plans to purchase the mortgage. There are different mortgage rates for delivery at different times (30 days, 60 days, or 90 days).

The Risks Associated with Mortgage Origination

The loan applications being processed and the commitments made by a mortgage originator together are called its pipeline. *Pipeline risk* refers to the risks associated with originating mortgages. This risk has two components: price risk and fallout risk.[4]

Price risk refers to the adverse effects on the value of the pipeline if mortgage rates rise. If mortgage rates rise, and the mortgage originator has made commitments at a lower mortgage rate, it will either have to sell the mortgages when they close at a value below the funds lent to homeowners or retain the mortgages as a portfolio investment earning a below-market mortgage rate. The mortgage originator faces the same risk for mortgage applications in the pipeline where the applicant has elected to fix the rate at the time the application is submitted.

Fallout risk is the risk that applicants or those who were issued commitment letters will not close (complete the transaction by purchasing the property with funds borrowed from the mortgage originator). The chief reason that potential borrowers may cancel their commitment or withdraw their mortgage application is that mortgage rates have declined sufficiently so that it is economic to seek an alternative source of funds. Fallout risk is the result of the mortgage originator giving the potential borrower the right but not the obligation to close (that is, the right to cancel the agreement). This is why we say that the mortgage originator has effectively sold the potential borrower an option. There are reasons other than a decline in mortgage rates to cause a potential borrower to fall out of the pipeline. There may be an unfavorable property inspection report, or the purchase could have been predicated on a change in employment that does not occur.

Mortgage originators have several alternatives to protect themselves against pipeline risk. To protect against price risk, the originator could get a

---

[4] For a more detailed discussion of pipeline risk and the methods mortgage originators can use to protect against it, see John Scowcroft, Andrew S. Davidson and Anand K. Bhattacharya, "Pipeline Risk Management," Chapter 33 in *The Handbook of Mortgage-Backed Securities*, second edition; Laurie Goodman and Judith Johnson, "Managing a Mortgage Pipeline: Instruments and Alternatives," in Frank J. Fabozzi (ed.), *Mortgage-Backed Securities: New Strategies, Applications and Research* (Chicago, IL: Probus Publishing, 1987); and Chapter 12 in Mark Pitts and Frank J. Fabozzi, *Interest Rate Futures and Options* (Chicago, IL: Probus Publishing, 1989).

commitment from the agency or the private conduit to whom the mortgage originator plans to sell the mortgage.[5] This sort of commitment is effectively a forward contract; the mortgage originator agrees to deliver a mortgage at a future date, and another party (either one of the agencies or a private conduit) agrees to buy the mortgage at that time at a predetermined price (or mortgage rate).

Consider what happens, however, if mortgage rates decline and potential borrowers elect to cancel the agreement. The mortgage originator has agreed to deliver a mortgage with a specified mortgage rate. If the potential borrower does not close, and the mortgage originator has made a commitment to deliver the mortgage to an agency or private conduit, the mortgage originator cannot back out of the transaction. As a result, the mortgage originator will realize a loss—it must deliver a mortgage at a higher mortgage rate in a lower mortgage rate environment. This is fallout risk.

Mortgage originators can protect themselves against fallout risk by entering into an agreement with an agency or private conduit for optional rather than mandatory delivery of the mortgage. In such an agreement, the mortgage originator is effectively buying an option that gives it the right, but not the obligation, to deliver a mortgage. The agency or private conduit has sold that option to the mortgage originator and therefore charges a fee for allowing optional delivery. Recall that fallout risk is the result of mortgage originators selling options to potential borrowers. Therefore, it makes economic sense for a mortgage originator to protect itself against fallout risk by buying an option.

THE TRADITIONAL MORTGAGE

Some Historical Background

Both mortgage design and the origin of the funds financing housing mortgages have, since the Great Depression, undergone revolutionary changes and been affected by spectacular innovations. Until the Depression, mortgages were not fully amortized, as they are now, but were of the nature of balloon instruments where the principal is not amortized, or only partially amortized, at maturity, leaving the debtor with the problem of refinancing the balance. Sometimes the bank could even ask for repayment of the outstanding balance on demand or relatively short notice, even if the mortgagor was fulfilling its obligations. This system of mortgage financing proved disastrous

---

[5] This commitment that the mortgage originator obtains to protect itself should not be confused with the commitment that the mortgage originator gives to the potential borrower.

during the Great Depression, and contributed to its depth and personal distress, as banks that were afflicted by loan losses and depositor withdrawals found it necessary to liquidate their mortgage loans, and debtors found it impossible to refinance their debt.

This experience led, in the middle of the 1930s, to the widespread adoption of a much superior instrument called the fixed-rate, level-payment, fully amortized mortgage (level-payment fixed-rate mortgage, for short). This development was encouraged by the newly created Federal Housing Administration (FHA), whose assignments include providing for affordable insurance to protect the lender's claim against non-performance by the borrower. This insurance is desirable not only for the lender but also for the borrower who with insurance would usually be able to secure better terms. The FHA specified the kind of mortgages it was prepared to insure; one of the requirements was that the instrument had to be a level-payment fixed-rate mortgage.

Characteristics of the Fixed-Rate, Level-Payment, Fully Amortized Mortgage

The level-payment fixed-rate mortgage is also referred to as a *traditional mortgage*. Some historical background is useful to help understand the shortcomings of the traditional mortgage.

The basic idea behind the design of the traditional mortgage is that the borrower pays interest and repays principal in equal installments over an agreed-upon period of time, called the maturity or term of the mortgage. Thus at the end of the term, the loan has been fully amortized. The interest rate is generally above the risk-free rate because of servicing costs, default risk that is present despite the collateral, and some further risks discussed below. The frequency of payment is typically monthly, and the prevailing term of the mortgage is 20 to 30 years; in recent years an increasing number of 15-year mortgages have been originated.

Each monthly mortgage payment for a level-payment fixed-rate mortgage is due on the first of each month and consists of:

1. interest of 1/12th of the fixed annual interest rate times the amount of the outstanding mortgage balance at the beginning of the previous month, and

2. a repayment of a portion of the outstanding mortgage balance (principal).

The difference between the monthly mortgage payment and the portion of the payment that represents interest equals the amount that is applied to reduce the outstanding mortgage balance. The monthly mortgage payment is designed so that after the last scheduled monthly payment of the loan is made, the amount of the outstanding mortgage balance is zero (i.e. the mortgage is fully repaid).

To illustrate a level-payment fixed-rate mortgage, consider a 30-year (360 month), $100,000 mortgage with a 10% mortgage rate. The monthly mortgage payment would be $877.57.[6] Table 17-2 shows how each monthly mortgage payment is divided between interest and repayment of principal for the first 36 months. At the beginning of Month 1, the mortgage balance is $100,000, the amount of the original loan. The mortgage payment for Month 1 includes interest on the $100,000 borrowed for the month. As the interest rate is 10%, the monthly interest rate is 0.0083333 (0.10 divided by 12). Interest for Month 1 is therefore $833.33 ($100,000 times 0.0083333). The $44.24 difference between the monthly mortgage payment of $877.57 and the interest of $833.33 is the portion of the monthly mortgage payment that represents repayment of principal. This $44.24 in Month 1 reduces the mortgage balance.

The mortgage balance at the end of Month 1 (beginning of Month 2) is then $99,955.76 ($100,000 minus $44.24). The interest for the second monthly

---

[6] Calculation of the monthly mortgage payment is just a basic application of the present value of an annuity. It can be determined as follows:

$$\text{Monthly mortgage payment} = \frac{\text{Amount of funds borrowed}}{\text{Present value of an annuity of \$1 per month}}$$

The present value of an annuity of $1 per month can be calculated as follows:

$$\text{PV of an annuity of \$1 per month} = \frac{1 - \dfrac{1}{(1 + r)^n}}{r}$$

where n = number of months of the mortgage
$\quad\ r$ = simple monthly interest rate (annual interest rate/12)

For example, consider the $100,000, 30-year, 10% mortgage. Then, the monthly mortgage payment is:

$$\frac{\$100,000}{\text{Present value of an annuity of \$1 per month}}$$

As $n = 360$ and $r = 0.0083333$ (=0.10/12), the present value of an annuity of $1 per month is:

$$\frac{1 - \dfrac{1}{(1.0083333)^{360}}}{0.008333} = 113.95119$$

The monthly mortgage payment is then:

$$\frac{\$100,00}{113.95119} = \$877.57$$

TABLE 17-2 AMORTIZATION SCHEDULE FOR A LEVEL-PAYMENT FIXED-RATE MORTGAGE (FIRST 36 MONTHS)

Mortgage Loan = $100,000
Interest Rate = .10
Term of Loan = 30 years (360 months)

(1)	(2) BEGINNING MORTGAGE-BALANCE	(3) MONTHLY MORTGAGE PAYMENT	(4) INTEREST FOR MONTH	(5) PRINCIPAL REPAYMENT	(6) ENDING MORTGAGE BALANCE
MONTH					
1	$100,000.00	$877.57	$833.33	$44.24	$99,955.76
2	99,955.76	877.57	832.96	44.61	99,911.16
3	99,911.16	877.57	832.59	44.98	99,866.18
4	99,866.18	877.57	832.22	45.35	99,820.83
5	99,820.83	877.57	831.84	45.73	99,775.10
6	99,775.10	877.57	831.46	46.11	99,728.99
7	99,728.99	877.57	831.07	46.50	99,682.49
8	99,682.49	877.57	830.69	46.88	99,635.61
9	99,635.61	877.57	830.30	47.27	99,588.34
10	99,588.34	877.57	829.90	47.67	99,540.67
11	99,540.67	877.57	829.51	48.06	99,492.61
12	99,492.61	877.57	829.11	48.46	99,444.14
13	99,444.14	877.57	828.70	48.87	99,395.27
14	99,395.27	877.57	828.29	49.28	99,346.00
15	99,346.00	877.57	827.88	49.69	99,296.31
16	99,296.31	877.57	827.47	50.10	99,246.21
17	99,246.21	877.57	827.05	50.52	99,195.69
18	99,195.69	877.57	826.63	50.94	99,144.75
19	99,144.75	877.57	826.21	51.36	99,093.39
20	99,093.39	877.57	825.78	51.79	99,041.60
21	99,041.60	877.57	825.35	52.22	98,989.37
22	98,989.37	877.57	824.91	52.66	98,936.71
23	98,936.71	877.57	824.47	53.10	98,883.62
24	98,883.62	877.57	824.03	53.54	98,830.08
25	98,830.08	877.57	823.58	53.99	98,776.09
26	98,776.09	877.57	823.13	54.44	98,721.65
27	98,721.65	877.57	822.68	54.89	98,666.77
28	98,666.77	877.57	822.22	55.35	98,611.42
29	98,611.42	877.57	821.76	55.81	98,555.61
30	98,555.61	877.57	821.30	56.27	98,499.34
31	98,499.34	877.57	820.83	56.74	98,442.59
32	98,442.59	877.57	820.35	57.22	98,385.38
33	98,385.38	877.57	819.88	57.69	98,327.69
34	98,327.69	877.57	819.40	58.17	98,269.52
35	98,269.52	877.57	818.91	58.66	98,210.86
36	98,210.86	877.57	818.42	59.15	98,151.71

mortgage payment is $832.96, the monthly interest rate (0.008333) times the mortgage balance at the beginning of Month 2 ($99,955.76). The difference between the $877.57 monthly mortgage payment and the $832.96 interest is $44.61, representing the amount of the mortgage balance paid off with that monthly mortgage payment. Notice that the last monthly mortgage payment is sufficient to pay off the remaining mortgage balance. When a loan repayment schedule is structured in this way, so that the payments made by the borrower will completely pay off the interest and principal, the loan is said to be *self-amortizing*. Table 17-2 is referred to as an *amortization schedule*.

As Table 17-2 clearly shows, *the portion of the monthly mortgage payment applied to interest declines each month, and the portion applied to reducing the mortgage balance increases*. The reason for this is that as the mortgage balance is reduced with each monthly mortgage payment, the interest on the mortgage balance declines. Because the monthly mortgage payment is fixed, a larger part of the monthly payment is applied to reduce the principal in each subsequent month.

In contrast to a mortgage loan where the monthly payments over the life of the mortgage are sufficient to pay interest and the original mortgage principal is a *balloon mortgage*. With this mortgage, only interest is paid over the life of the mortgage. No payments are made to reduce the original mortgage balance. At the end of the term of the mortgage, the original principal must be paid (this is the so-called balloon payment).

For example, suppose that $100,000 is borrowed to purchase a home, the term of the mortgage is seven years, and the mortgage rate is 10%. The annual dollar interest for each of the seven years will be $10,000. The monthly mortgage payment will then be $833.33 ($10,000 divided by 12). At the end of the seventh year, the homeowner must repay the principal of $100,000.

Investment Risks

The principal investors in mortgage loans (called whole loans) include thrifts and commercial banks. Pension funds and life insurance companies also invest in whole loans, but their ownership is small compared to banks and thrifts. Table 17-3 shows the net funds provided by investor category. By "net funds" we mean the total amount of mortgage originations and purchases less the amount of sales.

Investors are exposed to four main risks by investing in whole loans: (1) credit risk, (2) marketability risk, (3) price risk, and (4) prepayment risk.

Credit Risk. Credit risk is the risk that the homeowner/borrower will default. For FHA- and VA-insured mortgages, this risk is minimal. For privately insured mortgages, the risk can be gauged by the credit rating of the private insurance company that has insured the mortgage. For conventional

TABLE 17-3 SOURCES OF CREDIT FOR MORTGAGE ORIGINATIONS: NET FUNDS PROVIDED BY INVESTORS (MILLIONS OF DOLLARS)					
THRIFTS	COMMERCIAL BANKS	PENSION FUNDS	LIFE INSURANCE COMPANIES	OTHERS[a]	TOTAL
PART A: NET ACQUISITION OF MORTGAGE LOANS[b]					
1986	124,124	78,714	741	6,901	27,584	238,064
1987	158,581	104,643	959	6,451	(398)	270,236
1988:Q1	25,626	12,911	286	701	(5,891)	33,633
PART B: NET ACQUISITION OF MORTGAGE-RELATED SECURITIES[c]					
1986	78,428	60,761	22,224	22,488	146,355	330,256
1987	63,430	35,132	52,802	17,528	133,382	302,274
1988:Q1	799	7,581	10,294	4,243	22,643	45,560
PART C: TOTAL SOURCES OF NEW HOUSING CREDIT					
1986	202,552	139,475	22,965	29,389	173,939	568,320
1987	222,011	139,775	53,761	23,979	132,984	572,510
1988:Q1	26,425	20,492	10,580	4,944	16,752	79,193

[a]Others include mortgage bankers, households, corporations, and other insurance companies.

[b]The net acquisitions figure is the sum of mortgage originations and purchases less sales.

[c]Net acquisitions of mortgage-related securities equal purchases less sales.

Source: Reprinted from *Secondary Mortgage Markets,* Summer 1988, by permission of Freddie Mac. All rights reserved.

mortgages without private insurance, the credit risk depends on the borrower. The LTV provides a useful measure of the risk of loss of principal in case of default. Furthermore, when LTV is high, default is more likely, as there is more inducement for the debtor to walk away.

Marketability Risk.   While there is a secondary market for whole loans, which we shall discuss further below, the fact is that bid–ask spreads are large compared to other debt instruments. That is, mortgage loans tend to be rather illiquid because they are large and indivisible.

Price Risk.   Because a mortgage is a debt instrument, and a long-term one at that—indeed one of the longest—its price will move in an opposite direction from market interest rates. We discussed this relationship between price and interest rates in Chapter 11.

Prepayments and Cash Flow Uncertainty.   Our illustration of the cash flow from a level-payment fixed-rate mortgage assumes that the homeowner would not pay off any portion of the mortgage balance prior to the scheduled due date. But homeowners do pay off all or part of their mortgage balances prior to the maturity date. Payments made in excess of the scheduled principal repayments are called *prepayments.*

Prepayments occur for one of several reasons. First, homeowners prepay the entire mortgage when they sell their house for any number of reasons that require moving. Second, the borrower has the right to pay off all or part of the mortgage balance at any time. Effectively, those who invest in mortgages grant the borrower an option to prepay the mortgage, and the debtor will have an incentive to do so as market rates fall below the rate in the particular contract. Third, if homeowners cannot meet their mortgage obligations, the property is repossessed and sold, with the proceeds from the sale used to pay the lender in the case of a conventional mortgage. For an insured mortgage, the insurer will pay off the mortgage balance. Finally, if property is destroyed by fire, or another insured catastrophe occurs, the insurance proceeds are used to pay off the mortgage.

The effect of the prepayment right is that the cash flow from a mortgage is not known with certainty. This is true not only for level-payment fixed-rate mortgages but also for all the mortgages we discuss in this section.

The Level-Payment Fixed-Rate Mortgage before the 1970s

The level-payment fixed-rate mortgage was initially a great success. It contributed to the recovery of housing after the Great Depression, and continued to perform a valuable role in financing residential real estate in the first two decades of the postwar period until the inception of the era of high inflation, just before the middle of the seventies.

In this golden period, the organization that played the central role in providing mortgage loans was the thrift institution, especially savings and loan associations (S&Ls). There are several reasons for this, the first of which has to do with differentiated interest rates offered on deposits. One of the financial reforms introduced in the early days of the New Deal was imposition of deposit ceilings. These included a mandatory ceiling of zero interest on demand deposits—then held only at commercial banks—and authorization to the Federal Reserve Bank to impose and regulate ceiling rates on savings and related deposits (Regulation Q). The justification for this regulation was basically that, in its absence, banks would be induced to outbid each other for deposits, to the point of impairing the safety of depositors—indeed it was believed that the lack of such ceilings had contributed to the collapse of the banking system during the Depression. The important point, however, is that ceiling rates did *not* extend to thrift institutions.

As the economy came buoyantly out of the war, there was a large demand for housing and mortgages, especially in view of the low construction rate of the previous two decades. At the same time, the Federal Reserve Bank kept interest rate ceilings down below market levels. That gave the S&Ls, unencumbered by ceilings, an opportunity to attract deposits and to grow heftily by outbidding banks and still earning a comfortable margin. This growth was facilitated by favorable legislation in terms of tax treatment, inspired by the notion that S&Ls were to be the pillar of the housing market, as well as provide an attractive, highly liquid investment for the middle and upper classes. S&Ls accepted deposits that were universally regarded as demand liabilities, although in theory notice was required before withdrawal. At the same time they were making mortgage loans of 20 to 30-year maturities, and were further required to give the borrowers the right to prepay the loan at their option. This is equivalent to giving the borrowers a valuable option, in case interest rates should fall. The lender, on the other hand, had no recourse if interest rates rose.

Nobody seemed to appreciate, at the time, the highly speculative and risky position these institutions were taking by borrowing short and lending very long; in essence they took on commitments to make 20 to 30-year loans at the current long-term market rate, which they would have to cover later by attracting deposits at whatever short-term market rate might then prevail. Still, S&Ls were seen as solid; they had no difficulty securing deposits. The result was an explosive growth of S&L financing of housing, as can be seen in Table 17-4. Beginning with 1950, the share of mortgages held by savings institutions grew from 32% to 47% in the short space of 14 years. As one would expect, the explosion was in good measure at the expense of commercial banks, who were losing in the competition for funds, and of insurance companies, for whom the competition of S&Ls was reducing the attractiveness of mortgages as an investment. Thereafter, with the emerging problems of the S&Ls, the share of savings institutions stabilized and eventually began declining in the late seventies, mostly through the secondary market benefits from the explosive growth of mortgage pools, as explained in the next chapter.

The first sign of trouble came in the sixties. First the Federal Reserve, perhaps concerned with the shrinkage of its domain, the banking system, started cautiously to lift the interest rate ceilings, and to allow innovations such as certificates of deposit (CDs) that provided a partial way to circumvent ceiling regulations. Then in the mid-sixties, short-term rates began to rise quickly, first because of the economic boom, and later because of the Vietnam

TABLE 17-4 SHARE OF MORTGAGES HELD BY MAIN FINANCIAL INTERMEDIARIES BETWEEN 1950 AND 1988				
	1950	1964	1977	1988
Total of all holders	73	306	1,000	3,260
Share held by:				
Commercial banks	18	14	18	21
Savings institutions, primarily S&Ls	32	47	46	30
Insurance	22	20	11	8
Mortgage pools	0	3	6	25
All of the above	72	84	81	84

Source: Board of Governors of the Federal Reserve System, *Flow of Funds in the United States 1939–1953.* Other years, Board of Governors, *Flow of Funds Accounts: Financial Assets and Liabilities.*

war and resulting budget deficit. The rise in short rates squeezed the profits of the unhedged S&Ls and threatened to play havoc with an industry so essential to housing. The reaction of the authorities was to attempt to protect the S&Ls from the market by extending to them the ceilings previously applying only to banks. But S&Ls were allowed to keep some advantage by being granted a ceiling rate somewhat higher than that of banks. Thus began the disruptive practice of generalized ceilings that came to an end in the 1980s.

The ceilings were but a short-term palliative, which helped the S&Ls by shielding them from a rush by their immediate competitors to offer depositors interest rates matching the higher market rates. But the ceiling could not solve the basic problem created by low-yielding long-term assets in the face of much higher short-term market rates. By looking at ceilings from the point of view of what S&Ls could pay their depositors rather than being concerned with their relation to market rates, the Fed opened the door to disintermediation— that is, the transfer of funds by investors from the low-paying depository institutions toward direct investment in final lending and other intermediaries, in response to higher market rates. Disintermediation was encouraged further by financial innovations designed to circumvent the interest rate ceilings, such as the money market funds, which offered at market rates services providing a close substitute to those of the depository institutions. These bouts of disintermediation, with low growth of the thrift institutions, were reflected in repeated financial difficulties in the housing market. Problems were only magnified by other serious shortcomings of the level-payment fixed-rate mortgage in the presence of inflation.

THE MISMATCH PROBLEM AND THE CREATION OF VARIABLE-RATE MORTGAGES

In the presence of high and variable inflation, the fixed-rate, level-payment, fully amortized mortgage suffers from two basic and serious shortcomings: these may be labeled the "mismatch" problem and the "tilt" problem. The mismatch problem explains why traditional mortgages are unattractive to investors during times of significant inflation. This has led to the development of variable-rate or adjustable-rate mortgages. The tilt problem is behind the development of other types of mortgage instruments that we describe in the next section.[7]

Nature of the "Mismatch" Problem

This problem, to which we have alluded before, has been with us in the U.S. during most of the postwar period, because mortgages—a very long-term asset—have been financed largely by depository institutions that obtain their funds through deposits that are primarily, if not entirely, of a short-term nature. These institutions have engaged inevitably in highly speculative activity: borrowing short and lending very long. Speculation on the term structure will prove a losing proposition if interest rates rise, as is bound to happen in the presence of significant inflation (Fisher's Law). The institution may be earning the contractual rate, but to attract the deposits needed to finance the loan, it will have to pay the current higher market rate. Considering that the intermediation margin or spread is modest—some 100 to 200 basis points—it will not take much inflation or rise in interest rates before an institution runs into a loss.

Another way to put the matter is in terms of the balance sheet rather than the income statement. The difference between lending and borrowing rates will cause the lending institutions to become technically insolvent, in the sense that the market value of their assets will be insufficient to cover their liabilities. The reason for this is that the institution's liabilities are related to the *face* value of its mortgage assets, but the *market* value of these assets (which is the present value of the cash flow due by the debtor, discounted at the current high rate) will be below the face value by a factor that is not too far from the ratio of the contractual rate to the current market rate. For these reasons both losses and technical insolvencies have occurred on a large scale since the late 60s, especially in the 70s and early 80s.

---

[7] We do not provide a survey of all alternative mortgage instruments in this chapter. Mortgage instruments not covered are growing equity mortgages, balloon/reset mortgages, two-step mortgages, and reverse mortgages.

But, you might ask, why have there not been more bankruptcies? The basic reason is that a losing institution does not have to close so long as it can manage to pay depositors interest and principal, using reserves, liquidation of assets, and most important, the so-called Ponzi technique of attracting more deposits. Similarly, technical bankruptcy need not lead to bankruptcy so long as the depositors did not ask to be repaid. And on the whole they do not. If anything, they might look at the book value of assets, perhaps inflated through some "creative financing" that has been tolerated by the regulatory agencies that were anxious to keep things going and hide the disaster.

Of course some institutions did collapse or were taken over by other institutions, with subsidies provided by the now defunct Federal Saving and Loan Insurance Corporation (FSLIC). This did not help much, as both old and new institutions became engaged in highly speculative undertakings on the ground that successful speculation might let management reap part of the profits, and if the speculation were to turn out poorly, there would be no cost to depositors because they were covered by the deposit insurance, which had just been raised to $100,000.

Thus the gangrene progressed, until finally, in 1989, the administration launched a $150 billion rescue plan. It is interesting that although this plan involves a complete overhaul of the regulatory system, there is so far no indication of any new regulation requiring the kind of investment policy that would have worked against the tragedy of the last 20 years, namely, "match maturities!"

How could this requirement be achieved? One obvious way is for the institution that primarily finances fixed-rate mortgages to lengthen its liabilities through term deposits or analogous instruments. Actually, this has been done in recent years, but only to a modest extent. In fact, it is doubtful that this approach could go very far in meeting the problem, for what has made S&Ls so popular is unquestionably the highly liquid, riskless nature of their deposits. If they were allowed to finance mortgages only by long-term deposits, we might expect a substantial decline in the volume of funds available to them for mortgage financing.

A second approach consists in redesigning the traditional mortgage so as to produce an asset whose return would match the short-term market rates, thus better matching the cost of the liabilities. One instrument satisfying these requirements, and that has won considerable popularity, is the so-called adjustable-rate mortgage.

Characteristics of the Adjustable-Rate Mortgage

The adjustable-rate mortgage (ARM) calls for resetting the interest rate periodically, in accordance with some appropriately chosen index reflecting short-term market rates. It represents an approach applied to many other instruments, e.g., bank loans, especially of the Eurodollar market. By using a short-term rate as the index, S&Ls are able to improve the matching of their returns to their cost of funds. Equivalently, an instrument earning the market rate could be expected to remain close to par whether interest rates rise or fall, thus avoiding the problems of technical insolvency that have plagued the S&Ls relying on the traditional mortgage. Note also that, with high and variable rates of inflation, an adjustable-rate, in principle, reduces risk for the borrower—reduced inflation generally is accompanied by a fall in interest rates, which will benefit borrowers with an adjustable-rate contract. The adjustable-rate contracts currently popular in the U.S. call for resetting the interest rate either every month, six months, year, two years, or three years. The interest rate at the reset date is equal to a benchmark index plus a spread. The spread is between 100 and 200 basis points.

The two most popular indexes are the one-year Treasury rate and the 11th District Cost of Funds. The latter index is a calculation based on the monthly weighted average interest cost for liabilities of thrifts in the 11th Federal Home Loan Bank Board District.[8] This district includes the states of California, Arizona, and Nevada. While most thrifts will argue that the 11th District Cost of Funds is an appropriate index because it fairly represents their cost of funds, this is not quite accurate. In fact, the 11th District Cost of Funds is typically higher than the cost of funds in most regions in the country.

ARMs have been popular with lenders because they shift interest rate risk from the lender to the borrower. To be sure, the risk resulting from falling rates tends to be shifted from the borrower to the lender, but then this risk is born by the lenders anyway, at least in part, because of the prepayment option given to the borrower. Thrifts accordingly prefer to hold ARMs in their portfolios rather than fixed-rate mortgages such as level-payment and graduated-payment mortgages (discussed below), because ARMs provide a better matching with their liabilities. As liabilities are closely tied to the calculated cost of funds index, thrifts prefer ARMs benchmarked to the 11th District Cost of Funds. ARMs are used as collateral for the pass-through securities that we describe in the next chapter.

To encourage borrowers to use ARMs rather than fixed-rate mortgages, mortgage originators generally offer an initial mortgage rate that is lower than the prevailing market mortgage rate. This below-market initial mortgage rate, which the mortgage originator sets in recognition of competitive market conditions, is commonly referred to as a *teaser rate*. At the reset date, the

---

[8] The cost of funds is calculated by first computing the monthly interest expenses for all thrifts included in the 11th District. The interest expenses are summed and then divided by the average of the beginning and ending monthly balance.

benchmark index plus the spread determines the new mortgage rate. For example, suppose that one-year ARMs typically offer a 100 basis point spread over the one-year Treasury rate. Suppose also that the current one-year Treasury rate is 6.5%, so that the initial mortgage rate should be 7.5%. The mortgage originator might set an initial mortgage rate of 6.75%, a rate 75 basis points below the current index rate plus the spread.

The basic ARM is one that resets periodically and has no other terms that affect the monthly mortgage payment. Typically, however, the monthly mortgage payment, and hence, the investor's cash flow, are affected by other terms. These include: (1) periodic caps, and (2) lifetime rate caps and floors.

Periodic Caps.   Periodic caps limit the amount that the interest rate may increase or decrease at the reset date. The periodic rate cap is expressed in percentage points. The most common rate cap on annual reset loans is 2%.

Looking at this provision from the perspective of option theory, what is a periodic cap on the interest rate? Effectively the lender or investor has given the homeowner the right to borrow money at a below-market interest rate, should the rate rise more than the periodic cap. Thus, the lender or investor has sold the homeowner an option on an interest rate. In fact, because the cap goes into effect each year, the lender or investor has not sold one option but a package of options. Similarly, the homeowner has given the lender or investor the right to earn an above-market interest rate should the rate fall more than the periodic cap.

Lifetime Caps and Floors.   Most ARMs have an upper limit on the mortgage rate that can be charged over the life of the loan. This lifetime loan cap is expressed in terms of the initial rate, the most common lifetime cap being 5% to 6%. For example, if the initial mortgage rate is 7% and the lifetime cap is 5%, the maximum interest rate that the lender can charge over the life of the loan is 12%. Many ARMs also have a lower limit (floor) on the interest rate that can be charged over the life of the loan.

Once again, looking at the lifetime cap as an option, the lender or investor has effectively sold the homeowner an option on an interest rate. What about a lifetime floor? In this case, the homeowner is compensating the lender or investor should the interest rate fall below the floor. Therefore, the homeowner has sold the lender or investor an option. From the lender's or investor's perspective, an ARM with a lifetime cap and floor is equivalent to a "collar"—a maximum interest rate and a minimum interest rate. This, then, is equivalent to selling an option (the cap) at one interest rate and buying an option (the floor) at a lower interest rate.

Hybrid Mortgages

There are ARMs that can be converted into fixed-rate mortgages called *convertible ARMs*. Approximately three-quarters of ARMs originated in recent years have been convertible ARMs. There are also fixed-rate mortgages whose mortgage rate can fall if interest rates drop by some predetermined level. These are called *reducible fixed-rate mortgages* (FRMs). Unlike convertible ARMs, reducible FRMs have not been a popular financing vehicle to borrowers. Convertible ARMs and reducible FRMs are hybrid mortgages with built-in refinancing options, motivated by the high refinancing rates since 1983, particularly in late 1986 and early 1987. These hybrid mortgage instruments reduce the cost of refinancing.[9]

A convertible ARM gives the borrower the choice of converting to a fixed-rate mortgage. But what will the new rate be? It could be either (1) a rate determined by the lender, or (2) a market-determined rate. As an example of the latter, the rate could be some interest rate spread over the mortgage commitment rates established by one of the agencies that purchase mortgages. The trend today is toward a market-determined rate. A borrower typically can convert at any date between the first and the fifth times that the mortgage rate is reset. The lender charges a nominal fee for conversion.

In the case of a fixed-rate mortgage that may be adjusted downward, the borrower can exercise the option to have the mortgage adjusted only if some predetermined index rate falls below a certain level (called the *trigger rate*). Usually this option is not granted for the entire life of the mortgage, but typically only for the first five or six years.

Hybrid mortgage instruments reduce the cost of refinancing substantially. At the same time, investors in convertible ARMs and reducible FRMs must be compensated for holding them because they have effectively sold an option to borrowers. Investors must therefore determine whether they are receiving fair compensation for selling these options.

Assessment of Variable-Rate Mortgages

On the whole, the variable-rate mortgage and its variants have the merit of providing a manageable solution to the problem of mismatch of maturities. To borrowers, these mortgages reduce the risk associated with uncertain inflation. Unfortunately, the merits of the ARM have been significantly impaired by arbitrary and misguided regulatory rules, particularly interest rate caps. These caps, meant to protect the borrower, might make sense if

---

[9] For a more detailed discussion of these instruments, see Arnold Kling, "Refinancing Express," *Secondary Mortgage Markets* (Spring 1988), pp. 2–6.

rates were unilaterally set by the lender, but they do not make sense when they are tied to an objective market rate, or to the cost of funds to the lending institution. Furthermore, we know that an increase in nominal rates tends to occur when there is an appreciable rise in inflation, in which case the borrower, in general, can afford to pay the higher interest rate while it lasts.

The main effect of caps is to increase the risk of inflation to intermediary lenders who have no way of putting a cap on the rate they have to pay. Nor is a lower cap adequate compensation, because borrowers have the right to repay. Of course, some of the expected loss will tend to be recouped by a higher spread, and thus finally unloaded on some borrowers; even so, it would be best to leave the matter of caps to private bargaining.

Unfortunately, regulators have still not grasped these simple principles. Nor have they understood that in many cases the consumer generally pays for "consumer protection" in the form of higher rates or other less favorable terms. Finally, the variable-rate mortgage is not a satisfactory answer to inflation-swollen interest rates because it does not address the tilt problem.

THE TILT PROBLEM AND THE CREATION OF OTHER MORTGAGE INSTRUMENTS

Nature of the Tilt Problem

The fixed-rate level-payment fully amortized mortgage was designed so that the borrower would repay the debt in constant nominal installments. This form of repayment would seem highly desirable from the debtor's point of view, so long as inflation was zero or small, because a level nominal repayment rate in that case implies a level *real* rate of repayment. But when there is significant inflation, the traditional mortgage turns into a malfunctioning, very undesirable vehicle for home financing. The reason is not, as frequently supposed, that inflation increases interest rates. To be sure, with a 10% rate of inflation we would expect nominal interest rate to rise by roughly 10 percentage points—say, from 5% to 15%. But this rise does not, per se, make the lender any better off or the borrower any worse off, as the increase is offset by inflation losses and gains, leaving the real rate largely unchanged. The higher interest rate is, by and large, compensated for by the erosion of the principal in terms of purchasing power. (In nominal terms, the higher rate is offset by the rise in the value of the property.)

Rather, the reason for the unsatisfactory performance of the traditional mortgage lies in the "tilt" effect: with 10% steady inflation, if the nominal payment is level, then the real payment will decrease at 10% per year. By the twentieth year, it will be down to some 15% of the initial installment payment. If the creditor is to receive the same real amount as in the absence of inflation, the gradual erosion of the repayments in terms of purchasing power will have to be made up by sufficiently high initial real (and hence nominal) payments. Indeed, with the interest rate rising from 5% to 15%, the first payment on a long-term mortgage will rise roughly threefold.

The nature of the distortion or tilt in the real payment path is illustrated in Figure 17-1 for different rates of inflation. Notice that for an 8% rate of inflation, the path starts at more than twice the no-inflation level, to terminate at well below half. The high initial payment caused by inflation has the effect of foreclosing home ownership to large segments of the population, or forcing buyers to scale down their demands. Indeed, not many people would be able to pay a multiple of what they were paying in the preinflation period for the same facilities. This is especially true in the case of young people who have little asset accumulation.

The first thing to note about this problem is that it is not addressed by the adjustable-rate mortgage. That mortgage uses throughout a nominal interest rate comparable to the fixed-rate mortgage. In particular, the critical early payment will be roughly as high as with a traditional mortgage. Actually, one can show that the adjustable rate is, in some ways, even worse for borrowers than the traditional mortgage. It starts with a rate as high as the traditional mortgage independently of inflation, and will make a substantial jump every time the interest rate is adjusted and the payment shifts from one nominal level to another—even though the rate of payment is level as long as the interest rate does not change.

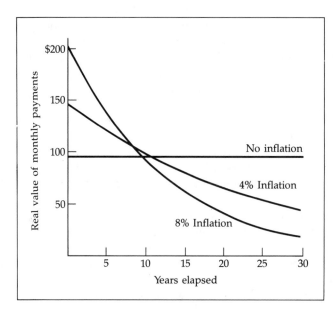

FIGURE 17-1
Nature of Tilt Problem: Real Value of Monthly Payments.
Source: D. Tucker, "The Variable-Rate Graduated Payment Mortgage," *Real Estate Review* (Spring 1975), p. 72.

Can the tilt problem be remedied? It is clear that in principle a solution must involve reducing the interest rate used in the early payments and recouping later. Three major approaches (with many variants) have been offered.

The Graduated-Payment Mortgage

The original graduated-payment mortgage (GPM) exploited an interesting property of the traditional mortgage payment formula. If in that formula the fixed interest rate R is replaced with a lower rate, say R minus x, and at the same time the level stream is replaced with one that grows at the rate of $x\%$ per year, then the new stream has the same present value, when discounted at R, as the level stream. If the rate of inflation over the life of the contract were roughly, say, $p\%$ per year, and known with certainty, then the GPM could provide a very satisfactory answer to the inflation tilt problem. By choosing x equal to p, one could offer a mortgage whose first payment was at the "real" rate R minus p, and whose subsequent payments grew in nominal terms at the rate of inflation p while staying level in real term terms.

Note that if x is large enough (larger than beginning amortization as a percent of principal), in the early years the nominal payments might be insufficient to cover interest at $R\%$ plus amortization. In this case nominal principal would initially rise. That is, there would be "negative amortization." However, as payments keep growing at x per year, amortization must eventually turn positive, and will necessarily (by construction) be completed by the end of the contract. The initial negative amortization, if any, will be larger, the longer the contract (because then the share of amortization in the payment declines with maturity), and the larger x is (and hence p).

Unfortunately, the rate of inflation is most unlikely to be constant over a couple of decades, and in any event it is unforeseeable with any degree of accuracy. Under these conditions the GPM is not likely to succeed in assuring the debtor anything approaching a level real repayment stream. In particular, if p is chosen below realized inflation, the real payments will decline in time, and thus start too high and end too low; if p is overestimated, the payments will start too low.

The original GPM described above is no longer in use. What is popular instead are modified versions introduced by the FHA in 1976, under which the nominal payment grows at a constant rate during a portion of the life of the contract, thereafter leveling off. The main reason why these modified plans are the ones most in use is that they are the ones that the FHA has declared eligible for their insurance—presumably because the mortgages are deemed less risky in nominal terms—and insurance is highly desirable for the borrower as well as for the lender.

The terms of a GPM plan include (1) the mortgage rate, (2) the term of the mortgage, (3) the number of years over which the monthly mortgage payment will increase (and when the level payments will begin), and (4) the annual percent increase in the mortgage payments. The most popular 30-year GPM plan calls for monthly payments that increase by 7.5% for five years, then at the beginning of the sixth year remain constant for the remaining 25 years. The monthly mortgage payments under this GPM program for a $100,000, 30-year, 10% mortgage would be: (1) $667.04 per month in the first year, (2) $717.06 per month in the second year, (3) $770.84 in the third year, (4) $828.66 in the fourth year, (5) $890.80 in the fifth year, and (6) $957.62 for the remaining term of the mortgage, beginning with the sixth year.

Table 17-5 compares the amount of the outstanding mortgage balance at the end of each year for this particular GPM and a level-payment fixed-rate mortgage. Notice that there is negative amortization of the GPM for the first four years. It is not until Year 10 that the outstanding mortgage balance is below the original mortgage balance.

It should be apparent from our description of the GPM's terms that it cannot solve the mismatching problem or provide a satisfactory answer to the tilt problem, at least as long as inflation is high and unpredictably variable. This shortcoming has probably contributed to the decreasing popularity of GPMs in recent years. In fact, the only two basic mortgage designs that can provide a more or less foolproof solution to both problems are the price-level-adjusted mortgage (PLAM) and the dual-rate mortgage (DRM).

The Price-Level-Adjusted Mortgage (PLAM)

The price-level-adjusted mortgage is similar to the traditional mortgage except that monthly payments are designed to be level in purchasing power terms rather than in nominal terms, and that the fixed rate is in the "real" rather than the nominal rate.

The real rate, it will be recalled from Chapter 11, is the interest rate that one could expect to prevail if there were no inflation in the economy. It can be estimated by taking the market nominal rate and subtracting the expected inflation rate, which might in turn be approximated by the recent inflation experience. The evidence suggests that in the U.S., the real rate, in contrast to the nominal one, tends to remain fairly stable in time around a value of, say, 3% to 4%.

To compute the monthly payment under a PLAM, we must first establish the terms of the contract, namely: (1) the real interest rate, (2) the term of the loan, and (3) the index to be used to measure the price level, usually the Consumer Price Index (CPI). One can then compute, from an ordinary mortgage table, the annual payment and the unpaid balance at the end of each year, corresponding to the stipulated real interest and maturity. These figures represent payments and balances in real terms. To compute the

---

TABLE 17-5   COMPARISON OF OUTSTANDING MORTGAGE BALANCE FOR A LEVEL-PAYMENT FIXED-RATE MORTGAGE AND A POPULAR GPM

Term of mortgage: 30 years
Original balance: $100,000
Mortgage rate: 10%

GPM: Monthly mortgage payment increases by 7.5% per year for 5 years

	OUTSTANDING MORTGAGE BALANCE AT END OF YEAR	
YEAR	LEVEL-PAYMENT FIXED RATE	GPM
1	$99,444	$102,090
2	98,830	103,769
3	98,152	104,949
4	97,402	105,526
5	96,574	105,383
6	95,660	104,385
7	94,649	103,282
8	93,533	102,064
9	92,300	100,719
10	90,938	99,233
11	89,433	97,591
12	87,771	95,777
13	85,934	93,773
14	83,906	91,559
15	81,665	89,113
16	79,189	86,412
17	76,454	83,427
18	73,432	80,130
19	70,094	76,488
20	66,407	72,464
21	62,333	68,019
22	57,833	63,108
23	52,862	57,684
24	47,370	51,691
25	41,303	45,071
26	34,601	37,757
27	27,197	29,678
28	19,018	20,752
29	9,982	10,892
30	0	0

payments actually due in each year, we simply multiply the real payment by an inflation correction factor equal to the ratio of the stipulated index in the last year to the value of the index in the initial year. Similarly, to compute the actual debt, we multiply the real debt by the inflation correction factor.

Table 17-6 (on pp. 558–559) illustrates the required computations for a PLAM with a 4% real rate, 30 year maturity, and relying on the CPI. Columns (2) and (3) report the real payments and the real ending balance, which correspond to those for a traditional mortgage with the same specifications. Column (4) shows the inflation correction factor based on actual experience for the years 1977 through 1987, and fictitious figures thereafter. Note that the figures in this column are the ratio of the price index in the current year to that in the *initial* year; it is not the rate of inflation but its accumulated rate plus one. We see that for Year 1 the correction is 1.076, implying an inflation rate of 7.6%. This figure is used to correct the ending balance for Year 1, which is reported in column (6). It cannot be used to correct the Year 1 payment because the information is available too late to use. Thus in column (5), which shows the corrected payments, the figures for the first two years are the same as the uncorrected ones in column (2), but the payment for Year 2 is corrected by using the correction factor for Year 1 (477.4) (1.076) = 513.7. Similarly, for every subsequent row, the figure in column (5) is the product of column (1) and column (4) lagged one year. By the end of the contract, in the thirtieth year, the debt has been fully amortized—a necessary consequence of the fact that the underlying contract in real terms is fully amortized by then (see, for example, the last row in columns (3) and (6)).

Calculation of the periodic payment can be accomplished in an alternative way that may be instructive in terms of our discussion of the dual-rate mortgage. In this alternative procedure, the ending balance for each year is computed as above, but the payment for each year is the level payment corresponding to a 4% mortgage rate, a maturity equal to the remaining life of the PLAM, and a debt equal to the balance for the previous year as given in column (6). To illustrate, consider the calculation of the payment for Year 10. At this point the mortgage has 20 years of remaining life. Using this maturity and an interest rate of 4%, the level annuity factor per month is 0.005873. (This can be found from a mortgage table or can be inferred from Table 17-6 as the ratio of the monthly payment rate in column (2) to the balance at the end of the year before, in column (3).) Multiplying this factor by the balance at the end of the year before in column (6), 146,824, we arrive at a payment for the year of $862, which coincides with the figure in column (5).

The behavior of the monthly payment and of the ending balance in columns (5) and (6) may raise questions about the desirability of this type of instrument, considering that by the end of the contract the payment is over six times as large as at the start—an increase of 500%. Similarly, because of negative amortization, the ending balance keeps growing through the first half of the mortgage life; by the fifteenth year the debt has just about doubled. In other words, the debtor, instead of repaying, has kept getting deeper and deeper in debt. In reality, these results are simply the consequence of the prevailingly high and persistent inflation assumed in the illustration, which causes the price level to rise by some six and a half times.

We know from columns (2) and (3) that in fact the real payment stays perfectly flat, and that is the only feature of the contract that should be relevant. In fact, the data on the behavior of average nominal income from 1977 to 1987, columns (7) and (8), show that it rose even faster than inflation, and that, accordingly, the ratio of the monthly nominal payment to monthly income actually would have decreased if such a mortgage had been outstanding in this period. Similarly, column (9), relying on estimates of the average value of a house, implies that the house's market value was rising substantially faster than the debt; by the fifteenth year when the debt is at its peak, the debt-to-value ratio has declined from 0.80 to 0.57.

It may be objected that "average experience" is of no help to an individual borrower; for many people income may not keep up with inflation and hence with the payment. While this risk exists, and may affect the probability of default, exactly the same risk exists with the traditional mortgage in the absence of significant inflation; in both cases the payment is level in real terms, and while most people may be expected to enjoy rising (or at least non-decreasing) real income, many fall short. But let's remember that insufficient real income is, generally, not a cause of default costly to the lender; as long as the market value of property exceeds the debt balance, it will pay the owner who cannot afford it any longer to sell the house and settle the debt, rather than default. Thus what matters most is the loan-to-value ratio; here again, the risk is no more than for a traditional mortgage with a stable price level. It may in fact be less, as it is not uncommon in times of inflation for house prices to rise faster than the general price level.

It is of course true that a PLAM provides less protection to the lender than does a traditional mortgage in the presence of significant inflation, because a traditional mortgage amortizes the debt faster. But that is because inflation, through the unintended tilt or front-loading effect, affords extra protection to the lender that was not intended by the designers of the traditional mortgage, or required by the lender, in the absence of inflation. It would seem that rational investors, if they are prepared to invest in a traditional mortgage with stable prices, should be equally willing to invest in a PLAM. In fact, the PLAM has distinct advantages for any investor interested in the real rather than in the nominal outcome of the investment, for it protects the investor as well as the borrower against purchasing power uncertainty.

Some difficulty might arise if thrift institutions wanted to offer a PLAM, for they would be earning the real rate while having to pay their depositors

TABLE 17-6   HYPOTHETICAL 30-YEAR $100,000 PLAM

| | ZERO INFLATION | | BASED ON 1977–1987 INCOMES, HOUSE PRICES, AND INFLATION | | | | | | |
(1) YEAR	(2) MONTHLY PAYMENT	(3) ENDING BALANCE	(4) CPI RATIO	(5) MONTHLY PAYMENT	(6) ENDING BALANCE	(7) MONTHLY INCOME	(8) CURRENT PTI* RATIO	(9) HOUSE VALUE	(10) CURRENT LTV
0	$477.42	$100,000	1.000	$ 477.42	$100,000	$ 2,388	20.0	$125,000	80.0
1	477.42	98,239	1.076	477.42	105,705	2,657	18.0	140,750	75.1
2	477.42	96,406	1.198	513.70	115,455	2,928	17.5	160,455	72.0
3	477.42	94,499	1.359	571.75	128,449	3,210	17.8	175,698	73.1
4	477.42	92,514	1.499	648.93	138,702	3,524	18.4	191,160	72.6
5	477.42	90,448	1.591	715.77	143,877	3,707	19.3	195,556	73.6
6	477.42	88,297	1.642	759.43	144,951	3,941	19.3	199,467	72.7
7	477.42	86,059	1.712	783.74	147,352	4,292	18.3	205,451	71.7
8	477.42	83,730	1.772	817.44	148,382	4,528	18.1	209,150	70.9
9	477.42	81,307	1.806	846.05	146,824	4,772	17.7	212,705	69.0
10	477.42	78,784	1.873	862.12	147,533	4,977	17.3	217,597	67.8
11	477.42	76,159	2.015	894.02	153,455	5,540	16.1	245,015	62.6
12	477.42	73,426	2.243	961.97	164,668	6,105	15.8	279,317	59.0

13	477.42	70,582	2.545	1,070.67	179,660	6,691	16.0	305,852	58.7
14	477.42	67,623	2.808	1,215.21	189,856	7,347	16.5	332,767	57.1
15	477.42	64,543	2.979	1,340.38	192,262	7,729	17.3	340,420	56.5
16	477.42	61,337	3.074	1,422.14	188,560	8,216	17.3	347,229	54.3
17	477.42	58,001	3.206	1,467.65	185,971	8,947	16.4	357,646	52.0
18	477.42	54,529	3.319	1,530.76	180,957	9,439	16.2	364,083	49.7
19	477.42	50,915	3.382	1,584.33	172,176	9,949	15.9	370,273	46.5
20	477.42	47,154	3.507	1,614.43	165,358	10,376	15.6	378,789	43.7
21	477.42	43,240	3.773	1,674.17	163,157	11,549	14.5	426,516	38.3
22	477.42	39,167	4.200	1,801.41	164,486	12,727	14.2	486,229	33.8
23	477.42	34,927	4.767	2,004.96	166,484	13,949	14.4	532,420	31.3
24	477.42	30,515	5.258	2,275.64	160,434	15,316	14.9	579,273	27.7
25	477.42	25,923	5.578	2,510.03	144,606	16,112	15.6	592,597	24.4
26	477.42	21,144	5.757	2,663.14	121,722	17,127	15.5	604,449	20.1
27	477.42	16,170	6.004	2,748.36	97,092	18,651	14.7	622,582	15.6
28	477.42	10,994	6.214	2,866.54	68,322	19,677	14.6	633,789	10.8
29	477.42	5,607	6.333	2,966.87	35,505	20,740	14.3	644,563	5.5
30	477.42	0	6.567	3,023.24	0	21,632	14.0	659,388	0.0

Table assumes a 4% real interest rate, 80% initial LTV, 20% PTI ratio, and 1% annual house depreciation relative to a new house.

*Payment-to-income.

Source: Susan E. Woodward and David A. Crowe, "A Power-Packed Mortgage," *Secondary Mortgage Markets* (Fall 1988), pp. 2–7.

the market nominal rate. Actually there need be no problem in that what the institution would earn is the real rate plus the annual revaluation of the subject property, and the sum of the two might be expected to be close to the nominal market rate (Fisher's Law). In addition, the intermediaries, if the contract real rate had been correctly chosen, could undertake to offer a new type of "indexed deposit" earning a real fixed rate on an indexed principal, although this might require appropriate changes in regulation.

The PLAM is not a new concept; it has been used for decades in many countries with high inflation, where the housing industries could not possibly have survived with the traditional mortgage. These include Finland right after World War II, many South American countries, and Israel. Somewhat surprisingly, it has not been used to any significant extent in the United States. This is largely explained because no innovation in home financing has been possible without some sanction of government regulators, and regulators have been unimaginative, and rather disinclined toward real indexation of any type. Critical in this respect has been HUD's lack of approval for FHA insurance. Quite recently, however, HUD seems about ready to change this attitude and to issue regulations to standardize these mortgages. PLAM may soon be making its debut in the U.S.

The Dual-Rate Mortgage (DRM)

This instrument, which has also been referred to as the *inflation-proof mortgage* (IPM), is similar in spirit and objective to the PLAM: payments start low—at current mortgage rates of around 10%, payments would start around 30% to 40% below those required by the traditional mortgage or by the ARM. They then rise smoothly at the rate of inflation, if any, achieving, like the PLAM, annual payments approximately level in terms of purchasing power. Finally, by construction, the debt is fully amortized by the end of the contract.

The DRM differs from the PLAM in that the amount owed by the borrower is computed on the basis of a floating short-term rate. This has several important consequences. First, just as in the case of other instruments where a fluctuating rate is indexed to short-term market rates, the market value of the instrument is not subject to interest rate risk but should instead remain close to par, except of course for credit risk. Second, there is little danger of prepayment risk, i.e., of the borrower taking the option to repay when rates fall, for the DRM rate would automatically fall. And finally, it can be financed through the existing institution of short-term nominal deposits.

A DRM requires specification of three parameters: (1) the "payment" rate; this is a "real" rate of interest fixed for the life of the loan, much as with a PLAM. The purpose of this rate is not to establish *how much* the debtor will pay but rather *how* the amount will be paid, i.e., to make possible a desirable and affordable distribution of payments over the life of the instrument; (2) the "effective" or "debiting" rate, a short-term rate that, as in the ARM, determines how much the borrower effectively pays (or is debited for) and how much the creditor earns; it changes periodically, say, once a year, on the basis of an agreed-upon reference short-term rate (say, the one-year Treasury bill); and (3) the life of the mortgage, just as for any other fully amortized mortgage contract.

Given these three parameters, calculation of the periodic payment is straightforward, as illustrated in Table 17-7. In any year the payment, shown in column (3), is obtained exactly as for the PLAM, i.e., by multiplying the balance outstanding at the beginning of the year, reported in column (1), by the annuity factor appropriate to a mortgage contracted at the *payment* rate and with maturity equal to the number of years remaining until the end of the contract. The calculations in the table are based on a payment rate of 7% and a 20-year life, so the annuity factor reported in column (2) turns out to be 0.0943. Multiplying by the initial balance of column (1), we obtain the first-year annual payment of $9,439 in column (3), implying a monthly payment of $787. To compute the balance at the beginning of the second year (1973), we take the first-year balance and subtract amortization in the first year.

Now recall that amortization of the debt is equal to the annual payment less the amount of interest for which one is liable (whether paid in cash or added to the debt). The essential feature of the DRM is that the interest for which the debtor is liable in a given year is calculated by multiplying the initial balance by the *effective* rate, and not the payment rate. In Table 17-7, the chosen debiting rate is the one-year Treasury bill rate for the first week of each year, plus 2%. Its value for year t is reported in column (4)—for the first year it is 6.28%. Thus the amount of interest due for the first year is $6,280 [column (5)], and the amortization in column (6) is the difference between the first-year payment [column (3)] and the interest due [column (5)]. Subtracting the amortization from the initial balance, we arrive at the initial balance for the second year [column (1), second row], which is used in turn to compute the second-year payment, and so on. To summarize:

1. The annual payment [column (3)] equals the initial balance [column (1)] times the annuity factor [column (2)].

2. The initial balance equals the previous year's balance less the previous year's amortization [column (6)].

3. Amortization [column (6)] equals the annual payment [column (3)] less interest due [column (5)].

4. Interest due equals the previous balance [column (1)] times the debiting or effective rate [column (4)].

TABLE 17-7 PERFORMANCE OF A 20-YEAR DRM BEGINNING IN 1972 WITH A PAYMENT RATE OF 7%

	(1)	(2)	(3)	(4)	(5)	(6)	(7)	(8)	(9)	(10)	(11)	(12)	(13)
YEAR	OUTSTANDING PRINCIPAL	PAYMENT FACTOR	TOTAL ANNUAL PAYMENT	EFFECTIVE INTEREST RATE	INTEREST CHARGED	AMORTIZATION (3)-(5)	PRINCIPAL YEAR END (1)-(6)	DEFLATOR	INFLATION RATE	PAYMENT OVER DEFLATOR (3)/(8) × 100	PAYMENT OVER PER CAPITA DISPOSABLE INCOME 1972 = 100	PRINCIPAL OVER DEFLATOR (7)/(8)	PAYMENT OVER RESIDENTIAL RENT INDEX 1972 = 100
1972	100000.00	0.09439	9439.00	0.0628	6280.00	3159.00	96841.00	100.00	—	9439.00	100	96841.00	100
1973	96841.00	0.09675	9369.37	0.0789	7640.75	1728.61	95112.39	105.70	0.06	8864.11	89	89983.34	95
1974	95112.39	0.09941	9455.12	0.0942	8959.59	495.54	94616.85	116.40	0.10	8123.20	81	81288.40	91
1975	94616.85	0.10243	9691.60	0.0883	8354.67	1336.94	93279.92	125.30	0.08	7734.68	78	74444.87	89
1976	93279.92	0.10586	9874.61	0.0781	7285.16	2589.45	90690.47	131.70	0.05	7497.67	74	68860.15	86
1977	90690.47	0.10979	9956.91	0.0729	6611.33	3345.57	87344.89	139.30	0.06	7147.85	68	62703.03	82
1978	87344.89	0.11434	9987.02	0.0928	8105.61	1881.41	85463.49	149.10	0.07	6698.21	62	57319.62	77
1979	85463.49	0.11965	10225.71	0.1241	10606.02	-380.31	85843.80	162.50	0.09	6292.71	57	52826.65	73
1980	85843.80	0.12590	10807.73	0.1406	12069.64	-1261.90	87105.70	179.00	0.10	6037.84	55	48662.40	71
1981	87105.70	0.13336	11616.42	0.1608	14006.60	-2390.18	89495.88	194.10	0.08	5984.76	53	46108.13	70
1982	89495.88	0.14238	12742.42	0.1632	14605.73	-1863.30	91359.19	205.30	0.06	6206.73	56	44500.33	72
1983	91359.19	0.15349	14022.72	0.0178	9848.52	4174.20	87184.99	214.00	0.04	6552.67	56	40740.65	77
1984	87184.99	0.16747	14600.87	0.1000	8718.50	5882.37	81302.61	226.84	0.06	6436.64	54	35841.39	75
1985	81302.61	0.18555	15085.70	0.1000	8130.26	6955.44	74347.18	240.45	0.06	6273.93	52	30919.96	74
1986	74347.18	0.20980	15598.04	0.1000	7434.72	8163.32	66183.86	254.88	0.06	6119.82	50	25966.94	73
1987	66183.86	0.24389	16141.58	0.1000	6618.39	9523.20	56660.66	270.17	0.06	5974.60	49	20972.22	72
1988	56660.66	0.29523	16727.93	0.1000	5666.07	11061.86	45598.80	286.38	0.06	5841.16	47	15922.47	71
1989	45598.80	0.38105	17375.42	0.1000	4559.88	12815.54	32783.26	303.56	0.06	5723.83	46	10799.49	70
1990	32783.26	0.55309	18132.09	0.1000	3278.33	14853.77	17929.49	321.78	0.06	5634.99	45	5572.03	70
1991	17929.49	1.10000	19722.44	0.1000	1792.95	17929.49	0.00	341.08	0.06	5782.29	46	0.00	72
TOTALS			260572.70		160572.70	100000.00							

A few observations are appropriate here. First, as the table reveals, negative amortization is possible with a DRM instrument because the debiting rate can exceed the annuity factor if inflation is high enough. Second, in principle, the DRM resembles the PLAM in several ways:

1. For both instruments the current payment is the previous balance times the same annuity factor.
2. In the PLAM the balance in year t is the balance at $t - 1$ times (1 − an amortization factor corresponding to the real rate and remaining life + rate of inflation). For the DRM the balance at t is the balance at $(t - 1)$ times (1 − an amortization factor as above + debiting rate − real rate). If we choose a real rate for a PLAM that is the same as the payment rate for a DRM, the only difference between the two instruments is that the PLAM's balance tends to be driven up through inflation, while the DRM balance grows through the difference between the nominal and the real rate. Thus, if Fisher's Law holds precisely, the two instruments would be identical. Deviations will arise because Fisher's Law may fail to hold, especially in the short run. In this case we can show that the PLAM debtor will end up paying precisely the real rate set in the contract, while the DRM borrower will end up paying the average effective real rate over the period. In the period covered by the example, the borrower would have fared somewhat better with a DRM.

If the DRM and the PLAM are so similar, why does the annual payment in Table 17-7 decline so steadily in real terms? The reason is that the real rate used in Table 17-6 is much higher than the 4% used in Table 17-7. There are two reasons for this choice. The first is that, once we allow for the intermediation spread, we believe that the 4% is too low. The second is that we have allowed the lender some extra protection by assuming a payment rate higher than the best guess of the real rate. Notice that raising the payment rate will result in faster amortization, tilting the payment schedule down, as in the table.

Despite their overall similarity, the DRM appears to have several advantages over the PLAM. One is the opportunity to reduce the lender's credit risk without increasing total interest costs, by raising the payment rate above the estimated real rate, thus accelerating the amortization in real terms. A second advantage is that it reduces the price risk for lenders. The PLAM is, after all, a fixed-rate contract, and although the real rate has turned out to be relatively stable, significant movements cannot be ruled out over a 20- to 30-year span. The DRM, by contrast, as a variable rate instrument should tend to remain always close to par (aside from credit risk). A further important advantage is that because the lender always earns the short-term market rate, the mortgage can be financed through short-term deposits without violating the principle of matching maturities.

So far the DRM has had rather limited application in the U.S., in good measure because it has not yet received FHA approval for insurance. It has had some application abroad and should have a future also in the U.S. after the PLAM has been introduced. There are a number of variants of the DRM that improve the working of the instrument in some directions, at the cost of deterioration in other directions.[10]

SUMMARY

The major originators of mortgage loans are thrifts, banks, and mortgage bankers. The risks associated with originating mortgages (pipeline risk) include price risk and fallout risk. Various types of mortgages have different cash flow characteristics. There are level-payment fixed-rate mortgages, graduated-payment mortgages, adjustable-rate mortgages, hybrid mortgages, and price-level-adjusted mortgages.

There is uncertainty associated with investing in any of these mortgages; because of prepayments, the cash flow is not known with certainty. This uncertainty is called prepayment risk. In addition, by investing in mortgages an investor faces marketability risk and price risk and may be exposed to credit risk.

The traditional type of mortgage, characterized by a fixed rate, level (nominal) payment, and full amortization, performed well in the first years of the postwar period, becoming the dominant vehicle for house financing. But this method began to falter with high and variable inflation. First, it was financed mainly by depository institutions with very short-term funds, even though a mortgage is a very long-term instrument; this mismatch of maturities proved catastrophic when short-term rates rose sharply, leading to widespread insolvency of S&Ls, the major lenders. The borrower's prepayment option also contributed to the difficulties of lenders. Second, in the presence of inflation-driven high interest rates, mortgage repayment in real terms is no longer level, but instead starts high and ends low, shutting off many would-be borrowers.

Two remedies in use in the U.S. are the adjustable-rate mortgage (ARM) and the graduated-payment mortgage (GPM). The first addresses the mismatch problem, and the second (imperfectly) the tilt problem; neither

---

[10] For a further discussion, see Frank J. Fabozzi and Franco Modigliani, *Mortgage and Mortgage-Backed Securities Markets* (Boston: Harvard Business School Press, forthcoming 1992).

addresses both. Two other solutions, the price-level-adjusted mortgage (PLAM) and the dual-rate mortgage (DRM), address fairly effectively both problems, but neither of these instruments has yet been adopted on a large scale in the U.S.

QUESTIONS

1. What are the sources of revenue arising from mortgage origination?

2. What are the risks associated with the mortgage origination process?

3. a. Why is a fixed-rate, level-payment mortgage unattractive to a depository institution?

   b. What types of mortgage instruments have been developed to overcome the unattractive features of the fixed-rate, level-payment mortgage?

4. What is meant by the "tilt problem" associated with mortgages?

5. a. Why is the cash flow of a mortgage unknown?

   b. In what sense has the investor in a mortgage granted the borrower (homeowner) a call option?

6. What features of an adjustable-rate mortgage will affect its cash flow?

7. What is the motivation for the design of price-level-adjusted mortgages and dual-rate mortgages?

8. What is meant by a conforming mortgage and a non-conforming mortgage?

CHAPTER

18

THE MARKET FOR MORTGAGE POOLS AND OTHER SECURITIZED ASSETS

LEARNING OBJECTIVES

After reading this chapter you will understand:

- the development of the current mortgage market, and the role of public and private conduits.

- what is meant by the securitization of assets.

- the investment characteristics of mortgage pass-through securities.

- the importance of prepayments to the valuation of mortgage-backed securities.

- why a collateralized mortgage obligation is created.

- the different types of collateralized mortgage obligation structures.

- the investment characteristics of stripped mortgage-backed securities.

- the different types of asset-backed securities.

- the benefits to issuers, investors, and borrowers of securitization.
- potential implications of securitization for the financial system.

Wₑ noted in the previous chapter that in the sixties and seventies the majority of all mortgages originated in depository institutions. These institutions kept the mortgages they originated in their portfolio. Some difficulties were inevitable even then, as the depository institutions, especially the S&Ls, were encouraged by legislation and regulation to confine their deposit-seeking and lending activities to their local market. As depository institutions obtained their funds from local citizens, there tended to be a poor allocation of capital; some regions had an excess supply of funds and low rates, and others had shortages and high rates.

This problem found a partial remedy with the entrance of a new participant—the mortgage bankers discussed in the previous chapter. Unlike thrifts and commercial banks, mortgage bankers did not provide funds from deposit taking. Instead, they originated mortgages and sold them, not just to life insurance companies but to thrifts in other parts of the country looking for a mortgage investment. They provided a *brokerage function*, laying the foundation for a national market. This would seem more like an adequate market, bringing mortgage rates throughout the country closer, and reducing the shortage of mortgage money in high-demand regions of the country.

While the mortgage market operated this way through the late 1960s, it had a major shortcoming—it was dependent on the availability of funds from thrifts and banks, whether local or national. With the inception of the period of high and variable inflation and interest rates in the late sixties, disintermediation, induced by ceiling rates, led to wide shortfalls in the funds available to all depository institutions. To counter or at least limit this problem, what was needed was a mortgage market that was not dependent on deposit-taking institutions. This could be accomplished by developing a strong secondary mortgage market that would attract institutional investors besides deposit-taking institutions and life insurance companies.

The driving force in the development of a strong secondary market was a financial innovation which involved the packaging (or "pooling") of mortgages and the issuance of securities collateralized by these mortgages.

This system of lending is referred to as *asset securitization* because securities are created whose collateral is the cash flow from the assets. Our focus in this chapter is on the market for securitized assets. By far the largest part of the market is the mortgage-backed securities market, where the assets collateralizing the securities are mortgage loans. The basic mortgage-backed security is the mortgage pass-through security. From this security, derivative mortgage-backed securities are created: collateralized mortgage obligations and stripped mortgage-backed securities. Securitized assets backed by non-real estate mortgage loans are a small but growing part of the market. These securities are commonly referred to as *asset-backed securities.* Asset securitization has various benefits for issuers, borrowers, and investors as well as far-ranging implications for the U.S. financial system.

This system is radically different from the traditional system for financing the acquisition of assets, which called for one financial intermediary, such as a commercial bank, thrift, or insurance company, to: (1) originate a loan; (2) retain the loan in its portfolio of assets, thereby accepting the credit risk associated with the loan; (3) service the loan (i.e., collect payments and provide tax or other information to the borrower); and (4) obtain funds from the public with which to finance its assets (except for the small amount representing the institution's equity).

With asset securitization more than one institution may be involved in lending capital. Consider mortgage activities. A lending scenario can look like this: (1) a thrift or commercial bank can originate a mortgage loan; (2) the thrift or commercial bank can sell its mortgages to an investment banking firm that creates a security backed by the pool of mortgages; (3) the investment banker can obtain credit risk insurance for the pool of mortgages from a private insurance company; (4) the investment banker can sell the right to service the loans to another thrift or a company specializing in serving mortgages; and (5) the investment banking firm can sell the securities to individuals and institutional investors.

Besides the original bank or thrift, an investment bank, an insurance company, another thrift, an individual, and other institutional investors participate. The bank or thrift in our example does not have to absorb the credit risk, service the mortgage, or provide the funding. Also notice that there is no government agency involved in this process. While we have specified mortgage loans, this system can be applied to automobile and boat loans, credit card loans, credit sales by finance companies and manufacturing firms, senior bank loans, and lease receivables.

We begin this chapter with a brief review of the development of the secondary mortgage market.

DEVELOPMENT OF THE SECONDARY MORTGAGE MARKET

The foundations for the secondary mortgage market can be traced back to the Great Depression and the legislation that followed. Congress's response to the Depression and its effects on financial markets was to establish several public purpose agencies. The Federal Reserve provided better liquidity for commercial banks through the Federal Reserve discount window. Liquidity for thrifts was provided by the creation of the Federal Home Loan Banks (FHLBs), which were granted the right to borrow from the Treasury.

Another creation of Congress, the Federal Housing Administration (FHA), addressed the problems with the balloon mortgage. It was this government agency that developed and promoted the fixed-rate level payment, fully amortized mortgage. The FHA also reduced credit risk for investors by offering insurance against mortgage defaults. Not all mortgages could be insured, however—the mortgage applicant had to satisfy FHA underwriting standards, which made the FHA the first to standardize mortgage terms. While we may take this for granted today, standardization was essential for the development of a secondary mortgage market. In 1944, the Veterans Administration began insuring qualified mortgages.

But who was going to invest in these mortgages? Thrifts could do so, especially with the inducement provided by several advantages reviewed earlier. But the investment would be illiquid in the absence of a market to trade mortgages in. Congress thought of that, too. It created another government-sponsored agency, the Federal National Mortgage Association (FNMA). This agency, popularly known as "Fannie Mae," was charged with the responsibility to create a liquid secondary market for FHA- and VA-insured mortgages, which it tried to accomplish by buying mortgages. Fannie Mae needed a funding source in case it faced a liquidity squeeze. Congress provided this by giving Fannie Mae a credit line with the Treasury.

Despite the creation of Fannie Mae, the secondary mortgage market did not develop to any significant extent. During periods of tight money, Fannie Mae could do little to mitigate the housing crisis. In 1968, Congress divided Fannie Mae into two organizations: (1) the current Fannie Mae, and (2) the Government National Mortgage Association (popularly known as "Ginnie Mae"). Ginnie Mae's function is to use the "full faith and credit of the U.S. government" to support the FHA and VA mortgage market. Two years later in 1970, Congress authorized Fannie Mae to purchase conventional mortgage loans (i.e., those not insured by the FHA or VA) and created the Federal Home Loan Mortgage Corporation (popularly known as "Freddie Mac") to provide support for FHA/VA insured mortgages and conventional mortgages.

Ginnie Mae accomplished its objective by guaranteeing securities issued by private entities who pooled mortgages together and then used these mortgages as collateral for the security sold. Freddie Mac and Fannie Mae purchased mortgages, pooled these mortgages, and issued securities using the pool of mortgages as collateral. The securities created are called *mortgage pass-through securities*. They are purchased by many types of investors (domestic and foreign) who had previously shunned investment in the mortgage market. In the 1980s, private issuers of mortgage pass-through securities who did not use the backing of the three agencies but instead some form of private credit enhancement began issuing pass-through securities backed by conventional family mortgages and commercial real estate mortgages.

We'll have more to say about all these securities in the following sections of this chapter. What is important to understand here is that it was the process of securitizing mortgages that resulted in the strong secondary mortgage market that exists today.

MORTGAGE PASS-THROUGH SECURITIES

As we noted in the previous chapter, investing in mortgages exposes the investor to default risk, price risk, liquidity risk, and prepayment risk. A more efficient way is to invest in a mortgage pass-through security. This is a security created when one or more holders of mortgages form a collection (pool) of mortgages and sell shares or participation certificates in the pool. A pool may consist of several thousand or only a few mortgages. The first mortgage pass-through security was created in 1968.

Risk-averse investors should prefer investing in a fraction of a pool to investing a single mortgage, just as investors prefer to hold a diversified portfolio of stocks rather than an individual stock. Individual mortgages expose the investor to unique (or unsystematic) risk and systematic risk. The risks in this case are the risk that the homeowner will prepay the mortgage at some unfavorable time and that the borrower may default on the loan. One reason that prepayments occur is because of changes in mortgage interest rates. The other reason is unrelated to the movement of mortgage interest rates.

Unsystematic prepayment risk is the risk of an adverse change in the speed at which prepayments are made that is not attributable to a change in mortgage interest rates. Systematic prepayment risk is an unfavorable change in prepayments attributable to a change in mortgage interest rates. Systematic risk in the case of default rates represents widespread default rates perhaps because of severe economic recession. Holding a diversified portfolio of mortgages in the form of a mortgage pass-through security reduces most unsystematic risk, leaving only systematic risk. In addition, a mortgage pass-through security is considerably more liquid than an individual mortgage.

When a mortgage is included in a pool of mortgages that is used as collateral for a mortgage pass-through security, the mortgage is said to be *securitized*. More than one-third of one- to four-family mortgages have been securitized. Only 22% of conventional mortgages have been securitized, but 85% of FHA/VA insured mortgages have been. Only 7% of multifamily mortgages have found their way into a mortgage pool backing a mortgage pass-through security.

Cash Flow Characteristics

The cash flow of a mortgage pass-through security depends on the cash flow of the underlying mortgages. As we explained in the previous chapter, the cash flow consists of monthly mortgage payments representing interest, the scheduled repayment of principal, and any prepayments.

Payments are made to securityholders each month. The amounts and the timing of the cash flow from the pool of mortgages and the cash flow passed through to investors, however, are not identical. The monthly cash flow for a pass-through security is less than the monthly cash flow of the underlying mortgages by an amount equal to servicing and other fees. The other fees are those charged by the issuer or guarantor of the pass-through security for guaranteeing the issue (discussed later).[1] Typically, the coupon rate on a pass-through security is 0.5% less than the mortgage or coupon rate on the underlying pool.

The timing of the cash flow is also different. The monthly mortgage payment is due from each mortgagor on the first day of each month, but there is a delay in passing through the corresponding monthly cash flow to the securityholders. The length of the delay varies by the type of pass-through security.

Grantor Trust Structure

An entity issuing a mortgage pass-through security wants to make sure that it is not taxed on the interest payments when they are received from homeowners, because it is simply acting as a conduit to pass those payments

---

[1] Actually, the servicer pays the guarantee fee to the issuer or guarantor.

through to the securityholders. Under the tax law, the issuer is not treated as a taxable entity if the pass-through security is issued through a legal structure known as a *grantor trust*.

Issuers of Mortgage Pass-Through Securities

The three major types of pass-through securities are guaranteed by agencies created by Congress to increase the supply of capital to the residential mortgage market and to provide support for an active secondary market: Government National Mortgage Association ("Ginnie Mae"), Federal Home Loan Mortgage Corporation ("Freddie Mac"), and Federal National Mortgage Association ("Fannie Mae").

While Fannie Mae and Freddie Mac are commonly referred to as "agencies" of the U.S. government, both are corporate instrumentalities of the U.S. government. The stock of these two entities trades on the New York Stock Exchange; therefore they are effectively quasi-private corporations. They do not receive a government subsidy or appropriation, and are taxed like any other corporation. Fannie Mae and Freddie Mac are more appropriately referred to as federally sponsored agencies or government sponsored entities. Their guarantee does not carry the full faith and credit of the U.S. government. In contrast, Ginnie Mae is a federally related institution because it is part of the Department of Housing and Urban Development. As such, its guarantee carries the full faith and credit of the U.S. government.

The securities associated with these three entities are known as *agency pass-through securities*. About 98% of all pass-through securities are agency pass-through securities. The balance of mortgage pass-through securities are privately issued. These securities are called *conventional mortgage pass-through securities*. While the major portion of pass-through issues have residential mortgages as their collateral, pass-throughs collateralized by mortgages on commercial property also have been issued.

Agency Pass-Through Securities

Government National Mortgage Association (GNMA).   Ginnie Mae mortgage-backed securities represent the largest proportion of mortgage pass-through securities outstanding. They are guaranteed by the full faith and credit of the United States Government with respect to timely payment of both interest and principal. That is, the interest and principal will be paid when due even if mortgagors fail to make their monthly mortgage payment.

While Ginnie Mae provides the guarantee, it is not the issuer. Pass-through securities are issued by lenders it approves, such as thrifts, commercial banks, and mortgage bankers. These lenders receive approval only if the underlying mortgages satisfy the underwriting standards established by Ginnie Mae. When it guarantees securities issued by approved lenders, Ginnie Mae permits these lenders to convert illiquid individual mortgages into liquid securities backed by the U.S. government. In the process Ginnie Mae accomplishes its goal to supply funds to the residential mortgage market and provide an active secondary market. For the guarantee, Ginnie Mae receives a fee, called the *guaranteeing fee*.

The security guaranteed by Ginnie Mae is called a *mortgage-backed security* (MBS); they are sold in minimum denominations of $25,000 and in increments of $5,000 thereafter. The first MBS was issued in 1968. Only mortgages insured or guaranteed by either the Federal Housing Administration, the Veterans Administration, or the Farmers Home Administration can be included in a mortgage pool guaranteed by Ginnie Mae.

Different mortgage-backed securities with different types of collateral are issued. Mortgage pass-through securities are backed by single-family (SF) mortgages, graduated-payment mortgages (GPM), growing-equity mortgages (GEM), and mobile or manufactured home loans. The large majority of GNMA MBS are backed by single-family mortgages (a loan for a one- to four-family primary residence with a level payment and a fixed rate). Within the single-family MBS, there are pools that consist of 30-year mortgages and 15-year mortgages that collateralize the security.

Mortgage-backed securities backed by adjustable-payment mortgages (APM) are issued. An APM's monthly mortgage payment changes periodically according to some index. One example is the adjustable-rate mortgages (ARM) described in the previous chapter.

The Federal Home Loan Mortgage Corporation. The second largest category of agency pass-through securities are those issued by the Federal Home Loan Mortgage Corporation (FHLMC). The security issued by Freddie Mac is called a *participation certificate* (PC). The first PCs were issued in 1971.

Most of the pools of mortgages underlying Freddie Mac participation certificates consist of conventional mortgages, although participation certificates with underlying pools consisting of FHA-insured and VA-guaranteed mortgages have been issued. While there are participation certificates that guarantee the timely payment of both interest and principal, most Freddie Mac participation certificates guarantee only the timely payment of interest. The scheduled principal is passed through as it is collected, with Freddie Mac guaranteeing only that the scheduled payment will be made no later than one year after it is due. A Freddie Mac guarantee is not a guarantee by the U.S. government. Most market participants, though, view Freddie Mac participation certificates as similar in creditworthiness to Ginnie Mae pass-throughs, which are fully guaranteed by the U.S. government.

Freddie Mac has two programs from which it creates PCs: the *Cash Program* and the *Guarantor/Swap Program.* The underlying loans for both programs are conventional mortgages (i.e., mortgages not backed by a government agency). Conventional Regular PCs are issued under the Cash Program. In this program the mortgages that back the PC include *individual* conventional one- to four-family mortgage loans that Freddie Mac purchases from mortgage originators, pools, and sells. Under the Conventional Guarantor/Swap Program, Freddie Mac allows originators to swap pooled mortgages for PCs in those same pools. For example, a thrift may have $50 million of mortgages. It can swap these mortgages for a Freddie Mac PC whose underlying mortgage pool is the $50 million mortgage pool the thrift swapped for the PC.

Both programs provide capital to the residential mortgage market and foster a secondary mortgage market. The Guarantor/Swap Program was designed specifically to provide liquidity to the troubled thrift industry. It allows thrifts to swap mortgages trading below par (mortgage rates lower than the current mortgage rate) without recognizing an accounting loss for financial reporting purposes. The PC that the thrift gets in exchange for the mortgage pool can then be either (1) held as an investment, (2) used as collateral for either short-term or long-term borrowing, or (3) sold. The Guarantor/Swap program has been a huge success and is one of the reasons for the significant growth of the amount of PCs issued.

There are 30-year and 15-year Freddie Mac Regular and Swap PCs. Freddie Mac also issues PCs with underlying mortgage loans of FHA/VA loans, adjustable-rate mortgages, and multifamily mortgages.

ARMs were first purchased in 1985 by Freddie Mac for its own portfolio under the ARM Cash Program. ARM PCs were first issued in early 1986. Freddie Mac began an ARM Guarantor/Swap Program in October 1987.

In the fall of 1990, Freddie Mac introduced its *Gold PC*, which it issues in both its Cash Program and Guarantor/Swap Program. The Gold PC is the only type of pass-through it will issue in the future. Gold PCs are guaranteed with respect to timely payment of both interest and principal. Non-Gold PCs can be converted into Gold PCs at the option of the investor upon payment of a conversion fee.

Federal National Mortgage Association. While it was created by Congress in 1938, the Federal National Mortgage Association (FNMA), in its current form, is the newest player in the agency pass-through securities market. Fannie Mae was charged by Congress with promoting a secondary market for conventional and FHA/VA single- and multifamily mortgages. To meet that obligation, since 1972 it has purchased these mortgages and held them as investments. It was not until 1981 that Fannie Mae pooled these mortgages and issued its first mortgage pass-through securities, called *mortgage-backed* *securities* (MBS). These pass-throughs are guaranteed with respect to the timely payment of both interest and principal. Like Freddie Mac participation certificates, Fannie Mae mortgage-backed securities are not the obligation of the U.S. government. Fannie Mae also has a swap program similar to that of Freddie Mac. It provides liquidity to mortgage originators such as thrifts.

Fannie Mae was the first to issue ARM pass-through securities in late 1984, with the underlying ARMs tied to the 11th District Cost of Funds. Fannie Mae ARMs indexed off the 11th District Cost of Funds are the most popular type of agency ARMs, with approximately $16 billion outstanding in 1988, because thrifts have found them more attractive for asset/liability management. To understand why, recall that a thrift's investment objective is to lock in a spread between its investments and its cost of funds. An adjustable-rate mortgage offers an investment with an interest rate that will change with some index. A thrift's cost of funds likewise will change with some index. If the indexes are the same, a thrift can lock in the difference between the ARM rate and the cost of funds. For example, if an ARM pays 100 basis points above some index, and the thrift's cost of funds is on average 30 basis points above the same index, the thrift will lock in an average spread of 70 basis points regardless of how interest rates change. Because the 11th District Cost of Funds more closely tracks a thrift's cost of funds than one-year Treasury rates, thrifts prefer ARMs where the underlying mortgages are indexed off the 11th District Cost of Funds.

Conventional Pass-Through Securities

Conventional pass-through securities, also called *private label pass-through securities*, are issued by thrifts, commercial banks, and private conduits. Private conduits may purchase non-conforming mortgages, pool them, and then sell pass-through securities whose collateral is the underlying pool of non-conforming mortgages. The underlying pool may be fixed-rate or adjustable-rate mortgages.

While the amount of conventional pass-through securities is small relative to agency pass-through securities, this market can be expected to grow significantly. The private conduits that issue conventional pass-through securities effectively are doing what the government created the agency conduits to do, without any guarantees (implicit or explicit) from the U.S. government. In this case, they are providing a secondary market for non-conforming mortgages.[2]

---

[2] Several legislative acts and regulatory changes helped foster the development of the private mortgage-backed securities market. The Secondary Mortgage Market Enhancement Act of 1984 included provisions to improve the marketability of mortgage-related securities earning a double-A quality rating or better from one of the nationally-recognized commercial rating companies.

Unlike agency pass-through securities, conventional mortgage pass-through securities are rated. Often they are supported by credit enhancements so that they can obtain a high rating. Most conventional mortgage pass-through securities have a rating of at least double A. The development of private credit enhancement is the key to the success of this market and, indeed, the key to the development of all asset securitization. Credit enhancement may take the form of either (1) corporate guarantees, (2) pool insurance from a mortgage insurance company, or (3) senior/subordinated interests.

In the case of a corporate guarantee, the issuer of a conventional pass-through uses its own credit rating to back the security. Under the second approach to credit enhancement, a mortgage pool policy is obtained to cover defaults up to a specified amount. The rating of the mortgage insurance company that writes the policy must be equal to or higher than the rating that the issuer seeks for the pass-through security. For example, if an issuer seeks a double-A rating for the pass-through, it cannot obtain a pool insurance policy from a single-A rated mortgage insurance company.

The third credit enhancement is the senior/subordinated structure, also known as the *A/B pass-through*. In this structure a mortgage pool is partitioned into senior certificates and subordinated certificates. The senior certificate holder has priority on the cash flow from the underlying collateral. It is the senior certificates that are rated and sold to investors as conventional pass-throughs. The subordinated certificates absorb the default risk. The amount of subordinated certificates relative to senior certificates that a mortgage pool is divided into will determine its credit rating. The greater the portion of subordinated certificates relative to senior certificates, the higher the credit rating that can be obtained.[3]

Unlike agency pass-through securities, conventional mortgage pass-through securities must be registered with the Securities and Exchange Commission.

Measuring Yields on Pass-Through Securities

Recall from Chapter 11 that the yield of any investment is the interest rate that will make the present value of the expected cash flow equal to the market price (plus accrued interest). The difficulty with computing the yield on any mortgage-backed security is that the cash flow is unknown because of the possibility of mortgage prepayments.

---

[3] For a more detailed description of this structure, see Anand K. Bhattacharya and Peter J. Cannon, "Senior-Subordinated Mortgage Pass-Throughs" in Frank J. Fabozzi (ed.), *Advances and Innovations in the Bond and Mortgage Markets* (Chicago, IL: Probus Publishing, 1989).

The only way to calculate a yield is to make some assumption about the prepayment rate over the life of the underlying mortgage pool. Then given the estimated cash flow, a *cash flow yield* can be computed. Cash flow yields are typically based on the Public Securities Association (PSA) standard prepayment benchmark.[4] Although it was developed initially for projecting the cash flow of collateralized mortgage obligations (discussed later in this chapter), it can be applied to project the cash flow of any mortgage-backed security. The benchmark is expressed as a monthly series of annual constant prepayment rates (CPR). A CPR is a measure of the percentage of the outstanding mortgage balance of a pool that is expected to prepay in a year. For example, a CPR of 6% assumes that 6% of the mortgage balance at the beginning of the year will prepay by the end of the year. Since a CPR is an annual rate, it must be converted to a monthly constant prepayment rate in order to calculate the monthly prepayments and thereby monthly cash flow.[5]

The PSA standard prepayment benchmark assumes prepayments will occur less often for newly originated mortgages, and then become more frequent as the mortgages become seasoned. More specifically, the PSA standard prepayment benchmark assumes the following pattern for annual CPRs for 30-year mortgages: (1) 0.2% for the first month, increased by 0.2% per month for the next 29 months, when it reaches 6%, and (2) 6% for the remaining months (at which time it is said that the mortgages become "fully seasoned").

This standard prepayment benchmark is referred to as "100% PSA." Slower or faster prepayment rates (or, prepayment "speeds") are then referred to as some percentage of the standard prepayment benchmark. For example, 50% PSA means one-half the CPR of the PSA standard prepayment benchmark; 300% PSA means three times the CPR of the PSA standard prepayment benchmark. The speed selected by an investor to project the cash flow for a pass-through often is estimated using an econometric (statistical) model that projects prepayments based on particular characteristics of the underlying mortgage pool and macroeconomic data.[6]

---

[4] The Public Securities Association is an organization that represents dealers in U.S. government securities and mortgage-backed securities.

[5] A monthly CPR is commonly called a *single monthly mortality* (SMM) rate. Technically, it is not found by dividing the annual CPR by 12 because each month the mortgage balance is being reduced. Consequently, the SMM will be a figure higher than the annual CPR divided by 12. For more explanation and an illustration of how a cash flow schedule is computed, see Chapter 16 in Frank J. Fabozzi, *Fixed Income Mathematics* (Chicago: Probus Publishing, 1988).

[6] For a discussion of prepayment models, see Lakhbir S. Hayre, Kenneth Lauterbach, and Cyrus Mohebbi, "Prepayment Models and Methodologies," in Fabozzi, *Advances and Innovations in Bond and Mortgage Markets*.

The PSA prepayment benchmark is *not* a model for forecasting prepayments. It is a market convention. While it has helped standardize quotations on mortgage-backed securities, critics have noted that the actual behavior pattern of prepayments has deviated significantly from the behavior indicated by the PSA standard prepayment benchmark. Specifically, it has taken longer than 30 months for mortgages to become fully seasoned.[7]

Bond Equivalent Yield.   Once the cash flow is projected, we can determine the interest rate that makes the present value of the cash flow equal to the price. As the cash flow from a pass-through security is monthly, the interest rate found is also a monthly rate. To compare the yield estimated for a pass-through security to a Treasury or corporate bond yield, it is not enough to multiply the monthly yield by 12; a Treasury coupon security and a corporate bond pay interest semiannually, while a pass-through has a monthly cash flow. This gives investors in pass-throughs opportunity to generate greater annual interest. They can reinvest monthly cash flows; bond investors who receive coupon payments semiannually will reinvest only twice a year. Therefore, the yield on a pass-through security must be calculated so as to make it comparable to the yield to maturity for a bond.

This is done by computing the *bond equivalent yield*[8] for a pass-through security assuming that the monthly cash flows from the pass-through are reinvested at the cash flow yield until the end of each semiannual period. The formula used is:

$$\text{Bond equivalent yield} = 2\,[(1 + r_M)^6 - 1]$$

where r_M = the monthly interest rate that will equate the present value of the monthly cash flow to the price of the pass-through security, and

$[(1 + r_M)^6 - 1]$ = the bond equivalent semiannual yield on the monthly pay pass-through security.

For example, if r_M is 1%, then the bond equivalent yield is:

$$\text{Bond equivalent yield} = 2\,[(1.01)^6 - 1]$$

$$= 2\,[1.06152 - 1] = 0.1230 = 12.30\%$$

---

[7] See David Jacob, Clark McGranery, Sean Gallop, and Lynn Tong, "The Seasoning of Prepayment Speeds and Its Effect on the Average Lives and Values of MBS," in Frank J. Fabozzi (ed.), *The Handbook of Mortgage-Backed Securities*, third edition (Chicago: Probus Publishing, 1992).

[8] Bond equivalent yield is explained in Chapter 11.

Obtaining Prepayment Estimates. The major dealers in pass-through securities and some vendors offer econometric models that estimate prepayment rates. These models take into account the economic and specific geographic factors that influence prepayment rates. The major dealers provide their projected prepayment rates by coupon for newly issued and seasoned pass-through securities on Reuters, Telerate, and Knight–Ridder.

Secondary Market

The secondary market for instruments issued as part of the more popular agency programs is highly liquid. Pass-throughs are quoted in the same manner as U.S. Treasury coupon securities. A quote of 94-05 means 94 and 5/32nd of par value, or 94.15625% of par value.

The yield corresponding to a price must be qualified by an assumption concerning prepayments. While yields are frequently quoted, remember that the yield is based on some underlying prepayment assumption. Consequently, a yield of 9% based on 150% PSA means that the bond equivalent yield is 9%, assuming that the underlying mortgages will prepay at a rate equal to 150% PSA. A yield number without qualification as to the prepayment assumption is meaningless.

In fact, even with specification of the prepayment assumption, the yield number is meaningless in terms of the relative value of a pass-through. For an investor to realize the yield based on some PSA assumption, a number of conditions must be met: (1) the investor must reinvest all the cash flows at the calculated yield, (2) the investor must hold the pass-through security until all the mortgages have been paid off, and (3) the assumed prepayment rate must actually occur over the life of the pass-through. Now, if all this is likely, then we can trust the yield numbers. Otherwise, investors must be cautious in using yield numbers to evaluate pass-through securities.[9]

There are many seasoned issues of the same agency with the same coupon rate outstanding at any given time. Each issue is backed by a different pool of mortgages. For example, there are many seasoned pools of GNMA 8's. One issue may be backed by a pool of mortgages all for California properties, while another may be backed by a pool of mortgages for primarily New York City homes. Others may be backed by a pool of mortgages on homes in several regions of the country.

Which pool are dealers referring to when they talk about, say, GNMA 8's? They are not referring to any specific pool but they mean a "generic" security

---

[9] A better procedure for evaluating pass-through securities is described in Chapter 16 of Fabozzi, *Fixed Income Mathematics.*

even though the prepayment characteristics of pass-throughs of underlying pools from different parts of the country are different. Thus, the projected PSA prepayment rates for pass-through securities reported by dealer firms are for generic pass-throughs. A particular pool purchased may have a materially different prepayment speed from the generic benchmark. Moreover, when an investor purchases a pass-through without specifying a pool number, the seller can deliver the worst-paying pools from the securities it holds.[10]

Prepayment Risks Associated with Pass-Through Securities

An investor who owns pass-through securities does not know what the cash flow will be because that depends on prepayments. The risks associated with prepayments are called *prepayment risks*.

To understand prepayment risk, suppose an investor buys a 10% coupon Ginnie Mae at a time when mortgage rates are 10%. Let's consider what will happen to prepayments if mortgage rates decline to, say, 6%. There will be two adverse consequences. First, we know from the basic property of fixed-income securities in Chapter 11 that the price of an option-free bond will rise, because the present value of the future stream of payments discounted at a lower rate will be greater. The new valuation will be such that the owner of the security could by selling the instrument secure the initial cash flow despite the lower returns now available in the market. But in the case of a pass-through security, the rise in price will not be as large as that of an option-free bond because a fall in interest rates will increase the probability that the market rate will fall below the rate the borrower is paying. This gives the borrower an incentive to prepay the loan and refinance the debt at a lower rate. To the extent that this happens, the securityholder will be repaid not at a price incorporating the premium but at the face value of the debt. The holder risks capital loss, which reflects the fact that the anticipated reimbursements at par will not yield the initial cash flow.

The adverse consequences when mortgage rates decline are the same as those faced by holders of callable corporate and municipal bonds. As in the case of those instruments, the upside price potential of a pass-through security is truncated because of prepayments. This characteristic, as we stated in Chapter 15, is referred to as "negative convexity." This should not be

---

[10] Instead of a generic pool, an investor can purchase a specific pool. For a further discussion, see Chuck Ramsey and J. Michael Henderson, "Specified Pools," Chapter 6 in Frank J. Fabozzi (ed.), *The Handbook of Mortgage-Backed Securities,* second edition (Chicago: Probus Publishing, 1988).

surprising, because a mortgage loan effectively grants the borrower the right to call the loan at par value. The adverse consequence when mortgage rates decline is referred to as *call risk* or *contraction risk.*

Now let's look at what happens if mortgage rates rise to 15%. The price of the pass-through, like the price of any bond, will decline. But again it will decline more because the higher rates will tend to slow down the rate of prepayment, in effect increasing the amount invested at the coupon rate, which is lower than the market rate. Prepayments will slow down, because homeowners will not refinance or partially prepay their mortgages when mortgage rates are higher than the contractual rate of 10%. Of course this is just the time when investors want prepayments to speed up so that they can reinvest the prepayments at the higher market interest rate. This adverse consequence of rising mortgage rates is called *extension risk.*

Therefore, prepayment risk encompasses contraction risk and extension risk. Prepayment risks make pass-throughs unattractive for certain financial institutions to hold from an asset/liability perspective. Let's look at why particular institutional investors may find pass-throughs unattractive:

1. Thrifts and commercial banks, as we explained in Chapter 2, want to lock in a spread over their cost of funds. Their funds are raised on a short-term basis. If they invest in fixed-rate pass-through securities, they will be mismatched because a pass-through is a longer-term security. In particular, depository institutions are exposed to extension risk when they invest in pass-through securities.

2. To satisfy certain obligations of insurance companies, pass-through securities may be unattractive. More specifically, consider a life insurance company that has issued a four-year GIC. The uncertainty about the cash flow from a pass-through security and the likelihood that slow prepayments will result in the instrument being long-term, make it an unappealing investment vehicle for such accounts. In such instances, a pass-through security exposes the insurance company to extension risk.

3. Consider a pension fund that wants to fund a 15-year liability. Buying a pass-through security exposes the pension fund to the risk that prepayments will speed up and the maturity of the investment will shorten to considerably less than 15 years. Prepayments will speed up when interest rates decline, thereby forcing reinvestment of prepayments at a lower interest rate. In this case, the pension fund is open to contraction risk.

We can see that some institutional investors are concerned with extension risk and others with contraction risk when they purchase a pass-through security. Is it possible to alter the cash flow of a pass-through so as to reduce the contraction risk and extension risk for institutional investors? This can be done, as we shall see later in this chapter.

Yield Spread to Treasuries

While we have explained that it is not possible to calculate a yield with certainty, it has been stated that pass-through securities offer a higher yield than Treasury securities. Typically, the comparison is between Ginnie Mae pass-through securities and Treasuries, for both are free of default risk. Presumably, the difference between the two yields primarily represents prepayment risk. The question should be whether the premium the investor receives in terms of higher yield for bearing prepayment risk is adequate. This is where option-pricing models applied to pass-through securities have been used.[11] Option-pricing models let us determine if the pass-through security is offering the proper compensation for accepting prepayment risk.

The yield spread between conventional pass-through securities and agency pass-through securities reflects both credit risk and prepayment risk. The reason for the difference in prepayment risk lies in the nature of the underlying mortgages. For example, in the case of Ginnie Mae pass-through securities, the underlying mortgages are FHA- or VA-insured mortgages. Borrowers who obtain such government guarantees have different prepayment characteristics compared to holders of non-government insured mortgages. Specifically, when interest rates decline, prepayments on FHA/VA-insured mortgages do not increase as fast as those for non-FHA/VA-insured mortgages. This reflects the fact that borrowers who obtain government-guaranteed mortgages typically do not have the ability to take on refinancing costs as rates decline. There are similar differences between the prepayment patterns of Ginnie Mae pass-through securities and the two other agency pass-through securities.

When we speak of comparing the yield of a mortgage pass-through security to a comparable Treasury, what does "comparable" mean? The stated maturity of a mortgage pass-through security is an inappropriate measure because of prepayments. Instead, market participants have used two measures: Macaulay duration and average life. As we explain in Chapter 12, Macaulay duration is a weighted-average term to maturity where the weights

---

[11] See David J. Askin, Woodward C. Hoffman, and Steven Meyer, "Evaluation of the Option Component of Mortgages," Chapter 28, and H. Gifford Fong, Ki-Young Chung, and Eric M. P. Tang, "The Valuation of Mortgage-Backed Securities: A Contingent Claims Approach," Chapter 30, in Fabozzi, *The Handbook of Mortgage-Backed Securities*, second edition.

are the present value of the cash flows. Average life is the average time to receipt of principal payments (scheduled principal payments and projected prepayments), weighted by the amount of principal expected.[12]

COLLATERALIZED MORTGAGE OBLIGATIONS

We have noted that any mortgage pass-through security is subject to considerable uncertainty about what its actual maturity will be. Consequently, market participants interested in purchasing a short-term security for, say, one to four years, find these securities unattractive; some long-term investors likewise find these securities unattractive because a fast-pay pass-through security could substantially reduce its maturity. A collateralized mortgage obligation (CMO) reduces the uncertainty concerning the maturity of a mortgage-backed security, thereby providing a risk/return pattern not available with typical mortgage pass-through securities.

A CMO is a security backed by a pool of pass-through securities or mortgages (whole loans). Because CMOs derive their cash flow from the underlying mortgage collateral, they are referred to as "derivative" securities. CMOs are structured so that there are several classes of bondholders with varying *stated* maturities. The principal payments from the underlying collateral in the earlier CMO structures are used to retire the bonds sequentially.

A "plain vanilla" CMO may be structured with four classes of bonds, which we shall refer to as Class A, Class B, Class C, and Class Z. (The classes are commonly referred to as *tranches*.) The first three classes, with Class A representing the shortest maturity bond, receive periodic interest payments from the underlying collateral; Class Z is an accrual bond that receives no periodic interest until the other three classes are retired. When principal payments, both scheduled and through prepayment, are received by the CMO trustee, they are applied to retire the Class A bonds. After all the Class A bonds are retired, all principal payments received are applied to retire the Class B bonds. Once all the Class B bonds are retired, Class C bonds are paid off from all principal payments. Finally, after the first three classes of bonds are retired, the cash flow payments from the remaining underlying collateral are used to satisfy the obligations on the Z-bonds (original principal plus accrued interest).

---

[12] Mathematically, the average life is expressed as follows:

$$\text{Average life} = \sum_{t=1}^{T} t \, \frac{(\text{Principal received at time } t)}{\text{Total principal}}$$

where T is the number of months.

TABLE 18-1 SUMMARY INFORMATION FOR M.D.C. MORTGAGE FUNDING, SERIES J

CLASS	PAR (IN MILLIONS)	STATED MATURITY	COUPON	PRICE
A	$35.5	5/99	8.05%	99.87500
B	15.5	2/02	8.75	99.84575
C	40.5	2/07	9.35	99.71875
Z	9.0	8/16	9.50	93.15625

CLASS	EXPECTED MATURITY	AVERAGE LIFE (YEARS)	DURATION	PROJECTED YIELD	BENCHMARK TREASURY	SPREAD OVER TREASURY
A	5/91	2.30	2.10	7.87%	2 year	120 bp
B	8/93	5.80	4.61	8.72	5	160
C	11/99	10.10	6.58	9.38	10	210
Z	8/11	18.50	17.05	10.00	20	235

Consider one of the early CMO issues as an example: the M.D.C. Mortgage Funding Corporation, Series J CMO, a $100 million issue priced on July 7, 1986.[13] This issue had four classes. The underlying collateral is GNMA pass-throughs with a weighted average coupon of 9.5% and 297 months remaining to maturity. The original maturity for the GNMA pass-throughs was 360 months. Basic information for each class is summarized in the upper panel of Table 18-1.

The cash flow for each class can be derived only by assuming some prepayment rate for the underlying mortgage collateral. The prepayment benchmark used by mortgage-backed securities dealers to quote CMO yields is the PSA standard prepayment model that we discussed earlier. Issue pricing depends on the issuer's expectations for the prepayment rate. For the M.D.C. Mortgage Funding CMO in the illustration, the issuer assumed a prepayment rate of 110% PSA. The expected maturity, average life, duration, projected yield, and spread to Treasuries based on 110% PSA are summarized in the lower panel of Table 18-1. The spread over Treasuries for each class of

---

[13] This information is taken from Lakhbir S. Hayre, David Foulds, and Lisa Pendergast, "Introduction to Collateralized Mortgage Obligations," Chapter 14, in Fabozzi, *The Handbook of Mortgage-Backed Securities*, second edition.

				TYPE OF ISSUER					TYPE OF COLLATERAL	
	TOTAL	FREDDIE MAC	FANNIE MAE	BUILDERS	THRIFTS	PRIVATE THRIFT CONDUITS	DEALERS	OTHER	WHOLE LOANS	PASS-THROUGH SECURITIES
1986	48,067	1,573	0	9,914	3,533	2,480	23,163	7,404	3,016	45,051
1987	59,053	0	916	6,002	1,530	794	40,002	9,809	2,590	56,463
1988	76,751	14,985	10,782	7,096	885	350	32,949	9,704	2,712	74,039
1989	100,504	39,731	44,043	220	899	0	9,898	5,713	4,214	96,290
1990	118,559	38,676	58,819	1,095	96	300	13,509	6,063	5,806	112,754

TABLE 18-2   ISSUERS OF CMOs: 1986–1990 (MILLIONS OF DOLLARS)

Source: Goldman, Sachs & Co. Includes public offerings of collateralized mortgage obligations and REMICs, but excludes strips issued under a grantor trust. Reprinted from *Secondary Mortgage Markets,* Summer 1991, by permission of Freddie Mac. All rights reserved.

this CMO issue represents compensation for prepayment risk and credit risk. The prepayment risk is lower than for a mortgage pass-through security.

The CMO market has seen phenomenal growth since the first publicly issued CMO was introduced in June of 1983 by Freddie Mac. Table 18-2 shows the issuance of CMOs from 1986 to 1990. Types of issuers are also shown in Table 18-2. The overwhelming bulk of CMOs are backed by pass-through securities.

Considerations in Constructing a CMO

The issuer faces three problems in constructing a CMO. First, the CMO must be structured to ensure that the cash flow structure will satisfy the bond obligations even under adverse prepayment conditions. This is necessary in order to obtain a high quality rating from the commercial rating companies. Second, the issuer wants to be sure that the trust is not treated as a taxable entity so that taxes will not be paid at the pool level. If the issuer pays taxes at the pool level, the payments made to securityholders are treated as dividends and not tax-deductible. The third problem is that the issuer wants the CMO to be considered as a sale of assets so that it will not appear as debt on its balance sheet.

With respect to taxation, recall from our earlier discussion of mortgage pass-through securities that an entity structuring a pass-through using a grantor trust is not treated as a taxable entity. Prior to the Tax Reform Act of 1986, however, the IRS ruled that multiple-class pass-throughs such as CMOs were taxable entities even if structured as a grantor trust. To circumvent this provision in the tax code, issuers designed cash flow structures so that they would be classified as debt payments for tax purposes. One result was that the CMO would be treated as debt on the balance sheet, failing to satisfy the issuer's objective of avoiding this adverse financial reporting consequence.

One provision of the Tax Reform Act of 1986, the Real Estate Mortgage Investment Conduit (REMIC), allowed issuers to issue multiple pass-through securities without being treated as a taxable entity. This means that a CMO can now be structured so that the issuer can treat it as a sale of assets for tax purposes but not as debt for financial reporting purposes. The issuer does this by electing to have the CMO treated as a REMIC. A REMIC CMO is not a new security but a tax election made by an issuer.

Credit Risk and Yield Spreads

Credit quality of most CMOs is high enough for the asset to be rated triple-A by the major commercial rating agencies. The credit risk depends on the way the CMO is structured and the quality of the underlying mortgage collateral, generally not the creditworthiness of the issuer of the CMO.

With respect to the collateral, CMOs backed by agency pass-through securities or FHA/VA-guaranteed mortgages expose the investor to minimal credit risk. CMOs issued by Freddie Mac and Fannie Mae carry their guarantee and are perceived to have low credit risk. CMOs that do not fall into one of these two categories typically carry pool insurance that guarantees the timely payment of interest and principal.

The other key element in determining the credit quality of the CMO is the manner in which the cash flows are structured. In order to receive a triple-A quality rating, cash flows must be sufficient to meet all obligations under any prepayment scenario. Also, the reinvestment rate assumed to be earned on the cash flow until it is distributed to bondholders must be low.

Because of the safeguards built into a CMO structure, a triple-A rating assigned to a CMO generally is viewed as a higher quality rating than that for a corporate bond with a triple-A rating. Even though CMOs have lower credit risk, they generally offer a higher yield relative to comparable credit-rated corporate bonds. The yield spread is due primarily to prepayment risk. Once again, the question is whether the size of the yield spread is sufficient to compensate for the prepayment risk.

Other CMO Structures

So far we have discussed the "plain vanilla" CMO structure. Other CMO structures introduced since June 1983 include CMOs with a floating-rate class and CMO planned and targeted amortization class (PAC and TAC) bonds that, under all but extreme prepayment rates, provide a more stable cash flow.

Floating-Rate CMOs.   In September 1986 Shearson Lehman Brothers introduced a CMO (SLB CMO Trust D, $150 million) where one class received interest that was reset quarterly at a spread of 37.5 basis points over the three-month London Interbank Offered Rate (LIBOR). The structure of such a floating-rate CMO appealed to financial institutions and foreign investors who sought investments whose yield varied with the rate on their liabilities. To indicate the popularity of this structure, almost one-half of the 150 CMOs issued in the six-month period following its introduction included a floating-rate class.[14] The design of the floating-rate CMO has evolved to make the class comparable in investment characteristics to other short-term instruments that attract funds from financial institutions.

One feature of the floating-rate CMO necessary to assure that the collateral is sufficient to meet all obligations of the CMO issue is a cap placed on the maximum lifetime interest rate that could be paid on the floating-rate class. This feature made floating-rate CMOs a less attractive vehicle for financial institutions and foreign investors using them for asset/liability management. To overcome this drawback, an inverse floating-rate class structure developed.[15]

Inverse Floater.   In October 1986, a CMO class was introduced in which the coupon rate floated in the opposite direction of the change in interest rates. This CMO class is called an inverse floating-rate class, or simply, inverse floater. When an inverse floater is included in a CMO structure along with a floating-rate class, the maximum coupon rate that can be paid to the floating-rate class is higher than in the absence of an inverse floater.

To illustrate the inverse floater and how it affects the cap on a floating-rate class, we will use an actual CMO deal. The FHLMC Series 128 CMO was issued in January of 1990. The coupon rate on the underlying collateral was 9% and the principal amount at the time of issuance was $1 billion. As part of the CMO structure there was a floating-rate class with a principal of $64

---

[14] Ravi Dattatreya and Lakhbir S. Hayre, "Floating-Rate Collateralized Mortgage Obligations," Chapter 15, in Fabozzi, *The Handbook of Mortgage-Backed Securities,* second edition.

[15] In September 1987, a new type of floating-rate bond class was introduced. This bond class, developed by PaineWebber and Franklin Savings Bank, has a coupon rate that changes by a multiple of the change in LIBOR; it is referred to as a *super floater.* For an illustration of a superfloater used in hedging applications, see Frank J. Fabozzi and Franco Modigliani, *Mortgage and Mortgage-Backed Securities Markets* (Boston: Harvard Business School Press, 1992).

million and an inverse floater with a principal of $16 million. Therefore, the floater and inverse floater represented $80 million of the $1 billion structure.
The coupon rate for the floating-rate class is:

LIBOR + 0.65

For the inverse floater the coupon rate is:

42.4 − 4 × LIBOR

The weighted-average coupon rate is:

$$\frac{60}{80} \text{ (Floater coupon rate)} + \frac{16}{80} \text{ (Inverse floater coupon rate)}$$

The weighted-average coupon rate is 9% regardless of the level of LIBOR. For example, if LIBOR is 10%, then

floater coupon rate = 10 + 0.65 = 10.65

inverse floater coupon rate = 42.4 − 4 × 10 = 2.4

The weighted average coupon rate is:

$$\frac{64}{80} (10.65) + \frac{16}{80} (2.4) = 9$$

Consequently, the coupon rate on the underlying collateral, 9%, can support the aggregate interest payments that must be made to these two classes.

Since LIBOR is always positive, the coupon rate paid to the floating-rate class cannot be negative. However, if there are no restrictions placed on the coupon rate for the inverse floater, it is possible for the coupon rate for that class to be negative. To prevent this, a floor is set on the coupon rate for the inverse floater. In this deal, the floor was set at zero. By imposing this floor, a restriction was placed on the maximum coupon rate that could be paid to the floating-rate class. The maximum coupon rate was 11.25%. This is found by substituting zero for the coupon rate for the inverse floater in the formula for the weighted-average coupon rate and setting the formula equal to 9.

Notice also that in the absence of the inverse floater, the coupon rate that the floating-rate class could be paid could not go far above 9%, the coupon rate on the underlying collateral. The reason that it can be slightly above 9% will be explained later when we discuss the CMO residual.

How can an inverse floater be used for asset/liability management? An inverse floater can be used to hedge portfolios with fixed-rate assets that mature sooner than fixed-rate liabilities. For example, if an asset matures in two years, but the corresponding liability matures in three years, this asset/liability mismatch represents risk of a fall in market interest rates that would cause the value of the liabilities to rise more than that of the asset. The danger is that when the asset matures the proceeds will be reinvested at a lower rate. The spread between the yield on the asset and the liability will then narrow and possibly become negative. Purchasing an inverse floater lets the investor receive a higher interest rate should rates decrease. The higher rate on the inverse floater can be used to offset the lower rate earned when the proceeds are reinvested.

Floater and inverse floater classes in a CMO structure allow conversion of a fixed-rate instrument into two instruments that satisfy two different asset/liability objectives.

PAC and TAC Bonds. In March 1987, the M.D.C. Mortgage Funding Corporation, CMO Series 0, included a class of bonds referred to as "stabilized mortgage reduction term bonds" or "SMRT" bonds. The same company included in CMO Series P a class referred to as "planned amortization class bonds" or "PAC" bonds. The Oxford Acceptance Corporation III, Series C, CMOs included a class of bonds referred to as "planned redemption obligation bonds" or "PRO" bonds. A characteristic common to these three bonds is that, within a specified range of prepayment rates, the cash flow pattern is known with greater certainty than the cash flow for other classes in a typical CMO issue.

The greater predictability of the cash flow for these classes of bonds, referred to generically as PAC bonds, occurs because there is a specified schedule to retire the obligations of this class (much like a sinking fund schedule for a corporate bond). The PAC class bondholders therefore have priority over all other classes in the CMO issue in receiving principal payments from the underlying collateral when prepayments are within the prespecified prepayment range. The greater certainty of the cash flow for the PAC bonds comes at the expense of the non-PAC bond, called *companion bond* or *support bond*, classes. Should the actual prepayment speed be faster than the upper limit of the PAC range, then the companion bonds receive the excess. This means that the companion bonds absorb the contraction risk. Should the actual prepayment speed be slower than the lower limit of the range, then in subsequent periods the PAC bondholders have priority on principal payments (both scheduled and through prepayments). This reduces extension risk, which is absorbed by the companion bondholders.

In 1988, PaineWebber introduced a variant of the PAC bond in its PaineWebber CMO Trust Series L, with a class called the "targeted amortization class," or TAC bond. A TAC bond is designed to provide protection against contraction risk but exposes the investor to extension risk. This is done by specifying a narrower prepayment range or just a single prepayment rate over which the principal is guaranteed.[16]

Because more than one class of bondholder may be paid principal at the same time, CMO structures with PAC and TAC bonds are called *simultaneous-pay* CMOs.

CMO Residuals

The excess of the cash flow generated by the underlying collateral over the amount needed to pay interest, retire the bonds, and pay administrative expenses is called the *CMO residual*. Investors can purchase an equity position in this residual cash flow. The amount of the excess cash flow depends on several factors: (1) current and future interest rates, (2) the coupon rate on the underlying mortgage collateral, (3) the type of collateral, (4) the prepayment rate on the underlying collateral, and (5) the structure of the CMO issue.

The three most common sources of CMO residual cash flow are (1) premium interest, (2) bond coupon differential, and (3) reinvestment income.[17] The first and most important component is the cash flow generated from premium interest. This represents the difference between the coupon rate on the collateral and the coupon rate paid on the highest coupon rate bond in the CMO structure. For example, if the coupon rate on the collateral is 11%, and 10% is the highest coupon rate paid on a bond class, the premium interest is 1%. The bond coupon differential arises because a CMO structure is designed to support bond payments assuming that each bond class has a coupon rate equal to the highest coupon rate bond class. For example, if the coupon rate on the highest coupon rate bond is 10%, and there are three other classes with coupon rates of 8%, 8.5%, and 9%, the bond coupon differential would be generated from 200-, 150-, and 100-basis point differentials, respectively. The third source of residual cash flow is the income generated from the reinvestment of cash flow payments from the collateral between the time they are received and the time that payments must be made to bondholders.

The CMO residual is an interesting instrument because its value moves in the same direction as the change in interest rates, not in the opposite

---

[16] For a more detailed explanation of TACs, see William J. Curtin and Paul T. Van Valkenburg, "CMO PAC and TAC Bonds: Call Protected Mortgage Securities," in Frank J. Fabozzi (ed.), *Managing Institutional Assets* (New York: Harper & Row, 1990).

[17] Mark Stanley, Helene Halperin, Robert Kulason, and William Calan, "CMO Residuals: Structure and Performance," Merrill Lynch Capital Markets, January 1988.

direction. To understand why, consider what happens when interest rates/mortgage rates fall. There are two adverse affects. First, prepayments are expected to speed up. The result is that the classes receiving the lower coupon rate will be paid off faster. This reduces the cash flow to the investor in the CMO residual resulting from the premium income and bond coupon differential. Second, the cash flow that is reinvested until it is paid to each CMO class will be invested at a lower interest rate. Together, these two effects will result in a lower expected cash flow for the CMO residual owners and a lower price for the CMO residual.[18] If interest rates/mortgage rates rise, the expected cash flow for the CMO residual will increase because prepayments will slow down, and cash flow before payout to CMO bondholders will be reinvested at a higher interest rate. The result should be an increase in the price of the CMO residual.

Because the price of a CMO residual moves in the same direction as the change in interest rates, institutions can use the CMO residual for hedging portfolios of mortgage pass-through securities.

STRIPPED MORTGAGE-BACKED SECURITIES

Stripped mortgage-backed securities, introduced by Fannie Mae in 1986, are another example of derivative mortgage securities. A mortgage pass-through security divides the cash flow from the underlying pool of mortgages on a pro rata basis to the securityholders. A stripped mortgage-backed security is created by altering that distribution of principal and interest from a pro rata distribution to an *unequal* distribution. The result is that some of the securities created will have a price/yield relationship that is different from the price/yield relationship of the underlying mortgage pool. Stripped mortgage-backed securities, if properly used, provide a means by which investors can hedge prepayment risk.

The first generation of stripped mortgage-backed securities were "partially stripped." We can see this by looking at the stripped mortgage-backed securities issued by Fannie Mae in mid-1986.[19] The Class B stripped mortgage-backed securities were backed by FNMA pass-through securities with a 9% coupon. The mortgage payments from the underlying mortgage pool are distributed to Class B-1 and Class B-2 so that both classes receive an equal amount of the principal, but Class B-1 receives one-third of the interest payments while Class B-2 receives two-thirds.

---

[18] The cash flow will be discounted at a lower interest rate, but typically the overall effect means a lower price.

[19] For a further discussion, see Richard Roll, "Stripped Mortgage-Backed Securities," Chapter 18 in Fabozzi, *The Handbook of Mortgage-Backed Securities*, second edition.

In a subsequent issue, Fannie Mae distributed the cash flow from the underlying mortgage pool in a far different way. Using FNMA 11% coupon pools, Fannie Mae created Class A-1 and Class A-2. Class A-1 was given 4.95% of the 11% coupon interest, while Class A-2 received the other 6.05%. Class A-1 was given almost all of the principal payments, 99%, while Class A-2 was allotted only 1% of the principal payments.

In early 1987, stripped mortgage-backed securities began to be issued where all the interest is allocated to one class (called the *interest only* or *IO* class) and all the principal to the other class (called the *principal only* or *PO* class). The IO class receives no principal payments.

The PO security is purchased at a substantial discount from par value. The yield an investor realizes depends on the speed at which prepayments are made. The faster the prepayments, the higher the investor's yield. For example, suppose there is a mortgage pool consisting of only 30-year mortgages, with $400 million in principal, and that investors can purchase POs backed by this mortgage pool for $175 million. The dollar return on this investment will be $225 million. How quickly that dollar return is recovered by PO investors determines the yield that will be realized. In the extreme case, if all homeowners in the underlying mortgage pool decide to prepay their mortgage loans immediately, PO investors will realize the $225 million immediately. At the other extreme, if all homeowners decide to remain in their homes for 30 years and make no prepayments, the $225 million will be spread out over 30 years, which would result in a lower yield for PO investors.

Let's look at how the price of the PO would be expected to change as mortgage rates in the market change. When mortgage rates decline below the coupon rate, prepayments are expected to speed up, accelerating payments to the PO holder. Thus, the cash flow of a PO improves (in the sense that principal repayments are received earlier). The cash flow will be discounted at a lower interest rate because the mortgage rate in the market has declined. The result is that the PO price will increase when mortgage rates decline. When mortgage rates rise above the coupon rate, prepayments are expected to slow down. The cash flow deteriorates (in the sense that it takes longer to recover principal repayments). Couple this with a higher discount rate, and the price of a PO will fall when mortgage rates rise.

An IO has no par value. In contrast to the PO investor, the IO investor wants prepayments to be slow. The reason is that the IO investor receives interest only on the amount of the principal outstanding. When prepayments are made, less dollar interest will be received as the outstanding principal declines. In fact, if prepayments are too fast, the IO investor may not recover the amount paid for the IO.

Let's look at the expected price response of an IO to changes in mortgage rates. If mortgage rates decline below the coupon rate, the prepayments are expected to accelerate. This would result in a deterioration of the expected cash flow for an IO. While the cash flow will be discounted at a lower rate, the net effect typically is a decline in the price of an IO. If mortgage rates rise above the coupon rate, the expected cash flow improves, but the cash flow is discounted at a higher interest rate. The net effect may be either a rise or fall for the IO. Thus, we see an interesting characteristic of an IO: its price tends to move in the same direction as the change in mortgage rates: (1) when mortgage rates fall below the coupon rate, and (2) for some range of mortgage rates above the coupon rate.[20]

This can be seen in Figure 18-1, which shows for various mortgage rates the price of (1) a 9% pass-through security, (2) a PO created from this pass-through security, and (3) an IO created from the pass-through security. Notice that, as mortgage rates decline below 9%, the price of the pass-through security does not respond much. This is the price compression (or negative convexity) property of pass-through securities that we discussed earlier in the chapter. For the PO security, the price falls monotonically as mortgage rates rise. For the IO security, at mortgage rates above approximately 10%, the price declines as mortgage rates rise; as mortgage rates fall below about 10%, the price of an IO falls as mortgage rates decline.

Both POs and IOs exhibit substantial price volatility when mortgage rates change. The greater price volatility of the IO and PO compared to the pass-through security can be seen by the steepness of a tangent line to the curves at any given mortgage rate.[21]

It has been suggested that stripped mortgage-backed securities can be used to hedge a portfolio of mortgage-backed securities[22] and to create a synthetic pass-through security with a risk/return pattern that better fits the needs of an institutional investor.[23]

---

[20] For a more detailed discussion of the price characteristics of IOs and POs and their valuation, see Andrew S. Carron, "Mortgage Strips," Chapter 19; Steven J. Carlson and Timothy D. Sears, "Stripped Mortgage Pass-Throughs: New Tools for Investors," Chapter 21; and R. Blaine Roberts, "The Relative Valuation of IO/PO Stripped Mortgage-Backed Securities," Chapter 20, in Fabozzi, *The Handbook of Mortgage-Backed Securities,* second edition.

[21] CMOs have been issued with PO and IO classes. Because of the substantial volatility of these classes, they are popularly referred to as *super POs* and *super IOs*. For a more detailed discussion of super POs see Blaine Roberts, Sarah Keil Wolf, and Nancy Wilt, "Advances and Innovations in the CMO Market," in Fabozzi, *Advances and Innovations in the Bond and Mortgage Markets.*

[22] Illustrations of hedging are provided in Carlson and Sears, "Stripped Mortgage Pass-Throughs: New Tools for Investors," Chapter 19 in Fabozzi, *The Handbook of Mortgage-Backed Securities,* second edition.

[23] For illustrations of how this can be done, see Marilyn J. Dicks and Janet Piez, "Using Stripped Mortgage-Backed Securities to Create Customized Mortgage Pass-Throughs," Chapter 22 in Fabozzi, *The Handbook of Mortgage-Backed Securities,* second edition.

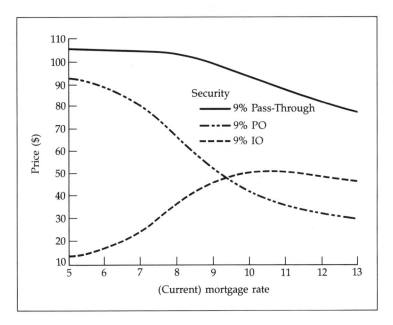

FIGURE 18-1
Relationship between Price and Mortgage Rates for a Pass-Through, PO and IO.
Source: Exhibit 3a, Steven J. Carlson and Timothy D. Sears, "Stripped Mortgage
Pass-Throughs: New Tools for Investors," Chapter 21 in Frank J. Fabozzi (ed.), *The
Handbook of Mortgage-Backed Securities,* second edition (Chicago: Probus Publishing,
1988).

ASSET-BACKED SECURITIES

Asset-backed securities are securities collateralized by assets that are not
mortgage loans. While the two most common types of asset-backed securities
are those backed by automobile loans and credit card receivables, there are
securities backed by boat loans, recreational vehicle loans, computer leases,
accounts receivable, Small Business Administration (SBA) loans, and leveraged buyout loans. At the time of this writing, investment bankers are
attempting to securitize highly leveraged transaction (HLT) loans and
non-performing loans.[24]

---

[24] Asset-backed securities backed by senior bank loans are called *collateralized loan obligations.* For
a discussion of these securities, see Peter J. Carril Jr. and Frank J. Fabozzi, "Collateralized Loan
Obligations," in Frank J. Fabozzi and John H. Carlson (eds.), *Trading and Securitization of Senior
Bank Loans* (Chicago: Probus Publishing, 1992).

As of December 31, 1989, the cumulative issuance of asset-backed securities was $55 billion, with $15 billion issued in 1988 and $20 billion in 1989. The par value of asset-backed securities outstanding as of December 31, 1989, was $35.6 billion. Of this, $13.7 billion (38.3%) was backed by automobile loans and $20 billion (56.0%) by credit card receivables. Only $2.0 billion (5.7%) was backed by the other loans or receivables mentioned above.[25]

While this market is small at the moment, it has tremendous potential for growth. This can be seen by the outstanding amounts of consumer installment credit and credit card borrowing. According to Federal Reserve statistics, the total consumer installment credit as of February 1989 is $674.8 billion. Of this total, $294.2 billion are automobile loans, with commercial banks and finance companies lending more than two-thirds of this amount. The credit card market has been estimated at $150 billion. Thus, the potential size of this market is $444.2 billion, of which less than 10% has been securitized. This excludes other types of consumer credit and corporate assets such as lease-backed notes, accounts receivable, SBA loans, and leveraged buyout debt.

In structuring an asset-backed security, issuers have drawn from the structures used in the mortgage-backed securities market. Asset-backed securities have been structured as pass-throughs and as structures with multiple bond classes just like a CMO. This last structure is called an *asset-backed obligation*. Credit enhancement is provided by letters of credit, recourse to the issuer, overcollateralization, or senior/subordination (or A/B pass-through). All issues backed by automobile loans and credit card receivables have received ratings of at least double-A.

Asset-Backed Securities Backed by Automobile Loans

The first public offering of an asset-backed security was in March 1985 by Sperry Lease Finance Corporation (now Unisys). The issue was collateralized by $192 million of lease-backed notes. Two months later, in May 1985, the first asset-backed securities backed by automobile loans were issued by Marine Midland. These issues are referred to as Certificates for Automobile Receivables or CARs.

The five largest issuers of automobile loan-backed securities between 1985 to 1987 in order of the principal amount outstanding are General Motors Acceptance Corporation (16 issues, principal amount $11.4 billion), Chrysler

---

[25] These data were reported in Andrew S. Carron, "Asset Backed Securities," Chapter 31, in Frank J. Fabozzi (ed.), *The Handbook of Fixed Income Securities,* third edition (Homewood, IL: BusinessOne-Irwin, 1991).

Financial Corporation (3 issues, principal amount $1.8 billion), Marine Midland Bank (3 issues, principal amount $1.1 billion), Western Financial Savings Bank (4 issues, principal amount $0.53 billion), and Bank of America (1 issue, $0.51 billion).[26]

Cash flow for automobile loan-backed securities is either monthly or quarterly. Stated final maturities range from three to five years, but have average lives of one to three years.

The first asset-backed obligation was offered by Asset Backed Securities Corporation, a subsidiary of First Boston Corporation. This issue also goes down in the record books as the largest non-government debt issue in history: $4 billion. General Motors Acceptance Corporation originated the automobile loans used as collateral. The credit enhancement included a limited guarantee from GMAC, a letter of credit from Credit Suisse, and the equity of the issuer (Asset Backed Securities Corporation). There were three bond classes with average lives of 1.1, 2.2, and 3.0 years. Borrowers pay regularly scheduled monthly loan payments (interest and scheduled principal repayments) and may make prepayments. For securities backed by automobile loans, prepayments result from: (1) sales and tradeins requiring full payoff of the loan, (2) repossession and subsequent sale of the automobile, (3) loss or destruction of the vehicle, (4) payoff of the loan with cash to save interest cost, and (5) refinancing of the loan at a lower interest cost.

While refinancings may be a major reason for prepayments of mortgage loans, they are of minor importance for automobile loans. Moreover, the interest rates for the automobile loans underlying several issues are substantially below market rates if they are offered by manufacturers as part of a sales promotion. There is good historical information on the other causes of prepayments. Therefore, the cash flow of securities backed by automobile loans do not have a great deal of uncertainty despite prepayments. Uncertainty is reduced even further in the asset-backed obligation structure.

Yields offered on these securities are typically higher than those on short-term corporate obligations with similar credit ratings, and liquidity in the secondary market is improving. There are several bellwether issues that market makers use as a pricing guide.[27]

Asset-Backed Securities Backed by Credit Card Receivables

The first two public issues of credit card asset-backed securities were by RepublicBank Delaware (a subsidiary of RepublicBank Corporation of Texas) and Bank of America in January and February 1987, respectively. The first

---

[26] William Haley, "Securitizing Automobile Receivables," Chapter 3 in Philip L. Zweig (ed.), *The Asset Securitization Handbook* (Homewood, IL: Dow Jones-Irwin, 1989).

[27] Haley, "Securitizing Automobile Receivables," p. 84.

offering was collateralized by $200 million of 227,000 Visa and MasterCard accounts that were seasoned three months. The second offering by Bank of America (California Credit Card Trust 1987-A) was a $400 million issue backed by 840,000 Visa accounts. These issues were called CARDs (Certificates for Amortizing Revolving Debts). The first credit card-backed securities not collateralized by Visa and/or MasterCard accounts were issued in early 1988 by the retailers Sears, Montgomery Ward, and J.C. Penney.

The yield an investor realizes depends on the credit card borrower's rate of repayment of the amount borrowed. Historical data on credit card borrower repayments indicate that repayments are high. For example, the Bank of America's $300 million California Credit Card Trust 1987-B had a projected cash flow of $2.05 million per month for the first 18 months and a constant monthly repayment rate of 18.5%.

Interest to holders of credit card-backed issues is paid monthly. Most issues have a fixed interest rate, but there are floating-rate issues.

BENEFITS OF SECURITIZATION AND IMPLICATIONS FOR FINANCIAL MARKETS

Securitization of mortgage loans, consumer loans, and commercial loans can be beneficial to issuers, investors, and borrowers.

Benefits to Issuers

The most commonly cited benefits of securitization are (1) obtaining a lower cost of funds, (2) more efficient use of capital, (3) managing rapid portfolio growth, (4) better asset/liability management, (5) enhanced financial performance, and (6) diversification of funding sources.[28]

Obtaining a Lower Cost of Funds.   Segregating assets and using them as collateral for a security offering lets lower funding costs be obtained. The cost of funding for a mortgage-related entity such as a thrift, commercial bank, or home builder depends on its credit rating. The lower the credit rating, the higher the cost of funding. By using mortgage loans as collateral and properly structuring a security, a mortgage-related institution can obtain a credit rating on the security that is higher than its own credit rating. This will result in a lower cost of funds.

This is also true in the asset-backed securities market, as can be seen in two examples. The Sperry Lease Financial Corporation asset-backed security backed by lease receivables was structured so that the cash flow from the underlying leases would be sufficient to satisfy the interest and principal

---

[28] Haley, "Securitizing Automobile Receivables," p. 75.

payments; the security as a result received a triple-A rating. At the time, Sperry Lease Financial Corporation had a lower credit rating. Bank of America issued asset-backed securities backed by credit card receivables. The securities received a triple-A rating, a rating higher than Bank of America's. It has been estimated that Bank of America saved at least 150 basis points over what it would have had to pay by issuing debt with a similar maturity.[29]

More Efficient Use of Capital.   For financial institutions that must meet capital guideline requirements, the sale of assets can free up capital. Recall from Chapter 2 that current capital guideline requirements for banks require a certain percentage of capital for each asset category a bank has. The percentage is supposed to reflect the credit risk associated with the asset. Often, however, the capital requirements are higher than the actual risks associated with the asset. By securitizing assets and selling these securities, the capital required will reflect the actual risks associated with the assets. This will result in a reduction of excess capital requirements.[30]

Manufacturing corporations or their captive finance companies gain through securitization the opportunity to obtain greater leverage than the credit rating companies might judge acceptable otherwise. As an example, consider General Motors Acceptance Corporation or Chrysler Financial Corporation. These finance companies might have a ratio of automobile receivables-to-liabilities (a measure of financial leverage) of 8 or 10 to 1, acceptable for this industry according to the credit rating companies. Proper structure of an asset-backed security would allow reduction of credit risk exposure so that the financing companies retain only a fraction of the credit risk associated with the assets.

Shifting the credit risk from the originator of the loan to another party reduces the issuer's return together with its risk. At the same time, the issuer may keep or sell the rights to service the loans. Earnings from the business thus come from fee income rather than interest rate spread income.

Managing Rapid Portfolio Growth.   As the business of a financial or non-financial entity grows, growth potential will be limited by capital constraints. Selling assets through securitization provides a means for quickly raising capital while keeping the asset, and hence the debt, off the balance sheet, avoiding capital requirements. The risk-based capital guidelines for

---

[29] Lowell L. Bryan, "Introduction," Chapter 1 in Zweig, *The Asset Securitization Handbook,* p. 18.

[30] For a discussion of the role of asset securitization for asset/liability management of depository institutions, see Anand Bhattacharya and Krishnan Kandapani, "Asset Securitization: Prospects and Issues," Chapter 12 in Frank J. Fabozzi and Atsuo Konishi (eds.), *Asset/Liability Management for Depository Institutions* (Chicago: Probus Publishing, 1991).

banks discussed in Chapter 2 encourage the practice of securitization of assets.

Better Asset/Liability Management. Because mortgages and consumer installment loans expose financial institutions to prepayment risk, it can be difficult to establish a liability structure consistent with the structure of the uncertain cash flow of these assets. Securitization passes the prepayment risk to the investor. This gives the financial institution a means for funding assets whose maturity matches that of the asset.

Enhancing Financial Performance. When loans are sold via securitization at a yield lower than the interest rate on the loan, the originator realizes the spread. This spread partially reflects the fee for servicing the loans and partially reflects conversion of an illiquid loan into a more liquid security backed by loans and with credit enhancements. This is most obvious with the CMO structure. The issuer of the CMO owns the residual cash flow. If the issuer chooses not to sell the CMO residual, the cash flow will be received over time. Alternatively, the issuer can capture the spread (in the case of a CMO this is the premium income and the bond coupon differential) immediately by selling the CMO residual. This source of spread will of course tend to be eroded by competition, which will tend to reallocate the abnormal spread between final borrowers and final lenders.

Diversification of Sources. Investors who ordinarily could not make mortgage loans, consumer loans, and/or commercial loans can invest in these securities. This provides more sources of capital for both financial and non-financial entities.

Benefits to Investors

Securitization converts illiquid loans into securities with greater liquidity and reduced credit risk. Credit risk is reduced because (1) it is backed by a diversified pool of loans, and (2) there is credit enhancement or, in the case of an agency mortgage pass-through security, an agency guarantee. This permits investors to broaden their universe of investment opportunities. It also tends to improve returns through the reduction of the cost of intermediation.

Benefits to Borrowers

Because a financial or non-financial entity can securitize a loan it originates, or sell it to some entity that will securitize it, the lender now has a more liquid asset that it can sell if capital is needed. This should reduce the spread between lending rates and safe assets such as Treasury securities. We have seen this in the mortgage market and, to some extent, in the automobile loan market. As the market matures, competition among originators should produce lower lending rate spreads in other loan markets.

Implications of Securitization for Financial Markets

Securitization has major implications for financial markets as well as the structure of financial institutions such as banks and thrifts. Securitization eventually may replace the traditional system of indirect financing. To understand why, let's briefly review the role of financial intermediaries, particularly banks and thrifts, that we explained in Chapter 1.

In Chapter 1, we explained that financial intermediaries act as conduits in bringing savers and borrowers together. They perform this function in several ways. First, banks and thrifts are in a better position than individual investors to assess credit risk. After evaluating credit risk, they may agree to grant a loan and hold the loan as an investment. Furthermore, being in a position to distribute their assets over many different borrowers and industries, they achieve risk reduction through diversification. The returns to investors are further made safe by government-guaranteed liabilities (e.g., their insured certificates of deposit).

Second, the maturities of loans sought by borrowers may be different from those that investors want. Thrifts and banks acquire short-term funds and grant loans with longer maturities. This satisfies the objective of investors who may want shorter-term investments and borrowers who want longer-term funds; that is, the institution provides maturity intermediation—though at their risk. Finally, the amount of funds sought by borrowers is typically greater than any one individual investor would be willing to lend. Thrifts and banks make large-denomination loans to borrowers and offer investors investments with smaller denominations. That is, they provide denomination intermediation, transforming very large assets into quite divisible ones.

Securitization provides direct financing between borrowers and investors, short-circuiting the traditional intermediaries. Pooling of assets reinforced by private credit enhancement reduces credit risk to more acceptable levels for investors. Recasting cash flows such as in CMOs and asset-backed obligations provides varying maturities acceptable to a wide range of investors. Thus, securitization serves a role similar to maturity intermediation while shifting its risk to the lenders. The availability of securities with smaller denominations than the underlying loans accomplishes denomination intermediation. All of this happens without the need for any government guarantees (although such guarantees may enhance the value of securitized instruments). The success of securitization indicates that it is a more efficient method for linking borrowers and investors than traditional financing through intermediaries. Consequently, the role of banks and thrifts may have to be reassessed.

The true innovations in this market are not really the securities themselves but (1) reduction of risk through pooling of assets and private credit enhancement, and (2) repackaging of the cash flows from assets in a way that relieves the intermediary of reliance on its own assets to finance the credit—i.e., that permits off-balance sheet financing. This is not an entirely new approach, as it underlies such instruments as bankers acceptances, mortgage bonds (popular in many foreign countries), and to some extent letters of credit. The current wave of applications, however, goes well beyond past practice in the magnitude and nature of innovative approaches, and it is already spreading to other countries.[31]

SUMMARY

The mortgage market at one time was primarily a local market: members of the community made deposits in local thrifts, which loaned the funds to local citizens who wanted to purchase a home. Because of imbalance between local supply and demand, mortgage bankers came into being to provide funds to regions of the country that needed funds from regions with surplus funds. This system, however, remained dependent on deposits at thrifts and banks, which became unstable due to interest rate ceilings that were imposed. A secondary market has developed to securitize mortgages, thereby allowing other investors to provide a steadier supply of funds to the mortgage market.

In this chapter we have discussed the market for mortgage-backed securities and other "securitized" assets. The basic mortgage-backed security is the mortgage pass-through security. The types of mortgage pass-through securities are agency, conventional, and commercial pass-through securities. The non-agency pass-through securities require private credit enhancements in order to receive a high credit rating. Mortgage pass-through securities can be backed by either fixed-rate or adjustable-rate mortgage loans. To address the prepayment risks associated with investing in mortgage pass-through securities—contraction risk and extension risk—collateralized mortgage obligations (CMOs) were created. Another derivative mortgage-backed security, the stripped mortgage-backed security, was created for hedging purposes.

---

[31] Securitization of personal loans occurred in France in 1980. The first public asset-backed deal in Canada, issued in May 1991, was for 350 million Canadian dollars backed by automobile loans purchased from Chrysler Credit Canada.

Asset-backed securities are backed by non-real estate mortgage loans. The most common type of asset-backed securities is backed by automobile loans, followed by securities backed by credit card receivables. Issuers have used pass-through structures and a multiple class structure similar to a CMO. The latter structures are referred to as asset-backed obligations. Credit enhancements are also used. While prepayment risk is a key element in the cash flow of a mortgage-backed security, it is less of a factor for some asset-backed securities.

Securitization of assets—that is, pooling loans and selling securities backed by the pool of loans—benefits issuers, investors, and borrowers alike. Securitization may be the wave of the future, as it appears to be a more efficient mechanism for bringing borrowers and investors together than traditional financing through intermediaries. Moreover, it can be done without any government guarantees.

QUESTIONS

1. a. What is a mortgage pass-through security?

    b. Describe the investment characteristics of a mortgage pass-through security.

    c. How has securitization enhanced the liquidity of mortgages?

2. What are the different types of agency pass-through securities?

3. a. What is a conventional pass-through security?

    b. Describe various ways that issuers have enhanced the credit quality of a conventional pass-through security.

4. a. What is meant by the cash flow yield of a mortgage pass-through security?

    b. What are the limitations of cash flow yield measures for a mortgage pass-through security?

    c. A cash flow yield typically is based on some prepayment benchmark to project the cash flow. Describe the benchmark.

5. a. What is meant by prepayment risk, contraction risk, and extension risk?

    b. How does a collateralized mortgage obligation alter the cash flow from mortgages so as to shift the prepayment risk across various classes of bondholders?

c. "By creating a CMO, an issuer eliminates the prepayment risk associated with the underlying mortgages." Do you agree with this statement?

6. This quotation is taken from a 1991 issue of *Bondweek:*

> First Interstate Bank of Texas will look into buying several different types of collateralized mortgage obligation tranches when it starts up its buy program sometime after the second quarter of 1991, according to Jules Pollard, v.p. Pollard said he will consider replacing maturing adjustable-rate mortgage pass-throughs with short companion tranches and planned and targeted amortization classes because the ARMS have become rich. . . . Pollard did not provide a dollar figure on the planned investments, which will be made to match fund the bank's liabilities. When he does invest he said he prefers government-guaranteed securities or those with implied guarantees.

a. Explain the types of securities that Pollard is buying and selling.

b. Given the preference stated in the last sentence of the quotation, what issuers is he likely to prefer? What issuers would he reject?

7. a. What is a principal-only security? An interest-only security?

b. How is the price of an interest-only security expected to change when interest rates change?

8. This quotation appeared in the October 22, 1990, issue of *Corporate Financing Week:*

> Asset-backed securities issuers in the fourth quarter have experienced a record widening of spreads to Treasuries and higher yields, but will continue to finance in that market because of the need for immediate capital and even higher rates in the alternative markets, Street asset-backed officials said.

a. For computing a spread to Treasuries for an asset-backed or mortgage-backed security, what is usually used as a "comparable" Treasury security?

b. Explain what is meant by "even higher rates in the alternative markets." Why does this make asset-backed issuance attractive?

9. The quotation below appeared in an article entitled "Burlington Uses New Structure in Lease Deal," that appeared in *Bondweek:*

> Burlington Northern Railroad was expected to hit the market last Friday with the first issue of pass-through securities backed by leases

from railroad equipment lease pools, according to Karl Essig, head of asset-backed securities structuring and origination at sole-manager Morgan Stanley. The pass-through structure made the deal more marketable and channeled cashflow enabled the deal to obtain a higher rating, he noted. "The structure was a very significant advance in obtaining ratings," Essig said.

Most of the leases' average lives were too long to qualify for the target Aa3/A+ rating. By channeling the different cashflows together, Burlington was able to add lease diversity and create an aggregate average life of an acceptable level for the desired rating, said Steven Schiffman, director of corporate finance at Burlington. . . .

The $117 million public offering, Burlington Northern Railroad Pass-through Trust 1990-A, was offered in two pass-through tranches, which had average lives of 8.8 and 16.7 years, respectively. . . . They were backed by seven different leases for automobile racks, new covered hoppers, new gondola cars, box cars, new locomotives and two for remanufactured locomotives, according to Schiffman.

a. At the time of issuance, Burlington Northern Railroad was rated A3/BBB+. Explain how this structure enabled Burlington to issue debt at a lower cost than would be possible by issuing traditional bonds.

b. Why do you think the issue was structured to have two classes of pass-throughs?

c. Why is this structure classified as an asset-backed obligation?

CHAPTER

19

INTEREST RATE FUTURES AND OPTIONS

LEARNING OBJECTIVES

After reading this chapter you will understand:

- the features of interest rate futures contracts.

- the Treasury bond and note futures contract.

- the delivery options embedded in the Treasury bond and note futures contract and their impact on the futures price.

- what a forward rate agreement is.

- the features of interest rate options contracts.

- why institutional investors use over-the-counter interest rate options.

- what futures options are, their trading mechanics, and the reasons for their popularity.

- the empirical evidence on the pricing efficiency of futures options.

- the limitations of applying the Black–Scholes option-pricing model to options on fixed-income securities.
- an overview of more appropriate models for pricing interest rate options.
- potential applications of interest rate futures and options by institutional money managers and borrowers.

This is the first of two chapters that describe derivative contracts or instruments that investors and issuers can use to control interest rate risk. Basically, the underlying economic variable for these derivative contracts is some interest rate. The derivative contract either is based directly on an interest rate, or it is based indirectly on an interest rate by making a debt obligation the underlying instrument for the contract. In this chapter we describe four derivative contracts to control interest rate risk: interest rate futures, forward rate agreements, interest rate options, and options on futures. We cover portfolio strategies using these contracts, unique features for pricing them, and considerations of pricing efficiency.

Futures contracts are products created by exchanges. Options on futures, a new derivative product that we will introduce you to in this chapter, are also created by exchanges. Options, however, can be exchange-traded products or customized products created by dealer firms. The latter are called over-the-counter options. While market agents rely almost exclusively on exchange-traded products in the case of options on common stocks and options on stock indexes, institutional investors and issuers make greater use of the over-the-counter options market to create tailor-made contracts to control interest rate risk. Forward rate agreements are also over-the-counter products. Agreements such as OTC options and forward rate agreements are two examples of *customized interest rate agreements.* Other customized interest rate agreements will be discussed in the next chapter.

INTEREST RATE FUTURES CONTRACTS

In October 1975, the Chicago Board of Trade (CBT) pioneered trading in a futures contract based on a fixed-income instrument—Government National Mortgage Association certificates. Three months later, the International Monetary Market (IMM) of the Chicago Mercantile Exchange began trading futures contracts based on 13-week Treasury bills. Other exchanges soon followed with their own interest rate futures contracts. The more actively traded interest rate futures contracts are described below.

Features of Actively Traded Contracts

Treasury Bill Futures.   Treasury bill futures and Eurodollar futures contracts are futures whose underlying instrument is a short-term debt obligation. The Treasury bill futures contract, which is traded on the IMM, is based on a 13-week (three-month) Treasury bill with a face value of $1 million. More specifically, the seller of a Treasury bill futures contract agrees to deliver to the buyer at the settlement date a Treasury bill with 13 weeks remaining to maturity and a face value of $1 million. The Treasury bill delivered can be newly issued or seasoned. The futures price is the price at which the Treasury bill will be sold by the short and purchased by the buyer. For example, a nine-month Treasury bill futures contract requires that nine months from now the short deliver to the long $1 million face value of a Treasury bill with 13 weeks remaining to maturity. The Treasury bill could be a newly-issued 13-week Treasury bill or a Treasury bill that was issued one year prior to the settlement date and therefore at the settlement has only 13 weeks remaining to maturity.

As we explain in Chapter 13, Treasury bills are quoted in the cash market in terms of the annualized yield on a bank discount basis, where

$$Y_D = \frac{D}{F} \times \frac{360}{t}$$

where Y_D = annualized yield on a bank discount basis (expressed as a decimal);

D = dollar disount, which is equal to the difference between the face value and the price of a bill maturing in t days;

F = face value; and

t = number of days remaining to maturity.

The dollar discount (D) is found by

$$D = Y_D \times F \times \frac{t}{360}$$

In contrast, the Treasury bill futures contract is not quoted directly in terms of yield but instead on an index basis that is related to the yield on a bank discount basis as follows:

Index price $= 100 - (Y_D \times 100)$

For example, if Y_D is 8%, the index price is

$100 - (0.08 \times 100) = 92.$

It will be seen that the "index price" of an instrument differs from its actual price because it is the price of an instrument with the same annual yield but maturing in a year. The primary purpose of this convention is that all instruments with the same annual yield will have the same price, regardless of maturity. Conversely, instruments with the same price will have the same yield to maturity and bank discount basis. This clearly facilitates comparison of annual yields across maturities.

Given the price of the futures contract, the yield on a bank discount basis for the futures contract is determined as follows:

$$Y_D = \frac{100 - \text{Index price}}{100}$$

To see how this works, suppose that the index price for a Treasury bill futures contract is 92.52. The yield on a bank discount basis for this Treasury bill futures contract is:

$$Y_D = \frac{100 - 92.52}{100} = 0.0748 \text{ or } 7.48\%$$

The invoice price that the buyer of $1 million face value of 13-week Treasury bills must pay at settlement is found by first computing the dollar discount, as follows:

$$D = Y_D \times \$1,000,000 \times \frac{t}{360}$$

where t is either 90 or 91 days.

Typically, the number of days to maturity of a 13-week Treasury bill is 91 days. The invoice price is then:

Invoice price = $1,000,000 − D

For example, for the Treasury bill futures contract with an index price of 92.52 (and a yield on a bank discount basis of 7.48%), the dollar discount for the 13-week Treasury bill to be delivered with 91 days to maturity is:

$$D = 0.0748 \times \$1,000,000 \times \frac{91}{360}$$
$$= \$18,907.78$$

The invoice price is:

Invoice price = $1,000,000 − $18,907.78
$$= \$981,092.22$$

The minimum index price fluctuation or "tick" for this futures contract is 0.01. A change of 0.01 for the minimum index price translates into a change in the yield on a bank discount basis of one basis point (0.0001). The change in the value of one basis point will change the dollar discount, and therefore the invoice price, by:

$$0.0001 \times \$1,000,000 \times \frac{t}{360}$$

For a 13-week Treasury bill with 91 days to maturity, the change in the dollar discount is:

$$0.0001 \times \$1,000,000 \times \frac{91}{360} = \$25.28$$

For a 13-week Treasury bill with 90 days to maturity, the change in the dollar discount would be $25. Despite the fact that a 13-week Treasury bill typically has 91 days to maturity, market participants commonly refer to the value of a basis point for this futures contract as $25.

Eurodollar CD Futures. As we explained in Chapter 10, Eurodollar certificates of deposit (CDs) are denominated in dollars but represent the liabilities of banks outside the United States. The rate paid on Eurodollar CDs is the London Interbank Offered Rate (LIBOR). The three-month Eurodollar

CD is the underlying instrument for the Eurodollar CD futures contract. As with the Treasury bill futures contract, this contract is for $1 million of face value and is traded on an index price basis with a minimum price fluctuation (tick) of 0.01 (or 0.0001 in terms of LIBOR). The contract is traded on both the International Monetary Market of the Chicago Mercantile Exchange and the London International Financial Futures Exchange.

The unique feature of the Eurodollar CD futures contract is that the settlement procedure requires that the parties settle in cash for the value of a Eurodollar CD based on LIBOR at the settlement date. Of the two futures contracts based on short-term instruments, Eurodollar CD futures are more commonly employed by institutional investors than Treasury bill futures.

Treasury Bond Futures.   The underlying instrument for a Treasury bond futures contract is $100,000 par value of a hypothetical 20-year, 8% coupon bond. While prices and yields of the Treasury bond futures contract are quoted in terms of this hypothetical Treasury bond, the seller of the futures contract has the choice of several actual Treasury bonds that are acceptable to deliver. The Chicago Board of Trade allows the seller to deliver any Treasury bond that has at least 15 years to maturity from the date of delivery if not callable; in the case of callable bonds, the issue must not be callable for at least 15 years from the first day of the delivery month. To settle the contract an acceptable bond must be delivered. That is, the contract is not a cash-settlement contract.

The minimum price fluctuation for the Treasury bond futures contract is a 32nd of one percent. The dollar value of a 32nd for a $100,000 par value (the par value for the underlying Treasury bond) is $31.25. Thus, the minimum price fluctuation is $31.25 for this contract.

The delivery process for the Treasury bond futures contract makes the contract interesting. At the settlement date, the *seller* of a futures contract (the short) is required to deliver the buyer (the long) $100,000 par value of an 8%, 20-year Treasury bond. Since no such bond exists the seller must choose from other acceptable deliverable bonds that the exchange has specified. Suppose the seller is entitled to deliver $100,000 of a 6%, 20-year Treasury bond to settle the futures contract. The value of this bond of course is less than the value of an 8%, 20-year bond. If the seller delivers the 6%, 20-year, this would be unfair to the buyer of the futures contract who contracted to receive $100,000 of an 8%, 20-year Treasury bond. Alternatively, suppose the seller delivers $100,000 of a 10%, 20-year Treasury bond. The value of a 10%, 20-year Treasury bond is greater than that of an 8%, 20-year bond, so this would be a disadvantage to the seller.

How can this problem be resolved? To make delivery equitable to both parties, and to tie cash to futures prices, the CBT has introduced *conversion factors* for determining the invoice price of each acceptable deliverable

Treasury issue against the Treasury bond futures contract. The conversion factor is determined by the CBT before a contract with a specific settlement date begins trading. The conversion factor is based on the price that a deliverable bond would sell for at the beginning of the delivery month if it were to yield 8%. The conversion factor is constant throughout the trading period of the futures contract. The short must notify the long of the actual bond that will be delivered one day before the delivery date.

The invoice price paid by the buyer of the Treasury bonds delivered by the seller is determined using the formula:

Invoice price = Contract size × Futures contract settlement price ×
    Conversion factor

Suppose the Treasury bond futures contract settles at 96 (0.96 in decimal form) and that the short elects to deliver a Treasury bond issue with a conversion factor of 1.15. As the contract size is $100,000, the invoice price is:

$100,000 × 0.96 × 1.15 = $110,400

The invoice price in the formula is just for the principal. The buyer of the futures contract must also pay the seller accrued interest on the bond delivered.

In selecting the issue to be delivered, the short will select from all the deliverable issues the one that is cheapest to deliver. This issue is referred to as the *cheapest-to-deliver* or the *most deliverable* issue; it plays a key role in the pricing of this futures contract. The cost to deliver is the difference between the cost of purchasing the Treasury issue and the invoice price for the principal. That is,

Cost to deliver = Cost of purchasing issue − Invoice price

This is equivalent to selecting the issue that would generate the greatest profit as measured by the invoice price for the principal minus the cost of purchasing the issue. Notice that computation of the cost of delivery does not consider the accrued interest that the seller (short position) must pay to acquire the issue. The reason is that the cost would be offset by the long when the issue is purchased from the short.

In addition to the option of which acceptable Treasury issue to deliver— sometimes referred to as the *quality or swap option*—the short position has two more options granted under CBT delivery guidelines. The short position is permitted to decide when in the delivery month delivery actually will take place. This is called the *timing option*. The other option is the right of the short position to give notice of intent to deliver up to 8:00 p.m. Chicago time after the closing of the exchange (3:15 p.m. Chicago time) on the date when the futures settlement price has been fixed. This option is referred to as the *wild card option*. The quality option, the timing option, and the wild card option (in sum referred to as the delivery options), mean that the long position can never be sure of which Treasury bond will be delivered or when it will be delivered.

Treasury Note Futures. Modeled after the Treasury bond futures contract, the underlying instrument for the Treasury note futures contract is $100,000 par value of a hypothetical 10-year, 8% Treasury note. There are several acceptable Treasury issues that may be delivered by the short. An issue is acceptable if the maturity is not less than 6.5 years and not greater than 10 years from the first day of the delivery month. The delivery options granted to the short position and the minimum price fluctuation are the same as for the Treasury bond futures contract.

Bond Buyer's Municipal Bond Index Futures. Traded on the CBT, the underlying product for this contract is a basket, or index, of 40 municipal bonds. The Bond Buyer, publisher of *The Bond Buyer* (a trade publication of the municipal bond industry), serves as the index manager for the contract and prices each bond in the index based on prices received between 1:30 and 2:00 p.m. (Central Standard Time) from five municipal bond brokers. It is necessary to obtain several independent prices from brokers because municipal bonds trade in the over-the-counter market.

Once the prices are received from the five pricing brokers for a given issue, the lowest and the highest prices are dropped. The remaining three prices then are averaged, and the resulting value is referred to as the *appraisal value*. The appraisal value for each issue then is divided by a conversion factor that equates the bond to an 8% issue. This gives a *converted price* for each issue. The converted prices then are summed and divided by 40, for an average converted price on the index. The index is revised bimonthly, when newer issues are added, and older issues or issues that no longer meet the criteria for inclusion in the index are dropped.[1] A smoothing coefficient is calculated on the index revision date so that the index will not change merely because of changes in the composition of the index. The average converted dollar price for the index is multiplied by this coefficient to get the index value for a particular date.

As delivery on all 40 bonds in the index is not possible, the contract is a

---

[1] The inclusion criteria, as well as the revision process and pricing of the index, are spelled out in a publication entitled "The Chicago Board of Trade's Municipal Bond Futures Contract," 1987.

cash settlement contract, with settlement price based on the value of the index on the delivery date.

The contract is quoted in points and 32nds of a point. For example, suppose the settlement price for the contract is 93-21. This translates into a price of 93 and 21/32, or 93.65635. The dollar value of a contract is equal to $1,000 times the Bond Buyer Municipal Bond Index. For example, the dollar value based on the settlement price is:

$$\$1,000 \times 93.65635 = \$93,656.35$$

Pricing of Interest Rate Futures Contracts

In Chapter 6, we explained how the price of a futures contract can be determined based on arbitrage arguments. We showed that the theoretical futures price depends on the cash market price, the financing cost, and the cash yield on the underlying instrument. In the case of stock index futures, the cash yield on the underlying instrument is the expected stream of cash dividends earned until the settlement date. For interest rate futures, the cash yield is the coupon interest earned until the settlement date, *not* the yield to maturity. Therefore, for an interest rate futures contract, the theoretical futures price is:

Futures price = Cash market price +
Cash market price × (Financing cost − Cash yield on bond)

The futures price can trade at a discount or a premium to the cash price, depending on whether the cost of carry (carry for short) is positive (i.e., the cash yield on the bond is greater than the financing cost) or negative (i.e., the cash yield on the bond is less than the financing cost). In the case of interest rate futures, the financing cost is determined by rates at the short end of the yield curve. The cash yields for Treasury bonds and Treasury notes will be determined by yields at the long-term and intermediate-term maturity sectors of the yield curve, respectively. Therefore, the shape of the yield curve will determine carry and, in turn, whether the futures price will trade at a premium, at a discount, or equal to the cash market price. This is summarized below:

SHAPE OF YIELD CURVE	CARRY	FUTURES PRICE WILL
Normal	Positive	Sell at a discount to cash price
Inverted	Negative	Sell at a premium to cash price
Flat	Zero	Be equal to the cash price

The shape of the yield curve also influences when the short will choose to deliver (i.e., exercise the timing option). If carry is positive, it will be beneficial for the short to delay delivery until the last permissible settlement date. If carry is negative, the short will deliver on the first permissible settlement date.

To derive the theoretical futures price in Chapter 6 using the arbitrage argument, several assumptions had to be made. We explained in that chapter the implications of these assumptions for the divergence between the actual futures price and the theoretical futures price for any futures contract. In Chapter 10, we highlighted the limitations as applied to stock index futures. Here we will do the same for interest rate futures.

Interim Cash Flows.   In Chapter 6, we explained that the model assumes no interim cash flows due to variation margin or coupon interest payments but that these can be incorporated. The unique aspect of interest rate futures is that if interest rates rise, the short will receive margin as the futures price decreases; the margin can then be reinvested at a higher interest rate. If interest rates fall, there will be variation margin that must be financed by the short, but because interest rates have declined, this can be financed at a lower cost. Thus there seems to be an advantage to the short as interest rates change. Correspondingly, there is a disadvantage to the long.

Deliverable Bond Is Known.   In the pricing model based on arbitrage arguments that we presented in Chapter 6, it is assumed that only one instrument is deliverable. But the futures contracts on Treasury bonds and Treasury notes are designed to allow the short the choice of delivering one of a number of deliverable issues (the quality or swap option).

Because there may be more than one deliverable, market participants track the price of each deliverable bond and determine which bond is the cheapest to deliver. The futures price will then trade in relation to the cheapest-to-deliver bond. As we explained earlier, the cheapest to deliver is the bond or note that will result in the smallest loss or the greatest gain on delivering by the short.[2]

There is the risk that while an issue may be the cheapest to deliver at the time a position in the futures contract is taken, it may not be the cheapest to deliver after that time. A change in the cheapest-to-deliver can dramatically alter the futures price.

---

[2] An alternative procedure is to compute the implied (break-even) repo rate. This rate is the yield that would produce no profit or loss if the bond is purchased and a futures contract is sold against the bond. The cheapest-to-deliver bond is the one with the lowest implied repo rate.

What are the implications of the quality (swap) option on the futures price? Because the swap option is an option granted by the long to the short, the long will want to pay less for the futures contract. Therefore, the theoretical futures price after adjusting for the quality option granted to the short should be less than the theoretical futures price given above.

Delivery Date Is Known.   In the pricing model based on arbitrage arguments, a known delivery date is assumed. For Treasury bond and note futures contracts, the short has a timing and wild card option, so the long does not know when the securities will be delivered. The effect of the timing and wild card options on the theoretical futures price is the same as with the quality option. These delivery options should result in a theoretical futures price that is lower than the one suggested above.

Deliverable Is Not a Basket of Securities.   The municipal index futures contract is a cash settlement contract based on a basket of securities. The difficulty in arbitraging this futures contract is that it is too expensive to buy or sell every bond included in the index. Instead, as we explained in Chapter 10 in our discussion of the pricing of stock index futures, a portfolio containing a smaller number of bonds may be constructed to "track" the index. The arbitrage, however, is no longer risk-free because there is tracking error risk.

Tax Considerations.   In our discussion of stock index futures contracts, we explained how the different tax treatment of futures and cash market transactions will affect the theoretical futures price. This applies equally to interest rate futures contracts. Moreover, for the municipal index futures contract, consideration must be given to the tax-exempt income from municipal bonds.[3]

Pricing Efficiency of Interest Rate Futures

Market observers have noted consistently that futures prices for Treasury bonds have been less than their theoretical price. Earlier observers concluded that this meant the market is inefficient. Yet researchers have been quick to point out that divergence between actual and theoretical futures prices was

---

[3] The lower and upper bounds for the municipal index futures contracts that take taxes into consideration are presented in Marcelle Arak, Philip Fischer, Laurie Goodman, and Raj Daryanani, "The MOB: Pricing and Arbitrage," in Frank J. Fabozzi and T. Dessa Garlicki (editors), *Advances in Bond Analysis and Portfolio Strategies* (Chicago, IL: Probus Publishing, 1987).

due to the delivery options granted to the short.[4] The empirical question then becomes what is the value of these options.

In two separate studies Kane and Marcus examine the value of the quality option and the wild card option.[5] Using a simulation approach to analyze these two delivery options, they find that each had a significant influence on the price of Treasury bond futures; each option reduces the value of the futures contract by roughly $0.20 (based on a futures price of $72). Hemler finds that the quality option has somewhat less of an effect for Treasury bond futures contracts.[6]

Portfolio Strategies with Interest Rate Futures

There are at least six strategies for which institutional investors can employ interest rate futures:

- speculating on the movement of interest rates
- controlling the interest rate risk of a portfolio (altering duration)
- hedging against adverse interest rate movements
- enhancing returns when futures are mispriced
- allocating funds between stocks and bonds
- portfolio insurance (dynamic hedging)

Speculating on the Movement of Interest Rates. The price of a futures contract moves in the opposite direction from interest rates: when rates rise (fall), the futures price will fall (rise). An investor who wants to speculate that interest rates will rise (fall) can sell (buy) interest rate futures. Before interest rate futures were available, investors who wanted to speculate on interest rates did so with the long-term Treasury bond: shorting it if they expected interest rates to rise, and buying it if they expected interest rates to fall. There are three advantages of using interest rate futures instead of the cash markets

---

[4] See Gerald D. Gay and Steven Manaster, "The Quality Option Implicit in Futures Contracts," *Journal of Financial Economics* (September 1984), pp. 353–370, and "Implicit Delivery Options and Optimal Delivery Strategies for Financial Futures Contracts," *Journal of Financial Economics* (May 1986), pp. 41–72.

[5] Alex Kane and Alan Marcus, "The Quality Option in the Treasury Bond Futures Market: An Empirical Assessment," *Journal of Futures Markets* (Summer 1986), pp. 231–248, and "Valuation and Optimal Exercise of the Wild Card Option in the Treasury Bond Futures Market," *Journal of Finance* (March 1986), pp. 195–207.

[6] Michael J. Hemler, "The Quality Delivery Option in Treasury Bond Futures Contracts," doctoral dissertation, Graduate School of Business, University of Chicago, March 1988.

(trading long-term Treasuries themselves). First, transactions costs are lower for futures compared to cash markets. Second, margin requirements are lower for futures than for Treasury securities; using futures thus permits greater leverage. Finally, it is easier to sell short in the futures market than in the Treasuries market. We repeat here what we said when we discussed the use of stock index futures to speculate on stock price movements, however: making speculation easier for investors is not the function of interest rate futures contracts.

Controlling the Interest Rate Risk of a Portfolio.   Stock index futures can be used to change the market risk of a diversified stock portfolio, that is, to alter the beta of a portfolio. Likewise, interest rate futures can be used to alter the interest rate sensitivity of a portfolio. As we explained in Chapter 11, duration is a measure of the interest rate sensitivity of a bond portfolio.

Investment managers with strong expectations about the direction of the future course of interest rates will adjust the durations of their portfolios so as to capitalize on their expectations. Specifically, if a manager expects rates to increase, the duration will be shortened; if interest rates are expected to decrease, the duration will be lengthened. While investment managers can alter the durations of their portfolios with cash market instruments, a quick and inexpensive means for doing so (on either a temporary or permanent basis) is to use futures contracts.

In addition to adjusting a portfolio based on anticipated interest rate movements, a portfolio must be adjusted periodically in the structured portfolio strategies such as immunization that we described in Chapter 12 and can be used in constructing a portfolio with a longer duration than is available with cash market securities. As an example of the latter, suppose that in a certain interest rate environment a pension fund manager must structure a portfolio to have a duration of 15 years to accomplish a particular investment objective. Bonds with such a long duration may not be available. By buying the appropriate number and kind of interest rate futures contracts, a pension fund manager can increase the portfolio's duration to the target level of 15.

Hedging against Adverse Interest Rate Movements.   Interest rate futures can be used to hedge against adverse interest rate movements by locking in either a price or an interest rate. Because in most applications the bond or the rate to be hedged is not identical to the bond or the rate underlying the futures contract, hedging with interest rate futures involves cross hedging. Here are some examples of hedging with interest rate futures:

1. Suppose that a pension fund manager knows that bonds must be liquidated in 40 days to make a $5 million payment to the beneficiaries of the pension fund. If interest rates rise in 40 days, more bonds will have to

be liquidated to realize $5 million. The pension fund manager can hedge by selling bonds in the futures market to lock in a selling price. This is an example of a sell or short hedge.[7]

2. A pension fund manager may use a long hedge when substantial cash contributions are expected and the pension fund manager is concerned that interest rates may fall. Also, a money manager who knows that bonds are maturing in the near future and who expects that interest rates will fall can employ a long hedge. In both cases, interest rate futures are used to hedge against a fall in interest rates that would cause cash flows to be invested at an interest rate lower than desired.

3. A corporation plans to sell long-term bonds two months from now, so to protect itself against a rise in interest rates, the corporation can sell interest rate futures now.[8]

4. A thrift or commercial bank can hedge its cost of funds by locking in a rate using the Eurodollar CD futures contract.[9]

5. A corporation plans to sell commercial paper one month from now. Treasury bill futures or Eurodollar CD futures can be used to lock in a commercial paper rate.[10]

6. Investment banking firms can use interest rate futures to protect both the value of positions held by their trading desks and positions assumed by underwriting bonds. An example of the latter is a 1979 Salomon Brothers underwriting of $1 billion of IBM bonds. To protect itself against a rise in interest rates, which would reduce the value of the IBM bonds, Salomon Brothers sold (shorted) Treasury futures. In October 1979, interest rates rose upon an announcement by the Federal Reserve Board that it was allowing interest rates more flexibility to move. While the value of the

---

[7] For evidence of the effectiveness of hedging corporate bonds with interest rate futures, see Joanne Hill and Thomas Schneeweis, "Risk Reduction Potential of Financial Futures for Corporate Bond Positions," in Gerald Gay and Robert W. Kolb (eds.), *Interest Rate Futures: Concepts and Issues* (Richmond, VA: Dame, 1982), pp. 307–323. For an illustration of hedging a corporate bond with Treasury futures, see Mark Pitts and Frank J. Fabozzi, *Interest Rate Futures and Options* (Chicago: Probus Publishing, 1989), Chapter 9. For evidence on the effectiveness of hedging municipal bonds with the municipal bond index futures contract, see Richard Bookstaber and Hal Heaton, "On the Hedging Performance of the New Municipal Bond Futures Contract," in *Advances in Bond Analysis and Portfolio Strategies*.

[8] See Richard W. McEnally and Michael L. Rice, "Hedging Possibilities in the Flotation of Debt Securities," *Financial Management* (Winter 1979), pp. 12–18.

[9] See Michael Smirlock, "An Analysis of Hedging Certificates of Deposit with Interest Rate Futures: Bank and Contract Specific Evidence," in *Advances in Futures and Options Research*, Vol. 2, Part B, 1986, pp. 153–170.

[10] For an illustration, see Chapter 9 in Pitts and Fabozzi, *Interest Rate Futures and Options*.

IBM bonds held by Salomon Brothers declined in value, so did the Treasury bond futures contracts, but because Salomon Brothers sold these futures it realized a gain, reducing the loss on the IBM bonds it underwrote.

Enhancing Returns When Futures Are Mispriced. In Chapter 10, we explained that institutional investors look for the mispricing of stock index futures to create arbitrage profits and thereby enhance portfolio returns. We referred to this strategy as index arbitrage because it involves a stock index. If interest rate futures are mispriced even after considering the pricing problems we discussed earlier, institutional investors can enhance returns in the same way that they do in equities.

Allocating Funds between Stocks and Bonds. A pension sponsor may wish to alter the composition of the pension's funds between stocks and bonds, that is, change its asset allocation. Suppose that a pension sponsor wants to shift a $1 billion fund from its current allocation of $500 million in stocks and $500 million in bonds to $300 million in stocks and $700 million in bonds. This can be done directly by selling $200 million of stocks and buying a like amount of bonds. The costs associated with shifting funds in this manner are: (1) the transactions costs with respect to commissions and bid–ask spreads, (2) the market impact costs, and (3) the disruption of the activities of the money managers employed by the pension sponsor.

An alternative course of action is to use interest rate futures and stock index futures. Assume the pension sponsor wants to shift $200 million from stocks to bonds. Buying an appropriate number of interest rate futures and selling an appropriate number of stock index futures can achieve the desired exposure to stocks and bonds. Futures positions can be maintained or slowly liquidated as funds invested in the cash markets are actually shifted. The advantages of using financial futures contracts are: (1) transactions costs are lower, (2) market impact costs are avoided or reduced by allowing the sponsor time to buy and sell securities in the cash market, and (3) activities of the money managers employed by the pension sponsor are not disrupted.[11]

---

[11] See Roger Clarke, "Asset Allocation Using Futures," Chapter 16 in Robert Arnott and Frank J. Fabozzi (eds.), *Asset Allocation* (Chicago, IL: Probus Publishing, 1988), and Mark Zurak and Ravi Dattatreya, "Asset Allocation Using Futures Contracts," Chapter 20 in Frank J. Fabozzi and Gregory Kipnis (eds.), *The Handbook of Stock Index Futures and Options* (Homewood, IL: Probus Publishing, 1988).

Portfolio Insurance (Dynamic Hedging).   In Chapter 10, we explained that a put option on a portfolio can be created synthetically with a portfolio of Treasury bills and stock index futures. This strategy requires rebalancing, or dynamic hedging, of the portfolios. While dynamic hedging is employed more commonly in the case of stock portfolios, bond portfolio managers have shown some interest in this strategy.[12]

There is some survey evidence on the use of interest rate futures. In the summer of 1987, Figlewski surveyed life insurance companies to assess their use of financial futures and options.[13] Fifteen respondents classified as larger firms had average assets of $33.4 billion; 16 firms in the smaller firm group had average assets of $4.4 billion. Ninety-three percent of the larger firms and 76% of the smaller firms indicated that they currently used futures on Treasury bonds and notes or were likely to use them in the future. The corresponding responses for the use of futures where the underlying instrument is a money market instrument were 60% and 25%, respectively. The most frequent use for both larger and smaller firms was for hedging. The next most frequent use was for immunization and duration matching, 73% for larger firms and 12% for smaller firms.

In the summer of 1985, Block and Gallagher surveyed the use of interest rate futures and options by the Fortune 500 largest U.S. corporations.[14] The authors do not report responses separately for futures and options, so our discussion covers both derivative instruments. Only 19% of the 193 corporations in their survey reported using interest rate futures and options. The firms that did use derivative instruments actually used interest rate futures more frequently. In fact, the most popular futures contracts used were the Treasury bill and Eurodollar CD futures contracts. Users of futures and options indicated that 96% of the time hedging was the primary reason for using derivative instruments. About half the users suggested that they used these contracts for hedging the rate on commercial paper issuance. Thirty-

---

[12] For an explanation and illustration of portfolio insurance for fixed-income portfolios, see Colin Negrych and Dexter Senft, "Portfolio Insurance Using Synthetic Puts—The Reasons, Rewards, and Risks," Chapter 12 in Frank J. Fabozzi (ed.), *The Handbook of Fixed Income Options* (Chicago: Probus Publishing, 1989), or Erol Hakanoglu, Robert Kopprasch, and Emmanuel Roman, "Portfolio Insurance in the Fixed Income Market," Chapter 11 in Frank J. Fabozzi (ed.), *Fixed Income Portfolio Strategies* (Chicago: Probus Publishing, 1989).

[13] Stephen Figlewski, "The Use of Financial Futures and Options by Life Insurance Companies," Salomon Brothers Center for the Study of Financial Institutions, Working Paper Series No. 460, June 1988.

[14] Stanley B. Block and Timothy J. Gallagher, "Use of Interest Rate Futures and Options by Corporate Financial Managers," *Financial Management* (August 1986), pp. 73–78.

three percent used interest rate futures to lock in a short-term interest rate on excess funds to be invested. Hedging long-term interest rates for a planned bond offering was reported by fewer than 10% of the users.

FORWARD RATE AGREEMENT

A forward rate agreement (FRA) is a customized agreement between two parties (one of whom is a dealer firm—a commercial bank or investment banking firm) where the two parties agree at a specified future date to exchange an amount of money based on a reference interest rate and a reference principal amount. The latter is referred to as the *notional principal amount.*

To illustrate an FRA, suppose that Industrial Products Company and an investment bank enter into the following three-month FRA whose notional principal amount is $10 million: if one-year LIBOR three months from now exceeds 9%, the investment banking firm must pay the Industrial Products Company an amount determined by the following formula:

(1-year LIBOR 3 months from now − 0.09) × $10,000,000

For example, if one-year LIBOR three months from now is 12%, Industrial Products Company receives:

(0.12 − 0.09) × $10,000,000 = $300,000

If one-year LIBOR three months from now is less than 9%, Industrial Products Company must pay the investment banking firm an amount based on the same formula.

Borrowers and investors can use FRAs to hedge against adverse interest rate risk by locking in a rate. To see how a borrower can use an FRA, consider the hypothetical FRA above. Suppose that the management of Industrial Products Company plans three months from now to borrow $10 million for one year. The firm can borrow funds at some spread over one-year LIBOR, which is currently 9%. The risk that the firm faces is that three months from now one-year LIBOR will be greater than 9%. Suppose further that management wishes to eliminate the risk of a rise in one-year LIBOR by locking in a rate of 9%. By entering into the hypothetical FRA, the management of Industrial Products Company has done so. Should one-year LIBOR rise above 9% three months from now, under the terms of the FRA the investment banking firm is obligated to make up the difference. If one-year LIBOR three months from now is below 9%, the Industrial Products Company does not benefit from the lower rate because it must pay the investment banking firm an amount such that the effective cost of borrowing is 9%.

INTEREST RATE OPTIONS

Interest rate options can be written on cash instruments or futures. At one time, there were several exchange-traded option contracts whose underlying instrument was a debt instrument. These contracts are referred to as *options on physicals*. The most liquid exchange-traded option on a fixed-income security at the time of this writing is an option on Treasury bonds traded on the Chicago Board Options Exchange. For reasons explained later, options on futures have been far more popular than options on physicals. In recent years, market participants have made increasingly greater use of over-the-counter options on Treasury and mortgage-backed securities.

Over-the-Counter Options on Treasury and Mortgage-Backed Securities[15]

Certain institutional investors who want to purchase an option on a specific Treasury security or a Ginnie Mae pass-through can do so on an over-the-counter basis. There are government and mortgage-backed securities dealers who make a market in options on specific securities.

Over-the-counter (or dealer) options typically are purchased by institutional investors who want to hedge the risk associated with a specific security. For example, a thrift may be interested in hedging its position in a specific mortgage pass-through security.[16] Typically, the maturity of the option coincides with the time period over which the buyer of the option wants to hedge, so the buyer is typically not concerned with the option's liquidity.

Besides options on fixed-income securities, there are OTC options on a yield spread (such as the spread between mortgage pass-through securities and Treasuries or between double-A corporates and Treasuries). These can be used by money managers or corporate treasurers. In the latter case, consider a corporation that plans to sell bonds in two months. The rate that the corporate issuer will pay in two months is the Treasury rate plus the spread to Treasuries. If the corporate treasurer is satisfied with the spread but not the Treasury rate, the firm can buy an option on the spread.

---

[15] For a more detailed discussion of over-the-counter options, see Chapter 2 of Pitts and Fabozzi, *Interest Rate Futures and Options.*

[16] For a detailed discussion of over-the-counter options on mortgage-backed securities, see William A. Barr, "Options on Mortgage-Backed Securities," in Frank J. Fabozzi (ed.), *The Handbook of Mortgage-Backed Securities,* third edition (Chicago: Probus Publishing, 1992).

Exchange-Traded Futures Options

An option on a futures contract, commonly referred to as a *futures option*, gives the buyer the right to buy from or sell to the writer a designated futures contract at a designated price at any time during the life of the option. If the futures option is a call option, the buyer has the right to purchase one designated futures contract at the exercise price. That is, the buyer has the right to acquire a long futures position in the designated futures contract. If the buyer exercises the call option, the writer (seller) acquires a corresponding short position in the futures contract.

A put option on a futures contract grants the buyer the right to sell one designated futures contract to the writer at the exercise price. That is, the option buyer has the right to acquire a short position in the designated futures contract. If the put option is exercised, the writer acquires a corresponding long position in the designated futures contract.

There are futures options on all the interest rate futures contracts reviewed in the previous section.

Mechanics of Trading Futures Options.   As the parties to the futures option will realize a position in a futures contract when the option is exercised, the question is: what will the futures price be? That is, at what price will the long be required to pay for the instrument underlying the futures contract, and at what price will the short be required to sell the instrument underlying the futures contract?

Upon exercise, the futures price for the futures contract will be set equal to the exercise price. The position of the two parties is then immediately marked to market based on the then-current futures price. Thus, the futures position of the two parties will be at the prevailing futures price. At the same time, the option buyer will receive from the option seller the economic benefit from exercising. In the case of a call futures option, the option writer must pay the difference between the current futures price and the exercise price to the buyer of the option. In the case of a put futures option, the option writer must pay the option buyer the difference between the exercise price and the current futures price.

For example, suppose an investor buys a call option on some futures contract in which the exercise price is 85. Assume also that the futures price is 95 and that the buyer exercises the call option. Upon exercise, the call buyer is given a long position in the futures contract at 85 and the call writer is assigned the corresponding short position in the futures contract at 85. The futures position of the buyer and the writer is immediately marked to market by the exchange. Since the prevailing futures price is 95 and the exercise price is 85, the long futures position (the position of the call buyer) realizes a gain of 10 while the short futures position (the position of the call writer) realizes a loss of 10. The call writer pays the exchange 10 and the call buyer receives from the exchange 10. The call buyer who now has a long futures position at 95 can either liquidate the futures position at 95 or maintain a long futures position. If the former course of action is taken, the call buyer sells a futures contract at the prevailing futures price of 95. There is no gain or loss from liquidating the position. Overall, the call buyer realizes a gain of 10. If the call buyer elects to hold the long futures position, then he will face the same risk and reward of holding such a position. But he still has realized a gain of 10 from the exercise of the call option.

Suppose instead that the futures option is a put rather than a call, and the current futures price is 60 rather than 95. Then if the buyer of this put option exercises it, the buyer would have a short position in the futures contract at 85; the option writer would have a long position in the futures contract at 85. The exchange then marks the position to market at the then-current futures price of 60, resulting in a gain to the put buyer of 25 and a loss to the put writer of the same amount. The put buyer who now has a short futures position at 60 can either liquidate the short futures position by buying a futures contract at the prevailing futures price of 60 or maintain the short futures position. In either case the put buyer realizes a gain of 25 from exercising the put option.

There are no margin requirements for the buyer of a futures option once the option price has been paid in full. Because the option price is the maximum amount that the buyer can lose, regardless of how adverse the price movement of the underlying instrument, there is no need for margin.

Because the writer (seller) of an option has agreed to accept all of the risk (and none of the reward) of the position in the underlying instrument, the writer (seller) is required to deposit not only the margin required on the interest rate futures contract position if that is the underlying instrument, but, with certain exceptions, also the option price that is received for writing the option. In addition, as prices adversely affect the writer's position, the writer would be required to deposit variation margin as it is marked to market.

Reasons for the Popularity of Futures Options.   There are three reasons why futures options on fixed-income securities have largely supplanted options on physicals as the options vehicle used by institutional investors.[17] First, unlike options on fixed-income securities, futures options on Treasury coupon futures do not require payments for accrued interest to be made. Consequently, when a futures option is exercised, the call buyer and the put writer need not compensate the other party for accrued interest.

---

[17] Laurie Goodman, "Introduction to Debt Options," Chapter 1 in Frank J. Fabozzi (editor), *Winning the Interest Rate Game: A Guide to Debt Options* (Chicago, IL: Probus Publishing, 1985), pp. 13–14.

Second, futures options are believed to be "cleaner" instruments because of the reduced likelihood of delivery squeezes. Market participants who must deliver an instrument are concerned that at the time of delivery the instrument to be delivered will be in short supply, resulting in a higher price to acquire the instrument. As the deliverable supply of futures contracts is more than adequate for futures options currently traded, there is no concern about a delivery squeeze.

Finally, in order to price any option, it is imperative to know at all times the price of the underlying instrument. In the bond market, current prices are not as easily available as price information on the futures contract.

Portfolio Strategies with Interest Rate Options

There are no new strategies using interest rate options beyond what we explained in Chapters 7, 9, and 10. An institutional investor can use interest rate options to speculate on fixed-income security price movements based on expectations of interest rate movements. Because a call option increases in price if interest rates decline, an investor can buy call options if he or she expects interest rates to move in that direction. Alternatively, because the writer of a put option will benefit if the price increases, an investor who expects interest rates to fall can write put options. Purchasing put options and/or selling call options would be appropriate for an investor who expects interest rates to rise. Remember that unlike speculation in interest rate futures, interest rate options limit downside risk while reducing upside potential by the amount of the option price.

Institutional investors can use interest rate options to hedge a price or rate. Here are a few examples.

Hedging against Adverse Interest Rate Movements. Interest rate options can be used to hedge against adverse interest rate movements but still benefit from a favorable interest rate movement by setting a floor or ceiling on a rate. We'll use the illustrations given earlier for interest rate futures to explain how this works and to compare the outcomes using futures and options:

1. Suppose that a pension fund manager knows that bonds must be liquidated in 40 days to make a $5 million payment to the beneficiaries of the pension fund. If interest rates rise in 40 days, more bonds will have to be liquidated to realize $5 million. The hedger will buy put options. Should interest rates rise, the value of the bonds to be sold will decline, but the put options purchased will rise in value. If the transaction is properly structured, the gain on the put options will offset the loss on the bonds. The cost of the safety bought by this strategy will then be the option price paid. If, instead, interest rates decline, the value of the bonds will rise. The pension fund manager will not exercise the put option. A

gain equal to the rise in the bond value minus the put option price will be realized. As we explained in Chapter 9, a strategy of buying put options on securities held in a portfolio is called a protective put buying strategy.

2. Suppose a pension fund manager knows there will be substantial cash contributions flowing into the fund and is concerned that interest rates may fall. Or, suppose a money manager knows that bonds are maturing in the near future and expects interest rates to fall. In both cases, proceeds will be reinvested at a lower interest rate. Call options can be purchased in this situation. Should interest rates fall, the call options will increase in value, offsetting the loss in interest income that will result when the proceeds must be invested at a lower interest rate. The cost of this hedge strategy is the call option price. Should interest rates rise instead, the proceeds can be invested at a higher rate. The benefit of the higher rate will be reduced by the cost of the call option, which expires worthless.

3. A corporation plans to issue long-term bonds two months from now. To protect itself against a rise in interest rates, the corporation can buy put options. If interest rates rise, the interest cost of the bond issued two months from now will be higher, but the put option will have increased in value. Buying an appropriate number of put options yields a gain on the put options sufficient to offset the higher interest cost of the bond issue. Again, the cost of this strategy is the price of the put options. Should interest rates decline instead, the corporation will benefit from a lower interest cost when the bonds are issued, a benefit reduced by the cost of the put options.

4. A thrift or commercial bank wants to make sure that the cost of its funds will not exceed a certain level. This can be done by buying put options on Eurodollar CD futures.

5. A corporation plans to sell commercial paper one month from now. Buying put options on Treasury bill futures or Eurodollar CD futures lets the corporation set a ceiling on its commercial paper interest cost.

Allocating Funds between Stocks and Bonds.   A pension sponsor may wish to alter the composition of the pension funds between stocks and bonds. Stock index options and interest rate options can be used rather than transacting in the cash market.[18]

In his survey of life insurance companies, Figlewski found that 87% of the larger firms and 68% of the smaller firms currently used or planned to use

---

[18] For an explanation and illustration, see Ravi Dattatreya, "Asset Allocation Using Futures and Options," Chapter 50 in Frank J. Fabozzi (ed.), *The Handbook of Fixed Income Securities* (Homewood, IL: BusinessOne Irwin, 1991, Third Edition).

options on Treasury bonds and notes.[19] The corresponding percentages for options on Treasury bills and Eurodollar CDs were 50% and 25%, respectively. The most frequent use cited was hedging.

Option-Pricing Models

In Chapter 9, we discussed two models popularly used for valuing options: the Black–Scholes model and the binomial model. For options on interest rate futures, we can use a model developed by Black to value options on commodity futures.[20]

To illustrate the problem with the Black–Scholes option-pricing model if applied to the pricing of interest rate options, consider a three-month European call option on a three-year zero-coupon bond.[21] The maturity value of the underlying bond is $100, and the strike price is $120. Suppose further that the current price of the bond is $75.13, the three-year risk-free rate is 10% annually, and expected price volatility is 4%. What would be the fair value for this option? Do you really need an option-pricing model to determine the value of this option?

Think about it. This zero-coupon bond will never have a price above $100 because that is the maturity value. As the strike price is $120, the option will never be exercised; its value is therefore zero. If you can get anyone to buy such an option, any price you obtain will be free money. Yet an option buyer armed with the Black–Scholes option-pricing model will input the variables we assume above and come up with a value for this option of $5.60! Why is the Black–Scholes model off by so much? The answer lies in the underlying assumptions.

There are three assumptions underlying the Black–Scholes model that limit its use in pricing options on interest rate instruments. First, the probability distribution for the prices assumed by the Black–Scholes option pricing model is a lognormal distribution, which permits some probability—no matter how small—that the price can take on any positive value. But in the case of a zero-coupon bond, the price can take on a value above $100. In the case of a coupon bond, we know that the price cannot exceed the sum of the coupon payments plus the maturity value. For example, for a five-year 10% coupon bond with a maturity value of $100, the price cannot be greater than $150 (five coupon payments of $10 plus the maturity value of $100).

[19] Figlewski, "The Use of Financial Futures and Options by Life Insurance Companies."

[20] Fischer Black, "The Pricing of Commodity Contracts," *Journal of Financial Economics* (January–March 1976), pp. 167–179.

[21] This example is given in Lawrence J. Dyer and David P. Jacob, "Guide to Fixed Income Option Pricing Models," in Fabozzi, *The Handbook of Fixed Income Options*, pp. 81–82.

Thus, unlike stock prices, bond prices have a maximum value. The only way that a bond's price can exceed the maximum value is if negative interest rates are permitted. This is not likely to occur, so any probability distribution for prices assumed by an option-pricing model that permits bond prices to be greater than the maximum bond value could generate nonsensical option prices. The Black–Scholes model does allow bond prices to exceed the maximum bond value (or, equivalently, allows negative interest rates). That is one of the reasons why we obtained the nonsensical option price for the three-month European call option on the three-year zero-coupon bond.

The second assumption of the Black–Scholes option-pricing model is that the short-term interest rate is constant over the life of the option. Yet the price of an interest rate option will change as interest rates change. A change in the short-term interest rate changes the rates along the yield curve. Therefore, to assume that the short-term rate will be constant is inappropriate for interest rate options. The third assumption is that the variance of prices is constant over the life of the option. Recall from Chapter 12 that as a bond moves closer to maturity its price volatility declines. Therefore, the assumption that price variance is constant over the life of the option is inappropriate.

While we have illustrated the problem of using the Black–Scholes model to price interest rate options, we can also show that the binomial option-pricing model based on the price distribution of the underlying bond suffers from the same problems. A way around the problem of negative interest rates is to use a binomial option-pricing model based on the distribution of interest rates rather than prices and construct the binomial tree shown in Figure 7-6 of Chapter 7 using interest rates.[22] Once a binomial interest rate tree is constructed, it can be converted into a binomial price tree by using the interest rates on the tree to determine the price of the bond. Then we use the same procedure as described in Chapter 7 for calculating the option price by working backward from the value of the call option at the expiration date.

While the binomial option-pricing model based on yields is superior to models based on prices, it still has a theoretical drawback. All option-pricing models to be theoretically valid must satisfy the put–call parity relationship explained in Chapter 7. The problem with the binomial model based on yields

---

[22] For example, in constructing the binomial tree based on interest rates, we can use the formula:

If yield increases:	If yield decreases:
$Y_{t+1} = Y_t \, e^s$	$Y_{t+1} = Y_t \, e^{-s}$

where Y_{t+1} = yield to maturity in time period $t + 1$
Y_t = yield to maturity in time period t
s = expected interest rate volatility
e = 2.7182818

is that it does not satisfy this relationship. It violates the relationship in that it fails to take into consideration the yield curve, thereby allowing arbitrage opportunities.

The most elaborate models that take the yield curve into consideration and as a result do not permit arbitrage opportunities are called *yield curve option-pricing models* or *arbitrage-free option-pricing models*. These models can incorporate different volatility assumptions along the yield curve. While they are theoretically superior to the other models we have described, they require extensive computer time to solve.[23]

Pricing Efficiency of the Options Markets

In our review of the pricing efficiency of the common stock options market, we explained that there were two types of tests: (1) tests based on violations of boundary conditions and put–call parity, and (2) tests based on an option-pricing model. There have been studies of options on interest rate futures in both categories.

Jordan and Seale employ a large transactions data base (21,402 observations) for Treasury bond futures and futures options to test for both the lower boundary condition and put–call parity.[24] The time period studied is October 5, 1982 (when futures options began trading) through March 26, 1985. They find that actual prices conformed closely to the theoretical prices specified by the lower boundary and put–call parity. The deviations from put–call parity that are found were not sufficiently large to be exploitable by even the lowest-cost traders. Therefore, the findings of Jordan and Seale provide virtually no evidence for rejecting the hypothesis that the market is efficient.

Merville and Overdahl empirically examine the mispricing bias and market efficiency for call options on Treasury bond futures from December 1982 through June 1985 using several option-pricing models.[25] They find that the pricing efficiency of call options improved only marginally with the inception of futures option trading. According to their option-pricing model,

---

[23] For a discussion of yield curve or arbitrage-free option-pricing models see: Chapter 7 of Pitts and Fabozzi, *Interest Rate Options and Futures*; Dyer and Jacob, "Guide to Fixed Income Option Pricing Models," *The Handbook of Fixed Income Options*; and Ravi E. Dattatreya and Frank J. Fabozzi, "A Simplified Model for the Valuation of Debt Options," Chapter 4 in *The Handbook of Fixed Income Options*.

[24] James V. Jordan and William E. Seale, "Transactions Data Tests of Minimum Prices and Put–Call Parity for Treasury Bond Futures Options," *Advances in Futures and Options Research,* Vol. 1, Part A, 1986, pp. 63–87.

[25] Larry J. Merville and James A. Overdahl, "An Empirical Examination of the T-Bond Futures (Call) Options Markets Under Conditions of Constant and Changing Variance Rates," *Advances in Futures and Options Research*, Vol. 1, Part A (1986), pp. 89–118.

they find that in-the-money options tend to be underpriced and at- and out-of-the-money options tend to be overpriced. These results, however, may be due simply to the lack of a good theoretical model to price the options.

SUMMARY

In this chapter we have reviewed the markets for interest rate futures and options contracts. Currently traded interest rate futures contracts include: Treasury bill futures, Eurodollar CD futures, Treasury bond and note futures, and the Bond Buyer municipal index futures. Interest rate futures are also traded on foreign exchanges where the underlying fixed-income security is foreign debt.

The Treasury bond and note futures contracts give the short several delivery options (quality or swap option, timing option, and wild card option). All three delivery options will reduce the futures price below the theoretical futures price suggested by the standard arbitrage model.

The Bond Buyer municipal bond index futures contract is based on a basket of 40 municipal bonds priced daily by five brokers and is a cash settlement contract.

Interest rate futures can be used by institutional investors to speculate on interest rate movements, to control a bond portfolio's exposure to interest rate changes (altering duration), to enhance returns when futures are mispriced, to allocate funds between stocks and bonds (in combination with stock index futures), and to create synthetic put options (portfolio insurance or dynamic hedging). The most popular use of interest rate futures by institutional money managers and corporate financial managers is for hedging—locking in an interest rate or a price.

Interest rate options include options on fixed-income securities and options on interest rate futures contracts. The latter, more commonly called futures options, are the preferred vehicle for implementing investment strategies. Because of the difficulties of hedging particular bond issues or pass-through securities, many institutions find over-the-counter options more useful; these contracts can be customized to meet specific investment goals.

The Black model is commonly used to price futures options. The assumptions underlying the Black–Scholes pricing model and the binomial model based on prices limit their application to options on fixed-income instruments. The binomial option model based on yields is a better model, but it still suffers from the problem that it does not satisfy the put–call parity relationship. More sophisticated models called yield curve or arbitrage-free pricing models overcome this drawback by incorporating the yield curve into the pricing model. Strategies using interest rate options include speculating on interest rate movements and hedging.

QUESTIONS

1. **a.** Explain how the shape of the yield curve influences the theoretical price of a Treasury bond futures contract.

    b. How does the shape of the yield curve affect the decision of a person short a bond futures contract as to when to deliver the underlying bond?

2. As the corporate treasurer of a major corporation, you envision that the firm will have to borrow $125 million in three months' time.

    a. How could you use a Treasury bond futures contract to hedge against increased interest rates over the next quarter?

    b. Why might this not work out to be a perfect hedge?

3. Consider a hypothetical scenario:

    Treasury Bond Futures Price: 95

    Bond A: Coupon = 12%, conversion factor = 0.85

    Bond B: Coupon = 10%, conversion factor = 0.75

    Bond C: Coupon = 6.5%, conversion factor = 1.25

    Bond A is selling at 105%, Bond B at 102%, and Bond C at 95%.

    a. Ignoring accrued interest, calculate the invoice price for each of the three bonds.

    b. Which bond is the cheapest to deliver?

4. What arguments would be given by those who feel that the Black–Scholes model does not apply in pricing interest rate options?

5. Here are some excerpts from an article entitled "It's Boom Time for Bond Options As Interest-Rate Hedges Bloom," published in the November 8, 1990, issue of *The Wall Street Journal.*

    a. The threat of a large interest-rate swing in either direction is driving people to options to hedge their portfolios of long-term Treasury bonds and medium-term Treasury notes, said Steven Northern, who manages fixed-income mutual funds for Massachusetts Financial Services Co. in Boston.

    Why would a large interest rate swing in either direction encourage people to hedge?

    b. If the market moves against an option purchaser, the option expires worthless, and all the investor has lost is the relatively low purchase price, or "premium," of the option.

Comment on the accuracy of this statement.

c. Futures contracts also can be used to hedge portfolios, but they cost more, and there isn't any limit on the amount of losses they could produce before an investor bails out.

Comment on the accuracy of this statement.

d. Mr. Northern said Massachusetts Financial has been trading actively in bond and note put options. "The concept is simple," he said. "If you're concerned about interest rates but don't want to alter the nature of what you own in a fixed-income portfolio, you can just buy puts."

Why might put options be a preferable means of altering the nature of a fixed-income portfolio?

6. Suppose an institutional investor wants to hedge a portfolio of mortgage pass-through securities using Treasury bond futures contracts. What are the risks associated with such a hedge?

7. What is the difference between an option on a bond and an option on a bond futures contract?

8. **a.** What is the motivation for the purchase of an over-the-counter option?

b. Does it make sense for an investor who wants to speculate on interest rate movements to purchase an over-the-counter option?

9. Three months from now the Summit Manufacturing Company plans to borrow $100 million for one year. The interest rate at which Summit Manufacturing expects to borrow is LIBOR plus 100 basis points. Currently, LIBOR is 10%.

a. What is the funding risk that Summit Manufacturing faces?

b. Suppose that Summit Manufacturing enters into a three-month forward rate agreement with an investment banking firm for a notional principal amount of $100 million. Terms of the FRA are as follows: If one-year LIBOR exceeds 10% three months from now, the investment banking firm must pay Summit Manufacturing; if one-year LIBOR is less than 10% three months from now, Summit Manufacturing must pay the investment banking firm. How can this FRA eliminate the risk that you identified in part a?

CHAPTER

20

CUSTOMIZED INTEREST RATE CONTROL CONTRACTS

LEARNING OBJECTIVES

After reading this chapter you will understand:

- what an interest rate swap is.

- how an interest rate swap can be used by institutional investors and corporate borrowers.

- why the interest rate swap market has grown so rapidly.

- the relationship between an interest rate swap and forward contracts.

- the various types of interest rate swaps and reasons for their development.

- what an option on a swap is, and how it can be used.

- what an interest rate agreement (cap or floor) is, and how these agreements can be used by institutional investors and corporate borrowers.

- the relationship between an interest rate agreement and options.

- how an interest rate collar can be created.
- what a compound option is and its use.

In the previous chapter we discussed interest rate futures and options and how they can be used to control interest rate risk. Commercial banks and investment banks also customize for their clients other contracts useful for controlling such risk. These include interest rate swaps and options on swaps, interest rate agreements (caps and floors) and options on these agreements, and compound options. These contracts are relatively new. In this chapter we will review each of them and explain how they can be used by borrowers and institutional investors. While there are no regulations governing customized interest rate control contracts, there is a pending bill in Congress to regulate interest rate swaps.

INTEREST RATE SWAPS

An interest rate swap is an agreement whereby two parties (called counterparties) agree to exchange periodic interest payments. The dollar amount of the interest payments exchanged is based on some predetermined dollar principal, which is called the *notional principal amount*. The dollar amount each counterparty pays to the other is the agreed-upon periodic interest rate times the notional principal amount. The only dollars that are exchanged between the parties are the interest payments, not the notional principal amount. In the most common type of swap, one party agrees to pay the other party fixed interest payments at designated dates for the life of the contract. This party is referred to as the *fixed-rate payer*. The other party agrees to make interest rate payments that float with some index and is referred to as the *floating-rate payer*.

For example, suppose that for the next five years party X agrees to pay party Y 10% per year, while party Y agrees to pay party X six-month LIBOR. Party X is a fixed-rate payer/floating-rate receiver, while party Y is a floating-rate payer/fixed-rate receiver. Assume that the notional principal amount is $50 million, and that payments are exchanged every six months for the next five years. This means that every six months, party X (the fixed-rate payer/floating-rate receiver) will pay party Y $2.5 million (10% times $50 million divided by 2). The amount that party Y (the floating-rate payer/fixed-rate receiver) will pay party X will be six-month LIBOR times $50 million divided by 2. For example, if six-month LIBOR is 7%, party Y will pay party X $1.75 million (7% times $50 million divided by 2). Note that we divide by two because one-half year's interest is being paid.

The interest rate benchmarks that are commonly used for the floating rate in an interest rate swap are those on various money market instruments: Treasury bills, London Interbank Offered Rate (LIBOR), commercial paper, bankers acceptances, certificates of deposit, federal funds rate, and prime rate.

As we illustrate later, market participants can use an interest rate swap to alter the cash flow character of assets or liabilities from a fixed-rate basis to a floating-rate basis or vice versa.

Risk/Return Characteristics of a Swap

As explained later in this chapter, there is a secondary market for swaps. The value of an interest rate swap will fluctuate with market interest rates. To see how, let's consider our hypothetical swap. Suppose that interest rates change immediately after parties X and Y enter into the swap. First, consider what would happen if the market demanded that in any five-year swap the fixed-rate payer must pay 11% in order to receive six-month LIBOR. If party X (the fixed-rate payer) wants to sell its position, say, to party A, then party A will benefit by only having to pay 10% (the original swap rate agreed upon) rather than 11% (the current swap rate) to receive six-month LIBOR. Party X will want compensation for this benefit. Consequently, the value of party X's position has increased. Thus, if interest rates increase, the fixed-rate payer will realize a profit and the floating-rate payer will realize a loss.

Next, consider what would happen if interest rates decline to, say, 6%. Now a five-year swap would require the fixed-rate payer to pay 6% rather than 10% to receive six-month LIBOR. If party X wants to sell its position to party B, the latter would demand compensation to take over the position. In other words, if interest rates decline, the fixed-rate payer will realize a loss, while the floating-rate payer will realize a profit.

The risk/return profile of the two positions when interest rates change is summarized below:

	INEREST RATES DECREASE	INTEREST RATES INCREASE
Floating-rate payer	Gain	Loss
Fixed-rate payer	Loss	Gain

Comparison of Interest Rate Swaps to Futures/Forward Contracts

Contrast the position of the counterparties in an interest rate swap to the position of the long and short futures (forward) contract discussed in the previous chapter. The long futures position gains if interest rates decline and loses if interest rates rise—this is similar to the risk/return profile of a floating-rate payer. The risk/return profile of a fixed-rate payer is similar to that of the short futures position: a gain if interest rates increase and a loss if interest rates decrease. By taking a closer look at the interest rate swap we can understand why the risk/return relationships are similar.

Consider party X's position. Party X has agreed to pay 10% and receive six-month LIBOR. More specifically, based on a $50 million notional principal amount, X has agreed to buy a commodity called "six-month LIBOR" for $2.5 million. This is effectively a six-month forward contract where X agrees to pay $2.5 million in exchange for delivery of six-month LIBOR. If interest rates increase to 11%, the price of that commodity (six-month LIBOR) is higher, resulting in a gain for the fixed-rate payer, who is effectively long a six-month forward contract on six-month LIBOR. The floating-rate payer is effectively short a six-month forward contract on six-month LIBOR. There is therefore a forward contract corresponding to each exchange date.

Now we can see why there is a similarity between the risk/return relationship for an interest rate swap and a forward contract. If interest rates increase to, say, 11%, the price of that commodity (six-month LIBOR) increases to $2.75 million (11% times $50 million divided by 2). The long forward position (the fixed-rate payer) gains, and the short forward position (the floating-rate payer) loses. If interest rates decline to, say, 9%, the price of our commodity decreases to $2.25 million (9% times $50 million divided by 2). The short forward position (the floating-rate payer) gains, and the long forward position (the fixed-rate payer) loses.

Consequently, *interest rate swaps can be viewed as a package of more basic interest rate control tools, such as forwards.* The pricing of an interest rate swap will then depend on the price of a package of forward contracts with the same settlement dates and in which the underlying for the forward contract is the same index.

While an interest rate swap may be nothing more than a package of forward contracts, it is not a redundant contract for several reasons. First, for forward or futures contracts, the longest maturity does not extend out as far as that of an interest rate swap; an interest rate swap with a term of 15 years or longer can be obtained. Second, an interest rate swap is a more transactionally efficient instrument. By this we mean that in one transaction an entity can effectively establish a payoff equivalent to a package of forward contracts. The forward contracts would each have to be negotiated separately. Third, the liquidity of the interest rate swap market has grown since its beginning in 1981; it is now more liquid than forward contracts, particularly long-dated (i.e., long-term) forward contracts.

Applications

So far we have merely described an interest rate swap and looked at its characteristics. We explain now how they can be used, with the help of two illustrations. While these show basic or "plain vanilla" swaps, the illustrations will help us understand why other types of interest rate swaps have been developed.

Illustration 1.   In the first illustration we look at how an interest rate swap can be used to alter the cash flow characteristics of an institution's assets so as to provide a better match between assets and liabilities. The two institutions are a commercial bank and a life insurance company.

Suppose a bank has a portfolio consisting of five-year term commercial loans with a fixed interest rate. The principal value of the portfolio is $50 million, and the interest rate on all the loans in the portfolio is 10%. The loans are interest-only loans; interest is paid semiannually, and the principal is paid at the end of five years. That is, assuming no default on the loans, the cash flow from the loan portfolio is $2.5 million every six months for the next five years and $50 million at the end of five years. To fund its loan portfolio, assume that the bank is relying on the issuance of six-month certificates of deposit. The interest rate that the bank plans to pay on its six-month CDs is the six-month Treasury bill rate plus 40 basis points.

The risk that the bank faces is that the six-month Treasury bill rate will be 9.6% or greater. To understand why, remember that the bank is earning 10% annually on its commercial loan portfolio. If the six-month Treasury bill rate is 9.6%, it will have to pay 9.6% plus 40 basis points to depositors for six-month funds, or 10%, and there will be no spread income. Worse, if the six-month Treasury bill rate rises above 9.6%, there will be a loss; that is, the cost of funds will exceed the interest rate earned on the loan portfolio. The bank's objective is to lock in a spread over the cost of its funds.

The other party in the interest rate swap illustration will be a life insurance company that has committed itself to pay a 9% rate for the next five years on a guaranteed investment contract (GIC) it has issued. The amount of the GIC is $50 million. Suppose that the life insurance company has the opportunity to invest $50 million in what it considers an attractive five-year floating-rate instrument in a private placement transaction. The interest rate on this instrument is the six-month Treasury bill rate plus 160 basis points. The coupon rate is set every six months.

The risk that the life insurance company faces is that the six-month interest rate will fall so that it will not earn enough to realize a spread over the 9% rate that it has guaranteed to the GIC holders. If the six-month Treasury bill falls to 7.4% or less, no spread income will be generated. To understand why, suppose that the six-month Treasury bill rate at the date the floating-rate instrument resets its coupon is 7.4%. Then the coupon rate for the next six months will be 9% (7.4% plus 160 basis points). Because the life insurance company has agreed to pay 9% on the GIC policy, there will be no spread income. Should the six-month Treasury bill rate fall below 7.4%, there will be a loss.

We can summarize the asset/liability problem of the bank and life insurance company as follows:

Bank:

1. has lent long term and borrowed short term
2. if the six-month Treasury bill rate rises, spread income declines

Life insurance company:

1. has effectively lent short term and borrowed long term
2. if the six-month Treasury bill rate falls, spread income declines

Now let's suppose that an intermediary offers a five-year interest rate swap with a notional principal amount of $50 million to both the bank and life insurance company. The terms offered to the bank are as follows:

1. every six months the bank will pay 10% (annual rate) to the intermediary
2. every six months the intermediary will pay the six-month Treasury bill rate plus 155 basis points to the bank

The terms offered to the insurance company are as follows:

1. every six months the life insurance company will pay the six-month Treasury bill rate plus 160 basis points per year to the intermediary
2. every six months the intermediary will pay the bank 10% (annual rate)

What has this interest rate contract done for the bank and the life insurance company? Consider first the bank. For every six-month period for the life of the swap agreement, the interest rate spread will be as follows:

Annual interest rate received:
From commercial loan portfolio	= 10%
From interest rate swap	= 6-month T-bill rate + 155 b.p.
Total	= 11.55% + 6-month T-bill rate

Annual interest rate paid:
To CD depositors	= 6-month T-bill rate + 40 b.p.
On interest rate swap	= 10%
Total	= 10.40% + 6-month T-bill rate

Outcome:
To be received	= 11.55% + 6-month T-bill rate
To be paid	= 10.40% + 6-month T-bill rate
Spread income	= 1.15% or 115 basis points

Thus, regardless of what happens to the six-month Treasury bill rate, the bank locks in a spread of 115 basis points.

Now let's look at the effect of the interest rate swap on the life insurance company:

Annual interest rate received:
From floating-rate instrument	= 6-month T-bill rate + 160%
From interest rate swap	= 10%
Total	= 11.6% + 6-month T-bill rate

Annual interest rate paid:
To GIC policyholders	= 9%
On interest rate swap	= 6-month T-bill rate + 160%
Total	= 10.6% + 6-month T-bill rate

Outcome:
To be received	= 11.6% + 6-month T-bill rate
To be paid	= 10.6% + 6-month T-bill rate
Spread income	= 1.0% or 100 basis points

Regardless of what happens to the six-month Treasury bill rate, the life insurance company locks in a spread of 100 basis points.

The interest rate swap has allowed each party to accomplish its asset/liability objective of locking in a spread.[1] It permits the two financial institutions to alter the cash flow characteristics of its assets: from fixed to floating in the case of the bank, and from floating to fixed in the case of the life insurance company. This type of transaction is referred to as an *asset swap*. Alternatively, the bank and the life insurance company could have used the swap market to change the cash flow nature of their liabilities. Such a swap

---

[1] Whether the size of the spread is adequate is not an issue to us in this illustration.

is called a *liability swap*. While in our illustration we used a bank, an interest rate swap obviously would be appropriate for savings and loan associations that, because of regulation, borrow short-term (i.e., floating-rate basis) and lend long-term (i.e., on fixed-rate mortgages).

Of course there are other ways that the two institutions could have chosen to accomplish the same thing. The bank might refuse to make fixed-rate commercial loans. If borrowers could find another source willing to lend on a fixed-rate basis, though, the bank has lost these customers. The life insurance company might refuse to purchase a floating-rate instrument. But suppose that the terms offered on the private placement instrument were more attractive than what would have been offered on a comparable credit risk floating-rate instrument, and that by using the swap market the life insurance company can earn a yield higher than if it invests directly in a five-year fixed-rate security. For example, suppose the life insurance company can invest in a comparable credit risk five-year fixed-rate security with a yield of 9.8%. Assuming that it commits itself to a GIC with a 9% rate, this would result in spread income of 80 basis points—less than the 115-basis point spread income it achieved by purchasing the floating-rate instrument and entering into the swap.

Consequently, not only can an interest rate swap be used to change the risk of a transaction by changing the cash flow characteristics of assets or liabilities, but under certain circumstances, it also can be used to enhance returns. Obviously, this depends on the existence of market imperfections.

Before we leave this illustration, look back at the floating-rate payments that the life insurance company makes to the intermediary and the floating-rate payments that the intermediary makes to the bank. The life insurance company pays the six-month Treasury bill rate plus 160 basis points, but the intermediary pays the bank the six-month Treasury bill rate plus only 155 basis points. The five-basis point difference represents the fee to the intermediary for the services of intermediation.

Illustration 2.   Our second illustration considers two U.S. entities, a triple A-rated commercial bank and a triple B-rated non-financial corporation; each wants to raise $100 million for 10 years. The bank wants to raise floating-rate funds, while the non-financial corporation wants to raise fixed-rate funds. The interest rates available to the two entities in the U.S. bond market are as follows:

Bank: Floating rate = 6-month LIBOR + 30 b.p.

Non-financial corporation: Fixed rate = 12%

Suppose instead that both entities could issue securities in the Eurodollar bond market (discussed in Chapter 22). For now, suffice it to say that this is a market for U.S. dollar-denominated bonds underwritten by a syndicate of international banks and securities firms. The buyers in this market are typically non-U.S. investors. The criteria used by these investors to assess the default risk of bonds historically have been different from those used in the U.S.

Suppose that the following terms are available in the Eurodollar bond market for 10-year securities for these two entities:

Bank: Fixed rate = 10.5%

Non-financial corporation: Floating rate = 6-month LIBOR + 80 b.p.

Notice that we indicate the terms that the bank could obtain on fixed-rate financing and that the non-financial corporation could obtain on floating-rate securities. You'll see why we did this shortly. First, let's summarize the situation for the two entities in the U.S. domestic and Eurodollar bond markets:

FLOATING-RATE SECURITIES

ENTITY	BOND MARKET	RATE
Bank	U.S. domestic	6-month LIBOR + 30 b.p.
Non-financial corp.	Eurodollar	6-month LIBOR + 80 b.p.
		Quality spread = 50 b.p.

FIXED-RATE SECURITIES

ENTITY	BOND MARKET	RATE
Bank	Eurodollar	10.5%
Non-financial corp.	U.S. domestic	12.0%
		Quality spread = 150 b.p.

Notice that the quality spread for floating-rate securities (50 basis points) is narrower than the quality spread for fixed-rate securities (150 basis points). This provides an opportunity for both entities to reduce the cost of raising funds. To see how, suppose each entity issued securities in the Eurodollar bond market, and then simultaneously entered into the following 10-year interest rate swap with a $100 million notional principal amount offered by an intermediary:

Bank:
  Pay floating rate of 6-month LIBOR + 70 b.p.
  Receive fixed rate of 11.3%

Non-financial corp.:
  Pay fixed rate   = 11.3%
  Receive floating rate = 6-month LIBOR + 45 b.p.

The cost of the issue for the bank would then be:

Interest paid:
    On fixed-rate Eurodollar bonds issued = 10.5%
    On interest rate swap   = 6-month LIBOR + 70 b.p.
        Total   = 11.2% + 6-month LIBOR

Interest received:
    On interest rate swap   = 11.3%

Net cost:
    Interest paid   = 11.2% + 6-month LIBOR
    Interest received   = 11.3%
        Total   = 6-month LIBOR − 10 b.p.

The cost of the issue for the non-financial corporation would then be:

Interest paid:
    On floating-rate Eurodollar bonds issued = 6-month LIBOR + 80 b.p.
    On interest rate swap   = 11.3%
        Total   = 12.1% + 6-month LIBOR

Interest received:
    On interest rate swap   = 6-month LIBOR + 45 b.p.

Net cost:
    Interest paid   = 12.1% + 6-month LIBOR
    Interest received   = 6-month LIBOR + 45 b.p.
        Total   = 11.65%

The transactions are diagrammed in Figure 20-1. By issuing securities in the Eurodollar bond market and using the interest rate swap, both entities are able to reduce their cost of issuing securities. The bank was able to issue floating-rate securities for six-month LIBOR minus 10 basis points rather than issue floating-rate securities in the U.S. domestic bond market for six-month LIBOR plus 30 basis points, thereby saving 40 basis points. The non-financial corporation saved 35 basis points (11.65% versus 12%) by issuing floating-rate bonds in the Eurodollar bond market and using the interest rate swap.

The point of this illustration is that if differences in quality spreads exist in different sectors of the bond markets, borrowers can use the interest rate swap to arbitrage the inconsistency. Whether they do exist is another question, which we will address below.

Finally, let's look once again at the intermediary in this transaction. The intermediary pays a floating rate of six-month LIBOR plus 45 basis points to the non-financial corporation, and receives six-month LIBOR plus 70 basis points, realizing 25 basis points for its intermediary services.

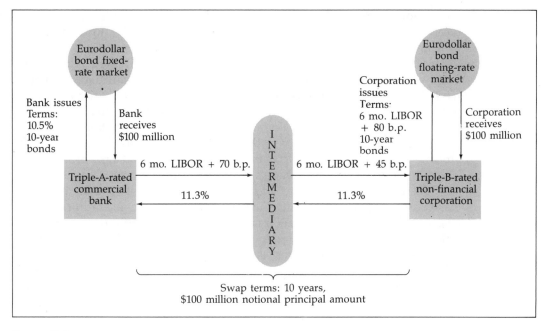

FIGURE 20-1
Diagram of Interest Rate Swap for Illustration 2

Development of the Interest Rate Swap Market

The interest rate swap was first developed in late 1981. By 1987, the market had grown to more than $500 billion (in terms of notional principal amount). What is behind this rapid growth? As our two illustrations have demonstrated, an interest rate swap is a quick way for institutional investors and corporate borrowers to change the nature of assets and liabilities or to exploit any perceived capital market imperfection.

Initial motivation for the interest rate swap market was borrower exploitation of what were perceived to be "credit arbitrage" opportunities because of differences between the quality spread between lower- and higher-rated credits in the U.S. and Eurodollar bond fixed-rate market and the same spread in these two floating-rate markets. Note that our second illustration assumes a spread of 50 basis points in the floating-rate markets and 150 basis points in the fixed-rate markets. Publications by dealer firms[2]

---

[2] See, for example, a January 1986 Salomon Brothers publication: T. Lipsky and S. Elhalaski, "Swap-Driven Primary Issuance in the International Bond Market."

and academic research have suggested this credit arbitrage motivation.[3] Basically, the argument for swaps was based on a well-known economic principle of comparative advantage in international economics. The argument in the case of swaps is that even though a high credit-rated issuer could borrow at a lower cost in both the fixed-rate and floating-rate markets (that is, have an absolute advantage in both), it will have a *comparative* advantage relative to a lower credit-rated issuer in one of the markets (and a comparative disadvantage in the other). Under these conditions, each borrower could benefit from issuing securities in the market in which it has a comparative advantage and then swapping obligations for the desired type of financing. The swap market was the vehicle for swapping obligations.

Several observers have challenged the notion that "credit arbitrage" exists. It should be evident that the comparative advantage argument, while based on arbitrage, is not based on the existence of an irrational mispricing, but on assumptions of equilibrium in segmented markets. If two completely separate markets are each perfectly competitive unto themselves, but set different prices for risk, a transactor in both markets simultaneously sees an imperfectly competitive market and can make money. Those who challenge the "credit arbitrage" notion argue that the differences in quality spreads in the fixed-rate and floating-rate markets represent differences in the risks that lenders face in these two markets. For example, the interest rate for a floating-rate note effectively represents a short-term interest rate. The quality spread on floating-rate notes therefore represents a spread in the short-term market. In contrast, the quality spread on fixed-rate medium- and long-term notes represents the spread in that maturity sector. There is no reason why the quality spreads have to be the same.[4]

Despite arguments that credit arbitrage opportunities are rare in reasonably efficient international capital markets, and that, even if they did exist, they would be eliminated quickly by arbitrage, the number of interest rate swap transactions has grown substantially. Another explanation is suggested in a May 1984 contribution sponsored by Citicorp that appeared in *Euromoney:*

> The nature of swaps is that they arbitrage market imperfections. As with any arbitrage opportunity, the more it is exploited, the smaller it becomes. . . .

---

[3] See, for example, James Bicksler and Andrew Chen, "An Economic Analysis of Interest Rate Swaps," *Journal of Finance* (July 1986), pp. 645–655.

[4] Two researchers demonstrate that differences in quality spreads between the fixed-rate and floating-rate markets are consistent with option-pricing theory. See Ian Cooper and Antonio Mello, "Default Spreads in the Fixed and in the Floating Rate Markets: A Contingent Claims Approach," *Advances in Futures and Options Research*, Vol. 3 (1988), pp. 269–290.

But some of the causes of market imperfections are unlikely to disappear quickly. For example, insurance companies in many countries are constrained to invest mainly in instruments that are domestic in that country. That requirement will tend to favour domestic issuers artificially, and is unlikely to be changed overnight. And even in the world's most liquid markets there are arbitrage opportunities. They are small and exist only briefly. But they exist nevertheless.[5]

As this opinion demonstrates, as early as 1984 it was argued that the difference in quality spreads in the two markets may be attributable to differences in regulations in two countries. Similarly, differences in tax treatment across countries also create market imperfections that can be exploited using swaps.[6] Thus, swaps can be used for regulatory or tax arbitrage.

Rather than relying exclusively on an arbitrage argument, one study suggests that the swaps market grew because it allowed borrowers to raise a type of financing that was not possible prior to the introduction of interest rate swaps.[7] To understand this argument, let's look at the instruments available to borrowers prior to the introduction of interest rate swaps. They include:

1. long-term fixed-rate instruments
2. long-term floating-rate instruments
3. short-term debt

The interest rate for a borrower is composed of the risk-free rate for the relevant maturity plus a credit spread. Consider borrowers with the following expectations:

- Borrower A believes that the risk-free rate will rise in the future, and its credit will weaken. This borrower will want to borrow long-term with a fixed rate to lock in the prevailing risk-free rate and credit spread.

---

[5] "Swap Financing Techniques: A Citicorp Guide," Special Sponsored Section, *Euromoney* (May 1984), pp. S1–S7.

[6] This applies even more so to currency swaps, which we discuss in the next chapter. Several examples of how swaps can be used to exploit differences in taxes are given in Clifford W. Smith, Charles W. Smithson, and Lee MacDonald Wakeman, "The Evolving Market for Swaps," *Midland Corporate Finance Journal* (Winter 1986), pp. 20–32.

[7] Marcelle Arak, Arturo Estrella, Laurie Goodman, and Andrew Silver, "Interest Rate Swaps: An Alternative Explanation," *Financial Management* (Summer 1988), pp. 12–18.

- Borrower B believes that the risk-free rate will fall in the future, but that its credit will weaken. In this case, the borrower will prefer to issue a long-term floating-rate instrument in order to lock in the credit spread but at the same time to take advantage of an anticipated decline in the risk-free rate.

- Borrower C believes that the risk-free rate will fall in the future, but that its credit will strengthen in the future. The instrument of choice for this borrower is short-term floating debt. This is because its cost of funds in the future will be lower because of the expected decline in the risk-free rate and the lower credit spread that will be imposed by the market.

- Borrower D believes that the risk-free rate will rise in the future, and that its credit will strengthen in the future. This borrower would want to fix the risk-free rate but let the credit spread float. Which instrument will this borrower prefer to issue? None of the three instruments listed above can be used by D to take advantage of its expectations.

D can use an interest rate swap, however, to fix the risk-free rate for the term of the swap but allow the credit spread to float.[8] In essence, this particular reason for the growth of the interest rate swap market is based on asymmetric information. That is, the borrower possesses information (or a belief) that the market does not possess, namely, that the borrower's credit will improve.

Finally, another argument suggested for the growth of the interest rate swap market is the increased volatility of interest rates that has led borrowers and lenders to hedge or manage their exposure. Even though risk/return characteristics can be replicated by a package of forward contracts, interest rate forward contracts are not as liquid as interest rate swaps. And entering into or liquidating swap transactions has been facilitated by the standardization of documentation published by the International Swap Dealers Association in early 1987. Moreover, a swap to hedge or manage a position costs less than a package of interest rate forward contracts.

Role of the Intermediary.   The role of the intermediary in an interest rate swap sheds some light on evolution of the market. Intermediaries in these transactions have been commercial banks and investment banks, who in the early stages of the market sought out end users of swaps. That is, they found in their client bases those entities that needed the swap to accomplish a funding or investing objective, and they matched the two entities. In essence, the intermediary in this type of transaction performed the function of a broker.

---

[8] For an explanation of how this can be done, see Eileen Baecher and Laurie S. Goodman, *The Goldman Sachs Guide to Hedging Corporate Debt Issuance* (N.Y.: Goldman Sachs & Co., 1988).

The only time that the intermediary would take the opposite side of a swap (that is, would act as a principal) was to balance out the transaction. For example, if an intermediary had two clients that were willing to do a swap but one wanted the notional principal amount to be $100 million while the other wanted it to be $85 million, the intermediary might become the counterparty to the extent of $15 million. That is, the intermediary would warehouse or take a position as a principal to the transaction to make up the $15 million difference between client objectives. To protect itself against an adverse interest rate movement, the intermediary would hedge its position.

There is another problem in an interest rate swap that we have yet to address. The parties to the swaps we have described had to be concerned that the other party would default on its obligation. While a default would not mean any principal was lost because the notional principal amount had not been exchanged, it would mean that the objective for which the swap was entered into would be impaired. As the early transactions involved a higher and a lower credit-rated entity, the former would be concerned with the potential for default of the latter. To reduce the risk of default, many early swap transactions required that the lower credit-rated entity obtain a guarantee from a highly rated commercial bank.

As the frequency and the size of the transactions increased, many intermediaries became comfortable with the transactions and became principals instead of acting as brokers. As long as an intermediary had one entity willing to do a swap, the intermediary was willing to be the counterparty. Consequently, interest rate swaps became part of an intermediary's inventory of product positions. Advances in quantitative techniques and futures products for hedging complex positions such as swaps made the protection of large inventory positions feasible.

Yet another reason encouraged intermediaries to become principals rather than brokers in swaps. As more intermediaries entered the swap market, bid–ask spreads on swaps declined sharply. To make money in the swaps market, intermediaries had to do a sufficient volume of business, which could be done only if an intermediary had (1) an extensive client base willing to use swaps, and (2) a large inventory of swaps. This necessitated that intermediaries act as principals. For example, a survey by *Euromoney* asked 150 multinationals and supranationals to identify the characteristics that make a swap house efficient.[9] The results indicated that the speed at which a swap could be arranged for a client was the most important criterion. That speed depends on client base and inventory. The same survey also revealed clients to be less interested in brokered deals than in transactions in which the intermediary is a principal.

---

[9] Special Supplement on Swaps, *Euromoney* (July 1987), p. 14.

Consequently, we can describe the development of the swap market as one that originated to exploit real or perceived imperfections in the capital market, but that involved into a transactionally efficient market for accomplishing asset/liability objectives.

Terminology, Conventions, and Market Quotes

We've now explained the basics of a swap, its applications, and development of the swap market. Here we review some of the terminology used in this market and explain how swaps are quoted.

The date that the counterparties commit to the swap is called the *trade date*. The date that the swap begins accruing interest is called the *effective date*, while the date that the swap stops accruing interest is called the *maturity date*.

While our illustrations assume that the timing of the cash flows for both the fixed-rate payer and floating-rate payer will be the same, this is rarely the case in a swap. In fact, an agreement may call for the fixed-rate payer to make payments annually but the floating-rate payer to make payments more frequently (semiannually or quarterly). Also, the way interest accrues on each leg of the transaction differs, because there are several day count conventions in the fixed-income markets.

The counterparty to an interest rate swap is either a fixed-rate payer or floating-rate payer. There are a number of ways to describe these positions:[10]

Fixed-rate payer
- pays fixed rate in the swap
- receives floating in the swap
- is short the bond market
- has bought a swap
- is long a swap
- has established the price sensitivities of a longer-term liability and a floating-rate asset

Floating-rate payer
- pays floating rate in the swap
- receives fixed in the swap
- is long the bond market

---

[10] See Robert F. Kopprasch, John Macfarlane, Daniel R. Ross, and Janet Showers, "The Interest Rate Swap Market: Yield Mathematics, Terminology, and Conventions," Chapter 58 in Frank J. Fabozzi and Irving M. Pollack (eds.), *The Handbook of Fixed Income Securities* (Homewood, IL: Dow Jones-Irwin, 1987).

- has sold a swap
- is short a swap
- has established the price sensitivities of a longer-term asset and a floating-rate liability

The first two expressions to describe the position of a fixed-rate payer and floating-rate payer are self-explanatory. To understand why the fixed-rate payer is viewed as short the bond market, and the floating-rate payer is viewed as long the bond market, consider what happens when interest rates change. Those who borrow on a fixed-rate basis will benefit if interest rates rise because they have locked in a lower interest rate. But those who have a short bond position will also benefit if interest rates rise. Thus, a fixed-rate payer can be said to be short the bond market. A floating-rate payer benefits if interest rates fall. Because a long position in a bond benefits if interest rates fall, terminology describing a floating-rate payer as long the bond market has been adopted.

The most common convention that has evolved for quoting swaps levels is for a swap dealer to set the floating rate equal to the index and then quote the fixed rate that will apply. To illustrate this convention, let's use the swap in our second illustration. The terms for the 10-year swap are repeated below:

Bank:
    Pay floating rate of 6-month LIBOR + 70 b.p.
    Receive fixed rate of 11.3%
Non-financial corporation:
    Pay fixed rate   = 11.3%
    Receive floating rate = 6-month LIBOR + 45 b.p.

The offer price that the dealer would quote the non-financial corporation (the fixed-rate payer) would be to pay 10.85% and receive LIBOR "flat." (The term "flat" means with no spread.) The 10.85% is obtained by subtracting from the fixed rate to be paid the 45-basis point spread over LIBOR that we use in the illustration. The bid price that the dealer would quote the commercial bank would be to pay LIBOR flat and receive 10.6%. The 10.6% represents the payment to be received of 11.3% minus the 70-basis point spread to LIBOR. The bid–offer spread is 25 basis points.

The fixed rate is some spread above the Treasury yield curve with the same term to maturity as the swap. In our illustration, suppose that the 10-year Treasury yield is 10.35%. Then the offer price that the dealer would quote to the fixed-rate payer is the 10-year Treasury rate plus 50 basis points versus receiving LIBOR flat. For the floating-rate payer, the bid price quoted would be LIBOR flat versus the 10-year Treasury rate plus 25 basis points. The difference between the Treasury rate paid and received is the bid–offer spread. Note that the terms of the swap as executed are not those quoted, but those with the applicable spread added. The method of quoting the swap bid and offer terms is a simplification enabling potential parties to evaluate different swap opportunities on a comparable basis.

Secondary Market for Swaps

There are three general types of transactions in the secondary market for swaps. These include (1) a swap reversal, (2) a swap sale (or assignment), and (3) a swap buy-back (or close-out or cancellation).

In a swap reversal, the party that wants out of the transaction will arrange for a swap in which (1) the maturity on the new swap is equal to the time remaining of the original swap, (2) the index is the same, and (3) the notional principal amount is the same. For example, suppose party X enters into a five-year swap with a notional principal amount of $50 million in which it pays 10% and receives LIBOR, but that two years later, X wants out of the swap. In a swap reversal, X would enter into a three-year interest rate swap, with a counterparty different from the original counterparty, let's say Z, in which the notional principal amount is $50 million, and X pays LIBOR and receives a fixed rate. The fixed rate that X receives from Z will depend on prevailing swap terms for floating-rate receivers at the initiation of the three-year swap.

While party X has effectively terminated the original swap in economic terms, there is a major drawback to this approach: party X is still liable to the original counterparty Y, as well as to the new counterparty, Z. That is, party X now has two offsetting interest rate swaps on its books instead of one, and as a result it has increased its default risk exposure.

The swap sale or swap assignment overcomes this drawback. In this secondary market transaction, the party that wishes to close out the original swap finds another party that is willing to accept its obligations under the swap. In our illustration, this means that X finds another party, say, A, that will agree to pay 10% to Y and receive LIBOR from Y for the next three years. A might have to be compensated to accept the position of X, or A might have to be willing to compensate X. Who will receive compensation depends on the swap terms at the time. For example, if interest rates have risen such that, to receive LIBOR for three years, a fixed-rate payer would have to pay 12%, then A would have to compensate X because A has to pay only 10% to receive LIBOR. The compensation would be equal to the present value of a three-year annuity of 2% times the notional principal amount.[11] If, instead, interest rates

---

[11] It is three years because this is the time remaining for the swap. The 2% represents the difference between the prevailing rate of 12% and the fixed rate of 10% on the swap.

have fallen so that, to receive LIBOR for three years, a fixed-rate payer would have to pay 6%, then X would have to compensate A. The compensation would be equal to the present value of a three-year annuity of 4% times the notional principal amount.

Once the transaction is completed, it is then A not X that is obligated to perform under the swap terms. (Of course an intermediary could act as principal and become party A to help its client X.)

In order to accomplish a swap sale, the original counterparty, Y in our example, must agree to the sale. A key factor in whether Y will agree is whether it is willing to accept the credit of A. For example, if A's credit rating is triple-B while X's is double-A, Y would be unlikely to accept A as a counterparty.

A buy-back or close-out sale (or cancellation) involves the sale of the swap to the original counterparty. As in the case of a swap sale, one party might have to compensate the other, depending on how interest rates and credit spreads have changed since the inception of the swap.

These methods for getting out of or into a swap leave much to be desired for market participants. It is this illiquidity in the secondary market that will hamper swap market growth. There have been proposals to create a swap clearing corporation, similar to the clearing corporations for futures and options, in which case swaps could be marked to market and credit exposure to a swap reduced.

Beyond the "Plain Vanilla" Swap

Thus far we have described the "plain vanilla" or generic interest rate swap. Non-generic or individualized swaps have evolved as a result of the asset/liability needs of borrowers and lenders, and some are described below.

Amortizing, Accreting, and Roller Coaster Swaps.   In a generic swap, the notional principal amount does not vary over the life of the swap. Thus, it is sometimes referred to as a *bullet swap*. In contrast, for amortizing, accreting, and roller coaster swaps, the notional principal amount varies over the life of the swap.

To explain an amortizing swap, we can use our first illustration of the interest rate swap between the commercial bank and the life insurance company. Recall that it was the fixed-rate commercial loans that were generating the cash flow that the bank was using to make the fixed-rate payment on the interest rate swap.

We assumed that the loans were interest-only loans and that the principal would be repaid at the end of five years. Suppose, instead, that the loan was a level-payment, fully amortized one, meaning that the principal outstanding would decline over the five years, and therefore the interest would decline over time. In such an instance, the amount received every six months from the commercial loans would be less than the fixed-rate payments to be made on the interest rate swap, if interest rates decline. This is because the principal repaid every six months would have to be reinvested at an interest rate less than 10% (the interest on the original loan balance).

An amortizing swap can be used to solve this problem. An amortizing swap is one in which the notional principal amount decreases in a predetermined way over the life of the swap. In situations where a liability to be funded increases over time, an *accreting swap* can be employed. An accreting swap is one in which the notional principal amount increases at a predetermined way over time. An accreting swap could be used by a lending institution that has committed to lend increasing amounts to a customer for a long-term project.

In a *roller coaster swap*, the notional principal amount can rise or fall from period to period according to an institution's liability structure.

Zero-Coupon Swaps. In a zero-coupon swap, the fixed-rate payer does not make any payments until the maturity date of the swap but receives floating-rate payments at regular payment dates. This type of swap exposes the floating-rate payer to significant credit risk because this party makes regular payments but does not receive any payments until the maturity date of the swap.

Basis Rate Swap. The terms of a typical interest rate swap call for the exchange of fixed- and floating-rate payments. In a basis rate swap, both parties exchange floating-rate payments based on a different money market index. As an example, assume a commercial bank has a portfolio of loans in which the lending rate is based on the prime rate, but the bank's cost of funds is based on LIBOR. The risk the bank faces is that the spread between the prime rate and LIBOR will change. This is referred to as *basis risk*. The bank can use a basis rate swap to make floating-rate payments based on the prime rate and receive floating-rate payments based on LIBOR.

Forward Rate Swaps. A forward swap is simply a forward contract on an interest rate swap. The terms of the swap are set today, but the parties agree that the swap will begin at a specified date in the future.

Deferred Rate Setting Swaps. In a deferred rate setting swap, the swap can begin at any time up to a specified date in the future. The fixed-rate payer has the right to select the date that the swap begins. The fixed-rate payer can use this option to defer the determination of the fixed rate that it must pay over the life of the swap to take advantage of a drop in interest rates.

Options on Swaps

The second generation of products in the interest rate swap market is options on interest rate swaps referred to as *swaptions*. The buyer of this option has the right to enter into an interest rate swap agreement on predetermined terms by some specified date in the future. The buyer of a put or call swaption pays the writer a premium.

A *put swaption* is an option allowing the buyer to enter into an interest rate swap in which the buyer pays a fixed rate and receives a floating rate, and the writer receives a fixed rate and pays a floating rate. A *call swaption* is an option that allows the buyer to enter into an interest rate swap where the buyer pays a floating rate and receives a fixed rate, while the writer receives a floating rate and pays a fixed rate. Swaptions may be exercised at any time prior to the expiration date (i.e., American type) or only at the expiration date (i.e., European type).

A callable or a putable swap is a swap with an embedded option. A putable swap effectively allows one of the parties to terminate the swap; it is therefore referred to as a *cancelable* or *terminable* swap. Putable swaps can be used in asset-based swaps when the cash flow of the fixed-rate asset enabling the fixed-rate payments is uncertain. The cash flow of the asset would be uncertain if it is (1) callable, as in the case of a callable corporate bond, a mortgage loan or pass-through security, or a loan that can be prepaid, and/or (2) exposes the investor/lender to default risk.[12]

To illustrate the use of a putable swap, suppose a savings and loan association enters into a four-year swap in which it agrees to pay 11% fixed and receive LIBOR. The fixed-rate payments will come from a portfolio of mortgage pass-through securities with a coupon rate of 11%. Suppose that one year after the swap begins, mortgage rates decline to 6%, resulting in large prepayments. The prepayments received will have to be reinvested at a rate less than 11%, but the S&L must still pay 11% under terms of the swap. A putable swap would give the S&L the right to pay LIBOR and receive 11%. This effectively terminates the swap.

A callable swap effectively lets one of the parties extend the terms of a swap. The party in a putable or callable swap that has the right to exercise the option pays for this right. The option price can be either an upfront payment, as in the case of the options we have discussed throughout this book, or it can be an amount paid over the life of the swap by adjusting the payments exchanged.

---

[12] For an explanation of how putable swaps can be used to manage a portfolio of callable bonds, see Robert M. Stavis and Victor J. Haghani, "Putable Swaps: Tools for Managing Callable Assets," Chapter 20 in Frank J. Fabozzi (ed.), *The Handbook of Fixed Income Options* (Chicago: Probus Publishing, 1989).

INTEREST RATE AGREEMENTS

An interest rate agreement is an agreement between two parties whereby one party, for an upfront premium, agrees to compensate the other if a designated interest rate, called the *reference rate*, is different from a predetermined level. When one party agrees to pay the other when the reference rate exceeds a predetermined level, the agreement is referred to as an *interest rate cap* or *ceiling*. The agreement is referred to as an *interest rate floor* when one party agrees to pay the other when the reference rate falls below a predetermined level. The predetermined interest rate level is called the *strike rate*.

The terms of an interest rate agreement include:

1. the reference rate
2. the strike rate that sets the ceiling or floor
3. the length of the agreement
4. the frequency of settlement
5. the notional principal amount

For example, suppose that C buys an interest rate cap from D with terms as follows:

1. the reference rate is six-month LIBOR
2. the strike rate is 8%
3. the agreement is for seven years
4. settlement is every six months
5. the notional principal amount is $20 million

Under this agreement, every six months for the next seven years, D will pay C whenever six-month LIBOR exceeds 8%. The payment will equal the dollar value of the difference between six-month LIBOR and 8% times the notional principal amount divided by two. For example, if six months from now six-month LIBOR is 11%, then D will pay C 3% (11% minus 8%) times $20 million divided by 2, or $300,000. If six-month LIBOR is 8% or less, D does not have to pay anything to C.

As an example of an interest rate floor, assume the same terms as the interest rate cap we just illustrated. In this case, if six-month LIBOR is 11%, C receives nothing from D, but if six-month LIBOR is less than 8%, D compensates C for the difference. For example, if six-month LIBOR is 7%, D will pay C $100,000 (8% minus 7%, times $20 million divided by 2).

Interest rate caps and floors can be combined to create an *interest rate collar*. This is done by buying an interest rate cap and selling an interest rate floor. Some commercial banks and investment banking firms now write options on interest rate agreements for customers. Options on caps are called *captions;* options on floors are called *flotions.*

Risk/Return Characteristics

In an interest rate agreement, the buyer pays an upfront fee, which represents the maximum amount that the buyer can lose and the maximum amount that the writer of the agreement can gain. The only party that is required to perform is the writer of the interest rate agreement. The buyer of an interest rate cap benefits if the underlying interest rate rises above the strike rate because the seller (writer) must compensate the buyer. The buyer of an interest rate floor benefits if the interest rate falls below the strike rate, because the seller (writer) must compensate the buyer.

How can we better understand interest rate caps and interest rate floors? In essence these contracts are equivalent to a package of interest rate options. As the buyer benefits if the interest rate rises above the strike rate, an interest rate cap is similar to purchasing a package of put options; the seller of an interest rate cap has effectively sold a package of put options. The buyer of an interest rate floor benefits from a decline in the interest rate below the strike rate. Therefore, the buyer of an interest rate floor has effectively bought a package of call options from the writer of the option. An interest rate collar is equivalent to buying a package of put options and selling a package of call options.

Once again, a complex contract can be seen to be a package of basic contracts, or options in the case of interest rate agreements.

Applications

To see how interest rate agreements can be used for asset/liability management, consider the problems faced by the commercial bank and the life insurance company we used in the first illustration to demonstrate use of an interest rate swap.[13]

Recall that the bank's objective is to lock in an interest rate spread over its cost of funds. Yet because it borrows short term, its cost of funds is uncertain. The bank may be able to purchase a cap such that the cap rate plus the cost

---

[13] For additional applications in the insurance industry, see David F. Babbel, Peter Bouyoucos, and Robert Stricker, "Capping the Interest Rate Risk in Insurance Products," Chapter 21 in Frank J. Fabozzi (ed.), *Fixed Income Portfolio Strategies* (Chicago: Probus Publishing, 1989). For other applications of interest rate agreements, see Victor J. Haghani and Robert M. Stavis, "Interest Rate Caps and Floors: Tools for Asset/Liability Management," in Frank J. Fabozzi (ed.), *Advances and Innovations in Bond and Mortgage Markets* (Chicago: Probus Publishing, 1989).

of purchasing the cap is less than the rate it is earning on its fixed-rate commercial loans. If short-term rates decline, the bank does not benefit from the cap, but its cost of funds declines. The cap therefore allows the bank to impose a ceiling on its cost of funds while retaining the opportunity to benefit from a decline in rates. This is consistent with the view of an interest rate cap as simply a package of call options.

The bank can reduce the cost of purchasing the cap by selling a floor. In this case, the bank agrees to pay the buyer of the floor if the underlying rate falls below the strike rate. The bank receives a fee for selling the floor, but it has sold off its opportunity to benefit from a decline in rates below the strike rate. By buying a cap and selling a floor, the bank has created a range for its cost of funds (i.e., a collar).

Recall the problem of the life insurance company that has guaranteed a 9% rate on a GIC for the next five years and is considering the purchase of an attractive floating-rate instrument in a private placement transaction. The risk that the company faces is that interest rates will fall so that it will not earn enough to realize the 9% guaranteed rate plus a spread. The life insurance company may be able to purchase a floor to set a lower bound on its investment return, yet retain the opportunity to benefit should rates increase. To reduce the cost of purchasing the floor, the life insurance company can sell an interest rate cap. By doing so, however, it gives up the opportunity of benefiting from an increase in the six-month Treasury bill rate above the strike rate of the interest rate cap.

COMPOUND OR SPLIT-FEE OPTIONS

A compound or split-fee option is an option to purchase an option. We can explain the elements of a compound option by using a long call option on a long put option. This compound option gives the buyer of the option the right but not the obligation to require the writer of the compound option to sell the buyer a put option. The compound option would specify the following terms:

1. the day on which the buyer of the compound option has the choice of either requiring the writer of the option to sell the buyer a put option or allowing the option to expire. This date is called the *extension date.*

2. the strike price and the expiration date of the put option that the buyer acquires from the writer. The expiration date of the put option is called the *notification date.*

The payment that the buyer makes to acquire the compound option is called the *front fee.* If the buyer exercises the call option in order to acquire the put option, a second payment is made to the writer of the option. That payment is called the *back fee.*

An option that allows the option buyer to purchase a put option is called a *caput*. A *cacall* grants the option buyer the right to purchase a call option. We've already seen an example of a rather complicated compound option. As a cap is a package of options, a caption is an option on a package of options; a floor as a package of options means that a flotion is an option on a package of options.

Compound options are most commonly used by mortgage originators to hedge pipeline risk.[14] They can also be used in any situation when the asset/liability manager needs additional time to gather information about the need to purchase an option.

SUMMARY

In this chapter we have covered customized interest rate control contracts created by commercial banks and investment banks for their customers. Markets for these instruments have grown explosively in the 1980s.

An interest rate swap is an agreement specifying that the parties exchange interest payments at designated times. In a typical swap, one party will make fixed-rate payments, and the other will make floating-rate payments, with payments based on the notional principal amount. Participants in financial markets use interest rate swaps to alter the cash flow characteristics of their assets or liabilities, or to capitalize on perceived capital market inefficiencies. A swap has the risk/return profile of a package of forward contracts.

A number of types of swaps have been developed to satisfy various needs of market participants. These include swaps in which the notional principal amount varies over the life of the swap (amortizing, accreting, and roller coaster swaps), zero-coupon swaps, basis rate swaps, forward rate swaps, and deferred rate setting swaps. The second generation of swaps is options on swaps: put and call swaptions, and putable and callable swaps.

An interest rate agreement allows one party for an upfront premium the right to receive compensation from the writer of the agreement if a designated interest rate is different from a predetermined level. An interest rate cap calls for one party to receive a payment if a designated interest rate is above the predetermined level. An interest rate floor lets one party receive a payment if a designated interest rate is below the predetermined level.

---

[14] Pipeline risk is discussed in Chapter 17. For a discussion of how compound options can be used to hedge pipeline risk, see Anand K. Bhattacharya, "Compound Options on Mortgage-Backed Securities," Chapter 22 in *The Handbook of Fixed Income Options*.

An interest rate cap can be used to establish a ceiling on the cost of funding; an interest rate floor can be used to establish a floor return. Buying a cap and selling a floor creates a collar. There are also options on interest rate caps (called captions) and on floors (called flotions).

An option that allows a party the right to enter into an option is called a compound or split-fee option. These options are used primarily by mortgage originators to hedge pipeline risk.

QUESTIONS

1. The following quotation appeared in an article entitled "Recent Developments in Corporate Finance," published in the August 1990 issue of the *Federal Reserve Bulletin:*

   > Before the 1980s, it was reasonable in aggregate analysis to characterize commercial paper and bank loans as short-term debt and corporate bonds and mortgages as long-term debt. Such characterizations often were used to gauge corporate exposure to interest rate and liquidity risk, under the assumption that interest rates on short-term debt were variable whereas those on long-term debt were fixed.
   >
   > Financial developments and innovations in the past decade have made this classification of debt less useful.

   What financial developments and innovations do you think this article is referring to? Why have they made the classification between short-term and long-term debt less useful?

2. Here is a quotation from the March 25, 1991, issue of *Bank Letter:*

   > Intense negotiations are underway involving regulatory officials, interested bank and brokerage industry representatives and Senate Staff to try to fashion a compromise floor amendment for a bill that would potentially put interest rate and currency swaps and forward foreign exchange agreements under the regulatory authority of the Commodity Futures Trading Commission, sources said. . . . Industry forces involved in the $2 trillion market are fighting to block Commodity Futures Trading Commission jurisdiction, arguing that the pending bill, if enacted, would scare the business overseas. . . .

   a. Why is an interest rate swap similar to a futures (or forward) contract?

   b. Why do you think opponents of regulation feel that the bill "would scare the business overseas"?

3. a. Why would a depository institution use an interest rate swap?

b. Why would a corporation that plans to raise funds in the debt market use an interest rate swap?

4. Suppose that a life insurance company has issued a three-year GIC with a fixed rate of 10%. Under what circumstances might it be feasible for the life insurance company to invest the funds in a floating-rate security and enter into a three-year interest rate swap in which it pays a floating rate and receives a fixed rate?

5. The excerpt following is from the March 4, 1991, issue of *Corporate Financing Week:*

> Merrill Lynch and Morgan Stanley are aggressively pitching deals to corporate issuers with a swap attached to take advantage of narrow spreads between LIBOR funding rates and short-term Treasury bills, Street officials said.

What type of interest rate swap would this be?

6. Give an example of why a market participant would want to use a swaption.

7. What is the relationship between an interest rate agreement and an interest rate option?

8. We state in the chapter that compound options are most commonly used by mortgage originators to hedge pipeline risk. Why do you think compound options are used to hedge pipeline risk?

9. The quotation following is taken from the January 28, 1991, issue of *Bank Letter:*

> The surge in the use of derivatives, their lengthening terms and growing complexity all spell greater credit risks for the banks and securities firms that fashion these instruments, according to a recent report by Moody's Investors Service. . . .
>
> The derivatives business includes creating, underwriting, trading and selling instruments including options, swaps, futures, swaptions related to debt and equity securities, commodities and foreign exchange. . . .
>
> Creating "over-the-counter derivatives," with other firms as counterparties also creates new credit risks compared to the use of traded, listed instruments. . . .

This quotation refers to two types of credit risk that banks and investment banking firms face as a result of their activities in the "derivatives business." Explain these two credit risks.

LEARNING OBJECTIVES

After reading this chapter you will understand:

- what is meant by a foreign exchange rate.

- the different ways that a foreign exchange rate can be quoted (direct versus indirect).

- the conventions for quoting foreign exchange rates.

- what foreign exchange risk is.

- a cross rate and how to calculate a theoretical cross rate.

- what triangular arbitrage is.

- the foreign exchange market structure.

- what the European Currency Unit is.

- the fundamental determinants of exchange rates: purchasing power parity and interest rate parity.

- the different instruments for hedging foreign exchange risk: forwards, futures, options, and swaps.

- the limitations of forward and futures contracts for hedging long-dated foreign exchange risk.

- how a forward exchange rate is determined, and covered interest arbitrage.

- the basic currency swap structure and the motivation for using currency swaps.

In previous chapters we have concentrated on the various sectors of the U.S. financial market. Clearly U.S. borrowers and investors need not look solely to domestic financial markets to accomplish their financial goals. Nor need foreign entities depend solely on their domestic markets. As a result, payments for liabilities made by borrowers and cash payment received by investors may be denominated in a foreign currency. In Chapter 22 we present an overview of the global financial markets. In this chapter, we provide a review of the spot (or cash) foreign exchange market and markets for hedging foreign exchange risk (forwards, futures, options, and swaps).

FOREIGN EXCHANGE RATES

An *exchange rate* is defined as the amount of one currency that can be exchanged per unit of another currency, or the price of one currency in terms of another currency. For example, let's consider the exchange rate between the U.S. dollar and the Swiss franc. The exchange rate could be quoted in one of two ways:

1. the amount of U.S. dollars necessary to acquire one Swiss franc, or the dollar price of one Swiss franc

2. the amount of Swiss francs necessary to acquire one U.S. dollar, or the Swiss franc price of one dollar.

Exchange rate quotations may be either *direct* or *indirect*. To understand the difference, it is necessary to refer to one currency as a local currency and the other as a foreign currency. For example, from the perspective of a U.S. participant, the local currency would be U.S. dollars, and any other currency, such as Swiss francs, would be the foreign currency. From the perspective of a Swiss participant, the local currency would be Swiss francs, and other currencies, such as U.S. dollars, the foreign currency.

A direct quote is the number of units of a local currency exchangeable for one unit of a foreign currency. An indirect quote is the number of units of a foreign currency that can be exchanged for one unit of a local currency. Looking at this from a U.S. participant's perspective, a quote indicating the number of dollars exchangeable for one unit of a foreign currency is a direct quote. An indirect quote from the same participant's perspective would be the number of units of the foreign currency that can be exchanged for one U.S. dollar. Obviously, from the point of view of a non-U.S. participant, the number of U.S. dollars exchangeable for one unit of a non-U.S. currency is an indirect quote; the number of units of a non-U.S. currency exchangeable for a U.S. dollar is a direct quote.

Given a direct quote, we can obtain an indirect quote (the reciprocal of the direct quote), and vice versa. For example, suppose that a U.S. participant is given a direct quote of dollars for Swiss francs of 0.7880. That is, the price of a Swiss franc is $0.7880. The reciprocal of the direct quote is 1.2690, which would be the indirect quote for the U.S. participant; that is, one U.S. dollar can be exchanged for 1.2690 Swiss francs, which is the Swiss franc price of a dollar.

In the financial press, a quote can be reported either way. Figure 21-1, taken from *The Wall Street Journal* on October 22, 1990, for quotes on October 19, 1990, shows this. All the exchange rates in the figure are between the country indicated in the first column and the U.S. dollar. Look down the first column that shows the countries until you get to "Switzerland (Franc)." Switzerland has four lines devoted to it. The first of the four lines refers to the spot or cash market exchange rate. We explain the other three lines ("30-Day Forward," "90-Day Forward," and "180-Day Forward") later in the chapter.

The first two columns show the U.S. dollar equivalent (labeled in Figure 21-1 "U.S. $ equiv.") on two different days. That is, it indicates how many U.S. dollars are exchangeable for one Swiss franc. So, from a U.S. participant's perspective, it is a direct quote; from that of a Swiss participant,

EXCHANGE RATES

Friday, October 19, 1990
The New York foreign exchange selling rates below apply to trading among banks in amounts of $1 million and more, as quoted at 3 p.m. Eastern time by Bankers Trust Co. Retail transactions provide fewer units of foreign currency per dollar.

Country	U.S. $ equiv. Fri.	U.S. $ equiv. Thurs.	Currency per U.S. $ Fri.	Currency per U.S. $ Thurs.
Argentina (Austral) ...	.0001890	.0001859	5292.00	5380.00
Australia (Dollar)	.7756	.7705	1.2893	1.2979
Austria (Schilling)	.09456	.09483	10.57	10.55
Bahrain (Dinar)	2.6532	2.6532	.3769	.3769
Belgium (Franc)				
Commercial rate	.03231	.03240	30.95	30.86
Brazil (Cruzeiro)	.01068	.01097	93.61	91.18
Britain (Pound)	1.9590	1.9701	.5105	.5076
30-Day Forward	1.9495	1.9602	.5130	.5102
90-Day Forward	1.9323	1.9438	.5175	.5145
180-Day Forward	1.9093	1.9214	.5238	.5205
Canada (Dollar)	.8525	.8540	1.1730	1.1710
30-Day Forward	.8493	.8508	1.1775	1.1754
90-Day Forward	.8439	.8450	1.1850	1.1835
180-Day Forward	.8361	.8375	1.1960	1.1940
Chile (Official rate)	.003046	.003046	328.35	328.35
China (Renmimbi)	.211864	.211864	4.7200	4.7200
Colombia (Peso)	.001912	.001912	523.00	523.00
Denmark (Krone)	.1743	.1750	5.7378	5.7156
Ecuador (Sucre)				
Floating rate	.001168	.001168	856.00	856.00
Finland (Markka)	.28019	.28149	3.5690	3.5525
France (Franc)	.19853	.19906	5.0370	5.0235
30-Day Forward	.19826	.19877	5.0440	5.0309
90-Day Forward	.19765	.19818	5.0595	5.0459
180-Day Forward	.19670	.19723	5.0840	5.0703
Germany (Mark)	.6649	.6671	1.5040	1.4990
30-Day Forward	.6648	.6670	1.5042	1.4992
90-Day Forward	.6642	.6665	1.5055	1.5003
180-Day Forward	.6629	.6653	1.5085	1.5031
Greece (Drachma)	.006601	.006623	151.50	151.00
Hong Kong (Dollar) ...	.12850	.12858	7.7820	7.7770
India (Rupee)	.05556	.05556	18.00	18.00
Indonesia (Rupiah)	.0005365	.0005365	1864.00	1864.00
Ireland (Punt)	1.7845	1.7890	.5604	.5590
Israel (Shekel)	.5089	.5089	1.9650	1.9650
Italy (Lira)	.0008874	.0008901	1126.86	1123.51
Japan (Yen)	.007940	.008016	125.95	124.75
30-Day Forward	.007942	.008019	125.92	124.71
90-Day Forward	.007938	.008018	125.97	124.72
180-Day Forward	.007933	.008015	126.06	124.77
Jordan (Dinar)	1.5485	1.5485	.6458	.6458
Kuwait (Dinar)	z	z	z	z

Country	U.S. $ equiv. Fri.	U.S. $ equiv. Thurs.	Currency per U.S. $ Fri.	Currency per U.S. $ Thurs.
Lebanon (Pound)	.000947	.000947	1055.97	1055.97
Malaysia (Ringgit)	.3706	.3709	2.6985	2.6965
Malta (Lira)	3.3445	3.3445	.2990	.2990
Mexico (Peso)				
Floating rate	.0003442	.0003442	2905.00	2905.00
Netherland (Guilder) .	.5901	.5919	1.6945	1.6895
New Zealand (Dollar) .	.6060	.6010	1.6502	1.6639
Norway (Krone)	.1708	.1715	5.8560	5.8315
Pakistan (Rupee)	.0462	.0462	21.65	21.65
Peru (Inti)	.00000225	.00000225	445037.83	445037.83
Philippines (Peso)	.04032	.04032	24.80	24.80
Portugal (Escudo)	.007536	.007450	132.70	134.22
Saudi Arabia (Riyal) ..	.26667	.26667	3.7500	3.7500
Singapore (Dollar)	.5845	.5865	1.7110	1.7050
South Africa (Rand)				
Commercial rate	.3938	.3947	2.5394	2.5336
Financial rate	.2688	.2674	3.7202	3.7397
South Korea (Won)	.0013985	.0013985	715.05	715.05
Spain (Peseta)	.010599	.010633	94.35	94.05
Sweden (Krona)	.1789	.1794	5.5900	5.5750
Switzerland (Franc) ..	.7880	.7933	1.2690	1.2605
30-Day Forward	.7882	.7935	1.2687	1.2602
90-Day Forward	.7883	.7936	1.2685	1.2601
180-Day Forward	.7878	.7931	1.2694	1.2608
Taiwan (Dollar)	.037313	.037327	26.80	26.79
Thailand (Baht)	.03995	.03995	25.03	25.03
Turkey (Lira)	.0003690	.0003700	2710.00	2703.00
United Arab (Dirham) .	.2723	.2723	3.6725	3.6725
Uruguay (New Peso)				
Financial	.000733	.000733	1365.00	1365.00
Venezuela (Bolivar)				
Floating rate	.02119	.02119	47.20	47.20
SDR	1.44202	1.44588	.69347	.69162
ECU	1.36477	1.36524	....	....

Special Drawing Rights (SDR) are based on exchange rates for the U.S., German, British, French and Japanese currencies. Source: International Monetary Fund.
European Currency Unit (ECU) is based on a basket of community currencies. Source: European Community Commission.
z-Not quoted.

Figure 21-1
Exchange Rates Reported in *The Wall Street Journal* for October 19, 1990.
Source: The Wall Street Journal, October 22, 1990.

it is an indirect quote. Look at the Friday number: "0.7880." This means that 78.80 cents can be exchanged for one Swiss franc, i.e., this is the price of one Swiss franc. The last two columns show how much of the foreign currency it is necessary to exchange for one U.S. dollar—the foreign currency price of a dollar. Thus, it is an indirect quote if taken from a U.S. participant's position, but a direct quote from the perspective of a non-U.S. participant. Once again, focusing on the Friday value, we see "1.2690." This means that 1.2690 Swiss francs can be exchanged for one U.S. dollar.

If the number of units of a foreign currency that can be obtained for one dollar—the price of a dollar or indirect quotation—rises, the dollar is said to *appreciate* relative to the foreign currency, and the foreign currency is said to *depreciate.* Thus appreciation means a decline in the direct quotation.

Foreign Exchange Risk

From the perspective of a U.S. investor, the cash flows of assets denominated in a foreign currency expose the investor to uncertainty as to the cash flow in U.S. dollars. The actual U.S. dollars that the investor gets depend on the exchange rate between the U.S. dollar and the foreign currency at the time the non-dollar cash flow is received and exchanged for U.S. dollars. If the foreign currency depreciates (declines in value) relative to the U.S. dollar (i.e., the U.S. dollar appreciates), the dollar value of the cash flows will be proportionately less. This risk is referred to as *foreign exchange risk.*

Any investor who purchases an asset denominated in a currency that is not the medium of exchange of the investor's country faces foreign exchange risk. For example, a Greek investor who acquires a yen-denominated Japanese bond is exposed to the risk that the Japanese yen will decline in value relative to the Greek drachma.

Foreign exchange risk is a consideration for the issuer too. Suppose that IBM issues bonds denominated in Japanese yen. IBM's foreign exchange risk is that at the time the coupon interest payments must be made and the principal repaid, the U.S. dollar will have depreciated relative to the Japanese yen, requiring that IBM pay more dollars to satisfy its obligation.

SPOT MARKET

The spot exchange rate market is the market for settlement within two business days. Since the early 1970s, exchange rates between major currencies have been free to float, with market forces determining the relative value of a currency.[1] Thus, each day a currency's price relative to that of another currency may stay the same, increase, or decrease.

A key factor affecting the expectation of changes in a country's exchange rate is the relative expected inflation rate. Spot exchange rates adjust to

---

[1] In practice, national monetary authorities can intervene in the foreign exchange market for their currency for a variety of economic reasons, so the current foreign exchange system is sometimes referred to as a "managed" floating rate system.

compensate for the relative inflation rate between two countries. This is the so-called *purchasing power parity* relationship. It says that the exchange rate—the domestic price of the foreign currency—is proportional to the domestic inflation rate, and inversely proportional to foreign inflation.

Let's look at the exchange rate reported in Figure 21-1 between the U.S. dollar and the Australian dollar. The exchange rate in U.S. dollar equivalents on Thursday was 0.7705; on Friday it was 0.7756. Consequently, on Thursday, one Australian dollar cost 0.7705 U.S. dollars. On Friday, it cost more U.S. dollars, 0.7756. Thus, the Australian dollar appreciated relative to the U.S. dollar, or, equivalently, the U.S. dollar depreciated relative to the Australian dollar. Figure 21-1 shows that the U.S. dollar appreciated relative to the Swiss franc between Thursday and Friday in the cash market. In terms of U.S. dollar equivalents, one Swiss franc cost 0.7933 U.S. dollars on Thursday; on Friday it cost fewer U.S. dollars, 0.7780.

While quotes can be either direct or indirect, the problem is defining from whose perspective the quote is given. Foreign exchange conventions in fact standardize the ways quotes are given. Because of the importance of the U.S. dollar in the international financial system, currency quotations are all relative to the U.S. dollar. When dealers quote, they either give U.S. dollars per unit of foreign currency (a direct quote from the U.S. perspective) or the number of units of the foreign currency per U.S. dollar (an indirect quote from the U.S. perspective). Quoting in terms of U.S. dollars per unit of foreign currency is called "American terms," while quoting in terms of the number of units of the foreign currency per U.S. dollar is called "European terms." The dealer convention is to use European terms in quoting foreign exchange with a few exceptions. The British pound, the Irish pound, the Australian dollar, the New Zealand dollar, and the European Currency Unit (discussed later) are exceptions that are quoted in American terms.

Cross Rates

Barring any government restrictions, riskless arbitrage will assure that the exchange rate between two countries will be the same in both countries. The theoretical exchange rate between two countries other than the U.S. can be inferred from their exchange rate with the U.S. dollar. Rates computed in this way are referred to as *theoretical cross rates*. They would be computed as follows for two countries, X and Y:

$$\frac{\text{Quote in American terms of currency X}}{\text{Quote in American terms of currency Y}}$$

To illustrate how this is done, let's calculate the theoretical cross rate between German marks and Japanese yen using the exchange rates shown in Figure 21-1 for Friday, October 19, 1990. The exchange rate for the two currencies in American terms is $0.6649 per German mark and $0.007940 per Japanese yen. Then: number of units of Japanese yen (Y) per unit of German marks (X)

$$\frac{\$0.6649}{\$0.007940} = 83.74 \text{ yen/mark}$$

Taking the reciprocal gives the number of German marks exchangeable for one Japanese yen. In our example, it is 0.01194.

In the real world, there are rare instances where the theoretical cross rate as computed from actual dealer dollar exchange rate quotes will differ from the actual cross rate quoted by some dealer. When the discrepancy is large enough after transactions costs, a riskless arbitrage opportunity arises. Arbitraging to take advantage of cross rate mispricing is called *triangular arbitrage,* so named because it involves positions in three currencies—the U.S. dollar and the two foreign currencies. The arbitrage keeps all rates in line.

Dealers

Exchange rates reported in *The Wall Street Journal* are indications of the rate at which a foreign currency can be purchased in the spot market. They are the rates for which the dealer is willing to sell foreign exchange. Foreign exchange dealers, however, do not quote one price. Instead, they quote an exchange rate at which they are willing to buy a foreign currency and one at which they are willing to sell a foreign currency. That is, there is a bid–ask spread. Consequently, a U.S. investor who has received Swiss francs and wants to exchange those francs into U.S. dollars will request a quote on the bid price for Swiss francs. Another U.S. investor who wants to purchase Swiss francs in order to, say, buy a bond denominated in that foreign currency will request an offer quote.

Dealers in the foreign exchange market are large international banks and other financial institutions that specialize in making markets in foreign exchange. The former dominate the market. There is no organized exchange where foreign currency is traded, but dealers are linked by telephone and cable, and by various information transfer services. Consequently, the foreign exchange market can best be described as an interbank over-the-counter market. Most transactions between banks are done through foreign exchange brokers. Brokers are agents who do not take a position in the foreign currencies involved in the transaction. The normal size of a transaction is $1 million or more.

Dealers in the foreign exchange market realize revenue from one or more sources: (1) the bid–ask spread, (2) commissions charged on foreign exchange transactions, and (3) trading profits (appreciation of the currencies that dealers hold a long position in or depreciation of the currencies that they have a short position in) or trading losses (depreciation of the currencies that they hold a long position in or appreciation of the currencies that they have a short position in).

The European Currency Unit

Since the inception of floating exchange rates in the early 1970s, there have been several attempts to develop a currency unit composed of a basket of foreign currencies that would be accepted as the unit of denomination for capital market transactions. Until early 1981, the composite currency unit that had the greatest support was the Special Drawing Right (SDR). This composite currency unit initially consisted of 16 currencies, not all of them important in global financial markets. While the SDR was subsequently redefined in 1986 to include only five major currencies, its use as an international currency unit has diminished.[2]

The most widely used composite currency unit for capital market transactions today is the European Currency Unit (ECU), created in 1979 by the European Economic Community. The currencies included in the ECU are those that are members of the European Monetary System (EMS). The weight of each country's currency is figured according to the relative importance of a country's economic trade and financial sector within the European Economic Community.[3]

Exchange rates between the ECU and those countries not part of the EEC float freely. The exchange rate between countries in the EEC, however, may fluctuate only within a narrow range.

The increased use of ECU-denominated loans, and, more recently, the issuance of ECU-denominated government bonds by some members of the EMS, suggests the growing importance of this composite currency in international capital market transactions.

The last row under the exchange rate column in Figure 21-1 indicates that on Friday, October 19, 1990, one unit of an ECU was quoted at $1.36477.

---

[2] For a review of other composite currency units, see P. L. Gilibert, "The International ECU Primary Bond Market: Structure and Competition," *Cahiers BEI/EIB Papers*, European Investment Bank, Luxembourg, December 1989, pp. 23–48.

[3] The countries whose currencies are included in the ECU are Germany, the United Kingdom, France, Italy, the Netherlands, Belgium, Luxembourg, Denmark, Ireland, Greece, Spain, and Portugal.

INSTRUMENTS FOR HEDGING FOREIGN EXCHANGE RISK

There are four instruments that borrowers and investors can use to protect against adverse foreign exchange rate movements: (1) currency forward contracts, (2) currency futures contracts, (3) currency options, and (4) currency swaps.

Currency Forward Contracts

Earlier we talked about the spot rate for the Swiss franc, which appears on the first line in Figure 21-1. Now let's look at the other three lines for the Swiss franc in that figure. Each line represents the exchange rate for a forward contract.

Recall that a forward contract is one in which one party agrees to buy "something," and another party agrees to sell that same "something" at a designated date in the future. Each line indicates a different number of days until settlement: 30-day settlement for the first line below "Switzerland (Franc)," 90-day settlement for the second line below, and 180-day settlement for the third. Consider the quote for Friday for the 90-day forward exchange rate. In the U.S. dollar equivalent column, the quote is "0.7882." This means that an American selling to Switzerland in Swiss francs with payment 90 days from now can, by selling forward francs, be assured of receiving 0.7882 U.S. dollars per franc. Similarly, a Swiss wanting to convert U.S. dollars into francs 90 days from now can count on paying $0.7882 for francs.

Most forward contracts have a maturity of less than two years. For longer-dated forward contracts, the bid–ask spread for a forward contract increases; that is, the size of the spread for a given currency increases with the maturity. Consequently, forward contracts become less attractive for hedging long-dated foreign currency exposure.

Also recall from Chapter 6 that forward and futures contracts can be used to lock in a foreign exchange rate. In exchange for locking in a rate, the user forgoes the opportunity to benefit from any advantageous foreign exchange rate movement but eliminates downside risk. Futures contracts which are creations of an exchange, have certain advantages over forward contracts in the case of stock indexes (Chapter 10) and Treasury securities (Chapter 18). For foreign exchange, however, the forward market is the market of choice. As the foreign exchange forward market is an interbank market, data on the amount of open interest are not public.

Pricing Currency Forward Contracts.   In Chapter 6, we showed the relationship between spot prices and forward prices. Arbitrage arguments can also be used to derive the relationship.[4] Consider a U.S. investor with a one-year investment horizon who has two choices:

Alternative 1: Deposit $100,000 in a U.S. bank that pays 7% compounded annually for one year.

Alternative 2: Deposit the U.S. dollar equivalent of $100,000 in German marks (deutschemarks) (DM) in a German bank that pays 9% compounded annually for one year.

The two alternatives and their outcome one year from now are depicted in Figure 21-2. Which is the best alternative? It will be the alternative that produces the largest number of U.S. dollars one year from now. Ignoring U.S. and German taxes on interest income or any other taxes, we need to know two things in order to determine the best alternative: (1) the spot exchange rate between U.S. dollars and German marks, and (2) the spot exchange rate one year from now between U.S. dollars and German marks. The former is known; the latter is not. We can determine, however, the spot rate one year from now between U.S. dollars and German marks that will make the investor indifferent between the two alternatives.

For alternative 1: The amount of U.S. dollars available one year from now would be $107,000 ($100,000 times 1.07).

For alternative 2: Assume that the spot rate is $0.6400 for one deutschemark. Then, ignoring commissions, $100,000 can be exchanged for DM 156,250 ($100,000 divided by 0.6400). The amount of German marks available at the end of one year would be DM 170,312.50 (DM 156,250 times 1.09).

The number of U.S. dollars that the DM 170,312.50 can be exchanged for depends on the exchange rate one year from now. Let F denote the exchange rate between these two currencies one year from now. Specifically, F will denote the number of U.S. dollars that can be exchanged for one German mark. Thus, the number of U.S. dollars at the end of one year from the second alternative is:

Amount of U.S. dollars one year from now = DM 170,312.50 $\times F$

---

[4] Recall that the relationship is not exact for futures prices because of the marked-to-market requirement.

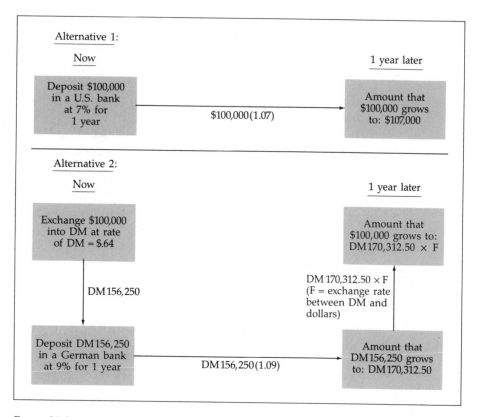

Figure 21-2
Outcome of Two Investment Alternatives: Determination of Theoretical Forward Rate.

The investor will be indifferent between the two alternatives if the number of U.S. dollars is $107,000; that is,

$$\$107,000 = DM\ 170,312.50 \times F$$

Solving, we find that F is equal to $0.6283.

Thus, if one year from now the spot exchange rate is $0.6283 for one German mark, then the two alternatives will produce the same number of U.S. dollars. If more than $0.6283 can be exchanged for one German mark, then there will be more than $107,000 at the end of one year. An exchange rate of $0.6300 for one German mark, for example, would produce $107,296.88 (DM 170,312.50 times $0.6300). The opposite is true if less than $0.6283 can be exchanged for one German mark. For example, if the future exchange rate is $0.6200, there will be $105,593.75 (DM 170,312.50 times $0.6200).

Let's look at this from a German investor's perspective. Suppose that the German investor with a one-year investment horizon has two alternatives:

Alternative 1: Deposit DM 156,250 in a German bank that pays 9% compounded annually for one year.

Alternative 2: Deposit the German mark equivalent of DM 156,250 in U.S. dollars in a U.S. bank that pays 7% compounded annually for one year.

Once again, assume that the spot exchange rate is $0.6400 for one German mark. The German investor will select the alternative that generates the largest number of marks at the end of one year. The first alternative would generate DM 170,312.50 (DM 156,250 times 1.09). The second alternative requires that deutschemarks be exchanged for U.S. dollars at the spot exchange rate. Given the spot exchange rate assumed, DM 156,250 can be exchanged for $100,000 (DM 156,250 multiplied by $0.6400). At the end of one year, the second alternative would generate $107,000 ($100,000 times 1.07). Letting F continue to denote the number of U.S. dollars needed to purchase one German mark one year from now, the German investor will realize the following amount of deutschemarks one year from now:

Amount of German marks one year from now = $107,000/F$

The investor will be indifferent between the two alternatives if

$107,000/F$ = DM 170,312.50

The equation above yields a value for F of $0.6283, the same exchange rate that we found when we sought the exchange rate one year from now that would make the U.S. investor indifferent between the two alternatives facing that investor.

Now suppose that a dealer quotes a one-year forward exchange rate between the two currencies. The one-year forward exchange rate fixes today the exchange rate one year from now. Thus, if the one-year forward exchange rate quoted is $0.6283 for one German mark, investing in the German bank will provide no arbitrage opportunity for the U.S. investor. If the one-year forward rate quoted is more than $0.6283 for one German mark, the U.S. investor can arbitrage the situation by selling German marks forward (and buying U.S. dollars forward for marks).

To see how this arbitrage opportunity can be exploited, suppose that the one-year forward exchange rate is $0.6300 for one German mark. Also assume that the borrowing and the lending rates within each currency are the same.

Suppose that the U.S. investor borrows $100,000 for one year at 7% compounded annually and enters into a forward contract agreeing to deliver DM 170,312.50 one year from now at $0.6300 per German mark. That is, one year from now the investor is agreeing to deliver DM 170,312.50 in exchange for $107,296.88 (DM 170,312.50 multiplied by $0.6300). The $100,000 that was borrowed can be exchanged for DM 156,250 at the spot rate of $0.6400 to one German mark, which can be invested in Germany at 9%. One year from now the U.S. investor will have DM 170,312.50 from the investment in Germany, which can be delivered against the forward contract. The U.S. investor will receive $107,296.88 and repay $107,000 to satisfy the bank loan, netting $296.88. Assuming that the counterparty to the forward contract does not default, this is a riskless arbitrage situation, because a $296.88 profit is generated with no initial investment.[5] This will result in the U.S. dollar rising relative to the German mark in the forward exchange rate market, or possibly some other adjustment.[6]

On the other hand, if the one-year forward exchange rate quoted is less than $0.6283, a German investor can arbitrage the situation by buying German marks forward (and by selling U.S. dollars forward). The forward exchange rate of U.S. dollars relative to German marks will therefore fall.[7] The conclusion is that the one-year forward exchange rate must be $0.6283 because any other forward exchange rate would result in an arbitrage opportunity for either the U.S. or the German investor.

Thus, the spot exchange rate and the interest rates in two countries will determine the forward exchange rate. The relationship among the spot exchange rate, the interest rates in two countries, and the forward rate is called *interest rate parity*. It says that an investor, after hedging in the forward exchange rate market, will realize the same sure domestic return whether investing domestically or in a foreign country. The arbitrage process that forces interest rate parity is called *covered interest arbitrage*.

---

[5] A German investor could also arbitrage this situation.

[6] Actually, a combination of things may occur when U.S. investors attempt to exploit this situation: (1) the spot exchange rate of U.S. dollars relative to German marks will fall as U.S. investors sell dollars and buy marks; (2) U.S. interest rates will rise in the U.S. as investors borrow in the U.S. and invest in Germany; (3) German interest rates will fall as more is invested in Germany; and (4) the one-year forward rate of U.S. dollars relative to German marks will fall. In practice, the last will dominate.

[7] A combination of things may occur when German investors attempt to exploit this situation: (1) the spot exchange rate of U.S. dollars relative to German marks will rise as German investors buy dollars and sell marks; (2) German interest rates will rise as investors borrow in Germany and invest in U.S.; (3) U.S. interest rates will fall as more is invested in the U.S.; and (4) the one-year forward rate of U.S. dollars relative to German marks will rise. In practice, the last will dominate.

Mathematically, interest rate parity can be expressed as follows for two countries, A and B:

> *Let I =* amount of A's currency to be invested for a time period of length *t*
>
> *S =* spot exchange rate: price of foreign currency in terms of domestic currency (units of domestic currency per unit of foreign currency)
>
> *F =* *t*-period forward rate: price of foreign currency *t* periods from now
>
> i_A = interest rate on an investment maturing at time *t* in country A
>
> i_B = interest rate on an investment maturing at time *t* in country B

Then:

$$I (1 + i_A) = (I/S) (1 + i_B) F$$

To illustrate, let country A be the U.S. and country B represent Germany. In our example we have:

> I = $100,000 for one year
>
> S = $0.6400
>
> F = $0.6283
>
> i_A = 0.07
>
> i_B = 0.09

Then according to interest rate parity this relationship holds:

$$\$100,000 (1.07) = (\$100,000/\$0.6400) (1.09) (\$0.6283)$$
$$\$107,000 = \$107,000$$

Equivalently, interest rate parity can be expressed as:

$$(1 + i_A) = (F/S) (1 + i_B)$$

Rewriting the equation, we obtain the theoretical forward exchange rate:

$$F = S \frac{(1 + i_A)}{(1 + i_B)}$$

While we have referred so far to investors, we could use borrowers as well to illustrate interest rate parity. That is, a borrower has the choice of obtaining funds in a domestic or foreign market. Interest rate parity provides that a borrower who hedges in the forward exchange rate market will realize the same domestic borrowing rate whether borrowing domestically or in a foreign country.

To derive the theoretical forward exchange rate using the arbitrage argument, we made several assumptions. When the assumptions are violated, the actual forward exchange rate may deviate from the theoretical forward exchange rate. First, in deriving the theoretical forward exchange rate we ignored commissions and the bid–ask spread when exchanging in the spot market today and at the end of the investment horizon. Second, we assumed that the borrowing and lending rates in each currency are the same. Dropping this unrealistic assumption means that there is not a single theoretical forward exchange rate, but a band around a level reflecting borrowing and lending rates. Third, the divergence between actual and theoretical forward exchange rates can be the result of the different tax structures of the two countries. Finally, any restrictions on foreign investing or borrowing in each country by impeding arbitrage may cause a divergence between actual and theoretical forward exchange rates.

Link between Eurocurrency Market and Forward Prices. In deriving interest rate parity, we looked at the interest rate in both countries. But the interest rate in each market that participants look to in order to perform covered interest arbitrage so that interest rate parity will hold is the interest rate in the Eurocurrency market. This is the market for bank deposits and bank loans denominated in a currency other than that of the country where the bank initiating the transaction is located. Examples of transactions in the Eurocurrency market are a British bank in London that lends U.S. dollars to a French corporation, and a Japanese corporation that deposits Swiss francs in a German bank. An investor seeking covered interest arbitrage will accomplish the short-term borrowing and lending in the Eurocurrency market.

The largest sector of the Eurocurrency market is the market for bank deposits and bank loans in U.S. dollars. This sector is called the *Eurodollar market*. (We discussed the Eurodollar CD market in Chapter 13.) The seed for the Eurocurrency market was, in fact, the Eurodollar market. As international capital market transactions increased, the market for bank deposits and bank loans in other currencies developed.

Currency Futures Contracts

There are U.S.-traded foreign exchange futures contracts for the major currencies traded on the International Monetary Market (IMM), a division of the Chicago Mercantile Exchange. The futures contracts traded on the IMM are for the Japanese yen, the German mark, the Canadian dollar, the British pound, the Swiss franc, and the Australian dollar. The amount of each foreign currency that must be delivered varies by currency. For example, each British pound futures contract is for delivery of 62,500 pounds, while each Japanese yen futures contract is for delivery of 12.5 million yen.

The maturity cycle for currency futures is March, June, September, and December. The longest maturity is one year. Consequently, as in the case of a currency forward contract, currency futures are limited with respect to hedging long-dated foreign exchange risk exposure.

Other exchanges trading currency futures in the U.S. are the Midamerica Commodity Exchange (a subsidiary of the Chicago Board of Trade) and the Financial Instrument Exchange (a subsidiary of the New York Cotton Exchange). The latter trades a futures contract in which the underlying is a U.S. dollar index. Outside the U.S., currency futures are traded on the London International Financial Futures Exchange, Singapore International Monetary Exchange, Toronto Futures Exchange, Sydney Futures Exchange, and New Zealand Futures Exchange.

Currency Option Contracts

In contrast to a forward or futures contract, an option gives the option buyer the opportunity to benefit from favorable exchange rate movements but establishes a maximum loss. The option price is the cost of establishing such a risk/return profile.

There are two types of foreign currency options: options on the foreign currency, and futures options. The latter is an option to enter into a foreign exchange futures contract. We described the features of futures options in Chapter 19. Futures options are traded on the IMM, the trading location of the currency futures contract.

Options on foreign exchange have been traded on the Philadelphia Exchange since 1982. The foreign currencies underlying the options are the same as for the futures. There are two sorts of options traded on the Philadelphia Exchange for each currency: an American-type option and a European-type option. Recall from Chapter 7 that the former permits exercise at any time up to and including the expiration date, while the latter permits exercise only at the expiration date. The amount of foreign currency underlying each option contract traded on the Philadelphia Exchange is one-half the amount of the futures contract. For example, the Japanese yen option is for 6.25 million yen and the British pound option is for 31,250 pounds. There are also options on currencies traded on the London Stock Exchange and the London International Financial Futures Exchange.

There is also an over-the-counter market for options on currencies. The markets for these products are made by commercial banks and investment banking firms. As we explained in Chapter 19, over-the-counter options are tailor-made products to accommodate the specific needs of clients. Only options on the major currencies are traded on the exchange. An option on any other currency must be purchased in the over-the-counter market.

One type of over-the-counter currency option created by some major dealers is a *lookback option*.[8] This is an option where the option buyer has the right to obtain the most favorable exchange rate that prevailed over the life of the option. For example, consider a two-month lookback call option to buy yen when the exchange rate between the U.S. dollar and Japanese yen is $1 for 126 yen on Day 0. Suppose that the next day, Day 1, the exchange rate changes to $1 for 130 yen. The option buyer has the right to exchange $1 for 130 yen. Suppose that on Day 2 the exchange rate changes to $1 for 127 yen. The option buyer still has the right to exchange $1 for 130 yen. Regardless of what happens to the exchange rate over the 60 days, the option buyer gets to exercise the option at the exchange rate that prevailed that gave the largest number of yen for $1 (or, equivalently, at the lowest price per yen).

Pricing Currency Options. The factors that affect the price of any option were discussed in Chapter 7. One of the key factors is the expected volatility of the underlying instrument or commodity over the life of the option. In the case of currency options, it is the expected volatility of the exchange rate between the two currencies from the present time to the expiration of the option. The strike price also affects the option value: the higher it is, the lower the value of a call, and the higher the value of a put. Another factor that affects the option price is the relative risk-free interest rate in the two countries. To understand why, recall the portfolio we created in Chapter 7 to replicate the payoff of a call option on an asset. A portion of the asset is purchased with borrowed funds. In the case of a currency option, this involves purchasing a portion of the foreign currency underlying the option. However, the foreign currency acquired can be invested at a risk-free interest rate in the foreign country. Consequently, the pricing of a currency option is similar to the pricing of an option on an income earning asset such as a dividend-paying stock or an interest-paying bond.[9] At the same time the

---

[8] For a further discussion of these options, see Mark Garman, "Recollection in Tranquility," *Risk* (March 1989), pp. 16–19.

[9] More detail on the pricing of currency options can be found in Nahum Biger and John Hull, "The Valuation of Currency Options," *Financial Management* (Spring 1983), pp. 24–28; Mark B. Garman and Steven W. Kohlhagen, "Foreign Currency Option Values," *Journal of International Money and Finance* (December 1983), pp. 231–237; and J. Orlin Grabbe, "The Pricing of Call and Put Options on Foreign Exchange," *Journal of International Money and Finance* (December 1983), pp. 239–253.

amount that must be set aside to meet the strike price depends on the domestic rate. Thus the option price, just like interest rate parity, reflects both rates.

Currency Swaps

In the previous chapter, we discussed interest rate swaps—a transaction where two counterparties agree to exchange interest payments with no exchange of principal. In a currency swap, there is an exchange of both interest and principal. The best way to explain a currency swap is with an illustration.

Assume two companies, a U.S. company and a Swiss company. Each company seeks to borrow for 10 years in its domestic currency; that is, the U.S. company seeks $100 million U.S. dollar-denominated debt, and the Swiss company seeks SF 127 million Swiss franc-denominated debt. For reasons that we will explore later, let's suppose that both want to issue 10-year bonds in the bond market of the other country, denominated in the other country's currency.[10] That is, the U.S. company wants to issue the Swiss franc equivalent of $100 million in Switzerland, and the Swiss company wants to issue the U.S. dollar equivalent of SF 127 million in the U.S.

Let's assume the following:

1. at the time that both companies want to issue their 10-year bonds, the spot exchange rate between U.S. dollars and Swiss francs is one U.S. dollar for 1.27 Swiss francs.
2. the coupon rate that the U.S. company would have to pay on the 10-year Swiss franc-denominated bonds issued in Switzerland is 6%.
3. the coupon rate that the Swiss company would have to pay on the 10-year U.S. dollar-denominated bonds issued in the U.S. is 11%.

By the first assumption, if the U.S. company issues the bonds in Switzerland, it can exchange the SF 127 million for $100 million. By issuing $100 million of bonds in the U.S., the Swiss company can exchange the proceeds for SF 127 million. Therefore, both get the amount of financing they seek. Assuming the coupon rates given by the last two assumptions, and assuming for purposes of this illustration that coupon payments will be made annually,[11] the cash outlays that the companies must make for the next 10 years are summarized below:

---

[10] In the next chapter, we will discuss the bond market in a country in which foreign borrowers issue bonds.

[11] In reality U.S. coupon payments are made semiannually. The practice for bonds issued in Europe is to pay coupon interest once per year.

YEAR	U.S. COMPANY	SWISS COMPANY
1-10	SF 7,620,000	$ 11,000,000
10	127,000,000	100,000,000

Each issuer faces the risk that at the time the liability payment must be made its domestic currency will have depreciated relative to the other currency, requiring more of the domestic currency to satisfy the liability. That is, both are exposed to foreign exchange risk.

In a currency swap, the two companies will issue bonds in the other's bond market. The currency swap agreement will require that:

1. the two parties exchange the proceeds received from the sale of the bonds.
2. the two parties make the coupon payments to service the debt of the other party.
3. at the end of the termination date of the currency swap (which coincides with the maturity of the bonds), both parties agree to exchange the par value of the bonds.

In our illustration this means:

1. the U.S. company issues 10-year, 6% coupon bonds with a par value of SF 127 million in Switzerland and gives the proceeds to the Swiss company. At the same time, the Swiss company issues 10-year, 11% bonds with a par value of $100 million in the U.S. and gives the proceeds to the U.S. company.
2. the U.S. company agrees to service the coupon payments of the Swiss company by paying $11,000,000 per year for the next 10 years to the Swiss company; the Swiss company agrees to service the coupon payments of the U.S. company by paying SF 7,620,000 for the next 10 years to the U.S. company.
3. at the end of 10 years (this would be the termination date of this currency swap because it coincides with the maturity of the two bond issues), the U.S. company agrees to pay $100 million to the Swiss company, and the Swiss company agrees to pay SF 127 million to the U.S. company.

This is illustrated in Figure 21-3.

Now let's assess what this transaction has done. Both parties received the amount of financing they sought. The U.S. company's coupon payments are in dollars, not Swiss francs; the Swiss company's coupon payments are in Swiss francs, not U.S. dollars. At the termination date, both parties will receive an amount sufficient in their local currency to pay off the holders of

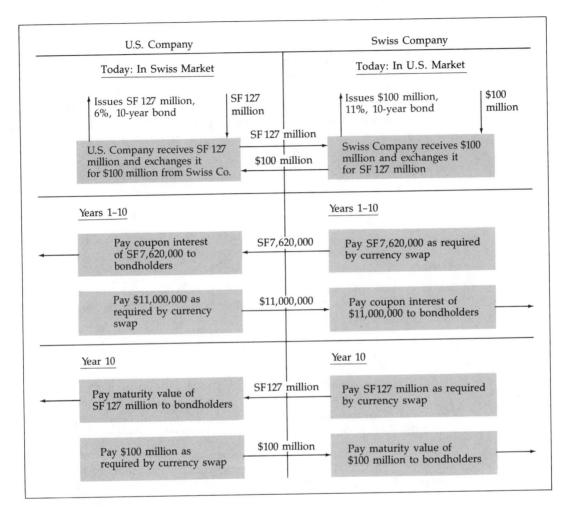

FIGURE 21-3
Illustration of a Currency Swap.

their bonds. With the coupon payments and the principal repayment in their local currency, neither party faces foreign exchange risk.

In practice, the two companies would not deal directly with each other. Instead, either a commercial bank or investment banking firm would be involved as an intermediary in the transaction either as a broker or a dealer. As a broker, the intermediary simply brings the two parties together, receiving a fee for the service. If instead the intermediary serves as a dealer, it not only brings the two parties together, but also guarantees payment to both parties. Thus, if one party defaults, the counterparty will continue to receive its payments from the dealer. Of course, in this arrangement, both parties are concerned with the credit risk of the dealer. When the currency swap market started, transactions were typically brokered. The more prevalent arrangement today is that the intermediary acts as a dealer.

As we explained in the previous chapter, an interest rate swap is nothing more than a package of forward contracts. The same is true for a currency swap; it is simply a package of currency forward contracts.

Motivation for Currency Swaps. Now we turn to the question of why both companies may find a currency swap beneficial. In a global financial market where there are no market imperfections because of regulations, taxes, and transactions costs, the cost of borrowing should be the same whether the issuer raises funds domestically or in any foreign capital market. In a world with market imperfections, it may be possible for an issuer to reduce its borrowing cost by borrowing funds denominated in a foreign currency and hedging the associated exchange rate risk. This is what is meant by an arbitrage opportunity. The currency swap allows borrowers to capitalize on any such arbitrage opportunities.

Prior to the establishment of the currency swap market, capitalizing on such arbitrage opportunities required use of the currency forward market. The market for long-dated forward exchange rate contracts is thin, however, which increases the cost of eliminating foreign exchange risk. Eliminating foreign exchange risk in our U.S.-Switzerland illustration would have required each issuer to enter 10 currency forward contracts (one for each cash payment that the issuer was committed to make in the foreign currency). The currency swap provides a more transactionally efficient means for protecting against foreign exchange risk when an issuer (or its investment banker) has identified an arbitrage opportunity and seeks to benefit from it.

As the currency swap market has developed, arbitrage opportunities for reduced funding costs available in the early days of the swap market have become less common. In fact, it was the development of the swap market that reduced arbitrage opportunities. When these opportunities do arise, they last for only a short period of time, usually less than a day.

There is another motivation for currency swaps. Some companies seek to raise funds in foreign countries as a means of increasing their recognition by foreign investors, despite the fact that the cost of funding is the same as in the U.S. The U.S. company in our illustration might have been seeking to expand its potential sources of future funding by issuing bonds today in Switzerland.

Currency Coupon Swap. In our illustration, we assumed that both parties made fixed cash flow payments. Suppose instead that one of the parties sought floating-rate rather than fixed-rate financing. Returning to the same illustration, assume that instead of fixed-rate financing, the Swiss company wanted LIBOR-based financing. In this case, the U.S. company would issue floating-rate bonds in Switzerland. Suppose that it could do so at a rate of LIBOR plus 50 basis points. Because the currency swap would call for the Swiss company to service the coupon payments of the U.S. company, the Swiss company will make annual payments of LIBOR plus 50 basis points. The U.S. company will still make fixed-rate payments in U.S. dollars to service the debt obligation of the Swiss company in the U.S. Now, however, the Swiss company will make floating-rate payments (LIBOR plus 50 basis points) in Swiss francs to service the debt obligation of the U.S. company in Switzerland.

Currency swaps in which one of the parties pays a fixed rate and the counterparty a floating rate are called *currency coupon swaps.*

Swaptions.   In our discussion of the interest rate swap in the previous chapter, we explained the motivation for the development of the option on an interest rate swap, called swaptions. It is not difficult to see why swaptions would be attractive in the case of currency swaps. Suppose that the 10-year bonds of either issuer are callable and that interest rates decline sufficiently in the U.S. so that the Swiss company will find it economic to call the bonds. The Swiss company will still be responsible for making the payments as specified in the currency swap. An option to exit the currency swap would be needed to offset these obligations.

SUMMARY

We have reviewed the spot foreign exchange market and markets for hedging foreign exchange risk. An exchange rate is defined as the amount of one currency that can be exchanged for another currency. A direct exchange rate quote is the domestic price of a foreign currency; an indirect quote is the foreign price of the domestic currency. Given a direct quote, an indirect quote can be obtained by the reciprocal of the direct quote, and vice versa. An investor or issuer whose cash flows are denominated in a foreign currency is exposed to foreign exchange risk.

The spot exchange rate market is the market for settlement of a currency within two business days. In the developed countries, and some of the developing ones, exchange rates are free to float. According to the purchasing power parity relationship, the exchange rate between two countries—the price of the foreign currency—is proportional to the domestic price level and inversely proportional to the price level in the foreign country. Exchange rates are typically quoted in terms of the U.S. dollar.

The foreign exchange market is an over-the-counter market dominated by large international banks that act as dealers. Foreign exchange dealers quote one price at which they are willing to buy a foreign currency and one at which they are willing to sell a foreign currency.

Today, the European Currency Unit is the most widely used composite currency unit for capital market transactions. It is continuing to grow in importance as an increasing number of loans have been denominated in ECU, and some members of the Economic Monetary System have been issuing ECU-denominated government bonds.

Currency forward contracts, currency futures contracts, currency options, and currency swaps are four instruments that borrowers and investors can use to protect against adverse foreign exchange rate movements.

Interest rate parity gives the relationship among the spot exchange rate, the interest rates in two countries, and the forward rate. The relationship is assured by a covered interest arbitrage. Interest rate parity implies that investors and borrowers who hedge in the forward exchange rate market will realize the same domestic return or face the same domestic borrowing rate whether investing or borrowing domestically or in a foreign country.

In implementing covered interest arbitrage, the relevant interest rates are those in the Eurocurrency market, the market for bank deposits and bank loans denominated in a currency other than that of the country where the bank initiating the transaction is located. The Eurodollar market is the largest sector of this market.

There are exchange-traded options on major foreign currencies and futures options on the same currencies traded in the U.S. An option on any other currency must be purchased in the over-the-counter market. A lookback option is an over-the-counter product granting the option buyer the right to obtain the most favorable exchange rate that prevailed over the life of the option.

A currency swap is effectively a package of currency forward contracts, with the advantage that it allows hedging of long-dated foreign exchange risk and it is more transactionally efficient. Currency swaps are used to arbitrage opportunities in the global financial market for raising funds at less cost than in the domestic market. Arbitrage opportunities have become rare.

QUESTIONS

1. What risk is faced by a U.S. life insurance company that buys British government bonds?

2. These foreign exchange rates were reported on February 8, 1991:

	GERMAN MARK	JAPANESE YEN	BRITISH POUND
U.S. $	0.6874	0.00779	1.9905

The exchange rates indicate the number of U.S. dollars necessary to purchase one unit of the foreign currency.

a. From the perspective of a U.S. investor, are the foreign exchange rates above direct or indirect quotes?

b. How much of each of the foreign currencies is needed to buy one U.S. dollar?

c. Calculate the theoretical cross rates between: (i) the German mark and the Japanese yen; (ii) the German mark and the British pound; and (iii) the Japanese yen and the British pound.

3. On February 8, 1991, the U.S. dollar/British pound spot rate was U.S. $1.9905 per pound and U.S. dollar/Japanese yen spot rate was U.S. $0.0079 per yen. The forward rates following were also quoted:

	BRITISH POUND	JAPANESE YEN
30 days	1.9908	0.007774
60	1.9597	0.007754
90	1.9337	0.007736

a. Explain what someone who enters into a 30-day forward contract to deliver British pounds is agreeing to do.

b. Explain what someone who enters into a 90-day forward contract to buy Japanese yen is agreeing to do.

c. What can you infer about the relationship between U.S. and German short-term interest rates and U.S. and Japanese short-term interest rates?

4. a. What is the European Currency Unit?

b. The Economic Monetary Community expects to revise the weights of the currencies comprising the ECU every five years. Why is it necessary to revise the weights?

5. What is the drawback of using currency forward contracts for hedging long-dated positions?

6. Why are the interest rates in the Eurocurrency market important in covered interest arbitrage?

7. Consider this quotation from *Euromoney* of September 1989:

    Enterprise Oil itself recently purchased what it claims to be the biggest currency option obtained by a corporate client. In March it spent over $15 million as the premium on a 90-day currency option. . . .

    The Chemical [Bank]-arranged option was used to lock in exchange rate protection on $1.03 billion of a $1.45 billion liability incurred in the acquisition of US-based gas transmission company, Texas Eastern. . . .

    The need for the option arose since Enterprise Oil was paying for a dollar liability by raising sterling-denominated equity. The option is a dollar-call option which gives the company the right to buy dollars at a dollar/sterling exchange rate of $1.70 for a 90-day period.

    Enterprise bought the option out-of-the-money on March 1 with dollar/sterling exchange rates at $1.73. It reduced its premium on currency options by taking the option a long way out-of-the-money.

    Discuss Enterprise Oil's financing strategy and rationale for the purchase of the currency options.

8. The quotation following is from a 1991 issue of *Corporate Financing Week:*

    To purchase additional aircraft, a major international carrier needed to borrow $105 million and then convert its dollar liability to a currency matching its passenger revenues. . . .

    SBCM [Sumitomo Bank Capital Markets] executed an amortizing cross-currency swap in which the carrier pays a monthly yen amount in return for a semi-annual U.S. dollar Libor-based payment. The fixed-yen payments on the swap represent interest plus amortization of principal on the yen equivalent of the U.S. dollar borrowing, and the floating Libor payments represent semi-annual interest plus amortization of the U.S. dollar principal amount.

    a. Discuss the rationale for this currency swap transaction.

    b. What alternative hedging techniques might have been used to achieve the same end?

9. The excerpt following appeared in the January 14, 1991, issue of *Wall Street Letter:*

    The Philadelphia Stock Exchange plans to list the first non-dollar denominated options to trade in the United States, according to sources at the exchange. The Phlx will list cross-currency options based on the relationships between the Deutsche mark and the Japanese yen, as well as British pound/yen and pound/mark options, a spokesman confirmed. . . .

The exchange currently lists currency options that are based on the relationship between that currency and the dollar, one Phlx member explained. "If you're not American," he added, "then the dollar doesn't do it for you." The three new cross-currency options should be attractive to the same banks and broker-dealers that currently trade dollar-based currency options, as well as non-U.S. entities that have interests in other currencies.

Cross-currency options are "a very big part of international trade and international capital markets," and are big over-the-counter products, but none currently trade on an exchange. The advantage of exchange-traded options, the Phlx member said, is that "99% of the customers don't have the credit" to trade such a product over-the-counter with a big bank.

a. What does the spokesman for the Philadelphia exchange mean when he says: "If you're not American then the dollar doesn't do it for you."?

b. Why is the credit of customers critical in the over-the-counter market but not for an exchange-traded contract?

c. When the Philadelphia Stock Exchange filed with the SEC to list cross-currency options, the exchange indicated that the demand for this product has been "spawned by recent large fluctuations and dramatic increases in volatility levels for cross-rate options." Why would this increase the demand for cross-currency options?

CHAPTER

22

GLOBAL
FINANCIAL MARKETS

LEARNING OBJECTIVES

After reading this chapter you will understand:

- the factors leading to the globalization of financial markets.
- the distinction between external and internal bond markets.
- characteristics of the Eurobond market.
- the types of securities issued in the Eurobond market.
- the sectors of the Japanese and German bond markets and the key institutional characteristics of these markets.
- the importance of the Euroclear and Cedel clearing systems.
- the market structures and trading procedures in non-U.S. stock markets.
- the Euroequity markets.
- the characteristics of the Japanese stock market.

- Non-U.S. stock index and interest rate derivative contracts, particularly those traded in Japan.

Globalization of financial markets means the integration of financial markets throughout the world into a universal financial market. In a discussion of globalization of financial markets, William Schreyer, Chairman and Chief Executive Officer of Merrill Lynch & Co., Inc., wrote:

> Suppose this is the mid-1990s. And suppose a German investment banker en route from a meeting with clients in Beijing to an international money managers' convention in Teheran turns off his portable pocket Quotron long enough to scan the day's copy of the *Global Wall Street Journal*.
>
> A headline catches his eye:
> *U.S.–USSR Global Underwriting*
> NEW YORK/MOSCOW—Merrill Lynch and Moscow's Norodny Securities today announced agreement to lead-manage a joint $20 billion bond underwriting, the proceeds of which will be used to finance commercial applications of technologies developed in the forthcoming joint U.S.–Soviet mission to Mars. The bonds will be offered simultaneously in 56 countries, including China and Poland, in denominations as small as $1,000. Calling it "the world's first global bond," a Norodny spokesman declared that it "marks another step forward in the free flow of capital throughout the world's markets."
>
> That isn't likely to happen tomorrow, of course. And some aspects may sound far-fetched. But the development of the world's capital

markets has been so sweeping and so swift that even stranger things probably will.[1]

In this chapter, we present an overview of the global financial markets: bond markets, equity markets, and derivative markets. We begin with an explanation of the factors that have led to the integration of financial markets throughout the world.

FACTORS LEADING TO THE GLOBALIZATION OF FINANCIAL MARKETS

We can classify the factors leading to the globalization of financial markets as: (1) deregulation or liberalization of financial markets and activities of market participants, especially with respect to foreign transactions in key financial centers of the world; (2) technological advances for monitoring world markets, executing orders, and analyzing financial opportunities; and (3) increased institutionalization of financial markets. These factors are not mutually exclusive.

Deregulation

Deregulation of foreign exchange markets and global competition have forced governments to deregulate (or liberalize) various aspects of their financial markets so that their financial-oriented entities can compete effectively in global financial markets. Two sorts of deregulation have led to increased integration of global financial markets: (1) *market deregulation,* and (2) *institutional deregulation.*[2]

The first refers to deregulation of the basic structure of the market. Within major national financial markets, this has taken the form of eliminating interest rate ceilings and fixed commissions on security transactions. Other deregulation measures to open up a country's financial market to global market participants include:

- eliminating foreign exchange controls
- reducing or eliminating withholding taxes or transfer taxes imposed on foreign investors

---

[1] William A. Schreyer, "The Globalization of Financial Markets," Chapter 2 in Robert Lawrence Kuhn (ed.), *Investing and Risk Management,* Volume I in The Library of Investment Banking (Homewood, IL: Dow Jones-Irwin, 1990), p. 27.

[2] Schreyer, "The Globalization of Financial Markets," p. 31.

- relaxing restrictions on:
  1. the purchase of domestic securities by foreign investors
  2. the issuance of bonds by foreign borrowers
  3. foreign commercial banks' participation in local loan markets[3]
  4. involvement of foreign investment banks and commercial banks in underwriting bonds sold in the domestic market
  5. foreign financial institutions' participation in that country's government bond market

With respect to the U.S. financial markets, we've discussed these deregulation measures throughout this book. In October 1986, the United Kingdom liberalized its domestic equities and government securities markets. The comprehensive changes made in the U.K.—referred to as the "Big Bang"—forced other European countries to liberalize their markets. Several deregulation measures in Japan and Germany are discussed later.

Institutional deregulation involves the liberalization or elimination of restrictions on the financial activities of domestic and foreign financial institutions. Examples include lifting restrictions on the activities that commercial banks and investment banks can undertake, and relaxing restrictions on the types of investments in which regulated financial institutions may invest.

Technological Advances

Technological advances have increased the integration of financial markets and the efficiency of the global financial market. Advances in telecommunication systems link dealers throughout the world so that orders can be executed within seconds. Advances in computer technology, coupled with advanced telecommunication systems, allow the transmission of real-time information on security prices. Such key financial information allows market participants to monitor global markets and simultaneously assess how information will impact the risk/return profile of their portfolios. Improved computing power allows the instant manipulation of real-time market information so that arbitrage opportunities can be identified. Telecommunication systems permit the rapid execution of orders to capture any opportunities.

---

[3] The international activities of commercial banks are discussed in Chapter 2.

Institutionalization of Financial Markets

In our discussion of the stock market in Chapter 8, we explained how the market has changed from a market dominated by retail investors to one dominated by financial institutions, particularly pension funds, insurance companies, and mutual funds. The bond markets also are dominated by institutional investors. We refer to this phenomenon as the institutionalization of financial markets, and it has occurred in other industrialized countries as well. Unlike a retail investor-dominated market, financial institutions have been more willing to transfer funds across national borders to improve portfolio diversification and/or exploit perceived mispricing of securities in foreign countries. Retail investors willing to invest in a particular foreign country or globally can do so through mutual funds that specialize in a particular country (such as the Japanese fund and the Canada fund) or that invest in more than one country (such as the Pacific Basin fund, the Europe fund, and the International Opportunities fund).

The potential portfolio diversification benefits associated with global investing have been documented in numerous studies.[4] These studies have alerted investors to the virtues of global investing. The underlying theory for international diversification is that because international capital markets are less than perfectly correlated, including securities from other countries allows an increase of expected return without increasing risk.

GLOBAL BOND MARKETS

In recent years, lending and borrowing activities in the international financial markets have shifted from traditional syndicated bank loans to some type of marketable security (such as a bond) or securitized instrument (such as an asset-backed security).

While there is no uniform system for classifying the global bond markets, we think it is appropriate to classify the global bond market into an *internal bond market* and an *external bond market* (from the perspective of a given country).

The internal bond market is also called the *national bond market*. It can be decomposed into two parts: the domestic bond market and the foreign bond market. The domestic bond market is where issuers domiciled in the country issue bonds and where those bonds are subsequently traded. The foreign bond market of a country is where bonds of issuers not domiciled in the

---

[4] For a review of these studies, see Bruno Solnik, *International Investments* (Reading, MA: Addison-Wesley, 1988), Chapter 2.

country are issued and traded. For example, in the U.S. it is the market where bonds are issued by non-U.S. entities and then subsequently traded. Bonds traded in the U.S. foreign bond market are nicknamed *Yankee bonds*. In Japan, a yen-denominated bond issued by a British corporation and subsequently traded in Japan's bond market is part of the Japanese foreign bond market. Yen-denominated bonds issued by non-Japanese entities are nicknamed *Samurai bonds*. Foreign bonds in the United Kingdom are nicknamed *Bulldog bonds*, in the Netherlands *Rembrandt bonds*, and in Spain *Matador bonds*.

Regulatory authorities in the country where the bond is issued impose certain rules governing the issuance of foreign bonds. These may include (1) restrictions on the bond structures that may be issued (e.g., unsecured debt, zero-coupon bonds, convertible bonds, etc.), (2) restrictions on the minimum or maximum size of an issue and/or the frequency with which an issuer may come to market, (3) how long an issuer must wait to bring the issue to market (imposed to avoid an oversupply of issues), (4) a minimum-quality standard (credit rating) for the issue or issuer, (5) disclosure and periodic reporting requirements, and (6) restrictions on the types of financial institutions permitted to underwrite issues. The 1980s have been characterized by government relaxation or abolition of these restrictions so as to open up their bond markets to issuers.

The *external bond market*, also called the *international bond market*, includes bonds with several distinguishing features: (1) they are underwritten by an international syndicate, (2) at issuance they are offered simultaneously to investors in a number of countries, (3) they are issued outside the jurisdiction of any single country, and (4) they are in unregistered form. The external bond market is commonly referred to as the *offshore bond market*, or, more popularly, the *Eurobond market*.[5] The Eurobond market is divided into different sectors based on the currency in which the issue is denominated. For example, when Eurobonds are denominated in U.S. dollars, they are referred to as Eurodollar bonds.

In recent years, it has become increasingly difficult to classify a bond issue as a foreign bond or Eurobond.[6] First, the most important characteristic of a Eurobond offering is the composition of the underwriting syndicate. Yet "bought deals"—when there is only one underwriter—are becoming increasingly common. A bond offering in which there is only one underwriter, and in which the issue is placed primarily outside the national market of both the issuer and underwriter, is not traditionally classified as a Eurobond offering. Another characteristic of a Eurobond is that it is not

---

[5] The classification we use is by no means universally accepted. Some market observers refer to the external bond market as consisting of the foreign bond market and the Eurobond market.

[6] Michael Bowe, *Eurobonds* (Kent, U.K.: Square Mile Books, 1988), pp. 16–17.

regulated by the country whose currency is being used to pay bondholders. In practice, however, only the U.S. and Canada do not place restrictions on U.S. dollar- or Canadian dollar-denominated issues sold outside these two countries. Regulators of other countries whose currencies are used in Eurobond issues have closely supervised such offerings. Their power to regulate Eurobond offerings comes from their ability to impose foreign exchange and/or capital restrictions.

Although Eurobonds are typically registered on a national stock exchange, the most common being the Luxembourg, London, or Zurich exchanges, the bulk of all trading is in the over-the-counter market. Listing is purely to circumvent restrictions imposed on some institutional investors who are prohibited from purchasing securities that are not listed on an exchange. Some of the stronger issuers privately place issues with international institutional investors.

In September 1989 the first true "global bond" was issued. This was a 10-year $1.5 billion offering of the World Bank. What made this issue a global bond is that it was offered simultaneously in the U.S. Yankee bond market and in the Eurobond market. This was the first attempt to surmount the fragmented market for U.S. dollar-denominated bonds.

Securities Issued in the Eurobond Market

The Eurobond market has been characterized by new and innovative bond structures to accommodate particular needs of issuers and investors. There are, of course, the "plain vanilla," fixed-rate coupon bonds, referred to as *Euro straights.* Because they are issued on an unsecured basis, they are usually issued by high-quality entities.

Coupon payments are made annually, rather than semiannually, because of the higher cost of distributing interest to geographically dispersed bondholders. There are also zero-coupon bond issues, deferred-coupon issues, and step-up issues, all of which we described in Chapter 15. There are issues that pay coupon interest in one currency but pay the principal in a different currency. Such issues are called *dual currency issues.* For example, the coupon interest payments can be made in Swiss francs, while the principal may be paid in U.S. dollars. In 1989, such *dual currency issues* represented about 3% of all foreign and international bonds issued, about 50% of which were yen-denominated.[7] There are many variants of the basic dual currency issues.

---

[7] "The International Capital Market in 1989," *Cahiers BEI/EIB Papers,* European Investment Bank, Luxembourg, March 1990, p. 38.

In Chapter 15 we also described convertible and exchangeable bonds. A convertible Eurobond is one that can be converted into another asset. The convertible bond structure was introduced into the Eurobond market in 1965 with an offering by Monsanto.

Bonds with attached warrants represent a large part of the Eurobond market. A warrant grants the owner of the option the right to enter into another financial transaction with the issuer if the owner will benefit as a result of exercising. Most warrants are detachable from the host bond; that is the bondholder may detach the warrant from the bond and sell it.

There are a wide array of bonds with warrants: equity warrants, debt warrants, and currency warrants. An *equity warrant* permits the warrant owner to buy the common stock of the issuer at a specified price. A *debt warrant* entitles the warrant owner to buy additional bonds from the issuer at the same price and yield as the host bond. The debt warrant owner will benefit if interest rates decline because a bond with a higher coupon can be purchased from the same issuer. A *currency warrant* permits the warrant owner to exchange one currency for another at a set price (i.e., a fixed exchange rate). This feature protects the bondholder against a depreciation of the foreign currency in which the bond's cash flows are denominated. There are also *gold warrants*, which allow the warrant holder to purchase gold from the issuer of the bond.

There are a wide variety of floating-rate Eurobond notes. In the Eurobond market, almost all floating-rate notes are denominated in U.S. dollars with non-U.S. banks being the major issuers. Floating-rate notes were first issued in 1970 by ENEL, an Italian utility company. In 1970, the floating-rate note market represented about 21% of the Eurodollar bond market. By 1984, Eurodollar floating-rate notes made up almost 50% of Eurodollar bond financing, but the share of floating-rate notes has declined dramatically since the mid 1980s.[8] The amount of outstanding issues in 1989 exceeded $150 billion.

The coupon rate on a Eurodollar floating-rate note is some stated margin over the London Interbank Offered Rate (LIBOR), the bid on LIBOR (referred to as LIBID), or the arithmetic average LIBOR and LIBID (referred to as LIMEAN).[9] The size of the spread reflects the perceived credit risk of the issuer, margins available in the syndicated loan market, and the liquidity of the issue. Typical reset periods for the coupon rate are either every six months

---

[8] Sarah Allen and Beth L. Palumbo, "Eurodollar Floating Rate Notes," Chapter 5 in Frank J. Fabozzi (ed.), *Floating Rate Instruments: Characteristics, Valuation, and Portfolio Strategies* (Chicago: Probus Publishing, 1986).

[9] A less commonly used index is the Singapore Interbank Offered Rate (SIBOR).

or every quarter, with the rate tied to a six-month or three-month LIBOR, respectively. That is, the length of the reset period and the maturity of the index used to establish the rate for the period are matched.[10]

Many issues have either a minimum coupon rate (or floor) that the coupon rate cannot fall below and a maximum coupon rate (or cap) that the coupon rate cannot rise above. An issue that has both a floor and a cap is said to be *collared*. There are some issues that grant the borrower the right to convert the floating coupon rate into a fixed coupon rate at some time. There are some issues referred to as *drop-lock bonds*, which automatically change the floating coupon rate into a fixed coupon rate under certain circumstances.

A floating-rate note issue will either have a stated maturity date, or it may be a *perpetual*, also called *undated*, issue (i.e., with no stated maturity date). The perpetual issue was introduced into the Eurobond market in 1984. For floating-rate notes that do mature, the term is usually greater than five years, with the typical maturity being between 7 and 12 years. There are callable and putable floating-rate notes; some issues are both callable and putable.

Major Non-U.S. Bond Markets

Table 22-1 shows the size of the major non-U.S. national government bond markets. We discuss the two largest non-U.S. bond markets, Japan and West Germany, because they typify the trend toward deregulation of financial markets that began in the 1980s.

Japan.   Regulation of the Japanese financial markets is the responsibility of the Ministry of Finance (MOF). All bond issues must be approved by the MOF; it plays a role similar to the SEC in the U.S. The Bank of Japan plays the same role in Japan as the Federal Reserve System in the U.S. The division of commercial banking and investment banking that was established in the U.S., and which we discussed in Chapter 2, has been followed by the architects of

---

[10] In 1984, "mismatched" Eurodollar floating-rate notes were issued. With a mismatched floater, the frequency at which the coupon is reset is generally shorter than the frequency of the coupon payment. When the yield curve is steep in the one-month to six-month portion of the yield curve, there is an opportunity for investors to enhance return by buying mismatched floaters with funds borrowed at the one-month rate and earning the higher coupon rate offered on the basis of the six-month rate determined monthly. This is in fact what occurred in the first quarter of 1985, which explains why the issuance of mismatched Eurodollar floating-rate notes exceeded that of other Eurodollar floating-rate notes in that period. Recognizing that the risk investors face with such a strategy is that the yield curve may become inverted in the short-term sector (that is, short-term money market rates may exceed long-term money market rates), issuers included protection for investors by having the coupon rate reset at the maximum of a short-term and long-term money market rate.

TABLE 22-1   SIZE OF THE MAJOR NON-U.S. NATIONAL GOVERNMENT BOND MARKETS   (AS OF JUNE 1, 1990, IN BILLIONS OF U.S. DOLLARS)

SECTOR	PRINCIPAL AMOUNT	MARKET VALUE	MARKET WEIGHT
Japan	$ 472.1	$ 460.4	37.34%
U.K.	167.1	155.6	12.62
West Germany	213.7	201.6	16.35
France	153.1	155.2	12.58
Canada	101.8	101.6	8.24
Netherlands	100.1	97.2	7.88
Denmark	33.3	34.0	2.76
Australia	21.8	21.1	1.71
Switzerland	7.1	6.6	0.53
Total	$1,270.1	$1,233.3	100.00%

Source: Salomon Brothers Inc.

the Japanese financial system. Japan's securities and exchange law prohibits non-securities companies from dealing in any securities except government or government-related bonds. As the wall between commercial banking and investment banking is being chiseled away in the U.S., similar issues are facing Japan's MOF, and reforms are under consideration there too.

While there are more than 200 securities companies in Japan, four dominate the market: Nomura, Daiwa, Nikko, and Yamaichi. These four firms are referred to as the "Big Four," or *Yondai Shoken*. Second- and third-tier securities houses are referred to as *Sho Shoken*. Banks in Japan are classified as either city banks, local banks, long-term credit banks, trust banks, mutual banks, institutions for agriculture and forestry, and credit associations. The most powerful in terms of financial clout are the 13 city banks, so-named because they are headquartered in major Japanese metropolitan areas. These are the primary lenders to private companies. Following city banks in terms of assets are the 64 local banks.

Legally there is no distinction between city banks and local banks. The distinction is based on size and business focus, with city banks targeting large industrial companies, and local banks focusing on individuals and locally based, medium-sized companies. The three long-term credit banks (Industrial Bank of Japan, Long-Term Credit Bank of Japan, and Nippon Credit Bank) provide long-term financing for Japanese industry. The seven trust banks in Japan conduct both banking business and trust activities (investment management of accounts and custodial activities).

An interesting institutional feature of the Japanese bond market is the

Bond Flotation Committee (*Kisaikai*). This committee, consisting of 43 institutions, plays an important role in the Japanese corporate bond market by (1) establishing eligibility standards to qualify to issue bonds, (2) monitoring the terms and amount of issues, and (3) controlling the coming of new issues to market to avoid flooding the market with issues. The central administration of this committee is implemented by a group consisting of seven banks (Industrial Bank of Japan, Dai-ichi Kangyo, Fuji Bank, Sumitomo, Mitsubishi, Mitsui, and Sanwa)[11] and the Big Four securities companies.

There is an inherent conflict between the banks and the securities houses. Corporations that issue bonds are substituting this form of borrowing for bank borrowing. As banks are not permitted to underwrite non-government bonds, corporate borrowing via the bond market reduces bank lending opportunities, which cannot be recouped in part from underwriting fees. Consequently, banks have a vested interest in establishing rigid standards to discourage corporate bond offerings; obviously, securities houses want the issuing rules liberalized. It must be emphasized that the rules established by the committee are voluntary rules. The power of this committee is expected to diminish with the further liberalization of the Japanese bond market.

Several key financial regulatory changes have liberalized the Japanese bond markets. Many of these changes represent attempts to foster the development of the Japanese foreign bond market (the Samurai bond market) and the Euroyen bond market (that is, yen-denominated Eurobonds).[12] For example, while the Bank Flotation Committee required that all bonds be secured, in 1979 Sears Overseas Finance N.V. issued an unsecured bond in the Samurai bond market, which helped foster the replacement of collateral requirements in the domestic bond market with a credit rating system for bonds. In 1987, Japan introduced the equivalent of the U.S. shelf-registration rule.[13] This rule permits issuers to come to market faster than would be possible by going through the standard issuing procedure. Motivation for shelf registration was to allow foreign issuers to issue securities in the Samurai bond market. Bought deal underwriting was introduced into Japan in mid-1986 with the thirty-fourth World Bank Samurai bond issue.[14] New and innovative bond structures were permitted in the second half of the

---

[11] This group is referred to as *"Hachikokai,"* which translated means a committee of eight banks. The group consists of only seven banks because Dai-ichi Bank and Nippon Kangyo Bank merged in 1971.

[12] For a more detailed description of the development of the Japanese bond market, see Issen Sato and E. M. Kanovsky, "Historical Development of the Japanese Bond Market," Chapter 13 in Frank J. Fabozzi (ed.), *The Japanese Bond Markets* (Chicago: Probus Publishing, 1990).

[13] See Chapter 3.

[14] Issen Sato and E. M. Kanovsky, "The Foreign Bond Market in Japan," Chapter 13 in *The Japanese Bond Markets*, p. 435.

1980s, and rules were also relaxed for the issuance of convertible bonds in 1985 and 1987.

The internal Japanese bond market includes the following sectors: government bonds, government-related organization bonds, local government bonds, bank debentures, and corporate bonds. By far, the largest sector is the Japanese government bond (JGB) market.

There are three types of JGBs: medium-term government bonds, 10-year government bonds (called long-term government bonds), and 20-year government bonds (called super long-term government bonds). There are two types of medium-term notes: discount five-year notes, and coupon bonds with two, three, or four years to maturity. All coupon bonds pay semiannual interest, just as in the U.S. The Japanese government also issues Treasury bills, which are issued at a discount and have 180 days to maturity.

Two unique features of the JGB market are worth noting. The first has to do with the benchmark or bellwether bond issue. It is this issue that is most actively traded and therefore has the greatest liquidity of all issues of similar maturity. In the U.S. Treasury market, the on-the-run issues, that is, the most recently auctioned issue for a given maturity, are the benchmark issues for each maturity. The on-the-run 30-year Treasury issue is the issue in which there is the most trading activity because investors use it to speculate on interest rates in the long-term end of the bond market. In Japan, the benchmark issue is basically the issue that the Big Four securities houses designate as being such.

The second unique feature is the method of quoting yields on JGB issues, which carries over to other types of Japanese bonds. As we explained in Chapter 11, the yield to maturity is the measure used in the U.S. to quote bond yields. We explained the deficiency of this measure because it assumes that the coupon payments can be reinvested at the calculated yield to maturity. In Japan, bond yields are quoted on a "simple yield" basis. The calculation is as follows:

$$\text{Simple yield} = \frac{\text{Annual coupon interest} + \dfrac{(\text{Par value} - \text{Price})}{\text{Years to maturity}}}{\text{Price}}$$

While this method for calculating yield may seem naive, we think in fact it is more suitable, because use of the term "simple" yield forewarns the investor that this yield measure may leave a great deal to be desired as a measure of relative value. Regrettably, in the U.S. many (too many) market participants view yield to maturity as a "scientific" measure of value. Nothing could be farther from the truth.

The Japanese government-related organization bond sector includes bonds issued by public corporations and special-purpose companies established under Japanese law. There are two types of issues: those with principal and interest guaranteed by the Japanese government, and those that are not. Each year the amount of guaranteed bonds that may be issued must be approved by the Japanese Diet (the legislative body). The Japanese government at one time used government-guaranteed bonds of government-related organizations to finance various projects rather than issuing its own bonds. In fact, the Japanese government did not issue any government bonds until 1966. The first, and largest, issuers of government-guaranteed bonds were the Japanese National Railways and the Nippon Telegraph and Telephone Public Corporation in 1953. Both of these organizations are now private corporations. Government-guaranteed bonds may be publicly offered or privately placed. The volume of government-guaranteed bonds has declined as a result of privatization in Japan.

The local government bond market sector consists of debt instruments issued by various Japanese cities, prefectures, towns, and villages of Japan. There are 23 entities that now publicly issue bonds. A few local governments (Tokyo, Osaka, Kobe, and Yokohama) have issued non-yen-denominated bonds outside Japan.[15]

Japanese law permits *certain* banks to issue bonds to raise funds. These issues are called *bank debentures* and represent the second largest sector of the Japanese bond market. The banks permitted to issue these debentures are the Industrial Bank of Japan, the Long-Term Credit Bank of Japan, the Nippon Credit Bank, the Norinchukin Bank, the Shoko Chukin Bank, and the Bank of Tokyo.

The corporate bond sector represents yen-denominated bonds issued by Japanese domestic corporations. As explained earlier, the Bond Flotation Committee supervises the issuance of these securities. A formal corporate bond rating system was introduced in 1977. Equity-linked bonds (convertible bonds and bonds with warrants) have been the most important type of bonds issued by corporations. Prior to 1983, Japanese corporations found it more attractive to issue convertible bonds overseas. Since 1983, the relaxation of restrictions on convertible bond issuance in Japan, coupled with a decline in domestic interest rates at that time, made domestic issuance more attractive.

The Japanese foreign bond market includes both yen-denominated and non-yen-denominated issues. There are three types of foreign bonds that are yen-denominated: Samurai bonds, Daimyo bonds, and Shibosai bonds. Samurai bonds are publicly offered issues. The primary issuers of Samurai bonds are supranational institutions (e.g., the Asian Development Bank and

---

[15] Such a practice is not new. In 1899, the city of Kobe issued British pound-denominated bonds, which were privately placed; in 1902 Yokohama and Osaka issued British pound-denominated bonds that were publicly offered. (David C. Lee and Kenji Sakagami, "Japanese Local Government Bonds," Chapter 8 in *The Japanese Bond Markets*, p. 279.)

the World Bank), followed by sovereign governments such as the Commonwealth of Australia, or by foreign municipal governments. Daimyo bonds were introduced in 1987 to improve liquidity. These publicly issued bonds are listed on the Luxembourg Exchange, and rather than being settled in Japan, they are settled through the Euroclear or Cedel systems (discussed later) as are Euroyen bonds. Shibosai bonds are privately placed bonds issued by foreigners that are yen-denominated.

Germany.   The third largest bond market is the German bond market. The Bundesbank is responsible for maintaining an orderly monetary system and establishing regulations for new bond issues. The Federal German Civil Code requires that domestic issuers obtain permission to issue new bonds.

There are several noteworthy features of the German bond market. First, more than in any other country with a well-developed capital market, the German capital market is more interdependent with its banking system. This is because most intermediation of funds is via banks. Consequently, in the German capital markets, banks are the largest group of investors. There are two types of banks in Germany: *universal banks* and "special" banks. The activities of universal banks include the usual commercial banking business and any kind of securities business. The latter activity includes the underwriting, trading, and investing in securities. Thus, there is no separation of the banking and securities businesses in Germany. The secondary market for both stocks and bonds as a result is mainly an interbank market. The three major universal banks are Deutsche Bank, Dresdner Bank and Commerzbank. The special banks provide financing for specific needs such as mortgage financing and consumer financing.

A second feature of the German capital market is that it is one of the most liberal in the world, with a number of measures adopted since 1985 that have opened up the German bond market to foreign entities. In April 1985, the Bundesbank granted subsidiaries of foreign banks domiciled in Germany permission to be lead managers of deutschemark-denominated Eurobonds, called Euro-deutschemark bonds or simply Euro-DM bonds. Also in April 1985, the Bundesbank authorized the issuance of a wide array of Euro-DM issues not previously permitted, such as floating-rate notes, zero-coupon bonds, and dual currency notes. Moreover, banks and investors were permitted to participate in currency swaps, an instrument that we discussed in the previous chapter.

There are three sectors in the German national bond market: (1) public authority bonds, (2) bank bonds, and (3) non-bank corporate bonds. Public authority bonds include bonds issued by the Federal Republic of Germany (Bund issues), its special agencies—the federal post office (Bundespost issues) and the federal railways (Bundesbahn issues)—and German state governments (Lander) and local authorities (Gemeinden).

Bund, Bundespost, and Bundesbahn issues are all guaranteed by the full faith and credit of the Federal Republic of Germany. Bundesobligationen is a Bund issue with five years to maturity that can be purchased only by German residents. No such restrictions are imposed on Bundekassenobligationen, a Bund issue with two to six years to maturity. All coupon payments are annual rather than semiannual, as in the U.S. and Japan; this is the convention followed in the European bond market overall. The German government also issues a zero-coupon note (U-Schaetze), which has a maturity of up to two years.

Typically the maturity of a public authority bond at issuance is between eight to 10 years; however, in 1986 Bundesobligationen with a 30-year maturity was issued. The underwriting of public authority bonds is done by the Federal Bond Syndicate, which at the end of 1988 consisted of 67 German and 20 foreign banks.

The second largest sector, roughly 40% of the German national bond market, is the market for bank bonds. Within this sector, the two major types of bank bonds are municipal bonds (Kommunalobligationen) and mortgage bonds (Pfandbriefe). Municipal bonds are debt obligations issued by banks but secured by public authorities. By far the smallest sector of the German national bond market is the non-bank corporate market. Borrowing by German corporations is done primarily via bank loans rather than through issuance of bonds. The German foreign bond market is also a small part of the national bond market. Most issues are privately placed.

Clearing Systems

Global financial markets require an effective system for the settlement of transactions. That is, buyers must receive the securities purchased and sellers must receive cash payment, which is complicated when buyer and seller may be in two different countries. Moreover, the broker or dealer firms involved in a transaction may also be in different countries from the buyer and seller. Geographical separation of parties increases the potential for fails (that is, the failure of the seller to deliver securities or of the buyer to make cash payment).

In response to such problems, two clearing systems have developed to handle international transactions: Euroclear, started in December 1968 by Morgan Guaranty Trust Company of New York, and Cedel, started in Luxembourg in September 1970. Their original objective was to handle Eurobond transactions. Now they handle a wide variety of securities and settle international primary and secondary equity transactions. In addition, they provide important services for the effective functioning of global market transactions beyond the settlement of transactions. First, they offer financing services for dealers so that they can finance their positions. Second, they provide a securities borrowing service so that dealers who are short securities can borrow them to cover their position.

GLOBAL EQUITY MARKETS

Table 22-2 provides a comparative analysis of the size, measured in U.S. dollars, of the equity markets of the world. The stock markets of the United States and Japan are the largest in the world. As the markets are measured in

TABLE 22-2	SIZE OF NATIONAL EQUITY MARKETS AS OF DECEMBER 31, 1990 (IN BILLIONS OF U.S. DOLLARS)

AREA OF COUNTRY	ESTIMATED MARKET VALUE
Europe	2,321.8
United Kingdom	882.4
West Germany	341.7
Switzerland	162.6
France	296.5
Netherlands	114.3
Sweden	93.0
Italy	148.2
Spain	105.1
Belgium	65.2
Denmark	39.5
Norway	25.7
Austria	24.5
Finland	22.9
Pacific Area	3,070.6
Japan	2,805.5
Australia	105.9
Hong Kong	83.5
Singapore/Malaysia	67.7
New Zealand	8.0
North America	3,035.9
United States	2,813.5
Canada	222.4
World	8,428.3*

*Excludes South African Gold Mines.

Source: Adapted from *Morgan Stanley Capital International Perspective,* January 1991 issue, p. 5.

U.S. dollars, the relative size of the U.S. and Japanese market varies as the value of the yen changes against the dollar; U.S. share increases when the yen depreciates and decreases when the yen appreciates. The third largest market, but trailing considerably behind the U.S. and Japan, is the U.K. market.

Trading activity by major national stock markets is shown in Table 22-3. Effective transactions costs (commissions and taxes) are higher in stock markets outside the United States, as can be seen in Table 22-4. Deregulation in many countries, however, is reducing the gap between transactions costs in stock markets outside the U.S.

TABLE 22-3 TURNOVER ON MAJOR STOCK EXCHANGES IN (1990)

COUNTRY	EXCHANGE	TOTAL VALUE OF TURNOVER (BILLIONS OF U.S. DOLLARS)	PERCENT OF TOTAL
Japan	Tokyo 1st Section	1,203.9	35.5
United States	NYSE	1,070.6	31.6
Germany	All Exchanges	497.8	14.7
United Kingdom	London	150.8	4.5
France	Paris	114.7	3.4
Canada	All Exchanges	68.0E	2.0E
Italy	Milano	42.9	1.3
Spain	Main Exchanges	40.4E	1.2E
Netherlands	Amsterdam	40.2	1.2
Australia	All Exchanges	37.9	1.1
Hong Kong	All Exchanges	35.2	1.0
Singapore	Singapore	18.8	0.6
Sweden	Stockholm	15.7	0.5
Norway	Oslo	14.1	0.4
Denmark	Copenhagen	11.9	0.4
Austria	Vienna	9.7	0.3
Belgium	Brussels	9.4	0.3
Finland	Helsinki	3.8	0.1
New Zealand	All Exchanges	0.7E	<0.1E
Total Major Stock Markets		3,386.5	100.0

The annual figures for turnover values in U.S. dollars are calculated by converting monthly values at month-end exchange rates.
E = estimate.

Source: Morgan Stanley Capital International Perspective, Monthly Issue 3, 1991, p. 14.

TABLE 22-4	EFFECTIVE TRANSACTIONS COSTS IN NON-U.S. EQUITY MARKETS (BASIS POINTS)*

COUNTRY	BUY	SELL	AVERAGE
Australia	80	80	80
Belgium	70	70	70
Canada	60	60	60
France	58	58	58
Germany	58	58	58
Hong Kong	107	107	107
Italy	72	72	72
Japan	45	100	73
Netherlands	40	40	40
Singapore	120	100	110
Spain	100	100	100
Sweden	136	136	136
Switzerland	55	55	55
U.K.	75	25	50
Weighted Non-U.S. Average	59	74	67
U.S.	20	20	20

*Transaction size assumed to be $500,000.

Source: Gary P. Brinson and Richard C. Carr, "International Equities and Bonds," Chapter 19 in Frank J. Fabozzi (ed.), *Portfolio and Investment Management: State-of-the-Art Research, Analysis and Strategies* (Chicago: Probus Publishing, 1989), Table 12, p. 437.

Stocks may be listed in more than one country. Arbitrage assures that the price is the same on all exchanges after adjusting for exchange rates and transactions costs.

In the United States, shares of some foreign companies can be traded through American Depositary Receipts (ADRs), which are instruments denominated in U.S. dollars that pay dividends in U.S. dollars. ADRs are issued by banks as evidence of ownership of the underlying stock of a foreign corporation that the U.S. bank holds. ADRs are traded on the NYSE, AMEX, and OTC. Examples of ADRs listed on the New York Stock Exchange are Honda Motor Co. (a Japanese company listed since February 1977), Club Med (a British West Indies company listed since September 1984), Royal Dutch

Petroleum Co. (a Netherlands company listed since July 1954), and British Petroleum Company (a U.K. company listed since March 1970). There may be more than one share of the foreign stock underlying an ADR. The American Stock Exchange trades an option on an index it has created, International Market Index, which is a broad-based, international stock index consisting of 50 leading foreign stocks that trade in the U.S. either directly or in the form of ADRs.

Euroequity issues, just like Eurobond issues, are those issued simultaneously in several national markets by an international syndicate. The Euroequity markets began in 1980. By 1986, issuance of Euroequities was between $8 and $10 billion.[16] This growth has been fueled by rising stock prices throughout the world, the desire of investors to diversify their portfolios internationally, the need for corporations to expand their sources of equity funding, and by governments seeking international investors for entities that have been privatized. The market crash of October 1987 slowed the growth of this market. While in 1987 issuance of Euroequities was about $15 to $18 billion (privatization offerings representing about half of this amount), it declined to about $8 billion in 1988 (with only a small amount resulting from privatization offerings). In 1989, Euroequities issuance rebounded to approximately $15 billion.[17] The Euroequities market is considerably smaller than the Eurobond market.

National Market Structures

In Chapter 8 we described the structure of the U.S. equity markets. While the stock exchanges in the U.S. are regulated by the SEC, they are privately owned entities. Activities of members of the exchange are regulated by the exchanges, and commissions are fully negotiable. Thus, the U.S. equity markets can be characterized as private markets whose activities while regulated at the federal level are basically self-regulated.

There are other countries that have a similar market structure: Japan, the

---

[16] P. L. Gilibert, B. Lygum, and F. Wurtz, "The International Capital Market in 1986," *Cahiers BEI/EIB Papers*, European Investment Bank, Luxembourg, March 1987.

[17] These statistics are obtained from: Bjorn Lygum, Jacques Girard, Danield Ottolenghi, Pier-Luigi Gilibert, and Alfred Steinherr, "International Capital Markets in 1988," *Cahier BEI/EIB Papers*, Luxembourg, European Investment Bank, March 1989, p. 38; and I. Drummond, P. L. Gilibert, B. Lygum, and E. Peree, "International Markets in 1989," *Cahier BEI/EIB Papers*, Luxembourg, European Investment Bank, March 1990, p. 23. Unfortunately, good data are not available for the Euroequities market. Annual market surveys of the European Investment Bank report inconsistent Euroequities issuance data from one year to the next.

United Kingdom, Canada, and Australia. In Japan, for example, there are eight major exchanges, three of which handle more than 98% of the trades (Tokyo Stock Exchange, Osaka Exchange, and Nagoya Exchange). In contrast, in the United Kingdom, the one dominant exchange is the London Stock Exchange. This exchange has predominated not because of any regulation but through absorption or attrition of its competitors. In many countries deregulation has resulted in commissions that are either fully or partially negotiable.

In some other countries, the stock exchange is a public institution. Brokers are selected by the government, and the commission rate structure is fixed by the government. Thus, the broker has a monopoly over all stock transactions. In some countries with this structure, all transactions are required to go through the exchange, even if they are consummated privately between a buyer and seller without the assistance of a broker. In such cases, a broker is paid a fee. European countries where the stock market is a public market include France, Belgium, Spain, Italy, and Greece. The last type of market structure is one where the majority of trading is done through banks. We described earlier how in Germany the universal banks dominate securities transactions. Other countries with this type of structure include Switzerland and the Netherlands.

Trading Procedures

In Chapter 8 we explained the difference between continuous and call markets. In the former, prices are determined continuously throughout the trading day as buyers and sellers submit orders. U.S. equity markets are continuous markets. Equity markets in Canada, in the Far East and most of Europe have a continuous market structure. A call market is one in which orders are batched for simultaneous execution at the same price. The equity markets in Germany, Belgium, Austria, and Israel have a call market structure. In several countries, electronic technology is being used to incorporate a call market structure into a continuous market structure.[18]

The U.S. stock markets are continuous markets. On the stock exchanges, the specialist is the market maker or dealer who has the role of providing liquidity; in the over-the-counter market there may be more than one market maker or dealer. On the Amsterdam Stock Exchange there is also only one specialist, the *hoekman*. On the London Stock Exchange there are more than one specialist, called *jobbers*.

---

[18] For a discussion of how this is being done and the advantages of this approach, see Chapter 10 of Robert A. Schwartz, *Reshaping the Equity Markets: A Guide for the 1990s* (N.Y.: HarperBusiness, 1991).

Stock Market Indexes

There are national indexes and international indexes. National indexes are those that measure stock market activity of a particular country. Where there is more than one stock exchange in a country, there is usually more than one stock market index, and often there are non-exchange constructed indexes. Examples of the former in the U.S. are the NYSE Composite Index and the AMEX Composite Index, while examples of the latter are the S&P 500 and the Dow Jones Industrial Average. In Japan, there is the Tokyo Stock Exchange Average (an exchange constructed index) and the Nikkei 225 Stock Average (a nonexchange constructed index).

To meet the increased interest in global equity investing, several international equity indexes have been developed. The international equity index followed most by U.S. pension funds is the Morgan Stanley Capital International Europe, Australia, Far East (EAFE) Index. This index, started by Capital International in 1968 and acquired by Morgan Stanley in 1986, covers more than 2,000 companies in 21 countries. Relatively new international equity indexes include: The Financial Times World Index (a joint product of the Institute of Actuaries in the U.K., Goldman Sachs & Co., and Wood MacKenzie & Co.), the Salomon Brothers–Russell Global Equity Index (a joint product of Salomon Brothers Inc and Frank Russell, Inc.), and the Global Index (a joint product of First Boston Corporation and London-based Euromoney).

STOCK INDEX INTEREST RATE DERIVATIVE CONTRACTS

In the U.S., the development of the markets for futures and options on stock indexes and debt obligations was a response to the need for an efficient risk-transference mechanism as stock price and interest rate volatility in the U.S. increased. Other countries have shared the U.S. experience with volatility and, as a result, developed derivative markets.

Many of these contracts are modeled after those developed in the U.S. futures and options markets. For example, many of the stock index futures and stock index options contracts are cash settlement contracts, which is the settlement procedure used in the U.S. In the case of bond futures on government securities, the short (the seller of the futures contract) has the right to deliver one of several acceptable government issues. Besides stock index derivative contracts, many countries have options on individual stocks.

The uses of derivative contracts that we discussed in Chapters 10 and 19 also coincide with the uses by most participants in other countries. Those who wish to invest in another country's stock market may find it more convenient to invest by buying stock index futures. Japanese derivative products are worth discussing at some length because of the size of this financial market.

Japanese Stock Index Futures and Options

There are three stock index futures contracts traded in Japan: the Nikkei 225 Stock Average (which began trading on the Osaka Stock Exchange in September 1988), the Tokyo Stock Price Index (TOPIX) (which began trading on the Tokyo Stock Exchange in September 1988), and the Osaka Stock Futures 50 (which began trading on the Osaka Stock Exchange in June 1987). In fact, the Osaka Stock Futures 50 began trading on the Singapore Exchange (SIMEX) in September 1986 before stock index futures trading was authorized in Japan.

Not all of the stock index futures contracts traded in Japan are cash settlement contracts. The first stock index futures contract to be traded in Japan, the Osaka Stock Futures 50, requires physical delivery of the 50 stocks in the index. Only when the other two contracts were introduced in September 1988 did a cash settlement contract become available.

As we explained in Chapter 10, one of the major reasons for using stock index futures is the significantly lower costs to transact in the futures market compared to the cash market. Total round-trip futures costs for the TOPIX futures contract are less than 5% of trading costs in the underlying stocks.[19] In Japan in particular there is another advantage of transacting in stock index futures rather than in the underlying stocks. Shorting stocks in Japan is difficult, so selling stock index futures is the only effective way of going short in the equities market.

In September of 1990, stock index futures and options on Japanese stock market indexes began trading on U.S. exchanges. The Chicago Mercantile Exchange trades stock index futures on the Nikkei 225 and options on futures based on the same index. For the futures contract, the dollar value is determined by multiplying $5 by the futures price. That is, the multiple for this contract is $5 (for the S&P 500, it is $500). Consequently, if the futures price is 27,000, the dollar value of the contract would be $135,000 ($5 times 27,000). The Chicago Board of Trade trades futures and futures options on the Tokyo Stock Price Index (TOPIX). In terms of yen, the multiple for the futures contract is 5,000 yen, so, if the index value is 2,450, the contract's yen value is 12,250,000 yen (5,000 yen times 2,450). The American Stock Exchange trades a European-type option on an index of Japanese stocks. The index is one that was created by the AMEX, which it calls the Japanese Index, consisting of 210 stocks actively traded on the Tokyo Stock Exchange.

---

[19] Gary L. Gastineau, Mark M. Arimura, Michael J. Belkin, Eric A. Clausen, Tak Kyokuta, Tatsuya Higashino, and Christopher M. Mitchinson, "Japanese Stock Index Futures— Structure and Applications" (New York: Salomon Brothers Inc, August 29, 1988), Figure 4.

Japanese Interest Rate Futures and Options

The Japanese government bond futures market opened on the Tokyo Stock Exchange in October 1985 with trading on the 10-year JGB (long-term government bond) and in July 1988 on the 20-year JGB (super-long government bond). Actually, the underlying JGBs for these two contracts are fictional 10-year and 20-year bonds with coupon rates of 6% and a face value of 100 million yen. By daily trading volume, the JGB futures contract is now the most actively traded contract in the world. In September 1990 the JGB futures contract began trading on the Chicago Board of Trade.

The options granted to the seller of a JGB futures contract are the same as those granted to the seller of a U.S. Treasury bond or note futures contract. Specifically, the seller has the right to select the JGB issue to deliver from among issues designated as acceptable for delivery by the exchange. The short seller also has delivery date and wild card options.[20]

Options on the 10-year JGB futures contract began trading on the Tokyo Stock Exchange in May 1990. In the first year of operation some 3 million contracts were traded, though volume has fallen off recently. Initially, securities companies dominated the trading, but recently banks have increased their share of total trading to 25%, from less than 15% in the first months of the market's operations.

Options on JGBs began trading on April 27, 1989. After approval by the MOF, dealers began making OTC markets on JGB options. At the same time, Japanese dealers began making OTC options on U.S. Treasury bonds.

SUMMARY

The increased integration of financial markets can be attributed to three factors: (1) deregulation or liberalization of major financial markets (market deregulation and institutional deregulation), (2) advances in telecommunications and computer technologies, and (3) institutionalization of financial markets.

The growth of bond markets throughout the world has been the result of a shift in lending and borrowing activities from traditional syndicated bank loans to some type of marketable security or securitized instrument. The global bond market can be classified into two markets: the internal or national bond market, which consists of a domestic bond market and a foreign bond market, and the external or international bond market (or Eurobond market).

---

[20] See Chapter 19.

The first true "global bond" was issued by the World Bank in September 1989.

Many innovative bond structures have been introduced in the Eurobond market such as dual currency issues and various types of convertible bonds and bonds with warrants. The floating-rate sector of the Eurobond market is dominated by U.S. dollar-denominated issues.

The Japanese bond market, the second largest bond market in the world, is regulated by the Ministry of Finance. The internal Japanese bond market includes government bonds (the largest sector), government-related organization bonds, local government bonds, bank debentures, and corporate bonds. The Japanese foreign bond market includes both yen-denominated (Samurai bonds, Daimyo bonds, and Shibosai bonds) and non-yen-denominated issues.

The third largest bond market is the German bond market. The German capital market, which is more interdependent with its banking system than any other developed capital market, has two types of banks: universal banks and special banks. Activities of universal banks include the usual commercial banking business and any kind of securities business. The three sectors in the German national bond market include public authority bonds, bank bonds, and non-bank corporate bonds.

Euroclear and Cedel are two clearing systems that handle Eurobond transactions as well as international primary and secondary equity transactions and provide dealer financing and a securities borrowing service.

The United States and Japanese stock markets are the two largest stock markets in the world, followed by the U.K. stock market. Outside the U.S., effective transactions costs (commissions and taxes) are higher; however, the gap has been closing as a result of deregulation in many countries. Stocks may be listed in more than one country. In the U.S., shares of some foreign companies can be traded through American Depositary Receipts (ADRs).

The Euroequities market includes stocks issued simultaneously in several national markets by an international syndicate. The Euroequities market is considerably smaller than the Eurobond market.

There are three types of stock market structures throughout the world: (1) private markets, whose activities while regulated by the government are basically self-regulated, (2) public institutions where brokers are selected by the government and the commission rate structure is fixed by the government, and (3) stock markets where the majority of trading is done through banks. A stock market may be a continuous market or a call market.

Futures and options on stock indexes and debt obligations throughout the world have developed as a response to the need for an efficient risk-transference mechanism as stock price and interest rate volatility increased. Many of the contracts mirror the delivery specifications in the U.S.

QUESTIONS

1. What types of regulations are imposed by regulators on the issuance of foreign bonds in a country's internal bond market?

2. The quotation following is from an article entitled "Spanish Bonds to be Tops," that appeared in the March 4, 1991, issue of *Bondweek:*

    > The Spanish bond market will be one of the best performing European markets this year due to its relatively high yields, a strong peseta [the Spanish currency] and moves by the Spanish government to liberalize the market, according to analysts. The Spanish government's recent move to lower short-term rates from 14.7% to 14.5%, hold monthly auctions and abolish the 25% withholding tax on *bonos* (government bonds) for non-residents has also helped increase liquidity in the market, they said.

    Explain why the relatively high yields, a strong peseta, and the government's liberalization policies will contribute to the projected favorable performance of the Spanish bond market cited in this quotation.

3. A withholding tax is a tax imposed by a country on interest or dividends to be paid to foreign (i.e., non-resident) investors who have purchased securities in that country. Foreign investors, of course, want to avoid withholding taxes. The excerpt below discussing withholding taxes is taken from the *International Capital Market in 1989* published by the European Investment Bank:

    > During 1989 changes in *withholding tax* regimes—actual and proposed—made for additional gyrations in securities prices. Speculation as to the permanence of the 10% withholding tax on coupon income of all domestically issued bonds in Germany was already alive when it was introduced on 1 January 1989. When the decision was finally taken in May to abolish the tax as from 1 July, yield relations between the euro-Deutsche Mark and the domestic markets had already begun to change. Yields on euro-Deutsche Mark bonds by supranational borrowers, for instance, which had traded below German Government bonds ("Bunds"), started to rise in early April and returned to their traditional level above those of "Bunds." Issuing patterns also fell back to those of the pre-withholding tax period: German entities reduced sharply their issuing activity in the euromarket. The heavy outflow of long-term funds from Germany which had preceded the introduction of the withholding tax was also partly reversed.

    a. What is a "euro-Deutsche Mark" bond?

    b. Why would proposed withholding taxes cause "gyrations in securities prices"?

    c. Explain why imposition of the German 10% withholding tax in January 1989 caused yields on Euro-Deutsche mark bonds issued by supranational borrowers to trade at a lower yield than German government bonds.

    d. Why did issuing patterns fall "back to those of the pre-withholding tax period"?

4. Define each of the following:

    a. LIBID

    b. LIMEAN

    c. drop-lock bonds

    d. Cedel

    e. Euroclear

    f. universal banks

5. This excerpt, which discusses dual currency bonds, is taken from the *International Capital Market in 1989* published by the European Investment Bank:

> The generic name of dual-currency bonds hides many different variations which are difficult to characterize in detail. These variations on the same basic concept have given birth to specific names like Index Currency Option notes (ICON), foreign interest payment bonds (FIPS), forex-linked bonds, heaven and hell bonds, to name but a few. Despite this diversity it is, however, possible to attempt a broad-brush classification of the various types of dual-currency bonds.
>
> The first category covers bond issues denominated in one currency but for which coupon and repayment of the principal are made in another designated currency at an exchange rate *fixed* at the time of issue. A second category comprises dual-currency bonds in which coupon payments and redemption proceeds are made in a currency different from the currency of denomination at the *spot* exchange rate that will prevail at the time of payment.
>
> Within this category, one finds the forex-linked bonds, foreign currency bonds and heaven and hell bonds. A final category includes bonds which offer to issuers or the holder the choice of the currency in which payments and/or redemptions are to be made at the future

spot exchange rate. ICONs fall into this latter category because there is an implicit *option* due to the exchange rate revision formula. Usually, these bonds are referred to as option currency bonds.

Irrespective of the above-mentioned categories, all dual-currency bonds expose the issuers and the holders to some form of foreign exchange risk . . . . Pricing dual-currency bonds is therefore an application of option pricing, as the bonds can be looked at as a combination of a straight bond and a currency option. The value of the straight bond component is obtained according to traditional fixed-rate bond valuation models. The pricing of the option component is, ex post, equal to the difference between the dual currency bond price and its straight bond component . . . .

There has been some considerable debate whether investors in dual-currency bonds have been properly compensated for the risks taken. This is a difficult question and one unlikely to draw a definitive conclusion.

a. Why do all currency bonds "expose the issuers and the holders to some form of foreign exchange risk" regardless of the category of bond?

b. Do you agree that the pricing of all dual-currency bonds is an application of option pricing?

c. Why should the price of the option component be "equal to the difference between the dual currency bond price and its bond component"?

d. Why is the debate over whether investors in dual-currency bonds have been properly compensated "one unlikely to draw a definitive conclusion"?

6. What are the three types of stock market structures observed throughout the world?

7. **a.** What is an American Depositary Receipt?

   b. What is a Euroequity issue?

8. Here is a quotation from the December 1988 issue of *Euromoney:*

   The proliferation of futures and options markets has created new opportunities for international investors. It is now possible to change investment exposure instruments, augmented by a limited number of individual securities. Asset allocation in most major markets is now feasible using futures and options.

State whether you agree or disagree with the quotation, and why.

INDEX